HANDYMAN
COMPLETE GUIDE TO
HOME MAINTENANCE

BANNER PRESS

NEW YORK, NEW YORK

CONTENTS

HANDTOOLS 1

POWER TOOLS 2

BUILDING MATERIALS 3

PAINTS AND FINISHES 4

WINDOWS, DOORS, CLOSETS, DRAWERS AND SHELVES

5

WALLS, FLOORS AND CEILINGS **6**

EXTERIOR MAINTENANCE **7**

PLUMBING AND TEMPERATURE CONTROL 8

WORKING WITH METAL 9

FASTENING TECHNIQUES 10

ELECTRICITY AND WIRING 11

REMODELING

12

FURNITURE REPAIR AND FINISHING

13

YOUR SHOP

14

WEIGHTS AND MEASURES

INDEX

1

HAND-TOOLS

HANDTOOLS

COLD CHISELS ■ HAMMERS ■ HANDSAWS ■ SCREWDRIVERS ■ WRENCHES
BORING TOOLS ■ PLIERS ■ FILES ■ PLANES ■ WOOD CHISELS AND GOUGES
SNIPS ■ VISES AND CLAMPS ■ SHARPENING ■ MEASURING TOOLS ■ ABRASIVES

In this day and age of instant conveniences, too many home handymen overlook the need for hand tools and think they must rely almost completely on power tools. The fact is, hand tools are basic and no home workshop is complete without them.

For example, to build a piece of furniture, you carefully and accurately cut the pieces. To assemble it, you need nails or screws and a good, well balanced hammer or the proper size screwdriver.

How do you choose hand tools? First determine your needs. If you are going to use the tools just for simple home maintenance, you may prefer to buy one of the many kits available. If you will use your tools for more than just maintenance, buy them individually to suit your needs.

Good hand tools are NOT cheap, but they are essential for the quick and efficient completion of even the simplest job. Remember too, that when properly cared for, good tools last a lifetime and will be worth the investment.

TOOL HABITS

"A place for everything and everything in its place" is just common sense. You cannot do an efficient, fast, repair job if you have to stop and look around for each tool you need.

Keep each tool in its proper place. A tool is useless if you cannot find it. If you return each tool to its proper place, it will be there the next time you need it.

Keep your tools in good condition. Protect them from rust, nicks, burrs and breakage.

Keep your selection of tools complete. The contents of your tool box should reflect your particular needs.

Use each tool only for the job for which it was designed. If you use the wrong tool to make an adjustment the results will not be satisfactory. For example, if you use a socket wrench that's a trifle too big, you'll round off the corners of the wrench or nut.

Keep your tools within easy reach. Avoid placing tools anywhere above machinery or electrical apparatus.

Never use damaged tools. A battered screwdriver may slip and spoil the screw slot, damage other parts, or cause painful injury. Always keep hand tools clean and free from dirt, grease and foreign matter.

HAMMERS

Every workshop needs a good selection of hammers. The right hammer for a particular job saves a lot of time, effort and temper. Too light a hammer requires added physical effort to get a job done, while one that's too heavy wears you out just lifting it and often damages the job.

Buy the very best hammer you can afford. Quite simply, you can't afford a cheap hammer. It will not have the "balance" of a good hammer, the face will not stand up under heavy use, and a very cheap hammer may even shatter. Flying pieces of head could cause a serious injury.

Before selecting the weight of a hammer, be sure you know how to use one correctly. Too many handymen "choke up" the handle, using only a short length close to the head. This requires a lot more work to drive a nail, and using a heavier head really doesn't compensate.

Hold the handle near the end where it narrows for an easy grip. Let the weight of the head do the work. Move your elbow and shoulder in a smooth easy swing so the head drops of its own weight. You can work for hours this way, as many professional carpenters do, without strain.

When you use a hammer correctly you can get by with a lighter head, as the swing and leverage do the work, rather than brute strength.

The face of a hammer is extremely important, and this is the part that causes the most trouble to the inexperienced. If you seem to be bending more nails than usual, look at the face. It may be scratched or covered with wood resin or glue. Place a piece of fine sandpaper flat on a workbench and polish the face on it. Never, never grind the face of a hammer. It is slightly rounded to permit driving a nail head evenly and almost flush with a wood surface without denting the wood.

Carpenters' Claw Hammer

One basic tool is a carpenters' claw hammer, which can weigh from 16 to 20 ounces; the size should be the one that you can most comfortably handle. Get a fairly heavy one for framing, but for inside finishing and trim work get one from 12 to 16 ounces. The slightly rounded face of a good finishing hammer allows you to drive a nail close to the surface of the wood before it is necessary to use a nail set to finish the job.

Curved claws generally are best, as they provide greater leverage for pulling nails. Straight claws are preferred by some carpenters who do mostly rough framing with heavy timbers.

Claw hammers can be obtained with the "conventional" wood handles, with steel or even fiber glass shanks. Shock-absorbing qualities of the three materials are not markedly different, so the selection of the type handle depends on you.

Ball-peen Hammer

The second most important hammer for any handyman is a ball-peen. This type hammer is used for metal work, for driving cold chisels, center punches and drift punches. Don't use a claw hammer for this work; it simply isn't designed for it.

Ball-peens come in various weights. A 2-pound model is best for general work. For lighter work, a 16-ounce size is handy. One use for the ball end is making gaskets for custom work. You simply place the sheet of gasket material over the surface of the work and tap gently around the edges of all openings in the work. Do not cut the pieces completely free; remove the gasket material and carefully push out the "perforated" pieces. If you tap these pieces loose on the work, they may fall into an opening where they are difficult to remove.

If the ball end of a ball-peen is kept clean and smooth, it can be used to emboss and shape soft metal, or create a peened pattern for craft work, as for ashtrays and the like.

Other Hammers

For heavy-duty work you'll want a blacksmiths' or sledge hammer. These hammers weigh from 2 to 20 pounds, depending on the use, which might be anything from shaping metal to driving stakes into the ground for a fence.

A good tack hammer is always needed around the house. It is used for upholstering, and for driving small brads and tacks when laying carpeting or inserting backing in picture frames. Get the magnetic type, with one end of the head split for the magnet. The type with the magnet cemented in a hole usually comes apart with use. You can pick up a tack with the magnet end, tap it in place, then reverse the hammer to drive it into the wood.

Every workshop should also have a wooden, leather or hard rubber mallet for working on surfaces that might be damaged by a metal hammer. For some jobs a plastic-headed hammer is best. The advantage of the latter is that the heads can be replaced when they are worn. Some types can be fitted with a screw-on lead or brass head in place of the plastic, when needed.

Not found in most workshops are two specialized hammers. One is the shingle hatchet that combines hammer and hatchet, with some models having an adjustable gauge for alignment. The other is the brick layers' hammer having a chisel on one end of the head that is used to score around bricks, blocks or other masonry work. The purchase of one of these hammers is a good investment.

Not exactly a hammer, but used as one, is a woodcarvers' mallet. This wooden mallet is shaped much like an old-fashioned potato masher and is used to drive carving chisels.

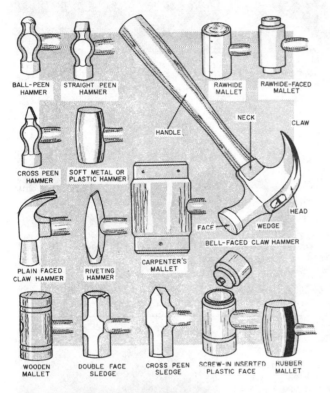

BALL-PEEN HAMMER · STRAIGHT PEEN HAMMER · RAWHIDE MALLET · RAWHIDE-FACED MALLET · CROSS PEEN HAMMER · SOFT METAL OR PLASTIC HAMMER · HANDLE · NECK · CLAW · HEAD · FACE · WEDGE · BELL-FACED CLAW HAMMER · PLAIN FACED CLAW HAMMER · RIVETING HAMMER · CARPENTER'S MALLET · WOODEN MALLET · DOUBLE FACE SLEDGE · CROSS PEEN SLEDGE · SCREW-IN INSERTED PLASTIC FACE · RUBBER MALLET

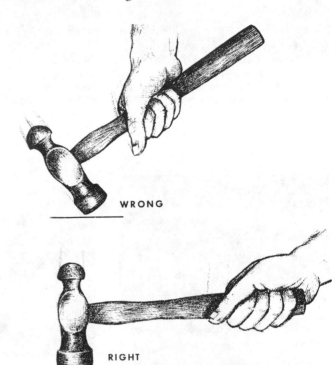

WRONG

RIGHT

Rough-framing hammer varies in weight from 16 to 20 oz. Straight claws are preferred by some.

Hammer for finishing work at a bench runs from 13 to 16 oz. in weight. This one weighs in at 13 oz.

When pulling long nails, or nails from surface you don't want to damage, use block under head for leverage.

Peen-type hammers are necessity in any shop. They come in ball, straight and cross-peens, generally used for riveting.

If ball end of ball-peen hammer is kept smooth and polished it can be used for creating peened surface on metals.

Bricklayers' hammer is flat and square on one end; other has chisel shape for scoring brick, block and masonry.

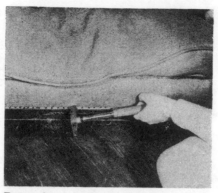

Every shop and home should have upholstery or tack hammer that has magnet on one end of head.

For heavy-duty work you'll need a small sledge or "blacksmiths'" hammer. They run from 2 to 3 lbs.

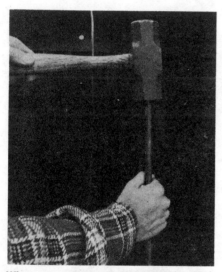

When you get into even heavier work you will require a sledge hammer; they run from 4 to 10 lbs.

Center punches, drift pins, other metalworking tools are driven with ball peen. Don't use a regular claw hammer.

Another builders' hammer is shingling hatchet that combines hatchet and hammer. Better ones have shingle gauge.

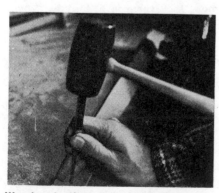

Wood or leather mallet is another hammer for delicate work; is often used for crafts such as leatherworking.

If you do any work that requires careful working of soft metals or fragile parts, a plastic-tipped hammer is a must.

Actually not a hammer, woodcarvers' mallet is used in same manner as hammer to drive carving chisels into wood.

6

HANDSAWS

Next to the hammer, a handsaw is the most important tool in a woodworker's tool box. If it is used just for home repairs there will probably be only one saw, a crosscut.

Crosscut Saws

As the name implies, a crosscut saws across the grain of the wood, cutting on both forward and backward strokes. These saws are available from coarse to fine "points-to-the-inch." A coarse crosscut will have 7- or 8-points-to-the-inch, while a fine will have as many as 11 or 12 points. A 7-point saw is about right for cutting green or wet wood, an 8-point is used for most normal crosscutting. The finer toothed blades cut slower and should be used only on light, dry wood. Saws are also described by length, running from 16 to 26 inches with a 24- or 26-inch blade best for most work. If properly maintained, a good crosscut saw will last a lifetime.

Using a Crosscut. To use a crosscut blade properly, be sure the work is well supported so the saw does not bind or twist. With the board properly positioned and supported, use a square to mark the cutting line. A right angle or 45-degree miter can be marked with a regular square; use an adjustable T-bevel for other angles. This mark will give you a point of reference and should not be removed. Cut outside the line.

Place the saw on the wood just outside the line. Pull back a few inches to make a starting notch, then make longer strokes. Use your thumb alongside the blade to help guide it and keep it vertical to the line. Pull your thumb out of the way when you begin the longer strokes. Don't force the saw; it will cut in both directions and you just have to pull it back and forth. When you near the end of the cut, grasp the waste with your free hand and support it so it does not fall and tear out a splinter from the main piece of the wood.

Ripsaws

A Ripsaw is similar to the crosscut, but cuts mostly on the forward stroke. It is used for ripping with the grain of the wood, has fewer teeth than a crosscut blade and makes a wider kerf. Ripsaws range from 4- to 6-points-to-the-inch, but are a standard 26 inches in length. Teeth on ripsaws

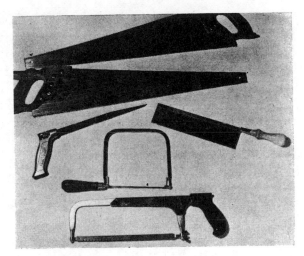

Top to bottom: crosscut saw, rip; left is keyhole saw, right is dovetail saw. Coping saw with deep frame and hacksaw.

are filed square across, rather than at an angle as on a crosscut saw.

Using a Ripsaw. Again, support the work solidly. Mark the rip line by drawing a pencil line along the end of a combination square set at the proper dimension, or use a marking gauge. With the line marked, position the work about knee high with your body directly over the line. Start the cut with the tip of the blade near the work, making short draw strokes to create a notch. Change to long, easy strokes to finish the cut. No forcing should be necessary; if the blade doesn't cut easily, sharpen it.

Cut the waste side of the line and keep moving so you are comfortable and can see the line. If the kerf closes up, slip a wedge or wood chisel in the cut to hold it open.

Maintenance

Whether a crosscut or a ripsaw, the important thing is proper maintenance. An occasional wiping with light oil will keep the blades free of rust. Sharpening and setting the teeth is the major maintenance required. While this job takes time, it is not difficult.

The teeth of the blade are "set" which means that alternate teeth are bent in opposite directions.

7

This set makes the saw kerf (groove created by the saw) wider at the teeth than the blade, which prevents the blade from dragging in the cut, and hence reduces sawing effort. The teeth need to be set every third or fourth sharpening.

Simple hand tools permit even a novice to sharpen a saw blade. Place the saw in a saw vise (or a couple of pieces of wood and a regular vise). If the teeth need setting, use a tooth setter, a tool shaped somewhat like pliers. After the teeth are set, file them with a three-cornered file. A saw filing tool is available. Ripsaw teeth are filed straight across, crosscut teeth at about 45 degrees. If some teeth are chipped or broken, file the length of the blade to get all teeth the same height, an operation called "jointing." Then file the individual teeth to renew the points and sharpen them.

Other Woodworking Saws

Saws with stiff backs are usually classified with crosscut saws, as they are made and used in a similar manner. There is less set in the teeth of a backsaw, and more points to the inch. This creates a blade that makes a fine cut, but a slow one. They also can cut no deeper than the width of the blade from teeth to the back. Backsaws are made in various sizes, from a big blade for a miter box to a small one for cutting dovetail joints. These blades are sharpened like a crosscut, only with a smaller file.

Coping saws use thin, disposable blades and are designed for cutting curves and scrollwork in thin stock. The blade can be removed and inserted in a starting hole.

Keyhole saws are for cutting holes in walls, plasterboard, and paneling for electrical boxes and the like. Fine to coarse blades fit this saw, which can even make a starting hole for itself. It is extremely handy for home maintenance work.

Hacksaws

Hacksaws are not woodworking tools, but they are "hand operated" and no workshop should be without one. The blades are disposable, but don't buy cheap ones. You'll wear out three or four cheap blades to one good one.

Hacksaws are used to cut metal that is too heavy for snips or boltcutters. Thus, metal bar stock can be cut readily with hacksaws.

There are two parts to a hacksaw: the frame and the blade. Common hacksaws have either an adjustable or solid frame. Most hacksaws are of the adjustable frame type. Adjustable frames can be made to hold blades from 8 to 16 inches long, while those with solid frames take only the length blade for which they are made. This length is the distance between the two pins that hold the blade in place.

Hacksaw blades are made of high-grade tool steel, hardened and tempered. There are two types, the all-hard and the flexible. All-hard blades are hardened throughout, whereas only the teeth of the flexible blades are hardened. Hacksaw blades have from 14 to 32 teeth per inch, and are from 8 to 16 inches long. The blades have a hole at each end which hooks to a pin in the frame. All hacksaw frames which hold the blades either parallel or at right angles to the frame are provided with a wingnut or screw to permit tightening or removing the blade.

The teeth of hacksaws may have one of four kinds of set. The teeth in the alternate set are staggered, one to the left and one to the right throughout the length of the blade. On the double alternate set blade, two adjoining teeth are staggered to the right, two to the left, and so on. On the raker set blade, every third tooth remains straight and the other two are set alternately. On the wave (undulated) set blade, short sections of teeth are bent in opposite directions.

Using Hacksaws. The hacksaw is often used improperly. Although it can be used with limited success by an inexperienced person, a little thought and study given to its proper use will result in faster and better work and less dulling and breaking of blades.

Good work with a hacksaw depends not only upon the proper use of the saw, but also upon the proper selection of the blades for the work to be done. Coarse blades with fewer teeth per inch cut faster and are less liable to choke up with chips. However, finer blades with more teeth per inch are necessary when thin sections are being cut. The selection should be made so that, as each tooth starts its cut, the tooth ahead of it will still be cutting.

To make the cut, first install the blade in the hacksaw frame so that the teeth point away from the handle of the hacksaw. (Hand hacksaws cut on the push stroke.) Tighten the wingnut so that the blade is definitely under tension. This helps make straight cuts.

Place the material to be cut in a vise. A minimum of overhang will reduce vibration, give a better cut, and lengthen the life of the blade. Have the layout line outside of the vise jaw so that the line is visible while you work.

The proper method of holding the hacksaw is to have the index finger of the right hand pointed forward. This aids in guiding the frame.

When cutting, let your body sway ahead and back with each stroke. Apply pressure on the forward stroke, which is the cutting stroke, but not on the return stroke. From 40 to 50 strokes per minute is the usual speed. Long, slow, steady strokes are preferred.

For long cuts rotate the blade in the frame so that the length of the cut is not limited by the depth of the frame. Hold the work with the layout line close to the vise jaws, raising the work in the vise as the sawing proceeds.

Metal which is too thin to be held can be placed between blocks of wood. The wood provides support for several teeth as they are cutting. Without the wood, teeth will be broken due to excessive vibration of the stock and because individual teeth have to absorb the full power of the stroke.

Cut thin metal with layout lines on the face by using a piece of wood behind it. Hold the wood and the metal in the jaws of the vise, using a C-clamp when necessary. The wood block helps support the blade and produces a smoother cut. Using the wood only in back of the metal permits the layout lines to be seen.

To remove a frozen nut with a hacksaw, saw into the nut starting the blade close to the threads on the bolt or stud and parallel to one face of the nut. Saw parallel to the bolt until the teeth of the blade almost reach the lockwasher. Lockwashers are hard and will ruin hacksaw blades, so do not try to saw them. Then, with a cold chisel and hammer, remove this one side of the nut completely by opening the saw kerf. Put an adjustable wrench across this new flat and the one opposite, and again try to remove the frozen nut. Since very little original metal remains on this one side of the nut, the nut will either give or break away entirely and permit its removal.

Hacksaw Safety. The main danger in using hacksaws is injury to your hand if the blade breaks. The blade will break if too much pressure is applied when the saw is twisted, when the cutting speed is too fast, or when the blade becomes loose in the frame. Additionally, if the work is not tight in the vise, it will sometimes slip, twisting the blade enough to break it.

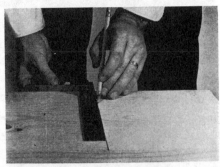

First step in cutting a board is to mark a line with sharp pencil, using a try square. Another important hand tool.

Place saw outside pencil line, use thumb as guide, pull saw back to start cut. Use short strokes at first, then longer.

Grip on saw should be firm, but not tight. Extended forefinger helps keep saw aligned with mark.

It's important to keep the cut just outside the line; this gives an accurate reference to the cut.

9

When finishing a cut, grasp the waste piece with your free hand to keep it from dropping and twisting out a splinter.

In making a "pocket" cut, or where two cuts meet, hold the saw vertical so the resulting corner is a neat 90-degrees.

Coping saw is indispensible for making curved and precise cuts for everything from cutting out toys to furniture.

Saw blades with stiff backs—this is dovetail saw—are accurate and handy to use.

Before filing handsaw to sharpen it, teeth are bent alternately with hand-operated saw-tooth setter.

Saw vise makes it easy to hold saw rigidly while you file the teeth at proper angle to sharpen them.

DIFFERENCE BETWEEN TEETH AND POINTS PER INCH

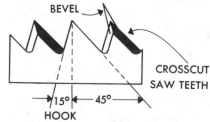

EXTRA-FINE BLADE
11 POINTS TO THE INCH

1"

COARSE BLADE
8 POINTS TO THE INCH

1"

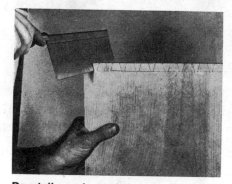

Dovetail saw is used to make that joint, or for any precision work that requires exact cut. Saw creates a narrow kerf.

Small kerf created by dovetail saw is required for many exacting jobs, as here where pistol grip is being fitted.

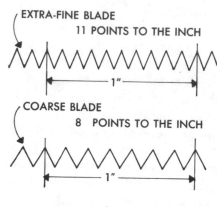

BEVEL

CROSSCUT SAW TEETH

15°   45°

HOOK

CROSS SECTION OF CROSSCUT TEETH

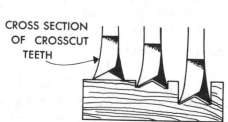

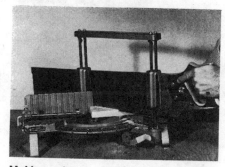

Making picture frames, cutting right angles and 45-degree miters on molding for trimming requires a miter box.

Keyhole saw is used to start and make openings in wallboard, lath-and-plaster walls for installing electrical boxes.

HOW CROSSCUT SAW CUTS

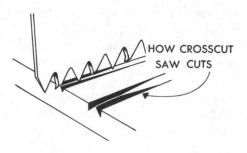

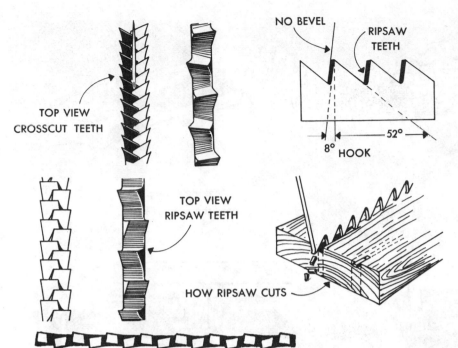

TOP VIEW
CROSSCUT TEETH

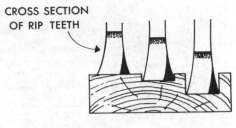

NO BEVEL

RIPSAW TEETH

8° HOOK

52°

CROSS SECTION
OF RIP TEETH

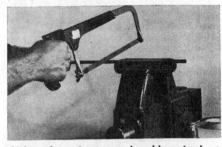

TOP VIEW
RIPSAW TEETH

HOW RIPSAW CUTS

Although not a woodworking tool, a hacksaw is a "must" tool in any shop. Buy only quality blades, clamp work.

ALTERNATE SET

RAKER SET

WAVE SET

"Set" of hacksaw
blade teeth.

ADJUSTABLE

SOLID
Hacksaws.

14 TEETH PER INCH

FOR LARGE SECTIONS
OF MILD MATERIAL

18 TEETH PER INCH

FOR LARGE SECTIONS
OF TOUGH STEEL

24 TEETH PER INCH

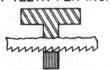

FOR ANGLE IRON, HEAVY
PIPE, BRASS, COPPER

32 TEETH PER INCH

FOR THIN TUBING

KEEP AT LEAST TWO TEETH CUTTING
TO AVOID THIS

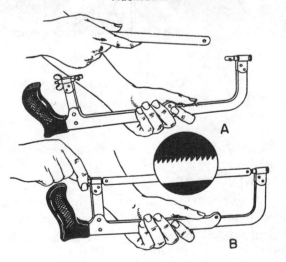

A

B

Installing a
hacksaw blade.

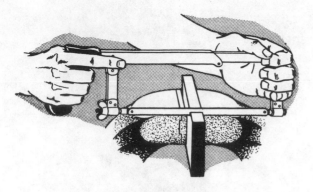

Proper way to
hold a hacksaw.

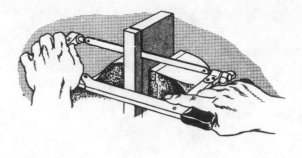

Making a long cut
near the edge of stock.

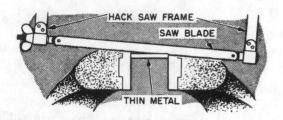

Cutting thin metal
with a hacksaw.

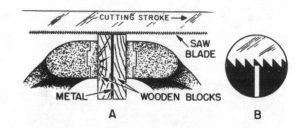

Cutting thin metal
between two wooden blocks.

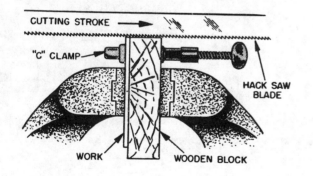

Cutting thin metal using
wood block with layout lines.

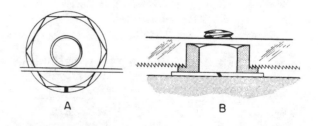

Removing a frozen
nut with a hacksaw.

SCREWDRIVERS

A screwdriver is one of the most basic of basic handtools. It is also the most frequently abused of all handtools. It is designed for one function only—to drive and remove screws. A screwdriver should not be used as a pry bar, a scraper, a chisel, or a punch.

Standard

There are three main parts to a standard screwdriver. The portion you grip is called the handle, the steel portion extending from the handle is the shank, and the end which fits into the screw is called the blade.

The steel shank is designed to withstand considerable twisting force in proportion to its size, and the tip of the blade is hardened to keep it from wearing.

Standard screwdrivers are classified by size, according to the combined length of the shank and blade. The most common sizes range in length from 2½ in. to 12 in. There are many screwdrivers smaller and some larger for special purposes. The diameter of the shank, and the width and thickness of the blade are generally proportionate to the length, but again there are special screwdrivers with long thin shanks, short thick shanks, and extra wide or extra narrow blades.

Screwdriver handles may be wood, plastic, or metal. When metal handles are used, there is usually a wooden hand grip placed on each side of the handle. In some types of wood- or plastic-handled screwdrivers the shank extends through the handle, while in others the shank enters the handle only a short way and is pinned to the handle. For heavy work, special types of screwdrivers are made with a square shank. They are designed this way so that they may be gripped

with a wrench, but this is the only kind on which a wrench should be used.

When using a screwdriver it is important to select the proper size so that the blade fits the screw slot properly. This prevents burring the slot and reduces the force required to hold the driver in the slot. Keep the shank perpendicular to the screw head.

Recessed

Recessed screws are now available in various shapes. They have a cavity formed in the head and may require a specially shaped screwdriver. The most common type found is the Phillips head screw. This requires a Phillips-type screwdriver.

The head of a Phillips-type screw has a four-way slot into which the screwdriver fits. This prevents the screwdriver from slipping. Three standard sized Phillips screwdrivers handle a wide range of screw sizes. Their ability to hold helps to prevent damaging the slots or the work surrounding the screw. It is a poor practice to try to use a standard screwdriver on a Phillips screw because both the tool and screw slot will be damaged.

BLADE HANDLE

HEAVY DUTY

SQUARE SHANK

CLUTCH TIP

SCREW HOLDING DRIVER

COMPRESSION OF SPRING HOLDS SCREW FIRMLY AGAINST TIP OF DRIVER

REED AND PRINCE DRIVER

PHILLIPS HEAD DRIVER

OFFSET DRIVER

RATCHET AND SPIRAL DRIVER

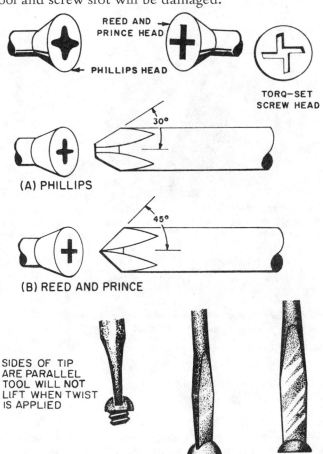

REED AND PRINCE HEAD

PHILLIPS HEAD

TORQ-SET SCREW HEAD

30°

(A) PHILLIPS

45°

(B) REED AND PRINCE

SIDES OF TIP ARE PARALLEL TOOL WILL NOT LIFT WHEN TWIST IS APPLIED

PLIERS

You can have as many as 30 pairs of pliers in your workshop and find regular use for every one of them, as each size and kind does a particular job better than any of the others.

There are pliers that double as hammers, others that can substitute for pipe wrenches, some even can be used as clamps. Both cutting and gripping are possible with some types of pliers, cutting only is done by others. Some types strip insulation from wires and crimp fittings onto the stripped wires, some can be adjusted to various sizes, others are one size only, but can fit objects of different sizes.

Common "gas" pliers, also called "slip-joint" pliers, can be adjusted to two sizes. They range in length from 5 to 10 in., with jaw capacities from about ¾ to 1½ in. Most pliers of this type also have a wire cutter at the pivot end of the jaw, but it is not the most efficient of devices. While most of these pliers have straight jaws, some are made with a "bent nose," that is angled about 30 deg. so your hand stays clear of a flat surface while working with the tool.

Maintenance

Nearly all sidecutting pliers and diagonals are designed so that the cutting edges can be reground. Some older models of pliers will not close if material is ground from the cutting edges. When grinding the cutting edges never take any more material from the jaws than is necessary to remove the nicks. Grind the same amount of stock from both jaws.

When jaws on pliers do not open enough to permit grinding, remove the pin that attaches the two halves of the pliers so that the jaws can be separated.

The serrations on the jaws of pliers must be sharp. When they become dull, the pliers should be held in a vise and the serrations recut by using a small 3-corner file.

Pliers should be coated with light oil when they are not in use. They should be stored in a tool box in such a manner that the jaws cannot be injured by striking hard objects. Keep the pin or bolt at the hinge just tight enough to hold the two parts of the pliers in contact and always keep the pivot pin lubricated with a few drops of light oil.

Special round-nose pliers have no flats on jaws, are used just for twisting wire for connections.

Commonly known as electrician's pliers, and usually fitted with insulated handles, these both grip and cut.

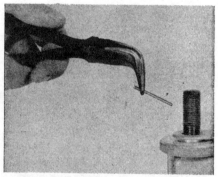

Even round-nose pliers are made with angled jaws. These are almost 90 deg., are used for inserting keys, etc.

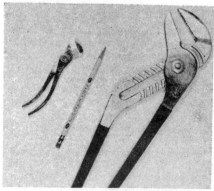

Available from small to large, these pliers are adjustable with aid of grooves; jaws are always parallel.

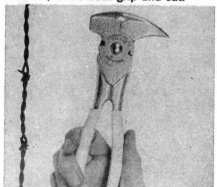

Half hammer, half plier, this tool is used for installing fencing. Jaws have cutters, projection is used for twisting.

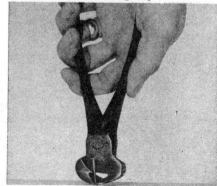

Sometimes used for cutting flush to a surface, these end cutters are more useful for pulling nails, staples.

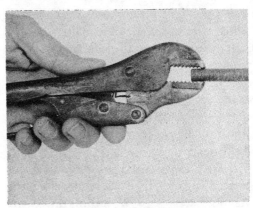

Clamp-type pliers grip with a locking action, are available with straight, curved and special-shape jaws.

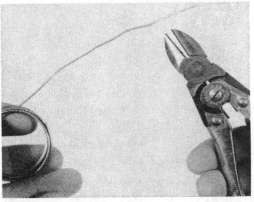

Another kind of diagonal cutters has a compound action that produces tremendous leverage.

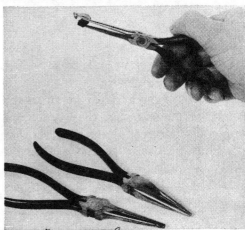

Long-nose, round-nose, needle-nose are names given for various configurations of this type.

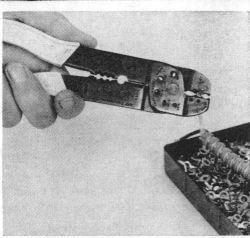

These specialty pliers strip insulation from wire, will rethread small screws and crimp fittings on wire.

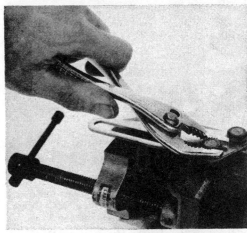

Slip-jaw pliers are made with both straight and angled jaws. The latter provide hand clearance.

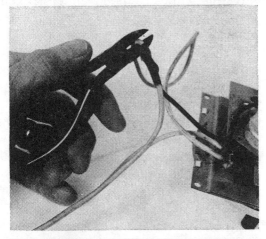

Diagonal-cutting pliers, "dykes" is the common term, are a must for almost any kind of wire work.

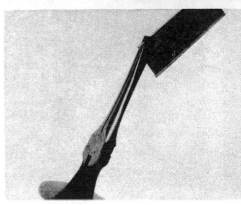

"Duck-bill" pliers are handy for holding and positioning flat work, for making bends in metal.

This type plier has two or more oval-shape openings for gripping brass, copper, aluminum tubing.

WRENCHES

A wrench is a basic tool that is used to exert a twisting force on bolt heads, nuts, studs and pipes.

The best wrenches are made of chrome vanadium steel. Wrenches made of this material are light in weight and almost unbreakable. This is an expensive material, however, so the most common wrenches are made of forged carbon steel or molybdenum steel. These latter materials make good wrenches, but they are generally built a little heavier and bulkier in order to achieve the same degree of strength as chrome vanadium steel.

The size of any wrench used on bolt-heads or nuts is determined by the size of the opening between the jaws of the wrench. The opening of a wrench is manufactured slightly larger than the bolt head or nut that it is designed to fit. Hexnuts (six-sided) and other types of nut or bolt heads are measured across opposite flats. A wrench that is designed to fit a 3/8-inch nut or bolt usually has a clearance of from 5 to 8 thousandths of an inch. This clearance allows the wrench to slide on and off the nut or bolt with a minimum of "play." If the wrench is too large, the points of the nut or bolt head will be rounded and destroyed.

Open-End Wrenches

Solid, nonadjustable wrenches with openings in one or both ends are called open-end wrenches. Usually they come in sets of from 6 to 10 wrenches with sizes ranging from 5/16 to 1 inch. Wrenches with small openings are usually shorter than wrenches with large openings. This proportions the lever advantage of the wrench to the bolt or stud and helps prevent wrench breakage or damage to the bolt or stud.

Open-end wrenches may have their jaws parallel to the handle or at angles anywhere up to 90 degrees. The average angle is 15 degrees. The angular displacement variation permits selection of a wrench suited for places where there is room to make only a part of a complete turn of a nut or bolt. If the wrench is turned over after the first swing, it will fit on the same flats and turn the the nut farther. After two swings on the wrench, the nut is turned far enough so that a new set of flats are in position for the wrench.

Handles are usually straight, but may be curved. Those with curved handles are called S-wrenches. Other open-end wrenches may have offset handles. This allows the head to reach nut or bolt heads that are sunk below the surface.

Box Wrenches

Box wrenches are safer than open-end wrenches since there is less likelihood they will slip off the work. They completely surround or box a nut or bolt head.

The most frequently used box wrench has 12 points or notches arranged in a circle in the head and can be used with a minimum swing angle of 30 degrees. Six and eight point wrenches are used for heavy, 12 for medium, and 16 for light duty only.

One advantage of the 12-point construction is the thin wall. It is more suitable for turning nuts which are hard to get at with an open-end wrench. Another advantage is that the wrench will operate between obstructions where the space for handle swing is limited. A very short swing of the handle will turn the nut far enough to allow the wrench to be lifted and the next set of points fitted to the corner of the nut.

Combination Wrenches

After a tight nut is broken loose, it can be unscrewed much more quickly with an open-end wrench than with a box wrench. This is where a combination box-open end wrench comes in handy. You can use the box-end for breaking nuts loose or for tightening them, and the open-end for faster turning.

The box-end portion of the wrench can be designed with an offset in the handle. The 15-degree offset allows clearance over nearby parts.

Using Wrenches. The correct use of open-end and box-end wrenches can be summed up in a few simple rules, most important of which is to be sure that the wrench properly fits the nut or bolt head.

When you have to pull hard on the wrench, as in loosening a tight nut, make sure the wrench is seated squarely on the flats of the nuts.

Pull on the wrench—do not push. Pushing a wrench is a good way to skin your knuckles if the wrench slips or the nut breaks loose unexpectedly. If it is impossible to pull the wrench, and you must push, do it with the palm of your hand and hold your palm open.

Only actual practice will tell you if you are using the right amount of force on the wrench. The best way to tighten a nut is to turn it until the wrench has a firm, solid "feel." This will turn the nut to proper tightness without stripping the threads or twisting off the bolt. This "feel" is developed by experience alone. Practice until you have mastered the "feel."

Socket Wrenches

The socket wrench is one of the most versatile wrenches in your tool box. Basically, it consists of a handle and a socket type wrench which can be attached to the handle.

The "Spintite" wrench is a special type of socket wrench. It has a hollow shaft to accommodate a bolt protruding through a nut, has a hexagonal head, and is used like a screwdriver. It is supplied in small sizes only and is useful for assembly and electrical work. When used for the latter purpose, it must have an insulated handle.

A complete socket wrench set consists of several types of handles along with bar extensions, adapters, and a variety of sockets.

Sockets. A socket has a square opening cut in one end to fit a square drive lug on a detachable handle. In the other end of the socket is a 6-point or 12-point opening very much like the opening in the box end wrench. The 12-point socket needs to be swung only half as far as the 6-point socket before it has to be lifted and fitted on the nut for a new grip. It can therefore be used in closer quarters where there is less room to move the handle. (A ratchet handle eliminates the necessity of lifting the socket and refitting it on the nut again and again.)

Sockets are classified for size according to two factors. One is the size of the square opening, which fits on the square drive lug of the handle. This size is known as the drive size. The other is the size of the opening in the opposite end, which fits the nut or bolt. The standard tool box can be outfitted with sockets having 1/4-, 3/8-, and 1/2-inch-square drive lugs. The openings that fit onto the bolt or nut are usually graduated in 1/16-inch sizes. Sockets are also made in deep lengths to fit over spark plugs and long bolt ends.

Socket Handles. There are four types of handles used with these sockets. Each type has special advantages; choose the one best suited for the job at hand. The square driving lug on the socket wrench handle has a spring-loaded ball that fits into a recess in the socket receptacle. This mated ball-recess feature keeps the socket engaged with the drive lug during normal usage. A slight pull on the socket, however, disassembles the connection.

The ratchet handle has a reversing lever which operates a pawl (or dog) inside the head of the tool. Pulling the handle in one direction causes the pawl to engage in the ratchet teeth and turn the socket. Moving the handle in the opposite direction causes the pawl to slide over the teeth, permitting the handle to back up without moving the socket. This allows rapid turning of the nut or bolt after each partial turn of the handle. With the reversing lever in one position, the handle can be used for tightening. In the other position, it can be used for loosening.

The hinged handle is also very convenient. To loosen tight nuts, swing the handle at right angles to the socket. This gives the greatest possible leverage. After loosening the nut to the point where it turns easily, move the handle into the vertical position and then turn the handle with fingers.

When using the sliding bar or T-handle, the head can be positioned anywhere along the sliding bar. Select the position which is needed for the job at hand.

The speed handle is worked like the woodworker's brace. After the nuts are first loosened with the sliding bar handle or the ratchet handle, the speed handle can be used to remove the nuts more quickly. In many instances the speed handle is not strong enough to be used for breaking loose or tightening the nuts. The speed socket wrench should be used carefully to avoid damaging the nut threads.

Accessories. To complete the socket wrench set, there are several accessory items. Extension bars of different lengths are made to extend the distance from the socket to the handle. A universal joint allows the nuts to be turned with the wrench handle at an angle. Universal sockets are also available. The use of universal joints, bar extensions, and universal sockets in combination with appropriate handles makes it possible to form a variety of tools that will reach otherwise inaccessible nuts and bolts.

Another accessory item is an adapter which

allows you to use a handle having one size of drive and a socket having a different size drive. For example, a 3/8-by 1/4-inch adapter makes it possible to turn all 1/4-inch square drive sockets with any 3/8-inch square drive handle.

Adjustable Wrenches

A handy all-round wrench that is generally included in every tool box is the adjustable open-end wrench. This wrench is not intended to take the place of the regular solid open-end wrench. Additionally, it is not built for use on extremely hard-to-turn items. Its usefulness is achieved by being capable of fitting odd-sized nuts. This flexibility is achieved although one jaw of the adjustable open-end wrench is fixed, because the other jaw is moved along a slide by a thumbscrew adjustment. By turning the thumbscrew, the jaw opening may be adjusted to fit various sizes of nuts.

Adjustable wrenches are available in varying sizes ranging from 4 to 24 inches in length. The size of the wrench selected for a particular job is dependent upon the size of nut or bolt head to which the wrench is to be applied. As the jaw opening increases the length of the wrench increases.

Using Adjustable Wrenches. Adjustable wrenches are often called "knuckle busters," because people frequently suffer these consequences as a result of improper usage of these tools. To avoid accidents, follow four simple steps. First, choose a wrench of the correct size; that is, do not pick a large 12-inch wrench and adjust the jaw for use on a 3/8-inch nut. This could result in a broken bolt and a bloody hand. Second, be sure the jaws of the correct size wrench are adjusted to fit snugly on the nut. Third, position the wrench around the nut until the nut is all the way into the throat of the jaws. If not used in this manner, the result is apt to be as bloody as before. Fourth, pull the handle toward the side having the adjustable jaw. This will prevent the adjustable jaw from springing open and slipping off the nut. If the location of the work will not allow for all four steps to be followed when using an adjustable wrench, then select another type of wrench for the job.

Pipe Wrench (Stillson). When rotating or holding round work an adjustable pipe wrench (Stillson) may be used. The movable jaw on a pipe

wrench is pivoted to permit a gripping action on the work. This tool must be used with discretion, as the jaws are serrated and always make marks on the work unless adequate precautions are observed. The jaws should be adjusted so the bite on the work will be taken at about the center of the jaws.

Chain Pipe Wrench. A different type pipe wrench, used mostly on large sizes of pipes is the chain pipe wrench. This tool works in one direction only, but can be backed partly around the work and a fresh hold taken without freeing the chain. To reverse the operation the grip is taken on the opposite side of the head. The head is double ended and can be reversed when the teeth on one end are worn out.

Strap Wrench. The strap wrench is similar to the chain pipe wrench but uses a heavy web strap in place of the chain. This wrench is used for turning pipe or cylinders where you do not want to mar the surface of the work. To use this wrench, the webbed strap is placed around the cylinder and passed through the slot in the metal body of the wrench. The strap is then pulled up tight and as you turn the wrench in the desired direction, the webbed strap tightens further around the cylinder. This gripping action causes the cylinder to turn.

Spanner Wrenches

Many special nuts are made with notches cut into their outer edge. For these nuts a hook spanner is required. This wrench has a curved arm with a lug or hook on the end. This lug fits into one of the notches of the nut and the handle turned to loosen or tighten the nut. This spanner may be made for just one particular size of notched nut, or it may have a hinged arm to adjust it to a range of sizes.

Another type of spanner is the pin spanner. Pin spanners have a pin in place of a hook. This pin fits into a hole in the outer part of the nut.

Face pin spanners are designed so that the pins fit into holes in face of the nut.

When you use a spanner wrench, you must ensure that the pins, lugs, or hooks make firm contact with the nut while the turning force is transferred from the wrench to the nut. If this is not done, damage will result.

Setscrew Wrenches (Allen and Bristol)

In some places it is desirable to use recessed heads on setscrews and capscrews. One type (Allen) screw is used extensively on office machines and in machine shops. The other type (Bristol) is used infrequently.

Recessed head screws usually have a hex-shaped (six-sided) recess. To remove or tighten this type screw requires a special wrench that will fit in the recess. This wrench is called an Allen-type wrench. Allen-type wrenches are made from hexagonal L-shaped bars of tool steel. They range in size up to 3/4 inch. When using the Allen-type wrench make sure you use the correct size to prevent rounding or spreading the head of the screw. A snug fit within the recessed head of the screw is an indication that you have the correct size.

The Bristol wrench is made from round stock. It is also L-shaped, but one end is fluted to fit the flutes of little splines in the Bristol setscrew.

Safety Rules for Wrenches

There are a few basic rules that you should keep in mind when using wrenches.

Always use a wrench that fits the nut properly.

Keep wrenches clean and free from oil. Otherwise they may slip, resulting in possible serious injury to you or damage to the work.

Do not increase the leverage of a wrench by placing a pipe over the handle. Increased leverage may damage the wrench or the work.

Provide some sort of kit or case for all wrenches. Return them to it at the completion of each job. This saves time and trouble and facilitates selection of tools for the next job.

Determine which way a nut should be turned before trying to loosen it. Most nuts are turned counterclockwise for removal.

Learn to select your wrenches to fit the type of work you are doing.

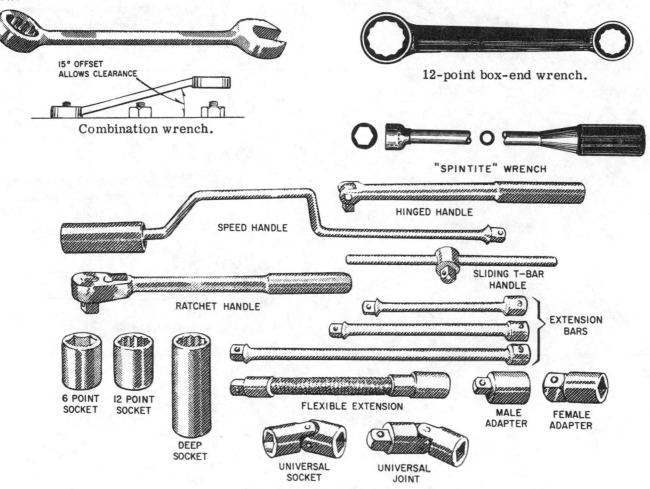

15° OFFSET ALLOWS CLEARANCE

Combination wrench.

12-point box-end wrench.

"SPINTITE" WRENCH

HINGED HANDLE

SPEED HANDLE

SLIDING T-BAR HANDLE

RATCHET HANDLE

EXTENSION BARS

6 POINT SOCKET   12 POINT SOCKET

FLEXIBLE EXTENSION

MALE ADAPTER   FEMALE ADAPTER

DEEP SOCKET

UNIVERSAL SOCKET   UNIVERSAL JOINT

Socket set components.

Socket end

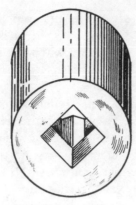

Drive end

12-point sockets.

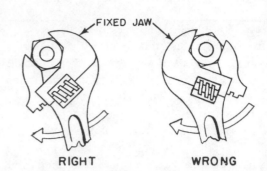

RIGHT WRONG

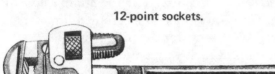

Adjustable pipe wrench.

Allen wrench.

Bristol wrench.

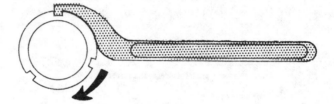

Hook Spanner.

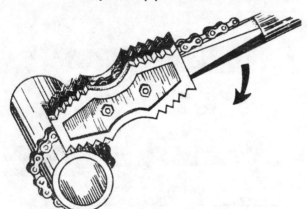

Chain pipe wrench.

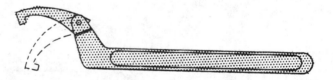

Adjustable Hook Spanner.

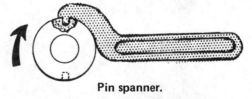

Pin spanner.

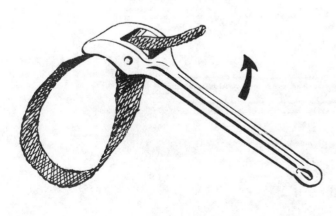

Strap wrench.

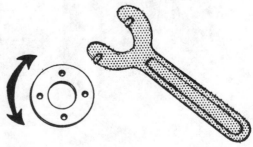

Face pin spanner.

20

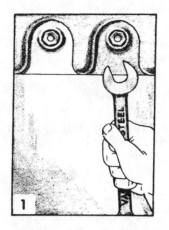

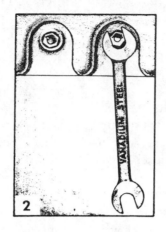

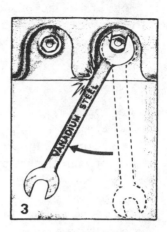

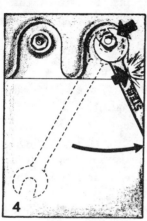

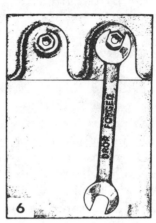

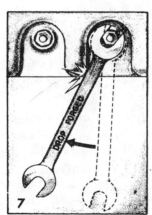

1. WRENCH, WITH OPENING SLOPING TO THE LEFT, ABOUT TO BE PLACED ON NUT.

2. WRENCH POSITIONED AND READY TO TIGHTEN NUT. NOTE THAT SPACE FOR SWINGING THE WRENCH IS LIMITED.

3. WRENCH HAS BEEN MOVED CLOCKWISE TO TIGHTEN THE NUT AND NOW STRIKES THE CASTING WHICH PREVENTS FURTHER MOVEMENT.

4. WRENCH IS REMOVED FROM NUT AND TURNED COUNTER CLOCKWISE TO BE PLACED ON THE NEXT SET OF FLATS ON NUT. BUT CORNER OF CASTING PREVENTS WRENCH FROM FITTING ONTO THE NUT.

5. WRENCH IS BEING FLOPPED OVER SO THAT WRENCH OPENING WILL SLOPE TO THE RIGHT.

6. IN THIS FLOPPED POSITION, THE WRENCH WILL FIT THE NEXT TWO FLATS ON THE NUT.

7. WRENCH NOW IS PULLED CLOCKWISE TO FURTHER TIGHTEN NUT UNTIL WRENCH AGAIN STRIKES CASTING. BY REPEATING THE FLOPPING PROCEDURE, THE NUT CAN BE TURNED UNTIL IT IS TIGHT.

BORING TOOLS

When working with wood, you will frequently be required to bore holes. It is important, therefore, that you know the proper procedures and tools used for this job. Auger bits and a variety of braces and drills are used extensively for boring purposes.

Auger Bits

Bits are used for boring holes for screws, dowels, and hardware, as an aid in mortising (cutting a cavity in wood for joining members) and in shaping curves and for many other purposes. Like saws and planes, bits vary in shape and structure with the type of job to be done.

Auger bits are screw-shaped tools consisting of six parts: the cutter, screw, spur, twist, shank, and tang. The twist ends with two sharp points called the spurs, which score the circle, and two cutting edges which cut shavings within the scored circle. The screw centers the bit and draws it into the wood. The threads of the screw are made in three different pitches: steep, medium, and fine. The steep pitch makes for quick boring and thick chips, and the fine or slight pitch makes for slow boring and fine chips. For end-wood boring, a steep- or medium-pitch screw bit should be used because end wood is likely to be forced in between the fine screw threads, and that will prevent the screw iron from taking hold. The twist carries the cuttings away from the cutters and deposits them in a mound around the hole.

The size of auger bits are indicated in sixteenths of an inch and are stamped on the tang. A number 10 stamped on the tang means 10/16 or 5/8 in.; number 5 means 5/16 in. and so on. The most common woodworkers auger bit set ranges in size from 1/4 to 1 in.

Ordinary auger bits up to 1 in. in diameter are from 7 to 9 inches long. Short auger bits that are about 3½ inches long are called dowel bits.

Expansive auger bits have adjustable cutters, for boring holes of different diameters. Expansive bits are generally made in two different sizes. The largest size has three cutters and cores holes up to 4 inches in diameter. A scale on the cutter blade indicates the diameter of the hole to be bored.

Braces and Drills

The auger bit is the tool that actually does the cutting in the wood; however, it is necessary that another tool be used to hold the auger bit and give you enough leverage to turn the bit. The tools most often used for holding the bit are the carpenter's brace, breast drill, and push drill.

Boring Through-Holes in Wood

To bore a hole in wood with an auger bit, first select the proper fit indicated on or near the square tang. Then you insert the auger bit into the chuck.

To chuck the bit, hold the shell of the chuck as you turn the handle to open the jaws. When the jaws are apart far enough to take the square tang of the bit, insert it until the end seats in the square driving socket at the bottom of the chuck. Then tighten the chuck by turning the handle to close the jaws and hold the bit in place.

With a chuck having no driving socket (a square hole which is visible if you look directly into the chuck), additional care must be taken to seat and center the corners of the tapered shank in the V grooves of the chuck jaws. In this type of chuck the jaws serve to hold the bit in the center and to prevent it from coming out of the chuck.

After placing the point of the feed screw at the location of the center of the hole you will bore, steady the brace against your body, if possible, with the auger bit square with the surface of the work.

To bore a vertical hole in stock held in a bench vise, hold the brace and bit perpendicular to the surface of the work.

Another way to bore a through hole without splitting out on the opposite face is to reverse the bit one or two turns when the feed screw just becomes visible through this opposite face. This will release the bit. Remove the bit while pulling it up and turning it clockwise. This will remove the loose chips from the hole. Finish the hole by boring from the opposite face. This will remove the remaining material which is usually in the form of a wooden disk held fast to the feed screw.

Twist Drill. An ordinary twist drill may be used to drill holes in wood. Select a twist drill of the size required. Secure the job to the table with a pair of C-clamps. Place a block of wood beneath the job. In drilling through wood, a backup block is used to ensure a clean hole at the bottom of the job.

A breast drill is used by turning the crank handle with one hand as you hold the side handle with the other hand. This will steady the breast drill while feed pressure is applied by resting your chest on the breast plate. When drilling a horizontal hole, apply feed pressure by resting your body against the breast plate.

In drilling a horizontal hole with the hand drill, operate the crank with the right hand and with the left hand guide the drill by holding the handle which is opposite the chuck end of the drill.

Push Drill. This drill can be used to drill· either horizontal or vertical holes when the accuracy of the right angle with the work is not critical.

The drill point used in push drills is a straight flute drill. Sharpen its point on the grinder and provide only slight clearance behind the cutting edge. It will drill holes in wood and other soft materials.

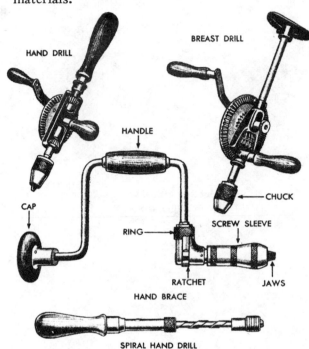

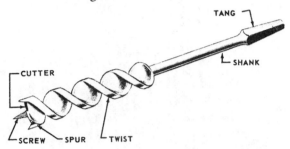

Nomenclature of an auger bit.

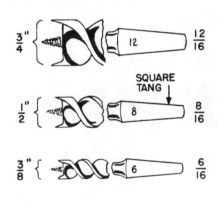

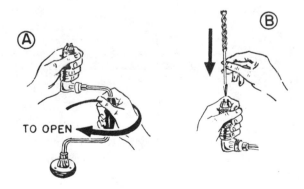

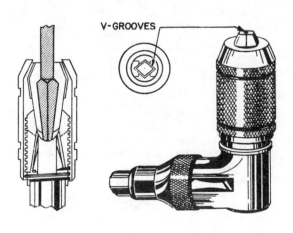

Placing an auger bit in a check.

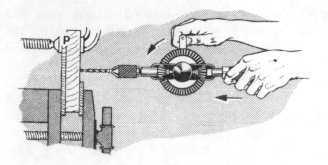

Drilling a hole
with a hand drill.

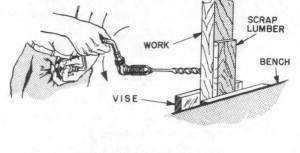

Using scrap lumber to prevent
splintering when boring.

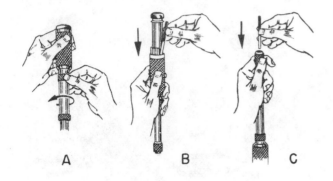

A   B   C

Selecting a drill for
use in a push drill.

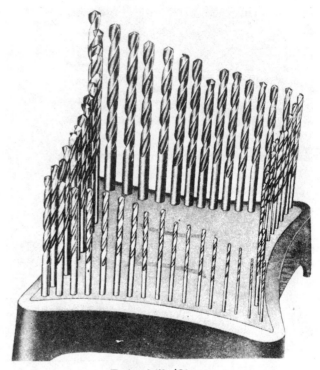

Twist drills (Sizes
No. 1 to No. 60).

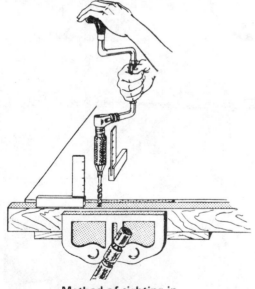

Method of sighting in
for perpendicular hole.

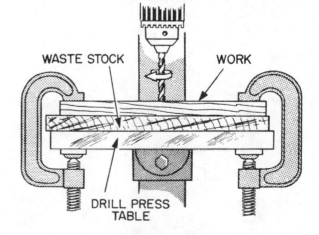

WASTE STOCK   WORK

DRILL PRESS
TABLE

Drilling a hole in
wood with a twist drill.

 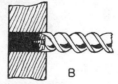

A   B

Boring a through hole
by reversing direction.

SNIPS

Snips are used for cutting sheet metal and steel of various thicknesses and shapes. Normally, the heavier or thicker materials are cut by shears.

One of the handiest tools for cutting light (up to 1/16 inch thick) sheet metal is the hand snip (tip snips). The straight hand snips have blades that are straight and cutting edges that are sharpened to an 85-degree angle. Snips like this can be obtained in different sizes ranging from the small 6-inch to the large 14-inch snip. Tin snips will also work on slightly heavier gauges of soft metals such as aluminum alloys.

Snips will not remove any metal when a cut is made. There is danger, though, of causing minute metal fractures along the edges of the metal during the shearing process. For this reason, it is better to cut just outside the layout line. This procedure will allow you to dress the cutting edge while keeping the material within required dimensions.

Cutting extremely heavy gauge metal always presents the possibility of springing the blades. Once the blades are sprung, hand snips are useless. When cutting heavy material use the rear portion of the blades. This procedure not only avoids the possibility of springing the blades but also gives you greater cutting leverage.

Many snips have small serrations (notches) on the cutting edges of the blades. These serrations tend to prevent the snips from slipping backwards when a cut is being made. Although this feature does make the actual cutting easier, it mars the edges of the metal slightly. You can remove these small cutting marks if you allow proper clearance for dressing the metal to size.

Safety and Care

Learn to use snips properly. They should always be oiled and adjusted to permit ease of cutting and to produce a surface that is free from burrs. If the blades bind, or if they are too far apart, the snips should be adjusted.

Never use snips as screwdrivers, hammers, or pry bars. They break easily.

Do not attempt to cut heavier materials than the snips are designed for. Never use tin snips to cut hardened steel wire or other similar objects. Such use will dent or nick the cutting edges of the blades.

Never toss snips in a toolbox where the cutting edges can come into contact with other tools. This dulls the cutting edges and may even break the blades.

When snips are not in use, hang them on hooks or lay them on an uncrowded shelf or bench.

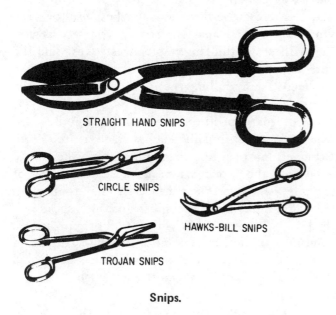

Snips.

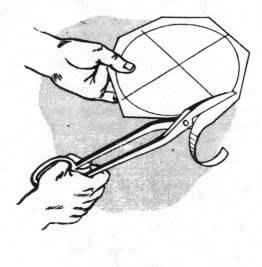

Cutting a disk out of sheet metal.

FILES

A tool box is not complete unless it contains an assortment of files. There are a number of different types of files in common use, and each type may range in length from 3 to 18 inches.

Grades

Files are graded according to the degree of fineness, and according to whether they have single- or double-cut teeth.

Single-cut files have rows of teeth cut parallel to each other. These teeth are set at an angle of about 65 degrees with the centerline. You will use single-cut files for sharpening tools, finish filing, and drawfiling. They are also the best tools for smoothing the edges of sheet metal.

Files with crisscrossed rows of teeth are double-cut files. The double cut forms teeth that are diamond-shaped and fast cutting. You will use double-cut files for quick removal of metal, and for rough work.

Files are also graded according to the spacing and size of their teeth, or their coarseness and fineness. The fineness or coarseness of file teeth is also influenced by the length of the file. (The length of a file is the distance from the tip to the heel, and does not include the tang or rough "handle."

You might like to compare the actual size of the teeth of a 6-inch, single-cut smooth file and a 12-inch, single-cut smooth file; notice the 6-inch file has more teeth per inch than the 12-inch file.

Shapes

Files come in different shapes. Therefore, in selecting a file for a job, the shape of the finished work must be considered.

Triangular files are tapered (longitudinally) on all three sides. They are used to file acute internal angles, and to clear out square corners. Special triangular files are used to file saw teeth.

Mill files are tapered in both width and thickness. One edge has no teeth and is known as a safe edge. Mill files are used for smoothing lathe work, drawfiling, and other fine, precision work. Mill files are always single-cut.

Flat files are general-purpose files and may be either single- or double-cut. They are tapered in width and thickness. Hard files are somewhat thicker than flat files. They taper slightly in thickness, but the edges are parallel.

The flat or hard files most often used are the double-cut for rough work and the single-cut, smooth file for finish work.

Square files are tapered on all four sides and are used to enlarge rectangular-shaped holes and slots. Round files serve the same purpose for round openings. Small round files are often called "rat-tail" files.

The half round file is a general-purpose tool. The rounded side is used for curved surfaces and the flat face on flat surfaces. When you file an inside curve, use a round or half-round file whose curve most nearly matches the curve of the work.

Kits of small files, often called "Swiss Pattern" or "Jewelers" files, are used to fit parts of delicate mechanisms, and for filing work on instruments. Handle these small files carefully because they break easily.

How to Use a File

Using a file is an operation that is nearly indispensable when working with metal. You may be crossfiling, drawfiling, using a file card, or even polishing metal.

When you have finished using a file it may be necessary to use an abrasive cloth or paper to finish the product. Whether this is necessary depends on how fine a finish you want on the work.

Crossfiling. Crossfiling means the file is being moved across the surface of the work in approximately a crosswise direction. For best results, keep your feet spread apart to steady yourself as you file with slow, full-length, steady strokes. The file cuts as you push it—ease up on the return stroke to keep from dulling the teeth. Keep your file clean.

Alternate positions of the file will be used when an exceptionally flat surface is required. Using either position first, file across the entire length of the stock again. Because the teeth of the file pass over the surface of the stock from two directions, the high spots and low spots will readily be visible after filing in both positions. Continue filing first in one position or direction and then the other until the surface has been filed flat. Test the flatness with a straight edge.

Using a File Card. As you file, the teeth of the file may "clog up" with some of the metal filings and scratch your work. This condition is known as pinning. You can prevent pinning by keeping the file teeth clean. Rubbing chalk between the teeth will help prevent pinning, too, but the best method is to clean the file frequently with a file card or brush. A file card has fine wire bristles. Brush with a pulling motion, holding the card parallel to the rows of teeth.

Always keep the file clean, whether you're filing mild steel or other metals. Use chalk liberally when filing nonferrous metals.

Drawfiling. Drawfiling produces a finer surface finish and usually a flatter surface than crossfiling. Small parts are best held in a vise. The cutting stroke is directed away from you when the handle of the file is held in the right hand. If the handle is held in the left hand, the cutting stroke will be toward you. Lift the file away from the surface of the work on the return stroke. When drawfiling will no longer improve the surface texture, wrap a piece of abrasive cloth around the file and polish the surface.

Care of Files

A new file should be broken in carefully by using it first on brass, bronze, or smooth cast iron. Just a few of the teeth will cut at first, so use a light pressure to prevent tooth breakage.

Do not break in a new file by using it first on a narrow surface.

Protect the file teeth by hanging your files in a rack when they are not in use, or by placing them in drawers with wooden partitions. Your files should not be allowed to rust—keep them away from water and moisture. Avoid getting the files oily. Oil causes a file to slide across the work and prevents fast, clean cutting. Files that you keep in your tool box should be wrapped in paper or cloth to protect their teeth and prevent damage to other tools.

Never use a file for prying or pounding. The tang is soft and bends easily. The body is hard and extremely brittle. Even a slight bend or a fall may cause a file to snap in two. Do not strike a file against the bench or vise to clean it—use a file card.

Safety

Never use a file unless it is equipped with a tight-fitting handle. If you use a file without the handle and it bumps something or jams to a sudden stop, the tang may be driven into your hand. To put a handle on a file tang, drill a hole in the handle, slightly smaller than the tang. Insert the tang end, and then tap the end of the handle to seat it firmly. Make sure you get the handle on straight.

SINGLE CUT

DOUBLE CUT

Single and double-cut files.

SINGLE CUT

BASTARD CUT   SECOND CUT   SMOOTH

DOUBLE CUT

BASTARD CUT   SECOND CUT   SMOOTH

Design and spacing of file teeth.

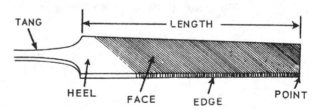

TANG   LENGTH

HEEL   FACE   EDGE   POINT

File nomenclature.

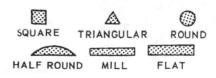

SQUARE   TRIANGULAR   ROUND

HALF ROUND   MILL   FLAT

Cross-sectional shapes of files.

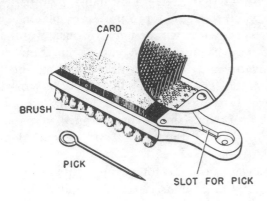

File cleaner.

Crossfiling a piece of mild steel.

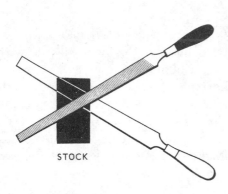

Alternating positions when filing.

Drawfiling a small part.

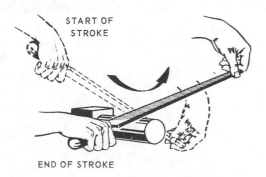

Filing round metal stock.

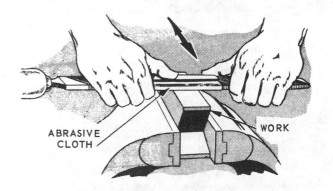

Polishing metal with abrasive
cloth wrapped around a file.

PLANES

While power tools are used for many of the jobs that used to be done with hand planes, there still are many operations that demand the muscle-powered wood trimmers.

Trimming a sticking door, for example, is quickly done with a few strokes of a plane. Fitting a piece of paneling in that odd-angled corner is another place where a pass or two of a hand plane is required. You plane that fraction of an inch away, at the proper angle, and the paneling slips easily into place.

We will not get into the debate on wooden versus metal planes, because in this country most craftsmen (yes, there are some exceptions) use metal planes. Our fellow craftsmen in England still use many of the wooden tools, and they have retained the skill to adjust the blade, then lock it in place with the wedge. It must be admitted that wood against wood is a better idea for fine furniture.

Types of Planes

If you don't have a powered jointer-planer, then a jointer plane is the tool for matching edges of stock to be edge-glued into larger panels.

If you want only one plane in your tool box, then a jack plane is the choice. With patience it can even be used to edge-fit.

Another handy tool is the smoothing plane about 9 in. long and used for final touch-up to get a glass-smooth finish. Note in the background that the sole of the jointer plane is grooved; this permits it to be used on green and gummy wood with less drag.

Easily slipped into even small "carryall" tool boxes is the block plane that can be used for making final adjustments, trimming doors and windows, jointing the ends of molding, etc.

If you do work with models, or miniatures such as doll furniture, a "shingle" plane is a must. Some modern versions use a double-edge razor blade as the plane "iron."

If you are working on antique furniture, or making reproductions, one type of plane that will be invaluable is a spokeshave. It can be used on both inside and outside curves, as on pediments. As its name implies, in the old days it was used for shaping wooden spokes for wheels.

One of the most versatile of the hundreds of planes available is the rabbet plane for which a variety of blades can be obtained for shaping and molding. They are still sold today. Another "antique" still being made is the router plane, generally used for making dadoes and grooves.

One type of rabbet plane is used just for cutting tongue-and-groove joints. You won't find these in just any store.

A modern type of plane is the "Surform" by Stanley. The one shown is a sort of block plane. There is a type definitely shaped like a plane. The cutting surface is readily changed; there is now a way to sharpen it.

Tips on Planing

One basic rule when using any type hand plane is that you must work with the grain. If you try to cut against the grain the result will be lifted chips and a rough surface. In a situation where you can't turn the work to permit going with the grain, reverse the plane and pull it toward you. A bit tricky at first, but with a little practice you can do a good job.

Another good tip when planing: plane across the grain first, then with the grain on the edge, so that chips are removed. Where the edge is not to be planed, clamp a wooden block snugly to the edge of the work. Chipping then will occur on the scrap block.

Cutting across end grain is best done with a "low-angle" iron, as is available in some block planes. If you do much end-grain work it would be worthwhile to get a low-angle unit.

There is no real mystery in removing a plane iron for sharpening. The first step is to lift the locking lever. Next lift out the plane iron and cap. On most planes you can use the end of the lever cap to turn the screw holding the iron to the cap.

A commercial, or shop-made jig can be used to hone the iron at the correct angle. When you reassemble the iron and cap, allow the cap to project 1/16 to 1/8 in. The adjusting nut lowers and raises the iron for depth of cut.

No matter how many power tools you have, one or more hand planes are a must for a complete set of tools. And good ones last a lifetime.

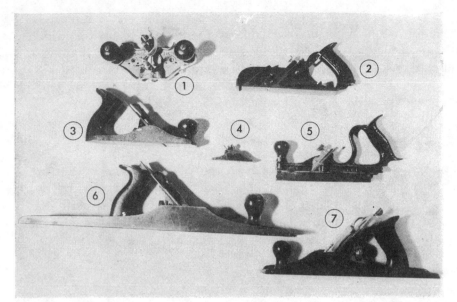

1. Router plane, 2. Rabbet plane, 3. Smoothing plane, 4. Shingle plane, 5. Tongue-and-groove plane, 6. Jointer plane, 7. Jack plane.

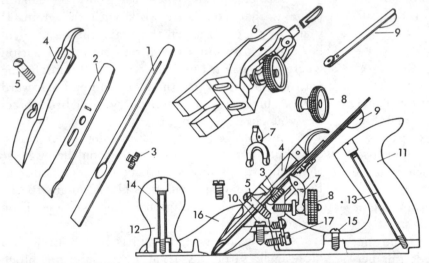

1. SINGLE PLANE IRON	7. "Y" ADJUSTING LEVER	13. HANDLE BOLT AND NUT
2. PLANE-IRON CAP	8. ADJUSTING NUT	14. KNOB BOLT AND NUT
3. CAP SCREW	9. LATERAL ADJUSTING LEVER	15. HANDLE SCREW
4. LEVER CAP	10. FROG SCREW	16. BOTTOM
5. LEVER-CAP SCREW	11. HANDLE	17. FROG-ADJUSTING SCREW
6. FROG COMPLETE	12. KNOB	

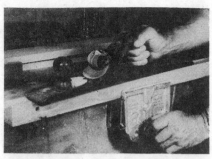

1. Largest hand plane is called a "jointer" and is the manual version of a powered jointer-planer.

2. Jack plane is moderate size, about 14 in. long. The tool for a "one-plane" workshop, can be used for variety of jobs.

3. Smoothing plane is about 9 in. long, used primarily for making those final "glass-smooth" cuts.

4. Small block plane is handy all-purpose tool that will fit in most "carry-all" tool boxes.

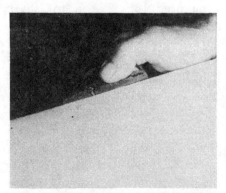

5. Smallest of planes is tiny "shingle plane," once used for fast shaping of wooden roof shingles.

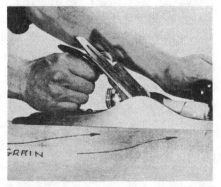

6. Plane must be used with the grain of wood; against the grain it will tear out chunks of wood, make rough surface.

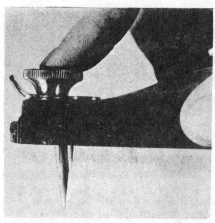

9. General-purpose block planes 6 or 7 in. long are available with both standard and "low-angle" irons.

7. Spokeshave is form of plane used for smoothing inside and outside curves. Once used for shaping wooden spokes.

8. When planing four sides of stock, cut across end grain first. Plane with grain to remove chipped areas.

12. On most planes, screw holding plane iron on plane-iron cap can be turned with end of lever cap, if not "frozen."

11. With lever cap removed, plane iron and plane-iron cap slip out easily, tipping assembly slightly to lift off.

10. First step in removing plane iron is to lift locking lever. Note that lever cap has a slot that fits lever-cap screw.

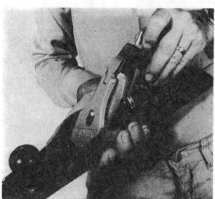

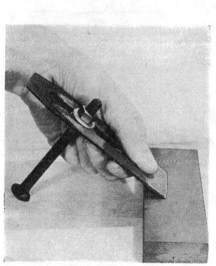

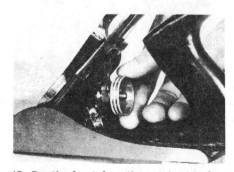

13. Plane iron is sharpened, maintaining angle. Ready-made jigs are available, but bolt is improvised angle jig.

14. Sharpened plane iron is attached to plane-iron cap, adjusted so blade projects about 1/16 in. Bevel is down.

15. Depth-of-cut is adjusted by turning depth-of-cut adjusting nut. This extends and retracts iron below surface.

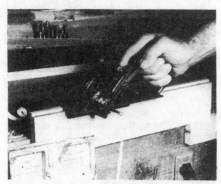

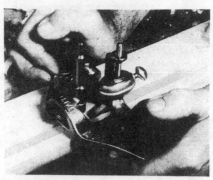

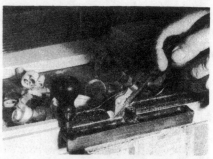

16. One of hundreds of types of planes is rabbeting plane, which cuts rabbets into the edges of stock.

17. Another unusual plane is routing plane, used for making dadoes. Used for dadoes in stairway stringers.

18. Old-time plane, not often seen, is this "tongue-and-groove" tool. Here it is being used to cut the tongue portion.

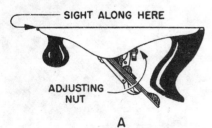

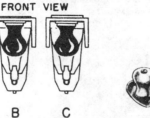

19. By loosening screw and reversing bottom guide, plane is adjusted to cut the groove that matches tongue it cuts.

20. Tongue-and-groove plane is held firmly against side of stock and groove is cut to match tongue.

21. While not a plane in the strictest sense of the term, this "Surform" by Stanley is used much like plane.

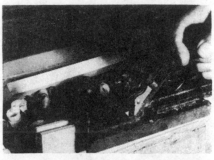

SIGHT ALONG HERE

ADJUSTING NUT

A

FRONT VIEW

B   C

Manipulation of the adjusting nut moves the plane iron up or down.

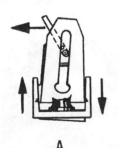

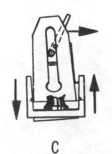

A   B   C

Effect of manipulation of the lateral adjustment lever.

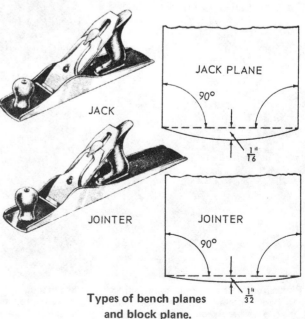

SMOOTHING

JACK

JOINTER

SMOOTH OR BLOCK

JACK PLANE
90°
$\frac{1"}{16}$

JOINTER
90°
$\frac{1"}{32}$

Types of bench planes and block plane.

COLD CHISELS (METAL CUTTING)

Chisels are tools that can be used for chipping or cutting metal. They will cut any metal that is softer than the materials of which they are made. Cold chisels, as they are sometimes called, are made from a good grade tool steel and have a hardened cutting edge and beveled head. Cold chisels are classified according to the shape of their points, and the width of the cutting edge denotes their size. The most common shapes of chisels are flat (cold chisel), cape, round nose, and diamond point.

The type chisel most commonly used is the flat cold chisel, which serves to cut rivets, split nuts, chip castings, and cut thin metal sheets. The cape chisel is used for special jobs like cutting keyways, narrow grooves and square corners. Round-nose chisels make circular grooves and chip inside corners with a fillet. Finally, the diamond-point is used for cutting V-grooves and sharp corners.

Using a Chisel

As with other tools there is a correct technique for using a chisel. Select a chisel that is large enough for the job. Be sure to use a hammer that matches the chisel; that is, the larger the chisel, the heavier the hammer. A heavy chisel will absorb the blows of a light hammer and will do virtually no cutting.

As a general rule, hold the chisel in the left hand with the thumb and first finger about 1 inch from the top. It should be held steadily but not tightly. The finger muscles should be relaxed, so if the hammer strikes the hand it will permit the hand to slide down the tool and lessen the effect of the blow. Keep the eyes on the cutting edge of the chisel, not on the head, and swing the hammer in the same plane as the body of the chisel. If you have a lot of chiseling to do, slide a piece of rubber hose over the chisel. This will lessen the shock to your hand.

When using a chisel for chipping, always wear goggles to protect your eyes. If other people are working close by, see that they are protected from flying chips by erecting a screen or shield to contain the chips. Remember that the time to take these precautions is before you start the job.

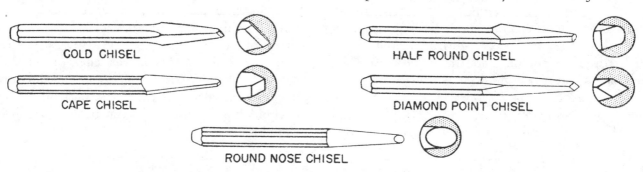

COLD CHISEL   CAPE CHISEL   ROUND NOSE CHISEL   HALF ROUND CHISEL   DIAMOND POINT CHISEL

WOOD CHISELS AND GOUGES

Wood chisels are an important and necessary part of any craftsman's tool collection. We are grouping gouges with chisels because they are a type of chisel and used for many woodworking jobs. Gouging the hollow for a wooden chair seat is one example of the work for which they can be used. In this case the gouge would have a U-shape cross section: others will be V-shape and they come in all sizes. Wood carving is where they are used most commonly, but they have many applications in furniture construction and even in house trimming.

You will need a special rounded stone, also called a "slip," for sharpening round gouges, and there are stones for honing the V-shape blades.

As with all tools, buy quality when you select chisels and gouges. They will last a lifetime, will hone to a razor edge and stay sharp a long time. That also means they are safer. Cheap chisels will dull quickly and require added effort to use, so your work will not be as accurate. Spoiled work can be expensive and you waste a lot of time. Buy quality.

Better chisels will have a one-piece blade and tang that extends through the handle of plastic or wood. Thus the force of hammer blows is directed right through the blade. The exceptions to this are quality wood chisels and gouges that have a V-pointed tang that is forced into a wooden handle. These chisels and gouges are for hand working only, and should not be struck with hammer or mallet.

Maintenance

Very little maintenance is required for quality chisels and gouges, but they should be honed frequently to keep the edges razor sharp. If the cutting edge of a chisel or gouge should ever become nicked, don't try to use it. Immediately grind the edge back to its proper shape, keeping the original angle of the bevel. When you have reshaped it, then hone it to razor sharpness.

Some high-carbon tool steel will rust readily in a damp environment, such as a basement workshop, so occasionally wipe your chisels with a rust-proofing oil.

Never store chisels loosely in a drawer. They will roll around and bang together and the cutting edges will become dulled. Instead, keep the chisels in a simple holder that will keep them upright and handy. Holes drilled in a board, or a simple assembly of strips to make openings can be used. In the holder shown in one photograph the chisels touch the workbench, so a strip of cork is tacked to the bench top to keep the blades clear of the dulling hardboard. Leather would do it as well.

Using Chisels and Gouges

Chisels and gouges can be used in two ways:

one is by pushing with the heel of one hand while the tool is guided with the fingers of the other hand. This method is used when only a small amount of material is to be removed and the finish must be smooth. A skilled craftsman can chamfer an edge or cut a shallow morise that appears to be "molded" in place, and there will be no need for sanding.

A second method of using chisels and gouges is with a mallet or hammer. Force is necessary when making vertical marking cuts for deep mortises, and when removing large chunks of wood. Square or round tenons also require the use of a hammer or mallet. The flat edge of the chisel is held against the cutting line, with the bevel on the "waste" side of the line.

Where possible, cuts should be made with the grain. Cutting is easier and the finish will be smoother. Generally the chisel will tend to ride up and out of the stock. When you cut against grain the the finish will be rough, and there usually is a tendency for the chisel to dig deeper. Against the grain take shallower "bites" and more of them.

Sharp chisels are safe when used properly, but those same sharp edges become dangerous when the tools are used improperly. Never cut toward yourself; a slip and you can cut yourself badly. Never hold the work in one hand and cut toward it with a chisel in the other hand. Clamp the work or hold it in a vise and keep both hands behind the chisel.

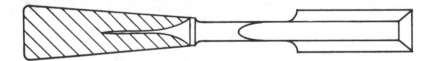

Of two types of chisels, best is one that has blade-tang-handle core and end cap; handle is molded plastic.

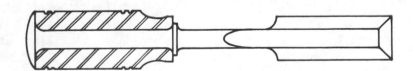

One important DON'T for wood chisels is not to push the tool toward any part of your body.

CUTTING MORTISE

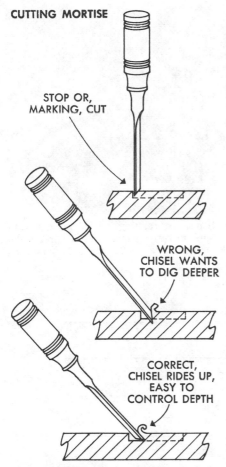

STOP OR, MARKING, CUT

WRONG, CHISEL WANTS TO DIG DEEPER

CORRECT, CHISEL RIDES UP, EASY TO CONTROL DEPTH

Whether job is horizontal or vertical, as in mortising a door frame, the chisel is held the same.

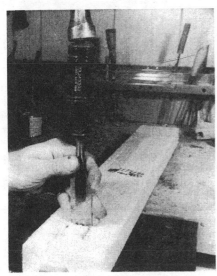

Mortise is started by first drilling series of holes inside lines marked for opening, then chisel is held vertical.

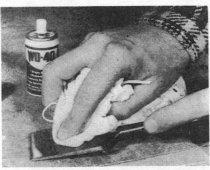

Good chisels are made of high-carbon tool steel that is susceptible to rust; wipe them occasionally with oil.

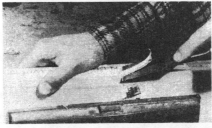

Another DON'T is holding the work with one hand and shoving the chisel toward that hand with the other; a certain cut.

Gouges are simply another form of wood chisel, the most common being curved in U-shape. Used for "scooping" seats.

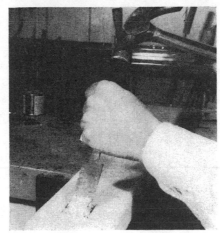

Cutting mortises is one of the most important jobs done with wood chisels. Note proper grip and use of the chisel.

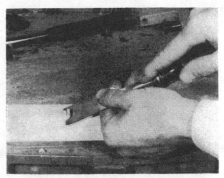

In many cases chisel is used without hammer. Heel of one hand is used to push chisel, other hand guides tool.

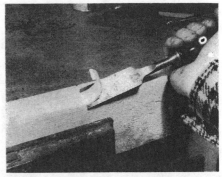

When you cut with the grain a nice curl is raised, or chip, and the surface under the cut will be smooth.

It sometimes will be necessary to cut across the grain of the wood, but the operation will tear the wood.

Handy storage at back of bench keeps chisels separated. Cork or leather on bench under them prevents dulling.

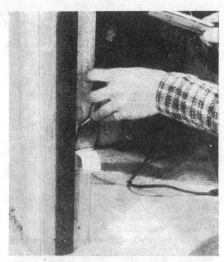

To cut recess (mortise) for door hinges, first mark outline with chisel cuts, then lift out wood, keeping bevel down.

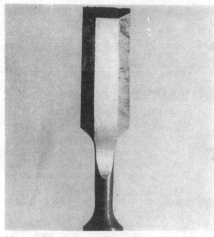

Most chisels can be honed for sharpness. This blade is badly nicked, so it will have to first be ground straight.

Use a sharpening stone frequently to hone chisel blades. This is "preventive maintenance" that assures sharp chisels.

When regrinding blades be sure to maintain existing angle, keep blade moving to prevent overheating the edge.

CORRECT ANGLE

HOLLOW GROUND

WRONG, BEVEL IS ROUNDED

Chisel blades should be ground flat at correct angle, or slightly hollow-ground. Never grind cutting edge round.

VISES AND CLAMPS

Vises are used for holding work when it is being planed, sawed, drilled, shaped, sharpened, or riveted, or when wood is being glued. Clamps are used for holding work which cannot be satisfactorily held in a vise because of its shape and size, or when a vise is not available. Clamps are generally used for light work.

Machinist's Bench Vise

This large vise has rough jaws that prevent the work from slipping. Most of these vises have a swivel base with jaws that can be rotated, while others cannot be rotated. A similar light duty model is equipped with a cutoff. These vises are usually bolt-mounted onto a bench.

Bench and Pipe Vise

The bench and pipe vise has integral pipe jaws for holding pipe from ¾ inch to 3 inches in diameter. The maximum working main jaw opening is usually 5 inches, with a jaw width of 4 to 5 inches. The base can be swiveled to any position and locked. These vises are equipped with an anvil and are also bolted onto a workbench.

Clamp Base Vise

This vise usually has a smaller holding capacity than the machinist's or the bench and pipe vise and is usually clamped to the edge of a bench with a thumbscrew. These type vises can be obtained with a maximum holding capacity varying between 1½ in. and 3 in. These vises normally do not have pipe holding jaws.

Blacksmith's Vise

Use a blacksmith's vise for holding work that must be pounded with a heavy hammer. It is fastened to a sturdy workbench or wall, and the long leg is secured into a solid base on the floor.

Pipe Vise

Specifically designed to hold round stock or pipe, this vise is also used on a bench. Some pipe vises are designed to use a section of chain to hold down the work. Chain pipe vises range in size from 1/8- to 2½-inch pipe capacity up to ½- to 8-inch pipe capacity.

C-Clamp

As the name implies, a C-Clamp is shaped like the letter C. It consists of a steel frame threaded to receive an operating screw with a swivel head. It is made for light, medium, and heavy service in a variety of sizes.

Hand Screw Clamp

A hand screw clamp consists of two hard maple jaws connected with two operating screws. Each jaw has two metal inserts into which the screws are threaded. The hand screw clamp is available in a variety of sizes.

Care

Keep vises clean at all times. They should be cleaned and wiped with light oil after using. Never strike a vise with a heavy object and never hold large work in a small vise, since these practices will cause the jaws to become sprung or otherwise damage the vise. Keep jaws in good condition and oil the screws and the slide frequently. Never oil the swivel base of swivel jaw joint; its holding power will be impaired. When the vise is not in use, bring the jaws lightly together or leave a very small gap. (The movable jaw of a tightly closed vise may break due to the expansion of the metal in heat.) Leave the handle in a vertical position.

Threads of C-clamps must be clean and free from rust. The swivel head must also be clean, smooth, and grit free. If the swivel head becomes damaged, replace it as follows: pry open the crimped portion of the head and remove the head from the ball end of the screw. Replace with a new head and crimp.

Safety Precautions

When closing the jaw of a vise or clamp, avoid getting any portion of your hands or body between the jaws or between one jaw and the work.

When holding heavy work in a vise, place a block of wood under the work as a prop to prevent it from sliding down and falling on your foot.

Do not open the jaws of a vise beyond their capacity, as the movable jaw will drop off.

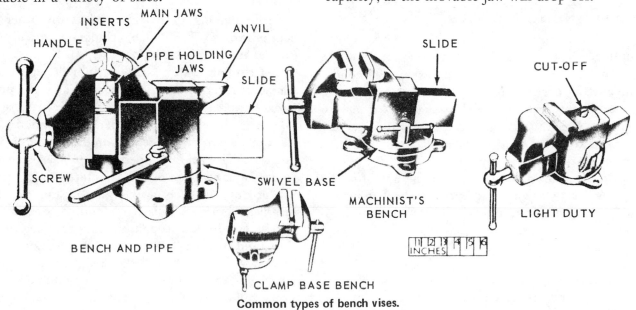

Common types of bench vises.

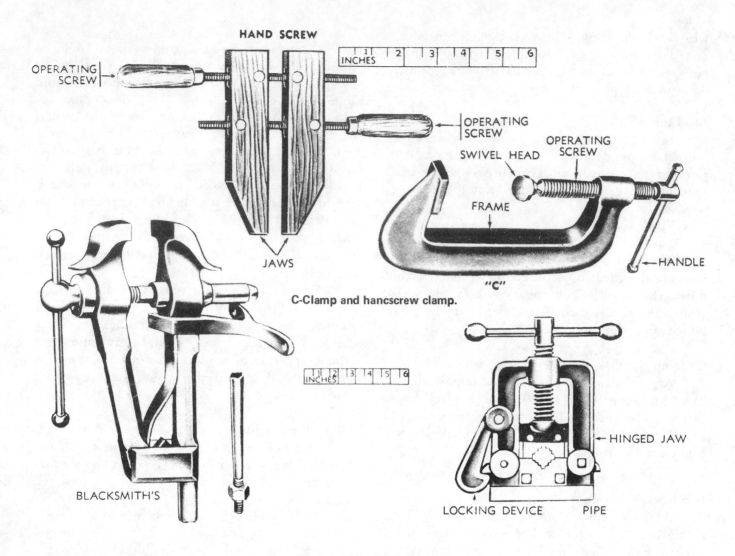

HAND SCREW

INCHES 1 2 3 4 5 6

OPERATING SCREW

OPERATING SCREW

SWIVEL HEAD

OPERATING SCREW

FRAME

JAWS

HANDLE

"C"

C-Clamp and hancscrew clamp.

BLACKSMITH'S

INCHES 1 2 3 4 5 6

HINGED JAW

LOCKING DEVICE   PIPE

Blacksmith's and pipe vises.

SHARPENING YOUR TOOLS

Grinding

To keep hand tools in the best usable condition, cutting edges must be sharpened frequently and certain other tools trued or shaped for special purposes. Chisels, punches, drills, tinsnips, screwdrivers, and other hand tools are shaped or sharpened on an abrasive grinding wheel.

Grinding may be defined as the act of shaping or wearing down a surface or sharpening an edge by means of the cutting action of thousands of abrasive grains on the surface of the grinding wheel. Excessive grinding shortens the useful life of a tool.

A variety of grinding machines are in use. Many of them are special machines used in tool and die making or machines used for other special purposes. The bench grinder is the type of grinder found in general use.

Grinding Safety. The grinding wheel is a fragile cutting tool which operates at high speeds. Great emphasis must be given, therefore, to the safe operation of bench and pedestal grinders.

What are the most common sources of injury during grinding operation? Hazards leading to eye injury caused by grit generated by the grinding process are the most common and the most serious. Abrasions caused by bodily contact with the wheel are quite painful and can be serious. Cuts and bruises caused by segments of an exploded wheel, or a tool "kicked" away from the wheel are other sources of injury. Cuts and abrasions can become infected if not protected from grit and dust from grinding.

Some guidelines for safe grinding practices are:

Study manufacturer's operating instructions.

Secure all loose clothing and remove rings or other jewelry.

Inspect the grinding wheel, wheel guards, the toolrest, and other safety devices to ensure they are in good condition and positioned properly.

Stand aside when starting the grinder motor until operating speed is reached. This prevents injury if the wheel explodes from a defect that has not been noticed.

Use light pressure when starting grinding; too much pressure on a cold wheel may cause failure.

Grind only on the face or outer circumference of a grinding wheel unless the wheel is specifically designed for side grinding.

Use a coolant to prevent overheating the work.

Wear goggles to protect your eyes from injury by grit and dust generated by grinding operations.

Grinding Wheels

A grinding wheel is composed of two basic elements: (1) the abrasive grains, and (2) the bonding agent. The abrasive grains may be compared to many single point tools embedded in a toolholder of bonding agent. Each of these grains extracts a very small chip from the material as it makes contact on each revolution of the grinding wheel.

An ideal cutting tool is one that will sharpen itself when it becomes dull. This, in effect, is what happens to the abrasive grains. As the individual grains become dull, the pressure that is generated on them causes them to fracture and present new sharp cutting edges to the work. When the grains can fracture no more, the pressure becomes too great and they are released from the bond, allowing new sharp grains to be presented to the work.

Grinding wheels come in various sizes and shapes. The size of a grinding wheel is given in terms of its diameter in inches, the diameter of the spindle hole, and the width of the face of the wheel. The shapes of grinding wheels are numerous. The specific job will dictate the shape of the wheel to be used.

Screwdrivers. To dress a common screwdriver, dress the sides so that the blade is symmetrical in shape. Then, square off the end. Check the squareness of the end by resting the tip on the handle of a trysquare and moving the shank of the screwdriver close to the blade of the square. If the blade and the shank appear to be parallel, the tip is square.

Tin Snips. To sharpen tin snips on a grinder, open the snips, resting the blade on the tool rest. Hold level the handle of the blade being ground and then rotate the other blade at whatever angle is necessary to grind the cutting edge to an included angle of 80º to 85º. Holding the blade lightly against the rotating wheel, move it from left to right across the face of the wheel. Sharpen first one blade of the snips and then the other.

Sharpening the snips requires close and careful attention; improper techniques may result in wrecking the snips or even in serious personal injury.

Cold Chisels. Never use a chisel whose head has been allowed to mushroom. You, or others, can be injured by chips or metal flying off the head when it is hammered.

Remove the ragged edges of such a head by grinding them off.

Using a Sharpening Stone

Sharpening stones are divided into two groups, natural and artificial. Some of the natural stones are oil treated during and after the manufacturing processes. The stones that are oil treated are sometimes called oilstones. Artificial stones are normally made of silicone carbide or aluminum oxide. Natural stones have very fine grains and are excellent for putting razorlike edges on fine cutting tools. Most sharpening stones have one coarse and one fine face. Some of these stones are mounted, and the working face of some of the sharpening stones is a combination of coarse and fine grains. Stones are available in a variety of shapes.

A fine cutting oil is generally used with most artificial sharpening stones; however, other lubricants such as kerosene may be used. When a tool has been sharpened on a grinder or grindstone, there is usually a wire edge or a feather edge left by the coarse wheel. The sharpening stones are used to hone this wire or feather edge off the cutting edge of the tool. Do not attempt to do a honing job with the wrong stone. Use a coarse stone to sharpen large and very dull or nicked tools. Use a medium grain stone to sharpen tools not requiring a finished edge, such as tools for working soft wood, cloth, leather, and rubber. Use a fine stone and an oilstone to sharpen and hone tools requiring a razorlike edge.

Prevent glazing of sharpening stones by applying a light oil during the use of the stone. Wipe the stone clean with wiping cloth or cotton waste after each use. If stone becomes glazed or gummed up, clean with aqueous ammonia or dry-cleaning solvent. If necessary, scour with aluminum oxide abrasive cloth or flint paper attached to a flat block.

At times, stones will become uneven from improper use. True the uneven surfaces on an old grinding wheel or on a grindstone. Another method of truing the surface is to lap it with a block of cast iron or other hard material covered with a waterproof abrasive paper, dipping the stone in water at regular intervals and continuing the lapping until the stone is true.

Stones must be carefully stored in boxes or on special racks when not in use. Never lay them down on uneven surfaces or place them where they may be knocked off a table or bench, or where heavy objects can fall on them. Do not store in a hot place.

Sharpening a Wood Chisel. To sharpen a wood chisel with a sharpening stone, use a common oilstone that has coarse grit on one side and fine grit on the other. Make sure the stone is firmly held so that it cannot move. Cover the stone with a light machine oil so that the fine particles of steel ground off will float and thus prevent the stone from clogging.

Hold the chisel in one hand with the bevel flat against the coarse side of the stone. Use the fingers of your other hand to steady the chisel and hold it down against the stone. Using smooth even strokes, rub the chisel back and forth parallel to the surface of the stone. The entire surface of the stone should be used to avoid wearing a hollow in the center of the stone. Do not rock the blade. The angle of the blade with the stone must remain constant during the whetting process.

After a few strokes, a burr, wire edge, or feather edge is produced. To remove the burr, first take a few strokes with the flat side of the chisel held flat on the fine grit side of the stone. Be careful not to raise the chisel even slightly; avoid putting the slightest bevel on the flat side, for then the chisel must be ground until the bevel is removed.

After whetting the flat side on the fine grit side of the stone, turn the chisel over and place the bevel side down and hold it at the same angle as used when whetting on the coarse side of the stone. Take two or three light strokes to remove the burr.

To test the sharpness of the cutting edge, hold the chisel where a good light will shine on the cutting edge. A keen edge does not reflect light in any position. If there are no shiny or white spots it is a good edge.

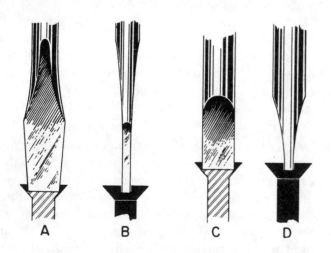

Shapes of screwdrivers when properly dressed.

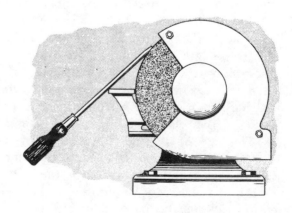

Brinding a screwdriver tip with a bench grinder.

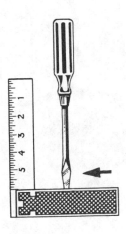

Checking the squareness
of the end of a screwdriver.

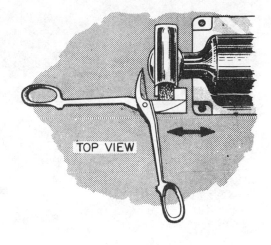

Sharpening snips
on a grinder.

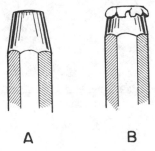

A   B

Good
and bad shaped
chisel heads.

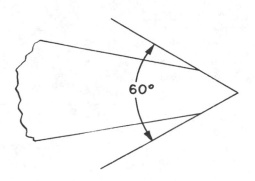

60°

Proper angle for
general use cold chisel.

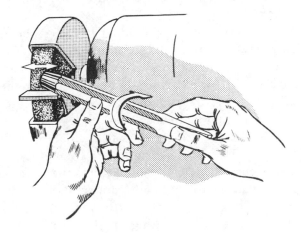

Grinding a chisel head
with a bench grinder.

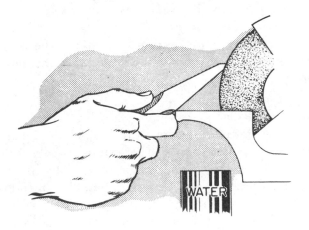

WATER

Sharpening a chisel
with a grinder.

41

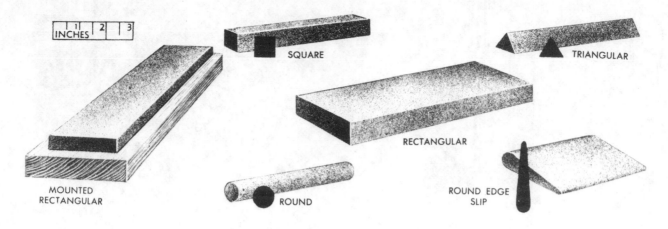

Shapes of sharpening stones and oilstones.

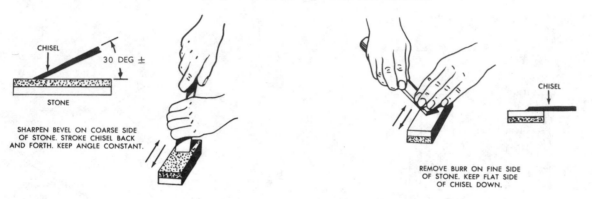

CHISEL

30 DEG ±

STONE

SHARPEN BEVEL ON COARSE SIDE
OF STONE. STROKE CHISEL BACK
AND FORTH. KEEP ANGLE CONSTANT.

REMOVE BURR ON FINE SIDE
OF STONE. KEEP FLAT SIDE
OF CHISEL DOWN.

CHISEL

Sharpening a woodworker's chisel.

MEASURING TOOLS

There are many different types of measuring tools. Where exact measurements are required, a micrometer caliper (mike) is used. Such a caliper, when properly used, gives measurements to within .001 of an inch accuracy. On the other hand, where accuracy is not extremely critical, the common rule or tape will suffice for most measurements.

Tapes and Rules

Of all measuring tools, the simplest and most common is the steel rule. This rule is usually 6 or 12 inches in length, although other lengths are available. Steel rules may be flexible or nonflexible, but the thinner the rule, the easier it is to measure accurately because the division marks are closer to the work.

There are many variations of the common rule. Sometimes the graduations are on one side only, sometimes a set of graduations is added across one end for measuring in narrow spaces, and sometimes only the first inch is divided into 64ths, with the remaining inches divided into 32nds and 16ths.

A metal or wood folding rule may be used for measuring purposes. These folding rules are usually 2 to 6 feet long. The folding rules cannot be relied on for extremely accurate measurements because a certain amount of play develops at the joints after they have been used for a while.

Steel tapes are made from 6 to about 300 ft. in length. The shorter lengths are frequently made with a curved cross section so that they are flexible enough to roll up, but remain rigid when extended. Long, flat tapes require support over their full length when measuring, or the natural lag will cause an error in reading.

The flexible-rigid tapes are usually contained in metal cases into which they wind themselves when a button is pressed, or into which they can be easily pushed. A hook is provided at one end to hook over the object being measured so one man can handle it without assistance. On some models, the outside of the case can be used as one end of the tape when measuring inside dimensions.

Measuring Procedures. To take a measurement with a common rule, hold the rule with its edge on the surface of the object being measured. This will eliminate parallax and other errors which might result due to the thickness of the rule. Read the measurement at the graduation which coincides with the distance to be measured, and state it as being so many inches and fractions of an inch. Always reduce fractions to their lowest terms, for example, 6/8 inch would be called 3/4 inch. A hook or eye at the end of a tape or rule is normally part of the first measured inch.

Bolts or Screws. The length of bolts or screws is best measured by holding them up against a rigid rule or tape. Hold both the bolt or screw to be measured and the rule up to your eye level so that your line of sight will not be in error in reading the measurement. Bolts or screws with countersink type heads are measured from the top of the head to the opposite end, while those with other type heads are measured from the bottom of the head.

Pipe Circumferences. To measure the circumference of a pipe, a flexible type rule that will conform to the cylindrical shape of the pipe must be used. A tape rule or a steel tape is adaptable for this job. When measuring pipe, make sure the tape has been wrapped squarely around the axis of the pipe (i.e., measurement should be taken in a plane perpendicular to the axis) to ensure that the reading will not be more than the actual circumference of the pipe. This is extremely important when measuring large diameter pipe.

Outside Dimensions. To measure an outside dimension using a tape rule, hook the rule over the edge of the stock. Pull the tape out until it projects far enough from the case to permit measuring the required distance. The hook at the end of the rule is designed so that it will locate the end of the rule at the surface from which the measurement is being taken. When taking a measurement of length, the tape is held parallel to the lengthwise edge. Read the dimension of the rule exactly at the edge of the piece being measured.

It may not always be possible to hook the end of the tape over the edge of stock being measured. In this case it may be necessary to butt the end of the tape against another surface or to hold the rule at a starting point from which a measurement is to be taken.

Distance Measurements. Steel or fiberglass tapes are generally used for making long measurements. Secure the hook end of the tape. Hold the tape reel in the hand and allow it to unwind while walking in the direction in which the measurement is to be taken. Stretch the tape with sufficient tension to overcome sagging. At the same time make sure the tape is parallel to an edge or the surface being measured. Read the graduation on the tape by noting which line on the tape coincides with the measurement being taken.

Care. Rules and tapes should be handled carefully and kept lightly oiled to prevent rust. Never allow the edges of measuring devices to become nicked by striking them with hard objects. They should preferably be kept in a wooden box when not in use.

To avoid kinking tapes, pull them straight out from their cases—do not bend them backward. With the windup type, always turn the crank clockwise—turning it backward will kink or break the tape. With the spring-wind type, guide the tape by hand. If it is allowed to snap back, it may be kinked, twisted, or otherwise damaged. Do not use the hook as a stop. Slow down as you reach the end.

Squares

Squares are primarily used for testing and checking trueness of an angle or for laying out lines on materials. Most squares have a rule marked on their edge. As a result they may also be used for measuring. There are several types of squares.

Carpenter's Square. The size of a carpenter's steel square is usually 12 inches x 8 inches, 24 inches x 16 inches, or 24 inches x 18 inches. The flat sides of the blade and the tongue are graduated in inches and fractions of an inch. (The square also contains information that helps to simplify or eliminate the need for computations in many woodworking tasks.) The most common uses for this square are laying out and squaring up large patterns, and for testing the flatness and squareness of large surfaces. Squaring is accomplished by placing the square at right angles to adjacent surfaces and observing if light shows between the work and the square.

One type of carpenter's square (framing) has additional tables engraved on the square. With the framing square, the craftsman can perform calculations rapidly and layout rafters, oblique joints and stairs.

Try Square. The try square consists of two parts at right angles to each other; a thick wood or iron stock and a thin, steel blade. Most try squares are made with the blades graduated in inches and fractions of an inch. The blade length varies from 2 inches to 12 inches. This square is used for setting or checking lines or surfaces which have to be at right angles to each other.

Sliding T-Bevel. The sliding T-bevel is an adjustable try square with a slotted beveled blade. Blades are normally 6 or 8 inches long. The sliding T-bevel is used for laying out angles other than right angles, and for testing constructed angles such as bevels. These squares are made with either wood or metal handles.

Combination Square. A combination square is equipped with movable heads called a square head, protractor head, and a center head. These combine the functions of several tools, and serve a wide variety of purposes. Normally, only one head is used at a time.

The square head may be adjusted to any position along the scale and clamped securely in place. The combination square can thus serve as a depth gauge, height gauge, or scribing gauge. Two of the faces of the head are ground at right angles to each other, and a third face at 45 degrees. A small spirit level is built into the head for checking whether surfaces are plumb, and a small scriber is housed in a hole in the end of the head for marking layout lines.

The center head can be slid on to the blade in place of the square head. This is a V-shaped member so designed that the center of the 90 degree V will lie exactly along one edge of the blade. This attachment is useful when locating the exact center of round stock.

The protractor head, commonly called a bevel protractor, can be attached to the scale, adjusted to any position on it, and turned and locked at any desired angle. Angular graduations usually read from 0 to 180 degrees both ways, permitting the supplement of the angle to be read.

A spirit level may be included on some models forming, in effect, an adjustable level to show any required degree.

Care of Squares. Make certain the blades, heads, dials, and all accessories are clean. Apply a light coat of oil on all metal surfaces to prevent rusting when not in use. Do not use squares for purposes other than those intended. When storing squares or bevels for long periods of time, apply a liberal amount of oil or rust-preventive compound to all surfaces, wrap in oiled paper or cloth, and place in containers or on racks away from other tools

Levels

Levels are tools designed to prove whether a plane or surface is true horizontal or true vertical. Some precision levels are calibrated so that they will indicate in degrees, minutes, and seconds, the angle inclination of a surface in relation to a horizontal or vertical surface.

The level is a simple instrument consisting of a liquid, such as alcohol or chloroform, partially filling a glass vial or tube so that a bubble remains. The tube is mounted in a frame which may be aluminum, wood, or iron. Levels are equipped with one, two, or more tubes. One tube is built in the frame at right angles to another. The tube is slightly curved, causing the bubble to seek always the highest point in the tube. On the outside of the tube are two sets of graduation lines separated by a space. Leveling is accomplished when the air bubble is centered between the graduation lines.

To level a piece of equipment, such as a workbench with a carpenter's level, set the level on the bench top parallel to the front edge of the bench. Notice that the level has several pairs of glass vials. Regardless of the position of the level, always watch the bubble in the bottom vial of a horizontal pair. Shim or wedge up the end of the bench that will return that bubble to the center of its vial. Recheck the first position of the level before securing the shims or wedges.

Levels must be checked for accuracy. This is readily accomplished by placing the level on a true horizontal surface and noting the vial indication. Reverse the level end for end. If the bubble appears on one side of the graduations with reference to the operator on the first reading and on the other side for the second reading, the level is out of true and must be adjusted.

Do not drop or handle a level roughly. To prevent damage, store it in a rack or other suitable place when not in use.

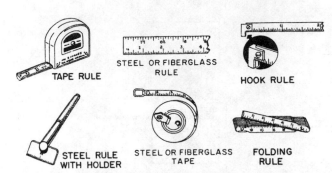

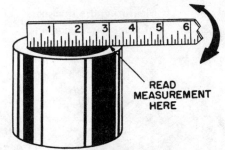

Some common types of rules.

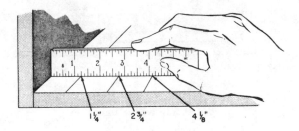

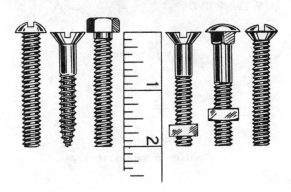

Measuring with and reading a common rule.

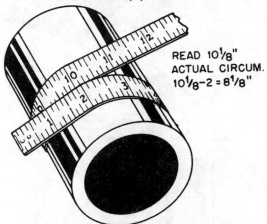

Measuring the inside diameter of a pipe.

Measuring the length of a bolt or screw.

READ 10⅛"
ACTUAL CIRCUM.
10⅛-2 = 8⅛"

Measuring the circumference of a pipe with a tape.

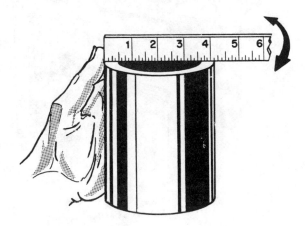

Measuring the outside diameter of a pipe.

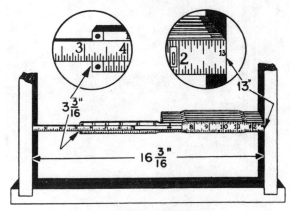

Using a folding rule to measure an inside dimension.

45

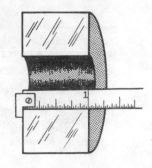

Measuring the thickness
of stock through a hole.

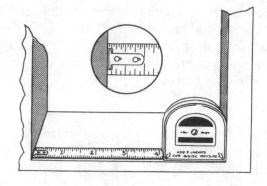

Measuring an inside
dimension with a tape rule.

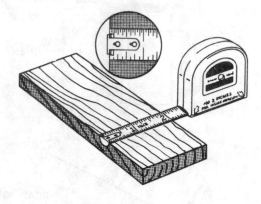

Measuring an outside
dimension using a tape rule.

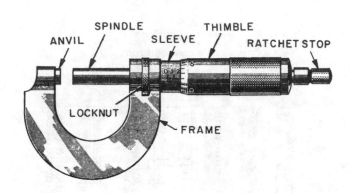

ANVIL   SPINDLE   SLEEVE   THIMBLE   RATCHET STOP

LOCKNUT   FRAME

Nomenclature of an
outside micrometer caliper.

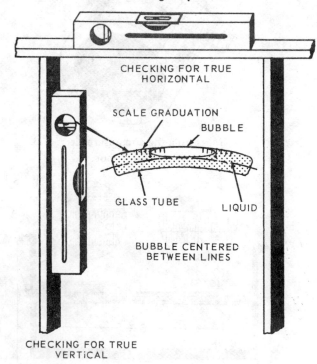

CHECKING FOR TRUE
HORIZONTAL

SCALE GRADUATION

BUBBLE

GLASS TUBE   LIQUID

BUBBLE CENTERED
BETWEEN LINES

CHECKING FOR TRUE
VERTICAL

Horizontal and vertical use of level.

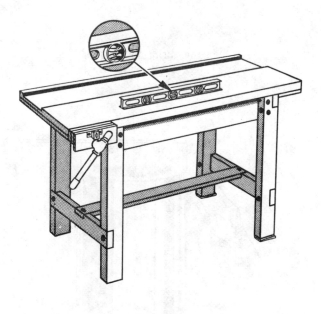

Leveling a bench.

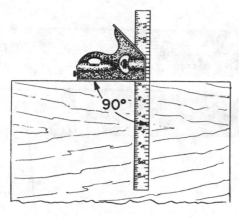

A—SQUARING A LINE ON STOCK.

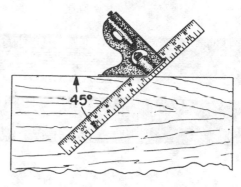

B—LAYING OUT A 45° ANGLE.

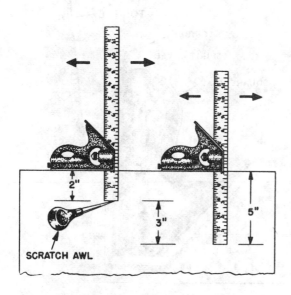

C—DRAWING PARALLEL LINES.

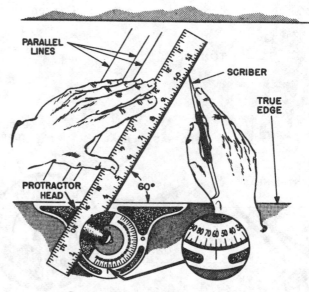

D—DRAWING ANGULAR LINES.

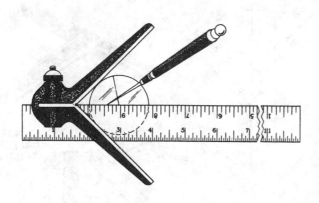

E—LOCATING A SHAFT CENTER.

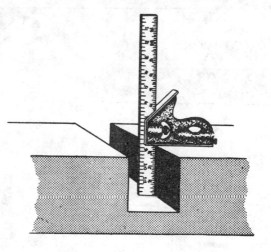

F—MEASURING THE DEPTH OF A SLOT.

Combination square applications.

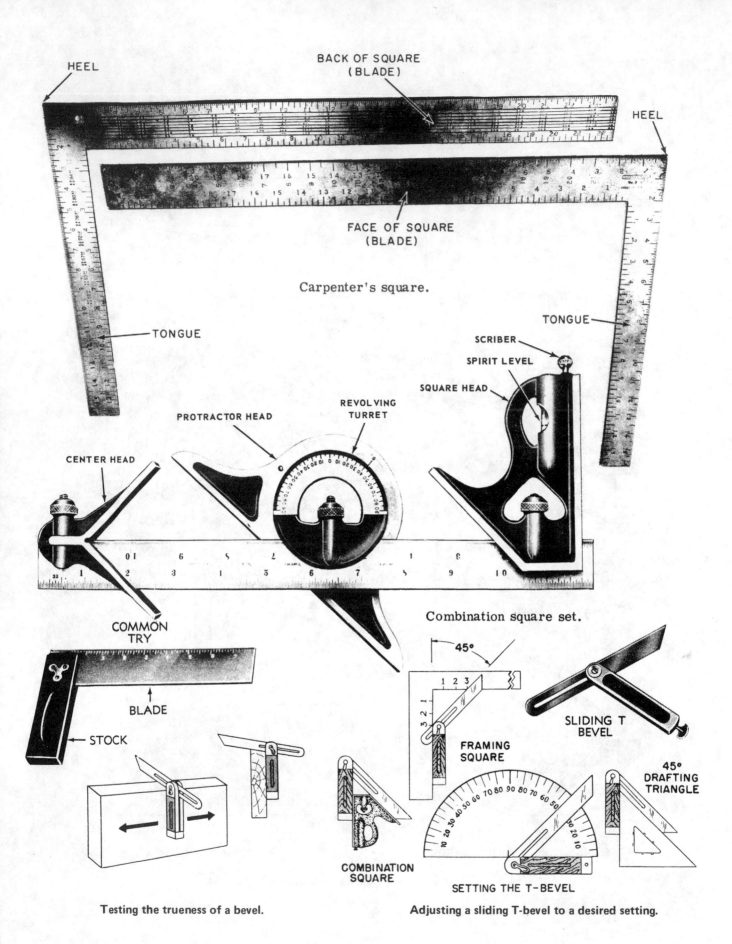

HEEL

BACK OF SQUARE
(BLADE)

HEEL

FACE OF SQUARE
(BLADE)

Carpenter's square.

TONGUE

TONGUE

SCRIBER

SPIRIT LEVEL

SQUARE HEAD

PROTRACTOR HEAD

REVOLVING
TURRET

CENTER HEAD

COMMON
TRY

Combination square set.

BLADE

STOCK

45°

FRAMING
SQUARE

SLIDING T
BEVEL

45°
DRAFTING
TRIANGLE

COMBINATION
SQUARE

SETTING THE T-BEVEL

Testing the trueness of a bevel.

Adjusting a sliding T-bevel to a desired setting.

ABRASIVES

Sandpaper

While there are thousands of kinds of abrasives, in a home workshop you need to consider only a few.

Flint paper is a natural quartz material a light tan in color. It is not durable and clogs quickly. You can use it for small jobs, but even at its low cost it's not a good buy.

Garnet paper is used for dry sanding, costs slightly more than flint, but lasts longer. It should not be used on power sanders because it lacks durability at power speeds.

Aluminum oxide can be obtained with either paper or cloth backing. This paper can be used for hand or machine sanding of wood, finishes, metals and plastics; it is used dry. Cloth-backed aluminum oxide will stand up to tough use and is the best abrasive for metal. It can be used either dry or with oil as a lubricant. Aluminum oxide costs more than flint or garnet, but because it is more durable, actually costs less to use.

Like aluminum oxide, silicon carbide is a man-made product, generally is a black color and can be used either wet or dry. Called by various names, silicon carbide has a paper back, but is waterproof. It's ideal for very fine work and is used for final sanding of auto-body repairs where a glass-smooth surface is required.

Emery cloth is a dull black, natural material used mostly on metal. It can be used with oil.

Crocus cloth comes in only one grit, very fine, and is used for polishing metal to a mirror-like finish, as on surfaces of bearings and where close tolerances are required. With its cloth backing it is long lasting.

Open-coat papers are relatively new, and are designed to be clog-resistant. Only about 50 to 70 per cent of the surface is covered with abrasive. They cut slower, but last longer.

There are three ways to designate the grit of coated abrasives: most accurate is mesh, or grit, number, which includes all 22 grit-particle sizes. The oldest way of describing grits is a system of numbers and fractions that include 19 of the 22 grits. Least accurate, but most commonly used, is the general listing of seven grades from extra fine to extra coarse.

GUIDE TO ABRASIVE SELECTION

TYPE	GRIT					USE
FLINT PAPER	Extra coarse	Coarse	Medium	Fine	Extra fine	Hand-sanding wood, removing paint, small miscellaneous jobs.
GARNET PAPER	Very coarse	Coarse	Medium	Fine	Very fine	General-use for hand sanding wood, furniture.
ALUM. OXIDE PAPER	Very coarse	Coarse	Medium	Fine	Very fine	Hand or machine-sanding hardwood, metal, plastic.
ALUM. OXIDE CLOTH	Very coarse	Coarse	Medium	Fine		Wood, metal, plastic, other materials with stationary, portable belt sanders.
PAPER SILICON WATERPROOF CARBIDE			Very fine	Extra fine	Super fine	Wet-sanding coats on wood, metal, other materials; used with oil and water.
EMERY CLOTH	Very coarse	Coarse	Medium	Fine		Polishing nonplated metal, cleaning off rust and scale.
CROCUS CLOTH	Very fine grade only					For polishing, creating glass-smooth finish on metal parts.

Common	Grit	Numbers
	600	
	500	
Extra fine	400	10/0
	360	
	320	9/0
	280	8/0
Very fine	240	7/0
	220	6/0
	180	5/0
Fine	150	4/0
	120	3/0
	100	2/0
Medium	80	1/0
	60	½
Coarse	50	1
	40	1½
	36	2
Very coarse	30	2½
	24	3
	20	3½
Extra coarse	16	4
	12	4½

Inexpensive flint or garnet papers clog rapidly when sanding soft material, as shown here. They are a poor buy.

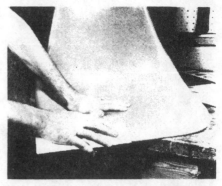
Newer open-grit papers do not clog easily even on plastics and other soft material. They do cut slower than closecoat.

Waterproof paper is used with water or oil to produce glossy or flat finish.

For power sanding, aluminum oxide cloth or paper should be used.

Various grits of paper or cloth-back abrasive are available for disk sanders.

Garnet paper is not bad for light hand-sanding of smaller jobs, as here where dowel is backing to sand cove molding.

Handy tool for any workshop is holder for hand-sanding wooden shapes. Standard sheet of paper is cut into strips.

For sanding irregular surfaces paper should have strong, but flexible backing. Only better grades of sandpaper will do.

Steel Wool

Steel wool is a versatile material that can be used wet or dry, to smooth or roughen, to apply or remove finishes and to polish or dull. And, it can be used as an improvised filter. For example, stuff a wad of fine wool in a funnel to filter liquids. Oiled steel wool is an effective air filter, and can be used as a temporary replacement filter in an exhaust fan, the lint trap in a clothes dryer and in other appliances.

The charts in this section tell about the seven readily available grades of steel wool, and how they are used. Experience may suggest finer or coarser grades for particular uses.

Steel wool is made by cutting V-shape shavings from strands of heat-treated steel wire. Leaving the shaving machine, the strands are spooled, then made into pads and other forms.

While steel wool competes with sandpaper in some areas, its main advantages are flexibility so it fits curved and sculptured surfaces; it does not "load up" because dust is tapped out of it and it can be used wet, which most sandpaper cannot. Because the finer grades of steel wool are "gentler" than the finest grades of sandpaper, it can be thought of as taking over where sandpaper leaves off.

Consulting the chart: steel wool can be used

for smoothing prior to finishing. On softwoods subject to grain-raising when finish is applied, sponge with water to raise the grain and let dry. Rub with wool to remove the fuzziness. Repeat as necessary. Steel wool can be used with wax, pumice, oil and other materials to either polish or dull a finish.

Try steel wool as a "power abrasive," utilizing simple arbors and other setups to polish and clean the inside of cups, tubes and other con- tainers. Handsome "engine turnings" can be done on metal with a pot of steel wool nailed to an arbor made from a dowel. Coarse wool stapled to a wood disk creates a pad that is effective for heavy cleaning of floor tile. Use the various de- vices at slow speed on a drill press, or in a variable- speed portable drill. Fine particles break off the wool, so wear a face mask and a filter over your nose to keep out dust.

APPLICATION CHART

Grade	Quality	Strand Size*	Cutting Action	Dry Uses
No. 3	Coarse	.003"	Severe	Initial smoothing of rough surfaces, Coarse rust removal, paint from glass, roughen surfaces for glue.
No. 2	Medium coarse	.0015"	Fairly severe	Remove old wax from linoleum, terrazo, tile, concrete floors. Remove paint, plaster, rust spots from ceramic tile. Remove grease from stove or range.
No. 1	Medium	.001"	Moderate	Clean soldering iron and gun tips, coarse cleaning of galvanizing or copper for sold- ering, brazing.
No. 0	Fine	.0008"	Medium light	Remove softwood raised grain, initial "sanding" of wood, remove alcohol stains from vinyl floors.
No. 00	Very fine	.0005"	Light	Clean, polish brass and copper, clean these metals prior to sweat-soldering, re- move slight burns from wood, leather, buff suede.
No. 000	Extra fine	.0003"	Very light	Intermediate "sanding" of wood.
No. 0000	Super fine	.0002"	Extra light	Final "sanding" of wood before finishing, buff waxed surfaces, buffing shellac be- tween coats, dulling sheen of lacquered or epoxied surfaces.

APPLICATION CHART

Grade	Quality	Strand Size*	Cutting Action	Wet Uses
No. 3	Coarse	.003"	Severe	Use with oil to remove rust on garden tools, shop tools, etc.
No. 2	Medium coarse	.0015"	Fairly severe	Remove rust from metal, with turpentine; clean discolored tile with water and scour- ing powder; clean whitewall tires with soap or scouring powder and water; remove gum and pitch from saw blades with turpentine or kerosene.
No. 1	Medium	.001"	Moderate	Clean stained aluminum with water and scouring powder; remove soot stains with trisodium phosphate and water; linseed oil to clean grimy antiques; with saddle soap to renew leather items.
No. 0	Fine	.0008"	Medium light	Polish aluminum with soap and water; clean zinc with scouring powder and water; renew rubber tile with mild soap suds; re- move tile stains with turpentine; take off paint and varnish with paint remover; clean vinyl floors with water.
No. 00	Very fine	.0005"	Light	Remove deep burns in leather with soap and water.
No. 000	Extra fine	.0003"	Very light	Rust from chrome with kerosene; clean stainless steel with scouring powder and water; tar from chrome with mineral spirits.
No. 0000	Super fine	.0002"	Extra light	Remove overspray from chrome with pol- ishing compound; apply paste furniture wax for final finish over penetrating sealer; "rub- out" between built-up coats of lacquer, us- ing auto rubbing compound; linseed oil to remove final nibs, and glare, after final coat of lacquer or varnish; create satin fin- ish on lacquer with pumice powder and mineral spirits.

*approximate

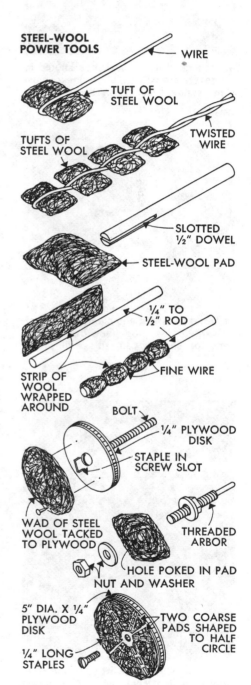

STEEL-WOOL POWER TOOLS — WIRE — TUFT OF STEEL WOOL — TWISTED WIRE — TUFTS OF STEEL WOOL — SLOTTED ½" DOWEL — STEEL-WOOL PAD — ¼" TO ½" ROD — FINE WIRE — STRIP OF WOOL WRAPPED AROUND — BOLT — ¼" PLYWOOD DISK — STAPLE IN SCREW SLOT — WAD OF STEEL WOOL TACKED TO PLYWOOD — THREADED ARBOR — HOLE POKED IN PAD — NUT AND WASHER — 5" DIA. X ¼" PLYWOOD DISK — TWO COARSE PADS SHAPED TO HALF CIRCLE — ¼" LONG STAPLES

Well-stocked home workshop should include steel wool, which is inexpensive and readily available in seven grades.

Secret of steel wool cutting action is in tiny triangular-shape wires. Thousands of cutting edges act as flexible scrapers.

Steel wool comes in pads, which can be refolded to expose fresh cutting surfaces. Less common, in tubes.

Powered polishing and cleaning is possible with these shop-made devices. Except for sander pad, use drill press.

Unfold pad of steel wool, twist it into a strong "rope" for stripping paint, "sanding" hard-to-reach places.

Use steel wool wet for tough jobs like removing gum from saw blades. Use lacquer thinner or kerosene.

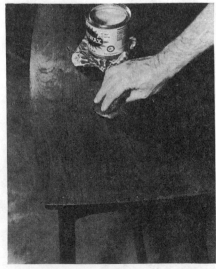

Apply wax with a pad of very fine steel wool as a final coat over a penetrating finish, to produce smooth surface.

Minimize the chance of steel particles lodging in wood pores by wiping surfaces with a tack rag before applying the finish.

New synthetic abrasive takes place of steel wool for cleaning off softened finish, does not leave residue.

2

POWER TOOLS

POWER TOOLS

2

ELECTRIC DRILLS ▪ BELT SANDERS ▪ FINISHING SANDERS

THE DRILL PRESS ▪ THE CIRCULAR SAW ▪ THE JIG SAW ▪ THE TABLE SAW

THE RADIAL-ARM SAW ▪ THE LATHE ▪ THE ROUTER ▪ THE CHAIN SAW

POWER TOOLS: TIMESAVERS

If you are a home handyman or woman, you may be thinking about buying your first power tools or purchasing companions to the ones you already own. Work goes faster when electric power replaces human effort and is often of high quality because a power tool has precise controls.

Before making any purchase, alert yourself to the safety, quality, and suitability features you should demand of any tool.

Certification

On the power tool itself, look for the symbol of an independent testing laboratory, such as Underwriters' Laboratories, Inc. It indicates that the tool is manufactured to conform to established electrical and mechanical safety standards.

On the carton you may find a manufacturers' association seal—for example, that of the Power Tool Institute. This particular seal shows that the tool not only meets safety standards but has been inspected under power at the factory and has instructions for safe use in the carton.

Motors

A power tool has either a rotary or a vibratory electric motor.

A rotary motor is durable and can be easily connected to gears and attachments to control power delivery. It also has brushes that eventually wear down to cause loss of power, excessive sparking, or even motor failure unless replaced.

A vibratory motor, used in some jib saws and finishing sanders, supplies back-and-forth motion that is not applied through gears or attachments. A tool with such a motor is moderately priced and has no brushes. It is best suited for light-duty applications.

Electrical Safety Systems

A tool may protect you from electric shock by either of two equally safe systems: by external grounding or double insulation.

THREE-PRONG PLUG

A tool with external grounding has a wire that runs from the housing through the power cord to a third prong on the power plug. When this third prong is connected to a grounded, three-hole electrical outlet, the grounding wire will carry any current that leaks past the electrical insulation of the tool away from you and into the ground of your home wiring.

A double-insulated tool has an extra layer of electrical insulation that eliminates the need of a three-prong plug and grounded outlet.

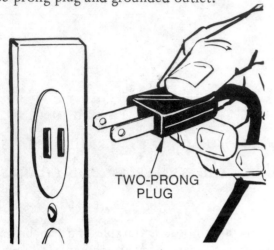

TWO-PRONG PLUG

Since the initial and servicing costs of the two systems are about the same, your choice of one over the other may depend on the availability of three-hole outlets in your home or workshop.

Ampere Ratings

The quantity of electric current a tool normally draws during operation is listed on the manufacturer's nameplate. Ratings on models for home use range from 2 to 13 amperes.

As a rule of thumb, the larger the drill, sander, or saw, the greater the ampere rating is likely to be. If two models are otherwise equal, the one with the higher ampere rating will generally have more power.

Remember, however, that a heavy-duty tool drawing 12 to 13 amperes should never be connected to an electrical circuit on which another appliance is operating. You may overload the circuit wiring and blow a fuse or trip a circuit breaker.

Tools drawing 8 to 10 amperes can be operated on household circuits except those carrying major appliances such as freezers and air conditioners.

Models with still lower ratings can be plugged into any circuit not overloaded with several small appliances in operation.

RECOMMENDED GAUGES

Ampere rating of tool	Gauge for 25-ft. cord	Gauge for 50-ft. cord	Gauge for 75-ft. cord	Gauge for 100-ft. cord
1-7	18	18	18	18
8-10	18	18	16	16
11-12	16	16	14	14

Using Power Tools Safely

Power hand tools are convenient aids, but they can be dangerous if misused. High-speed bits, blades, and abrasives can cut and tear hands and feet as well as wood and metal. Electric current can shock and burn. Heat and sparks from operating tools can cause fires.

You can help prevent power tool accidents by using common sense and following the suggestions below that apply to your tool and your situation.

Know Your Tool. Before you begin using a tool, learn how it operates and the care it should have. Read the owner's manual, and keep it handy for reference. Use the tool only on work for which it is suited and with recommended accessories. Familiarize yourself with its particular limitations.

Provide Electric Ground. If your tool is not double insulated, you need a three-hole, grounded outlet where you plan to use the tool. It should be installed by an electrician.

Creating a temporary three-hole outlet by means of an adapter plug is not recommended; often adequate grounding is not established. Without grounding, an electrical failure in the tool could give you a serious, or even fatal, shock. With grounding, any stray electricity would flow harmlessly away from you and into the ground of your home wiring.

No matter how well the tool is grounded or insulated, avoid using it in damp or wet locations. Moisture readily conducts electricity.

Protect Power Cords. Keep tool and extension cords away from heat, oil, and sharp edges that can damage electrical insulation. Don't carry a tool by the cord or jerk the cord to remove the plug from the outlet. You may break the wire or its insulation. A damaged cord should be replaced immediately.

Avoid Flammable Mixtures. Never operate a power tool near open containers of flammable solvents, cleaners, or varnishes. Fumes from such substances and air form a mixture that can burst into flame from a motor or friction spark.

Prevent Tool Overheating. When a tool overheats, its electrical insulation may break down and start a fire in the tool. Even if a fire does not start, the tool may be damaged and unsafe for future use.

Keep housing vents clear for good air flow. If the tool heats because of heavy work, turn it off until it cools. Never wrap a cloth around a hot tool to hold it; the cloth not only increases tool heat but may catch fire.

Make Tool Changes Correctly. Follow the directions in the owner's manual when changing bits, blades, wheels, or abrasives and observe these safety precautions:

Before doing anything else, put the tool switch in the "off" position and disconnect the power cord from the electrical outlet.

When you change a drill bit, never run the tool to release or fasten the chuck. Take out the chuck key before you start the drill so it won't be thrown out and hit someone.

When you are ready to use the tool, check to see that the switch is still at "off" or that your finger is not holding down a trigger switch. Then plug in the tool.

Guard Against Cuts and Bruises. Never work in loose clothing, wear long hair loose, or have on dangling jewelry that can catch in a tool's moving parts. If the job requires it, wear safety glasses, a dust mask, or other protection.

Clear the work area of anything that could cause you to slip or stumble, and do not let litter accumulate while you work.

Check the structural safety of any ladder you plan to use and be sure it is positioned so it won't slip when you climb it.

If you work on a small piece that could be thrown or hurled by tool action, use clamps or a vise to fasten it firmly to a bench or table.

Attach auxiliary handles to tools when doing heavy work so you can use both hands for control.

Be sure drill bits or saw blades are sharp. Worn blades or bits can stick and cause a saw or drill to jerk out of your control.

Be specially careful with circular saws. Keep blade guards in place and in working order. Clamp the workpiece to a bench or sawhorses whenever possible. Never support a saw on the portion of work to be cut off. Always let the blade reach full speed before beginning to cut and withdraw the blade immediately if it slows or begins to stick or bind. Stand to one side of the saw, not directly behind it; you are less likely to be cut if the saw jerks out of control.

Protect Children. Never let a child play with a power tool or be near one in operation. Never leave a tool running and unattended. Store tools out of a child's reach.

The Housing. The tool housing shields the motor, gears, and electrical parts from dirt and holds them in place. It may either have two halves or several interlocking parts. Some housings have portholes for inspecting or replacing motor brushes.

Materials commonly used are aluminum and plastic because they are light in weight yet sturdy.

Extension Cords. An extension cord used with a power tool should have a suitable gauge, or wire size, for its length and the ampere rating of the tool. Otherwise the working power supply to the tool may be decreased by a "voltage drop." If the drop is more than 10 percent, the tool motor cannot function properly and may be permanently damaged.

Remember also that you need a three-wire extension cord for use with grounded tools with three-prong plugs. Two-wire cords are suitable for use with double-insulated tools.

When you shop, match the gauge and cord type you need with the American Wire Gauge (AWG) number stamped on the cord. A 16-gauge, three-wire cord will be stamped "16/3," "16/3 AWG," "16 AWG/3," or "3 conductor 16 AWG."

Be sure the cord has a safety seal of approval by Underwriters' Laboratories, Inc. or a similar testing institution. A legitimate Underwriters' Laboratories label will read "Underwriters' Laboratories, Inc. listed."

If you need an outdoor cord, select one labeled "Suitable for use with outdoor appliances." Any other cord will be unsafe.

Suitability. Models for household use may be labeled "domestic" or "utility" on their literature or packaging. The words "industrial," "commercial," and "builders" usually indicate a tool designed for heavy or specialized use.

No matter what the label says, be sure to lift and handle the model. If possible, test operate it in the store. Is it comfortable to hold and easy to control? Can you clearly see your work when the tool is in operating position?

If you have any doubts about a particular model, try it from a rental shop before you make a purchase.

Warranties. Some warranties promise free repair of faulty materials and guarantee workmanship for one year; others guarantee replacement of a defective tool by the local dealer. Some have no time limit but are usually valid only to the original owner.

No company will repair a tool without charge if their examination indicates it failed owing to abuse or unauthorized service.

Service. If you buy a brand that has a nearby authorized service center, you will avoid paying postage for a tool to and from a distant factory if repairs are needed during the warranty period. Once the warranty expires, the same center will continue to be a reliable repair shop with replacement parts in stock.

At any shop, ask about the repair guarantee before you leave your tool for servicing. Most shops guarantee new parts and work for 90 days.

ELECTRIC DRILLS

An electric drill can do so many jobs that it may be the first power tool you want to buy. With it you can make holes in almost any material. By using its accessories and attachments you can sand, polish, grind, buff, stir paint, and drive screws.

Depending on quality, size, gearing, and special features, a drill for home use costs from $5 to $50 or more. Your best choice will be a model with the work capacity and special features you will regularly use.

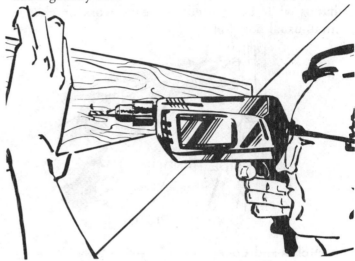

Work Capacity

The work capacity of a drill depends on its chuck size and rated revolutions per minute (RPM).

The chuck size is the diameter of the largest bit shank the drill chuck can hold. Home-use sizes are one-fourth, three-eighths, and one-half inch. Usually, the larger the chuck, the wider and deeper the holes the drill can bore.

The RPM rating is an indication of the number of gear sets in a model, its speed, and the type of work for which it is best suited. For example, a ¼-inch drill rated about 2,000 RPM usually has one gear set and is appropriate for rapid drilling in wood and use with sanding and polishing accessories. A model with more gears would have a lower RPM rating and work more slowly but could make bigger holes in hard metals or masonry without stalling or overheating.

Speeds and Versatility

For most jobs around a home, a single-speed drill is adequate. However, a two-speed or variable-speed model will be more suitable if you intend to drill material that requires a slow speed or if you want to use many accessories. A drill with both variable speed and reverse is effective for driving and removing screws.

Handles

Most drills have a pistol-grip handle. It should be comfortable and well balanced and have finger-holds in front for nonslip gripping. Some models include spade grips or side handles. These may be attached so that the drill can be grasped by both hands while being used for heavy work or while in an unusual position.

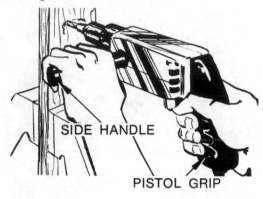

SIDE HANDLE

PISTOL GRIP

Switches and Locks

The trigger switch, which starts the drill, is on the pistol-grip handle, and many models include a switch lock for continuous operation. You activate the lock by pressing a button; the lock instantly releases if you tighten your squeeze on the trigger switch.

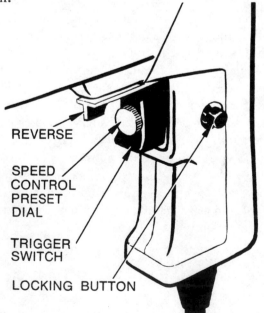

REVERSE

SPEED CONTROL PRESET DIAL

TRIGGER SWITCH

LOCKING BUTTON

Variable-speed drills have trigger switches that allow you to vary bit speed from almost nothing up to the maximum RPM by trigger-finger pressure. Some have controls that allow you to preset the maximum RPM.

Drills with reverse have separate reverse controls in different positions on different brands. To protect the motor on any brand, allow the drill to come to a full stop before reversing.

The Chuck

The front of the drill, where bits and other accessories are inserted and removed, is called the chuck. The three-jaw gear type is the most common. Its collar is first hand closed on the shank of a bit. Then a key is inserted into the chuck body and turned to tighten the three jaws simultaneously and with considerable force. Some models have a holder to make key loss less likely.

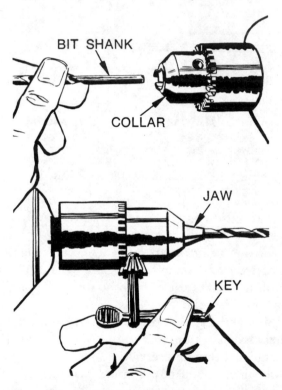

BIT SHANK

COLLAR

JAW

KEY

Some "bargain" drills have chucks that are hand tightened by means of knurled collars. They may either offer a poor hold on bits and accessories during work or be difficult to loosen when work is finished.

Examine chuck placement as well as quality. The higher the chuck on the front of the housing, the easier the drill will be to use in corners.

Drill Accessories

The common accessories that enable you to use a drill for many different jobs are explained below. See a manufacturer's catalog for information on the accessories available for particular drill brands and models.

Bits. A drill bit has a working end that makes holes and a smooth shank that is grasped by the jaws of a chuck. While bits can be bought individually, they cost less if purchased in sets.

CUTTING EDGE

The twist bit, the most commonly used, cuts cylindrical holes. It has a sharp point and two spiral-shaped cutting edges that lift chips out of the hole as the bit turns.

Carbon steel twist bits are suited to drilling wood and soft metals; high-speed steel bits cut wood, soft metals, and mild steel; tungsten carbide or carbide-tipped bits cut hard metals and masonry. Cutting diameters commonly available range from one-sixteenth to one-half inch.

The spade bit cuts large cylindrical holes in wood. It has a flat, spade-shaped driving end with a pointed tip. Common cutting diameters range from three-eighths inch to one inch.

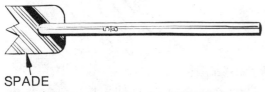

SPADE

The wood-screw pilot bit has three widths of cutting edge. The least wide drills a hole to give screw threads solid anchorage. The next makes a shaft for the unthreaded screw shank. The widest makes a hole, or countersink, for flat-headed screws. A detachable stop can make shallow or deep countersinks.

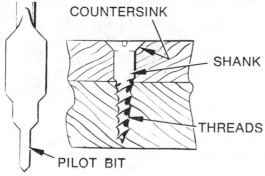

COUNTERSINK

SHANK

THREADS

PILOT BIT

The screw-driving bit attaches to drills with variable speed and reverse to drive and remove slotted and Phillipshead screws. On single or two-speed drills, the bit must be used with a screw-driving attachment.

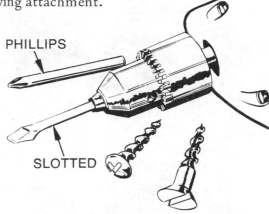

PHILLIPS

SLOTTED

Wheels and Discs. Polishing and sanding discs, grinding wheels, wire brush discs, and hole saws are usually secured to a drill by an arbor adapter. One end of the arbor goes through the center hole of the wheel or disc and is fastened by a washer and nut or by a screw and washer. A flange keeps the wheel from slipping down the shank that fits into the drill chuck.

Some discs and wire brushes have built-in shanks that fit the drill spindle when the chuck is removed.

Discs are used with either abrasive paper for sanding or with a soft bonnet for polishing.

Grinding wheels are for sharpening tools or smoothing metal.

Wire brushes remove paint, rust, and dirt from wood and metal.

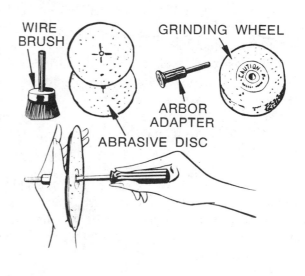

WIRE BRUSH

GRINDING WHEEL

ARBOR ADAPTER

ABRASIVE DISC

Hole saws cut round holes through boards or sheet materials by means of a rim saw blade and a centered pilot bit. Common diameters range from one-half inch to 4 inches.

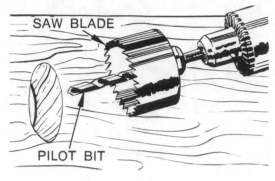

SAW BLADE

PILOT BIT

Stands. A drill stand holds an operating drill in place while you manipulate work pieces. It is permanently attached to a workbench but is designed so that the drill can be easily inserted or removed.

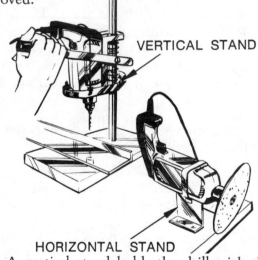

VERTICAL STAND

HORIZONTAL STAND

A vertical stand holds the drill with the bit pointing down. A handle lowers and raises the drill bit into the work. Adjustments allow you to drill precisely spaced and positioned holes.

The horizontal stand holds the drill so that the operator can conveniently control and position work against revolving accessories.

Kits. If you intend to buy several accessories as well as a drill, a kit may be a prudent purchase. It includes the drill plus assorted bits, other accessories, and a carrying case.

If you already have a drill, or decide to buy a model that does not include a case, you can purchase a carrying case separately. It will help keep your drill clean and be a handy container for bits and other accessories.

BELT SANDERS

A belt sander quickly sands large surfaces such as floors, walls, and planks. It can remove old paint, erase scratches, or smooth uneven workmanship. With the right abrasive belt, it can work on wood, metal, glass, ceramics, plastic, and stone. It should never be tilted or held in one spot while operating; it could damage the work. It is not suited to sanding most furniture or for extra-fine finishing.

Depending on quality, size, speed, and special features, a belt sander plus assorted belts costs between $40 and $150. Weights range from 5 to 25 pounds. Heavier sanders usually have greater work capacity, but they may also be beyond your strength to control or to hold vertically against walls and doors.

Work Capacity

The work capacity of a belt sander depends upon its size and belt speed. These are either noted on the tool itself or in the tool literature.

The size is listed as the width and circumference of the abrasive belt that fits a sander. Common belt sizes are 3 by 18, 3 by 21, 3 by 24, 4 by 21, and 4 by 24 inches. Generally, the larger the sander, the greater its work capacity.

The speeds of belts on different models, given in surface feet per minute (SFPM), range from 900 to 1600. The greater the SFPM, the greater the work capacity of the tool for its size, or the faster it removes material from the surface being sanded.

The Housing

The housing covers the motor, the upper surface of the abrasive belt, and one side of the sander.

The other side is mostly open to make belt changing easier. Check to see if the housing allows you to sand close to a wall. Areas the belt can't reach must be sanded by other means.

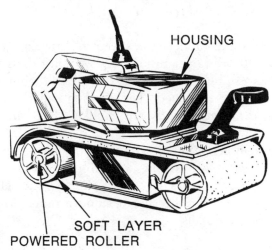

HOUSING

SOFT LAYER
POWERED ROLLER

Handles

Rear handles on most models are a contoured D shape for good grip. A few have pistol grips. An additional knob or bar handle in front is helpful for guiding the sander or applying even sanding pressure.

Switches and Locks

A trigger switch on the rear handle starts the sander, and most models have a button to lock the trigger switch "on" during prolonged sanding. The lock releases the instant the trigger switch is squeezed.

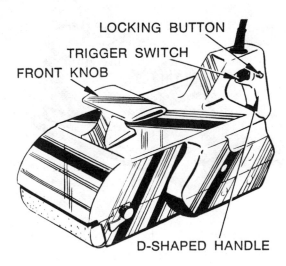

LOCKING BUTTON

TRIGGER SWITCH

FRONT KNOB

D-SHAPED HANDLE

A few models that offer two speeds have separate slide or toggle speed-selection switches.

Belt Traction

On some models the rear roller, powered by the motor, has a soft outer layer that grips the abrasive belt and helps prevent slippage. Other models provide a soft lining belt over which the abrasive belt is placed for good traction.

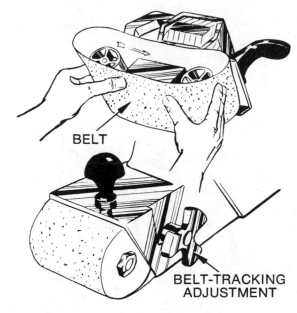

BELT

BELT-TRACKING
ADJUSTMENT

Belt Changing

To change a belt, you first retract the front, free-turning roller of a belt sander. Then, after the new belt is on and the front roller returned to operating position, you must align the belt so it won't run off to one side during sanding.

Consult the owner's manual about belt changing for the model you are considering for purchase. It should be simple to understand and easy to do. Ask the salesman to demonstrate belt changing and aligning; then try it yourself.

Dust Collection

A belt sander produces large quantities of waste, or dust, from a work surface. Any one of three systems of dust collection is recommended: a built-in dust bag; a bag bought separately that can be attached as required; an accessory flexible hose that connects to a vacuum cleaner. In the first two

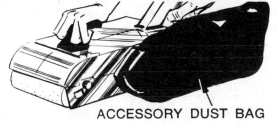

ACCESSORY DUST BAG

systems, dust collection is powered by a motor in the sander. In the third, the vacuum cleaner motor sucks dust away from the sander.

FINISHING SANDERS

A finishing sander makes a surface smooth and ready for a coating, if one is to be applied. It can be used on wood furniture and cabinets, metal, plastic, or plaster. It is not usually suitable for use on large areas or to remove deep dents, scratches, or paint.

Finishing sanders range in price from about $5 to $50 and more. The least expensive models commonly have vibratory motors and back-and-forth, or "reciprocal," sanding motion. Models that are moderately priced usually have rotary motors and a circular, or "orbital," sanding action. More expensive models with rotary motors are capable of both motions. Quality, special features, and size also affect price.

Work Capacity

The work capacity of a finishing sander depends on the size of its sanding pad and the speed and length of the sanding strokes. These specifications are found either on a model or in its sales literature.

The pad sizes of most models for home use range from 3½ by 7 inches to 4½ by 9 inches. Many catalogs and brochures list only the size of the abrasive sheet required to fit the pad. To determine the pad size, subtract 2 inches from the sheet length and about one-eighth inch from the width. Generally, a bigger pad means greater work capacity.

The speeds and lengths of sanding strokes are coordinated in three different ways in finishing sanders.

On some models the speed is between 3,000 and 4,500 orbits per minute (OPM); on others the speed is doubled to around 10,000 OPM but the stroke length is halved. The sanding capacities of the two arrangements are similar, but shorter strokes give a glossier surface.

Reciprocal sanders with vibratory motors have a speed of 7,200 strokes per minute (SPM), the equivalent of 7,200 OPM, and a short stroke. They can produce a fine finish but smooth more slowly than orbital models.

The Housing

If the housing extends beyond the edges of the sanding pad, hand sanding will be necessary close to perpendicular surfaces and in corners.

Handles

Most models have separate handles, but some simply have a housing palm grip. Try such a tool under power to find if it becomes uncomfortably hot to hold with extended use. Heavier units may have auxiliary handles, such as a front knob, to provide better control and more uniform pressure with two-handed use.

PALM GRIP

Switches and Locks

The "off-on" control on a finishing sander is either a slide or a trigger switch. A trigger switch usually has a locking button nearby. A slide switch locks "on" automatically.

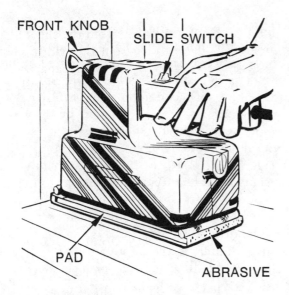

FRONT KNOB SLIDE SWITCH

PAD ABRASIVE

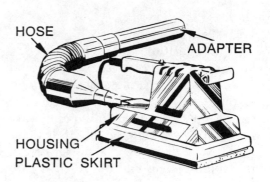

HOSE ADAPTER

HOUSING PLASTIC SKIRT

Abrasive Changing

To take a worn abrasive sheet off the pad of a finishing sander and replace it with a fresh one, you must operate a special mechanism. On some models a lever opens and closes clamps at the front and back of the sanding pad. On others you use a special key or a screwdriver to loosen and tighten pad clamps. Still others have spring-loaded clamps that must be held open while an abrasive sheet is inserted.

Before you purchase a model, test the ease of abrasive changing.

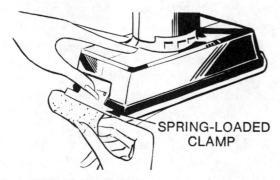

SPRING-LOADED CLAMP

Dust Collections

Finishing sanders produce less waste than belt models, but you may still want a dust-collection system to keep your work and work area clean. You can buy either a model with a built-in dust bag or one that will accept a kit. A kit contains a plastic skirt to fit over the sanding pad, a flexible hose, and an adapter to connect the hose to your vacuum cleaner. Some manufacturers make dust-collection kits to fit all their models; others make kits only for some styles.

Accessories

Accessories for both belt and finishing sanders include flexible pads to fasten under sheets or belts when sanding irregular or curved surfaces, felt or fabric pads or belts for use with loose abrasives and polishes, and carrying cases.

Accessories for belt sanders only are a canvas or felt belt for fine finishing and a bench stand that holds the sander while you touch small pieces of work to the moving belt. Belts can be changed without removing the sander from the stand.

RECOMMENDED ABRASIVE GRITS FOR COMMON USE ON SANDERS

Name	Grit Number	Use
Coarse	36	Removing paint and heavy rust.
	40	Rough sanding of wood, plastic, and
	50	metal.
Medium	60	Semifinish sanding on hard wood,
	80	plastic, and metal. Finish sanding on
	100	soft wood.
Fine	120	Finish sanding on hard wood, plastic,
	150	and metal.
Extra Fine	220	Final sanding for extra-smooth finish.
	320	
	400	

THE DRILL PRESS

With the multitude of ingeniously-designed and highly practical accessories available today, a drill press becomes a versatile tool that can be used to shape, rout, sand, buff, grind, rabbet, cut tenons and mortises, mill, spin rivets, mix paint, cut dovetails and, of course, do its basic job of drilling.

Basically, a drill press is a power-driven vertical shaft (spindle) one end of which is threaded to accept a chuck. The spindle is fitted in a moveable, hollow housing (quill), which in turn is mounted in a head that has a feed lever to control the up and down movement of the spindle and quill. The head assembly is on a stand, usually tubular, and below it is an adjustable table to hold the work. There is a locking device to hold the quill in a fixed position, a return spring that holds the quill in the full-up position when no pressure is exerted on the feed lever, and a depth control that can be set to limit the downward travel of the quill. On some presses the worktable can be tilted, as well as moved up and down on the column.

Whether your drill press is a table or floor model (usually the only difference is in column length) it should be carefully leveled and solidly anchored.

To prevent slipping or, even worse, undue wear on the spindle bearings, the drive belt should be adjusted so that it is just tight enough so it will not slip on the pulleys when pulled by hand.(1)

Spindle-return tension should be set to the individual taste of the operator, but it should always be strong enough to hold the quill in the full-up position. Adjustments can be made by loosening the locking screw and rotating the tensioning knob.(2)

Most drill presses are fitted with a Jacob's chuck which requires a special geared key to open and to lock it. In regard to this necessary key, you can save hours of frustration looking for it by either fitting an appropriate-size spring clip to the side of the drill-press head, the column or by attaching the key to a chain that is fastened to the underside of the motor mount.(3) The motor mount is suggested, because this location keeps the key well clear of the chuck when not in use, but still within easy reach.

Using a Drill Press

In everyday drilling operations, feed and speed are the two most critical factors in producing a good job, and in assuring the maximum life from drill bits. Speed, on most presses, is varied by moving the drive belt on step pulleys. The speeds produced by the various combinations will be shown either in your instruction manual, or on a small plate somewhere on the head of the press. Generally, a pulley setup will give speeds of 600, 1300, 2400 and 5000 r.p.m., close enough to handle most jobs. Some manufacturers, however, make a special speed-control unit which can be obtained as an accessory for most presses. The unit incorporates a series of pressure-variable pulleys, and the device not only eliminates the annoyance of constantly switching the belt around to change speeds, but will drive the press at the exact r.p.m. you need for any job.(4)

The table gives a range of recommended speeds for different operations and for different materials, but a good rule-of-thumb to keep in mind is that the larger the diameter of the cutter (drill bit, fly cutter, etc.) and the harder the material, the slower the drill press should be run.

The speed with which the cutter is fed into the work also is important. Too heavy a feed will force the tool beyond its cutting capacity and produce jammed or broken tools. At best, you will make rough cuts. On the other hand, feeding too slowly, particularly with metal and other hard materials, will cause overheating of the cutting edges of the tool and will dull and burn them. For best results, pick the right speed, then feed with a constant, even pressure that lets the tool cut easily through the material at a steady rate.

Accessories

Drilling tools are available in a wide variety of sizes, shapes and styles, but probably the most common are the center shaft with interchangeable cutter blades, the single-spur boring bit (power bit) and the common twist drill.

The first three are for wood, only, but the twist drill can be used in metal and other materials. The twist drill does not have outlining spurs as do the wood bits, so it is not a good choice for drilling neat holes in wood.

For those really big holes, you will need an adjustable fly cutter. This type cutter should always be operated at the lowest possible speed, and because of the leverage produced by the long cutting

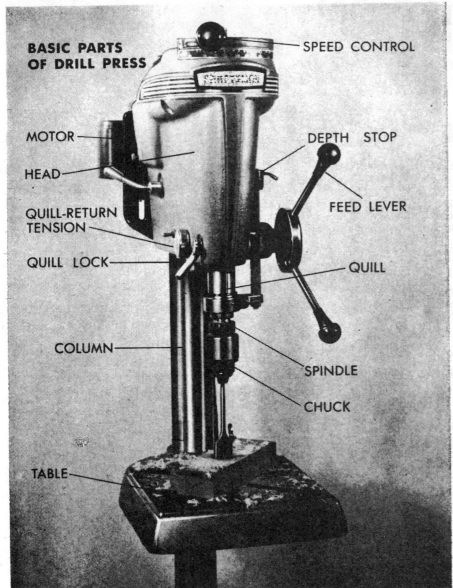

BASIC PARTS OF DRILL PRESS

SPEED CONTROL

MOTOR

HEAD

DEPTH STOP

FEED LEVER

QUILL-RETURN TENSION

QUILL LOCK

QUILL

COLUMN

SPINDLE

CHUCK

TABLE

1. To prevent slipping of belt, undue wear on spindle bearings, belt should be just tight enough not to slip easily.

2. Spindle-return tension is individual thing, but should be strong enough to assure quill stays in full-up position.

3. Avoid frustration of seeking lost key by fitting it in spring clip on column, or by attaching it to chain as here.

4. While a step pulley will give about four drilling speeds, a speed control accessory provides greater speed range.

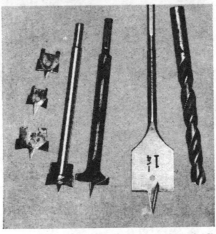

5. Common bits are, left to right, shaft with changeable blades, Forstner bit, power bit and common wood bit.

6. For really large holes, you will need an adjustable fly cutter. These are always operated at lowest possible speed.

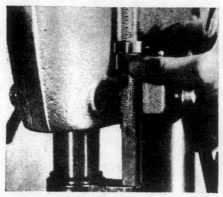
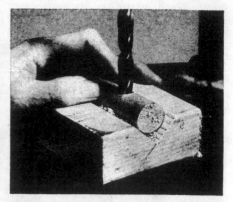

7. To drill to predetermined depth, mark stock, then lower bit to the mark, lock quill, set depth stop accordingly.

8. When setting depth stop, remember that numbers on stop are only relative, as position of table will affect depth.

9. For drilling round or irregular-shape work a simple fixture can be made by cutting a V-notch in a block of wood.

arm, the work should be solidly clamped.(6)

When you want to bore to a predetermined depth, the quickest way to set up is to measure and mark the edge of the work, then lower the bit to the mark and lock the quill.(7) You then set the depth stop accordingly.(8)

Quite often drilling operations will be in round or irregular-shape material that is difficult to hold on the press table by hand. To aid with this kind of work there are several basic fixtures you will want to include in your accessories. The most simple, and the one you can either buy or make yourself, is the V-block, used to hold round work. A simple one can be made by cutting a V-notch in a block of wood.(9)

Another type of hold-down resembles half of a C-clamp, but bolts to the press table.(10)

One of the most useful fixtures available, particularly when working with metal, is the drill-press vise. This can be secured to the table or used freehand to hold small parts or rounds. Most of these vises can be tilted for angle drilling.(11)

Drilling Holes

If you want to drill a series of holes on a common center line, you will save time and get a more accurate job if you use a fence. A simple one can be made by clamping a strip of straight lumber to the table.(12)

When you are drilling a series of equally-spaced holes on a common center line, you will gain accuracy and save time with a simple jig consisting of a piece of scrap with a short length of dowel fitted through it. The dowel is the same diameter as the holes to be drilled. When the first hole is located and bored, the work is slid along the fence until the dowel drops into the hole, locating the work for the next hole. Just repeat for as many holes as you need.(13)

Wood screws not only will drive easier, but will hold better when they are put in the proper-size pre-drilled holes. Profile drilling, as this is called, can be done by using three drills: a small one for the lead hole which allows the screw point to enter easily and provides good bite for the threads, a larger hole to accommodate the un-threaded shank of the screw, and a countersink that allows the head of the screw to lie flush or below the surface for filling or plugging.

The easiest way to profile-drill for screws is to use a set of specially-designed bits made just for this purpose. Some of these are set up with a series of marking rings on the shank, providing an accurate depth guide for flush setting or counter-boring the screws.(14)

Depth, of course, can be set with the depth stop on the drill press, or there are accessory stops available that fit over the shank of the bit. A tiny ballbearing collar, which allows the stop to remain stationary, even though the jaws of the chuck are rotating against it when it contacts the work, prevents the jaws from marring the work.(15)

Another handy accessory, if you need to plug counterbored screw holes, is a matching set of plug cutters. With these you can cut plugs from the same stock as the work, assuring a match of grain and color. Because the plug cutters are sized to match the profile bits, the plugs will fit the screw holes exactly, something you cannot be sure of when using dowels for plugs.(16)

Although it's not likely to become an every-day operation, there probably will come a time when you'll want to drill a hole in glass or ceramic material. It's really a simple job if you know how. Find a short length of brass tubing, such as used in lamps or curtain rods and cut several shallow slots in one end. Secure the rod in the drill-press chuck, then shape a dam of regular glazing putty around the area where you want the hole. Fill the dam with valve-grinding compound (available at auto-supply stores) thinned with turpentine. Set the press speed at about 600 and maintain a light, steady pressure. Lift the rod from time to time to let fresh abrasive flow into the ring being cut into the glass. A light weight on the feed-lever arm will reduce some of the arm fatigue.(17)

Drilling Mortises

It's no trick to drill mortises with a press, but it does take some special equipment. The regular chuck must be removed to permit fitting the housing that holds the mortising bit. A fence on the press table also is required. Carefully mark out the mortise on the work, place it on the table and adjust the hold-down on the fence so there is just enough clearance for the work to slide easily. Cut the two ends of the mortise first, then work across, overlapping each cut by about one-third the width of the chisel. Press speed should be about 3600 r.p.m. for a ¼-inch chisel, about 2800 r.p.m. for 3/8 and ½-inch chisels. (18)(19)

Drawer and Box Construction

For drawer or box construction with a professional touch, use a dovetail cutter and jig. The standard ½-inch cutter should be fitted in a collet chuck that replaces the regular chuck.(20) The boards are clamped in a fingered jig, with the ends to be mated butted together. Correct depth of cut

is set by adjusting the table, and the press speed is set at maximum to make the cuts.(21)

More Accessories and Tips

High on the list of inexpensive, but handy, accessories are the various rotary planers. Rough stock can be planed smooth, rabbets can be cut, and by tilting the table (or head, as on a radial-arm drill press) panel-raising can be done.(22-24)

While 6 or 8 inches is the maximum depth that the average drill bit will penetrate, there is a stunt that will double the effective length of a bit. First, clamp a piece of scrap to the press table and bore a hole almost through, using the bit to be employed.(25) Next, drop the table to accommodate the work, and locate and drill the hole to the limit of the bit.(26) Now, remove the work and insert a length of dowel, slightly longer than the work, into the hole you bored in the scrap. (The dowel is the same diameter as the bit.) Line up the top of the dowel with the bit.(27) Lock the table securely and remove the dowel. Finally, place a short length of dowel in the hole in the scrap, set your work over it so the dowel fits the hole first drilled in the work, to serve as a locating pin, then finish boring from the other end of the work.(28)

Another job your drill press can handle is shaping. Add an auxiliary plywood table to the press, clamp on a shaping fence and fit the special arbor to the spindle.(29) Curved-edge work can be easily handled with this setup by substituting conventional depth collars for the fence.(30)

Sanding drums of various sizes are another good item to have around. Used with a false top on the worktable, bored so the bottom edge of the drum is below the lower edge of the work, they can't be beat for irregular shapes.(31)

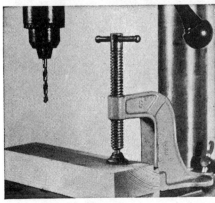

10. A handy hold-down resembles half a C-clamp, but the base is designed so a bolt fits through the slots in the table.

11. One of the most useful fixtures is a drill-press vise. It can be tilted at angle, is especially good for metal.

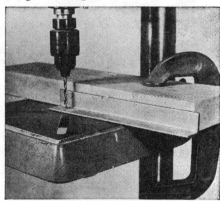

12. To drill a series of holes on a common center line, use a fence; this can be just a strip of clean lumber.

13. For a series of equally-spaced holes, use a jig that's a scrap of wood with a short length of dowel fitted through it.

14. The best way to drill for wood screws, either for countersinking or counterboring is to use special bits.

15. Other than using the depth stop on the press there are accessory stops that fit over the bit, have ball-bearing collar.

16. Another handy accessory if you want to plug screw holes is a set of plug cutters, cut plugs from same wood.

17. Length of brass tubing, the lower end notched, drills glass in pool of abrasive inside putty dam on table.

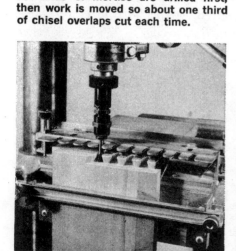

19. Ends of mortise are drilled first, then work is moved so about one third of chisel overlaps cut each time.

18. Special equipment is used to "drill" square holes to create mortise. Fence has hold-down to align work.

20. Collet chuck is used to hold router bit that shapes dovetail with aid of fixture that permits cutting two pieces.

21. Dovetail is still the classic in joints; neat, extremely strong, the sign of quality joinery in all woodworking.

22. Surface planer is inexpensive, very useful accessory for any drill press. Here it is being used to smooth stock.

23. Safe-T-Planer is handy for making rabbets in stock. It has three small knives, rather than conventional one.

24. Tipping table or quill at an angle permits planer to make raised-panel shapes for use as doors or plaques.

25. You can double usable length of a drill bit with this stunt: first, drill almost through a scrap block of wood.

26. Second step is to set up work, drill into it as far as the bit will reach. In this case hole is centered in block.

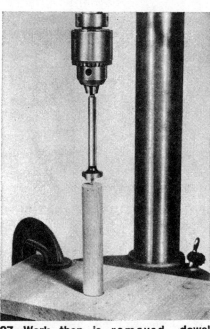

27. Work then is removed, dowel slightly longer than work is fitted in hole, moved so it is centered under drill.

28. Short dowel then is fitted in hole in scrap, work is fitted over it; will be automatically centered under drill bit.

29. Shaping is another job a drill press can handle. Special chuck is required, along with split shaper fence.

30. Conventional spacing collars can be used in place of shaper fence; they will regulate depth of cut.

31. Sanding drums are fine tools; fit them in hole in table so their lower edges are below edges of work.

Light surface grinding on metal parts is easily accomplished when the part is securely clamped in a drill-press vise and passed under a chucked emery wheel to make light cuts. Be sure the stone is turned at a speed within its limits; the maximum speed it can be driven will be stated on the label on the stone.(32)

32. A small emery wheel chucked in press will permit light surface grinding of metal. Turn stone at safe speed.

When working with a drill-press vise, a commercial fence or any other fixture that is clamped to the worktable, you can save a great deal of time and effort by making up a pair of hold-down bolts. These are readily made by sawing off the head of a heavy bolt (of a diameter that will fit through the slots in the table), drilling a hole in the shank of the bolt and driving in a rod. The bolt can be slipped through a table slot, turned 90 degrees so the rod locks under the table, then snugged down by a few turns of the wing nut, eliminating the need to remove the nut completely or turning it on, when using it.

Safety is a factor when using a drill press, as with any power tool. Wear goggles or a face shield when grinding, using a planer or a wire brush. Don't wear loose clothing or ties when operating a drill press; the spindle rotating at high speeds can seize a tie or loose material and wind it up in a fraction of a second, pulling the operator into the machine.

Keep tools sharp. Forcing a drill bit or planer into the work to make up for its dullness puts a strain on the bearings, and the operator, and it's easy to slip into the machine when you are trying to force it.

For most work you can clamp an auxiliary plywood table to the regular table. This will prevent metal-drill bits from scarring up the regular table, and will prevent wood-boring bits and planers from being dulled against the metal table.

RECOMMENDED DRILL-PRESS OPERATING SPEEDS

Material	Operation	Speed (rpm)
Wood	Drilling to ¼"	3800
Wood	Drilling ¼" to ½"	3100
Wood	Drilling ½" to ¾"	2300
Wood	Drilling ¾" to 1"	2000
Wood	Drilling over 1"	600
Wood	Expansion bit	600
Wood	Routing	Maximum
Wood	Plug cutting	3000
Wood	Carving	Maximum
Wood	Fly cutter	Minimum
Wood, hard	¼" Mortising chisel	2800
Wood, soft	¼" Mortising chisel	3600
Wood, hard	⅜" or ½" Mortising Chisel	2000
Wood, soft	⅜" or ½" Mortising Chisel	2800
Metal	Wire-brushing	3600
Glass, ceramic	Drilling	600

THE CIRCULAR SAW

Why use a portable electric saw? The two biggest reasons are accuracy and speed. Unless you're a real professional with a handsaw you can't begin to match the precision you'll get with a portable electric unit and, even if you are great on straight-line cutting, you'll have a tough time competing when it comes to miters and compound miters. You just can't beat a portable electric saw with its tilt base, built-in guides and accessories like the adjustable protractor. When it comes to speed, it's readily apparent that an electric unit will cut several times faster than a muscle-powered handsaw. While relatively new, as power tools go, the portable electric saw has become a sophisticated piece of machinery.

As with many power tools, it probably was the on-the-job professional carpenter who first realized the value of a lightweight, accurate, fast-cutting saw that could easily be carried up ladders, used on roofs, siding and for cutting studs to length when framing walls. The saw can slice off a section of 2x4 in just over 3 seconds, and that's a tough act to follow with a handsaw.

Portable electric saws are available in a wide variety of sizes, with a price spread to match. While some of the larger industrial models spin a blade as large as 12 inches in diameter, a unit that drives a blade 7 or 8 inches in diameter will cut 2½ inches deep, which is ample for the average home craftsman. A saw of this size with plenty of power to drive the blade can be purchased from about $40 on up. If you do only light work, you can get a portable saw as small as 5½ inches in diameter that will cut almost 2 inches deep.

Buying a Portable Saw

There are a couple of important points to keep in mind when buying a portable electric saw: get a blade big enough to cut the maximum depth you will encounter, when the blade is tilted a full 45 degrees, and be sure the motor is powerful enough to rotate that blade under all conditions. A saw with a 7½ or 8-inch blade usually will cut a depth of about 2 inches angled at 45 degrees which is adequate for the work done by most home craftsmen. To power a blade this size you will need a motor rated at about 1 HP or larger.

Preparation for Work

Once you have made a choice and have your new portable electric saw home, the first step is to fit the blade. This may sound basic, but many a craftsman has wondered why the saw wouldn't cut the way it was supposed to, and finally discovered that the blade was on backwards. The teeth on the blade of a portable electric saw should point toward the front of the tool, whether the blade is on the left or right of the motor.

To fit the blade, slip it on the arbor and turn the retaining nut or bolt by hand until it is snug. Retract the guard, rest the blade solidly on a piece of wood and snug up on the arbor nut with the special wrench that will be provided with the saw.(1)

Next, and this is very important, make sure the saw is properly grounded, which requires that it be fitted with a 3-wire cord. An exception here is a saw with a double-insulated motor and plastic case, such as the Rockwell Model 75. A short-circuit in an ungrounded tool can give you a tremendous electrical shock, and under some circumstances can kill you.

How to Use a Circular Saw

The "how" of using a portable electric saw starts with a straight-line cut. Mark off the line, then align the guide on the base of the saw with it, squeeze the trigger switch, and away you go. All portable saws have retractable blade guards that automatically swing up out of the way as you start your cut.(2)

Bevel cutting is a simple operation. Just set the saw to the angle you want and make the cut. Just follow the guide; the same applies to mitering and compound cuts. Follow the line, or use the accessory protractor available where portable electric circular saws are sold, and hardware stores.(3)

One of the few times you will have to touch the guard when actually sawing is when making a "pocket" cut. Use the handle on the guard to retract it, rest the saw on the front of its base, and slowly lower it into the work until the base rests flat on the stock.(4)

While a portable saw does best at cut-off work, it does perform well at ripping. If you are slicing off lengths of relatively narrow strips, use the rip fence or guide that fits on the base.(5)

There may be times when you will want to rip stock wider than the gauge will accommodate, and you want a more precise cut than possible following a pencil line. If so, clamp or tack-nail a length of straight stock to the work and run the saw base along it.(6)

To cut overlapping sheathing or other jobs where you want to cut only the top layer of material, use the depth control at the back of the saw.(7)

Dadoes and grooves can be cut with a portable electric saw. Just set the depth, then saw along the sides of the groove. Clear the groove with a succession of saw cuts between the side cuts, or use a

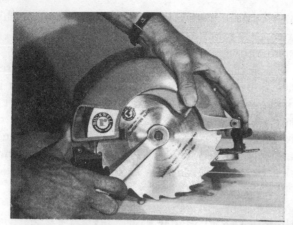

1.

2.

3.

4.

5.

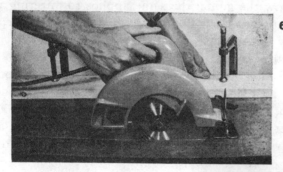

6.

7.

8.

9.

10.

74

chisel. A quick and accurate way of making the side cuts is to use the clamped fence with a second piece of stock, the width that the finished groove will be, fitted between the fence and the base of the saw.(8) After making the first cut, remove the stock and proceed with the second cut, using the fence as the guide.(9)

If you ever need to cut concrete or masonry, your portable saw can be a real time and labor saver. And the cuts will be clean and straight, not rough as they would be with a chisel. Fit the saw with an abrasive blade designed for cutting masonry and use it the same as when cutting wood. All operations are slower, however. Making a pocket cut in a concrete floor, for example, requires lowering the blade only as fast as the blade will cut into the concrete. Moving the saw along also is a much slower process than when cutting wood with a regular blade.(10)

Keep the blade sharp. Trying to force a dull blade through work is an invitation to trouble, and the added strain on the motor will shorten its life.

The portable electric circular saw is a time and labor saver. Keep it lubricated according to instructions, make sure you always have a sharp blade, and it will work for you for many years.

Safety. A face shield or goggles is a must when cutting masonry with an abrasive blade, as bits of stone and particles from the blade will be hurled in your face. For the same reason, keep other people away from the operation while you are doing the cutting. The bits of abrasive and concrete can be hurled several feet with considerable force.

We mentioned the guard that moves back automatically when you start a cut. The guard also should snap back up around the blade when a cut is complete. This permits setting the saw down immediately after using it, without worrying about the spinning blade causing damage to a surface or to itself. And mostly it prevents injuries to the user of the tool.

If the guard does not snap back immediately, clean the tool and lubricate the pivot of the guard so it does snap back readily. If the spring that controls the guard is weak or broken, replace it at once.

THE JIG SAW

Yes, you can cut out puzzles with a jig saw, but more important, you also can cut simple or intricate patterns in wood, metal, plastic, bone and other materials. The tool can be used to sand, file and do a host of other jobs that make it a worthwhile tool in any shop.

In appearance, the jig saw resembles a large letter "C," with the cutting blade supported between the extended arms of the letter. In the bottom portion of the machine there is an enclosed crankshaft that moves a vertically-positioned piston up and down. On the end of the piston is a chuck to hold the lower end of the blade. The upper end of the blade is held by another chuck, attached to a piston that is spring-loaded to maintain tension on the blade as it moves through its cycle. The unit shown in the photos in this section is a particular brand, but all jig saws are similar in design.

The crankshaft of a jig saw is in a crankcase, somewhat like an automobile engine; and like an engine requires that the case be filled with light oil.(1)

1. Crankshaft in lower part of jig saw runs in oil-filled crankcase.

Blades

There are two types of blades available for the tool, regular jig-saw blades and saber blades. (Very fine jig-saw blades, about .008 inches thick, are called jeweler's blades.) Both jig and saber blades are obtainable in a tremendous variety of widths, thicknesses and tooth sizes.(2)

The last three blades on the right are saber-saw blades. (The blade at the far right actually is a hacksaw blade, broken in half and ground down so it

JIG SAW BLADE SELECTION GUIDE

Blade Type	Type of Cut	Speed of Cut	Blade Length	Teeth per Inch
Flush Cutting	Rough	Fast	3"	7
Plaster Cutting	Rough	Fast	3⅝"	9
Double Cutting	Rough	Fast	3"	7
Double Cutting	Medium	Medium	3"	10
Skip Tooth	Rough	Fast	3"	5
Wood Cutting Coarse	Rough	Fastest	3"	7
Wood Cutting Fine	Medium	Medium	3"	10
Wood Cutting Hollow Ground	Smooth	Medium	3"	7
Metal Cutting	Medium	Medium	3"	14
Metal Cutting	Smooth	Medium	3"	18
Metal Cutting	Fine	Slow	3"	24
Metal Cutting	Very Fine	Slow	3"	32
Hollow Ground	Extremely Fine	Medium	4¼"	10
Hollow Ground	Smooth	Medium	4¼"	6
Hollow Ground	Smooth	Medium	4¼"	6
Hollow Ground	Fine	Medium	3"	10
Hollow Ground	Smooth	Medium Fast	3"	7
Hollow Ground	Medium	Fast	3"	5
Knife Blade	Smooth	Fast	3"	Knife Edge
Fleam Ground	Smooth	Medium	4"	10
Fleam Ground	Coarse	Fast	4"	6
Scroll Cut	Smooth	Medium	2½"	10
Wood Cutting Coarse	Rough	Fast	6"	3
Wood Cutting Medium	Medium	Medium	6"	7

2. Variety of jig and saber blades are available for jig saw.

will fit the lower chuck.) These blades are held by the bottom chuck only, as in a saber saw. To give the blades support at the point of contact with the work there is a lower guide that has a selection of slots of varying widths and depths. This notched disk is turned so it matches the particular blade you are using. The narrowest slot in which the blade will slide freely will assure that the blade will not twist and flex as the workpiece is turned during cutting.(3)

It is particularly important that the blade be mounted absolutely vertical. If it slants even slightly, forward or back, it will cut poorly, and often will cause the work to vibrate with each stroke, making it difficult to make an accurate cut. The fastest and safest way to fit blades, and be sure they are properly aligned, is to use a simple aligning block that you can make from a piece of scrap stock. Clamp the blade in the lower chuck first, making sure the chuck is at the top of its stroke. Then, lower the tension sleeve until the upper chuck is over the top of the blade. Tighten the chuck, then slide the sleeve up until the correct tension is on the blade, and lock the sleeve.(4)(5)

At the front of the lower-guide assembly there is a support roller. This should be adjusted so it just touches the back edges of the blade. This support keeps the blade from bending backward under the pressure of work being fed against it. The slotted lower guide, incidentally, should be adjusted so its forward edge comes just behind the bottom of the blade teeth.(6)

The last adjustment of the lower-guide assembly is to set the air-blower nozzle so that it is pointed at a spot just in front of the blade. This very handy device—not standard equipment on all jig saws—keeps the sawdust off the cutting line, and will save a lot of your time and breath, keeping the line easy to see.(6)

When it comes to using a saber blade, there are some differences in the setup, as opposed to using a regular jig saw. For a regular jig-saw blade, the flat jaws of the lower chuck are used, but for a saber blade you will have to loosen the locking screw on the lower chuck and rotate it 90 degrees so the blade can be clamped in the V-jaws of the chuck. The saber blades are held only by the lower chuck. Also, because saber blades often are used on heavier work, an auxiliary lower guide is fitted below the table. Used in conjunction with the upper

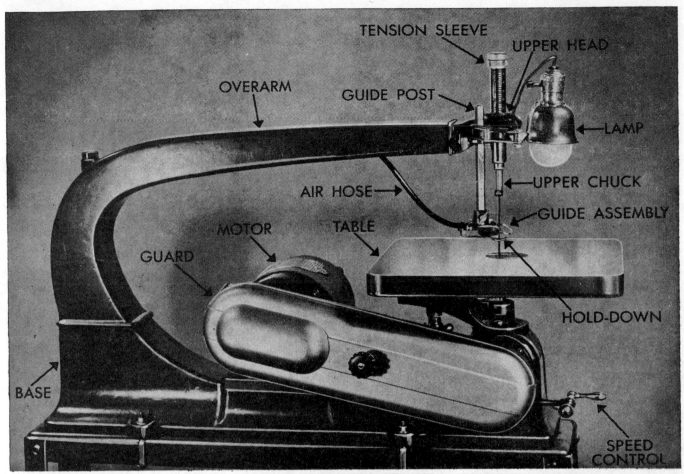

TENSION SLEEVE

UPPER HEAD

OVERARM

GUIDE POST

LAMP

AIR HOSE

UPPER CHUCK

MOTOR

TABLE

GUIDE ASSEMBLY

GUARD

HOLD-DOWN

BASE

SPEED CONTROL

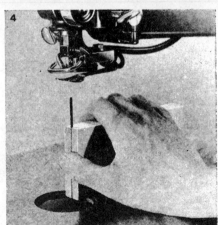

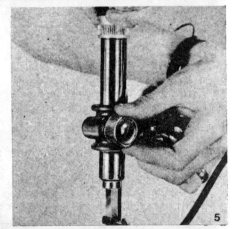

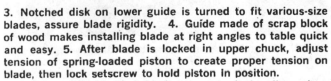

3. Notched disk on lower guide is turned to fit various-size blades, assure blade rigidity. 4. Guide made of scrap block of wood makes installing blade at right angles to table quick and easy. 5. After blade is locked in upper chuck, adjust tension of spring-loaded piston to create proper tension on blade, then lock setscrew to hold piston in position.
6. Support roller behind blade prevents it bending when work is pressed against it. Blower nozzle clears sawdust.

guide it makes the blade quite rigid and permits cutting a straight line with no worry about the blade flexing and twisting. Should the need arise to work on a piece of stock too large to fit in the throat of the saw, you can use a rigid saber blade and completely remove the overarm.(7-13)

Going to the opposite extreme, when doing very fine work, you may find a self-centering chuck invaluable. These slender "jeweler's" blades are just .008 inches thick and .035 inches wide, and break easily, especially if not properly aligned.(14)

There might also be times when you will find it handy to rotate the chucks and guides 90 degrees either way to permit cutting from the right or left, rather than in line with the arms of the machine. This is especially handy with long work that would run against the arm if the blade were aligned parallel to the arms.(15)

The table of a jig saw can be tilted up to 45 degrees by releasing a lock under the table and the saw used for bevel cutting. A quadrant in which the lock moves is calibrated in degrees for quick reference. This calibration should be checked occasionally, by using a square at 90 and 45 degrees, and the pointer moved accordingly. The upper guide of

a jig saw has no provision for tilting, but the spring hold-down always should be set at a matching angle to the table. This assures that the work is held firmly down on the table, and does not vibrate up and down with the movement of the blade. It is difficult to support the work on the slanting table while cutting intricate curves, and any added problem makes the job almost impossible.(16)(17)

There are many different blades that can be used on a jig saw. The wide variety of blades listed in the chart should handle just about any job that will be done in the average home workshop. A good rule-of-thumb when selecting blades for a job is "the heavier, rougher the work and the less intricate the cut, the coarser the blade."

To get the results you want from a particular blade, you must operate it at the proper speed. Most jig saws come with a constant-speed 1725 r.p.m. motor and cone pulleys. Varying the belt position produces speeds of 610, 910, 1255 and 1725 strokes per minute. Several makers of jig saws, and some accessory firms make a handy variable-speed unit as an accessory. Using spring-loaded, expanding V-pulleys, controlled by a crank, the speed control will produce any speed from 650 to 1700 r.p.m.(18)

7. Regular jig-saw blade is held by top, bottom chucks.
8. Saber blade is held only by lower chuck, against guide.

9. End of regular jig-saw blade is held between flat jaws of lower chuck, clamped firmly with setscrew of chuck.

10. For saber blade you have to loosen locking screw on lower chuck and rotate it 90 deg. so blade is held in V-jaws.

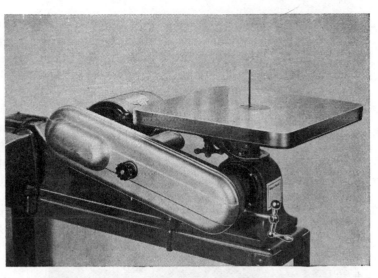

11. Firmer grip on saber blade is possible with V-jaws. 12. Additional support for saber blade is provided by optional guide that is fastened under the table.

13. When work is too large to fit inside arms of jig saw, upper arm can be removed completely. This can be done, of course, only when saber blades are used in saw, as they do not require use of upper chuck.

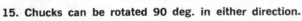

14. Self-centering chuck is indispensible for fine blades.

15. Chucks can be rotated 90 deg. in either direction.

16. Lock under table releases it for tipping up to 45 deg.

17. Hold-down on upper arm is angled to parallel surface.

18. Optional variable-speed unit permits speed from 650 to 1700 r.p.m.

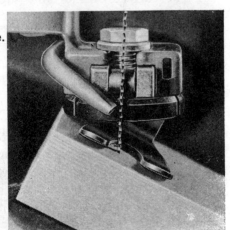

Saw Accessories

In addition to carrying cases, accessories for jig saws consist chiefly of blades for special tasks. They may be bought either separately or in sets.

While most jig saw blades fit most models, you can be certain of correct fit if you buy blades of the same brand as your saw.

The accompanying table briefly matches blades to use. For more detailed information, consult a manufacturer's catalogue or read the specifications on blade packages on a display rack in a store.

THE TABLE SAW

One of the most useful and basic tools in any woodworking shop is the table saw. It also is the easiest to use, if it is set up correctly and the operator has the knowhow to handle it properly and safely.

Care and Maintenance

A saw can only deliver top performance if it is in perfect alignment, and probably not one in ten does not not need at least minor adjustment.

First, keep the inside mechanism clean. A brush will remove loose sawdust before it cakes. Gum and pitch can be removed with commercial solvents made for that purpose. Debris in the works not only makes the controls hard to adjust, but can prevent the mechanism from seating against the stops and create inaccuracies.(1)

The surface of the table should not only be kept clean, but should be given a coat of paste wax periodically. This will prevent rust and allows work to slide more easily.(2)

The first step in checking alignment is to make sure the blade is square with the table. Crank the blade as high as it will go and mark one tooth. Position that tooth even with the top of the table and place the miter gauge opposite it. Fit a length of dowel against the gauge and butt it against the marked tooth. Mark the dowel at the end of the gauge. Now, rotate the blade so the marked tooth is at the opposite end of the table slot and measure again. If there is any variation in the two measurements, loosen the bolts that hold the arbor to the table and move the arbor until the blade is square with the table.(3)

To check for vertical alignment of the blade, crank the tilt mechanism until it hits its stop. Use a square to check the blade. If the blade isn't true,

first check to make sure sawdust or gum is not preventing the mechanism from going against the stop. If necessary, adjust the stop bolt. When the blade is square, set the pointer at "0" on the scale.(4)

Next, check the rip fence. Insert two blocks in the miter-gauge slot and slide the fence up against them. If the side of the fence does not fit snugly against both blocks when it is locked, adjust it. The rip fence also should be adjusted for vertical alignment.(5)(6)

Use a square to set the miter gauge, then adjust the pointer to "0" on the scale, and adjust indexing stops if the gauge has them. The final check is to use a square to see that the miter gauge is exactly at right angles to the blade, which it should be, if everything else has been correctly aligned.(7)(8)

Blades

Three types of blades are the most-commonly used in a home shop: the plywood blade with fine teeth and tempered to stand up under cutting the bonding adhesives used in plywood; the novelty combination with groups of teeth, used for ripping, mitering and crosscutting; and the hollow-ground combination that does the same work as the novelty combination, but makes a smoother cut.(9)

There are two ways to install a blade. One method is to mount the blade, washer and nut on the arbor and turn the nut on firmly by hand. Then, rest the wrench on the table and pull the blade toward you. The second method is to jam a block of wood against the teeth and turn the nut with the wrench. A similar method (10)(11) is used to remove the blade.

The blade of a table saw will cut well at almost any height, but it will cut most safely when it is set right. The position at which there is least chance of kickbacks is with the edge of the blade about ¼ inch above the top of the work.(12) The setup is correct for any type of blade. Cutting grooves or dadoes, however, does require the blade to be below the surface of the stock, and the chance of kickback is always present during this operation. Always stand to one side of the stock when using a table saw; a kickback can hurl the stock into your stomach and it can be somewhat painful.

Using the Table Saw

When ripping a short piece of stock, or finishing the cut on a long one, hook your two little fingers over the edge of the rip fence and hold the work with the thumb and two other fingers. Slide your hand along the fence as you feed the stock. If the material being cut is quite wide, your left hand can rest on it on the other side of the saw blade.(13)

If the fence is closer than a generous hand width to the blade, use a push stick. It is a good safety practice to use a push stick for any job where your hand will be close to the blade. The push stick is simply a piece of scrap stock with a V-notch cut in it to fit over the edge of the stock. On a short piece of stock, be sure to hold the front edge of the work down with the other hand (once it is well past the blade) so it will not kick up.(14)

Unless you use a rip blade with its more severely set teeth, you may have trouble with binding, particularly on thick or wild-grained stock. An easy way to avoid this—if you do not use a guard with a splitter—is to use a screwdriver or large nail to keep the kerf open when the cut is past the blade. A guard and splitter is a much better arrangement for this operation; a kickback could pull the blade where it would be hurled back at the operator.

For some operations the use of a guard and splitter is not practical, as when cutting angles or coving stock, but they should be used whenever possible. On hardwood, or any stock that splinters readily, a face shield will protect your eyes from flying fragments.

Special Problems

Now that you have your saw adjusted so it is in perfect alignment, and you have learned a few ways to simplify the job of making some saw cuts, let's tackle occasional problems that every craftsman will encounter:

You want to edge-groove a wide board. The standard fence is so low that the board will wobble and the cut will be inaccurate. What's the answer? Use a wide (high) auxiliary fence fastened to the regular rip fence. Your fence may have holes for such attachments, or you can drill through it to permit holding the auxiliary fence with wood screws.(16)

When you need to rip a piece of stock that is wider than the widest setting of the rip fence—a frequent problem with sheets of plywood—clamp a straightedge piece of stock to the underside of the work and let it ride along the edge of the table. The

strip is positioned, of course, the proper distance from the blade to the table edge. The same method is handy when ripping a wide board with an irregular edge, and you want to create a clean, straight edge.(17)

Another difficulty you will frequently encounter with wide stock is warping. When you have this situation, always make the cut with the concave side down and do not press down too strongly as you can bind the blade in the cut. If you try to make a cut in a bowed board with the concave side up, the workpiece will rock, and certainly cause the blade to bind.(18)

A safety tip too often ignored by beginning craftsmen is to never hold both ends of a piece of stock, particularly narrow material, when crosscutting. When you come to the edge of the work you will naturally force the kerf closed on the saw blade and cause either stalling of the motor or a kickback.(19)

When making miter cuts you will often find that the end of the miter gauge is so far from the blade that there is little stock in contact with it. Avoid this problem by fitting an auxiliary fence to the gauge. You can even extend the fence beyond the blade, making it high enough so the blade does not cut it off, and use the cut in the fence as a reference point in aligning a number of workpieces that are to be cut the same length.(20)

One method of preventing work from creeping on the miter gauge when cutting angles is to face the gauge with sandpaper. An even better way is to spend a few dollars for a hold-down clamp that is attached to the bar of the miter gauge. With one of these on the gauge even a difficult compound miter will be cut cleanly and the workpiece will not shift.(21)(22)

Crosscutting wide stock can be just as difficult on a table saw as ripping it. But you often can handle it by reversing the miter gauge in its slot and making the cut this way. In the reverse position there will be several inches of the miter-gauge bar in the slot of the table before the stock contacts the blade.(23)

When a number of identical pieces of stock are to be crosscut there are several ways the job can be done. One of the easiest is to use a stop rod fastened to the miter gauge. How the rod is located is important; never use the stop on the free end of the work as the freed portion will bind and kick

1. Keep the internal mechanism of the saw free of sawdust, gum and pitch. Also clean the motor housing.

4. Blade must be vertical with table; be sure sawdust or gum is not keeping mechanism from contacting stops.

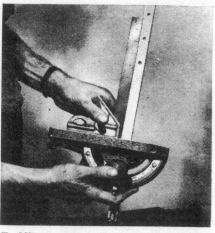

7. Miter gauge is used frequently, should be checked often for square. Indexing stops may require alignment.

2. Keep the saw table clean and free of rust with periodic applications of paste wax that lets work slide easily.

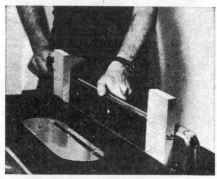

5. If fence is parallel with table slot it will contact blocks in slot. If it does not, adjustment of fence is necessary.

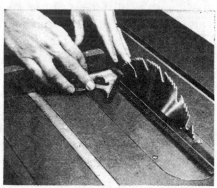

8. If you have aligned blade parallel to slots, and if miter gauge is set correctly, blade and gauge are 90°.

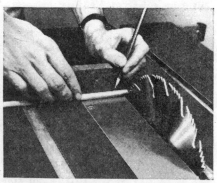

3. Dowel is used as measure to check on whether saw blade is parallel with table slots. Correction is simple.

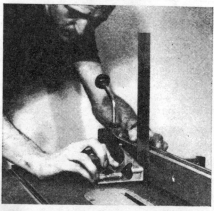

6. Rip fence also must be vertical to table. Combination square usually is the best tool for checking this.

9. Most commonly used blades in home workshop are plywood, novelty combination and straight combination.

10. Arbor nut must be tight; one way is to pull blade against wrench, the other is to hold blade with block.

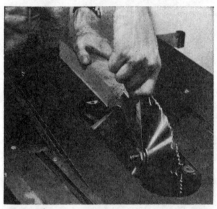

11. Teeth of blade are easily jammed into scrap of wood to permit using wrench to loosen arbor nut.

12. Safest height for blade, to minimize kickback, is a projection of about ¼ in. above top surface of the stock.

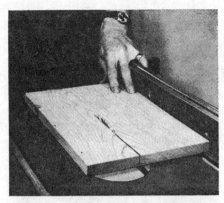

13. Safety first always; two fingers on rip fence will keep hand clear of the blade when ripping short stock.

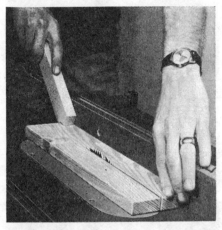

14. When hands must be close to blade, use a push stick. Just a scrap of wood with a V-notch cut in it.

15. Using a screw driver or nail to prevent kerf closing is all right, but better to use guard and splitter.

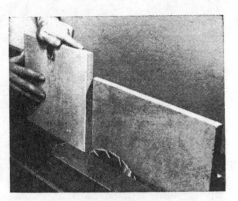

16. High auxiliary fence fastened to rip fence permits edge-grooving a wide board safely and accurately.

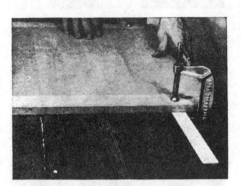

17. Straightedge board clamped to wide stock slides along table in place of rip fence that cannot adjust to fit.

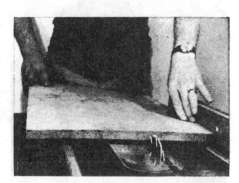

18. Always cut bowed stock with concave side down. With concave side up, stock will rock, cut will bind on blade.

back. The end of the stock held firmly against the miter gauge rests against the stop; the free end of the stock will simply be cut off and slide away from the saw blade.

When you have to cut a number of very short pieces, clamp a stop block on the rip fence, but locate it well back of the blade, then adjust the fence to get the correct length of cut. Never use the fence for a stop or the cut-off piece will jam between the blade and fence and probably will end up by being hurled back at you.(26)(27)

Cutting tenons and similar operations often require making cuts on the ends of long, narrow stock. Because there is very little support from the end riding the table, and especially when passing over the blade with its slot, clamp a piece of scrap to the work and let it ride along the top of the rip fence as a support and guide. Hold the work firmly down and against the fence to be sure of an accurate cut.(28)

If you do much tenoning you will find it worthwhile to invest in a tenoning jig.

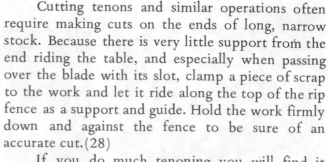

19. Never hold both ends of stock, especially narrow material, when crosscutting, or it will bind, kick back.

20. Auxiliary fence fitted to miter gauge permits mitering short stock, can even be used as a reference point.

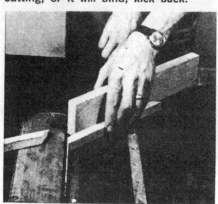

21. Hold-down clamp that attaches to bar of miter gauge will hold work firmly when it is to be mitered.

22. Hold-down is especially effective when cutting complex compound miters that tend to slip against miter gauge.

23. Crosscutting wide board sometimes makes it necessary to reverse miter gauge in its slot, as shown here.

24. Stop rod on miter gauge is fine way to cut a number of identical pieces, but not holding free end.

25. With stop rod against secured end of stock, free end is cut off and simply slides safely away from blade.

26. When using stop-block on rip gauge to determine lengths of short pieces, clamp block behind saw blade.

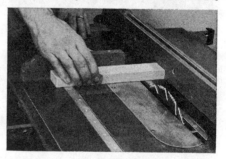

27. Never use the rip fence as a gauge without a stop-block. As with stop on miter gauge, you get kickback.

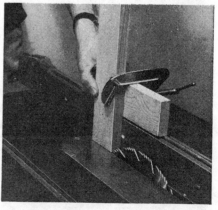

28. To tenon long, narrow stock, clamp scrap block to it and let it ride on rip fence to provide safety, accuracy.

THE RADIAL-ARM SAW

Although designed mainly for crosscutting and ripping, a radial-arm saw, even the smaller home-shop size, can be used for dadoing, rabbeting, mitering, making ornamental parts such as dentils of various types, moldings and shapes.

Preparation for Work

Proper adjustment of a radial-arm saw is a must if you want to get accurate work, and trouble-free performance.

The first step in setting up a new saw (and checking out one that is used frequently) is to make sure the blade is cutting at right angles to the fence. New units are factory-adjusted, but they can be misaligned in shipment. After the three parts of the table have been attached to the frame and the arm is in place, lock the arm. Raise the blade, slide it behind the rip fence and with the motor running, lower the blade until it cuts into the table about 1/8 inch. Now pull it forward the limit of its travel. Use a square to check the blade to be at right angles to the table and square to the fence. Make adjustments if necessary, then pull the running saw the full length of travel again. This may widen the groove in the table which is all right. Set the bevel pointer at "0."(1-4)

Next, turn the yoke 90 degrees and lower the blade so it cuts about 3/16 inch deep; this is done with the fence and back table removed. Start the blade behind the fixed table and pull it slowly forward. This makes a shallow cavity in the table so you can set the blade teeth slightly below the table surface at any point when in the rip position.(5)

Safety

If you are used to operating a table saw the "don'ts" and "carefuls" for a radial saw will require some memory jogging for a time until you keep in mind that the blade is above the table. This is not to say the radial saw is more hazardous, it just means the saw is more dangerous if you forget where your hands are. But this is a truism with any power tool: know the hazards and keep your mind on what you are doing!

Nearly all radial-arm saws have a "keyed" switch; pull out the key and the switch is locked. It cannot be turned on without the key.

If you have not used the saw for a time, check all controls; key switch, wing nuts, thumbscrews, lever-locks or whatever, to be sure they are tight so they hold things securely in place before you turn on the switch. Do all these checks if you have reason to suspect the machine has been bumped or moved around in the shop. The table may have been misaligned or the lever-locks and controls loosened by tampering or otherwise.(6)(7)

When working with the saw keep the table clear of everything except the piece being worked. Remove cutoffs, squares, any tools that could be hurled by the spinning blade.

When you set up for a rip cut, always use a push stick. Be sure the push stick will bear against the waste as well as the piece to be used. You can run the cut all the way through the work piece, cutting into the push stick, then slide the cut piece away with one hand well clear of the blade. This prevents either the waste or good piece being caught and damaged or thrown by the blade. Tables of radial-arm saws, especially the smaller ones such as shown, are relatively small, so provide an outboard support when cutting larger stock.(8)(9)

When ripping also be sure the antikickback unit is adjusted to ride on the work; this prevents the piece from being kicked back, or from lifting off the table while the cut is being made.

Using the Saw

All radials can cut right or left-hand angles by moving the arm. The simple angle jig is handy and somewhat faster when a number of pieces are to be mitered. Several such jigs can be made for the common angles, such as 30 and 22½ degrees. The jigs must be made accurately, of course. They are clamped to the table in use, and the cut is made on one end. The work piece then is turned end for end and the other cut made. Pieces must be marked for length beforehand.

You can use a dado blade on your radial saw for dadoing across the grain, grooving lengthwise or by tilting the motor 45 degrees you can run a neat cope cut. In running the latter to a given depth, make it in a series of cuts about 1/8 inch each pass. It's safer this way than running one deep cut, and the job will be smooth and require no sanding.(12)

When cutting across the grain with a dado you can cut to any reasonable depth in one pass, either square or at an angle. The parts of the dado blade must be sharp to produce neat, smooth work. Drill blades will cause splintering at the edges and "burning" and discoloration. When making cuts with a dado blade it's important to feed the stock, or blade, slowly and uniformly.(13)

Do you need to make a 180-degree bend in solid wood? You can do this trick on your radial-arm saw. Adjacent and parallel cuts are made almost, but not quite, through the stock.(14)(15)

Nearly all woods will bend with this operation if you are careful to select fairly straight-grained pieces. The spacing of the cuts must be accurate; a finish nail driven into the fence will help in accurate spacing, fitting into successive grooves.

Use a hollow-ground combination blade for this kerfing, as it makes narrow grooves that are more suitable for sharp bends.

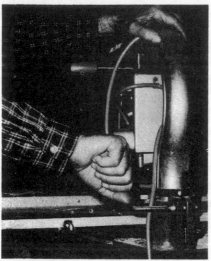

1. On this particular saw, arm is locked in position with "pinch" clamp operated by turning L-shape lever on base casting.

2. After arm is clamped, lower blade behind rip fence, turn on motor and pull blade forward so it cuts groove in table.

3. Check to see that blade is square with the fence. If not, adjust the arm and/or yoke square to fence, recut groove.

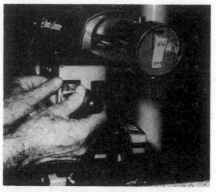

4. Also check with square to see that blade is at right angles to table. Set the bevel pointer at "O" on scale.

5. To cut the concavity in the table for setting the blade in rip position below table, remove fence, turn blade.

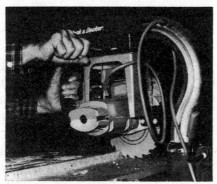

6. Before running tool after period of not using it, check all controls, lever-locks, etc. to make sure everything is tight.

7. Be sure guard is correctly positioned for thickness of stock being cut and that antikickback is adjusted and working.

8. When doing a ripping operation always use a push stick. It should be thinner than stock being cut, with handle.

PUSH STICK FOR RIP CUTS

HANDLE

ANGLE CUT

FIG. 9

¼" OR ⅜"

AT LEAST 10"

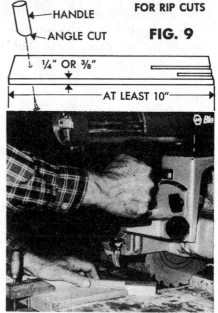

10. When cutting a number of pieces with identical angles you can make a jig to eliminate swinging arm.

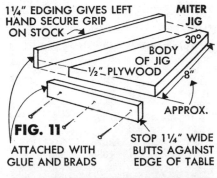

1¼" EDGING GIVES LEFT HAND SECURE GRIP ON STOCK

MITER JIG

BODY OF JIG

30°

½" PLYWOOD

8"

FIG. 11

APPROX.

ATTACHED WITH GLUE AND BRADS

STOP 1¼" WIDE BUTTS AGAINST EDGE OF TABLE

12. You can use a radial-arm saw to make a cope cut. This is made by lowering blade ⅛ in. for each pass.

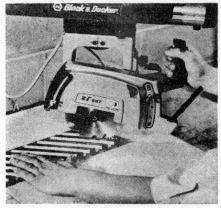

13. When cutting across the grain with a dado blade you can cut to any reasonable depth in one pass.

14. You can make a 180-deg. bend in wood by making adjacent cuts, not quite through the stock as shown.

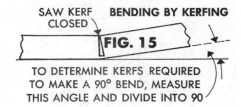

SAW KERF CLOSED

BENDING BY KERFING

FIG. 15

TO DETERMINE KERFS REQUIRED TO MAKE A 90° BEND, MEASURE THIS ANGLE AND DIVIDE INTO 90

THE LATHE

Of all the power tools in a woodworking shop, the lathe is the simplest, yet the most difficult to use. Simple, because even a beginner can use scraping chisels to create an attractive profile on his first try. Complicated, because it takes a lot of practice to learn to use chisels with a shearing and cutting action.

Three cutting actions are used. "Scraping" action is the one a beginner should use. The idea is to locate the cutting edge of the tool slightly above the center line of the work, then advance the tool slowly. You will duplicate (in reverse) the shape of the tool. Assuming that you are working with a round-nose chisel, you will form a cove. To enlarge the cove you just use the contact point between chisel and tool rest as pivot. To do smoothing, you advance the chisel until you are cutting about 1/16 inch deep, then move the chisel along the rest parallel to the work. Many experienced turners work this way (scraping) with all chisels except the gouge and skew. With these chisels a "cutting" or "shearing" action is best. Used skillfully in this manner, they work fast and leave a surface that hardly requires sanding.

Lathe speeds are important for both good work and safety. Notice that the rougher the cut and the larger the work, the slower the speed must be. In truth, this is mostly for safety. A large piece of work in the average lathe turning at high speed will rattle the machine all over the shop. It isn't always possible to set the speeds the chart calls for, but stay as close as you can. A good general rule is to start all work at slow speeds, then build up to the maximum suggested to make finishing cuts.

It's a good idea to wear goggles when doing lathe work, especially when you are making roughing cuts. Even better with some woods that chip and splinter badly is a face shield. Long-sleeve shirts are okay if the cuffs are tight around the wrists. The usual precaution about not wearing a loose-hanging tie seems rather silly, as the average woodworker would no more wear a tie in the shop than go to a formal dance in a bathing suit.

Mounting the Work

For spindle turnings you should locate a pretty true center at each end of the stock. If the work is square, all you have to do is draw intersecting diagonals at each end. If the work is not square, you can draw lines parallel to each edge and then judge the center. When the work is round to begin

1. Using chisels correctly is the way to become a "pro" with a lathe, but even a beginner will do well with scraping.

SPEED CHART			
Material and diameter	Roughing Cut r. p. m.*	Shaping Cut r. p. m.*	Finishing Cut r. p. m.*
wood to 2"	910	2590	4250
wood 2" to 4"	810	2375	3380
wood 4" to 6"	650	1825	2375
wood 6" to 8"	650	1200	1825
wood 8" to 10"	650	910	1025
wood over 10"	650	650	650
plastic to 3"	2200	3125	3875
plastic over 3"	1025	1200	1680
nonferrous metal to 3" (carbide-tipped tools)	650	1300	3125
*approx.			

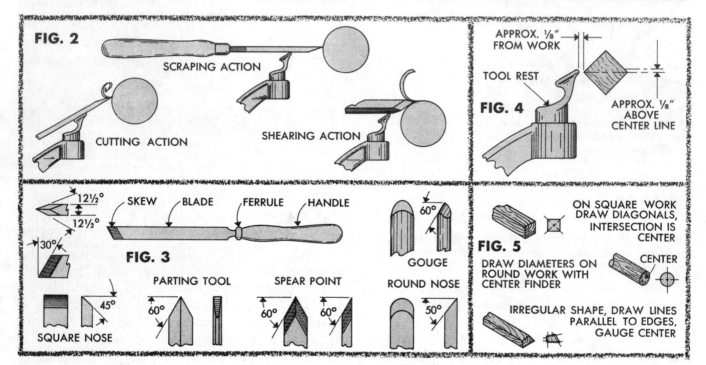

FIG. 2 — SCRAPING ACTION — CUTTING ACTION — SHEARING ACTION

FIG. 4 — APPROX. ⅛" FROM WORK — TOOL REST — APPROX. ⅛" ABOVE CENTER LINE

FIG. 3 — 12½° — 12½° — 30° — SKEW — BLADE — FERRULE — HANDLE — 45° — SQUARE NOSE — PARTING TOOL — 60° — SPEAR POINT — 60° — 60° — 60° — GOUGE — ROUND NOSE — 50°

FIG. 5 — ON SQUARE WORK DRAW DIAGONALS, INTERSECTION IS CENTER — DRAW DIAMETERS ON ROUND WORK WITH CENTER FINDER — CENTER — IRREGULAR SHAPE, DRAW LINES PARALLEL TO EDGES, GAUGE CENTER

with, you should use a center-finder. You may already have one of these that is mountable on the blade of a combination square.

Stock to be marked is placed in the V-notch and intersecting lines are drawn along the edge of the guide. Note that this tool may be used for square as well as round stock.

On softwood you can use an awl to mark the center point at each end. Most times, even the hardwoods, this is sufficient. If not, you can drill at the center and make light saw cuts for the spur center. The important thing is for the spur center to seat firmly. Best bet is to tap it firmly in position with a mallet while the center is out of the lathe. At the other end, seat the dead center firmly by advancing the ram in the tailstock. Don't overdo

this though, or the work and/or the dead center may burn. To avoid this problem, buy a ball-bearing live center which usually is an option for a lathe.

Thoughts on Design

Many woodworkers get a little shook here, but you can simplify the whole bit by relying heavily on classic forms. It's a serious mistake to start cutting into a blank mounted in a lathe without knowing what the end result should be. Better to do this on paper by drawing a center line, then applying those forms that are in the sketch. If you own a table saw and are equipped with a molding head, the molding knives can provide ready-made "templates" for tracing on your pattern. If you check through an assortment of molding knives,

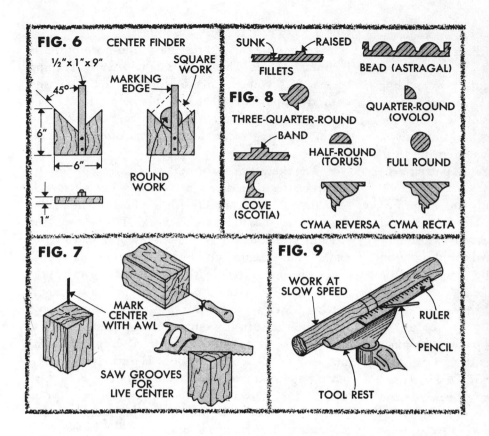

FIG. 6 CENTER FINDER

1/2"x 1"x 9"

45°

MARKING EDGE

SQUARE WORK

6"

6"

ROUND WORK

1"

SUNK — RAISED

FILLETS

BEAD (ASTRAGAL)

FIG. 8

THREE-QUARTER-ROUND

QUARTER-ROUND (OVOLO)

BAND

HALF-ROUND (TORUS)

FULL ROUND

COVE (SCOTIA)

CYMA REVERSA

CYMA RECTA

FIG. 7

MARK CENTER WITH AWL

SAW GROOVES FOR LIVE CENTER

FIG. 9

WORK AT SLOW SPEED

RULER

PENCIL

TOOL REST

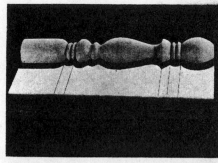

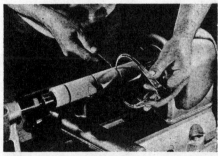

10. Template or pattern is good for complicated design, but a must when you need to turn duplicate pieces.

11. Next step after dimension marks on turning square is to locate maximum depth of cut at main points in design.

FIG. 12 SPINDLE TURNING

TEMPLATE

WORK

FIG. 13 FACEPLATE TURNING

WORK

TEMPLATE

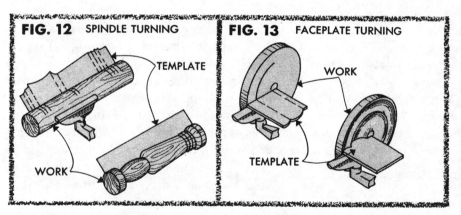

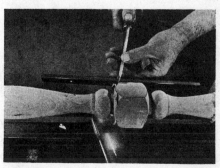

14. Gouge is best tool to use for all roughing cuts. It may be used with scraping action, or with shearing cut.

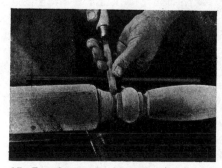

15. Forming coves is snap with round-nose tool. Chisel is moved slowly and directly into work.

16. It takes some practice to use skew well. Best bet is to work heel of blade into work, then move parallel to work.

17. Skew also can be used in kind of knife action as shown here where it produces clean edge square to round.

you will find that when used alone or in combination, it will be easy to duplicate the classic forms on almost any turning.

Another way to go, if you don't have molding knives, is to check through the catalog of any power-tool manufacturer. There you will find the profiles of shaper cutters as well as molding knives. By cutting these out and mounting them on thin, stiff cardboard, you'll have on-hand patterns of designs.

Another suggestion is to study the shapes of moldings. These too are based on classic forms. If you make it your business to amass an assortment of slim cross-sections from standard moldings, you will have no problem designing the project before you mount the stock in the machine.

The Basics of Layout

Once you have the design on paper, you must transfer it to the job. When the design is quite simple, you can get away with marking the essential points. This is just a matter of placing a ruler on the tool rest and using a pencil as if it were a chisel.

Then you work with a parting tool (in a scraping action) and a pair of outside calipers to cut down to maximum penetration at each of the points you marked. This looks like a "touchy" operation, but is really easy to do. Just work slowly; don't force the parting tool.

Most times it's better to make a full-size pattern on cardboard. Note that when the main points are carried across the pattern that the straight edge may be used for the basic dimensioning, and the profile for checking as you do the shaping. This procedure applies to faceplate work as well as spindle turning. The full-size pattern is good for any complicated turning, but it's a must when you require a number of similar pieces.

General Working

The gouge is the best tool to use for roughing stock from square to round. The corners of the wood should be removed with saw cuts (or jointer) before the work is mounted. This reduces considerably the amount of lathe-tool work you must do to get to a full-round shape. The chisel is held pretty much as shown and moved parallel to the work. The left hand rides the tool-rest edge, while the right hand does the actual tool positioning. If the gouge were held flat, it would be a scraping action. This

works okay too; it just takes longer.

In one of the figures the round-nose chisel is forming a cove. This is a straightforward scraping action, but you can make it go faster by starting with the point of the tool a bit below the center line and raising it gradually as you penetrate the work. You'll get the feel of this quickly if you practice a bit.

The skew is probably the most difficult tool to use in professional fashion. Your best bet is to work so that you make contact with the heel of the blade, then move parallel to the work. This is fine for straight cuts and for gentle curves. For ball shapes and similar designs, you must imagine that the cutting edge is following the shape you want. You don't do this in one "pass," but in slight stages, cutting away material just a bit at a time. Don't force the skew; in this cutting action it will dig in.

The skew can be used with a scraping action, and in a kind of knife action. Here it is making a sharp edge in a transition from square to round. It works fine, but do be careful by keeping your hands well away from the work. This square edge is difficult to see when it is spinning.

The spear point is used mostly in a scraping action. Here it is cleaning a shoulder. It's a good touch-up tool, but in a straight scraping action it does a fine job forming V-grooves.

You can use molding knives as turning tools. This is a simple scraping action with the cut started just slightly below the center line. Bring the tool up slowly as you penetrate the work. The secret here is to proceed slowly; don't allow the cutter to dig into the work. The handle for the knives is just a length of steel bar stock, drilled at one end so the molding knife can be bolted to it.

Long, slim turnings are flexible enough to require some support at the shaping point. You can provide this easily with a V-block affair mounted on a base that can be clamped to the lathe ways. The center of the V-notch must be on the center line of the work. Position it, as you work, close to where you are doing the cutting.

Drilling

No matter what the capacity of your lathe, there will be times when you must join spindles to get the length you need. Drilling for this joint can be done in the lathe. The chuck for the drill can be mounted in either the tailstock or head stock. As shown, the work is held still while the drill turns. The work is fed into the drill by using the tailstock ram.

If the drill is in the tailstock, the work is held against the spur center. This is not as easy to do, simply because the work is turning.

You can join spindles, and use turnings as shelf supports. In either case the tenon can be part of the turning, or holes can be drilled in each piece to accept a dowel.

When you need a hole completely through a piece it might be best to work simply, and a good glue joint will be almost invisible on the finished turning.

Other Mountings

Flat work; bowls, bases for spindles, etc., is mounted on a faceplate. The plate is a disk mounted in place of the spur center and attached to the work with screws.

For faceplate work, try to saw the work to full round before mounting it. Use a round-nose chisel in a scraping action; don't use the gouge. Position the tool rest for maximum support of the chisel point. Do this even for deep work, if you must locate it inside the work. Start at slow speeds; it's best to use a scraping action with any chisel as you are cutting across end grain.

Work too small to mount on a faceplate requires the use of a screw center. Everything about faceplate turning applies, except that speed is not critical, since you will be working with small pieces.

Finishing

Smooth work with progressively finer grits of sandpaper. After initial sanding, dampen the work and resand when it dries. You can apply stain or finish using slow speeds so the material is not hurled off. Dilute varnish and similar finishes and apply a couple of coats, rather than one heavy one. Don't rush finishing; if the material requires 24 hours drying, allow that time. Don't saturate the cloth or the project; excess material will coat you as well as the wood.

18. Spear-point chisel is always used with scraping action. Here it is forming and cleaning a shoulder.

20. Steady-rest is always required when turning a long, slender spindle. Support is clamped to lathe ways.

19. Molding knives are fine as lathe "chisels." Action is always scraping, feed is kept at minimum.

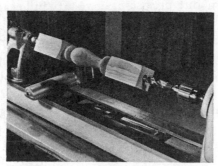

21. Best way to drill in lathe is to have bit in headstock end of lathe. Feed work into drill using tailstock ram.

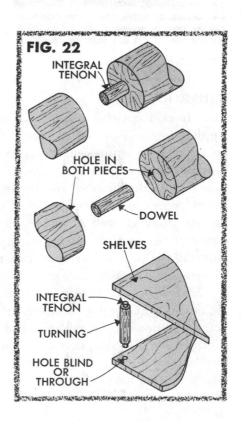

FIG. 22
INTEGRAL TENON
HOLE IN BOTH PIECES
DOWEL
SHELVES
INTEGRAL TENON
TURNING
HOLE BLIND OR THROUGH

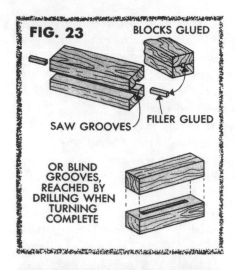

FIG. 23 BLOCKS GLUED

SAW GROOVES — FILLER GLUED

OR BLIND GROOVES, REACHED BY DRILLING WHEN TURNING COMPLETE

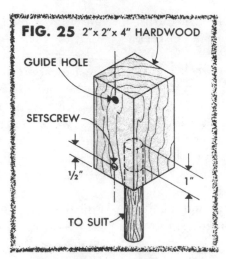

FIG. 25 2"x 2"x 4" HARDWOOD

GUIDE HOLE

SETSCREW

½" 1"

TO SUIT

27. Work too small for faceplate is mounted on screw center. This is the way for finials, drawer pulls.

24. Series of holes drilled on common center line removes stock for mortise. Remainder is cut out with sharp chisel.

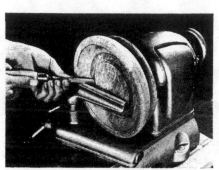

26. Faceplate is used when work can't be mounted between centers, as for bowls. Set tool rest for best support.

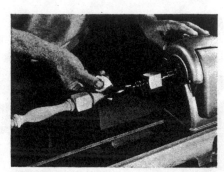

28. You can do almost any kind of finishing in the lathe. Use stain full strength, other materials diluted.

THE ROUTER

In concept the router is a simple tool, but in application it is one of the most flexible pieces of woodworking equipment you can own. By making a professional-type shaper table in which the router can be fitted, plus the wise buying of good accessories, you can run the gamut of the special jobs a shaper does as well as those which the portable router does so well. As an example, by buying a dovetail jig and cutter, you can turn out precise dovetails on par with any professional

With an assortment of other cutters you can do coving, chamfering, beading, etc. and make such joint components as rabbets, dadoes and grooves. Cutters can be one-piece or screw-on types. With the latter you use a single shaft for various profiles. Many cutters have pilots; an area of the shank below the cutter which rides on the edge of the work as a guide.

It's important for the pilot to have a substantial bearing surface against the edge, and it must be clean and smooth, to avoid burning and denting the wood.

Using the Router

Routers cut clockwise (looking down from the top of the motor), so feed the tool from left to right. Like all rules this one must occasionally be broken, especially with freehand work. Always grip the router firmly and feed just fast enough to cut at full capacity without having the cutter "choke up." If you have never used a router before, "play" with some scrap stock to get the feel of the tool before doing any finish work. The more powerful the router, the faster and deeper you'll be able to cut. Smaller routers (¼ to ½ HP) can do about as much as the big fellows (¾ to 1 HP), but will take longer. A small router may take two passes to cut a groove that can be done in one with a larger tool.

Straight cuts should be guided, and an easy way is to clamp a guide strip to the work. It should have a smooth edge and be fairly stiff so it does not

To turn out professional dovetail joints on a "production-line" basis all you need is a dovetail jig and template.

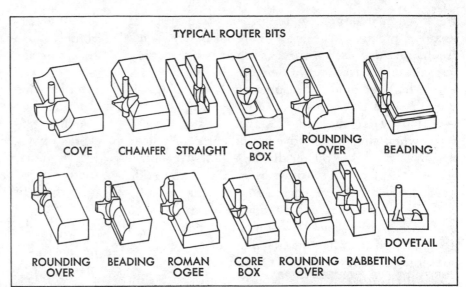

TYPICAL ROUTER BITS

COVE CHAMFER STRAIGHT CORE BOX ROUNDING OVER BEADING

ROUNDING OVER BEADING ROMAN OGEE CORE BOX ROUNDING OVER RABBETING DOVETAIL

Rigid strip of wood clamped to work makes good guide for straight cuts. Always feed so bits cut into the wood.

Edge guide is good for straight cuts when near an edge. Or, as here, when making series of parallel grooves.

When working along edge with pilot-tipped cutter, use a piece of scrap under the outboard edge of the router base.

GUIDE BLOCK CLAMPED TO WORK

ROUTER BASE ROUTER EDGE GUIDE

IN SOME SITUATIONS IT PAYS TO USE TWO GUIDE BLOCKS TO FORM A TRACK FOR ROUTER BASE

GUIDE CUT GUIDE

WHEN YOU NEED CUTS LIKE THIS SET UP LIKE THIS, CLAMP WORK BETWEEN BEARING BLOCKS

WORK

ALSO FOR CUTS LIKE THIS CUT INTO BEARING BLOCKS IF NECESSARY

Template can be any shape, but its edge must be smooth. Sleeve on template guide rides edge of template.

Template guides are economical accessories, but important for complete router use. These lock in place.

You can even cut out parts in quantity by making template and using template guides. All parts will be duplicates.

flex. When making a wide cut, use two strips to assure a precise cut; remove material between cuts freehand. Also use two tracks when it is necessary to make an accurate cut in one pass, as in a dovetail.

The edge guide that comes with the tool, or is purchased as an accessory, is fine for straight cuts, especially when they are close to an edge. It's also good when shaping an edge with a cutter that does not have a pilot. You set the edge guide to control the width of cut. You must be sure that the guide bears against the work edge throughout the pass.

On occasion you may find use for the edge guide when doing parallel grooves or dadoes. This is good procedure when making a number of equally-spaced cuts, as it guarantees correct spacing.

When working with a pilot-tipped cutter on the edge of stock it's a good idea to place a support strip under the outboard edge of the router to guard against accidental tipping of the tool.

You can work accurately on stock edges if you set up for the job. Bearing blocks support the router, and you guide the cut with an edge guide or, if the blocks are wide enough, by guide strips. This is a good way to make similar cuts on several pieces; merely "gang" them between the blocks.

Template guides are important accessories and are economical enough so you should not be without them. They provide a sleeve through which the cutter passes, while the router is used in the normal fashion, but with the sleeve riding against the edge of a template you make. The template can be a simple curved line, or an intricate pattern. It can even be the shape of a part required in quantity. The sleeve on the guide does have thickness, so the cutter is held away from the template by that

amount. On many jobs this is not critical; if it is, compensate by making the pattern that much larger for inside cuts, that much smaller for outside cuts.

You can use templates for incising or piercing; even for the shallow cuts required when inlaying. On thick stock several cuts will be required for piercing; generally a cut about ¼ inch on each pass works okay. Be sure the thickness of the template is a bit more than the projection of the sleeve from the router base. Make template edges smooth, and hold them firmly on the work with clamps or tack-nailing.

The fulcrum-pin setup permits freehand shaping on edges that can't ride the fence. The work is braced against the infeed pin and gradually brought forward to engage the cutter that has a pilot. Near the end of the cut you contact the outfeed pin. Precise dovetail work is almost entirely a matter of following the instructions that come with the jig. With sharp cutters and slow feed it's almost impossible to go wrong with this setup.

Perfect circles, or parts of circles are made by using a drill rod clamped in the holes normally used for the edge guide. A hole drilled in the rod accepts a nail.

Various cutters are used in a router for trimming plastic laminate. These bits provide both a guide and a cutting edge, so the projection of the bit is critical. These cutters take a beating on laminate, so buy the tungsten-carbide type, even though they do cost more. Generally the laminate is cut to project 1/16 to 1/8 inch, then is trimmed with the cutter to be squared or beveled. These laminate bits are a must when making counter tops.

Fulcrum pin setup lets you shape edges that can't feed along fence. Pins are ⅜-in. bolts with heads removed.

Start by bracing stock against infeed pin, then advance work to pilot cutter until end of work bears on outfeed pin.

Perfect dovetails can be created with dovetail jig if you follow instructions packaged with it. Jig matches router.

Pivot cutting requires rod to fit router-base hole. Nail fits through hole drilled in rod, acts as pivot for the router.

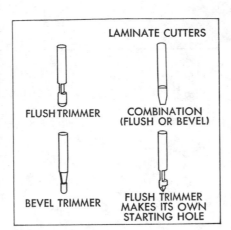

LAMINATE CUTTERS

FLUSH TRIMMER

COMBINATION (FLUSH OR BEVEL)

BEVEL TRIMMER

FLUSH TRIMMER MAKES ITS OWN STARTING HOLE

Laminate trimmers can be purchased in kits. Tungsten-carbide tools are not cheap, but are wise buy.

THE CHAIN SAW

The gasoline-powered chain saw is becoming more and more popular, as evidenced by an increasing amount of the new "Saturday-morning sound." Basically the reason more people are using chain saws is because manufacturers are turning out easier to use, lighter weight saws and yet with ample power. People are saving money by trimming their own trees, cutting their own firewood and removing storm-damaged trees.

Using the Chain Saw

One of the main jobs of the small saws is removing or felling small trees. Basically there are three easy steps to follow; the first wedge cut, the second wedge cut, and the back cut which fells the tree. However, before beginning the wedge cuts, low branches should be trimmed away if they are near enough from the ground to be reached easily.

On small, straight trees wedging the side of the tree in the direction you wish it to fall is not difficult. Sometimes larger trees lean or twist in a direction opposite to the way you want them to fall. In this case, it is wise to attach a guy rope to help pull in the direction of the notch to ensure that the tree will fall correctly.

Maintenance

Most people can neglect their hand and power tools and get away with it; but a chain saw is a more complex tool. It has many of the elements of an automobile, including a fuel and electrical system, rotating elements and lubricating and cooling systems.

In addition, chain saws work in a hostile environment, where the chain can be damaged by nails, stones, hard earth and wood, wire and other debris. Consequently, your chain saw needs regular maintenance and care, before and after use, and while you are cutting with it.

Before using your saw, there are a few things you can do to ensure trouble-free operation.

Check the oil level in the supply tank for the bar-chain lubrication; look for excessive moisture and foreign particles; change oil if needed.

Test the chain tension; too much will stretch the chain, too little causes excessive sprocket wear.

Clean the air cleaner and brush off the cooling fins, exhaust ports and muffler screen. Inspect the fuel filter and replace if it is dirty.

Examine the chain cutter teeth for sharpness. If they're dull, sharpen them. Check the built-in sharpening stone (if one is included) for wear; it pays to have a spare on hand.

Check the spark plug for dirt and gap. Adjust gap (per instruction book), using the proper tools, which should always be kept with the saw.

When using the saw in the field, most emergencies can be handled if you have a basic tool kit and vise. The kit should include: bar wrench, plug wrench, screwdriver, small socket set and special tools.

When you're through for the day, observe the following procedures; clean the fins and ports, remove sawdust and other particles, check the straightness of the bar, look for tooth wear and damage, make sure all nuts and bolts are tight, check air filter and wipe the saw clean.

To store the saw, oil the bar-chain system, run the engine dry of fuel and clean it. Wrap in newspaper to keep out dust and dampness.

As an extra measure of protection, you might want to make yourself an operator's maintenance checklist:

8 Hours of Operation
Check the oil tank for the bar-chain lubricating system.
Check chain tension.
Check chain-teeth sharpness.

Brush sawdust from cooling fins, exhaust ports and muffler screen.
Check wear on sharpening stone.
Check sparkplugs.

25 Hours of Operation
Clean air filter.

50 Hours of Operation
Clean fuel filter.

Trim away any low branches that will get in your way of felling the tree. Clear area around tree before felling.

Notch tree in the direction you wish it to fall. You may have to use guy ropes to guide the fall of a leaning tree.

Limbing branches of the fallen tree is a snap with the new saws. Stand clear and uphill of the fallen tree.

Clean air filter after 25 hours of operation. Brush off dirt, clean with kerosene, let dry, replace.

"Buck" the tree trunk into firewood size logs. Keep saw blade sharp and oiled according to directions.

Flying chips and sawdust can clog saw's air cleaner and lubricating system. Safety goggles are a must for operator.

Chain tension should be checked after 8 hours of use. Misadjustment can result in excessive wear, unsafe operation.

BUILDING
MATERIALS

3

BUILDING
MATERIALS

BUILDING MATERIALS

WOOD ■ FRAMING LUMBER

PLYWOOD ■ SHEET MATERIALS ■ PLASTIC

SELECTING THE PROPER MATERIAL

Today it is more important than ever to select the most appropriate wood product for each use in residential and farm construction. Wood products are now being made in more forms and from a greater variety of species than ever before. What was most suitable for a particular use a few years ago may not be so today.

About 25 billion board feet of wood products are used each year by the construction industry in the United States—much of this for homes and farm buildings. In addition, more than 6 billion board feet of lumber are used annually to maintain, repair, and remodel structures.

To select lumber and other wood-based material wisely, one must first single out the key requirements of the job. Then it is relatively easy to check the properties of the different woods to see which ones meet these requirements.

A builder or property owner may believe that he needs a strong wood for the siding of his house or barn when he really requires a wood that takes paint well, is resistant to weathering, and develops little or no warping. Or he may think he needs a wood with high bending strength for the joists of his house, whereas adequate stiffness is more important. Other considerations include the moisture content of the wood, its ability to resist distortion (warping), and its shrinkage characteristics.

In buying sheathing material, one should consider not only the original cost but cost of application as well. Such factors as relative nail-holding qualities, insulation values, and the possible elimination of corner bracing should also be considered.

It is not necessary to purchase only the best quality lumber or wood-based products. Lower and cheaper grades serve satisfactorily for many uses.

WOODS

Wood species are divided into two classes—hardwoods, which have broad leaves, and softwoods or conifers, which have scalelike leaves or needles. The terms "hardwood" and "softwood" do not denote hardness or softness of the wood. In fact, some "hardwoods" like cottonwood and aspen are less dense (or hard) than some "softwoods" like southern pine and Douglas-fir.

Most hardwoods differ substantially from softwoods in their properties (basic characteristics) and in their uses. As a class, hardwoods are heavier, harder, shrink more, and are tougher. Hardwoods and softwoods are similar in stiffness, so on a weight basis the softwoods are actually much stiffer. In strength as a post and in bending strength the two

Broad classification of woods according to characteristics and lar respect listed; B: Among woods intermediate in that respect; refer to lumber grades).

Kind of wood	Working and behavior characteristics											Strength properties			
	Hardness	Weight, dry	Freedom from shrinkage and swelling	Freedom from warping	Ease of working	Paint holding[1]	Nail holding	Decay resistance of heartwood	Proportion of heartwood[2]	Amount of figure	Freedom from odor and taste (dry)	Bending strength[3]	Stiffness[3]	Strength as a post	Toughness
1	2	3	4	5	6	7	8	9	10	11	12	13	14	15	16
Ash: Black	B	B	C	B	C	C	A	C	C	A	A	B	B	C	A
White	A	A	B	B	C	C	A	C	C	A	A	A	B	C	A
Aspen	C	C	B	B	A	A	A	C	B	A	A	C	B	C	C
Basswood	C	C	B	B	A	A	C	C	B	C	A	C	B	C	C
Beech	A	A	C	B	C	B	A	C	A	B	B	A	A	B	A
Birch	B	A	C	B	C	B	A	C	C	B	A	A	A	B	A
Cedar: Eastern red	B	B	A	B	B	A	B	A	C	B	A	B	C	B	B
Northern white	C	C	A	A	A	A	B	A	B	B	B	B	C	C	C
Southern white	C	C	A	A	A	A	C	A	A	C	B	C	C	C	C
Western red	C	C	A	A	A	A	C	A	A	B	C	C	C	B	C
Cherry	B	B	B	A	B	B	A	C	B	B	B	B	A	A	B
Cottonwood	C	C	B	C	B	A	C	C	C	C	B	A	B	C	C
Cypress	B	B	A	B	B	A	B	B	B	A	B	B	B	B	C
Douglas-fir	B	B	B	B	B	A	A	B	A	A	C	A	A	A	B
Elm: Rock	A	A	B	B	C	C	A	C	B	A	A	A	A	A	A
Soft	B	B	B	C	C	C	A	C	B	A	A	B	B	B	A
Fir: Balsam	C	C	B	B	C	C	C	C	B	A	A	C	C	C	C
White	C	C	A	B	B	C	C	C	C	C	A	B	A	B	C
Gum	B	B	C	C	B	C	A	B	B	B	B	B	A	B	B
Hackberry	B	B	C	B	C	C	A	C	C	A	A	B	C	C	A
Hemlock: Eastern	B	B	A	B	B	C	B	C	B	A	A	B	C	C	C
West coast	B	C	A	B	B	B	B	B	B	A	B	B	A	B	B
Hickory	A	A	A	B	C	C	A	C	B	A	A	A	A	A	A
Larch: Western	B	A	A	B	C	C	A	C	A	A	C	A	A	A	B
Locust	A	A	A	B	C	C	A	A	A	A	B	A	A	A	A
Magnolia	B	B	B	B	B	B	A	C	B·	B	B	B	B	B	B
Maple: Hard	A	A	C	B	C	B	A	C	C	B	A	A	A	B	A
Soft	B	B	B	B	C	B	A	C	C	B	A	B	B	B	A
Oak: Red	A	A	C	B	C	C	A	C	B	B	A	A	A	B	A
White	A	A	C	B	C	C	A	A	B	B	A	A	A	B	A
Pecan	A	A	B	B	C	C	A	C	B	A	B	A	A	A	A
Pine: Idaho white (western)	C	C	B	A	A	A	C	C	B	C	C	B	B	B	C
Lodgepole	C	C	B	A	B	A	B	C	B	C	C	B	B	B	C
Northern white (eastern)	C	C	A	A	A	A	C	B	B	C	C	C	C	C	C
Ponderosa	C	C	A	A	A	B	B	C	C	C	C	C	C	C	C
Southern yellow	B	C	A	B	A	C	A	C	C	A	C	A	A	A	C
Sugar	C	C	A	A	A	A	C	C	B	C	C	C	C	C	C
Poplar	C	B	B	A	B	A	B	C	B	B	A	B	B	B	B
Redwood	B	C	A	A	B	A	B	A	A	B	A	B	B	A	C
Spruce: Eastern	C	C	B	A	B	B	C	C	C	B	B	B	B	C	C
Engelmann	C	C	B	A	A	B	B	C	C	C	B	B	B	C	C
Sitka	C	C	A	A	B	B	B	C	C	B	A	B	A	B	B
Sycamore	B	B	B	C	C	B	A	C	B	B	A	B	B	B	B
Tupelo	B	B	B	C	C	B	A	C	B	C	A	B	B	B	B
Walnut	B	A	B	A	B	C	A	A	B	C	A	A	A	A	A

[1] Indicates general paintability and performance characteristics of edge-grained surfaces exposed to the weather.

[2] Exclusive of the all-heartwood grades that are available on special order in birch, cedar, cypress, Douglas-fir, gum, southern yellow pine, redwood, and walnut.

[3] Many of the softwood species are sold stress-graded for greater strength and stiffness.

properties (A: Among the woods relatively high in the particu-
C: Among woods relatively low in that respect. Letters do not

Surface characteristics of common grades					
Knots		Pitch defects	Other defects		
Freedom from	Acceptance as to size	Freedom from	Freedom from	Acceptance as to size	Distinctive and principal uses
17	18	19	20	21	22
A	B	A	B	B	Implements, cooperage, containers, furniture
A	B	A	B	B	Implements, containers, furniture, veener
A	B	A	B	B	Boxes, lumber, pulp, excelsior, veneer
A	B	A	A	A	Woodenware, boxes, veneer, excelsior, lumber
B	B	A	A	C	Flooring, furniture, woodenware, cooperage, veneer
A	B	A	B	B	Flooring, furniture, millwork, veneer
C	B	A	B	A	Posts, paneling, wardrobes, chests
B	B	A	B	B	Poles, posts, tanks, woodenware
A	B	A	A	A	Posts, poles, boat and tank stock, shingles, woodenware
A.	C	A	A	B	Shingles, siding, poles, millwork, boats, paneling
A	B	A	B	B	Furniture, woodenware, paneling, gunstocks
A	B	A	A	A	Pulpwood, excelsior, containers, woodenware, lumber, veneer
A	B	B	B	B	Millwork, siding, tanks, cooling towers, poles, shakes
B	B	B	B	B	Construction, plywood, millwork, flooring, piling, poles
B	B	A	C	C	Furniture, containers, veneer, cooperage
B	B	A	B	C	Containers, furniture, veneer
C	A	A	B	B	Light construction, pulpwood
B	B	A	B.	C	Light construction, containers, millwork
A	B	A	A	A	Millwork, containers, furniture, veneer, pulpwood
A	C	A	B	B	Furniture, veneer, containers
B	B	A	C	C	Construction, containers, pulpwood
B	B	A	B	B	Construction, pulpwood, containers, flooring
B	C	A	B	B	Handles, athletic goods, implements, flooring
C	A	A	C	A	Construction, poles, ties, millwork
B	A	A	B	B	Poles, posts, insulator pins, ties, fuel, containers
A	B	A	B	B	Furniture, veneer, containers, millwork
B	B	A	B	A	Flooring, furniture, veneer, woodenware
A	C	A	A	B	Furniture, woodenware, fuel, pulpwood
A	C	A	B	B	Flooring, furniture, veneer, posts, millwork
A	C	A	B	B	Furniture, cooperage, millwork, veneer, flooring, implements
A	C	A	C	C	Implement handles, flooring, pallets
C	A	A	C	A	Millwork, construction, siding, paneling, containers
C	B	A	B	B	Poles, lumber, ties, mine timbers
C	A	A	B	B	Millwork, furniture, containers, paneling, siding
B	B	B	B	B	Millwork, construction, poles, veneer, paneling
A	C	C	B	B	Construction, poles, siding, cooperage, ties, plywood
C	B	A	B	A	Millwork, patterns, construction, containers, siding
A	B	A	A	A	Furniture, plywood, containers, pulpwood, excelsior
A	C	A	A	B	Siding, tanks, millwork, cooling towers, outdoor furniture
C	A	A	B	B	Construction, pulpwood, millwork, containers
C	A	A	B	B	Light construction, poles, pulpwood, mine timbers
B	B	A	B	B	Construction, millwork, containers, pulpwood, cooperage
A	B	A	B	B	Furniture, veneer, cooperage, containers
A	B	A	A	A	Containers, furniture, veneer, cooperage
A	B	A	A	A	Furniture, gunstocks, interior finish, veneer

groups are more directly comparable than they are in weight, toughness, and hardness; nevertheless, more commercial hardwoods than softwoods can be rated high in bending strength.

The softwoods are used principally in construction work, whereas hardwoods furnish most of the wood for interior finish and flooring as well as for implements, furniture, and other industrial uses. In addition to normal construction uses, 2-inch and thicker lumber is also sold stress-graded for more carefully engineered components such as trusses.

Hardness

Hardness is the property that makes a surface difficult to dent, scratch, or cut. Generally, the harder the wood, the better it resists wear, the less it crushes or mashes under loads, and the better it can be polished. On the other hand, the harder wood is more difficult to cut with tools, harder to nail, and more likely to split in nailing.

Hardness is of particular concern in flooring, furniture, and tool handles. Hardness is also important in selecting interior trim such as door casings, base, and base shoe, as well as door jambs, sills, and thresholds. These portions usually receive the hardest wear in a house.

There is a pronounced difference in hardness between the springwood and the summerwood of woods such as southern yellow pine and Douglas-fir. In these woods the summerwood is the denser, darker colored portion of the annual growth ring. Differences in surface hardness thus occur at close intervals on a piece of such wood depending on whether springwood or summerwood is encountered. In woods like maple, which do not have pronounced springwood and summerwood, the hardness of the surface is quite uniform.

The classification of a species as a hardwood or softwood is not based on actual hardness of wood. Technically, softwoods are those cut from coniferous or evergreen trees, whereas hardwoods are those cut from broad-leaved and deciduous trees. Actually, some of the softwoods are harder than some of the hardwoods.

As a group, the hardwoods can be divided into (a) dense and (b) less dense. The softwoods can also be divided into two groups: (1) medium-density and (b) low-density.

A number of woods are strong favorites for building purposes largely because of their softness and uniformity rather than their hardness. Northern white pine (eastern) and Idaho white pine (western), poplar, white fir, and basswood are traditional examples. Others are ponderosa pine, sugar pine, and cedar. The ease with which these woods can be cut, sawed, and nailed has put them in a high position for general use. This is less important in present-day construction because portable power tools make it easier to handle such dense species as Douglas-fir and southern yellow pine. In fact, the use of these denser species allows greater spans for joists and rafters than can be used for equal-sized members of the softer woods.

Differences in hardness are great enough to affect the choice of woods for such uses as flooring and furniture on one hand, and for siding, millwork, and cabinets on the other.

Weight

Weight, in addition to being important in itself, is generally a reliable index of strength. A heavy piece of wood is generally stronger than a lighter piece of the same moisture content and size, whether it is of the same or of a different species.

Wood weights, as commonly expressed, are either in the green or in the air-dry condition. Green weight of wood is the weight before any drying takes place; air-dry weight of wood refers to the weight after drying by exposure to atmospheric conditions for a time, either outdoors or in unheated sheds.

Freedom From Shrinkage and Swelling

Most materials change in dimension with changes in temperature or moisture. Wood, like many other fibrous materials, shrinks as it dries and swells as it absorbs moisture. As a rule, however, much shrinking and swelling of wood in structures can be avoided by using wood that has been dried to a suitable moisture content.

For most species, the shrinkage or swelling in width of a flat-grained or plainsawed board is often approximately twice that of an edge-grained or quartersawed board of the same width. Edge-grained boards or other items cut from a species with high shrinkage characteristics will therefore prove as satisfactory as flat-grained boards or items cut from species with lower shrinkage characteristics. The normal wood of all species shrinks or swells very slightly along the grain (lengthwise).

Plywood is relatively free from shrinkage and swelling as compared to solid wood because its construction generally consists of alternate laminations of veneers laid with grain at 90 degrees to each other. From soaked to ovendry condition, the shrinkage of plywood in length and width is generally quite uniform and ranges from only about 0.2 to about 1.2 percent. After manufacture, plywood has a low moisture content and normally does not require drying out before use.

Methods of determining whether wood is dry enough for use are discussed later.

Freedom From Warping

The warping of wood is closely allied with shrinkage. Lumber that is crossgrained, or is from near the pith (core) of the tree, tends to warp when it shrinks.

The combined characteristics of warping and shrinkage determine the ability of wood to remain flat, straight, and not change size while in use. These qualities are desired in practically all uses. They are especially important in furniture, cabinetwork, window sash and frames, doors, and siding. Proper seasoning is important, but good construction details outlined later for preventing shrinkage also effectively prevent warping.

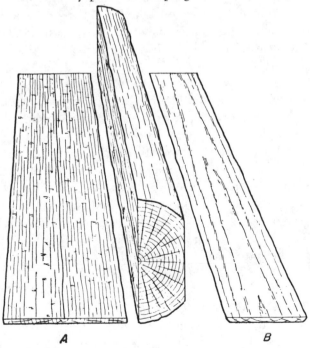

Grain depends on how lumber is cut from log. Board "A" is quartersawed or edge-grained. Board "B" is plainsawed or flat-grained.

Ease of Working

Wood is generally easy to cut, shape, and fasten with ordinary tools directly on the building site. For some purposes the difference between woods in ease of working is negligible, but for others it may decidedly affect the quality and cost of the finished job. In general, ease of working is of first importance to the worker and indirectly to the one who pays the bill. Fabrication and assembly at the factory of cabinets, windows, frames, doors, and other units have greatly reduced the time required for the skilled worker at the building site.

Harder and denser woods with high load-carrying capacity and wear resistance should not be passed over just because softer woods are easier to work; rather, a reasonable balance must be drawn in selecting wood for a specific use.

A skilled carpenter working with lumber that is well seasoned and manufactured can get good results from even the more difficult-to-work woods. An unskilled worker is more likely to get good results only from the softer woods. However, with portable power tools, jigs for installation of hinges and door locks, and other modern labor-saving methods, skill is no longer the major factor it was when hand tools were the only means of cutting and fitting on the job.

Nail Holding

As a rule, fastenings are the weakest link in all forms of construction and in all materials; therefore the resistance offered by the wood to the withdrawal of nails is important. Usually, the denser and harder the wood, the greater is the inherent nail-holding ability, assuming the wood does not split. The grouping of the commercial woods according to their inherent nail-holding ability is based on tests that measured the force required to pull nails from wood.

The size, type, and number of nails have a marked effect on the strength of a joint. Correct placement of the nails is as important as the size and number. If high winds are general during severe storms, special fastenings should be used to resist these pressures.

The resistance of nails to withdrawal increases almost directly with their diameter; if the diameter of the nail is doubled, the holding strength is doubled, providing the nail does not split the wood when it is driven. The lateral resistance of nails increases as the 1½ power of the diameter.

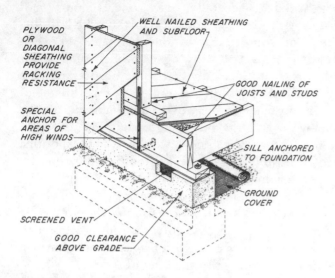

GOOD PRACTICE

PLYWOOD OR DIAGONAL SHEATHING PROVIDE RACKING RESISTANCE

WELL NAILED SHEATHING AND SUBFLOOR

GOOD NAILING OF JOISTS AND STUDS

SPECIAL ANCHOR FOR AREAS OF HIGH WINDS

SILL ANCHORED TO FOUNDATION

GROUND COVER

SCREENED VENT

GOOD CLEARANCE ABOVE GRADE

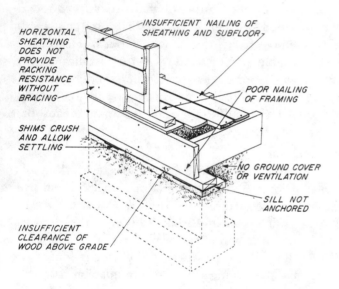

POOR PRACTICE

HORIZONTAL SHEATHING DOES NOT PROVIDE RACKING RESISTANCE WITHOUT BRACING

INSUFFICIENT NAILING OF SHEATHING AND SUBFLOOR

POOR NAILING OF FRAMING

SHIMS CRUSH AND ALLOW SETTLING

NO GROUND COVER OR VENTILATION

SILL NOT ANCHORED

INSUFFICIENT CLEARANCE OF WOOD ABOVE GRADE

Good and poor construction practices at foundation.

The nail most generally used in wood-frame construction is the common nail. However, galvanized and aluminum nails are used extensively in applying siding and exterior trim because these nails resist rusting. The galvanized nail is slightly better than the common bright nail in retaining its withdrawal resistance.

Superior withdrawal resistance has been shown by the deformed-shank nail, which is produced in two general forms, the annular-groove and the spiral-groove shanks. The annular-groove nail is outstanding in its resistance to static-withdrawal loads but not as good as the spiral-groove nail when subjected to racking loads. The spiral-groove nail is superior to the plain-shank nail in its resistance to withdrawal loads and is commonly used in construction of pole-type buildings.

Interior carpentry uses the small-headed finish nail, which can be set and puttied over.

The moisture content of the wood at the time of nailing is extremely important for good nail holding. If plain-shank nails are driven into wet wood, they will lose about three-fourths of their full holding ability when the wood becomes dry. This loss of holding power is so great that siding, barn boards, or fence pickets are likely to become loose when plain-shank nails are driven into green wood that subsequently dries. Thus the most important rule in obtaining good joints and high nail-holding ability is to use well-seasoned wood.

Prevention of Splitting. The splitting of wood by nails greatly reduces their holding ability. Even if the wood is split only slightly around the nail, considerable holding strength is lost. Because of hardness and texture characteristics, some woods split more in nailing than do others. The heavy, dense woods, such as maple, oak, and hickory, split more in nailing than do the lightweight woods such as basswood, spruce, and balsam and white fir.

Predrilling is good practice in dense woods, especially when large diameter nails are used. The drilled hole should be about 75 percent of the nail diameter.

Woods without a uniform texture, like southern yellow pine and Douglas-fir, split more than do such uniform-textured woods as northern and Idaho white pine, sugar pine, or ponderosa pine.

In addition to predrilling, the most common means taken to reduce splitting is the use of small diameter nails. The number of small nails must be increased to maintain the same gross holding strength as with larger nails. Slightly blunt-pointed nails have less tendency to split wood than do sharp-pointed nails. Too much blunting, however, results in a loss of holding ability.

FRAMING LUMBER

The homeowner or hobbyist who hasn't browsed through his local lumber yard, selected an appropriate grade and species of lumber, and brought a construction project or repair project to successful completion has a creative experience awaiting him.

The day of the skilled cabinet maker is said to be rapidly passing. Competent carpentry tradesmen are costly to employ. As a result, many of the amenities which make the older home or the custom home more attractive and more livable are beyond the means of the average home buyer.

Fortunately, most of the features that distinguish the custom home from one having only the bare essentials are well within the capabilities of the home craftsman. Lumber, the oldest yet in many respects the most modern and most readily workable building material, makes this possible.

Lumber was a more familiar item to our parents and grandparents when locally grown species were used and when grades and species selections were minimal. Softwood lumber of several species and from a number of regions is currently available in many communities, and dimension lumber grades have been developed on a more precise engineering basis.

For these reasons, any complete listing of all the grades and species of softwood lumber available throughout the nation tends to appear somewhat confusing at first. Not all the listed grades and species of lumber are available in every locality, however. Just as the builder must do, the home craftsman will quickly become familiar with the most commonly marketed species and grades in his community.

At the retail level, lumber is classified primarily by use and by size. It is also differentiated by the extent to which it has been manufactured, that is, rough sawn, dressed and worked (tongued and grooved, shiplapped or patterned).

Classification by Use

Yard Lumber. Yard lumber consists of those grades, sizes and patterns used in ordinary construction. It is broken down into Select and Common grades.

Select grades of yard lumber have the best appearance and are used where a clear or high grade of finishing is desired. Grade names such as "B and Btr" (Better), "C" and "D" are used for most species.

Common grades of lumber are suitable for general construction. The home craftsman will find even the lower common grades of boards yield many clearcuttings which can be used for furniture,

cabinetry and other household projects. Common grades of lumber are "No. 1," "No. 2," "No. 3," and "No. 4." Alternate names for common lumber, such as "Sel Merch" (Select Merchantable), "Merch," "Const." (Construction), "Std" (Standard), and "Util" (Utility), may also be encountered.

The common grades will frequently be found at the retail level as combination grades where the grade requirements for many uses make it practical to inventory and sell a "No. 2 and Btr" ("No. 1" and "No. 2" grades, combined), or "No. 3 and Btr" ("No. 3" and "No. 2" and possibly "No. 1," combined). The home craftsman can check the suitability of such combined grades for his purposes by inspecting several pieces of the material which is inventoried this way at the lumber yard.

Factory and Shop. Factory and shop lumber is produced primarily for industrial purposes such as the manufacture of windows and doors. It will not ordinarily be encountered by the home craftsman at the retail yard.

Structural. Structural lumber is 2 inches or more in nominal thickness (1¼ inches actual dressed thickness). It is also called stress graded lumber because each grade is assigned working stress values to permit its use in engineered structures.

Classification by Size

Lumber sizes are usually referenced for convenience and tally as nominal sizes, such as 1"x2", 2"x4", 4"x10", etc. Actual surfaced sizes are smaller in thickness and width. Lengths are actual lengths as specified or slightly longer.

Boards. Boards are less than 2 inches in nominal thickness and are 1 inch and larger in width. Boards less than 6 inches in nominal width may be called strips. Boards are used for fencing, sheathing, subflooring, roofing, concrete forms, box material and as a source of many smaller cuttings.

Dimension. Dimension is from 2 inches to, but not including, 5 inches in nominal thickness and 2 inches or more in width. Such lumber, depending upon use, may be called framing, studs, joists and planks, rafters, and the like.

Timbers. Timbers are 5 inches or more in their least dimension. According to use in construction, they are classified as beams and stringers, girders, purlins and posts.

Nominal sizes (2x4, etc.) are widely used in

Nominal and minimum-dressed sizes of boards, dimension, and timbers.

(The thicknesses apply to all widths and all widths to all thicknesses)

ITEM	THICKNESSES			FACE WIDTHS		
	NOMINAL	Minimum Dressed		NOMINAL	Minimum Dressed	
		Dry[1]	Green[1]		Dry[1]	Green[1]
		Inches	Inches		Inches	Inches
Boards[2]	1	¾	25/32	2	1½	1 9/16
	1¼	1	1 1/32	3	2½	2 9/16
	1½	1¼	1 9/32	4	3½	3 9/16
				5	4½	4 5/8
				6	5½	5 5/8
				7	6½	6 5/8
				8	7¼	7½
				9	8¼	8½
				10	9¼	9½
				11	10¼	10½
				12	11¼	11½
				14	13¼	13½
				16	15¼	15½
Dimension	2	1½	1 9/16	2	1½	1 9/16
	2½	2	2 1/16	3	2½	2 9/16
	3	2½	2 9/16	4	3½	3 9/16
	3½	3	3 1/16	5	4½	4 5/8
				6	5½	5 5/8
				8	7¼	7½
				10	9¼	9½
				12	11¼	11½
				14	13¼	13½
				16	15¼	15½
Dimension	4	3½	3 9/16	2	1½	1 9/16
	4½	4	4 1/16	3	2½	2 9/16
				4	3½	3 9/16
				5	4½	4 5/8
				6	5½	5 5/8
				8	7¼	7½
				10	9¼	9½
				12	11¼	11½
				14		13½
				16		15½
Timbers	5 & Thicker		½ Off	5 & Wider		½ Off

[1] "Dry" lumber has been dried to 19 percent moisture content or less; "green" lumber has a moisture content of more than 19 percent.

[2] Boards less than the minimum thickness for 1 inch nominal but ⅝ inch or greater thickness dry (11/16 inch green) may be regarded as American Standard Lumber, but such boards shall be marked to show the size and condition of seasoning at the time of dressing. They shall also be distinguished from 1-inch boards on invoices and certificates.

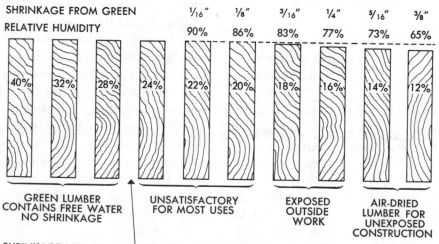

SHRINKAGE FROM GREEN   1/16"   ⅛"   3/16"   ¼"   5/16"   ⅜"

RELATIVE HUMIDITY   90%   86%   83%   77%   73%   65%

40%   32%   28%   24%   22%   20%   18%   16%   14%   12%

GREEN LUMBER CONTAINS FREE WATER NO SHRINKAGE   UNSATISFACTORY FOR MOST USES   EXPOSED OUTSIDE WORK   AIR-DRIED LUMBER FOR UNEXPOSED CONSTRUCTION

SHRINKAGE BEGINS AT FIBER SATURATION POINT

7/16″	15/32″	1/2″	17/32″	9/16″	5/8″	11/16″	3/4″
53%	50%	42%	34%	29%	18%	7%	0%
10%	9%	8%	7%	6%	4%	2%	0%

KILN-DRIED LUMBER
FOR INTERIOR WORK   OVERDRIED LUMBER

lumber tallying and, for simplicity, by the construction trades.

If the home craftsman buys what the trade calls a 2x4 and measures it, the dimensions will be found to be significantly less. Actually, the 2x4 surfaced size at 19 maximum percent moisture content is 1½″x3″.

Board and dimension lumber is generally sold by the board foot. This is a volume unit 1 inch in thickness, by 1 foot in length and 1 foot in width. To determine the number of board feet in a piece of lumber, multiply the thickness (in inches) by the width (in feet), by the length (in feet). For example, a 2″x4″ twelve feet long contains 2″x4″/12″x12′= 8 board feet.

The exception to the rule occurs where the nominal thickness is less than 1 inch. In this case it is only necessary to multiply the width in feet by the length in feet to obtain the board foot tally of the piece.

Select or finish lumber sizes apply at 19 or lower percent moisture content. Most finish lumber is manufactured at a maximum moisture content of 15 percent.

Board and dimension lumber may be surfaced "dry" at 19 percent maximum moisture content (marked S-DRY), at 15 percent maximum moisture content (marked MC15 or KD), or at the green condition (S-GRN). Dressed sizes for such lumber at the dry and green conditions are given in a table with this chapter. Timbers (over 4 inches in thickness) are produced at the green condition, permitting them to season in service.

Classification by Manufacture

Lumber may be manufactured rough, dressed, and worked (matched, shiplapped or patterned). Rough lumber has been sawed, edged and trimmed but not surfaced. Dressed lumber has been surfaced on one or more sides to remove saw marks and surface blemishes. The most common dressed lumber is surfaced on all sides or S4S.

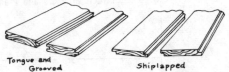

Tongue and Grooved   Shiplapped

Worked lumber has been tongued and grooved (T&G), shiplapped or patterned, in addition to being surfaced.

American Softwood Lumber Standard

With the issuance of the American Softwood Lumber Standard, PS 20-70, in September 1970, development of a National Grading Rule for dimension lumber became a reality.

Prior to development of the standard published by the U.S. Department of Commerce, each regional grade writing agency developed structural grades for dimension lumber based upon regional species or species groups. These grades took into consideration the characteristics of the species, i.e., knot size, size of timber, non-dimension uses of the species, etc. As a result, a great many different engineering stress levels were developed and an even greater number of allowable spans for joists and rafters were tabulated.

To simplify the multitude of structural grades and working stresses available to the designer and the user, the Softwood Lumber Standard PS 20-70 published in 1970 provided that a National Grading Rule Committee be established, "To maintain and make fully and fairly available grade strength ratios, nomenclature and descriptions of grades for dimension lumber." These grades and grade requirements, as developed, are now used by all regional grade writing agencies.

Dimension Lumber Grades
(National Grading Rule)

Grade
2″–4″ Thick, 2″–4″ Wide

Structural Light Framing	Sel Str (Select Structural)
	No. 1
	No. 2
	No. 3
Studs	Stud
Light Framing	Const (Construction)
	Std (Standard)
	Util (Utility)

2″–4″ Thick, 6″ and Wider

Structural Joists and Planks	Sel Str (Select Structural)
	No. 1
	No. 2
	No. 3

2″–4″ Thick, 2″ and Wider

Appearance Framing	A (appearance)

Since development of the National Grading Rule and the adherence of all regional and species rules to its requirements, a great deal more uniformity has resulted and use of dimension lumber by the architect and engineer has been materially simplified.

All softwood grade writing agencies which publish grading rules, certified by the American Lumber Standards Committee, adhere to this rule for dimension lumber. The rule provides for uniform grade names for all species and grades of structural lumber.

The National Grading Rule separates dimension lumber into two width categories. Pieces up to 4 inches wide are graded as "Structural Light Framing," "Light Framing," and "Studs." Pieces 6 inches and wider are graded as "Structural Joists and Planks." For special uses where a fine appearance and high bending strength are required, the national rule also provides a single "Appearance Framing" grade.

"Structural Light Framing" grades are available for those engineered uses where the higher bending strengths are required.

The four grades included in this category are "Sel Str" (Select Structural), "No. 1," "No. 2," and "No. 3."

"Light Framing" grades are available for those uses where good appearance at lower design level is satisfactory. Grades in this category are called "Const" (Construction), "Std" (Standard), and "Util" (Utility).

A single "Stud" grade is also provided under the National Grading Rule. It is intended specifically for use as a vertical bearing member in walls and partitions and is produced to a maximum length of 10 feet.

"Structural Joists and Plank" grades are available in widths 6 inches and wider for use as joists, rafters, headers, built-up beams, etc. Grades in this category are "Sel-Str" (Select Structural), "No. 1," "No. 2," and "No. 3."

Not all grades described under the National Grading Rule and listed in the last table will be available in all species or regions. The "Sel-Str" and "No. 1" grades are frequently used for truss construction and other engineered uses where high strength is required. For general construction, the grades normally encountered at the retail yard are "No. 2," or "No. 2 and Btr," or "Std and Btr." The "No. 3" and "Util" grades are also available and provide important economies where less demanding strength requirements are involved.

In selecting dimension lumber for load bearing

purposes, it is prudent to have engineering assistance and, where required, a building permit.

Span tables for joists and rafters are available from the National Forest Products Association and other lumber organizations.

Careful use of such tables and the assigned working stress for the various grades permits selection of the species and minimum grade to satisfy requirements of span and floor loadings.

Where severe use conditions require lumber to be frequently wet or exposed to damp soil, naturally durable species and pressure-treated lumber are available.

Choosing the Right Lumber

Lumber used for sleepers or sills resting on a concrete slab which is in direct contact with the earth, or joists closer than 18 inches to the ground, should be of naturally durable species or pressure-treated lumber. Where lumber is imbedded in the ground to support permanent structures, pressure-treated lumber should be used.

Naturally durable species most frequently encountered at the retail yard are California redwood, Western red cedar and tidewater red cypress. The Foundation grades of redwood and red cedar should be selected for ground contact. In cypress, a heart Structural grade should be selected for similar exposure.

Assume you have decided upon the species and grade of lumber required for a project, as well as the appropriate number of board feet you will need. Make a simple sketch showing the layout of framing members, furring strips, paneling, etc. and include it with the list of materials you will take to the lumber yard. At the yard, request the assistance of a clerk who can check your sketch, quantity and grade selections.

If at all possible, follow your order through the yard. Look at the types of material in stock, the grade marks and other identification. Inspect other wood items, such as windows, doors, moulding and trim. This is a part of the education process which will be most helpful in planning the next project and in providing a mental picture of the appearance of the various lumber grades and species.

PLYWOOD AND OTHER SHEET MATERIALS

While lumber is widely used in frame construction, sheet materials are also important. Wood-based panel materials are now broadly of three types—plywood, building fiberboard, and particle-board.

PLYWOOD

For everything from subfloors to roof decks to siding and built-ins, plywood is an all-round building material. Whether you're building, remodeling, adding on, or making furniture in your home workshop, plywood may be the material you need.

In residential construction, plywood's structural role extends to floor, wall, and roof systems. You can also use it for interior paneling, exterior siding, furniture, cabinets, shelving, fences, wind screens, patio decking, outdoor storage units, and hundreds of do-it-yourself projects.

Before employing plywood to do a task around the house, you should know the product, its capabilities and its limitations.

Plywood is a real wood. Although it is an engineered product, the natural wood is changed very little in the manufacturing process.

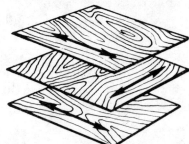

Plywood is a glued panel made up of layers of veneer (thin sheets of wood) with the grain of adjacent layers at right angles to each other. The kind of glue used determines whether it is interior or exterior type. Plywoods are classified by kinds and by qualities of faces. Those with hardwood faces are usually classed as decorative and those with softwood faces as construction. Exceptions for softwood plywood include, for example, face veneers of knotty pine or clear, cabinet grades, which are decorative. Plywood is graded on both front and back faces, in that sequence.

How Plywood is Made

When a log arrives at a plywood mill, it is peeled, placed in a giant lathe, and turned against a lathe knife. The veneer (thin sheet of wood) that flows from the lathe in a continuous ribbon is clipped into pieces of a convenient size for kiln drying and assembly into plywood panels.

Every plywood panel is a bulk-up board made of kiln dried layers of veneer. An odd number of layers is used for every panel so that the grain direction on the face and back run in the same direction.

The veneer layers are assembled at right angles to each other and united under high pressure with an adhesive. The resulting glue-bonds become as strong or stronger than the wood itself.

Since wood is stronger along the grain, this cross-lamination distributes wood's strength in both directions.

Peeling veneers from a log and reassembling them also provides a means for making panels much larger than those that could be produced by sawing. (Standard plywood panels are 4x8 feet, though wider and longer panels are also produced.)

Selecting Plywood

One basic thing to remember in selecting plywood is to look for the grade—trademark which identifies the product, subject to the quality inspection of an approved testing agency.

The grade and type of a panel should also be considered in the selection of plywood. Type refers to the durability of the glueline or the degree of exposure the panel should be subjected to. Letter grades N, A, B, C, D, refer to the quality of the face and back veneers. N represents the highest veneer quality.

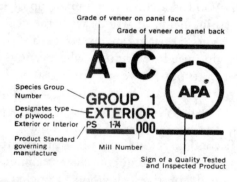

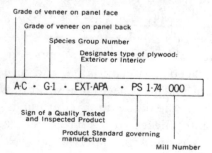

A two letter combination, for example, A-C, is used to indicate the quality of the panel face and back. "A" indicates the face quality and "C" describes the back.

Grades A-A, A-B, or A-D interior type sanded plywood are recommended for cabinet doors, furniture, built-ins, and other projects to be painted.

If you prefer a waxed, sealed, or varnished natural finish, select fine grain panels in A-A, A-B, or A-D grades.

For exterior siding, interior paneling and ceilings, textured plywood panels are available in many different species, surfaces, and patterns. Textured plywood sidings are best finished with stains, although some species may be left to weather naturally.

Good results for painted surfaces, interior or exterior, can also be achieved with Medium Density Overlaid (MDO) plywood. This grade has a smooth resin-treated fiber surface bonded to the panel face. It takes and holds paint well.

Plywood is available in both appearance and in engineered grades. Appearance grades are normally sanded. Engineered grades which are left unsanded are generally applied where a high degree of strength and rigidity are required.

You'll notice that the approved grade-trademark on appearance grades includes a group number. That number stands for one of the more than 70 wood species from which plywood is manufactured.

Since species vary in strength and stiffness, they have been classified into five groups under PS 1 (Product Standard 1). The strongest woods are found in Group 1.

Unsanded engineered grades of plywood bearing a grade-trademark carry an Identification Index which tells you the maximum support spacing to which the plywood can be applied in conventional construction.

The Identification Index appears as two number designations separated by a diagonal such as 24/0, 32/16, etc. The number to the left of the diagonal indicates the maximum spacing of supports in inches which should be used when the panel is applied as roof decking. The number designation to the right provides the same information for subflooring applications.

Unsanded grades designated as STRUCTURAL I and STRUCTURAL II are recommended for

heavy load application, where plywood's strength properties are of maximum importance.

Where to Use Plywood

Now that you've become a little better acquainted with plywood, we can move on to its role in residential construction.

Flooring. Starting with the basics, let's look at the part it plays in the area of flooring.

In a double layer system, your floor will be made up of plywood subflooring and a separate layer of underlayment. The underlayment plywood offers a high degree of dimensional stability that eliminates swelling and buckling. The result is a smooth, solid, stable base for any kind of finish flooring you desire.

One good way to save money and time is to use one layer of plywood as a combination subflooring and underlayment material. The plywood serves both as a structural subfloor and as an excellent base for resilient floorings, carpeting, and for other nonstructural floorings.

Plywood bearing the registered grade-trademark 2.4.1 can be used to provide both subflooring and an underlayment surface in a single 1-1/8 inch thick plywood panel. It's best to use 2 x joists spaced 32 inches on center or 4 x girders spaced 48 inches as the support system.

One excellent construction system you can use in building a floor is the APA Glued Floor System in which glue and nails are used to secure the structural underlayment to wood joists. This system was designed to produce floors that would be stronger and less apt to squeak.

The glues needed for this system are elastomeric adhesives meeting performance specification AFG-01. These glues, which may be applied even in below freezing weather, are available in cartridges designed for conventional caulking guns.

Specific recommendations on the APA Glued Floor System may be obtained from the American Plywood Association.

Walls. Plywood is also a key word in any discussion of wall construction. Performing structurally as wall sheathing, it covers large areas rapidly and supplies strength and rigidity. Neither let-in bracing nor building paper is required with it.

Plywood wall sheathing may be installed either vertically or horizontally. Horizontal application of panels will give you greater stiffness under loads perpendicular to the surface. So, if you're going to be nailing siding such as shingles directly into your wall sheathing, it would be wise to apply the sheathing horizontally.

The availability of many siding textures adds an aesthetic dimension to plywood's structural role as a wall material. Textured plywood can be used for interior paneling as well as exterior siding.

Although many builders and handymen still apply plywood siding in a two layer system, more and more are turning to the APA Single Wall System in which plywood siding is applied directly to studs.

Accepted by the Federal Housing Administration, the Farmers Home Administration, and most local building codes, the single wall system is designed to offer tight wall construction. All horizontal and vertical joints are backed with lumber framing members. Nails around the edges secure panels to the framing and provide draft stops at all points.

To insure weather tightness, single wall joints are shiplapped, battened, or backed with building paper.

When you're using the APA Single Wall System, you may apply plywood panel siding, or lap, or beveled siding. Specify 3/8, 1/2, or 5/8 inch, depending on your stud spacing.

Be sure to seal plywood edges. If you're going to paint the surface, the prime coat can serve as your sealer. If the plywood is to be stained, seal it first with a water-repellent preservative that's compatible with the finish.

Although plywood sidings are normally installed vertically, you may place panels horizontally with the face grain across supports.

Determining what is the allowable support spacing for the construction of single walls is a simple matter. Panels for single wall construction which are identified as 303 sidings have their maximum support spacing listed in their grade-trademark.

A 303 siding, for example, bearing a "303—24 in. o.c." may be applied vertically to studs 16 or 24 inches on center, while panels marked "303—16 in. o.c." may be applied vertically over studs spaced no more than 16 inches apart.

Texture 1–11, 1 5/8 inch thick exterior siding panel with a 3/8 inch wide vertical grooving spaced 2, 4, 6, or 8 inches on center may be used vertically over studs spaced 16 inches on center.

All edges of panel siding should be backed with framing or blocking. And to keep from staining siding with nails, use hot dip galvanized, aluminum, or other nonstaining nails. No extra corner bracing is needed with plywood panel siding.

Roof Construction. Moving along to roof construction, you'll find that plywood roof sheathing gives you the strength and rigidity you need while it makes a solid base for roofing material.

Plywood sheathing bears an Identification Index which tells you the recommended rafter spacing for a specific plywood thickness. For example, for roof systems with a 24 inch span (distance between rafters), plywood with a marking of 24/0 will do the job.

These Identification Index panels are available in thicknesses ranging from 5/16 through 7/8 inch.

Plywood roof sheathing has superior nail holding capabilities. Extensive laboratory and field tests have proven that even 5/16 inch plywood will hold shingle nails securely and permanently in place, in the face of hurricane force winds.

Your house plan will show either "open soffits" or "closed soffits." For a roof deck over closed soffits, you can use C-D Interior grade sheathing. To enclose the soffits, Medium Density Overlaid plywood is preferable because it has a superior painting surface.

With open soffits, panels will be exposed at the overhang. Thus, you'll want to select an Exterior type plywood. In addition to being an Exterior type plywood, the plywood you choose for an open soffit application should be a high enough appearance grade to permit painting or staining.

Textured plywood with the textured side down can be used for exposed soffits and ceiling applications. Staining is the only finishing required.

Working with Plywood

When you work with plywood, remember that the face and back are thin veneers. You can't drop a coarse-belted sander on a panel and work on it as though it were some rough-sawed lumber; you will simply cut through the veneers. Handle plywood carefully so that sanding can be kept to a

Plywood is real wood made by laminating an odd number of plies so that grain is at right angles.

Don't rush a cut, or wood will feather as at the left. Same blade used with slow feed made smooth cut on piece at right.

Cutting workpiece slightly oversize will permit making trim cut to remove imperfections when cutting dadoes.

Attic remodeling job is almost all fir-plywood panels. Big sheets make for fast construction, minimum finishing.

Saber saws should be used with special inserts that fit around blade, minimize opening. Saw cuts on up stroke.

If not possible to have face-veneer down with saber saw, apply tape along the cutting line to minimize feathering.

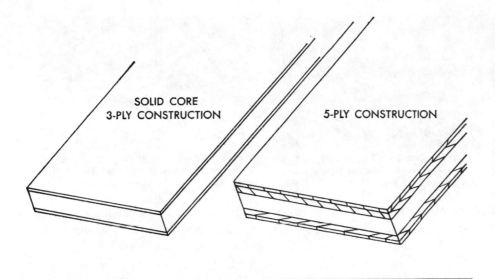

SOLID CORE
3-PLY CONSTRUCTION

5-PLY CONSTRUCTION

Sculptured effect is achieved after panels are assembled; giant wire brush removes the soft grain.

VENEER CUTS FROM LOG

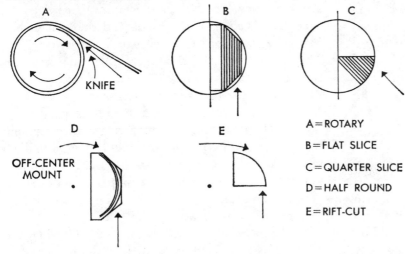

A

B

C

KNIFE

D

OFF-CENTER MOUNT

E

A = ROTARY

B = FLAT SLICE

C = QUARTER SLICE

D = HALF ROUND

E = RIFT-CUT

Plywood makes it possible to buy a 4 x 8-ft. piece of "oak." This is close-up of prefinished paneling with grooves.

EFFECTS OF VENEER CUTS

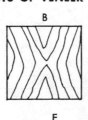

A

B

C

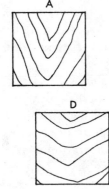

D

E

A = ROTARY

B = FLAT

C = QUARTER

D = HALF ROUND

E = RIFT-CUT

Offset rip fence eliminates "second-cutting" by back teeth of blade. Arrow shows where teeth might hit.

Yes, this is plywood, just ⅛-in. thick. Flush doors in your home probably have face veneers of this thin plywood.

Special plywood-cutting blade is excellent investment. Special-shape, no-set teeth leave an almost burnished edge.

Be careful when sanding. Pad sander does not remove much material, but it can work through face veneer.

minimum. This is not difficult, as most plywoods come already sanded. Don't handle panels so the edges get banged up—a good rule also for solid lumber.

Be especially careful when making initial layouts. This for two reasons: to plan grain direction for best appearance of the finished project, and to minimize waste. The best bet is to plan the cutting layout on a scale drawing; 1 inch to the foot is good, creating a 4x8-inch rectangle. It's cheaper and less frustrating to redo the job on another sheet of paper than it would be to cut another panel. Plywood has strength in either direction, so you are concerned mostly with grain direction on the face veneer. When butting pieces on the layout, be sure to allow for a saw kerf of about 1/8 inch.

As a general rule, you want the teeth of a saw blade to cut down into the face veneer. This means when working with a handsaw, table or radial-arm saw that the face veneer should be up. (When ripping with a radial-arm saw the good face should be down.) When cutting with a portable circular saw the good face should be down.

For the best cut you should use a blade with small teeth. For example, a good crosscut circular saw will produce a better edge than a deep-gulleted rip or combination blade. A handsaw should have 10 to 15 points to the inch, and the angle of cut should be less than you would use normally.

A slow feed and a sharp blade will produce an edge that requires little further attention. Consider getting a special plywood-cutting blade. Like a regular hollow-ground blade, these have no set, and so minimize feathering and splintering. They are specially tempered to hold up longer against the abrasive action of the many blue lines in plywood.

Rate of feed—how fast you push a piece of work past a saw blade—has much to do with the edge you get. In one photo we show a cut made by rushing the work, another shows a cut made with a slow, gentle feed. The difference, even though the "rush-cut" was deliberately exaggerated, is obvious. While the slow-feed techniques apply more specifically to plywood, they apply to any wood you are cutting.

Some craftsmen have a slight offset on a table-saw rip fence. That is, there is more space between the "back" edge of the blade and the fence, than from the front of the blade where the work is fed. This provides some clearance as the work passes the "back" teeth and avoids "second-cutting" that can damage the face veneer.

Like all work, plywood should be firmly supported. Use sawhorses when cutting with hand-held tools, and an extra pair of hands when making initial cuts on big panels on a table or radial-arm saw. Or, use an outboard support. Don't try to "muscle" big panels—it will be difficult to cut correctly and certainly will not be safe.

Use a regular dado blade for rabbeting and making dado cuts. It is a little difficult to avoid some feathering at the end of a wide cut, such as you would make with a dado, but you can minimize, if not eliminate it, by using a back-up block. Another method, which is a little more trouble, but which will guarantee good work for precision jobs, is to cut the workpiece just a little oversize. Then, after making the dado cuts, you make a slight trim cut which will remove any splintering or feathering at the end of dado cuts.

Some craftsmen wonder about whether to use veneered plywood, or lumber-core plywood for furniture. If you are making an especially fine piece of furniture, we would recommend lumber-core plywood: this is made with face veneers glued to a core of strips of solid stock; the strips of stock are arranged to minimize the tendency of solid stock to warp and twist. This plywood, however, is more expensive than the veneered type, and the latter is fine for most jobs.

The use of veneer tape for the edges will conceal the fact that plywood is used, and quite often will look exactly like solid lumber.

Hardwood-faced plywood comes with veneers of rare and exotic woods that would be much too expensive to buy as solid stock. Teak, ebony and rosewood, for example, are beautiful in panels of plywood. Panels of edge-glued solid stock might cost hundreds of dollars, and the ebony would be too heavy to lift.

OTHER SHEET MATERIALS

Building fiberboards are produced with fibers interfelted so the board has some natural bonding. Additives improve the bond and impart strength. Boards of this type are generally classified by density into structural insulating boards (with a density of between 10 and about 31 pounds per cubic foot), medium hardboards (with a density of between about 31 and 50 pounds per cubic foot), and high density or regular hardboard (with a density of over 50 pounds per cubic foot).

Structural Insulating Board

Many types of sheet materials in addition to plywood are being used for sheathing walls because they are easily applied and resist racking. Structural insulating board sheathing in 1/2- and 25/32-inch thicknesses is available in 2- by 8-foot and 4- by 8-foot sheets. The 2- by 8-foot sheets are applied horizontally and usually have shallow V or tongued-and-grooved edges. The 4- by 8-foot sheets are square-edged and applied vertically with perimeter nailing. These building boards are made water resistant by means of an asphalt coating or by impregnation.

When insulating board sheathing is applied with the 2- by 8-foot sheets horizontally, the construction normally is not rigid enough. Auxiliary bracing, such as 1- by 4-inch let-in bracing, is necessary.

A wall with enough rigidity to withstand wind forces can be built with 4- by 8-foot panels of three types—regular density sheathing 25/32 inch thick, intermediate density material 1/2 inch thick, or nail-base grades. Panels must be installed vertically and properly nailed. Each manufacturer of insulating board has recommended nailing schedules to satisfy this requirement.

Interior structural insulating board 1/2 inch thick and laminated paperboard in 1/2- and 3/8-inch thickness may be obtained in 4- by 8-foot sheets painted on one side, or in paneled form for use as an interior covering material. These materials are also produced in a tongue-and-grooved ceiling tile in sizes from 12 by 12 inches to 16 by 32 inches; thicknesses vary between 1/2 and 1 inch. They may be designed to serve as a prefinished decorative insulating tile or to provide acoustical qualities. The present practice of manufacturers is to furnish interior board either plain or acoustical with a flamespread-retardant paint finish.

Medium Hardboard

Medium hardboards are generally available in nominal 7/16- and 1/2-inch thicknesses in 4-foot-wide sheets or in the form of siding. This material provides good service when used as exterior coverage in sheet form or as lap siding. The 4- by 8-foot sheets are applied vertically, with batten strips placed over the joints and between for decorative effect.

High-Density Hardboard

High-density hardboard in standard or tempered form is commonly supplied in 1/8- and 1/4-inch-thick sheets of 4- by 8-foot size. It may be used for both interior and exterior covering material. As with plywood or medium hardboard, the high-density hardboard in the thicker types can be applied vertically with batten strips, or horizontally as a lap siding.

It is often used in the construction of barn doors and for interior lining of barns and other buildings. In perforated form, both types of hardboard are used as soffit material under cornice overhangs to ventilate attic spaces. In untreated form, high-density hardboard of special grade is also used as an underlayment for resilient flooring materials. Hardboards can be obtained with decorative laminated surfaces that provide a pleasing appearance as interior paneling.

Particleboard

Particleboard is a sheet material made up of small particles of wood glued together to form a panel. Hot-setting resins produce the bond necessary to give the panels form, stiffness, and strength.

They are generally classified as low density when the board has a density of less than 37 pounds per cubic foot, medium density when the density is between 37 and 50 pounds per cubic foot, and high density when the board weighs more than 50 pounds per cubic foot.

Particleboard is usually supplied in 4- by 8-foot sheets and in 3/8-inch thickness for paneling, in 5/8-inch thickness for underlayment, and in block form for flooring. It is also used for cabinet and closet doors, as core stock for table tops and other furniture, and is also adaptable as covering material for interior walls or other uses where exposure to moisture is not a problem.

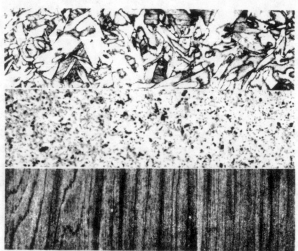

Examples of particleboards: Top: Particleboard surface showing large decorative flakes representative of products commonly used for interior paneling. Center: Particleboard with fine surface particles (a small percentage of bark included), commonly used as core stock for overlaying with veneers or other decorative materials, as in bottom photo.

WORKING WITH PLASTIC

Acrylic plastic and plastic laminate have become almost as important as wood to the domestic handyman. While acrylic plastic is used primarily as a construction material, plastic laminate is used as a covering for counter and table tops.

Acrylic Plastic

You will find that working with acrylic is much the same as working with wood. You can choose from every color and tint in the rainbow, clear or translucent acrylic, and a variety of thicknesses for different uses. Price varies according to thickness and color. You can even buy mirror backed acrylic which eliminates the scratch problem often encountered in working with mirrors.

The most commonly used thicknesses for acrylic are 1/4 inch and 1/8 inch; the difference in price between the two is minimal and both are easily handled. For thicknesses up to 1/8 inch you can score the plastic with a scribing tool making several passes along a straight edge. Now run a 3/4-inch dowel beneath the length of the cut and pressing firmly with both hands about two inches from the cut on either side, gently break the sheet. Do not try to break off pieces less than 1½ inches or they will splinter.

To cut acrylic with a saw, use your crosscut blade on a circular saw . . . the same blade you use

to cut plywood. Always leave the paper backing on the plastic until you are finished cutting. This will eliminate unnecessary scratches and give you some means of marking and measuring the acrylic sheet.

To drill through acrylic, any twist bit for hand or variable speed power drill will do. Drill slowly with a minimum of pressure.

Acrylic can be cemented at joints with special capillary cementing solvents available at plastic outlets. Sand, do not polish, the joints to be joined and apply solvent with an eyedropper or other such small applicator. Tape pieces together for 5 minutes, until cement hardens and be careful to immediately wipe up any solvent which accidentally spills onto the acrylic surface.

You can keep acrylic clean by using soap and water and a soft cloth, or a hard auto wax, but not a combination cleaner wax.

Plastic Laminate

Plastic laminate is an artificial paneling material made of paper layers which have been impregnated with synthetic resins. Panels come in unlimited patterns and colors and are extremely resistant to scratches, grease and moisture.

A base of 3/4-inch plywood is used under the laminate and the plastic is cemented down after being cut to exact size with a crosscut blade made for cutting plywood.

4

PAINTS AND FINISHES

PAINTS AND FINISHES

4

BRUSHES ■ INTERIOR PAINTS AND FINISHES ■ SURFACE PREPARATION
ROLLERS ■ CAUSES OF PAINT FAILURE ■ WATER-BASE PAINTS ■ HOUSE PAINTS
SPRAY GUNS ■ EXTERIOR PAINTS AND FINISHES ■ FINISHING WOOD SIDING AND TRIM
COLOR SCHEMES ■ MAINTENANCE OF FINISHES ■ PAINTING WINDOWS AND DOORS

PAINTS AND PAINTING

For an attractive, long-lasting paint job, there are some basic rules which you should follow:

Choose the proper tools with which to apply the paint.

Properly prepare the surface.

Use good quality paint.

Apply the paint correctly.

PAINTING TOOLS

In order to do a good job with a minimum of trouble, choose the right tools and learn how to handle them properly. The brush, the roller and the sprayer are the basic tools to work with.

Selecting a Brush

In selecting a brush you should choose one which is wide enough to cover the area in a reasonable amount of time. If you are painting large areas such as exterior or interior walls or a floor, you will want a wide brush—probably four to five inches in width. If you are painting windows or trim, you will want a narrower brush so that you can handle comparatively narrow surfaces—probably one to one and one-half inches in width.

The bristles should be reasonably long and thick so that they will hold a good load of paint;

and flexible, so that you can stroke evenly and smoothly.

Quality brushes are not necessarily expensive. Where the professional painter may spend $20 or more for his brushes, a home owner can get an excellent brush from $1.50 to about $7.50. A good brush picks up plenty of paint, applies it smoothly and does not spatter. It paints a clean-cut edge, and will last many years if given proper care.

The Code of Ethics of the American Brush Manufacturers' Association states that all subscribers to the Code list on the handle the material in the brush. It is unlikely you will find "100% pure China bristle" on a handle, but there are other natural bristles, and here is a check list you can use as a guide:

100% Undyed Natural Bristle. These brushes contain Asian black, gray and white bristles and give long service.

100% Pure Bristle. These bristles have been dyed black, being lightcolored European domestic hog bristles. Dyeing weakens bristles, not so they are decidedly inferior, but undyed bristles are a better value. Long bristles hold more paint, apply it more evenly. As a handy rule: a brush 1 inch wide should have bristles about 2 inches long; a 2-inch brush should have bristles 2½ inches long; a

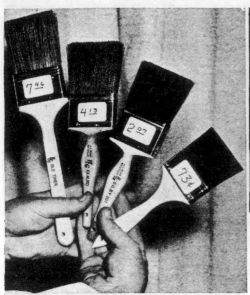

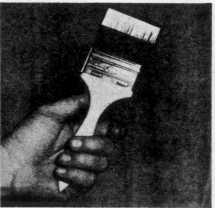

Low-price brush exhibits many shorter filaments, much shorter than the full-length of the brush they should be.

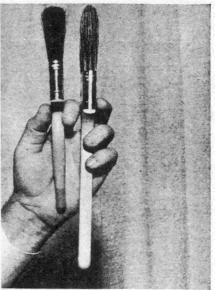

These paint brushes show a variety of prices; obviously there also is a variety of quality in the selection.

Machine-made "chisel" left, does not even compare to proper hand taper of the better, more expensive brush, right.

An evolution in design, "Ruff-Rider" does not even look like a paintbrush.

3-inch brush, 3-inch bristles and a 4-inch brush should have 3½-inch bristles.

Spotting Quality. The sides of a good brush should be straight or taper in at the end. Pressed flat, the bristles spread evenly and spring back when released. A quality brush has a tapered or "chisel" edge for clean "cutting." As exceptions, some wall brushes are flat-ended. A cheap brush looks sawed-off on the end. A quality brush has few short, cracked hairs; a cheap one has many, even less than half the length of the brush. Inside the heel of any brush is a plug that creates a paint-holding pocket. It should be one-fourth to one-third the thickness of the brush. Too large a plug causes the bristles to divide into two clumps.

Bristle tips should be tapered and flagged. This is true also of synthetic fibers, some of which will almost equal a natural-bristle tool, and will be superior for water-base paints, as natural bristles absorb water and lose resiliency.

Using a Brush

The use of a brush assures good contact of paint with pores, cracks and crevices. Brushing is particularly recommended for applying primer coats and exterior paints.

Paint should be brushed up and down, then across for even distribution. On a rough surface, however, it is wise to vary the direction of the strokes so that the paint will penetrate thoroughly.

The brush should be held at a slight angle when applying the paint, and pressure should be moderate and even. Excessive pressure or "stuffing" the brush into corners and cracks may damage the bristles.

Always start painting at the top and move downward. For interior painting, do ceilings and walls first, then the doors, windows and trim areas. If floors are to be painted, they should be last.

Always work toward the "wet edge" of the

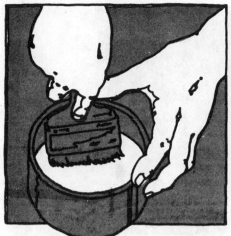

1 After removing excess paint with scraper, soak brush in proper thinner, work it against bottom of container.

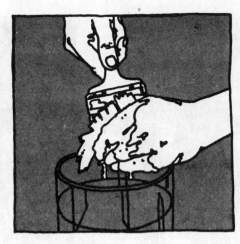

2 To loosen paint in center of brush, squeeze bristles between thumb and forefinger, then rinse again in thinner. If necessary, work brush in mild soap suds, rinse in clear water.

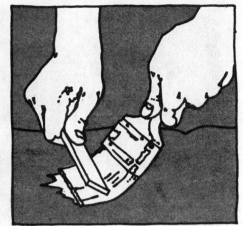

3 Press out water with stick.

4 Twirl brush — in a container so you won't get splashed!

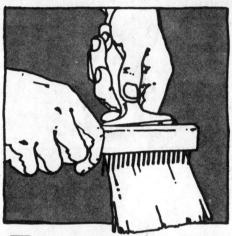

5 Comb bristles carefully — including those below the surface. Allow the brush to dry by suspending from the handle or by laying it flat on a clean surface. Then wrap the dry brush in the original wrapper or in heavy paper to keep the bristles straight. Store suspended by handle or lying flat.

previously painted area, making sure not to try to cover too large a surface with each brushload.

Care and Cleaning of Brushes

A good brush is a good tool, and it pays to invest the necessary time and effort to take care of it properly. Clean brushes immediately after use with a thinner or special brush cleaner recommended by your paint or hardware store. Use turpentine or mineral spirits to remove oil base paints, enamels and varnish; alcohol to remove shellac; and special solvents to remove lacquer. Remove latex paints promptly from brushes with soap and water. If any type paint is allowed to dry on a brush, a paint remover or brush-cleaning solvent will be needed.

Selecting a Paint Roller

Paint rollers are obtainable in a variety of sizes, shapes and naps to apply almost any kind of paint to any kind of surface. Extension handles permit painting a ceiling while standing on the floor, painting a soffit while standing on the ground. Long-nap covers allow painting a wire fence from one side, or doing the edges and filling irregularities in a wooden picket fence. Tapered rollers "cut in" edges and corners, divided types paint around corners and all surfaces of ornamental-iron work.

As with brushes, quality is important: a good roller will apply cheap paint well, the best paint in

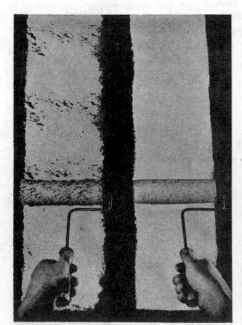

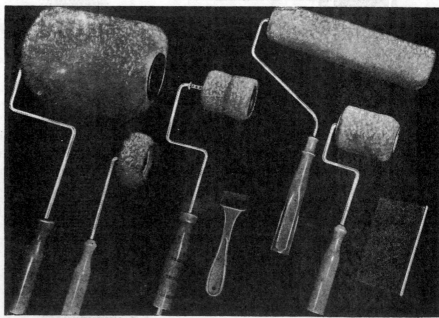

Difference between quality and cheap roller show in application of paint.

Rollers come in a variety of shapes and sizes, with long and short naps to handle every painting job, inside and out. Two of the items wipe on paint.

Inside ceilings, outside soffits are painted quickly with extension handle for roller. Hardware cloth makes "evener" for big roller.

Short extension handle is ideal when it's necessary to reach over shrubbery to paint siding. Narrow roller is for edges of siding.

Wire fence is painted from one side; long-nap Dynel® fibers wrap around wire. Faster painting of wooden picket fence also is possible with same type long-nap roller that gets edges, fills cracks. Short-nap roller of narrow width is great for painting porch railings. Divided, "split" roller easily follows contours of intricate pattern in porch column.

the world will go on poorly with a cheap roller. The old standby covers, mohair and lambs' wool, do poorly with water-base paints, matting and losing resiliency, applying the paint thinly and unevenly. Low-cost rollers are a poor bargain. Those made with synthetics cost slightly more, but can be used for any type paint, and will last for years.

Spotting Quality. Check that the roller you buy has an even nap and the fibers are closely spaced (the spiral seam will be almost invisible). There should be no loose nap and the ends will be beveled (this avoids streaks from the roller ends). The core should be resin-impregnated and absolutely waterproof.

Using a Paint Roller

For large, flat surfaces, painting by roller is easier than painting by brush for the average do-it-yourself painter. Select a roller with a comfortable-to-hold handle and try several dry sweeps across the surface until you get the hang of it.

When you buy a roller you may find that it comes as part of a set—the roller itself, and a sloping metal or plastic tray. Pour paint into the tray until approximately two-thirds of the corrugated bottom is covered. Dip the roller into the paint in the shallow section of the tray, and roll it back and forth until it is well covered. If the roller drips when you lift it from the tray, it is overloaded. Squeeze out some of the paint by pressing the roller against the upper part of the tray above the paint line.

Apply paint by moving the roller back and forth over the surface being painted, first up and down in long, even strokes, then across. Reload the roller with paint as needed.

Roller Care

Rollers used with alkyd or oil base paints should be cleaned with turpentine or mineral spirits. When latex paint has been used, soap and water will do a satisfactory cleaning job. If any kind of paint has been allowed to dry on the roller, a paint remover or brush-cleaning solvent will be needed.

SELECTING A SPRAY GUN

Every home shop should have a spray-painting outfit. And not just for spraying paint. The compressor can be used—with hose and attachments—for blowing up beach toys, inflating tires and blowing dust from work in the shop.

The gun itself, if cleaned thoroughly afterward, can be used for spraying insecticide in the garden, for coating grease-remover on lawn mowers, auto engines, etc. and dozens of other jobs.

Choose a compressor and gun to fit your needs. For the average home shop a low-cost diaphragm-type compressor is adequate. It will produce 30 to 50 pounds pressure, which is enough to spray most materials used around the home. The diaphragm-type compressor consists of a flexible diaphragm actuated by a connecting rod driven by an eccentric crankshaft. Because the compressed air is produced above the diaphragm, where there are no metal parts in contact, requiring lubrication, the air is free of oil that might contaminate the paint or other material being sprayed.

For heavy-duty work, where pressures of 50 pounds and above are required, a piston-type compressor is required. The piston-type compressor also will produce more cubic feet per minute (CFM) than the diaphragm-type compressor. Because oil is required to lubricate the sliding piston it is neces-sary to have a filter system to remove oil vapor from the compressed air. If you have a piston-type compressor, be sure to clean the filter frequently. (Also clean the intake-air filters on any type compressor, before each use. Paint vapor in the air will plug them quickly.)

Types of Spray Guns

Most spray guns used with smaller compressors are called "bleeder" guns. That is, the air flows through the gun constantly, while paint flows through the gun only when the trigger is pulled. This type gun is used with a compressor constantly supplying air, as it would quickly empty a tank of stored air. The trigger of a "nonbleeder" controls both paint and air. This type gun is used primarily with a container of air.

Methods of Liquid Feed

Two methods of liquid feed are used in spray guns. Pressure feed is created by the air supply forcing paint through the fluid tube to the nozzle. This generally is used for heavy liquids and fast spraying. In a siphon gun, the air is directed across the fluid tube creating a vacuum that pulls the paint up into the gun. There must be a vent in this type gun to allow atmospheric pressure to push down on the paint. The siphon gun is best for finer atomization of the liquid when an extra-fine finish is desired and rapid spraying is not essential.

In a gun fitted with an internal-mix nozzle air and paint are mixed inside. This type nozzle is used with pressure-feed guns for heavy-bodied liquids like house paint.

Paint and air flow separately from an external-mix nozzle and are combined just outside the nozzle. This type nozzle works equally well with pressure or siphon guns and is better suited for fast-drying materials such as lacquers, automobile finishes and water-base paints.

Selecting a Compressor

When you select a spray gun that will fit your needs, be sure to get a compressor that will match the gun. Most important, match the CFM rating of the gun to the CFM rating of the compressor. CFM delivered by a compressor is used as a measure of its capabilities. Compressors with higher CFM ratings force more air through the hose to the spray gun, and this added volume moves more

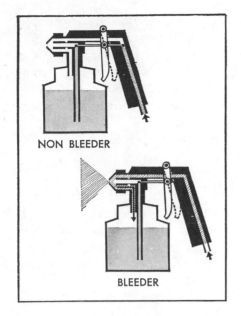

NON BLEEDER

BLEEDER

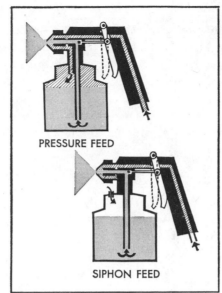

PRESSURE FEED

SIPHON FEED

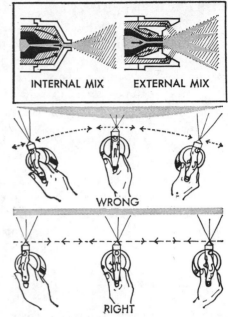

INTERNAL MIX EXTERNAL MIX

WRONG

RIGHT

paint faster, making the higher-capacity compressor better for bigger jobs.

Pounds per square inch (PSI) is the measure of the air pressure pumped to the nozzle of the spray gun. Compressors that deliver a higher PSI permit thicker paints to be used, with less thinning, and faster coverage. Higher PSI also permits you to have a wider range of spray-gun adjustment.

Using a Spray Gun

Spray painting is not difficult, but like any skill it does take practice. Basically, you hold the gun parallel to the surface being sprayed. Do not swing the gun in an arc, which is the natural motion of hand and arm; this will cause a build-up of the paint at the center of the stroke and a thinning at the ends. With the gun moved parallel to the surface the coating will be the same thickness the full length.

When spraying, overlap each pass. Aim the center of the spray pattern at the edge of the last pass. This will assure full coverage of the surface. Keep the gun about 6 to 9 inches from the surface. If you start to get runs and sagging, quite likely you are holding the gun too close. If you get "orange peel," a rough surface, you are holding the gun too far away and the paint has become a dry powder by the time it strikes the surface you are painting.

Start the stroke or motion of the hand holding the sprayer while the spray is pointed slightly beyond the surface to be painted. This assures a smooth, even flow when you reach the surface to be coated.

Adjust the width of the spray fan to the size of the surface to be coated. A narrow fan is best for spraying small or narrow surfaces; a wider fan should be used to spray table tops or walls.

Use a respirator to avoid inhalation of vapors.

One of the main problems with spray painting is thinning the paint so that it sprays properly, yet is not so thin that it covers poorly, or dries in the air before contacting the surface. One way of making sure of this is to use a viscosimeter. This device is a cup-like gauge that quickly tells you the viscosity (thickness, if you will) of the paint. It tells you how much to thin a paint so that it will spray properly. It costs only a couple of dollars, and will quickly pay for itself in better paint jobs, and paint saved.

When you do spray paint, be sure to mask the surrounding area, and remove the tape and masking as soon as you have finished painting.

A spray gun will let you paint faster, get a better finish, and save material while doing the job.

Paint Sprayer Care

Clean sprayer promptly before the paint dries. After using oil-base or alkyd paints, clean the sprayer with the same solvent used to thin the paint. After using latex paint, clean with detergent and water. Fill the sprayer tank with the cleaning liquid and spray it clean.

If the fluid tip becomes clogged, it can be cleaned with a broom straw. Never use wire or a nail to clear clogged air holes in the sprayer tip.

SURFACE PREPARATION

The finest paint, applied with the greatest skill, will not produce a satisfactory finish unless the surface has been properly prepared. The basic principles are simple. They vary somewhat with different surfaces and, to some extent, with different paints; but the goal is the same—to provide a surface with which the paint can make a strong, permanent bond.

The surface must be clean, smooth, and free from loose particles such as dust or old paint. Use sandpaper, a wire brush, or a scraper.

Oil and grease should be removed by wiping with mineral spirits. If a detergent is used it should be followed by a thorough rinse with clean water.

Chipped or blistered paint should be removed with sandpaper, a wire brush, steel wool, or a scraper.

Chalked or powdered paint should be removed with a stiff bristle brush, or by scrubbing with water mixed with household washing soda or TSP (trisodium phosphate, sold in hardware stores). If the old surface is only moderately chalked and the surface is relatively firm, an oil primer can be applied without the prior use of a stiff brush. The primer rebinds the loose particles and provides a solid base for the paint.

Loose, cracked or shrunken putty or caulk should be removed by scraping.

If new putty, glazing compound, caulking compounds and sealants are used, they should be applied to a clean surface and allowed to harden before paint is applied. If the caulk is a latex type, latex paint can be applied over it immediately without waiting for the caulk to harden.

Damp surfaces must be allowed to dry before paint is applied, unless you are using a latex paint.

Wood Surfaces

Scrape clean all areas where sap (resin) has surfaced on the wood, and sand smooth prior to application of "knot sealer." Small, dry knots should also be scraped and thoroughly cleaned, and then given a thin coat of knot sealer before applying wood primer.

Fill cracks, joints, crevices, and nail holes with glazing compound, putty or plastic wood and sand lightly until flush with the wood. Always sand in the direction of the grain—never across it.

New wood surfaces to be stain-finished should first be sanded smooth. Open grain (porous) wood should be given a coat of paste filler before the stain is applied (paste fillers come in various matching wood colors). The surface should then be resanded. Read manufacturer's instructions carefully before applying paste fillers.

Masonry Surfaces

Surfaces such as plaster, gypsum, cement and drywall should be dry and clean. If the surface is cracked, sand it smooth and then fill with spackling compound or some other recommended crack filler. After the repaired surface is dry, sand lightly until smooth—then wipe clean.

Allow new plaster to dry for 30 days before painting.

Roughen unpainted concrete and stucco with a wire brush to permit a good bond between the surface and the paint.

Wash new concrete surfaces with detergent and water to remove any film left over from oil, or from the compound used for hardening the concrete during the "curing" process.

Remove "efflorescence," the crystalline deposit which appears on the mortar between the bricks in a brick wall, by using undiluted vinegar or a 5-percent muriatic acid solution. After scrubbing with acid, rinse the surface thoroughly. CAUTION: When using muriatic acid, wear goggles and gloves for protection.

Metal Surfaces

Clean new metal surfaces such as galvanized steel, aluminum or tin with a solvent such as mineral spirits to remove the oil and grease applied to the metal as a preservative by manufacturers.

Remove rusted or corroded spots by wire-brushing or with coarse sandpaper. Chemical rust removers are also available from paint and hardware stores. Paint will not adhere well when applied over rusted or corroded surfaces.

Allow galvanized steel, such as that used for roof gutters, to weather for about six months before painting. If earlier painting is necessary, wash the surface with mineral spirits or VM&P (Varnish Makers & Painters) naphtha, then apply a primer recommended specifically for galvanized surfaces.

PREPARATION FOR PAINTING

Before you brush, roll or spray a drop of paint, there are certain preparations you should make to ensure a good job with a minimum of effort, errors and spattering. The precautions may seem obvious, but they are often overlooked.

Protect Other Surfaces

Cover floors and furnishings with drop cloths. You can use tarps, old sheets, or the inexpensive plastic sheets designed for the purpose.

Clean up as you paint. Wet paint is easy to remove; dry paint is hard to remove. Use turpentine or other thinner to remove oil paint; water to remove latex.

CAUTION! If paint is dropped on an asphalt tile floor, do not attempt to remove it with mineral spirits or turpentine since this may permanently damage the tile. If the paint will not come off with a dry cloth, let it dry and then scrape it off.

Rub protective cream onto your hands and arms. A film of this cream will make it easier to remove paint from your skin when the job is done. Old gloves or throwaway plastic gloves and aprons are also useful.

Check the Condition of the Paint

When you buy new paint of good quality from a reputable store, it is usually in excellent condition. However, after stirring the paint thoroughly (if it is a type which should be stirred), you should examine it for lumps, curdling, or color separation. Do not use the paint if there are still any signs of these conditions.

Old paints which, upon removal of the container lid, release a foul odor (especially latex paints) or show signs of lumps or curdling, are probably spoiled and should be discarded.

If there is a "skin" on the surface of the paint when you open the container, remove as much of the hardened film as possible with a spatula or knife and strain the paint through a cheesecloth or fine wire mesh such as window screening. If you fail to do this, bits of the skin will show up with exasperating frequency to spoil the appearance of your paint job.

Follow Directions on Mixing

New paints are usually ready for use when purchased and require no thinning except when they are to be applied with a sprayer. Get the advice of the paint store salesman when you buy the paint, and check the label before you mix or stir. Some manufacturers do not recommend mixing as it may introduce air bubbles. If mixing is required, it can be done at the paint store by placing the can in a mechanical agitator—or you can do it at home with a paddle or spatula.

If you open the can and find that the pigment has settled, use a clean paddle or spatula and gradually work the pigment up from the bottom of the can, using a circular stirring motion. Continue until the pigment is thoroughly and evenly distributed, with no signs of color separation. If the settled layer should prove to be hard or rubbery, and resists stirring, the paint is probably too old and should be discarded.

Protect the Paint between Jobs

Between jobs, even if it is only overnight, cover the paint container tightly to prevent evaporation and thickening, and to protect it from dust. Oil base and alkyd paints may develop a skin from exposure to the air.

When you finish painting, clean the rim of the paint can thoroughly and put the lid on tight. To ensure that the lid is air-tight, cover the rim with a cloth or piece of plastic film (to prevent spattering) and then tap the lid firmly into place with a hammer.

What's the Weather?

You can easily ruin your paint job if you forget to consider the weather. Excessive humidity, or extremely cold weather can cause you trouble. Good ventilation, regardless of the weather, is essential.

Unless you are using latex paint, you should not paint on damp days. Moisture on the painting surface may prevent a good bond. If humidity is high, check the surface before painting. If you can feel a film of moisture on the surface, wait for a better day. If you are painting inside and the area is airconditioned, however, neither rain nor humidity will affect the job.

Exterior painting is not recommended if the temperature is below 50 degrees or above 95 degrees Fahrenheit, since you may not be able to get a good bond. This is especially critical if you are using latex paint.

If conditions are borderline, good ventilation will help paint to dry. Allow more drying time in damp or humid weather. The label on the can will tell you the normal drying time, but test each coat by touch before you add another. When paint is thoroughly dry, it is firm to the touch and is not sticky.

Interior Priming

Previously painted surfaces usually do not require primer coats except where the old paint is worn through or the surface has been damaged.

Wood Surfaces. Unpainted wood to be finished with enamel or oil base paint should be primed with enamel undercoat to seal the wood and provide a better surface. If the unpainted wood is not primed, the enamel coat may be uneven. Unpainted wood to be finished with topcoat latex should first be undercoated. Water-thinned paint could raise the grain of the bare wood and leave a rough surface.

If clear finishes are used, soft woods such as pine, poplar and gum usually require a sealer to control the penetration of the finish coats. In using stain, a sealer is sometimes applied first in order to obtain a lighter, more uniform color.

Clear finishes used on open grain hard woods such as oak, walnut and mahogany require a paste wood filler, followed by a clear wood sealer.

Close grain hard woods such as maple and birch do not require a filler. The first coat may be a thinned version of the finishing varnish, shellac or lacquer.

Masonry Surfaces. Smooth, unpainted masonry surfaces such as plaster, plasterboard, and various drywall surfaces can be primed with latex paint or latex primer-sealer. The color of the first coat should be similar to the finish coat.

Coarse, rough or porous masonry surfaces, such as cement block, cinder block and concrete block cannot be filled and covered satisfactorily with regular paints. Block filler should be used as a

first coat to obtain a smooth sealed surface over which almost any type paint can be used.

Unpainted brick, while porous, is not as rough as cinder block and similar surfaces and can be primed with latex primer-sealer or with an exterior-type latex paint.

Enamel undercoat should be applied over the primer where the finish coat is to be a gloss or semi-gloss enamel.

Follow carefully the manufacturer's label instructions for painting masonry surfaces.

Metal Surfaces. Unpainted surfaces should be primed for protection against corrosion and to provide a base for the finish paint. Interior paints do not usually adhere well to bare metal surfaces, and provide little corrosion resistance by themselves.

Primer paints for bare metal surfaces must be selected according to the type of metal to be painted. Some primers are made especially for iron or steel; others for galvanized steel, aluminum or copper.

An enamel undercoat should be used as a second primer if the metal surface is to be finished with enamel; that is, apply the primer first, then the undercoat, and finally the enamel finish. Most enamel undercoats need a light sanding before the topcoat is applied.

INTERIOR PAINTS

Unless you are an experienced painter, shop for a salesman or a paint store owner before you shop for paint. Find one who is willing and able to help you match the paint to the job. Read labels and company leaflets carefully. They are usually well-written, accurate and helpful.

Paints for Light Wear Areas

Latex interior paints are generally used for areas where there is little need for periodic washing and scrubbing; for example, living rooms, dining rooms, bedrooms and closets.

Interior flat latex paints are used for interior walls and ceilings since they cover well, are easy to apply, dry quickly, are almost odorless, and can be quickly and easily removed from applicators.

Latex paints may be applied directly over semi-gloss and gloss enamel if the surface is first roughened with sandpaper or liquid sandpaper. If the latter is used, follow carefully the instructions on the container label.

Flat alkyd paints are often preferred for wood, wallboard and metal surfaces since they are more resistant to damage; also, they can be applied in thicker films to produce a more uniform appearance. They wash better than interior latex paints and are nearly odorless.

Paints for Heavy Wear Areas

Enamels, including latex enamels, are usually preferred for kitchen, bathroom, laundry room, and similar work areas because they withstand intensive cleaning and wear. They form especially hard films, ranging from flat to a full gloss finish.

Fast-drying polyurethane enamels and clear varnishes provide excellent hard, flexible finishes for wood floors. Other enamels and clear finishes can also be used, but unless specifically recommended for floors they may be too soft and slow-drying, or too hard and brittle.

Polyurethane and epoxy enamels are also excellent for concrete floors. For a smooth finish, rough concrete should be properly primed with an alkali resistant primer to fill the pores. When using these enamels, adequate ventilation is essential for protection from flammable vapors.

Paints, Properties, and Uses

Latex Primer-Sealer (water thinned). Simple to apply. Dries quickly and can be recoated in about two hours. Not flammable; almost odorless. One coat usually sufficient. Thinning unnecessary unless recommended by manufacturer. Unpainted interior walls and ceilings of wallboard, plaster, masonry and all types of drywall.

Enamel Undercoater (alkyd base-low odor type). Hard, tight films. Provides good base for enamel. Easy brushing, smooth leveling. Dries in about 12 hours. Undercoater for interior enamels.

Latex Wall Paint (water thinned). The most popular of the interior paints. Durable, excellent coverage, good washability, quick-drying, and easy to touch-up. Safe to use and store; nontoxic, practically no odor. Primer-sealer and also finish coat for interior walls and ceilings of wallboard, wallpaper, plaster, and other porous, absorptive materials. Use on primed wood but not on bare wood.

Flat Alkyd Enamel. Made with alkyd resins. Has flat finish practically free of sheen. Used same as latex wall paint but has slightly better washability and abrasion resistance. Dries in about four hours. Practically no odor. Primer-sealer and also finish coat on interior walls and ceilings of plaster, wallboard, masonry, and similar surfaces.

Semi-Gloss and Full-Gloss Enamel (alkyd base). Made with alkyd resins. Has good gloss retention, grease and oil resistance, and better washability and resistance to abrasion than flat alkyd enamel. On primed plaster and wallboard, and on suitably prepared wood trim and metal. Very useful for kitchens and bathrooms, and for decorative use on properly primed woodwork.

Semi-Gloss and Full-Gloss Latex Enamel (water thinned). Has most properties of alkyd enamels plus usual advantages of latex paints: easy application and cleanup, rapid drying, low odor, and nonflammable. Good leveling but lapping does not compare favorably with alkyd enamels. Walls and ceilings of wallboard, wallpaper, wood, and plaster. Very useful for kitchens, bathrooms, and for decorative use on properly primed woodwork.

Epoxy Enamel. Hard film, wide gloss range, low odor, ideal where vigorous and frequent cleaning is done. Has excellent adhesion and resistance to abrasion, water, solvents, greases, and dirt. Packaged in two containers—enamel in one and curing agent in the other. Contents of both containers mixed together prior to use. Cost comparatively high but durability is excellent. Highly effective in heavy wear areas such as hallways, kitchens, bathrooms, laundries and concrete floors.

Dripless Enamel (special alkyd base). Does not drip from brush or roller. Made with special alkyd resins to form a soft gel which liquefies with agitation but gels again on standing. Soft, buttery, easy brushing, low odor, self-sealing. Has excellent color retention; solvent and water resistant. Decorative enamel for properly primed walls and ceilings of plaster, wallboard, and similar surfaces; also, for wood trim and primed metal.

Interior Floor and Deck Enamel. Alkyd and latex used successfully but polyurethane types provide harder, more flexible and more abrasion-resistant surfaces. Polyurethane enamels are packaged in one and two-container forms. The latter has paint in one can and curing agent in the other. Contents of both are mixed together prior to use. When applying polyurethane enamel, follow manufacturer's instructions explicitly and also keep room

Product	Asphalt Tile (Masonry)	Concrete Floors	Kitchen & Bathroom Walls	Linoleum	New Masonry	Old Masonry	Plaster Walls & Ceiling	Vinyl & Rubber Tile Floors	Wall Board	Aluminum Windows (Metal)	Heating Ducts	Radiators & Heating Pipes	Steel Cabinets	Steel Windows	Floors (Wood)	Paneling	Stair Risers	Stair Treads	Trim	Window Sills
Latex Gloss & Semi-gloss			X•		X•	X•	X•		X•	X•	X•	X•	X•	X•		X•	X•		X•	
Latex (Wall) Flat		X			X	X	X		X	X•	X•	X•		X•		X•			X•	
Metal Primer										X	X	X	X	X						
Sealer or Undercoater			X		X	X	X		X										X	
Aluminum Paint						X	X			X	X	X		X						
Floor Paint or Enamel		X													X•			X		
Floor Varnish															X•			X		
Wood Sealer															X	X	X	X		
Stain		X•													X•	X	X	X	X	
Wax (Emulsion)	X	X•		X				X							X•					
Wax (Liquid or paste)		X•						X							X	X			X	
Shellac-Lacquer															X	X	X	X	X	
Interior Varnish															X	X			X	X
Gloss Enamel			X•																	
Semi-gloss Enamel			X•		X•	X•	X•		X•	X•	X•	X•	X•	X•		X•	X•		X•	
Flat Enamel					X•	X•	X•		X•	X•	X•	X•	X•	X•	X•	X•			X•	

X. Black dot indicates that a primer or sealer may be necessary before the finishing coat (unless surface has been previously finished).

well ventilated. General application to properly primed floors and covered decks.

Aluminum Paints. Resistant to water. Can be brushed or sprayed on new metal and wood surfaces. When brush is used, apply in one direction only for best results. As a sealer for wood surfaces (especially knots) and as a primer for metal surfaces. Can be used as a finish coat if color is not objectionable. Particularly useful for aluminum and steel windows, heating ducts, radiators and heating pipes.

INTERIOR FINISHES

Clear Finishes for Wood

Varnishes form durable and attractive finishes for interior wood surfaces such as wood paneling, trim, floors, and unpainted furniture. They seal the wood, forming tough, transparent films that will withstand frequent scrubbing and hard use, and are available in flat, semi-gloss or satin, and gloss finishes.

Most varnishes are easily scratched, and the marks are difficult to conceal without redoing the entire surface. A good paste wax applied over the finished varnish—especially on wood furniture—will provide some protection against scratches.

Polyurethane and epoxy varnishes are notable for durability and high resistance to stains, abrasions, acids and alkalis, solvents, strong cleaners, fuels, alcohol and chemicals. Adequate ventilation should be provided as protection from flammable vapors when these varnishes are being applied.

Shellac and lacquer have uses similar to most varnishes, and these finishes are easy to repair or recoat. They apply easily, dry fast, and are also useful as a sealer and clear finish under varnish for wood surfaces. The first coat should be thinned as recommended on the container, then sanded very lightly and finished with one or more undiluted coats. Two coats will give a fair sheen, and three a high gloss.

Wax Finishes

Liquid and paste waxes are used on interior surfaces. They provide a soft, lustrous finish to wood and are particularly effective on furniture and floors. Waxes containing solvents should not be used on asphalt tile; wax emulsions are recommended.

Waxes should be applied to smooth surfaces with a soft cloth. Rub with the grain. Brushes should be used to apply liquid waxes to raw-textured wood.

Wax finishes can be washed with a mild household detergent, followed by rinsing with a clean, damp cloth.

A wax finish is not desirable if a different type of finish may be used later, for wax is difficult to remove.

Finishes, Properties, and Uses

Clear Varnish Finishes for Wood. Provide durable and attractive finish; seal wood better than lacquer; and form tough, transparent coat that will withstand frequent scrubbings and hard use. Tend to darken the wood surface and give impression of visual depth. Readily show scratch marks which are difficult to conceal without redoing entire surface. Some varnishes turn yellow with age. Extra coat recommended on new work. Can be flat, satin, semi-gloss, or glossy finish. For all interior smooth wood. Recommended for washrooms, kitchens, or other areas exposed to dirt, grease, and moisture and subject to frequent scrubbing. A rubbed-in coat of paste wax will provide some protection against scratches.

Shellac. Available in clear and "orange" finishes. Fast drying. Thinned first coat provides excellent seal for new wood. Can be overcoated in about 30 minutes. Should be lightly sanded between coats. Paste wax, as final coat, provides lustre and some protection against scratches. For wood walls, trim, furniture, or any wood surface requiring only occasional dusting. Unsuitable for kitchens, washrooms, or other areas exposed to dirt, grease, and moisture

Lacquer. Fast drying; can be overcoated in about 30 minutes. Provides gloss or sheen when two or more coats are applied. Paste wax, as final coat, provides attractive lustre and some protection against scratches. Available in clear and a variety of color finishes. For wood walls, trim, furniture, or any wood surface requiring only occasional dusting. Unsuitable for kitchens, washrooms, or other areas exposed to dirt, grease, and moisture.

Stains. Available in natural finish and in a variety of colors which provide attractive, natural appearance. Several coats are required for bare wood, with light sanding between coats. Final coat of paste wax provides lustre and some protection against scratches, particularly on furniture. "Thick" stains can be thinned with turpentine or mineral spirits. For interior wood surfaces such as walls, trim, and furniture.

PAINTING EXTERIOR SURFACES

The durability of an exterior paint job depends greatly on surface preparation, the quality of paint selected, the skill of application, the proper spacing of repaintings, the protection of surfaces from the sun and rain, and climatic and local weather conditions.

As previously indicated, conditions must be right for exterior painting. The temperature should not be much below 50 degrees or above 95 degrees Fahrenheit, and surfaces must be free of moisture. Latex paints, however, can be used even if the surface is not bone dry. The best time for exterior painting is after morning dew has evaporated.

Before you start on the job, make a thorough inspection tour and check the surface condition of window and door frames and surrounding areas, bases of columns of porches and entranceways, steps, siding, downspouts, under-eave areas, and anywhere that moisture is likely to collect.

Exterior Priming

Wood Surfaces. The tendency of wood to expand and contract during changes in temperature and humidity makes it imperative that a good wood primer be applied to provide the necessary anchorage for the finish paint.

Surfaces such as wood siding, porches, trim, shutters, sash doors, and window sills should be primed with an exterior primer intended for wood. Application should be by brush to thoroughly dry surfaces.

Painted wood usually does not need priming unless the old paint has cracked, blistered or peeled. Defective paint must be removed by scraping or wire brushing—preferably down to bare wood—and then primed.

Scratches, dents, recesses, and raw edges should be smoothed and then touched-up with a suitable exterior primer.

Masonry Surfaces. New masonry surfaces should be primed with an exterior latex paint, preferably one specifically made for masonry.

Common brick is sometimes sealed with a penetrating type of clear exterior varnish to control efflorescence and spalling (flaking or chipping of the brick). This varnish withstands weather, yet allows the natural appearance of the surface to show through.

Coarse, rough and porous surfaces should be covered with a fill coat (block filler), applied by brush to thoroughly penetrate and fill the pores.

Old painted surfaces which have become a little chalky should be painted with an exterior oil primer to rebind the chalk. If there is much chalk, it should be removed with a stiff bristle brush or by washing with household washing soda or TSP (trisodium phosphate) mixed with water.

Metal Surfaces. Copper should be cleaned with a phosphoric acid cleaner, buffed and polished until bright, and then coated before it discolors. Copper gutters and downspouts do not, however, require painting. The protective oxide which forms on the copper surface darkens it or turns it green, but does not shorten the life of the metal. Copper is often painted to prevent staining of adjacent painted surfaces.

Zinc chromate type primers are effective on copper, aluminum and steel surfaces, but other types are also available for use on metal.

Galvanized steel surfaces, such as gutters and downspouts, should be primed with recommended special primers since conventional primers usually do not adhere well to this type of metal. A zinc-dust zinc-oxide type primer works well on galvanized steel. Exterior latex paints are sometimes used directly over galvanized surfaces, but not oil paints.

Unpainted iron and steel surfaces rust when exposed to the weather. Rust, dirt, oils and old loose paint should be removed from these surfaces by wire brushing or power tool cleaning. The surface should then be treated with an anti-corrosive primer.

Exterior Finishing

All exterior surfaces, properly primed or previously painted, can be finished with either exterior oil paint or exterior latex paint.

Latex paints are easy to apply, have good color retention, and can be used on slightly damp surfaces.

Oil or alkyd base paints have excellent penetrating properties. They provide good adhesion,

WHAT TO USE AND WHERE (Exterior Surfaces)

Product	MASONRY – Asbestos Cement	Brick	Cement & Cinder Block	Concrete/Masonry Porches And Floors	Coal Tar Felt Roof	Stucco	METAL – Aluminum Windows	Steel Windows	Metal Roof	Metal Siding	Copper Surfaces	Galvanized Surfaces	Iron Surfaces	WOOD – Clapboard	Natural Wood Siding & Trim	Shutters & Other Trim	Wood Frame Windows	Wood Porch Floor	Wood Shingle Roof
Water Repellent Preservatives		X																	X
House Paint (Latex)		X	X	X		X	X•	X•	X•	X•		X•	X•	X•		X•	X•		
Metal Primer							X	X•	X•	X		X•	X•						
Primer or Undercoater	X	X	X			X								X		X	X		
Porch and Deck Paint				X														X	
Trim Paint							X•	X•		X•		X•	X•			X•	X•		
Roof Coating					X														
Wood Stain															X				X
Aluminum Paint		X	X			X	X	X•		X•		X•	X•	X		X			
Exterior Clear Finish											X				X				
Cement Powder Paint		X	X			X													
House Paint (Oil or Oil-Alkyd)	X•	X•	X•			X•	X•	X•	X•	X•		X•	X•	X•		X•	X•		

X. Black dot (shown here as X•) indicates that a primer, sealer or fill coat may be necessary before the finishing coat (unless surface has been previously finished).

durability, and resistance to abrasion and blistering on wood and other porous surfaces.

Mildew, fungus, and mold growths on exterior surfaces are a problem in areas where high temperature and humidity are prevalent. Use paint which contains agents to resist bacterial and mold growth. The manufacturer's label will state whether the paint contains such inhibitors.

Exterior oil and latex paints can be applied by brush or by spraying; however, brush application generally provides a more intimate bond between surface and the paint film.

Colored exterior house paints must resist chalking so that colors will not fade and the erosion of the paint film will be minimized. The manufacturer's label will indicate whether the paint is a non-chalking type. Some white exterior house paints are expected to chalk slightly as a means of self-cleaning.

Exterior Finishes, Properties, and Uses

Oil Base Primers. Good adhesion and sealing; resistant to cracking and flaking when applied to unprimed wood; good brushing and leveling; controlled penetration; and low sheen. Unsuitable as a top coat and should be covered with finish paint within a week or two after application. As primer on unpainted woodwork or surfaces previously coated with house paint.

Anti-Rust Primers. Prevent corrosion on iron and steel surfaces. Slow-drying type provides protection through good penetration into cracks and crevices. Fast-drying types are used only on smooth, clean surfaces, and those which are water resistant are effective where surfaces are subject to severe humidity conditions or fresh water immersion. Priming of steel and other ferrous metal surfaces when good resistance to corrosion is required.

Galvanizing Primers. High percentage of zinc dust provides good anti-rust protection and adhesion. Galvanizing/zinc dust primers give excellent coverage, one coat usually being sufficient on new surfaces. Two coats are ample for surfaces exposed to high humidity. Priming of new or old galvanized metal and steel surfaces. Satisfactory as finish coat if color (metallic gray) is not objectionable.

House Paints (oil or oil alkyd base). Made with drying oils or drying oil combined with alkyd resin. Excellent brushing and penetrating properties. Provides good adhesion, elasticity, durability, and resistance to blistering on wood and other porous surfaces. Often modified with alkyd resins to speed drying time. Apply with brush to obtain strong bond, especially on old painted surfaces. General exterior use on properly primed or previously painted wood or metal surfaces.

House Paints (latex type). Exterior latex paints have durability comparable to oil base paints. Resistant to weathering and yellowing, and so quick-drying that they can be recoated in one hour. Can be applied in damp weather over a damp surface. Easy to apply and brush or roller can be cleaned quickly with water. Free from fire hazard. White latex paints usually offer better color retention than oil or oil-alkyd exterior paints. Covers properly primed or previously painted concrete, stucco, and other masonry and wood surfaces.

Trim Paint. Usually made with oil modified alkyds. Slow drying (over night). Made in high sheen, bright colors; have good retention of gloss and color. More expensive silicone-alkyd enamels are also available for trim painting. They are substantially more durable than conventional oil-alkyd enamels. Applied over primed wood and metal surfaces such as aluminum and steel windows, metal siding, shutters and other trim, and wood frame windows.

Clear Finishes (for wood). Not as durable as pigmented paint. Alkyd varnishes have good color and color retention but may crack and peel. Some synthetics such as polyurethane varnishes have good durability but may darken on exposure. Spar varnish (marine varnish) is quite durable but will also darken and yellow. Use thin penetrating coats on the bare wood, followed by the unreduced varnish. For clear finish on wood surfaces where natural appearance is desired.

Roof Coatings. Bituminous roof coatings are made of asphalt (chosen for good weather resistance), dissolved in a suitable solvent. Asbestos and other fillers are added to prevent sagging on sloping roofs and to permit application of relatively thick coatings. Basically made in gray and black; however, addition of aluminum powders provides for other colors. Asphalt emulsion roof coatings can be applied over damp surfaces. Special application techniques are usually required and manufacturer's instructions must be followed carefully. Used primarily for coal tar felt roofs.

SUGGESTED COLOR SCHEMES

If your house has shutters, paint the trim the same color as body of house—
or white. If not, use these suggested colors for trim.

If the roof of your house is	You can paint the body	. . . and the trim or shutters and doors															
		Pink	Bright red	Red-orange	Tile red	Cream	Bright yellow	Light green	Dark green	Gray-green	Blue-green	Light blue	Dark blue	Blue-gray	Violet	Brown	White
GRAY	White	x	x	x	x	x	x	x	x	x	x	x	x	x	x		
	Gray	x	x	x	x		x	x	x	x	x	x	x	x	x		x
	Cream-yellow		x		x		x		x	x							x
	Pale green				x		x		x	x							x
	Dark green	x				x	x	x									
	Putty			x	x					x	x		x	x		x	
	Dull red	x				x		x						x			x
GREEN	White	x	x	x	x	x	x	x	x	x	x	x	x	x	x		
	Gray		x			x	x	x									x
	Cream-yellow		x		x				x	x	x					x	x
	Pale green			x	x		x		x								x
	Dark green	x		x		x	x	x									x
	Beige						x		x	x	x		x	x			
	Brown	x				x	x	x									x
	Dull red			x			x			x							x
RED	White		x		x				x		x			x			
	Light gray		x		x				x								x
	Cream-yellow		x		x							x	x	x			
	Pale green		x		x												x
	Dull red					x	x			x	x						x
BROWN	White			x	x		x	x	x	x	x		x	x	x	x	
	Buff			x					x	x	x					x	
	Pink-beige			x					x	x						x	x
	Cream-yellow			x					x	x	x					x	
	Pale green								x	x						x	
	Brown			x		x	x										x
BLUE	White			x	x		x					x	x				
	Gray			x		x						x	x				x
	Cream-yellow			x	x									x	x		
	Blue			x		x	x					x					x

135

Water Repellent Preservative (silicone type).
Silicone water repellents are transparent liquids that help repel water without changing the surface appearance. Must be applied strictly in accordance with instructions to ensure adequacy of film and water repellency. Should not be topcoated with paint until surface has weathered for at least two years. For wood shingle roofs, brick walls, and other surfaces where some degree of water repellency is desired.

CAUSES OF PAINT FAILURE

Blistering

Causes: Inside and outside moisture from poor construction; e.g., unpainted openings, poor ventilation, inadequate insulation. Cooking, bathing, dishwashing, laundry, etc. (Daily evaporation in average home: 25 quarts.)

Treatment: Caulk and repair gutters, faulty siding, and roof flashings. Repair leaky roof. Provide attic louvres, exhaust fans, dehumidifiers, all possible ventilation. Scrape blisters; repaint with blister resistant paint.

Blistering

Excessive Chalking

Excessive Chalking

Causes: Paint applied in rain, fog, or mist. Paint applied too thin. Low quality paint.

Treatment: Remove chalk with a stiff bristle brush. Use nonchalking paint, or one with controlled rate of chalking if desirable to maintain clean surfaces.

Alligatoring

Causes: Low quality paint. Insufficient drying time between coats. A hard coating applied over a soft oil-base type paint.

Treatment: Scrape thoroughly and sand smooth. Apply good quality paint according to manufacturer's instructions.

Alligatoring

Checking

Checking

Causes: Oil paint applied over damp surface. Low quality paint. Improperly mixed paint. Unevenly applied paint. Excessive paint.

Treatment: Scrape paint to bare surface. Apply good quality paint over a clean, primed surface.

Mildew

Causes: Mildew producing fungi. Insufficient sunlight on surfaces in damp areas.

Treatment: Apply solution of trisodium phosphate (available in paint stores) mixed with household ammonia and water, followed by clean water rinse—OR wash down with a solution of 1 pint of household laundry bleach to 1 gallon of water, followed by a thorough clean water rinse. Use mildew resistant paint containing zinc oxide and a mildewcide.

Mildew

Peeling

Peeling

Causes: Paint applied over greasy or oily surface. Inadequately prepared and primed surfaces. Application of oil-base paint over damp surfaces.

Treatment: Scrape and sand peeled surfaces. Apply good quality paint, with brush.

ABOUT WATER-BASE PAINTS

Despite the widespread use of water-base paints for both inside and outside work, there still is some confusion as to how they are formulated and how they work, as opposed to the older oil-base paints.

First, water-base paints are emulsion formulations. An emulsion consists of microscopic particles or tiny globules of liquid, suspended in a liquid. This phenomenon exists in homogenized milk, where the globules of butter fat are suspended in the milk uniformly, rather than being allowed to rise to the top in the form of cream. In the case of water-base paints, generally called latex, small particles of film-forming materials are suspended in water, rather than being dissolved in turpentine or mineral spirits, as is the case with the older, oil-base paints. The film-forming material may be oil, oleoresinous varnish, resin or other emulsifiable natural or synthetic binders.

There are three types of latex paints. Named in the order of their development they are: butadiene-styrene ("rubber-base"), polyvinyl acetate (vinyl), and acrylic copolymers (acrylic). All offer certain improvements in application and performance over the long established oil-base materials. In general, they all share several major characteristics: they spread rapidly, dry quickly, are free of odor from solvents because they are water-thinned, and equipment used to apply them can be cleaned with soap and water.

History

Acrylic resins originally were formulated in the late 1930s and produced in the form of transparent-plastic tubes, rods and sheets. They were used—and still are—for making decorative objects such as candle holders, picture frames and other home-furnishing accessories. During World War II the plastic sheet was used largely as transparent enclosures for aircraft, such as bomber noses and turrets. After the war, acrylic polymers were developed and formulated as lacquers for auto finishes. Acrylic lacquers are used on about half the automobiles produced today. In 1959 two other acrylic applications were perfected, one being a baked-on finish for aluminum, the other a blister-resistant paint for exterior wood siding.

At first the paint was recommended only for use over bare wood on which a special primer first was applied. Product improvement, demonstrated by several years of actual consumer use, showed that it need not be used just over new or bare wood, but could be applied successfully to any sound substrate (surface to which paint is applied), and that it offered much longer life than conventional oil-base paints. Acrylic resin is quite inert chemically so that the paint resists fading and discoloration, does not oxidize and will not chalk to the extent that many oil-base paints do. There are some formulations, however, in which a chalking pigment is used for "self-cleaning."

Properties

The paint "breathes," that is, allows water vapor to pass through it, while keeping out rain. This means that water vapor from inside a house will pass through the wood of the siding, and on through the paint where it is discharged into the air. With oil-base paints the moisture would be trapped under the paint film.

When water-base paint is applied over a sound oil-base paint, and at a later date water vapor does cause the oil-base paint to blister, the tremendous elasticity of the acrylic paint will reduce the chances of the blisters rupturing and exposing the bare wood.

When an acrylic paint is applied over previously-painted surfaces that are not in good condition, the old paint should be washed to remove excessive chalk, dirt, oil or grease, then hosed with clear water. Blistered areas should be scraped or sanded down to bare wood, and well back from the immediate area of damage to assure that all failing paint is removed. Some latex paints require a special oil-base primer for bare wood, but the newest formulations can be applied without primers, or with a latex primer.

A home owner can make an effective paint cleaner by mixing a quart of household chlorine bleach (Clorox, Purex, etc.), one ounce of synthetic detergent (Fab, Tide, All, etc.) and three ounces of trisodium phosphate (Soilax, Spic 'n Span, other cleaners containing TSP) in enough water to make one gallon of cleaning solution. Do not use detergent containing ammonia for this solution because the reaction of ammonia and chlorine will produce a poisonous gas. This solution also will remove mildew that shows as dark spots and streaks.

The newest acrylic paint can be applied without primer over clean masonry surfaces such as brick, concrete, concrete block, stucco and even asphalt shingles, with a brush or roller. New masonry should be allowed to "cure" for 30 days before being painted. Dry masonry surfaces may

Product improvement, demonstrated by several years of consumer use, has shown that modern water-base formulations can be applied over bare wood without primer.

Where a wood surface is mahogany, cedar, redwood or fir plywood, a latex primer is used to seal in soluble dyes that otherwise can bleed through the paint, cause discoloration.

be so porous that they soak up the water in the paint too rapidly, so should be dampened with water, and the paint applied to the damp surface. Calsomine, powdery cement-water paints and whitewash should be removed by wirebrushing to assure good adhesion of the acrylic paint. There now is a special masonry primer that can be applied to penetrate whitewash and assure adhesion.

Mechanical failures of a home should be repaired before painting. Cracked boards, loose trim and the like should be renailed, the nails set and the heads covered with putty. Rotted wood should be replaced, joints around windows and doors caulked. Because of its lower surface tension, water-base paint will not bridge cracks and splits as oil-base paint does, so such damage should be caulked.

The latest formulations of latex paint require no primer for bare wood, except for mahogany, cedar, redwood or fir plywood, and then a special primer is used to seal in soluble dyes that otherwise would "bleed" and cause discoloration. Galvanized steel and aluminum require no primer when the newest latex paints are applied. Rusty steel should be wirebrushed and coated with special rust-inhibiting primer. Do this on recessed nail heads, then fill in recess with putty. Allow putty and caulking to set thoroughly before painting, as these oily materials tend to make paint "crawl." For best results, coat caulking with blister-resistant primer before painting. Acrylic paint dries fast, so avoid

painting on the sunny side of the house. Leave western and southern exposures for cloudy days, or mornings, while they are in the shade. If it rains, stop immediately; the paint will not spot-mark if it has a few minutes to set. When the rain stops, start to paint again as soon as free water evaporates.

Acrylic paint spreads easily, so do not brush it out too thin. You will feel a slight drag as the paint thins. Apply the paint against the lower edges of siding, then spread from there. Check for skips as you go along; if you miss a spot go back and feather the paint around the "patch." Feather the edge of the area you are working on, so the next area will blend in without lap marks. When you quit for a short period of time, put brushes and rollers in a pail of water. When you are ready to start, shake out the excess water before dipping in paint. Because acrylic paint dries quickly, open and close windows several times when painting around them to prevent them sticking.

Some gel-type paints used for interior painting also are made from acrylic water-base material, but with an added component that gives them the property chemists call thixotrophy. The motion of a brush or roller makes the paint more fluid and it applies smoothly. The thixotropic formulation keeps the various materials in suspension so the paint need not be stirred. Because the paint is thick, more can be carried on brush or roller, and less dipping is required. The thixotropic quality also causes fluid paint to return to a gel state a few moments after application, so there is less chance of dripping or running. The paint is quite opaque, and unless you are painting a light color over a dark, one coat is enough.

No matter what the "how" or "why" of water-base paints, the important factors are that they are easy to apply, cover well, are easily washed with soap and water when dry, and brushes or rollers can be cleaned with plain soap and water.

MORE ABOUT HOUSE PAINTS

House paint consists of two parts, a solid part (pigments) and a liquid part (the vehicle). The pigments include hiding (opaque) pigments and transparent (extending pigments). The vehicle of an oil-base paint consists generally of a drying oil (usually linseed oil) or an oil modified with an alkyd resin, a solvent (mineral spirits or turpentine), and a small amount of paint dryer to harden the paint promptly after application. The vehicle of latex paint consists of a suspension of resin particles, usually acrylic or vinyl, in water. The performance characteristics of a paint are dependent to a great extent on the nature of the pigment, the proportion of pigment to vehicle, and the kind of vehicle.

Oil-Base and Alkyd House Paints

In these the white house paints may be classified simply according to the kind of white pigments used in them. The white pigments used are white lead oxide, zinc oxide, and titanium dioxide.

Each type has some of the characteristics generally considered essential in good house paint. These include durability sufficient to last 4 to 6 years before needing renewal, a normal form of wearing that insures a good repaint surface with a minimum of preparatory work, and a normally fast rate of wear from the surface. The wear requirement prevents the accumulation of an excessively thick film of paint when a reasonable maintenance schedule is followed (a single coat every 4 or 5 years or two coats every 6 years). Paint should also have a clean, highly reflective color and ability to remain free from excessive dirt collection in service. It should be nonsensitive to moisture, and should not be stained by metal corrosion and wood extractives. Nor should it be discolored by hydrogen sulfide or organic sulfides. No one type of house paint on the market has all of these characteristics.

All types of paint have some desirable features and some that are not so desirable. To select the type of paint likely to give the most satisfactory service, the homeowner should be familiar with the conditions in his area to which house paints are subjected. He must also know the types of paint that will stand up best under these conditions—which of the various paint properties are important to him under the circumstances and which are relatively unimportant.

In terms of years of use, white lead paint is the oldest. It has been used on houses in this country since Colonial times, and is still preferred by some painters and houseowners to the other types of house paints. However, it accounts for only a very small fraction of the total house paint used in this country.

White lead paint is a durable paint that normally fails by chalking and crumbling. Probably the most important of its properties, however, is its nonsensitiveness to water. Even when exposed to water for a long time, it swells only about as much as wood does when wet. Consequently, it has little tendency to blister, and can be used where moisture blistering is an obvious paint problem. One of the more serious objections to white lead paint is its retention of dirt. Another objection is that it discolors on contact with hydrogen sulfide gases that cause the formation of black lead sulfide.

A few paints pigmented with a combination of white lead and titanium are sold as "titanized white lead." Paints of the titanium-lead type are nonsensitive to moisture, therefore very blister resistant. Because of this property, titanium and lead pigments were used universally for many years in house paint primers.

Paint with zinc oxide pigment usually has a brilliant and highly reflective color, remains uniformly clean in service, and is mildew resistant. It is generally hard, and wears away slowly. Paints of this type normally fail by cracking, curling, and flaking. With paints that fail in this manner, the coating on the wood must not be permitted to become too thick, and the cracking failure must not be permitted to advance too far before repainting. Because zinc-containing paints swell when wet, they blister more readily on contact with water than do the other types of paint.

Zinc-containing paints also are likely to become stained by nail rust and by the corrosion products of iron and copper screens reacting with zinc. House paints made with zinc oxide and titanium dioxide, often called "fume-proof" paint, do not discolor on exposure to hydrogen sulfide or organic sulfide gases.

Paints of titanium pigment combined with alkyd-oil resin vehicles are widely used. Alkyd paints are sold as "flat-alkyd, low-luster, breather-type, blister-resistant, and self-priming" paints. They may have little or no gloss, and also be very porous. The performance of alkyd paints relates to quality; the better the quality, the better the performance.

Titanium-alkyd paints normally fail by cracking and peeling, and may chalk excessively if formulated with an excessively low-vehicle content. The porous nature of the flat-alkyd type paints makes them quite susceptible to extractive staining over redwood and cedar. These paints should, therefore, be applied over a nonporous, zinc oxide-free primer, which will protect the wood surface from excessive moisture in the form of rain and dew. They resist sulfide discoloration.

Dark-color paints, sometimes called trim paints or trim-and-trellis paints, consist chiefly of dark-color pigments with little, if any, titanium dioxide, white lead, or zinc oxide. In most trim paints, the major part of the vehicle is varnish, usually an alkyd-resin varnish. Iron oxide paints—the familiar red barn paints—may also be classified as dark-color paints. Sometimes used on houses, they are very durable if of good quality. In general, good paints of dark colors are more durable than white or light-color paints.

Latex House Paints

Exterior latex white paints are usually based on suspensions of either acrylic or vinyl resins and titanium dioxide pigment. Latexes of this type may also be modified with alkyd-oil resins. These paints can have excellent adhesion to wood surfaces, blister resistance, tint retention, and durability. Their ease of application and cleanup with water makes them very popular. Like the flat-alkyd paints, however, they are porous, and should be applied over a nonporous oil-base primer on both new wood, which contains colored extractives, and old chalky oil-base paint.

Paint Primers

Some paints can be used as self-primers, whereas others require a special primer for the first coat on new wood. The proper choice of primer can do much to insure long-lasting, trouble-free paint performance. In particular, a primer should be nonporous, flexible, and blister resistant. It should therefore not contain zinc oxide pigment. Most paint manufacturers provide special, zinc-free house paint primers or undercoaters for use with their paints containing zinc. As a rule, it is wise to use primer and finish paint of the same brand.

The "breather-type" paints and titanium flat-alkyd resin paints are usually used as self-primers, but may be too porous to provide complete protection against moisture.

Very refractory wood surfaces, such as those of dense pine or fir, flat grain, wood with knots, and exterior plywood, may need the protection from moisture in many situations that only aluminum primer can provide. Aluminum paint for wood is the most impervious (nonporous) of the primers.

Selection of a particular type of house paint requires careful consideration. Where moisture troubles are widespread, a zinc-free paint of a high-quality latex is to be preferred. The construction of the house should also be considered. Does it have a wide roof overhang to shield the walls? Does it have adequate gutters and downspouts, and are they properly installed? Is there a good vapor barrier plus the insulation? Are the attic spaces well insulated and vented? If the answers are "yes," the probabilities for minimal maintenance and successful paint performance are very good.

FINISHING WOOD SIDING AND TRIM
Painting

Questions that arise for applying finish include: When to paint? Where to begin? How many coats?

Finish can be applied with a brush, a spray, or a roller. A brush is generally used, and, for purposes of this discussion, brush application is assumed.

The following are three simple steps in painting exterior wood:

(1) Apply water-repellent preservative by brush, roller, or squirt can to all joints (wherever two pieces of wood come together) and ends of boards. Dry 2 days before priming.

(2) Apply nonporous, zinc-free oil-base prim-

CLEAN OUT
ALL JOINTS.

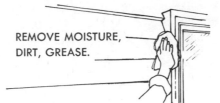
REMOVE MOISTURE,
DIRT, GREASE.

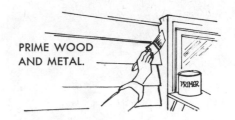
PRIME WOOD
AND METAL.

Chips and blisters must be scraped, edges smoothed to prevent future peeling. Clean surface well.

A propane torch with a flame spreader and a heavy-duty spatula removes most large blisters. Keep pail of water handy.

A sanding disk may be sufficient to smooth out small cracks and blisters, use scraper for large blisters.

Most of the old calking had peeled away from the wood, leaving openings where moisture seeped in.

Wire brushing is necessary before painting any brick or masonry to remove dust, dirt and loose particles.

Foundation walls were sprayed with water after wire brushing to wash away all loose particles.

141

Compare the difference in appearance of the newly-painted foundation wall and the unpainted portion.

Latex paints have more viscosity, do not run or sag on the wall surface, or cause annoying runs down your arm.

Test a sample of the stain on scrap of siding; different woods and stains will give different results when dry.

Protect valuable shrubs and trees by covering them with sheet plastic, tying back with ropes.

Stain only a few boards at a time, to maintain a wet working edge. This helps eliminate "lap" marks.

To assure uniformity of color, stir stain well before use. Stir often while working for consistent color.

Pour stain into work bucket for easier handling; less mess. It also prevents contamination of entire can from dirt.

142

er thick enough to cover the wood grain.

(3) Within 2 days to 2 weeks after applying primer, apply latex or oil-base topcoats. Two topcoats should be applied in areas fully exposed to the weather.

Finish is best applied during warm dry weather when several weeks of sunshine can be expected. This creates a problem for houses built during fall or winter; often builders let them stand with a prime coat until spring before finishing the job. This procedure can result in trouble. The better practice in these situations is to brush water-repellent preservatives on the siding, after which it can go without finish until spring.

The answer to the question "How many coats?" depends largely on the kind of paint selected. As a rule, three coats are recommended for new wood. Many builders apply only two. The third coat may be applied only to areas exposed to severe weathering. A first paint job of oil-base paint should be 4½ to 5 mils (thousandths of an inch) thick, which is about the thickness of a dollar bill. It is difficult, if not impossible, to apply that much by brush with one primer and one finish coat of today's average paints. Exceptionally heavy coats, where oil-base paint is applied at a rate of 450 to 500 square feet a gallon, are likely to result in wrinkling, loss of gloss, and slow drying during cold weather. The optimum thickness of a three-coat latex system is 3 to 3.5 mils.

With paint, an old craftman's rule is: "Follow the sun around the house." This means that the north side should be painted early in the morning, the east side late in the morning, the south side well after noon, and the west side during late afternoon.

Morning dew or the water of a brief shower should be wiped off, and painting can begin after half an hour of warm-weather sunshine. After many hours of hard rain, however, a day or two of drying is needed.

The amateur painter can learn to gauge spreading rates by applying a pint of paint evenly over a measured area. For example, at a spreading rate of 450 square feet to the gallon, a pint covers 55 square feet, or an area of 5 by 11 feet; at 550 square feet a gallon, a pint covers about 70 square feet, or an area of 5 by 14 feet. The average beginner tends to spread paint too thinly.

For modern oil paints of average composition, a total thickness of between 4½ and 5 mils results when one coat of housepaint primer is applied at 450 square feet a gallon and two coats of finish paint at 550 square feet a gallon each.

In warm dry weather, each coat of oil-base paint should dry a day or two before the next is applied. Cold or damp weather may make an extra day or two advisable, but more than 2 weeks between coats should be avoided. Coats of latex paint can be applied within a few hours of each other.

Staining

Penetrating stains are very easy to apply. For smooth surfaces that are not too absorptive, two coats of stain are not recommended because the second coat will not penetrate. This results in hold-out of the stain in certain areas to produce unsightly glossy spots. On smoothly planed wood surfaces a one-coat application will last about 3 years. Rough-sawn and weathered wood surfaces are much more absorptive than newly planed surfaces, and are finished best with two coats of penetrating stain. Two coats of stain on rough surfaces will last 8 to 10 years. The second coat of stain should be applied within an hour of the first so that both coats will penetrate. If the first is allowed to dry, it acts as a sealer, and the second coat cannot penetrate. Stain that has not penetrated after an hour should be wiped from the surface. Penetrating stain will "lap" badly if the front edge of stain area is permitted to dry. Stains should therefore be applied to only one or two courses of siding at a time, and the course should be completed before painting is stopped.

Because the stain penetrates, there is no coating on the surface that can later separate by peeling and flaking. Penetrating stains are therefore ideal finishes for wood surfaces considered difficult to paint and for those exposed to high-moisture conditions.

MAINTENANCE OF FINISHES
Repainting or Restaining

Hot summer sun, wind-driven rain, hail, dust, and winter snow and ice gradually take a toll on even the best finish. How frequently the finish should be renewed is governed by the rate at which it weathers away.

As pointed out, a paint maintenance program is determined by the kind of paint used in the first paint job. The basic rule is, paint only after most of the old paint film has weathered away. Always remember that coating thickness can build up dangerously if paint, especially oil base, is applied too frequently. Abnormal behavior spells trouble and possibly costly removal of old paint by blowtorch or by paint and varnish remover.

Paint that starts to crack and peel from the wood indicates that a serious moisture problem may be involved. It may indicate two conditions: (1) Either a primer was used that was sensitive to water and perhaps too porous to provide adequate protection from rain and dew or (2) moisture from cold weather condensation or ice dams is excessively wetting the walls and the siding.

Quality latex paints properly applied to old painted surfaces are proving excellent refinish systems. Latex does not always bond well to chalk surfaces, and because of its porosity, it holds rain and dew. In turn, this water can penetrate the paint film and produce an abnormal peeling problem. When repainting chalky surfaces with exterior latex, therefore, it is advisable either to remove the chalk by sanding, scrubbing, or steel wooling or to apply a new coat of oil-base primer over the chalk. Recent developments in latex paint formulation have greatly improved performance over old paint. Thus, it is important to read the directions on a label carefully before applying latex over old chalky paint.

Penetrating natural stains are easy to renew. Fresh finish is simply applied when the old finish appears to need it. As with the first finishing job, any excess of stain or oil should be wiped off, so that formation of a surface coat is prevented.

Eliminating Troubles

Paint troubles arise from various causes. Most common are porous finish systems that allow rain and dew to enter the coating; improper first priming of wood with wide summerwood bands; repainting too soon without washing; moisture vapor troubles in tightly built insulated houses that lack vapor barriers; or rain or other water getting behind the siding. Evidence of paint trouble usually comes in the form of cracking, blistering, and peeling.

Before repainting, the probable cause of the trouble should be ascertained. If it is due to springtime blistering on localized areas on the house in the colder northern states, a more effective vapor

barrier is needed. This can be obtained by painting the indoor side of the exterior walls. Two coats of aluminum paint plus two coats of decorative paint are best for sand-finish plaster. On smooth plaster, a primer-sealer and at least one coat of semigloss paint make a good barrier. Shutting off humidifiers will also help.

Where the trouble is due to water that gets inside the walls from the roof, leaks should be found. If the trouble is due to ice damming, the situation can be improved by increasing the insulation in the attic floor to a minimum thickness of 6 inches and by increasing the screened venting area of the attic to 1/225 of the ceiling area. If the gutters overflow during heavy rains, additional downspouts may be needed or the gutters may need to be cleaned and rehung with a greater pitch. If paint fails first at ends of boards, water is getting through the joints of the siding, and the lap and butt joints should be treated with water-repellent preservatives before repainting. This type of solution is highly penetrating, and creeps well into the joints to seal them against future inroads of rainwater.

"Snowflake" type peeling of paint, especially in protected areas, indicates that the old paint surface was not adequately washed before repainting.

Tan- to brown-discoloration stains on redwood and cedar siding on all sides of the house mean that the paint was too thin and porous, which allowed rain and dew to pass through the coating to dissolve the extractives. This type of paint condition frequently involves peeling because too much rain and dew penetrate the old paint layers. These failures occur on all sides of a building and on both heated and unheated buildings. These failures are usually corrected by priming all old paint surfaces with a good nonporous oil-base primer before the top coat is added.

Whatever the cause of a paint problem it should be found and corrected before the house is repainted. Then the repaint job should markedly reduce future recurrences of abnormal paint behavior.

SPECIAL PROBLEMS
Painting Windows and Trim

Most do-it-yourself painters find that, although the rest of the job is a snap, painting windows and trim presents a bit more of a problem. But with a system for painting, you won't waste time waiting

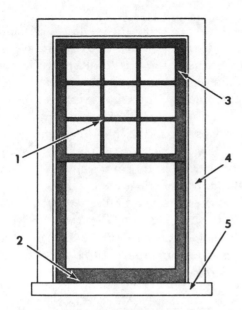

Paint windows in this order: (1) Mullions, (2) horizontal of sash, (3) verticals of sash, (4) verticals of frame, (5) horizontal frame and sill.

for various areas to dry and you'll be sure to cover every spot. On windows, paint the mullions first, and then the horizontals of the sash. Paint the verticals of the sash next, followed by the verticals of the frame. Your last step is painting the horizontal frame and sill.

It's a good idea to remove the hardware from your doors and windows before you begin to paint. This will make the painting job easier and will give you a chance to clean and polish the metal until it looks like new.

Masking tape is very helpful in keeping stray splatters away from the glass when painting window frames. Apply the tape along the window directly adjacent to the glass. Then brush the paint onto the frame, being careful not to use too thick a coat. Once the paint has dried, carefully cut the paint film between the tape and frame with a razor blade, then strip off the tape.

Even though you may be painting the walls with a handy flat paint, it's best to use a quality trim enamel for the windows and woodwork since they receive the most wear. The area of the sash and frame of a window is generally 35 square feet. Multiply this figure by the number of windows to get the area that has to be covered with trim enamel. Divide this amount by the coverage, and you'll know how much trim enamel to buy.

Outdoor wooden trim, such as window sashes, shutters and doors should be attractively coated with a colorful exterior trim paint or enamel. These coatings, which dry with a relatively glossy surface, are available in a variety of attractive colors.

When painting woodwork use a round 1-inch brush for window sash, and a 2- or 3-inch brush for the balance of the trim.

Painting Doors

Doors are subject to more close scrutiny by visitors than almost any other part of your home. People pass within a few inches of a door whenever they enter or leave a room, and when guests call, they have nothing to do but gaze at your door until you answer their ring.

More than the usual care must be taken, therefore, when painting a door. The job must be done quickly, 20 minutes should be enough time, but 30 minutes would be maximum, because the paint will start to set by then. Hard edges will form along the edges of painted sections and the brush will "pick up" a congealing paint film.

You will have to check your work frequently, going back to pick up misses and runs. You cannot wait until you have finished the whole door because the paint will have started to dry, and any touch-ups will show.

A first-class job on a door demands that you use your best brushes. For a flush door use a 3-inch brush, for a paneled door use a 2-inch brush. You may need a smaller one for moldings if they are quite narrow. A good used brush is best, as there will be less chance of loose bristles pulling out and depositing in the paint film.

The first step is to remove the knob and any hardware; this is a time-saver, as painting around hardware can be tedious, and you are almost bound to get a splash or two of paint on the knob.

Paint the frame around the door first. If you do splash paint, it will fall on the unpainted door and can be wiped up quickly.

For flush doors, start at one top corner by applying two or three vertical strokes about one-third the height of the door. This applies to all primers and finish coats, unless the paint has instructions saying that "brushing-out" is not necessary. Brush out the vertical strokes horizontally, using pressure to cut the paint film. Another few vertical strokes are applied, then brushed horizontally until you have gone all the way across the door. Now, brush the complete width with vertical strokes, then horizontal.

Now, "lay-off" with the tips of the bristles in a downward direction, lifting the brush lightly at the ends of the strokes. Move down and do the next third of the door in the same manner, but this time lay-off with upward strokes into the wet edge of the first area. The final third of the door is painted in the same way, the final brushing being upward.

Painting a paneled door requires a completely different procedure. You start by painting the molding in the upper panel. Use a fairly dry brush to minimize the amount of paint that will spread on the adjoining panel and rails. Next, paint the panel, going with the grain of the wood, and pick-ing up the overlaps from the molding. Brush out horizontally, then vertically and finally horizontally with the tips of the bristles. Repeat the operation on all moldings and panels. Now paint the vertical rails, picking up the overlaps from the moldings. Next, paint the horizontal rails, picking up the overlaps from the moldings and vertical center stiles. Lay-off horizontally, with the grain.

The final step is to paint the outside stiles, which will permit picking up overlaps from the moldings and the horizontal rails.

When brushing-out on the rails, move the brush to the edges to make sure they are properly coated. This does not apply to laying-off, where the brush is stroked with the grain.

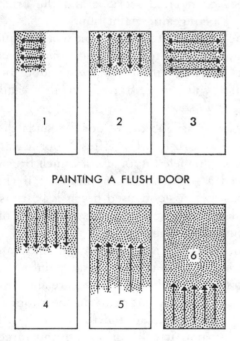

PAINTING A FLUSH DOOR

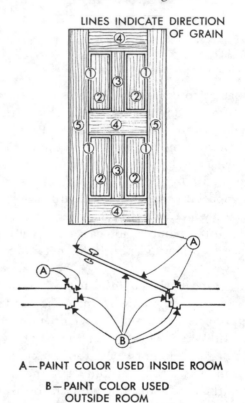

LINES INDICATE DIRECTION OF GRAIN

A—PAINT COLOR USED INSIDE ROOM

B—PAINT COLOR USED OUTSIDE ROOM

5

WINDOWS, DOORS, CLOSETS, DRAWERS AND SHELVES

WINDOWS, DOORS, CLOSETS, DRAWERS AND SHELVES

5

REPAIRING DRAWERS ■ INSTALLING A CYLINDER LOCK ■ BROKEN WINDOWS

CEDAR CLOSET ■ PROBLEM DOORS ■ FRAMING AND HANGING A DOOR ■ HINGES

BUILDING DRAWERS ■ SHELVING ■ STORM WINDOWS ■ REPAIRING SCREENS

STORM WINDOWS

Cold windows lower inside temperature and raise fuel bills. The remedy consists of insulating windows with a blanket of still air, also needed to keep out heat when using air conditioning in hot weather.

One answer to the problem is insulating glass. This consists of double panes hermetically sealed at their edges to enclose a space of dehydrated air. The heat loss of 115 square feet of this glass is no more than 65 feet of single glazing. Insulating glass can be used for most windows regardless of their method of operation. On metal windows, however, it will not stop condensation on the metal beyond the glass.

Another popular method of insulating windows and doors is storm sash and doors. The semi-annual, backbreaking chore of putting up and taking down old-style storm sash is eliminated with today's neat, compact combination storm sash and screens that are installed permanently. You merely push easy-sliding inserts up and down to suit the season.

In a realistic appraisal of modern storm sash you will find it highly convenient, and if used on all windows of a house it will save about 20 per cent of heating costs or more. This saving will re-pay the investment in just a few years. Other benefits are a 1 to 2-degree increase in temperature at floor level when the furnace is on, and savings in air conditioning costs. Also, storm sash properly installed on the outside of weatherstripped windows usually ends condensation troubles. When storm sash is fitted on the inside of metal windows such as casement, louver or awning types, they often do not cover the windows entirely and do allow condensation to take place at the uncovered areas.

Combination storm sash and screens are made in both metal and wood. A unit consists of a frame that fits against the blind stop of a window casing. Metal units may or may not have a flange at the top and sides to conceal the crack between the unit and the casing. On the inside of the frame there are tracks or channels holding two glass inserts and a screen. Each of the inserts equal about half the window area, and can be slid from end to end. This permits the entire window opening to be closed with the glass inserts or closed at the top half when the screen is in the lower half.

Most storm-screen units have inserts that are unlatched at their lower end so they can be tilted inward and then brought to a diagonal position for removal. Some units are prefinished, and can be

149

Permanently installed storm-screen units have tilting, removable inserts for easy washing. Are self-storing, slide up and down at fingertip control to suit season.

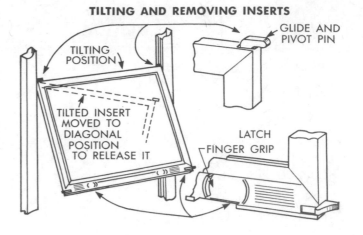

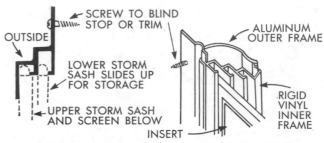

TYPICAL 2-TRACK FRAME   TYPICAL 3-TRACK FRAME

painted on the outside to match the house.

Purchasing Storm-Screen Units

Before purchasing you should know the basic difference between 1-, 2- and 3-track varieties. Low-cost single-track units usually have a glass insert located above the screen in the same channel. Both are removable from inside. The screen is replaced by a second glass insert when full storm-sash protection is desired. Some units have clips to hold the unused insert in the frame for storage, with others the insert must be stored separately. Units with 2 and 3 tracks are more convenient than 1-track types.

In 2-track units, one storm sash and a screen usually occupy the outer channel—sash above, screen below. The inner channel holds the other storm sash that is slid up for ventilation, down for storm-sash protection. The screen may be left in place permanently, or it can be removed and stored. In 3-channel units each storm sash and screen occupy separate tracks, the screen in the inside one where it can be slid up for storage, or entirely removed. The 2-track type costs less because of simpler construction, and the better grades of

this type offer just as much protection as the 3-track styles.

When purchasing combination storm sash and screens check for the following: 1. Metal is thick enough to produce a substantial frame. 2. Proper reinforcement at points of strain and the seams are interlocked. 3. All inserts can be self-stored in the frame. 4. Joints where two glass inserts, or glass and screen meet have a soft, tight seal. 5. Inserts slide easily, are well cushioned and are easy to tilt and remove. Some of the better grades have vinyl or nylon channels that minimize friction and noise usually created by metal-to-metal contact. Generally it is preferable to purchase units that can be repaired by any competent glazier instead of being sent back to the factory.

To attempt making a combination storm sash and screen that can be left in place permanently involves problems of which the solutions, if attained, will cost just as much in time and materials as the readymade product. Making these, therefore, is not advised.

Storm-screen units purchased from mail-order houses generally come preassembled. In ordering, follow the catalog instructions on measuring the

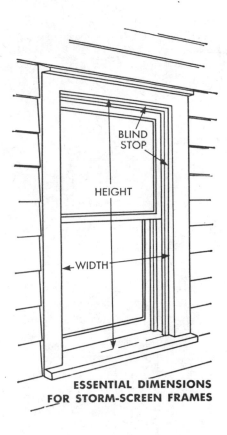

**ESSENTIAL DIMENSIONS
FOR STORM-SCREEN FRAMES**

windows to be fitted. It is important to give the exact width and height of the window casing just outside of the blind.

Only aluminum or stainless-steel screws should be used for attachment of metal units, as ordinary steel screws will rust. Caulking sometimes is recommended at the top of each unit, and for a distance of about 6 inches at the upper ends of the sides. More caulking than this results in too much restriction of the slight air leakage necessary to prevent condensation in the inside of the storm sash.

Divided Sash Units

If your pocketbook dictates a lesser expenditure than that for storm-screen units, you can use divided sash made of aluminum or wood. These can be put in place from inside. Stock to make aluminum storm sash with required fittings can be obtained at most larger hardware stores. There are two types of stock for frames. The stock comes in 5-, 6- and 8-foot lengths. To avoid waste, measure the windows and decide which lengths are most suitable. The maker of this product furnishes a sheet of detailed instructions on making and installing the sash.

In using the parts for assembly of a divided

sash made of the extruded frame, the sections should join in front of the window center rail, and generally will be of different heights. Measure the width and height of the window opening just outside the blind stop. Then determine the height of each sash. Horizontal parts of the frames are 3/8 inch less than the width of the opening, the length of the side members of both sections is 3/16 inch less than the distance from top or bottom of the window opening to the point where both sections join. The distances deducted allow for clearance of nuts on screws that hold corner braces, and also compensate for slightly out-of-square openings or slight errors in cutting stock.

Each frame member is mitered 45 degrees at the ends, and is drilled for attachment of L-braces that will clear the blind stop. Note the lower L-braces of the upper section are on the inside, all others on the outside. Sash hangers for both sections fit directly over the L-braces and are held by the same screws. There is an extra piece—meeting-rail and drip cap—bolted to the lower rail of the top section, using the bolts of the L-braces plus an added one at the center. One leg of the glass channel of the meeting rail is notched at each end to clear the blind stop and allow the two sections to lie flush against it. The lower rail of the bottom section is fitted with two hooks to fit eyes in the sill. Where it is desired to open the lower section for ventilation, a storm-sash adjuster is substituted for one hook.

Size of the glass, either single or double strength, is 1¾ inches less than the outside dimensions of each section. The frames are disassembled to install the glass. Friction tape is pressed over the edges of the glass, two thicknesses for single and one for double-strength. Notch the corners to keep the tape from doubling. Frames are pressed in place over the tape and after assembly excess tape is cut away. Matching parts of the hangers are screwed to the window casing. To install these sash, pass them out the fully opened lower window diagonally, hanging the upper section in place first, then the lower one.

Storm Sash and Screens Inside

Casement, louver and awning-type windows, all opening outward, take storm sash and screens inside. Makers of metal windows make storm sash and screens to fit their products, together with the

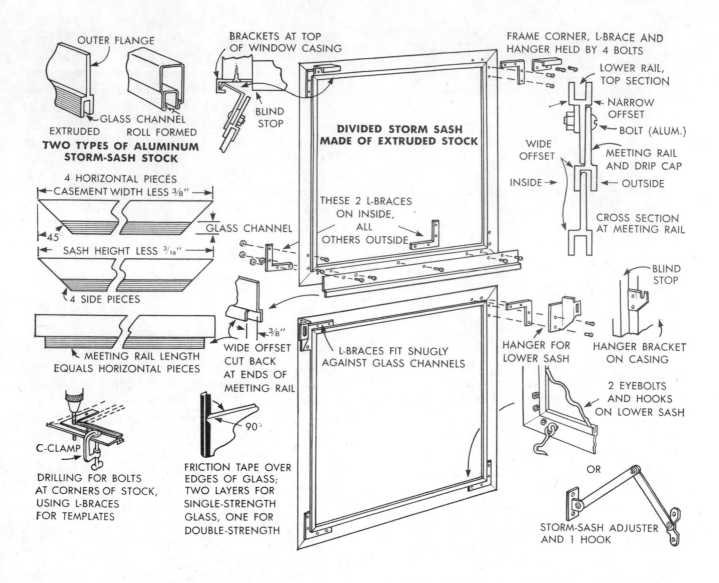

OUTER FLANGE

GLASS CHANNEL

EXTRUDED — ROLL FORMED

TWO TYPES OF ALUMINUM STORM-SASH STOCK

4 HORIZONTAL PIECES
CASEMENT WIDTH LESS ⅜"

45°

SASH HEIGHT LESS 3⁄16"

4 SIDE PIECES

MEETING RAIL LENGTH EQUALS HORIZONTAL PIECES

C-CLAMP

DRILLING FOR BOLTS AT CORNERS OF STOCK, USING L-BRACES FOR TEMPLATES

BRACKETS AT TOP OF WINDOW CASING

BLIND STOP

DIVIDED STORM SASH MADE OF EXTRUDED STOCK

THESE 2 L-BRACES ON INSIDE, ALL OTHERS OUTSIDE

GLASS CHANNEL

WIDE OFFSET CUT BACK AT ENDS OF MEETING RAIL

⅜"

90°

FRICTION TAPE OVER EDGES OF GLASS; TWO LAYERS FOR SINGLE-STRENGTH GLASS, ONE FOR DOUBLE-STRENGTH

L-BRACES FIT SNUGLY AGAINST GLASS CHANNELS

FRAME CORNER, L-BRACE AND HANGER HELD BY 4 BOLTS

LOWER RAIL, TOP SECTION

NARROW OFFSET

BOLT (ALUM.)

WIDE OFFSET

MEETING RAIL AND DRIP CAP

INSIDE →

← OUTSIDE

CROSS SECTION AT MEETING RAIL

BLIND STOP

HANGER FOR LOWER SASH

HANGER BRACKET ON CASING

2 EYEBOLTS AND HOOKS ON LOWER SASH

OR

STORM-SASH ADJUSTER AND 1 HOOK

fittings for attachment. To cover metal windows completely, eliminating condensation along the edges of uninsulated frames, you can make storm sash that fits snugly inside of the casings against blind stops. Unlike outside storm sash, those on the inside should be sealed with weatherstripping to keep out warm, humid air from inside. Where windows have an area of more than 9 square feet, homemade sash of aluminum should be divided into sections, one fitting above the other. The joint between sections can be sealed with neoprene roll or other stripping.

Weatherstripping

As every window sash is fitted to have slight clearance for easy movement, there are cracks through which air passes. Shrinkage of wood windows eventually makes cracks larger, and building

settling often distorts metal windows slightly so the sash no longer fits snugly. To seal these cracks use weatherstripping.

There are many kinds of weatherstripping. The surface-mounted type is easiest to install and comes in kit form. On swinging doors some kinds of surface-mounted stripping near the knob may be objectionable as it may cause bruised knuckles when opening and closing the door. The spring-metal variety often is used on double-hung and casement windows and on doors. It is nailed against window or door. Sash need not be removed from casings to install the metal; exposed ends of the strips are bent back so they do not catch when the sash slides over them. It is notched to fit around strike plates and latches, or special inserts are used. An objection to its use on door bottoms is that it traps dirt and loses its flexibility. Spring-

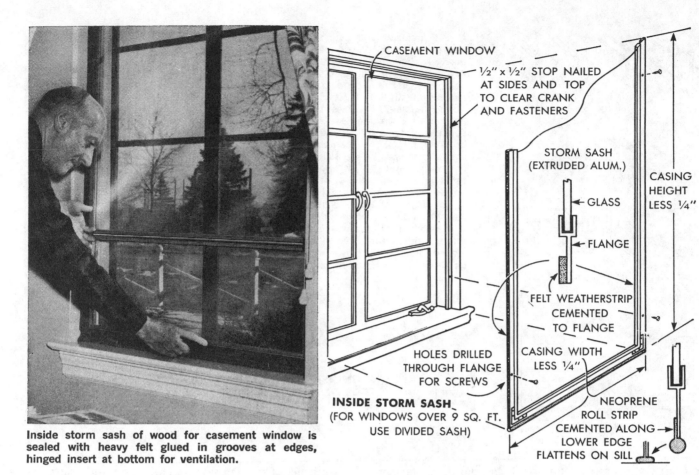

Inside storm sash of wood for casement window is sealed with heavy felt glued in grooves at edges, hinged insert at bottom for ventilation.

CASEMENT WINDOW

½" x ½" STOP NAILED AT SIDES AND TOP TO CLEAR CRANK AND FASTENERS

STORM SASH (EXTRUDED ALUM.)

GLASS

FLANGE

CASING HEIGHT LESS ¼"

FELT WEATHERSTRIP CEMENTED TO FLANGE

HOLES DRILLED THROUGH FLANGE FOR SCREWS

CASING WIDTH LESS ¼"

INSIDE STORM SASH (FOR WINDOWS OVER 9 SQ. FT. USE DIVIDED SASH)

NEOPRENE ROLL STRIP CEMENTED ALONG LOWER EDGE FLATTENS ON SILL

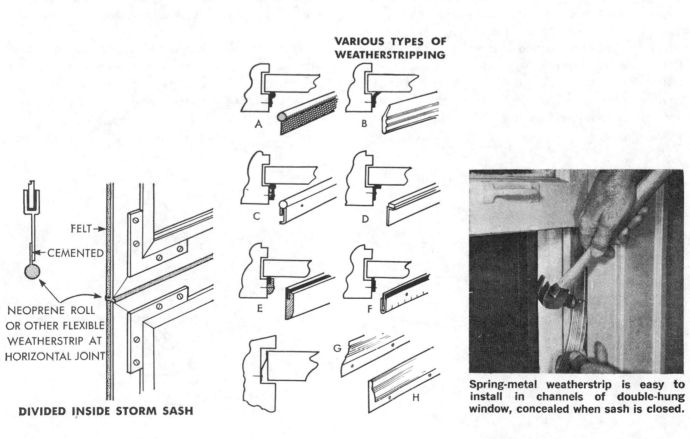

FELT

CEMENTED

NEOPRENE ROLL OR OTHER FLEXIBLE WEATHERSTRIP AT HORIZONTAL JOINT

DIVIDED INSIDE STORM SASH

VARIOUS TYPES OF WEATHERSTRIPPING

A

B

C

D

E

F

G

H

Spring-metal weatherstrip is easy to install in channels of double-hung window, concealed when sash is closed.

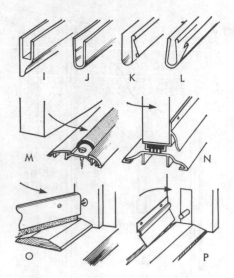

A to F inclusive show surface-mounted weatherstripping on double-hung windows. A shows a padded neoprene roll, B a molded vinyl strip, C a vinyl tube held on rigid metal strip. D is fabric on aluminum strip, E is felt recessed in wood molding, F shows felt held by aluminum strip, comes in roll. Two concealed spring-metal kinds are shown in G and H. For casements there is vinyl weatherstripping as in I and J, or spring-metal type, K and L. For bottoms of swinging doors, M shows aluminum threshold with flexible insert, N is vinyl strip with wipers held in aluminum angle that includes drip cap. O is mechanical type with plunger that forces felt on threshold when door is closed. P is vinyl strip brought down on threshold by short metal peg.

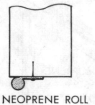
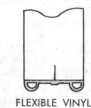

Caulking along outside edges of window frame seals cracks, eliminates air leakage and entrance of rain into wall.

WEATHERSTRIPS FOR LOWER EDGE OF GARAGE DOORS

NEOPRENE ROLL   FLEXIBLE VINYL   RUBBER

metal weatherstripping must be handled and installed with care to avoid bending or kinking it.

Weatherstripping for metal windows may be vinyl or spring metal and is made to fit snugly on the sash edge. For door bottoms you can get aluminum thresholds with the plastic inserts that bear against the door edge. Also, there are devices that are self-opening and closing that bear against the

threshold. These raise to clear carpeting when the door opens, are forced down when the door is closed.

To stop air leakage between cracks at joints between walls and window or door trim, and also exclude rain, caulk these joints on the outside. When repainting the inside walls, seal edges of trim with crack filler.

REPLACING BROKEN WINDOWS

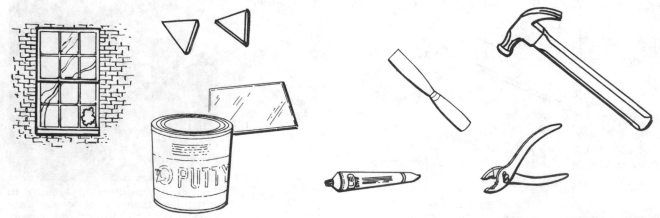

Tools you will need.

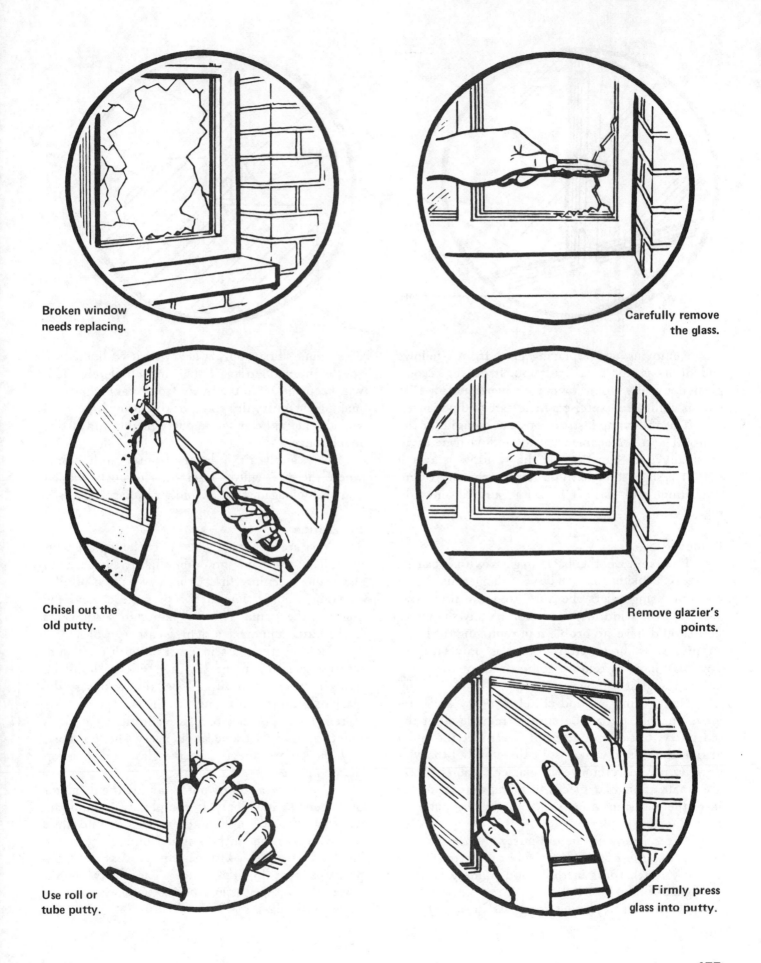

Broken window
needs replacing.

Carefully remove
the glass.

Chisel out the
old putty.

Remove glazier's
points.

Use roll or
tube putty.

Firmly press
glass into putty.

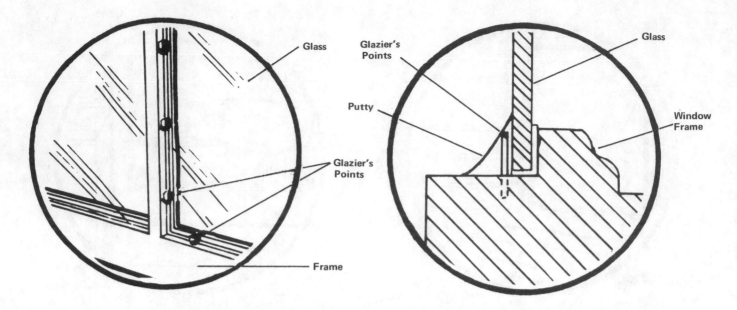

Removing and replacing glass from windows and doors is not a difficult job. It can be accomplished by any home owner or apartment dweller who is willing to exercise a little care and patience.

The following instructions can be used for the removal and replacement of a window pane of almost any size. However, if the window is a large one, it is suggested that you remove the entire window frame and place it on a flat surface for working.

Removal

First remove the broken glass with a pair of pliers. As broken glass can be very dangerous, if you are not using pliers, be sure to wear protective gloves. If the window pane is completely shattered, you should have no problem in removing the broken pieces. If, however, the glass is only cracked, you may have to remove some or all of the putty before the glass can be removed.

Next, using a wood chisel or putty knife, remove the old putty. Be sure to remove all of the old putty, but do not attempt to remove too much at one time or you may split the wood of the window frame. Also remove all glazier's points. These are small, triangular pieces of metal that are driven into the wooden frame underneath the putty to hold the glass in place.

After removing the old putty and the glazier's points, use the point of a chisel or knife to smooth out any rough spots in the wood frame where the new glass will be inserted.

If you are replacing the glass in an old window frame, first apply a heavy coat of linseed oil to the frame, letting it soak in completely. This will keep the oil in the putty from soaking out and making the putty dry too quickly. Using linseed oil will also aid in keeping the putty pliable and lasting much longer.

Now apply a thin layer of putty to the frame where the glass will be inserted. This putty will act as a cushion against shock and air leakage.

Installation

You are now ready to insert the replacement glass. The new pane should be slightly smaller than the frame opening. Insert the new pane carefully, exerting a slight amount of pressure around the edges of the frame. This will eliminate air pockets in the putty and make a tight, weatherproof seal.

Holding the glass in position with one hand, insert a glazier's point on each side to hold the glass in place. You should be able to insert the glazier's points with only a slight tap of your chisel. Then proceed to place additional glazier's points around the frame, about every 4 inches apart. Lay the points directly on the glass and then tap them in place.

Now take a roll of putty, about the diameter of a pencil, and apply it completely around the window pane. Using long, even strokes, smooth it out with a clean putty knife. Holding the putty knife at an angle, continue this process until the putty is neat in appearance. The putty should cover all of the glazier's points and be set at an angle to the glass.

Finishing

Use a single-edge razor blade to clean any excess putty on the window pane or in the corners of the frame. If you are going to paint the newly puttied area, let the putty cure for at least 48 hours. If you do not allow sufficient time for curing, the putty will not hold the paint.

Replacing Glass in Doors

Although window glass is most often held in place with putty, the glass on many doors is held in place with wood strips. These wood strips can be easily removed, the new glass inserted, and the strips replaced. There is no need to use putty.

Using a putty knife, screwdriver or some instrument for prying, first pry a strip of wood from the long side of the pane. The remaining three strips of wood will come out easily. Remove the small nails with a pair of pliers, insert the new glass, replace the wood strips, and nail in position.

FRAMING AND HANGING A DOOR

Framing a Door

The first step in framing and hanging a door is to decide where the door is to be located when you are installing studs, plates and shoes for a new wall. However, the same advice applies when you are cutting a door through an existing stud wall.

The "shoe" is the 2x3 or 2x4 nailed to the floor as a base for the studs. The "studs" are 2x4's placed in a vertical position that support the wall. The 2x4 which rests across the studs is the "plate."

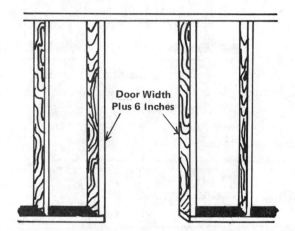

A single stud is added to each side of the door.

After measuring the height of the door you will be installing, cut 2x4's to this height plus one inch. These studs should be installed at the edge of the shoe, on both sides of the door opening.

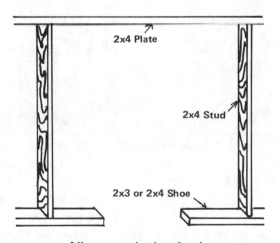

Allow space in shoe for door.

The average door opening is 2 feet eight inches wide, but cut the opening to fit the door you plan to use. Be sure to measure and cut carefully.

Next, cut and insert studs on each side of the door area. The distance between the studs should be the width of the door plus six inches, this allows for the width of the door facing.

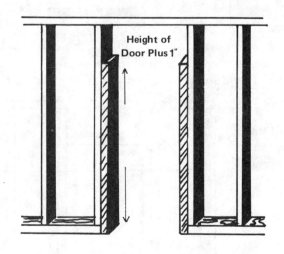

2x4 studs are added to each side of the door.

Cut 2x4's to the width of the original door opening (door width plus six inches) and place them above the door, as a header. Nail them together securely.

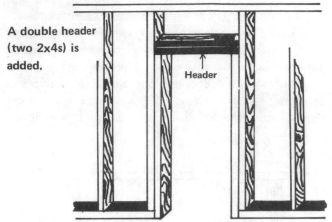

A double header (two 2x4s) is added.

Header

After measuring the distance from the top of this header plate to the ceiling plate, cut "cripple studs" to this length and insert them in the space above the door header. Toenail these studs to the header and plate.

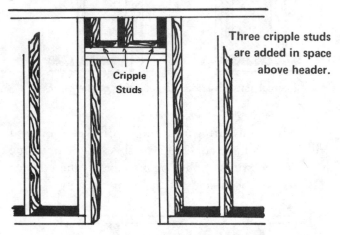

Cripple Studs

Three cripple studs are added in space above header.

Now you are ready to install the door jamb in the door space. You will most likely have purchased the door jamb ready-made for installation.

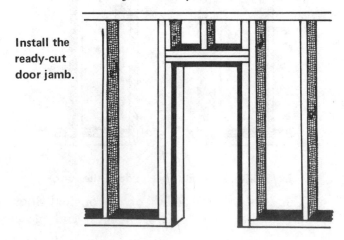

Install the ready-cut door jamb.

The casing on an outside door frame will be nailed either directly to the studs or over the sheathing. The thickness of the interior wallboard and the sub-sheathing will determine which method is used. If needed, a filler strip can be inserted to make the door jamb fit the installation.

Door jamb installation detail.

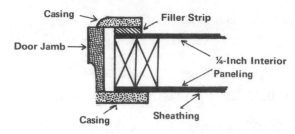

Casing

Filler Strip

Door Jamb

¼-Inch Interior Paneling

Casing

Sheathing

Finish framing is added after the paneling or wall material is installed. Head and side casings complete the opening which is now ready for the door.

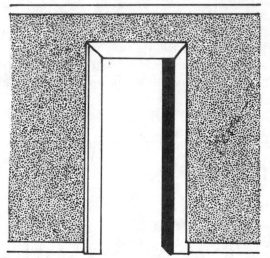

The finish framing is added after walls are in place.

Hanging a Door

When hanging a door you must first decide whether it is to be a right hand or a left hand door. The hand of a door is determined from the outside, that is, the street side for an exterior door; on an interior door it is the side from which the door opens away from you and the hinges are not available. On a right hand door the hinges are added to the right side; on a left hand door the hinges are on the left.

One tool that makes the hanging of doors easier is the butt gauge. Place the flange of this tool against the jamb or the side of the door. Mark the position where you will be attaching the hinge. Set

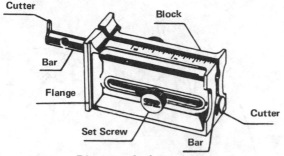

Diagram of a butt gauge.

the butt gauge to the width of the hinge being installed. Allow for a setback of about ¼ inch which will hide the hinge when it is recessed into the door. Applying the butt gauge to the jamb, mark this measurement on the jamb.

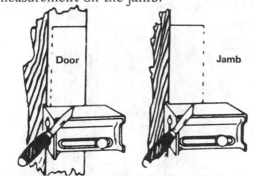

You can use the butt gauge on either doors or jambs.

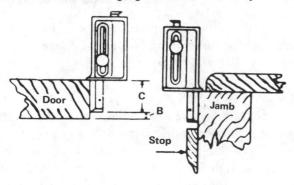

A small extension on the opposite end of the butt gauge allows for measuring the offset of swaged hinges. The swage of a hinge is the space

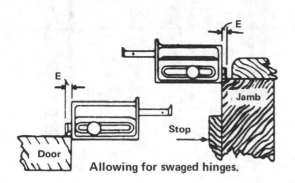

Allowing for swaged hinges.

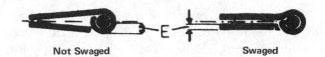

Not Swaged   Swaged

between the leaves which allows for clearance at the butt edge of a door. If a hinge is not swaged, then set the butt gauge for just less than half the thickness of the hinge barrel.

LOOSE PIN BUTT HINGE APPLICATION FOR WOOD DOORS
(doors more than 5 feet high take at least 3 butt hinges, one for every 2½ feet)

DOOR			BUTT HINGE
Size (inches)	Type	Width (inches)	Size (inches)
3/4, 7/8	Cupboard	up to 24	2½
7/8–1 1/8	Screen Door	" " 36	3
1 1/8–1 3/8	Doors	" " 32	3½
1 1/8–1 3/8	"	32 – 37	4
1 9/16, 1 3/4, 1 7/8	"	up to 32	4½
" " "	"	32 – 37	5
" " "	"	37 – 43	5 (ex. hvy.)
" " "	"	43 – 50	6 (")
2, 2¼, 2½	"	up to 43	5 (ex. hvy.)
" " "	"	43 – 50	6 (")

Mortising the Door

After marking the location of the hinge on the door, use a marking gauge to indicate the area of the door which the hinge will not cover. This area is known as the gain or setback.

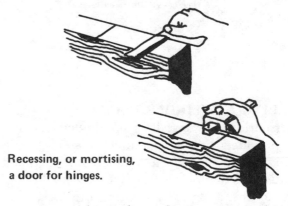

Recessing, or mortising, a door for hinges.

Score this indicated area using a chisel and a rubber or plastic hammer. Now make shallow cuts about ¼ inch apart in the marked area by tapping the chisel lightly with the hammer. Again, using the chisel, remove the surplus wood to the depth required to conceal the hinge.

Using a nail punch or a drill, start the screw holes in the door and door jamb. Now using a good screwdriver, pull the leaf of the hinge tightly into place on both the door and door jamb.

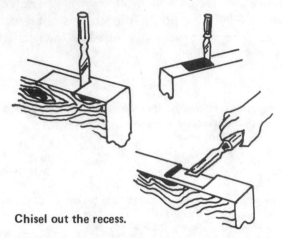

Chisel out the recess.

With the door in its correct position, insert the hinge pins and tap them into place with the rubber or plastic hammer. Swing the door back and forth a few times to check the alignment. You may have to make some adjustments in the hinges or plane or sand the door to make it fit properly.

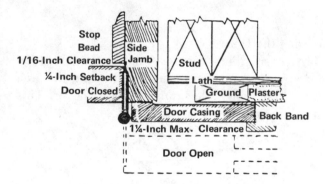

INSTALLING A CYLINDER LOCK

Instructions for installing a cylinder lock are usually provided by the manufacturer. These instructions should include a template for marking the position of the lock on the door before drilling the face of the door for mounting the lock. The hole for any lock is generally drilled about 38 inches from the floor.

You can purchase special adjustable drill bits for this job or use a cylinder-type hole drill which works with your power drill. In either case, the diameter of the hole to be drilled is most often about

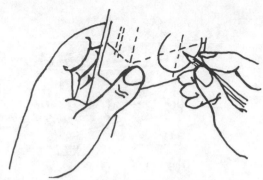

Use a template to position the lock on the door before you drill.

2-1/8 inches. Another hole, about 7/8 inch is drilled into the edge of the door at the spot marked with the template. Use a brace and bit for this job.

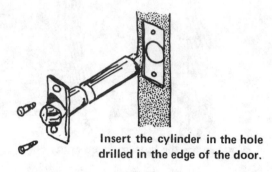

Insert the cylinder in the hole drilled in the edge of the door.

Now follow the manufacturer's instructions carefully for positioning the lock. Be sure you read and think before you cut!

MORE ABOUT HINGES

Most hinges are reversible, that is, they can be used with either end mounted in an upright position. Some hinges, however, are made especially for use on right or left hand doors. For instance, a loose pin hinge must be mounted in such a way

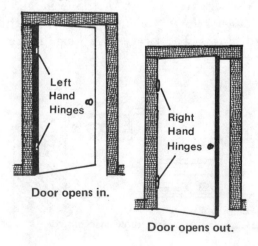

Door opens in.

Door opens out.

that the pin can be removed from the top. Therefore, it is not reversible.

Two doors may both be mounted on the same side, yet one will open in, while the other opens out. The door that opens in takes a left hand hinge; the door that opens out takes a right hand hinge.

In another case, the door that opens in takes a right hand hinge; the door that opens out takes a left hand hinge.

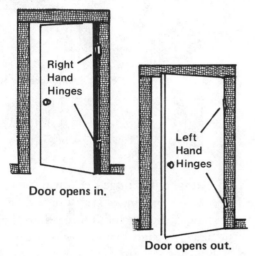

Door opens in.

Door opens out.

The outside of a door is the corridor side of an interior door; the street side of an exterior door. If it opens from you and to the right, it uses a right hand hinge. If it opens from you and to the left, it uses a left hand hinge.

Some Types of Hinges

Common Butt Hinges. Both the rigid and loose pin types are frequently used for mounting ordinary doors. The rigid butt hinge has a stationary pin and can be used for either right or left hand doors. The loose pin type has an easily removable pin, but must be selected carefully for either right or left hand mount. It does have an advantage, however, in that the door mounted with this type of hinge can be easily removed without actually removing the hinge.

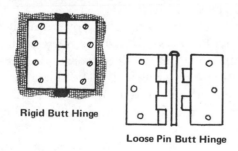

Rigid Butt Hinge

Loose Pin Butt Hinge

Loose Joint Butt Hinge. If the removal of a door is required with any frequency, the loose joint butt hinge is suggested, as it is possible to remove the door by simply lifting it high enough to clear the pin on the other section.

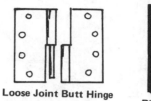

Loose Joint Butt Hinge

Rising Butt Hinge

Rising Butt Hinge. This type of hinge is used specifically where the type of floor covering interferes with the operation of a door. The unique design of this hinge causes the door to rise slightly as it is swung open.

Knuckle Hinge. This loose joint hinge is so called because only the knuckle of the hinge shows when the door is closed. Although principally decorative, it is capable of carrying a considerable weight.

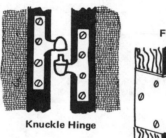

Flush Hinge

Knuckle Hinge

Flush Hinge. Intended for use only on light weight doors (such as cabinet doors), the barrel is the only portion of this hinge that is visible.

Ball Bearing Hinge. This is a permanently lubricated hinge that is best used on heavy exterior doors or on any door which receives an unusual amount of use.

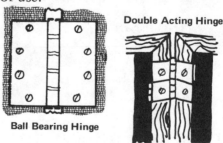

Ball Bearing Hinge

Double Acting Hinge

Double Acting Hinge. As the name implies, this hinge permits a door to be opened in either direction. It is most often used on folding doors.

Pivot Hinge. The advantage to using the pivot hinge is that it requires no door frame for mounting. It can be used for overlay, recessed, or flush doors.

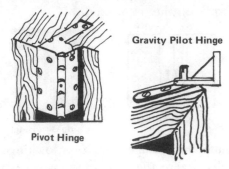

Gravity Pilot Hinge

Pivot Hinge

Gravity Pilot Hinge. This hinge is available with or without a stop that permits the door to be held open.

Offset Blind Hinge. The design of this hinge permits a full opening and swinging action of the door, as is required on screen or storm doors.

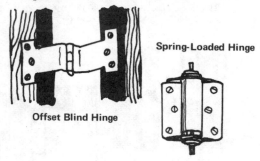

Spring-Loaded Hinge

Offset Blind Hinge

Spring Loaded Hinge. A built-in spring mechanism on this hinge automatically closes the door after it has been opened.

Parliment Hinge. For use where the projecting of the pin well beyond the face of the door is required.

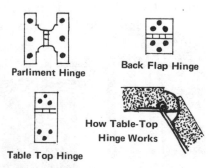

Parliment Hinge

Back Flap Hinge

Table Top Hinge

How Table-Top Hinge Works

Back Flap Hinge. This smaller version of the butt hinge is used principally as a furniture type hinge.

Table Top Hinge. This hinge can be used on any construction where one leaf in a section of wood needs to be dropped, as a table top.

Ornamental Hinges. Ornamental hinges are used primarily on cabinet work and on some types of furniture. The exposed portion of a rustic semi-concealed hinge has a very neat appearance, as do the H and HL hinges. You have chosen this type of hinge for its attractive appearance; be sure to match the other cabinet hardware.

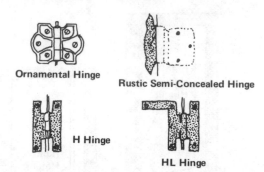

Ornamental Hinge

Rustic Semi-Concealed Hinge

H Hinge

HL Hinge

Strap Hinge, T Hinges, Continuous Hinge. These three types of hinges are designed for use in specific instances. Strap and T hinges are designed for use in heavy, rough installations. The continuous or piano hinge is used most often on lids of chests, cabinets, etc.

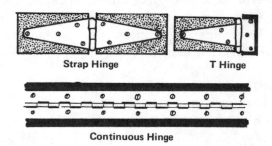

Strap Hinge

T Hinge

Continuous Hinge

INSTALLING HINGES

Most butt type hinges are installed in such a manner that only the knuckle of the hinge is visible. This is done by cutting a recess into both the door and the door facing.

It is very important that you carefully mark the area to be recessed. Lay the hinge against the edge of the door and the door facing. Mark its position carefully and accurately. The thickness of the knuckle should be marked on the side of the door; The width of the flange should be marked on the edge of the door.

Most often you will be recessing both the

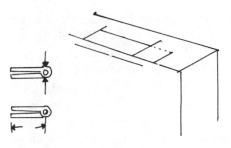

How to recess a hinge.

Usually hinges are recessed equally into both door and case.

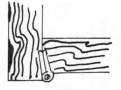

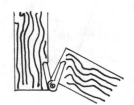

Or, the recess can be cut entirely into either door or door mount.

How you plan to mount the hinge will determine depth of cut.

The door can be installed flush or on the door mount.

Chisel out recess for hinge.

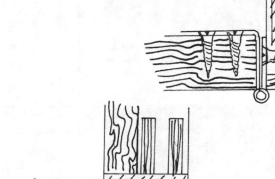

Secure the hinge with screws.

Surface hinges do not require recessing.

door and the door facing. In this case, the recess on both members will be equal in depth. You may, however, cut the recess entirely into the door or entirely into the door facing. It is most important that you make this decision before you begin; how you plan to mount the hinge will dictate the depth of the cuts.

After measuring the marking the areas to be cut, chisel out the area to be recessed with a wood chisel and a hammer. Be sure to use a sharp chisel. Now position the hinge and secure with screws.

You may also use a surface mount hinge. In this case, you need not recess the hinge on the door or door frame.

INSTALLING SLIDING GLASS DOORS

If you have an attractive view from a window, or wish access to a patio from a room, the installation of a sliding-glass door will open that room to the outdoors, provide light and give the room a new personality.

Following the instructions packaged with the door, any do-it-yourself home owner who has done any carpentry will have no problems. For those home owners who have not had the experience, step-by-step instructions follow.

Whether you are installing a wider door to replace an existing one, enlarging a window to become a door, or installing a door in what is now a blank wall, the first step is the same; and it is an important one. The ceiling must be supported, because any outside wall is a load-bearing structure. A shore, usually a 4 x 4, is located on each side of the proposed opening—far enough away to allow working clearance—to support a length of 2 x 10 or 2 x 12 placed against the ceiling. Jacks can be used under the shores, or wedges can be employed.

Mark position of new door on inside of wall. Use wide chisel to score plaster or plasterboard, then cut with saw.

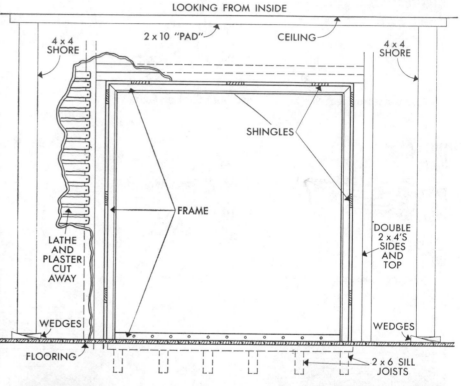

LOOKING FROM INSIDE

Four pieces of precut frame are easily fitted together on a flat surface. Top portion of frame is nailed together.

Yes, a rain storm as soon as the wall opening was cut. Tarp keeps workers dry. Frame is slipped in from outside.

Smooth bead of calking is run completely around outside edge of door and flange that fits over opening.

Removable grilles are an extra-cost item, but well worth the money. They are finished before installing.

Before and after views of outside of house reveal change new door made. Patio is more easily reached.

Before and after, inside views show that new door is focal point of room giving room more personality.

The shores are simply snugged against the ceiling firmly; you do not want to raise the ceiling, merely support it.

You now figure the rough opening for the door; this will be listed in the catalog sizes for the door you select. Plaster and lathe, or plasterboard, is cut and removed a distance equal to the width of the required rough opening. Your installation may require two new studs on each side, if the edges of the rough opening fall between existing studs.

For the height of the opening you may have to go all the way to the ceiling to install the header, which is a double 2 x 10 or 2 x 12 on edge. The studs above the opening are sawed off to allow inserting the header. Note that this inside work can be done without making an opening to the outside, keeping "exposure time" to a minimum. With the rough opening complete on the inside you now make the outside cuts. Siding can be cut with a saber saw. In the job shown it was necessary first to chisel away the stucco.

The assembly of the door frame should be done on a flat surface, such as a driveway or garage floor. The accurately precut pieces assemble easily, and a few nails fasten them together.

You can do the work for the rough opening by yourself, but for fitting the frame into the opening it is best to have a buddy to help. Also be prepared for rain; there is no surer way of causing rain than to cut an opening through a house wall.

The old sill is removed and a longer one fitted in the opening. This usually is a stock 2 x 8. Shingles were used to level the sill, then it was spiked to the floor joists. Two men now can slip the door frame into the opening from the outside. A flange on the frame fits snugly against the outside of the wall. Some last-minute trimming may be necessary to remove the stucco or siding so the flange fits tightly against the sheathing. Caulking is applied liberally on the back and edges of the flange, and the frame is pressed into place. While the buddy holds the frame, the home owner drives shingles around the sides and top to plumb and level it. It then is nailed temporarily in place, the nails being

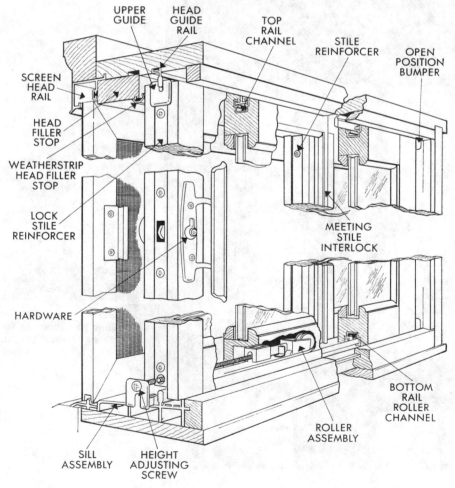

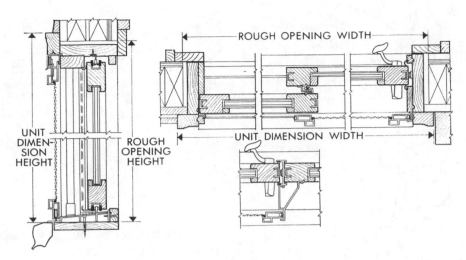

UNIT DIMENSION HEIGHT   ROUGH OPENING HEIGHT

ROUGH OPENING WIDTH

UNIT DIMENSION WIDTH

driven through the frame and shingles into the new studs.

The head filler stop now is removed from the top of the frame and the sliding door (it has the handle) is lifted into the frame, the head guide rail slipping in the inside top rail channel. The door now is lowered until the bottom rail roller channel fits into the roller assembly. If the door doesn't fit square, adjust the height with the adjusting screw. You also may need to shift the frame. When the door slides smoothly, permanently spike the frame into place. The fixed door panel goes in next, in the outside track. Fit the head filler stop in front of it and attach the hardware.

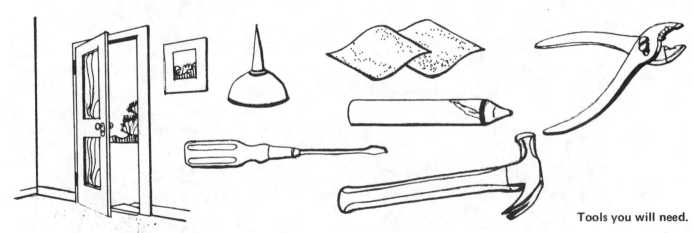

Tools you will need.

FIXING PROBLEM DOORS

The most common problems are doors that squeak, stick, drag or do not close because the door strikes the frame; door knobs that rattle and locks that will not catch. If you took a survey of all the doors in your home, chances are at least one of them would exhibit one or more of these symptoms. With some oil, graphite, a screwdriver and a hammer, sandpaper and a pair of pliers you can fix these problems as well as any experienced carpenter.

Eliminating Noise

More often than not you can stop a door from squeaking by applying a few drops of oil at the top of each hinge. Move the door back and forth to thoroughly work the oil into the hinge. If the squeaking does not stop, raise the pin and add more oil. Repeat this process as often as necessary.

Apply oil to top of hinge.

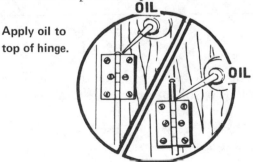

OIL

OIL

Place some newspaper on the floor directly beneath the hinges to catch any oil overflow.

Noisy or squeaking locks can be lubricated with graphite which you can purchase at any hardware store. This also works well for locks that refuse to turn or are tight.

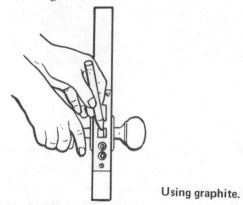

Using graphite.

To stop the rattle in the door knob, loosen the setscrew on the knob. Remove the knob and put a small piece of putty or modeling clay in it. Put the knob back on, pushing it as far as possible. Tighten the setscrew.

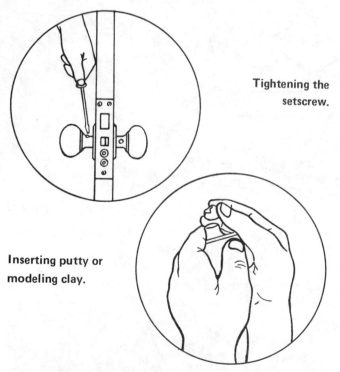

Tightening the setscrew.

Inserting putty or modeling clay.

For a door that is sticking or dragging, first check the condition of the screws in the hinges. If the screws are not holding, replace them, one at a time, with a longer screw. Or, insert a matchstick in the hole and use the old screw.

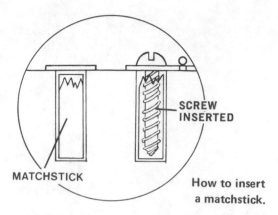

MATCHSTICK

SCREW INSERTED

How to insert a matchstick.

If loose hinges are not causing the dragging, then check the edges of the door for a shiny spot. Sand this spot down, but not too much or the door will not fit as tightly as it should.

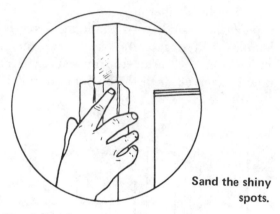

Sand the shiny spots.

If the door frame is badly out of shape you may have to remove the door and plane down the area that drags.

Remove the door and plane down the area that drags.

As part of your normal maintenance program, you should sand down the edges of the doors in your home every time you paint them. This will prevent the paint build-up that eventually causes doors to stick.

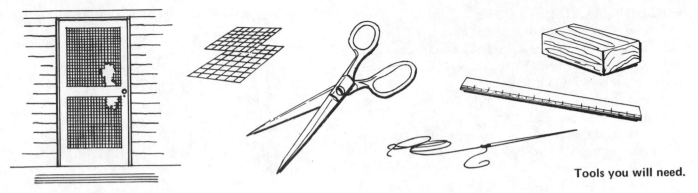

Tools you will need.

REPAIRING SCREENS

If you have been meeting an unusual number of insects in your home lately, check to see if there isn't a hole in the screening of a window or door. If you do locate a hole, it is best to repair it immediately as small holes have the tendency to become larger and repairing is cheaper than replacing an entire screen.

The job is simple enough and requires very little equipment. An additional piece of screening will probably be your only purchase as you will most likely already have a pair of shears, block of wood, ruler or straight edge, and some fine wire or nylon thread.

The first step is to trim the hole to make the edges smooth and square. Next, from your extra screening, cut a rectangular patch about one inch larger than the hole and remove the three outside wires from all four sides.

Place the patch over a block or straight edge and bend the ends of the wires to a right angle from the screening.

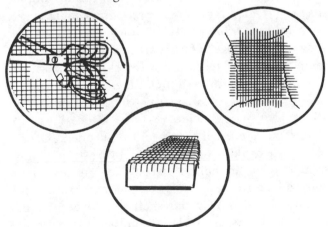

Put the patch over the hole from the outside of the screen. Hold it firmly against the screen so that the bent portions of the wires go through the screen.

Now, from the inside, bend the ends of the wires down and toward the center of the hole. In order to maintain the proper tension while you do this, it might be necessary to have someone hold the patch firmly against the screening.

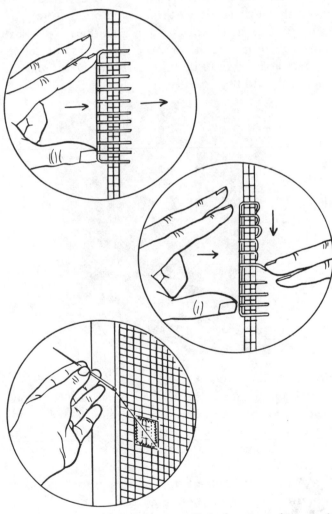

For mending very small holes merely stitch back and forth across the hole with a fine wire or a nylon thread. Be sure to use a matching color so your handiwork will not be quite so visible.

BUILDING A CEDAR CLOSET

The time to build a cedar closet, or line an existing closet with cedar, is before you find moth holes in your clothes. You can buy aromatic red cedar closet lining in lengths up to 8 feet; it is 3/8ths of an inch thick and comes in widths up to four inches. These cedar strips are packaged by their manufacturers so that each bundle contains 40 board feet. A bundle, allowing for waste, will cover 30 square feet.

To cedarize an existing closet, apply the cedar strips starting at the bottom. Each course or row of strips should be applied with the grooved edges facing downwards. Strips can be face-nailed into place or "blind" nailed. In either case, set the nails below the surface of the wood to prevent possible snagging of clothes. The joints need not occur over the wall studs as the tongue and groove pattern of the strips locks them together. To assure absolute moth-repellency, the door and the ceiling of the closet should be lined with the strips and the closet should be virtually air tight.

Free-Standing Cedar Chest

If you need more storage space for your clothes, you should consider building a free-standing cedar closet. Such a closet can be built in the attic, or basement, or wherever space in an out-of-the-way area of the house is available.

The first step—after deciding upon the location and buying the necessary cedar and lumber—is to build the framework for the closet. This framework will of course, depend upon the available space. Height inside should be at least 6½ feet so you can walk in without bumping your head. Make

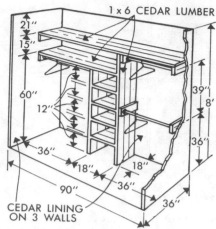

the framework out of 2 x 4 s spaced 16 inches apart. If the closet you are planning to build is more than six feet wide, you should use a doubled 2 x 4 at each corner. After completing the framework, install the floor, the sides, the back, and the ceiling. Use ¾-inch plywood, exterior grade if the installation is below grade. If the closet will be in the attic, ordinary plywood marked A-D (good one side) can be used.

You can make the doors out of plywood, or buy factory-made doors. The latter are recommended as they are less apt to warp. Mount the doors—one or two depending upon the width of your closet—to the 2 x 4s at each side.

The next step is to install the cedar strips. As mentioned before they come in random lengths and they should be applied in a random pattern for most pleasing results. Use four-penny finishing nails or brads and set them with a nail set below the surface of the cedar to avoid possible clothes snagging. Don't try to make the joints come over a stud in the framing. It is not necessary as the tongue-and-groove construction of the strips locks them together. The pole for the clothes consists of a dowel or a length of ¾-inch pipe.

Cut an elliptical opening in a piece of wood about four inches wide to form a recess for the pipe. Two pieces of wood will be needed. The recess in each piece of wood should be deep enough so that when a shelf is placed over the top, there will still be room enough to hang and remove the clothes. Incidentally, the shelf should be of cedar wood which is available at lumber yards. Cedar trim can be used if you have the urge to highlight the outside of the door, or any exposed edges of the closet.

Cedar should be left in its natural state—never

apply varnish, paint, or shellac—they will only seal in the cedar fumes and make the closet ineffective as a moth repeller. When the odor of cedar becomes faint, you can restore it by sanding. Remove the clothes when you do this and clean up by vacuuming before returning the clothes.

Rubber or vinyl weatherstripping applied along all door edges will help keep the cedar fumes in the closet where they will do the most good. The only maintenance a cedar closet requires is an occasional wiping with a slightly damp cloth to remove dust from the cedar so as to allow the fumes to escape more readily. Keep the door tightly closed with a secure latch. Make sure that the clothes you put into the closet have been well aired and are free of moths, since the cedar fumes do not kill the insects.

CEILING CLOSET

Do you live in a small home or apartment where you simply don't have enough storage space? Your solution might be "ceiling" closets. Fitted between the top of a door or window frame and the ceiling, such a closet will hardly be noticeable; most people never look up when entering a room.

You will have to stand on a chair or ladder to reach the closet, but it will be used mostly for "dead" storage: off-season clothes, blankets, and household items that are used only occasionally. These are the same items that now take up closet and drawer space.

The closet is a frame of 1 x 2s, covered with hardboard or plywood. One edge can rest on a door or window frame, the other on a cleat fastened to the adjacent wall. Screw anchors in the ceiling wall will support the edges away from the walls. When the closet is finished, paint it in the same as the walls, and fit molding around it to match the ceiling molding.

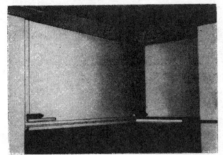

Ceiling closet is handy storage area and makes use of otherwise wasted space.

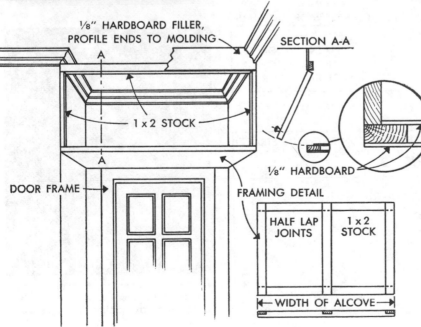

1/8" HARDBOARD FILLER, PROFILE ENDS TO MOLDING

SECTION A-A

1 x 2 STOCK

1/8" HARDBOARD

FRAMING DETAIL

DOOR FRAME

HALF LAP JOINTS | 1 x 2 STOCK

WIDTH OF ALCOVE

In some situations there may be a built-in wardrobe or other piece of furniture to add support.

BUILDING DRAWERS

Drawers are major components of many important furniture projects. Quite often, especially on factory-made units, the construction of the drawers denotes the general quality of the piece. You can look for dovetails, let-in bottoms and backs, quality hardwoods, etc. when you are examining expensive furniture.

As a home craftsman, however, you may be involved in constructing drawers that will hold anything from postage stamps to heavy shop tools, so you do not have to follow any set procedure. Rather, you base your design on what a drawer must do, its compatibility with the case in which it is enclosed and the tool you have to work with.

You can do a fine job, even with hand tools. Quite often the simple design saves time and money and results in respectable craftsmanship. (2)

Drawer Designs

One drawer design that can be used for many types of projects is shown. It can be made on a table saw, even if you lack a dado blade. The rabbets, dadoes and grooves can be done by making repeated passes with a regular saw blade. (1; 3)

Note the design is nothing more than a shallow butt-jointed box. When done with glue and nails (or screws) this drawer can take plenty of abuse; you can "pretty it up" with a false front. (3)

Joints. There are two major strain points in a

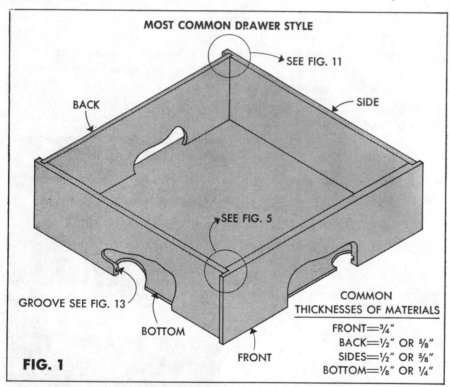

MOST COMMON DRAWER STYLE

SEE FIG. 11

BACK

SIDE

SEE FIG. 5

GROOVE SEE FIG. 13

BOTTOM

FRONT

COMMON THICKNESSES OF MATERIALS

FRONT = ¾"
BACK = ½" OR ⅝"
SIDES = ½" OR ⅝"
BOTTOM = ⅛" OR ¼"

FIG. 1

2. Box construction is simple to do, and functional. It also can be attractive with false front of appropriate material.

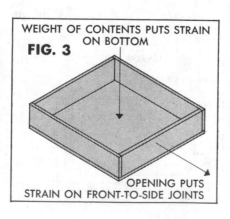

WEIGHT OF CONTENTS PUTS STRAIN ON BOTTOM

FIG. 3

OPENING PUTS STRAIN ON FRONT-TO-SIDE JOINTS

4. Dovetail is finest joint for drawer construction. Is used between front and sides, and for quality work, at back.

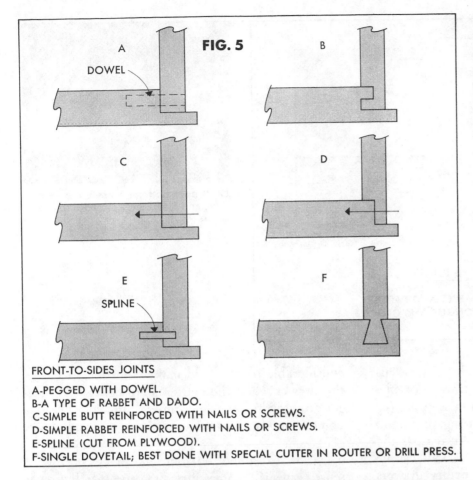

FIG. 5

DOWEL

SPLINE

FRONT-TO-SIDES JOINTS

A-PEGGED WITH DOWEL.
B-A TYPE OF RABBET AND DADO.
C-SIMPLE BUTT REINFORCED WITH NAILS OR SCREWS.
D-SIMPLE RABBET REINFORCED WITH NAILS OR SCREWS.
E-SPLINE (CUT FROM PLYWOOD).
F-SINGLE DOVETAIL; BEST DONE WITH SPECIAL CUTTER IN ROUTER OR DRILL PRESS.

8. Rabbet and dado is good joint for front-to-sides on drawer. It provides strength, is easily made.

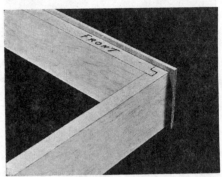

9. With false front added, rabbet-dado does a good job, does not detract from appearance. Attach pull through fronts.

6. Pegged joint is good substitute for dovetail. It resists pull when you open drawer, holds even if the glue fails.

7. Finger-lap (box) joint is excellent for drawers. Fingers provide maximum glue surface. Adding dowel increases strength.

10. Rabbet-dado also can be used for back-to-sides joints. On front or back, make dado half thickness of stock.

drawer: when you open it you stress the front-to-sides joint, while the contents stress the bottom joints. That's the reason the dovetail is so good for joining the front to the sides. It resists the pull when you open the drawer, and it has a locking feature that persists even if the glue fails. The dovetail can be shaped by hand, but it's a tedious job. A dovetail jig that can be used with a portable router, drill press or electric drill will permit you to produce dovetails on an "assembly-line."

There are other front to sides joints that will also resist the pull from the front. Even the simple C and D joints, with nails or screws driven into the sides, provides resistance. (5)

An excellent joint, one that substitutes for a dovetail, is the "pegged" joint which can be made easily with a table or radial-arm saw and a portable drill. You make the drawer parts first, then clamp them together while you drill the holes for the pegs. Make the pegs extra-length, so you can cut

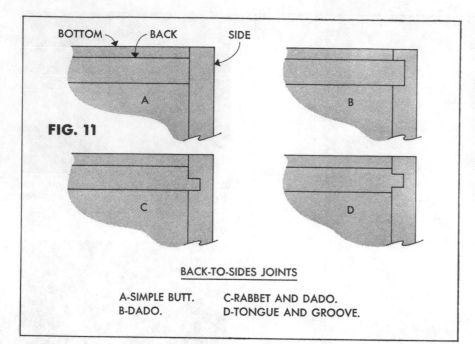

BOTTOM — BACK — SIDE

FIG. 11

A

B

C

D

BACK-TO-SIDES JOINTS

A-SIMPLE BUTT.   C-RABBET AND DADO.
B-DADO.   D-TONGUE AND GROOVE.

12. Drawer bottoms usually are let into sides and front. Stock for bottom generally is ¼ in., but ⅛ in. can be used.

them off and sand flush after the glue dries. This pegged joint can be done on lipped drawers or on a butt-jointed box to which you add a false front. (6)

Another joint that is very strong, if for no other reason than maximum glue surfaces, is the finger-lap (also called a "box joint"). This can be used on box-type construction for utility drawers or when you will add a false front. Drilling a hole through the fingers after they are joined and inserting a dowel makes this a "lock joint." (7)

A very common joint, and a good one, is no more than a rabbet in the drawer front and a dado in each drawer side. Always cut the dado about half the thickness of the stock and shape the rabbet to match. This can be done on a box drawer or on a lipped drawer or where you plan on adding a false front. (8; 9)

This same joint can be used to install the drawer back. It's about like taking the drawer front and flipping the assembly end-for-end. Other back-to-sides joints are shown. The drawer back is most important for holding together other drawer components. It does not take too much stress. (10; 11)

Generally, drawer bottoms are let into the drawer front and the sides. The drawer back is cut narrower so it sets on the drawer bottom. (12)

In other bottom joints, B is the simple butt joint; one problem here is that the drawer contents press on the entire bottom, forcing it down on the shelf on which the drawer rides. This can create

considerable friction and make it difficult to open the drawer when the contents are heavy. You can get around this by using runners. On wider drawers you can add runners between the two outside ones. (13)

The extended bottom, D, makes a lot of sense, especially on utility drawers. Installation is just a matter of cutting dadoes in the case sides. Avoid a tight fit, the drawer bottom must slide easily in the grooves.

Installation. Various methods of drawer installation are shown. Look at the frame as a horizontal divider between the case sides. This can be open, as shown, or a solid shelf. When the frame is open, thin plywood panels can be inserted in grooves cut in the frame edges. Such construction encloses individual drawers so they are more nearly dustproof. (14)

The guide is a strip of hardwood rabbeted at each end to fit between frame members. The slide attaches to the drawer bottom. These parts are not "strength" members. They serve merely to guide the drawer in and out of the enclosure. When they are used, the overall width of the drawer can be considerably less than the inside dimensions between the case sides. This cuts down quite a bit on friction and makes the drawer easier to use. (15; 16)

Dadoes cut in the drawer sides can ride on

cleats firmly attached to the case. You can, of course, reverse this by putting the dadoes in the case. Either way, remember that the weight of the drawer is on the cleat and this should be good hardwood, solidly attached. Here too, don't go for a precise fit: the drawer must slide easily. (17)

An example of the extended drawer bottom is shown. These are small-parts shop drawers that have seen many years of service. Be sure to allow clearance between the drawer sides and the case and also in the groove. (18)

A common type of ready-made installation hardware is all-metal slides with nylon rollers. Attachment is just a matter of location and driving some screws. Such slides have advantages: they are strong, easy to install and do cut down on drawer details you have to worry about. Also, you can install a series of drawers without having to worry about horizontal dividers between them. Disadvantage is that they can be expensive, costing anywhere from about three to ten dollars, depending on type and size. There are times when such hardware can do a job tough to duplicate otherwise. For example, some are made so you can pull the drawer out completely while it maintains its horizontal position. Some are made so even a drawer full of cast iron can be opened easily because the slides ride on rollers or bearings. Most hardware stores and lumberyards have a supply of this hardware on display, so you can check out samples. (19)

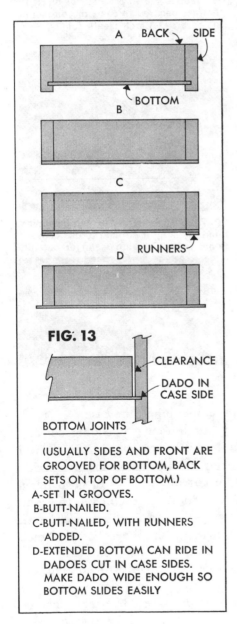

FIG. 13

BOTTOM JOINTS

(USUALLY SIDES AND FRONT ARE GROOVED FOR BOTTOM, BACK SETS ON TOP OF BOTTOM.)
A-SET IN GROOVES.
B-BUTT-NAILED.
C-BUTT-NAILED, WITH RUNNERS ADDED.
D-EXTENDED BOTTOM CAN RIDE IN DADOES CUT IN CASE SIDES. MAKE DADO WIDE ENOUGH SO BOTTOM SLIDES EASILY

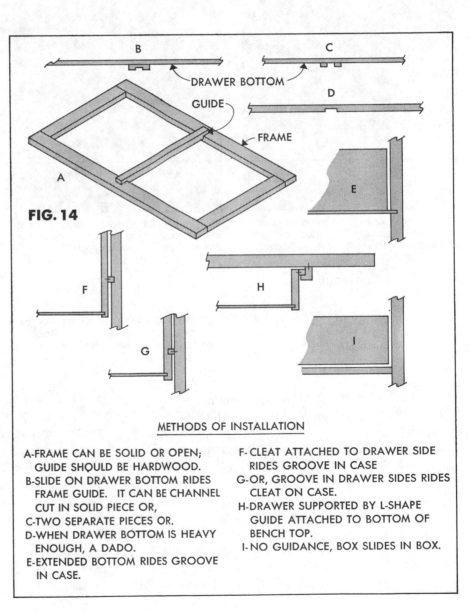

FIG. 14

METHODS OF INSTALLATION

A-FRAME CAN BE SOLID OR OPEN; GUIDE SHOULD BE HARDWOOD.
B-SLIDE ON DRAWER BOTTOM RIDES FRAME GUIDE. IT CAN BE CHANNEL CUT IN SOLID PIECE OR,
C-TWO SEPARATE PIECES OR.
D-WHEN DRAWER BOTTOM IS HEAVY ENOUGH, A DADO.
E-EXTENDED BOTTOM RIDES GROOVE IN CASE.

F-CLEAT ATTACHED TO DRAWER SIDE RIDES GROOVE IN CASE
G-OR, GROOVE IN DRAWER SIDES RIDES CLEAT ON CASE.
H-DRAWER SUPPORTED BY L-SHAPE GUIDE ATTACHED TO BOTTOM OF BENCH TOP.
I-NO GUIDANCE, BOX SLIDES IN BOX.

15. Drawer guide is strip of hardwood set between back and front pieces of frame. Use a nail or screw at each end.

16. Slide attaches to drawer bottom. Can be two separate pieces, as shown, or one piece with groove cut into it.

17. Dadoes in drawer sides ride on cleats that are secured to case, or you can do the reverse. Attach cleats solidly.

18. Extended drawer bottoms ride in dadoes cut into case sides. This is a functional method for installing drawers.

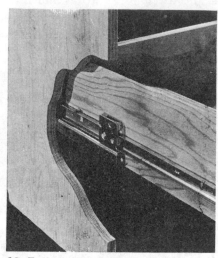

19. Typical sliding-drawer hardware has mating parts that attach to case and drawer. Unit shown supports 75 lbs.

20. These drawers are hidden by sliding doors, making it difficult to use conventional pulls. Solution is finger cut-out.

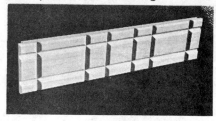

21. Attractive faceting for front is made on table or radial-arm saw. Router or router bits in a drill press can be used.

Many craftsmen are too precise when they size a drawer, figuring it should be a snug fit in its enclosure. This is a bad way to go, and can be frustrating everytime you try to open or close the drawer. A drawer must slide easily, therefore there must be clearance between it and the case. To provide this clearance at the top, the drawer sides may be lower than the front. When you want maximum height on the sides, chamfer or round off the top edges. When the drawer front is flush with the front of the case frame, allow a clearance of at least 1/16 inch between the top and sides of the drawer front and the opening in the case.

Drawers that are hidden by sliding conventional drawer pulls, without making the drawer shorter back-to-front to allow for the projection of the hardware, or cutting notches or grooves on the back sides of the doors. In such cases the solution is to provide finger room in the drawer front. This can be as shown, or simply a 1½- to 2-inch diameter hole bored in the drawer front. (20)

Drawer fronts can be plain or decorated, depending on how the treatment blends with the project as a whole. A faceted effect can be achieved by making intersecting V-cuts on a table or radial-arm saw, or by using a portable router, or router bits in a drill press. (21)

The most important thing is not to have any preconceived notion that a drawer must be built just one way. Design it for appearance and construction in relation to the job it must do. A heavy box on casters, that's a "drawer" under a workbench, is a good design if it's functional. The same goes for such a drawer under a bed.

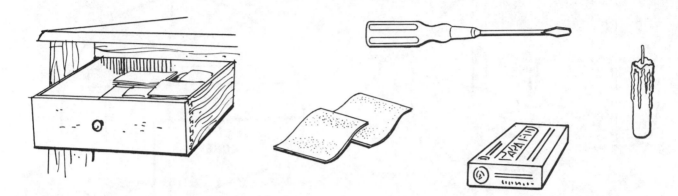

REPAIRING DRAWERS

Drawers that stick, come apart or have handles and knobs that are loose, broken or non-existent are more of a hindrance than a help. However, with the application of a good screwdriver, some sandpaper, and a little candle wax, soap or paraffin, you can solve all of these annoying problems.

Fixing Handles and Knobs

A loose handle or knob is the easiest of all problems to fix. Just tighten the offending fixture from the back with a screwdriver.

If a handle or knob is missing, you can walk into any hardware store and find a large selection from which to choose a new one. For the more economically-minded, painted thread spools make attractive knobs. Or, if you have a length of decorative molding left over from a project, you can cut it into three or four inch lengths, paint or otherwise finish the segments, and glue them to the drawer face as pulls.

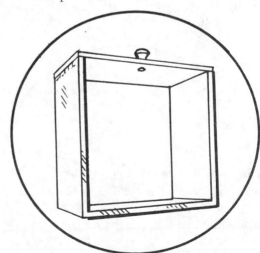

Look for the telltale shiny spots.

Fixing a Sticking Drawer

First remove the drawer and inspect it for a shiny spot on the top and bottom edges or somewhere along the sides. This telltale shiny spot is caused by additional friction and will indicate

SCREW

KNOB

exactly where the problem area is.

Sand down the shiny areas. Replace the drawer and check to see if it moves more easily. Repeat the sanding and checking process until the drawer no longer sticks.

Sand down the shiny spots.

Next, rub the drawer and frame, where they come in contact with one another, with candle wax, paraffin or household soap. The application of these substances reduces friction and makes the drawers glide more easily. This is especially important if the drawer is usually filled with heavy items.

To help drawers glide, apply lubricant.

If the glides are badly worn the drawer may not close completely. The drawer front strikes the frame. The answer here is to lift the drawer. Remove it and insert two or three large smooth-headed thumbtacks along the front of each glide. This should raise the drawer sufficiently to alleviate the problem.

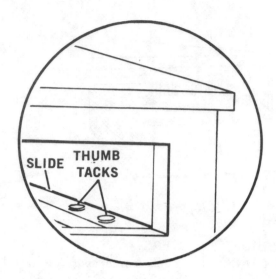

If your drawers stick, but only in damp weather, then the answer is to coat the unfinished wood with a penetrating sealer or wax. Sealing the wood will prevent it from absorbing moisture and swelling, causing the drawer to stick.

Apply sealer or wax to prevent swelling.

MEETING YOUR SHELVING NEEDS

No matter how well planned your home or apartment is, there inevitably comes a time when extra storage space is needed. Additional shelving is one answer to this problem and it can be added to your home easily, quickly and inexpensively.

Non-Adjustable Shelving

Solid boards of almost any size can be used to create basic non-adjustable shelving for normal storage and shelving requirements. The disadvantage is that some items may be too tall for the space between the shelves, while other items may be too short, thus wasting space. This problem can be partially alleviated by varying the heights between shelves. With a little planning you can make shelving that allows for the differences in heights of the items to be stored and is also attractive to the eye. Normally, however, non-adjustable shelving is used in closets, attics, basements, work rooms, and other areas were appearance is not a prime consideration.

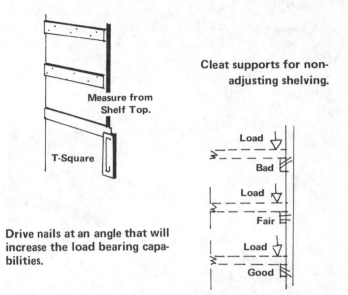

Measure from Shelf Top.

T-Square

Cleat supports for non-adjusting shelving.

Load
Bad
Load
Fair
Load
Good

Drive nails at an angle that will increase the load bearing capabilities.

Simple non-adjustable shelving.

One type of non-adjustable shelving uses cleats, or small pieces of wood, to support the shelves. Although this type of shelving allows for shelves to be as long or wide as necessary, shelves longer than 3 feet should have additional support. If you will require the shelving to carry exceptionally heavy loads, supports every 2½ feet are suggested. Take the time and care to make sure the cleats are level before nailing to the side boards.

The way in which you drive the nails into the cleats will affect the load-bearing abilities of the shelving. Nails driven at an upward angle provide very poor support and will probably pull out if subject to any degree of weight. Nails driven at a right angle to the cleat offer more support. Best

are nails driven at a downward angle. Nails driven in this manner greatly increase the ability of the shelving to withstand weight.

If you require an extra degree of structural strength, make the cleats wider and nail them firmly into position.

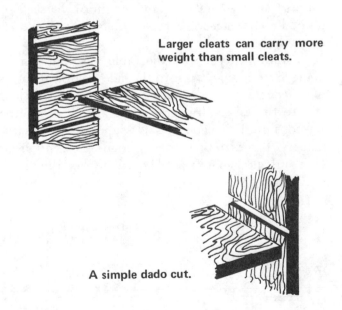

Larger cleats can carry more weight than small cleats.

A simple dado cut.

Adjustable Wood Shelving

Adjustable wood shelving can be made by making simple dado cuts in the side supports. You can make any number of dado cuts along the sides and therefore allow for as many adjustments as you may require. Make the dado cuts relatively deep.

Dado cuts can also be used for non-adjustable shelving; these can be made fairly shallow. If you do not want the dado cut to be visible from the front of the shelving, a concealed dado cut is recommended. This makes for a neater, cleaner looking joint.

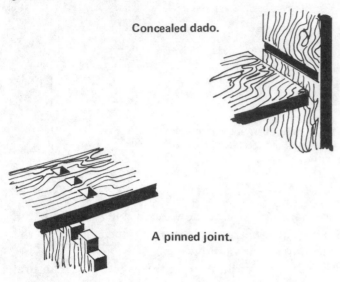

Concealed dado.

A pinned joint.

If your space requirements necessitate a long length of shelving, you should provide additional support somewhere along the length of the shelf. A pinned joint can solve this problem; it is also removable.

Another type of adjustable shelving can be made by making cuts into the side boards at angles of 90 degrees and 45 degrees. Then cut the shelf end to the same 45 degree angle and fit it into the sawed slot. This type of shelf support is not satisfactory for extremely heavy loads. A continuous series of cuts in the side boards makes this shelving adjustable.

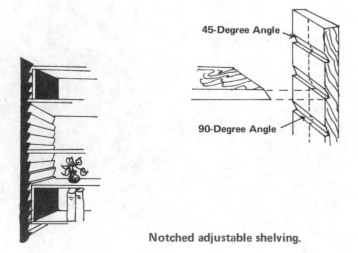

45-Degree Angle

90-Degree Angle

Notched adjustable shelving.

A third method of making adjustable shelving is to drill 1¾-inch holes in a 1-inch by 4-inch board at intervals of 1¾ inches. The board is then split down the middle and mounted on the side boards. Each 1 x 4 board makes two shelf supports that will more than adequately support one side of the shelf. When mounting the supports, be sure the two sides are even. For a neat appearance, carefully sand and finish the brackets. You must also round and sand the shelf edges so they will fit in the supports.

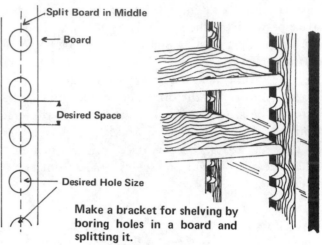

Split Board in Middle

Board

Desired Space

Desired Hole Size

Make a bracket for shelving by boring holes in a board and splitting it.

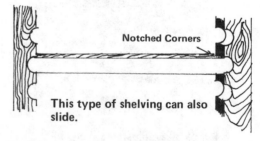

Notched Corners

This type of shelving can also slide.

Adjustable Metal and Wood Brackets

The most popular method of supporting adjustable shelves is with metal brackets. Such brackets are inexpensive and readily available.

For light shelving requirements you can purchase brackets that fit into small holes drilled into the side boards. Holes can be drilled at any interval, the brackets inserted, and shelves placed on the brackets. Shelving supported in this way is easily adjustable. Simple dowel pins can be used in place of the metal brackets. They are not suitable for heavy loads as they usually wear or give away under extended use.

There is a special flush-type of shelf bracket that is very inexpensive and easy to use. This type of shelving provides sufficient strength for average storage purposes. The only mounting requirement

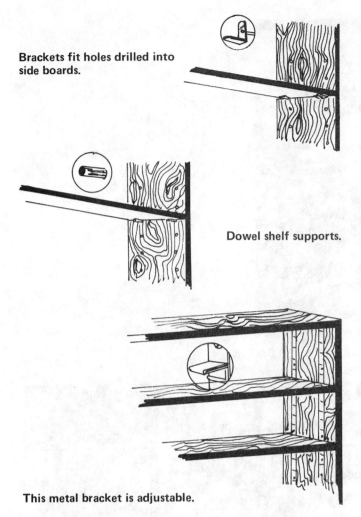

Brackets fit holes drilled into side boards.

Dowel shelf supports.

This metal bracket is adjustable.

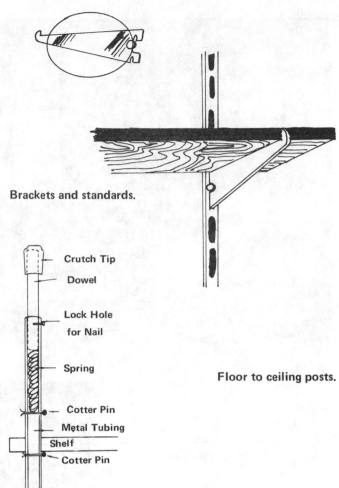

Brackets and standards.

Crutch Tip

Dowel

Lock Hole for Nail

Spring

Cotter Pin

Metal Tubing

Shelf

Cotter Pin

Floor to ceiling posts.

for this type of bracket is a dado cut for each bracket in the supporting end of the shelf.

Another type of metal shelf bracket is made to fit into holes drilled into a supporting wall. The bracket then drops into place.

The shelf bracket and standard has become increasingly popular. This type of shelving is now available in various lengths, widths and colors. It is easily installed and just as easily removed if no longer needed in a particular spot.

Shelf bracket fits into drilled holes.

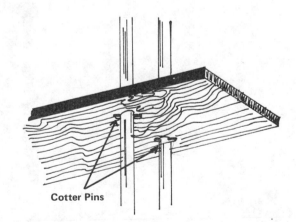

Cotter Pins

Load carrying capabilities are minimal.

Floor-to-ceiling posts are temporary shelf holders. A spring holds the pole in position between the floor and the ceiling. Special keys, such as a cotter pin, then provide the shelf support. This shelving is not designed to support any but light loads.

WALLS, FLOORS AND CEILINGS

WALLS, FLOORS AND CEILINGS

GYPSUM WALLBOARD ■ TAPING WALLBOARD ■ "BRICK" WALLS

DRYWALL TEXTURING ■ PATCHING HOLES ■ WALLPAPERING ■ FLOOR COVERINGS

CHOOSING CARPET ■ STICK-DOWN CARPETING ■ CARPET INSERTS

LAYING A TILE FLOOR ■ SELF-STICKING WOOD TILES ■ WOOD FLOOR FINISHING

LAYING ROLL GOODS ■ TILE REPAIRS ■ "PAINT" A FLOOR OR COUNTER TOP

PANELING ■ CEILING BEAMS ■ SUSPENDED CEILING ■ KEEP YOUR BASEMENT DRY

USING GYPSUM WALLBOARD

A little thought and planning before you start your project can result in a better appearing job and a savings in materials and time. Make a sketch of the areas to be surfaced with gypsum wallboard and lay out the board panels. Install the boards across (perpendicular to) the joists or studs. Use as long a board as can be handled to eliminate or reduce end joints. For example, in a 12-foot by 13-foot room where the ceiling joists run parallel to the 13 foot dimension, it is desirable to have the boards be 12 feet long. If they are 8 feet long, an end joint would be necessary in each course. Where end joints cannot be avoided, they should be staggered.

It is usually better to apply the board on the ceiling first, then the sidewalls.

It is often easier to use the adhesive/nail-on method of application. This method results in fewer nails to drive and conceal and makes a higher quality installation.

Using the sketch, determine the lengths and number of boards required. Estimate the quantity of nails. About 5¼ pounds of 1 5/8-inch coated type drywall nails are needed per 1000 square feet of 3/8-inch or ½-inch wallboard. The same number of pounds is required for 1 7/8-inch coated drywall nails for 5/8-inch wallboard.

After the wallboard is installed, the flat joints and inside corners are to be reinforced with a paper tape and joint compounds. The outside corners are to be reinforced with a drywall metal corner bead and joint compound.

In the adhesive nail-on method, adhesive is applied to the joists and studs before each piece of wallboard is positioned and nailed. The adhesive is applied to the framing member from a caulking gun in about a 3/8-inch diameter bead. For each 1,000 square feet of wallboard use eight quart size tubes of adhesive.

ESTIMATING MATERIALS		
NAILS		
Wallboard Thickness	Nail Type	Pounds per 1000 Sq. Ft. of Gypsum Wallboard (approx.)
3/8-inch or ½-inch	1 5/8-inch coated type drywall nail	5¼ pounds
5/8-inch	1 7/8-inch coated type drywall nail	5¼ pounds

JOINT COMPOUND TAPE		
Gypsum Wallboard (square feet)	Joint Compound (gallons)	Wallboard Tape
100-200	1	2 (60') rolls
300-400	2	3 (60') rolls
500-700	3	1 (250') roll
700-800	4	1 (250') roll
900-1000	5	1 (60') roll 1 (250') roll 2 (60') rolls or 1 (500') roll

Tools You Will Need

The basic tools you need are:

1. Wallboard cutting knife and heavy duty knife blade.
2. Wallboard hammer or regular crown head carpenters claw hammer.
3. 4 foot T-square or steel straight edge.
4. Steel tape measure.
5. Utility saw or keyhole saw.
6. Joint finishing knives—4-inch and 10-inch blades.
7. Plastic pan for joint compound.
8. Sandpaper (medium texture) for joint finishing.
9. Caulking gun.

Cutting the Wallboard

Use a T-square and wallboard knife for scoring. With the knife at right angles to the board, score completely through the face paper. Then apply firm even pressure to snap the board. Fold back the partially separated portion of the board and use the knife again to cut the back paper. Rough edges should be smoothed. Panels can be cut with a saw if desired.

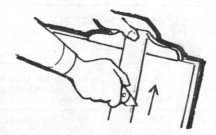

It will be necessary to cut holes in the wallboard for electrical outlets, light receptacles, etc. The distance of the opening from the end and edge of the board should be carefully measured and marked on the face of the wallboard. The opening should then be outlined in pencil and cut out with a keyhole saw. The cut-out must be accurate or the cover plate will not conceal the hole.

Ceiling Installation

It is more difficult to install the ceiling boards because of the overhead positioning. It is desirable to have T-braces to hold the board in place while it is being nailed. A satisfactory T-brace consists of a 2 foot piece of 1 x 4 nailed onto the end of a 2 x 4. The length should be about an inch longer than the floor to ceiling height. The nails should be 7 inches apart. When the adhesive nail-on method is used, the edges should be nailed, but only 1 nail per joist in the field of the board. All edges should be supported on framing. The nails should be driven to bring the board tight to the framing, then another blow struck to dimple the nail, being careful not to break the face paper.

T-braces hold board in position.

Wall Application

In horizontal application on sidewalls, install the top board first. Push the board up firmly against the ceiling and nail, placing nails 7 inches apart. One exception, however, is to keep all nails back 7 inches from interior ceiling angles. Nails in the interior angles are quite apt to pop. If the adhesive nail-on method is used, all of the field nailing can be eliminated. The nailing is around the edges of the board. If the board is bowed out in the center, it may be advisable to secure with a temporary nail until the adhesive sets.

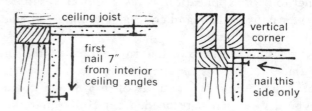

Wallboard application.

A vertical application places the long edges of the wallboard parallel to the framing members. This is more desirable if the ceiling height of your wall is greater than 8 feet 2 inches or the wall is 4 feet wide or less. Nailing recommendations are the same as for horizontal application.

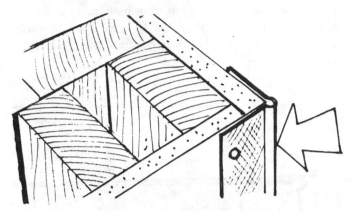

Metal cornerbead protects edges from damage.

To protect corners from edge damage, install metal cornerbead after you have installed the wallboard. Nail the metal cornerbead every 5 inches.

Joint Finishing

A pre-mixed joint compound is the easiest to use to finish joints, corners and nailheads. A minimum of three coats is recommended for all taped joints. This includes an embedding coat to bond the tape and two finishing coats over the tape. Each coat should dry thoroughly, usually 24 hours, so that the surface can be easily sanded. When sanding, wrap your sandpaper around a wood sanding block so you sand the surface evenly. Do not over-sand or sand the paper surface. This may outline the joint or nail head through the paint.

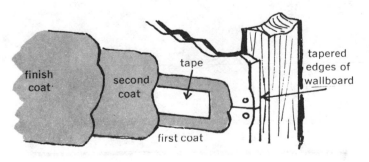

Joints are concealed by applying joint compound, tape and two more coats of compound.

Take your 4 inch joint finishing knife and apply the joint compound fully and evenly into the slight recess created by the adjoining tapered edges of the board.

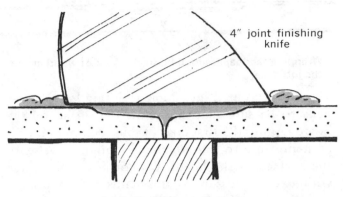

Applying joint compound.

Next, take your wallboard tape, center it over the joint and press the tape firmly, into the bedding compound with your wallboard knife held at a 45 degree angle. The pressure should squeeze some compound from under the tape, but enough must be left for a good bond.

Wallboard tape is pressed firmly into the bedding compound.

Finishing

When thoroughly dry, at least 24 hours, apply a fill coat extending a few inches beyond the edge of the tape and feather the edges of the compound. When the first finishing coat is thoroughly dry, use your 10-inch joint finishing knife and apply a second coat and feather the edges about 1½ inches beyond the first coat. When this coat is dry, sand lightly to a smooth even surface. Wipe off the dust in preparation for the final decoration. Total width should be 12 to 14 inches.

compound width should be 12 to 14 inches

sanding block

tape

Wrapping sandpaper around a small block of wood makes the job easier.

Draw your 4-inch joint finishing knife across nails to be sure they are below the surface of the board. Apply the first coat of joint compound with even pressure to smooth the compound level with the surface of the board. Do not bow knife blade with excess pressure as this tends to scoop compound from dimpled area. When dry, apply the second coat, let dry, sand lightly and apply the third coat. Sand lightly before applying your decoration. An additional coat may be needed depending on temperature and humidity.

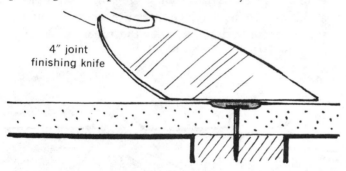

4″ joint finishing knife

Finishing nail heads.

You use basically the same steps with end or butt joints as you do with tapered edges. The end joints are not tapered so care must be taken not to build up the compound in the center of the joint. This encourages ridging and shadowed areas. Feather the compound well out on each side of the joint. Final application of joint compound should be 14 to 18 inches wide.

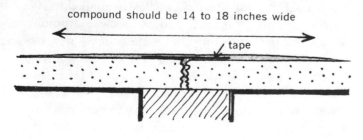

compound should be 14 to 18 inches wide

tape

End joint finishing.

Be sure the metal cornerbead is attached firmly. Take your 4-inch finishing knife and spread the joint compound 3 to 4 inches wide from the nose of the bead, covering the metal edges. When completely dry, sand lightly and apply second coat, feathering edges 2 inches to 3 inches beyond the first coat. A third coat may be needed depending on your coverage. Feather the edges of each coat 2 inches or 3 inches beyond the preceding coat.

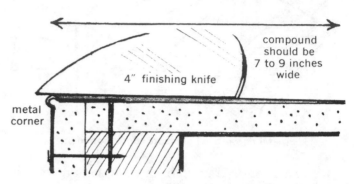

compound should be 7 to 9 inches wide

4″ finishing knife

metal corner

Metal cornerbead is also finished with compound.

Cut your tape the length of the inside corner angle you are going to finish. Apply the joint compound with your 4-inch knife evenly about 1½ inches on each side of the angle. Use sufficient compound to embed the tape. Fold the tape along the center crease and firmly press it into the corner. Use enough pressure to squeeze some compound under the edges. Feather the compound 2 inches from the edge of the tape. When the first coat is dry, apply a second coat. Feather the edge of the compound 1½ inches beyond the first coat. Apply a third coat if necessary. Let dry and sand to a smooth surface. Use as little compound as possible at the apex of the angle to prevent hairline cracking.

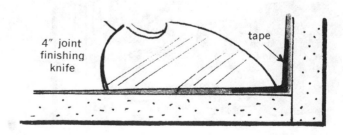

4″ joint finishing knife

tape

Inside corners are taped and finished with compound.

MORE ON TAPING WALLBOARD

You know that joints in plasterboard can be taped and filled so smoothly that they are invisible when painted, but when you try it you get a rough ridge that takes hours to sand flat. What is the secret of successful taping?

Mostly it is not using too much taping compound. Note in the photo of the first application of tape and compound that the tape still shows clearly. Here is where the amateur makes his mistake: he thinks the tape will fall off the wall, so he applies more compound. Don't, quite simply, don't, apply more compound. You want the tape to show.

When the compound is dry, sand lightly to remove any rough spots or excess, brush or wipe down to remove dust then apply another layer of taping compound, making it slightly wider than the first application. Get it as smooth as you can, even if depressions remain. It's easier to fill in the depressions with the next application than to sand down the excess after it is rock-hard.

When you are taping the "factory edges" they will be tapered to allow for the thickness of the tape and compound. Using a wider knife for each succeeding layer of compound spreads the joint to fill the recess created by the tapered edges, and goes slightly beyond. Note this in the photos.

When you must cut a piece of plasterboard there will be one, possibly both edges that will not be tapered. With this kind of joint you must be even more careful not to use too much compound.

On the first application, butter the joint with compound, then scrape your putty knife down the joint to remove all but a little. Press your tape against the joint and compound and use the knife to gently force it against the joint, sliding the knife down. Then, apply a little compound and slide it down the tape with the knife, making sure only that you thoroughly wet the tape and that there is some compound (not much) on all the tape. Let it dry!

When you go back the next day the tape will be firmly adhered to the joint and there will be only a few places to sand. Apply the next layer, going wider than the first, smooth it and let it dry another 12 hours or more. Sand lightly, then put on that third application. Just enough to fill the recesses and make the joint smooth. The final sanding will create a joint that will be almost invisible when painted.

Nails are handled much the same; dimple the nail head, but try not to break the paper. Apply three coats of compound, thinly, sanding between coats when dry. Use too little compound, rather than too much, you can always add more.

To cut wallboard, first mark cutting line with straightedge and pencil. Double-check your measurements.

Plasterboard knife, or ordinary linoleum knife, can be used to score the board. Don't try to cut all the way through.

Place scored line on straightedge, press down on both sides of the line and board will break cleanly.

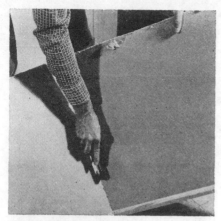

Use your knife to cut paper on the back of the board and your cut is complete. Keep the knife really sharp.

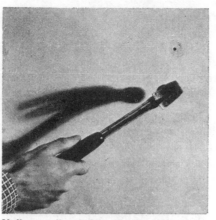

Nails are dimpled to accept compound, but do this gently; depress the nail-head, but try not to break the paper.

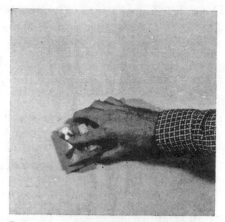

By using minimum of compound in first application there are only a few high spots to sand away.

First application of taping compound should barely cover the tape. Too much compound is the usual mistake.

For second application of compound use wider knife, again keep amount of material to minimum that will cover.

When second coat is dry it is sanded like first, then third and last layer is applied. Use wide knife.

Sanding of final layer of compound produces smooth, flat surface that will blend with wall when it is painted.

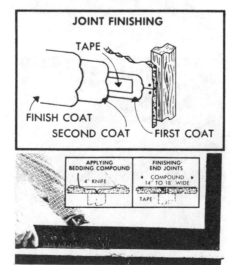

Factory edges of wallboard are tapered to allow for filling in with tape and compound. Broken edge has no taper.

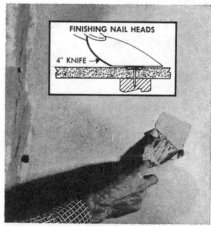

Two to three applications of compound are applied over nail heads, as on joints. Keep compound to a minimum.

METAL WALLBOARD TAPE

A new drywall tape has two ½-inch-wide galvanized-metal strips that assure straight, sharp corners for any wallboard job. The material is extremely versatile and can be used on any inside or outside corner, cathedral ceiling, arches, splay angles, drop ceilings, flat surfaces, and for reinforcing joints. The tape also can be used for joining drywall partitions to plastered walls in alteration work, or for repairing cracked inside corners and chipped outside corners on plaster walls. The tape has feathered edges that blend perfectly into the wall's surface, hiding any trace of irregularities.

Applying the tape is an easy three-step process. First, cut the tape to the desired length and shape. For the inside of curves and arches you cut V-notches; for outside curves you cut slits. The tape compound (called "mud" in the trade) is applied to the joint or corner, then the tape is pressed into the mud, with the metal strips against the surface. The rest of the application is the same as with any wallboard tape: you smooth the tape into the mud, forcing out all the air bubbles. When the first layer of mud is dry, you sand lightly where necessary, then apply another coat that is featheredged.

For easy handling the tape is packaged in 100-foot lengths, so you can pull out just the amount you need, while the rest stays clean.

The tape has been rigorously tested, and the metal does not delaminate from the paper under high humidity and temperature. The paper edges do not wrinkle.

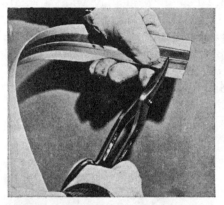

First step in using metal-lined tape is to cut it to length. It also can be notched to go around arches, curves, other shapes.

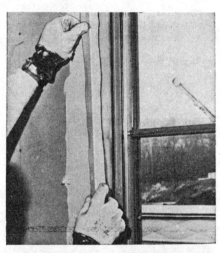

For outside corner, as here at window recess, tape is creased with metal toward wall, pushed into "mud."

For inside corner, whether more or less than right angle, as in this cove ceiling, tape is fitted in similar manner in mud.

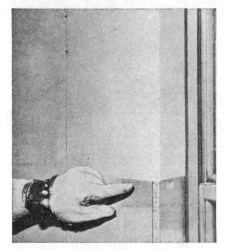

Once tape is applied it is finished as with any plasterboard tape. Here the corner is finished; metal is concealed.

Board breaks cleanly, as shown here, and there is no need to use hand or power saw, which some amateurs use.

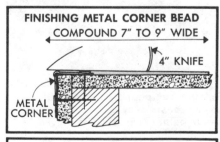

FINISHING METAL CORNER BEAD

COMPOUND 7" TO 9" WIDE

4" KNIFE

METAL CORNER

FINISHING INSIDE CORNERS

4" KNIFE

TAPE

DRYWALL TEXTURING

If you have installed some plasterboard lately and were not quite pleased with the flat, plain look of it, here is one method to make it look more like wet plaster applied over lath:

First, of course, the joints should be taped and concealed with joint compound. You can get by with just one coat of compound if it is applied thickly enough to conceal the tape, rather than using two or three applications as is normal. This is a help to the amateur installer, as it is the joints that take time.

You will need two tools for the job; one is a spring trowel, "skip" trowel it is called, and it can be purchased where plasterers' supplies are sold. The second item is a "mud" tray, which is a long, shallow plastic tray that has a metal edge on which the trowel is wiped.

Dry-wall texture compound is somewhat like joint compound, and is mixed with water to create a liquid about the consistency of thick paint. The solution can be mixed in any clean container. For the average-size room, mix up a couple of gallons, and to it add about 1 tablespoon of fine, clean sand for each gallon. The sand is what causes the trowel to skip over the surface, leaving the compound in streaks.

Put the mixture in the mud tray and pick up a small amount on the back (convex) side of the trowel. Apply it to the wall with a curved, sweeping motion. With a little practice you'll soon be moving rapidly along the wall. Do not try for a regular pattern, although professionals do all sorts of fancy designs. As to the amount of texture to apply, it is up to you. For surfaces to be enameled, as in the bath and kitchen, put the compound on rather lightly. For surfaces to be coated with latex paint, the compound can be applied quite heavily.

Don't try to cover every square inch of the wall surface. There will be many bare spots intermingling with the textured areas. On areas that are textured quite heavily you may want to flatten the material slightly by using a regular concrete-finishing trowel. Do this after the texture is pretty well set up, but not dry.

Allow the compound to dry thoroughly before applying either enamel or latex-base paint.

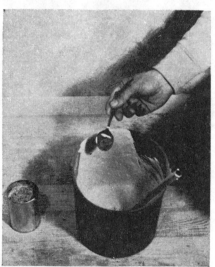

Texture compound is mixed with water to a consistency about like that of heavy paint. Then sand is stirred in.

Skip trowel has curved, springy blade about 10 in. wide. Plastic "mud" tray holds mix, permits scraping trowel.

Apply texture in long, curved, sweeping motions. Use a light touch, move trowel rapidly, don't cover all of surface.

PATCHING HOLES IN WALLS

Holes and cracks in walls are a common problem around homes and apartments. The settling of a house as well as the expansion and contraction that occurs during the various seasons of the year create stresses and strains which often result in cracks. Holes are left in the wall whenever you decide to move a picture or a wall hanging.

As part of your regular maintenance program, walls should be carefully inspected for holes and

Hole in plaster wall needs repair.

Tools you will need.

cracks and neatly repaired before each paint job.

Materials

Two types of patching compounds are commonly used and readily available at your local hardware store.

Spackling Compound. This material is convenient for small jobs but is more expensive. You can purchase it as a powder or ready-mixed. The ready-mixed variety must be tightly resealed after each use to prevent its drying out.

Patching Plaster. Patching plaster can be bought in larger packages and costs less. If you have a large job to tackle, this is your most economic choice. Both spackling powder and patching plaster need to be mixed with water.

Preparation

Surface preparation is the all important first step in the proper completion of this job. Remove any loose plaster. Using a knife, scrape out plaster from the back edges of the crack until the back of the crack is wider than the front surface.

Remove all loose plaster.

Thoroughly dampen the surface of the crack with a wet cloth or paint brush. Prepare the patching compound according to the directions on the package. Mix only a small amount the first time.

Dampen the surface of the hole or crack.

Prepare the patching mixture.

Patching

Small holes can be filled with the patching mixture in a single application. Press the mixture firmly, making sure it completely fills the hole. Carefully smooth the surface with a putty knife. After the patch has dried sand it smooth. Do not attempt to sand before the patching compound is completely dry, as you will only have to remove the compound and start all over again. Check the instructions on the packing for average drying times. To make sanding easier and obtain a smoother surface, wrap the sandpaper around a small block of wood.

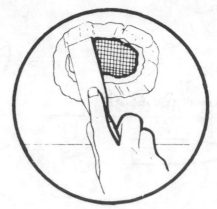

Larger holes should be filled a little at a time.

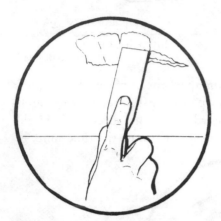

Press mixture firmly into hole.

Starting around the edges, apply the patching mixture in stages, working toward the center.

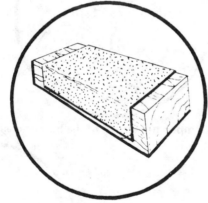

Sanding is easier if you use a piece of sandpaper wrapped around a hand-sized block of wood.

If you are patching a hole in a wall that has a textured surface, you will of course want to match the surface of your patch. To achieve this you will need a sponge, comb, or any instrument which will give you the desired effect. Work the plaster while it is still wet.

Larger holes and cracks should be filled step-by-step. First, partly fill the hole. Let the patch dry thoroughly. This gives a base for the final fill. Add a second batch of compound; let it dry thoroughly. Sand, following the directions previously given, until the surface is smooth.

Very large holes may require a fill of wadded newspaper. Start patching by working in from all sides. Again, let the patching compound dry thoroughly. Apply another layer around the new edge and let it dry. Repeat this process, building toward the center, until the hole is filled. After the patch has dried, sand it smooth.

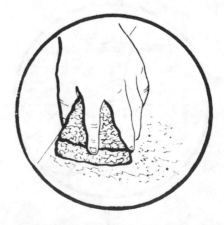

A sponge can be used to achieve a textured surface.

PANELING WALLS

Before you begin make a sketch of the room and locate various furnishings as you intend to arrange the room when the job is finished. This will give you an idea of how the paneling will appear and may suggest a different arrangement.

If you haven't made your paneling selection, think about color coordination with paint and floor coverings. Your dealer can offer assistance.

To determine the perimeter, or the total of the widths of each wall in the room, try to figure as accurately as possible. Purchase an extra panel above your calculations, to cover possible mis-cuts or other errors. This will eliminate an extra trip back to your dealer.

If your room walls measured 14 feet x 14 feet x 16 feet x 16 feet, this would equal 60 feet or 15 panels required (60 feet divided by the 4-foot panel width). To allow for areas such as windows, doors, fireplaces, etc., use these deductions listed below:

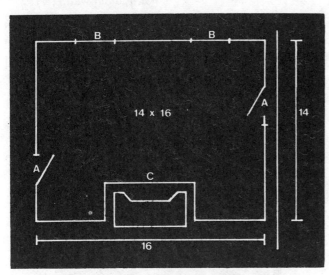

DIAGRAM OF ROOM DIMENSIONS

Deductions

Door	½ panel (A)
Window	¼ panel (B)
Fireplace	½ panel (C)

Thus, the actual number of panels for this room would be 13 pieces (15 pieces minus 2 total deductions). If the perimeter of the room falls in between the figures in the above table, use the next highest number to determine panels required. These figures are for rooms with 8-foot ceiling heights or less. For greater ceiling heights, consult your dealer or contractor.

Your panels should be stored prior to installation in a dry place. If possible, stack flat on a couple of two by fours in the room to be paneled. Do not store in a freshly plastered structure since this might impart moisture to the panels. Prefinished paneling is highly moisture resistant but like all laminated wood products, it is not waterproof and should neither be stored nor installed in areas where it will be subjected to moisture for long periods.

Panel Arrangement

No two wood panels are the same. That's the beauty of real wood paneling—nature's own harmonious balance of color and grain configurations. It provides your room an individuality all its own.

Place your panels around the room to achieve the best sequence and pleasing effect. Once you have them where you want them, number them on the back. The panels should remain standing in the room 48 hours prior to installation to acclimate to room conditions.

Tools

There is no need to purchase expensive woodworking tools—most common household tools are all you'll need. Here's a brief check list:

Hammer
Saw (hand or power)
Level
Large square
Tape measure
Nail set

You'll also find the following items handy for a real professional installation.

Chalk line
Small wooden block
Caulking gun (for installations using panel adhesive)
Keyhole saw or chisel
Shingle scraps
Small compass
Drill
Stud finder

Existing Walls

Most paneling installations over existing true walls require a minimum preliminary preparation. Simply sand out any rough or uneven spots, cut panels to fit, and nail or glue to the wall. Remove old molding and trim or, if desirable, leave in place and cut panels to fit. Measure wall height in several places to assure accurate fitting. (In older homes, height may vary due to settling so this step is very important.) For other types of existing or new walls, review the following:

Wallpapered or plastered walls which are uneven or not true require furring strips. Most common furring strips are 3/8-inch x 1-7/8-inch plywood strips or 1-inch x 2-inch lumber. It's a good idea to place bottom furring strip ½ inch from floor. Leave a ¼-inch space between the horizontal and vertical strips to allow for ventilation. Use shingle shims as necessary to "true" severe uneven areas.

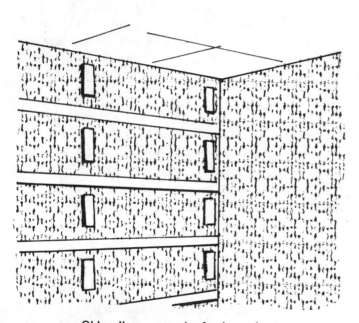

Old walls may require furring strips.

If you're paneling a basement or other areas which have masonry or cement walls, furring strips are an absolute necessity. Furring strips can be attached by drilling and inserting wood plugs or expansion shields; nail, bolt or adhesive anchors; or with a power gun using cement nails. In some cases, 2-inch x 3-inch studs may be required where shimming will not "flush out" the wall. Apply flat against wall to conserve space. Note: In below grade or basement applications, a polyvinyl vapor/moisture barrier film behind the furring strips is recommended. Rolls of this material can be obtained from your dealer.

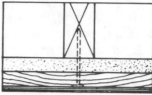

Nail furring through plaster to studs.

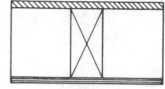

On masonry—screw or nail furring to shields or wood dowels inserted in wall.

On masonry—use Nail Anchors or adhesive anchors.

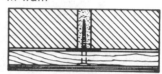

On masonry—2″ x 3″ framing wedged to ceiling and floor. (Alternate treatment—lay framing flat against wall.)

On masonry—Bolt Anchors may be used for attaching 1″ x 3″ sub-furring to wall then attach 1″ x 2″ furring to 1″ x 3″ as if to studs.

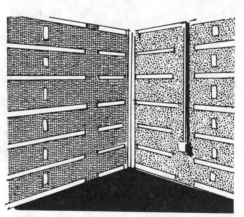

Furring strips are a necessity on cement or masonry walls.

New Walls

Paneling can be applied direct to studs. It is desirable, however, to use 3/8-inch or ½-inch gypsumboard as a backer for a solid installation. It will also help reduce sound transmission and enhance insulation properties. If stud spacing is greater than the normal 16 inches on center (do not space wider than 24 inches on center), use horizontal blocking between the studs and as necessary for solid backing behind all panel edges.

Stud Location

Your panels are random grooved with grooves also located on 16-inch centers. This means that most nailing can be accomplished in the grooves direct to studs behind the existing wall. Probe through the wall with a long nail to find stud location. A stud finder will be a great help in finding the location of studs. Check two or three places to determine exact spacing. (Studs are not always straight so it is a good idea to probe at several heights to assure accurate nailing.)

It's helpful, once stud spacing has been determined, to snap a chalk line floor to ceiling for nailing. Make a light small mark, floor and ceiling, to guide you for panel installation.

Cutting Panels

Measure the floor to ceiling height for your first panel. Normally, this will be at the corner of the room, next to adjacent wall. Allow ½ inch clearance, top to bottom. Molding will cover up this space.

If the corner is irregular, such as a brick or masonry wall, use a small compass to scribe the panel for perfect fitting.

Measure panel for cutting and mark dimensions in soft lead pencil. Use a straight edge to provide a clear, even line.

Applying Panels

Put the first panel into place and butt to adjacent wall in corner. Make sure the panel is completely plumb and outer edge is parallel with plumb line. If outer edge does not fall directly on a stud, scribe or mark the panel to the adjacent wall so outer edge of the panel comes to the center of the stud. This will provide room for nailing of your next panel. Note: Once joint location has been determined, it is helpful to paint a black or dark brown strip on the wall at this location. Any noticeable gap between the panel edges will thus be minimized.

Regular finishing nails can be used in any installation. These require countersinking and touch up with a putty stick to harmonize with the panel.

Or, you may desire to use colored nails to

For application direct to studs use 3d (1¼ inch) finish nails every 6 inches along panel edges and 12 inches elsewhere.

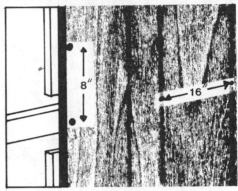

For application over furring, use 3d nails every 8 inches along panel edges and 16 inches (into horizontal furring) elsewhere.

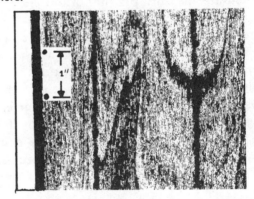

Over backer board or old wall, use 6d (2 inch) finish nails every 4 inches along panel edges and 6 inches elsewhere.

eliminate countersinking and putty stick. These are available to match most paneling color finishes; in 1-inch size for direct application to studs, and 1-5/8-inch size for application to backer board, furring strips or existing walls.

Use of panel adhesive is the professional way to apply paneling. Follow manufacturer's recommendations on application direct to studs or over existing walls. Make absolutely sure panels are properly cut and fitted prior to adhesive application. Once applied, it's hard to make adjustments. Make sure walls and panels are clean, free from dirt and particles.

Use shims or blocks to keep panel snug and in place while nailing or gluing. Butt the second panel into place next to the first, tapping up snug with small wooden block.

A wedge will keep the panel in place while nailing or gluing.

Windows and Doors

Accurate measuring is important here. Measure from your last applied panel edge to the trim. Measure up from bottom and from top to get accurate pattern for cut-out. Drill a ¾-inch hole from the panel surface side to provide a turning corner for your saw. (A keyhole or sabre saw is helpful for this kind of cutting.) If possible, your cut-out panels should meet close to the middle of the window or door. These panel sections are easier to work with than the one panel middle section cut almost entirely out.

Outlet Boxes

Again, accurate measurements are important. Many a good paneling job has been ruined by inaccurate cutting for outlet boxes or heat registers. One good way is that after the panel has been properly cut for fit, mark outlet box with chalk. Then, place panel on wall and tap at outlet location. This will transfer image to back of panel and indicate area for cutting. A ¼-inch space around this area will provide room for spacing and adjustment—the face plate will cover up the extra space. Drill ¾-inch holes from front side of panel, then

use keyhole or sabre saw from surface side to make cut-out.

Note: On an existing wall, adjust outlet box to meet panel thickness. Unscrew at top and bottom, wedge a small paneling scrap at screw locations and tighten.

Measuring for an outlet box.

Molding

Mitering joints is the first basic operation in working with molding. For accuracy, use a miter box and fine tooth saw. To assure a snug fit at corners, trim both pieces at 45 degree angles in opposite cuts so together they form a tight right angle.

To splice lengths of molding along the same wall, 45 degree cuts are made at the same angles on both pieces.

After molding has been cut properly, install with 3-penny finish nails, countersink 1/32 inch and cover with putty stick, or use colored nails to match the molding color.

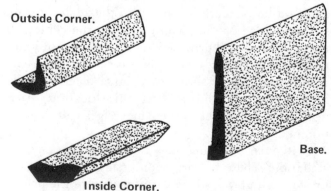

Outside Corner.

Inside Corner.

Base.

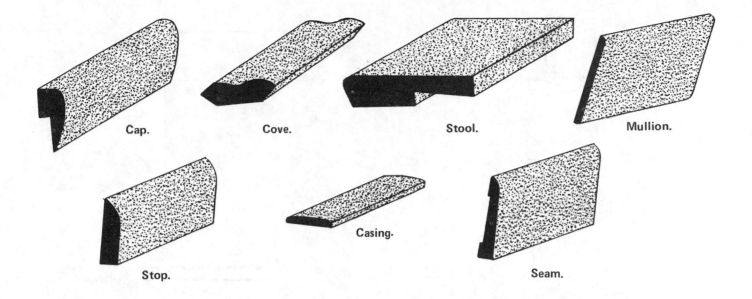

Cap.   Cove.   Stool.   Mullion.

Stop.   Casing.   Seam.

Cleaning

The finish on wood panels can be cleaned with a damp cloth in most cases. A quality liquid wax made by a number of manufacturers may also be used.

Pencil and crayon marks and other heavily soiled areas may be cleaned with a damp cloth or with a mild soap or detergent. Wipe with the grain. After soil is removed, rinse and allow to dry thoroughly, and then apply a clear wax to achieve the desired sheen. Cleansers which contain coarse abrasives are not recommended. Cleansers or waxes that will leave deposits in the pores of the wood should not be used. On the textured paneling, use a heavy cloth that will not catch in the wood grain.

If scratches or mars do occur, they can generally be removed if they are in the finish only and have not penetrated the wood. Use a clear wax on a damp cloth and rub the scratch area with the grain. You may want to wax the entire wall in order to make it more uniform. Continuous waxing, however, will not be necessary. If the scratch goes through the finish and into the wood, a partial re-finishing job is required. If there is major damage to the panels, it is recommended that you seek the services of a professional refinisher.

Light

Light has a tendency to mellow wood wall coloring except behind pictures hung flat against the wall. This can be minimized by holding the picture out ½ inch from the wall with nails placed in the back of the frames. This allows the light to seep in behind the picture eliminating the sharp contrasts, should the picture need to be removed.

Control of Humidity

Low or fluctuating relative humidity (amount of water vapor in the air) can adversely affect any wood product. This is readily apparent when dry air causes a feeling of chilliness—even when room temperature is 75 degrees F or more. For your own personal comfort and to keep your paneling looking its best, it is recommended that humidity control systems be considered—especially in known areas of wintertime dry air.

WALLPAPERING

As in painting, the first step in wallpapering is to prepare the walls. Patch all holes and cracks with a spackling compound and seal with a thin coat of shellac. Even though you can paper over old wallpaper, provided there are no loose areas, it is best to remove old paper by soaking it with a removal preparation and a scraper. Next, buy sufficient rolls of paper to cover the room. Most wallpaper or wallcovering is now made of vinyl with a

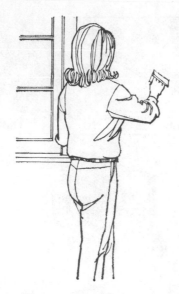

First step is to put walls in proper condition. Remove old wallpaper, fill cracks and holes with spackle, sand smooth.

To right of doorway snap plumb line 1 in. less than width of wall covering, for righthand side of the first strip.

Unroll wall covering, pattern side up, cut strips height of wall plus 2 in. at ceiling and baseboard. Mark tops.

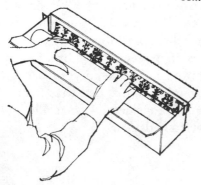

Half-fill water box, immersing one strip at a time in box about 30 seconds, threading 2 in. under the guide.

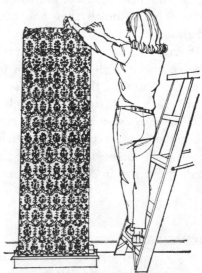

Set stepladder for easy climbing. Hold top of strip and gently pull up to about 2 in. above ceiling line, smooth.

Cut strips to height of wall plus 2 in. at both ceiling line and baseboard to allow for trimming to correct length.

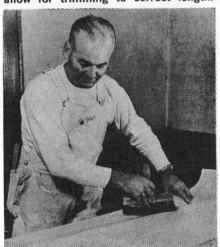

Mix paste according to directions. Spread paste from middle of sheet to edges and one end, sparingly, evenly.

Fold pasted portion from the end to the center, paste-to-paste, without creasing fold. Be especially careful with flocks.

Now, paste the remaining half of strip in the same manner, and fold so both ends of the strip meet in the center.

Carry strip ("top" side up) to wall. Unfold top half of strip and position about two inches above ceiling line.

Smooth strip in place with a dry smoothing brush, flattening out wrinkles, air pockets. Unfold bottom.

Paste and hang remaining strips in same way, being sure pattern matches and edges meet. Do not overlap seams.

Whether inside or outside, corners may not be perfectly plumb, so plan your strips to extend around the corners.

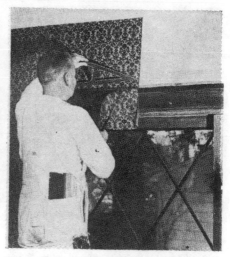

Next strip should overlap in the corner, but hang it only after snapping another chalk plumb line on the new wall.

Trim excess paper at ceiling, baseboard and casement or chair rail and around doors with a razor and straightedge.

Strategy around doors and windows is simple. Merely approximate size of strip. Slip into position, cut to fit.

cloth or paper backing, and comes in various size widths.

Start at a wall that has the fewest window and door openings and measure off a distance that is a half-inch less than the wallcovering width. Suspend a plumb line at this point and snap a chalk line on the wall. The chalk line is most important as it will determine the "straightness" of the first strip and all succeeding strips. If you don't have pre-pasted paper, the next step is to mix the paste. Use a bucket and keep stirring as you add the powder. (A special paste must be used to hang the heavy vinyl wallcoverings that come in 54-inch widths.) Keep adding the powder to the water in the bucket, and stirring all the time, until the paste has the consistency of sour cream. Break up all lumps with your fingers or strain the paste through some cheesecloth.

Cut several strips of paper, or wallcovering if you prefer, equal to the height of the wall you are going to cover, plus an overlap of two inches for top and two inches for the bottom. Apply the paste to the back of the paper with a wide brush, paying particular attention to the edges of the paper. An unpasted area will show up as a blister on the wall. Newspapers placed under the paper will keep your pasting table clean. If your table is too short to support a full length of paper, use a chair or a stool to hold the paper at either end to prevent creasing. Paste up half a length of paper (if your table is a short one) and fold up this half to

meet the middle of the strip. Do not crease the fold. Do the same thing with the other half and now fold both halves together. The paper is folded paste side to side and can be easily handled by the dry, patterned side. Bring the strip to the wall with the chalk line. Line up the strip with the chalk line and the ceiling, leaving a two-inch overlap at the ceiling. Unfold the paper, letting it drop free, and then carefully position the paper so that it lines up with the chalk line from top to bottom. Use a special paper-hanger's brush to force the paper into the corner of the room. You will wind up with a half-inch overlap into the adjacent corner wall. Apply the brush firmly over the entire surface of the paper, starting from the middle and working towards the edges. Make sure you have a good bond at the ceiling, baseboard, and along the edge.

Now cut and paste up the next strip. If the paper has a pattern that must be matched, you will have to make an allowance for it when you cut the paper (professional paper hangers will cut and paste up a half-dozen or more strips at a time!) Bring the second strip over and carefully butt it to the preceeding strip. Ease it in place by using the palms of your hands. Again use the brush to smooth out the paper. Wipe away any excess paste that oozes out between the seams with a sponge dampened with water. Use a seam roller to press down the seams. Press lightly with the roller to prevent the pattern of the wheel from being embossed on the paper.

Obstructions

Continue working around the room. Do not skip any "hard" areas with the expectation of coming back to them later. When you come to a switch plate or outlet, apply the paper right over it—after first removing the cover plate—and use a sharp trimming knife to cut away the paper over the opening. (Be careful not to touch a live wire.) Replace the cover plate after you have finished the entire papering job. When you come to a fireplace, mantelpiece, window, or door, remove as much as possible of the waste paper before smoothing it in place. You can do an exact trimming job around these obstructions if you crease a line with a putty knife on the paper following the outline of the window, door, etc. Then cut along this line with a pair of scissors and finish pressing the paper into place with your fingers, followed by the brush. Trimming away the excess paper at the ceiling and baseboard can be done with a sharp trimming knife as these are fairly long, straight cuts.

Are you working in an older house? If so, you may find that the corners are not plumb so that you may not be able to continue papering around corners. In this case, leave an overlap of about an inch on the next wall. Then snap a new plumb line on the next wall. You may need to snap a plumb line on all four walls.

"BRICK" WALLS

If you have been intrigued by the beauty of brick used indoors, but have shied away from it because of the problems involved—added foundation support, heavier wall construction—and the expense, then you should check out the modern products made of plastic. These materials look so much like brick that you have to tap them with a hammer to determine whether or not they are imitation or the real thing.

In the raised-hearth project described both real brick and plastic brick are used, and it is impossible to tell which is which.

The plastic bricks are ¼ inch thick, color-fast, nonporous and will resist flame up to temperatures of 350 degrees F. The biggest advantage of these bricks, other than their authentic appearance, is their light weight, which eliminates the need for a heavy foundation or any special support structures. Even a standard stud wall, covered with well-nailed sheets of ¼-inch plywood makes an excellent base for the application. The bricks also may be applied over plaster, plasterboard, concrete, concrete blocks, Styrofoam and many other materials.

Installation

The actual installation is fun, as you are not involved with the work of mixing mortar, and there is no worry about having a full kit of masonry tools. All you need is the special mastic, plus a putty knife. For cutting the bricks, use a hacksaw or a band saw fitted with an all-purpose blade, or a metal-cutting blade on a table or radial-arm saw.

The surface to which the brick is adhered must be sound, clean and free of any loose material; oil or grease will prevent adhesion. Dampening dry, porous surfaces with water will help the application. Use a 3 inch putty knife to pick up mastic directly from the can. Spread it evenly over the surface, but don't attempt to smooth it out like

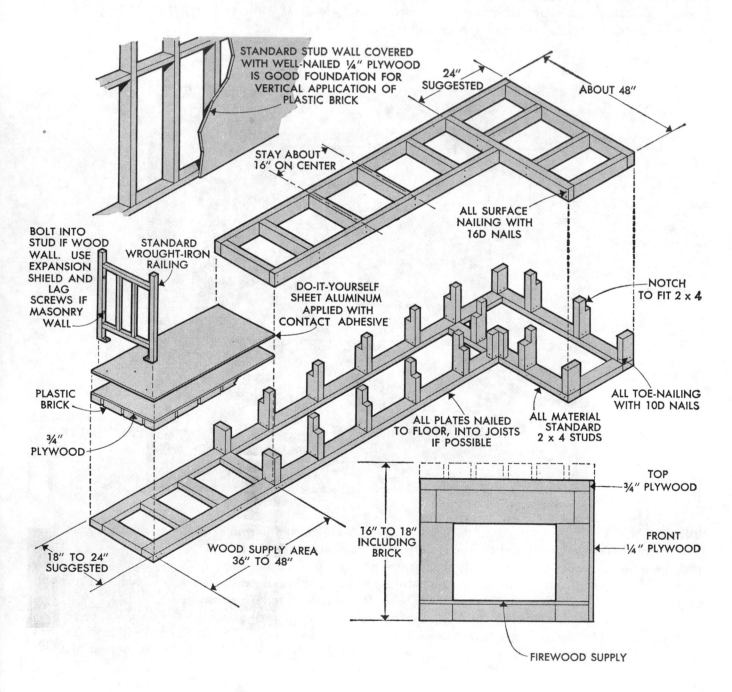

STANDARD STUD WALL COVERED WITH WELL-NAILED ¼" PLYWOOD IS GOOD FOUNDATION FOR VERTICAL APPLICATION OF PLASTIC BRICK

24" SUGGESTED

ABOUT 48"

STAY ABOUT 16" ON CENTER

ALL SURFACE NAILING WITH 16D NAILS

BOLT INTO STUD IF WOOD WALL. USE EXPANSION SHIELD AND LAG SCREWS IF MASONRY WALL

STANDARD WROUGHT-IRON RAILING

DO-IT-YOURSELF SHEET ALUMINUM APPLIED WITH CONTACT ADHESIVE

NOTCH TO FIT 2 x 4

PLASTIC BRICK

¾" PLYWOOD

ALL PLATES NAILED TO FLOOR, INTO JOISTS IF POSSIBLE

ALL MATERIAL STANDARD 2 x 4 STUDS

ALL TOE-NAILING WITH 10D NAILS

18" TO 24" SUGGESTED

WOOD SUPPLY AREA 36" TO 48"

16" TO 18" INCLUDING BRICK

TOP ¾" PLYWOOD

FRONT ¼" PLYWOOD

FIREWOOD SUPPLY

Use standard studding material for the understructure, but try to get dry material to eliminate shrinkage.

Mastic is applied with putty knife about 1/16 in. thick. Work about 2 sq. ft. at a time with mastic.

Blob of mastic is applied to back of each brick, then it is spread to cover full surface about 1/16 in. thick.

Special corner bricks permit turning corner with look of real brick. Best to start at corner to avoid cutting.

Versatile plastic bricks are rugged enough to be used on the floor. Mortar is made flush, floor sealed with urethane.

On kitchen walls the plastic brick is readily cleaned with a damp cloth, and most stains will not penetrate.

paint. A coating 1/16 inch thick is needed.

Before you apply each brick, put a blob of adhesive on the back, then spread it out with the putty knife until the entire surface is covered. Put the brick directly in place, but with a "squiggly" motion to settle it firmly in position. Continue adding brick in the same manner, maintaining a spacing that is compatible with the brick design you have chosen. In this area you can be a little careless if you are working with "used" brick. With more formal types of brick the spacing should be quite uniform. In these cases it helps to make a wooden spacer as a gauge.

Special shapes of brick are available so you can turn corners neatly and create the appearance of a real brick. These are applied the same as normal face pieces. The bond is quick and firm with the mastic, so you always start at the top of a surface and work down.

Even with its natural color, the mastic is the same shade as mortar, so "grouting" is not necessary. If you want smooth lines between the bricks, make a smoothing stick" the same width as the joint. You can even use a fingertip. Clean-up is with water; but before the mastic sets up on fingers and tools.

In the project shown, real brick was used on the flat surface of the hearth because of the closeness to the fire. This brick was adhered to the plywood platform with mastic, then the joints were filled with mortar. The bricks can be used as-is, or painted with two coats of latex-base finish as on the hearth shown.

Construction

Construction details of the project are shown in the drawing. Your best bet is to do some planning on paper to suit these details to your own needs. Construction will remain the same, even though dimensions probably will be different.

Start by using a chalk line to mark the outline of the hearth on the floor. Use a level to mark the height on the walls. It's a good idea to think in terms of brick sizes. Some slight adjustment in width or height can minimize the amount of bricks you will have to cut.

Cut the 2 x 4 plates to length and nail them solidly to the floor. If possible, try to hit the floor joists; this is not critical if the floor and subfloor are solid.

Next, cut the verticals. Most of these are notched to fit a standard 2 x 4. Others are cut square at each end. These later can be cut to fit after the notched vertical and upper plates have been installed.

If you turn a corner for added seating try to stay close to the suggested dimensions. If it is made wider or narrower it will be out of proportion and not be practical.

After the verticals and top plates are in, add the cross members. While 16 inches on center may seem like "over-designing," the finished project should have the feel of solid masonry. Your own requirements may necessitate some moves away from the design shown, but it makes sense to add verticals rather than eliminating them.

In corners, end with verticals cut square at each end. Then add another vertical behind it; this provides a nailing surface for the covering material.

For the top cover ¾-inch fir plywood was used. For vertical facings ¼-inch plywood was used. Heavier stock can be used if you have it handy. Just be sure joints fall on the studs.

FLOOR COVERINGS

Traditionally, people have used linoleum in areas such as the kitchen, ceramic tile in the bathroom, and wood floors throughout the rest of the house. With the variety of flooring materials available today—approximately 30 types and hundreds of varieties—there is little reason to be bound by tradition.

In making a choice, livability, esthetics, durability, maintenance, and cost should be considered. Remember, no one material is ideally suited to the requirements of every room in your home.

The principal kinds of floor coverings used as wearing or "finished" surfaces are: resilient, wood, ceramic tile, clay, and carpet. The first four will be considered here.

Resilient Floor Coverings

Resilient surfaces refer to a number of different types of water-resistant materials that range from the traditional linoleum available in rolls to thin sheets or tile materials differentiated according to their ingredients: asphalt, vinyl, vinyl asbestos, rubber, and cork.

They are dense and have non-absorbent surfaces. Their resilience aids in sound control and provides resistance to indentation. Density of the material usually provides long life and ease of maintenance. The most expensive material will usually give the most beauty and highest wear resistance. The lowest cost materials give the least wear and should be used only as a short term covering.

The sheet materials are more difficult to install than tile; however, in comparable materials, sheet usually costs less than tile. Most resilient surfaces are secured to the subfloor with an adhesive: linoleum paste, asphalt emulsion, latex, or epoxy. What you use is dictated by the flooring manufacturer's specifications.

Linoleum. This blend of linseed oil, pigments, fillers and resin binders is bonded to a backing of asphalt-saturated felt. It is available in solid colors or with inlaid, embossed, or textured patterns, simulating stone, wood, or tile. It is available in rolls eight feet or wider and tiles either 9 inches x 9 inches or 12 inches x 12 inches square with thicknesses of 1/16-inch, .090-inch, and 1/8-inch.

Linoleum provides fair wear resistance, and its color extends completely through to the backing material.

Inlaid linoleum has a hard durable surface, is greaseproof, and easy to clean; however it is damaged by cleaning products containing alkali solutions.

It should not be installed on a concrete slab on grade (the ground), since moisture permeating through the concrete from below will cause the material to rot.

Asphalt Tile. Asphalt tile is a combination of asbestos fibers, ground limestone, and mineral pigments with an asphalt binder. It is the least expensive and most commonly used tile. Its price depends on the color; dark colors are the least expensive, light colors and special patterns are the most expensive.

Asphalt tiles are manufactured with the pattern through the total thickness. Some tile patterns simulate other materials. In this case, the pattern does not penetrate its thickness and it will wear rapidly under heavy use.

Normal tile size is 1/8-inch thick and 9 inches x 9 inches square.

Asphalt tile will stain and break down if it contacts animal fats and mineral oils. It is brittle and breaks easily. Its recovery from indentation is negligible. It can, however, be used on concrete slabs on grade and where there may be a moisture problem.

Vinyl. This floor covering's chief ingredient is polyvinyl chloride (PVC). It also contains resin binders, with mineral filters, stabilizers, plasticizers, and pigments. The vinyl may be filler or clear.

Clear vinyl consists of a layer of opaque particles or pigments covered with a wearing surface of clear vinyl bonded to a vinyl or polymer-impregnated asbestos fiber or resin-saturated felt. The clear vinyl surface provides high resistance to wear.

Filled vinyl is made of chips of vinyl of varied color and shape immersed in a clear vinyl base and bonded by heat and pressure. When used in a basement, a vapor barrier or an epoxy adhesive should be used to install it.

Vinyl tile is the most costly, but also the most wear resistant and easily maintained of the various tiles. It is produced in standard size squares, 9 inches x 9 inches and 12 inches x 12 inches, in standard thicknesses of 1/16-inch, .080-inch, 3/32-inch, and 1/8-inch.

Sheet Vinyl. Sheet vinyl may be produced with a layer of vinyl foam bonded to the backing or between the finish surface and the backing. The result is a resilient flooring with good walking comfort and an effective sound absorbent quality.

The vinyl is produced in rolls eight feet wide or wider and can be installed over most subsurfaces. While the material has high resistance to grease, stains, and alkali, its surface is easily damaged by abrasion and indentation since it is, generally, a soft product.

Vinyl-Asbestos Tile. This resilient flooring consists of blended compositions of asbestos fibers, vinyls, plasticizers, color pigments, and fillers. The tiles, without backing, are 9 inches x 9 inches or 12 inches x 12 inches square and 1/16-inch, 3/32-inch, and 1/8-inch thick.

The tile may be obtained in marblized patterns, or textured to simulate stone, marble, travertine, and wood.

It is semiflexible and requires a rigid subfloor for support. The tile has high resistance to grease, oils, alkaline substances, and some acids. It is quiet underfoot and many forms can go without waxing for extended periods of time. It can be used almost anywhere, and can be obtained with a peel-and-stick backing.

Rubber Tile. Rubber tile is based on natural or synthetic rubber. Mineral fillers and nonfading organic pigments are used to produce a narrow range of colors and patterns.

The standard sizes are 9 inches x 9 inches and 12 inches x 12 inches. Larger sizes are available at higher cost. The thicknesses are 0.080-inch, 1/8-inch, and 3/16-inch.

Rubber tile is resilient and has high resistence to indentation. The material is softened by petroleum products and its resistance to grease and kitchen oils depends on its method of manufacture. Waxing and buffing are necessary to maintain a high gloss. The surface becomes slippery when wet.

Use of a vapor barrier or epoxy adhesive for a slab on grade installation is required.

Cork Tile. Cork tile consists of granulated

MATERIAL	CHARACTERISTICS	DIFFICULTY OF INSTALLATION	WHERE TO USE
Wood Strip Flooring	Long Wear Life Moderate Resiliency Moderate Care Required	Moderate	All areas except bath and utility
Wood Block Flooring	Moderate Long Wear Life Moderate Resiliency Moderate Care Required	Moderate	All areas except bath and utility
Linoleum	Moderate Wear Life Resilient Moderate Care Required	Moderate—Low	All areas
Sheet Vinyl	Long Wear Life High Resiliency Low Care Required	Moderate—Low	All areas
Vinyl Tile	Long Wear Life High Resiliency Low Care Required	Low	All areas
Vinyl Asbestos Tile	Long Wear Life Resilient Moderate Low Care Required	Low	All areas
Asphalt Tile	Moderate Wear Life Moderate Resiliency Moderate High Care	Low	Avoid areas where grease is used
Ceramic Tile	Long Wear Life No Resiliency Easy Care	Moderate—Difficult	Bathrooms, entrance areas, kitchens, halls
Clay Tile	Long Wear Life No Resiliency Easy Care	Moderate—Difficult	Bathrooms, entrance areas, kitchens, halls, utility rooms

cork bark combined with a synthetic resin as a binder. The best tile has a clear film of vinyl applied to improve its durability, water resistance, and ease of maintenance. Tile sizes are 6 inches x 6 inches and 12 inches x 12 inches with a range of thicknesses from 1/8-inch to ½-inch.

Cork floors are great for foot comfort and sound control. They wear rapidly and do not resist impact loads well. Maintenance is difficult since the material is broken down by grease and alkalies.

Wood Floorings. Many varieties of both hard and soft woods are available for flooring. Certain hardwoods, because of their high resistance to wear, are more often used than others. Two are oak and maple.

Wood flooring is finished with a combination of coatings such as a sealer and varnish, or a liquid plastic.

Wood flooring may be simply nailed to the subfloor or, when used over a concrete slab, nailed to wood "sleepers" fastened to the slab. In either case, the floor is sanded smooth, and finished with stain and sealer.

The most commonly used hardwood flooring is oak because of its beauty, warmth, and durability. Maple flooring is produced from the sugar, or rock, maple. It is smooth, strong, and hard. The grain of maple does not have as much contrast as oak; however, where a smooth polished surface is necessary, maple makes a superior floor.

Beech, birch, hickory, and several other hardwoods are also used.

Hardwood strip flooring is hollowed or has "V" slots cut into its back surface to minimize warping. It is produced in thicknesses of 3/8-inch, 1/2-inch, or 25/32-inch and widths varying from 1½-inch to 3¼-inches, with the most popular width being 2¼-inches, and is tongue and grooved to provide tight joints.

Hardwood flooring is graded on its appearance according to the number of defects, variations of color, and surface characteristics. Strength and wear are not dependent on grading since all grades are comparable in these respects.

Strip flooring is available prefinished. The finish is applied at the factory and the floor can be used right after installation. It comes as imitation peg style, random width, and simulated plank.

The softwood most used is southern yellow pine; Douglas fir is next, with western hemlock and larch following. Some woods such as redwood, cedar, cypress, and eastern white pine are used in areas where they are common and available.

Softwood flooring is available in several sizes and thicknesses; the most common is 25/32-inch thick and 4½-inches wide. The long edges of the flooring are tongue and groove or side matched in order to give tight joints. Similar to hardwood, the underside is hollowed or V-grooved to minimize warping.

Hardwood squares 9 inches x 9 inches or 12 inches x 12 inches by 5/16-inch or ½-inch thick can be purchased to produce a parquet floor. These squares are available in several types of wood such as oak, maple, mahogany, cherry, and teak.

Thin block flooring is normally produced in prefinished form. The blocks may be nailed to the subfloor or secured with a mastic. These materials, while costing more than strip flooring, require no finishing and are competitive in completed cost.

Non-Resilient Flooring

These include brick "pavers", ceramic, and clay tile, stone, and terrazzo. These materials are more difficult to install than other flooring materials and usually are the most expensive. However, they have a long life.

They may be installed using a special "thin-set" cement, or in the traditional ¾-inch bed of mortar. They require a "grout" (cement fill) between the tiles.

Glazed ceramic tile and terra cotta are relatively non-porous and as a result resist staining. These glazed tiles are, however, susceptible to scratching and crazing (formation of minute cracks) with age. Ceramic tiles range in size from what is called "mosaic" tile of 3/8-inch x 3/8-inch to a large 16 inches x 18 inches size.

Mosaic tiles commonly are sold on a backing sheet, making possible the installation of larger areas at one time. It is necessary to grout the joints between each tile after they are set in place.

Unglazed ceramic tile, slate, and flagstone are porous unless treated with special stain-resistant sealants.

Clay or quarry tile, usually unglazed, is produced from clays that result in a strong, long-wearing surface. It is relatively easy to maintain and withstands impact well.

The color range is reds, buffs, blacks, browns,

greys, and gold. A semiglazed type is produced in greys, browns, and greens. The product is available with a variety of surface patterns.

The tiles come in several thicknesses from ¼-inch, ½-inch, and up to 1½-inches depending on their width and length. They may be square, rectangular, or some geometric shape.

Terrazzo is made of marble chips in combination with portland cement mortar and is ground and polished to a smooth finish. It is very resistant to moisture and therefore relatively easy to maintain. It is very noisy and is a tiring walking and work surface.

Most non-resilient flooring is installed using a masonry mortar. This demands a higher degree of skill than other types of flooring and adds to the installed cost.

Cost of each type of flooring will vary depending on its quality and the manufacturer. As an example, asphalt tile may cost as little as 20¢ a square foot while high quality vinyl may reach $4 per square foot. If you consider that an oak floor may cost only 75¢ per square foot, it is obvious that a wide variety of options is available.

EASY PARQUET FLOORING

You can install a luxurious hardwood parquet floor in a matter of hours, and the cost will be less than wall-to-wall carpeting. A pad of foam plastic on the back of each piece of parquet tile reduces impact sound and adjusts to minor irregularities in the floor beneath it.

Installing the parquet tiles requires that the base shoe be removed from the molding. Then the center of the room is found and right-angle chalk lines are snapped. You measure along the lines in 12-inch steps (the tiles are 12 inches square) and adjust the lines to make sure the end tiles are the same size.

Using the lines as guides you place each tile. Stripping off the paper on the back of the tiles exposes dots of adhesive that quickly adhere to the subfloor. Tongues and grooves assure tight fits between each of the tiles.

There must be a 3/8-inch space on all four edges of the floor to allow for expansion and contraction. A portable electric jig saw makes quick work of trimming the tiles as necessary, or a handsaw can be used.

When all the tiles are in place you install a reducer strip in doorways to eliminate the toe-catching step created by the thickness of the tile. The final step in the job is to replace the base shoe, which covers the 3/8-inch expansion space on the edges of the floor.

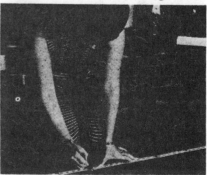

Starting operation in the tiling project is to remove shoe molding between base molding and the floor, using chisel.

Close-up photo of individual parquet tile shows tongue-and-groove details, backing of closed-cell foam that cushions.

As with any project, first step in installing parquet tiles is to carefully read instructions provided by manufacturer.

Measurements are made parallel to one wall, in multiples of 12 in., plus an allowance of 3/8 in. for expansion.

Two chalk lines are snapped at right angles to locate the center of the room for starting rows of the parquet tiles.

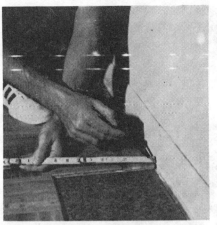

3/8-in border is left next to wall for expansion. Chemically-treated paper is peeled off, tile pressed in place.

Most time-consuming part of the installation is cutting end pieces to fit; next to walls and to provide 3/8 in. expansion.

Areas where parquet floor ends is handled with reducer strip cut to fit and adhered with double-face tape or glue.

Reducer strip is simply pressed into place, providing tapered edge to flooring, avoiding toe-catching step.

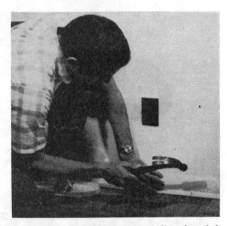

Base shoe is replaced and flooring job is done. Molding to match walls (as shown) can be used.

SPEEDY INSTALLATION OF RESILIENT FLOORING

If you're afraid of the mess and time involved in a do-it-yourself installation of resilient flooring, try the method shown. Fast, easy, economical, the secret is the use of double-face tape on the seams and perimeter. Best results can be had with a quality flooring as it will "lay-out" with few wrinkles. As with any installation, the floor to be covered must be sound and smooth.

Roll out the first width and scribe around the walls of the room. (To make the job even easier,

take up the quarter round). Roll out the second sheet of material and cut to length. Be sure to provide sufficient length for pattern matching and allow for an overlap of about 2 to 4 inches on each seam. Using a straightedge, cut through both thicknesses of flooring. Scribe and cut the second sheet to fit around the walls of the room. Apply double-face tape to the seams and around the perimeter of the room. Remove the tape backing and position the flooring. Roll or press the seams and replace the quarter-round.

Lift up flooring, remove scraps, and apply double-face tape, pressing it in place on one side as shown.

After determining pattern match and cutting widths of flooring to length, overlap about 2 to 4 in. and, using a straightedge, cut through both thicknesses.

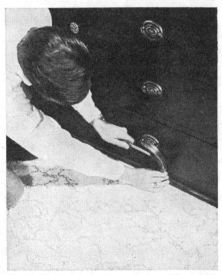

Remove backing from the double-face tape and press the first width of flooring in place as you go.

Roll or press the seams together. Pounding with the flat of your hand will shift the flooring somewhat.

Replace the quarter-round, nailing into the baseboard. Do not nail into flooring as this may cause it to buckle.

CHOOSING CARPET

Choosing carpet is one of the major decisions facing a homeowner when decorating a home. With today's hundreds of styles, fibers and colors, selection can be extremely confusing. With a little basic information you can be your own expert:

Carpet Fibers

Wool carpet has been in use for many years, but since the introduction of man-made fibers, its popularity has waned. It is quite high priced because the fibers are not as available in large quantities. Wool is not highly stain-resistant, and is still the victim of the moth.

Acrylic is used mostly in sculptured carpets and is a soft fiber, giving a rich appearance. It is extremely easy to care for and with a good stain resistance.

Polyester is a yarn with a lot of bulk. It gives the appearance of more yarn in a carpet than there actually is.

Nylon is probably the best buy in most carpets. It is particularly noted for its great strength and toughness. It has great resiliency and recovers quickly from furniture marks. Nylon is a great stain resister, being immune to practically all stains, including oil and chemicals. Many different carpet styles can be created from nylon, such as a high-luster yarn, or a silky effect of the more expensive plush.

Carpet Styles

Sculptured carpet can be used in almost any area of the home. Wool used to be the most popular in this carpet, but it has been replaced by the synthetic fibers, for cleanability. Sculptured carpet gives a soft, traditional look and a good choice of fibers would be nylon or acrylic.

Kitchen carpet has eliminated the housewife's chore of scrubbing and waxing. This carpet is soil and stain-resistant, so you don't have to worry about spills. It is virtually stainproof. Its cushioned back minimizes breakage and makes the kitchen much quieter. Kitchen carpet is not restricted to kitchen use only. It is ideal for any area of heavy traffic—a den, play room, utility room, or even for commercial use. Again, nylon is a good choice of fibers because of its toughness.

Shag carpet is one of the most beautiful yet practical of carpets. It can take the toughest traffic and never show the wear. One of the most important aspects in selecting a shag carpet is the twist of the yarn. A tightly twisted, yet full strand indicates a good, long lasting, resilient carpeting. Again, nylon is the toughest fiber, and the easiest to clean. Shag can be cleaned easily with an upright vacuum cleaner.

Plush or velvet-textured carpet gives your home that truly luxurious look. If you're looking for a more formal appearance, plush is your carpet. Plush is noted for its shading characteristics that gives a rich, almost two-color look. For a soft look, try acrylic fibers.

Sculptured plush shag is the one carpet that combines all—shag, sculpture, and plush. This carpet is beautifully embossed and is truly a quality carpet to meet the most discriminating taste. It is constructed of nylon, and in better carpets a special additive eliminates static electricity.

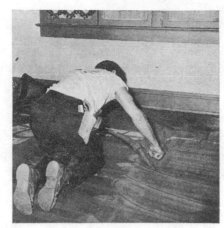

STICK-DOWN CARPETING

Indoor/outdoor carpeting can be installed several ways, including loose-laid, taped and full adhesive.

Carpet has been cut "oversize" to fit room, is carefully laid into position on the adhesive-covered floor.

Air bubbles and wrinkles are smoothed out towards the walls, carpeting should be smoothed out, but not stretched.

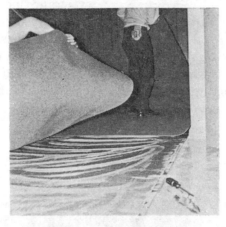
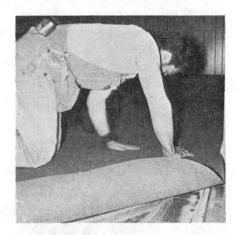

Carpeting is pushed up against joint of wall and floor, and a sharp knife drawn along the joint, molding replaced.

In full-adhesive carpet laying, the carpeting adhesive is quickly and smoothly spread with a notched trowel.

Carpeting is trimmed to fit down into carpet strip and smoothed up to strip then pushed in place.

Indoor/outdoor carpeting and family rooms go together like strawberries and ice cream, and when combined with vinyl-tile flooring, can help to make a room double purpose. The different floorings separate the room into use-areas much more effectively than partitioning it off, and yet the room is wide-open for large parties. The "living-in" portion of the room is covered with carpeting, to deaden sound, and provide comfort and warmth to playing children, while the "bar and dance floor" are covered with vinyl-tile flooring for easy care and party use.

Although indoor/outdoor carpeting can be installed by simply unrolling it and positioning, a seven-year-old cornering at high speeds, can move any loose-laid carpet. For a hard-use family recreation room, the carpeting should be installed with adhesive.

The most permanent job is a "full adhesive" carpeting installation, and can be an easy Saturday job, as the sheet carpeting goes down much the same as sheet vinyl.

You must, however, make certain the surface on which the carpeting is installed is clean, dry and free of dust before you apply the adhesive. The adhesive should be applied with a notched spreader, and the carpet should be "rolled" or pressed with a flat object.

For perfect seams, overlap the two edges of the carpet about 1 inch and cut through both thicknesses of carpet using a straightedge and a sharp linoleum knife.

Since rooms are seldom square, or walls parallel, cut the carpet oversize, then trim around the edges of the wall with a sharp knife. Pull the carpeting tight to remove all wrinkles and air bubbles, but do not stretch it, or you will create unsightly buckles.

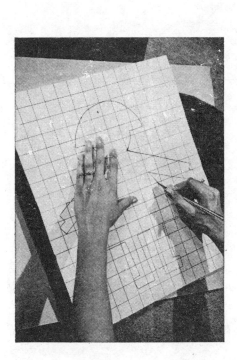

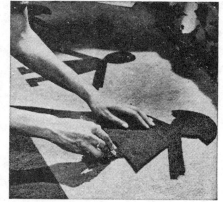

CARPET INSERTS

If you are going to install indoor/outdoor carpeting on your patio or in any room in your home you can create a custom floor. All you will need are a few pieces of flooring of a color to contrast with the carpet you are laying, a sharp knife and a pattern cut from hardboard.

You cut the pattern, which can be any motif you want: an eagle for an early-American living room, something in pop-art for a recreation room, then cut around it to make the insert. The pattern then is placed on the carpet and a cutout made. The section is removed and replaced by the figure you have cut out.

LAYING A TILE FLOOR

The first step in laying a tile floor is to remove all wax, grease or oil with a good chemical cleaner. This is necessary in order to provide a good contact for the cement.

The new tile will require a smooth surface. Plane down any high spots and renail any loose boards on wood floors. If this is not done these spots will show through and eventually wear through the tile flooring.

If the old floor is in very poor condition, it may be necessary to cover it with plywood or parchment board. This will provide a smooth substructure. If the laying of plywood is necessary, nail every four inches along the edge and in all directions. Use coated or ring-grooved nails. Be sure heads are even with the board level or they will also show through the tile floor.

Planning

The first tiles you lay should start from the exact center of the room. Do not guess! The only way to find the exact center of the floor is to measure, and do so carefully. It is really fairly simple. First, find the exact center of each wall and mark it. Ignore irregularities in the shape of the room. Hold a chalk line at the point you have marked and snap it on the floor. The point at which the two lines cross will indicate the exact center of the room. An easy check for accuracy is to mark a 3-foot point on one line and a 4-foot point on the line perpendicular to it. Then, measure the distance between the two points. This distance should be exactly 5 feet. If it is not, there is an error and you had best begin again.

Even if this check indicates that you have found the exact center of the room, check once more before actually installing the tile. Do this by laying loose tiles along the marked lines, starting at the center. After you have placed a full run of tiles from the center toward each wall, measure the distance between the edge of the last tile and the wall. If it is more than 8 inches or less than 2 inches, you will probably have difficulty in cutting a tile to fit this spot. At this point you should adjust for this problem by moving the centerline that is parallel to the wall closer to the wall.

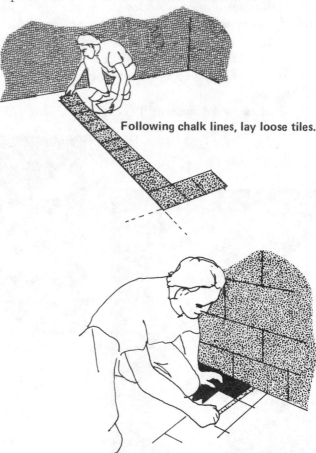

Following chalk lines, lay loose tiles.

If the end tile is more than 8 or less than 2 inches, remark.

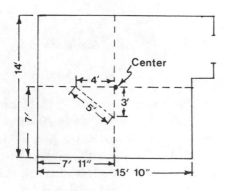

Checking the center point.

Move center line closer to parallel wall.

Preparation

All the tile you have purchased may not have been manufactured at the same time. It is to your advantage to open all cartons of tiles and use the tiles from each box on an alternating basis. This will ensure an even distribution of the tile colors, should there be any noticeable variation.

Consider whether you will be alternating grains, using more than one color tile, or laying the grain in only one direction. Plan before you proceed to lay any tile.

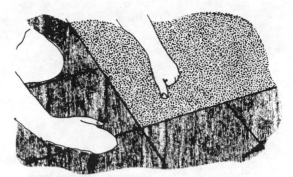

Cement should be tacky, but not stick to your thumb.

Variations in grain and pattern.

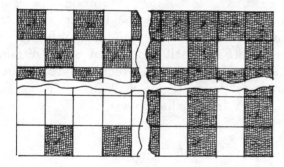

Applying Cement

Spread an even coat of brushing grade tile cement over one fourth of the room. Be sure to follow the manufacturer's directions. Cement for vinyl-asbestos tile can be applied with a brush.

Cement for embossed vinyl-asbestos tile should be applied with a trowel.

Usually the cement will dry to the proper consistency in about fifteen minutes, but variations in temperature and humidity can alter this. Check the consistency by placing your thumb in the cement. It should feel tacky, but should not stick to your finger. If it does stick, wait a little longer and test it again.

Laying the Tile

Start at the markings in the center of the floor. Be sure the first tile is square with the lines you have marked. If the first tile is placed incorrectly, all other tiles will be also, as the first tile serves as your guide.

Lay each tile firmly in position. Do not attempt to slide it. Each tile should be butted against the previous one. Tile should be laid alternately toward each wall. This will counteract the expansion and contraction of the tiles and also adds to the appearance.

Lay tiles, starting at center.

To cut the border tile use the following method. Place a loose tile over the last tile in the row. Then take another tile and butt it against the wall and mark the point where the two tiles overlap. Cut the tile along the line you have marked with a pair of scissors. The tile will cut more easily if it is warm.

The cut portion of the first tile will now slip into the border space. Be sure the tile to be cut is placed face up and at right angles to the grain of the tile below it. This ensures the correct pattern when it is laid.

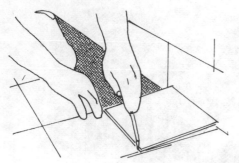

Measure, cut, and lay end tiles.

Border tile will fit exactly into place.

If you find it necessary to lay tiles around pipes or other odd-shaped obstructions, cut a paper pattern, trace the pattern onto the tile, and cut to fit.

A paper pattern will help in cutting tiles for pipes.

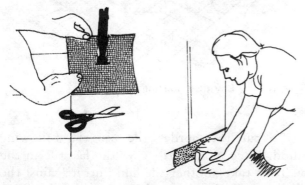

Vinyl cove base adds finishing touch.

Vinyl cove bases of matching or contrasting colors are also available. Not only does the cove base give a finished look to your new floor, but it also aids in cleaning.

To ensure a good bond between the tile and the cement, it is best not to wash the floor for at least a week after installation.

SELF-STICKING WOOD TILES

No nailing, or messy mastic is needed; simply peel off the tape and press in place; that's the appeal of these new hardwood floor tiles. Installation for an average-size room (12 x 15) should take no longer than an easy four hours. The secret is a tape-application method. An extremely strong, pressure-sensitive tape is utilized to permanently bond the tile to the floor.

The tiles can be installed over concrete, plywood, any kind of tile or old wood floors. Make sure the surface is free of dust, wax, oil, grease or moisture and reasonably level. On concrete that continues to "dust," a good grade of latex acrylic primer should be used.

If the room has a quarter-round baseboard molding, it should be carefully removed for later re-installation. Room temperature should not be below 60 degrees F. prior to and during installation. Avoid any pressure on the tiles until properly positioned. If they are stepped on before they're exactly in place, they may be pried up with a screwdriver and repositioned.

Proper installation requires an accurate beginning. After the floor is thoroughly cleaned, measure 36 inches from the longest wall in the room. Starting from the adjoining wall (wall B), measure off on chalk line X an exact distance, divisible by nine inches, which will reach somewhere near the center of chalk line X. Next, snap chalk line Y from wall A to wall C.

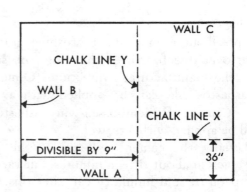

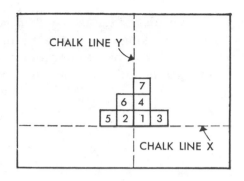

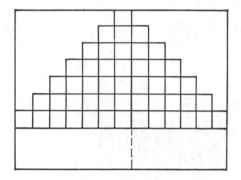

Strip the protective covering from the tape on the back of tile 1 and lay it at the point where the chalk lines intersect, with the grooved edge over line X. Then position tiles 2 and 3. Make certain these key tiles are perfectly aligned with the chalk line. Press tiles down with your hand. Now install tiles 4, 5, 6 and 7 around the center tiles in a pyramid pattern. Once the basic pyramid pattern has been established, start laying tiles accordingly, fitting the tongues into grooves. Continue until opposite wall is reached. Fill in the uncovered area. Return to the starting point and lay the blocks in a similar manner in the area between chalk line X and wall A. Replace the quarter round, and buff the tiles with a soft cloth.

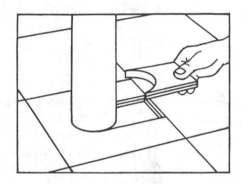

Self-sticking hardwood tiles are easy to install. Merely peel off tape, position tongue and grooves and press tile in place.

WOOD FLOOR FINISHING

Floor varnishes are available in high, medium and low glosses, the selection depending largely on personal preference. The newer urethane varnishes cost slightly more than the older types, but usually are longer wearing, so choose the varnish according to the wear the floor will receive.

A variety of floor finishes is available.

Obtaining a perfect finish takes time, most of it in preparing the floor. This usually is done with a power sander. The first cut can be made at a 45 degree angle across the grain, then successive cuts should be made with the grain. Use No. 2 or 2½ sandpaper on the first cut, 1 or 1½ on the second, ½ on the third and No. 0 or 00 on the final pass.

When the sanding is done, use a vacuum cleaner to remove all dust. It is important after sanding to immediately apply the varnish. Raw wood will collect moisture which may lift the

After sanding immediately vacuum all dirt and dust.

grain, and dirt or stains may damage the flooring. Work in stocking feet to avoid scuffing the floor.

Stain is the first step in finishing, and is used to change the color of the wood and accentuate grain. If the wood color is satisfactory, this step may be skipped. If stain is used, let it dry for 24 hours.

Using a stain, let it dry for 24 hours.

If the floor is oak, it will require the use of a paste or liquid filler, available at paint and hardware stores.

The next step is optional; the use of a sealer. This material penetrates the fibers of the wood to form a wear-resistant surface, and provide a good base for varnish. If varnish is to be applied, lightly sand the sealer.

Now you're ready to apply varnish. If you have not used sealer, two coats are required. Be sure both floor and brush are free of dust. Air bubbles may appear in varnish films, caused by bristles of the brush. To avoid them, don't brush too much. Apply the varnish with smooth, even strokes. If bubbles do appear, brush back into the area with light, feathering strokes.

Let the varnish dry for several hours. Some types dry faster than others so read the manufacturer's instructions carefully. Don't let dust settle on the wet varnish film, as this will cause a speckled appearance; keep doors and windows closed. Sand the first coat of varnish lightly before applying the second.

LAYING ROLL GOODS

Surface Preparation

The most common types of roll goods available today are vinyl sheet goods, rotovinyl sheet goods, linoleum or felt base. Although some of these materials are stiffer than others, these directions apply for installing any type of roll goods.

Sand or plane any high spots in the existing flooring; fill any low spots. This provides a smooth substructure for the new flooring. The floor base should also be clean and free of grease, oil and wax. Paint and varnish should also be removed. Allow a scrubbed floor to dry completely before applying the new floor covering. If the existing flooring is in very poor condition, it may be necessary to install a plywood base. Secure the plywood base with nails or cement. If you use nails, be sure that they are at the same level as the plywood, otherwise they will show through the new floor covering. Sand the edges of the plywood sheets to eliminate any rough spots.

Measuring and Cutting

Unroll a section of material in the same direction as you plan to lay it. Cut the roll goods approximately 2 to 3 inches longer than the length of the room.

Scribe along wall.

Position the strip, allowing about 1 inch of excess material to ride against the end wall. This surplus will be cut away in the trimming.

With the scribed edge set firmly against the side wall, draw a chalk line along the long edge of the material.

Using any straightedge, draw a line on the yard goods and out onto the floor. This line should be drawn approximately 2 inches from the end wall.

Unroll, measure, and cut roll goods.

Lay this first strip along one wall and scribe along that wall, using the heavy dividers held at right angles to the wall. Bear down heavily so you will transfer to the sheet goods any irregularities in the wall line. Trim the scribed side of the material with a linoleum knife. Be sure to follow the scribed line carefully.

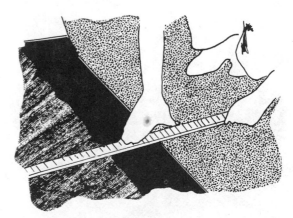

Mark lines along edge, across roll goods and onto floor.

Pull the surplus material down off the wall and butt the end of the roll goods tightly against the wall. Measure the offset between the two lines using the scriber. The amount you have just measured is the amount of material that you should cut away at the end of the run of yard goods.

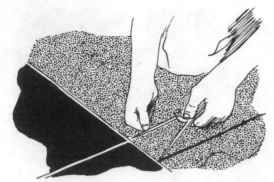

Butt ends of goods against wall and measure offset with scriber.

Now, at the end of the yard goods, scribe this measure along the wall. This procedure will tell you how much to cut away at the end of the roll and indicate any irregularities in the wall.

You can allow about 1/8 inch between the end of the yard goods and the wall, as the quarter round or other molding will conceal this space. You can now cut the end of the roll goods with a linoleum knife.

Repeat this process for each strip of roll goods needed to cover the floor.

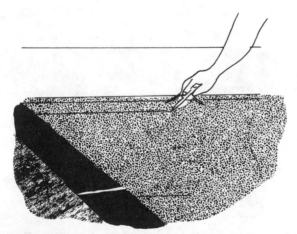

Scribe and cut end to the measurements you have marked.

Installation

Although most modern roll goods can be laid directly on any solid and even surface, in some cases a felt lining or base coat may be necessary.

Spread adhesive evenly across the floor, using a notched plasterer's trowel. Use the adhesive recommended by the manufacturer of the roll goods. Cover the entire floor surface evenly. This will eliminate the possibility of blisters in the finished job.

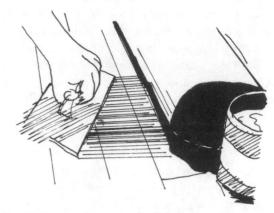

Adhesive is spread with a notched plastering trowel.

Usually you can safely spread adhesive on about 36 square feet of floor. Do not, however, spread a surface area so large that a skin forms on the adhesive before you can lay the material. Be sure to cover the adhesive container when not in use.

Unroll each sheet of roll goods as you need it and lay it firmly in place.

Roll goods are laid over area where adhesive has been applied.

If joints are necessary, use the overlapping technique. That is, lap the second sheet about ¾ inch over the end of the sheet you have laid. Adjust the straightedge and cut through the top sheet with enough pressure to mark the bottom one.

Overlap two sheets and cut through both to achieve a tight fit.

Lifting the top sheet, trim the bottom along the lines marked with the straightedge. This will give you a smooth and even fit. Use pressure to fit the roll goods at the seams. A hammer is an ideal tool for this purpose, but any heavy object with a smooth head will do the job equally well.

Be sure to clean up any excess adhesive before it dries.

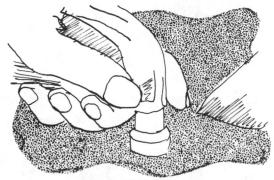

Use pressure to make seams fit.

If you have to make uneven cuts around doors or other offsets, use your dividers, setting them to slightly more than the width of the door facing. Using this dimension, scribe completely along the wall. This will transfer the shape of the door facing to the linoleum, which you can then cut to fit.

Use a scriber to transfer pattern to be cut to fit around doors, etc.

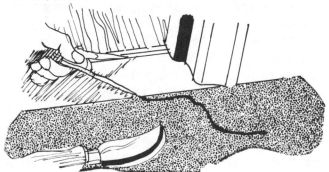

Use heavy dividers for cutting holes to fit pipes or posts. Mark the position of the pipe or post and place the center leg of the dividers direcly in the center of the area to be cut. Applying adequate pressure, use the outer leg to cut through the yard goods. After you have removed the circle, cut a slit to it that will enable you to place the roll goods around the pipe.

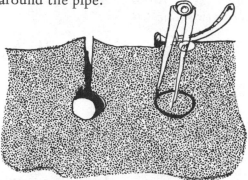

A divider can be used to cut holes for pipes.

When laying roll goods from one room to another, you might have to make adjustments for differences in the level of the two rooms. One method of easing the difference between the two levels is to feather-edge pieces of felt to widths of about 2, 4 and 6 inches. Then stack the pieces of felt in staircase fashion.

Finishing

Now you are ready to add a feature strip if desired. A feature strip is a section of goods of contrasting color or design which is installed along the edges of the roll goods. Using the dividers, determine the exact width of the feature strip you will be installing. With the dividers set to this exact dimension, use a straightedge to mark the area on the floor where the feature strip is to be inserted. It should be marked at a distance of 6 to 8 inches from the wall. Using a sharp linoleum knife and a straightedge, cut this strip out of the flooring and insert the feature strip.

Insert a trim of contrasting color if you desire.

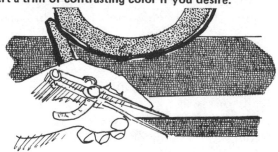

If you prefer, you can install a border around the edge of the roll goods instead of a feature strip. Make sure that the border you are installing is at least 6 inches wide. Miter the border at joints by overlapping two border pieces at the corner and cutting through the piece diagonally from the wall to the corner. Then cut the bottom piece along the same line. The two pieces will now fit snugly together at this joint.

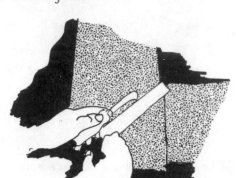

Or, you can use a border of a different color.

Cove type bases, usually molded from vinyl plastics, are also available for a do-it-yourself custom trim job. Special corner pieces are available for inside and outside corners. Although many people prefer to use quarter rounds, cove base molding is recommended for use in such rooms as kitchens where the floor will be subject to frequent washings.

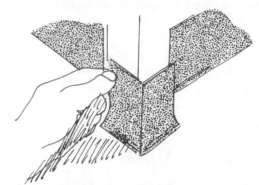

A cove base gives the new floor a neat look and aids in cleaning.

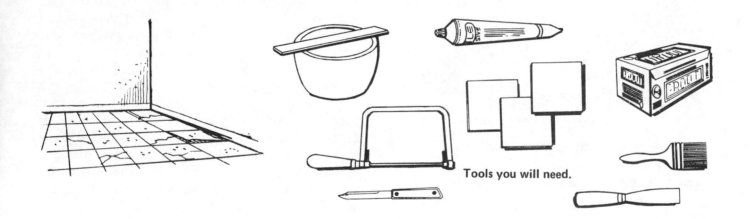

Tools you will need.

TILE REPAIRS

Tile that has come loose from walls or floors or is damaged should be replaced promptly. You will require the following tools to accomplish this job:

    Something to mix in.
    Adhesive.
    Paint brush or putty knife.
    Knife or saw.
    New tile (if needed).
    Grout—for ceramic or plastic tile.

Flexible Tile

First remove all loose or damaged tile. A warm iron will aid in softening the tile and making removal easier.

Scrape the old adhesive from the floor or wall and also from the tile if you will be reusing it. Be sure to fit the tiles carefully. Some tiles can be cut with a knife or a shears, others with a saw. Tile is less likely to break if it is warm.

Spread the adhesive on the wall or floor with a paint brush or putty knife.   Wait until it begins to set before installing the new tile. Position

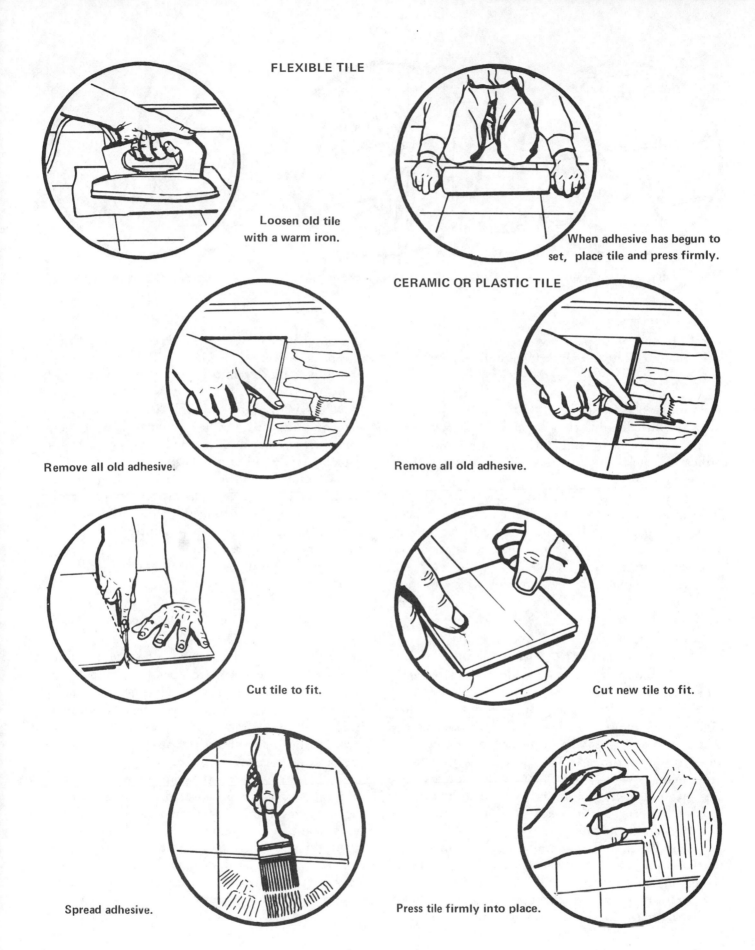

FLEXIBLE TILE

Loosen old tile with a warm iron.

When adhesive has begun to set, place tile and press firmly.

CERAMIC OR PLASTIC TILE

Remove all old adhesive.

Remove all old adhesive.

Cut tile to fit.

Cut new tile to fit.

Spread adhesive.

Press tile firmly into place.

Fill joints with grout.

Remove excess grout before it dries.

Clean tools immediately.

carefully and press it firmly into place. You might find that a rolling pin works well in helping you do this.

Ceramic or Plastic Tile

As with flexible tile, be sure the floor or wall surface is free of the old adhesive. Also remove the adhesive from the back of the old tile if you will be reusing it.

If you are using new tile you will need to fit it. Mark it carefully to size and cut with a saw. You can make straight cuts on tile by scoring it first. Then it will snap off if you press it on the edge of a hard surface.

Spread the adhesive on the wall or floor and on the back of the tile. Press the tile firmly into place.

Joints on ceramic tile should be filled with grout after the tile has firmly set. Mix the grout (powder) with water to form a stiff paste. Press the mixture into the joints with your fingers. Smooth the surface. For small jobs, grout is also available ready-mixed in tubes.

Carefully remove excess grout from the tile surface before it dries. Discard the excess grout mixture, but not down the drain! Be sure to clean all surfaces and tools promptly, as hardened grout is difficult to remove.

Let the grout cure over night before exposing it to moisture.

"PAINT" A FLOOR OR COUNTER TOP

Is the counter top in your kitchen scarred and scratched from years of use? Is the linoleum or tile on the floor dull and dingy from countless scrubbings? How about the tile on the bathroom floor; is it so old and worn that it never looks clean even when freshly scrubbed? The lavatory, is it dull and drab? You now can "paint" a new floor or counter top in almost any color, and with an infinite variety of patterns, from flakes of solid colors on to bits of gleaming metallic.

The basis of the system is a coat of either urethane or epoxy-based clear glaze into which flakes of material are tossed. The flakes settle into the partly-set glaze, then become firmly embedded when the glaze hardens. A light sanding smooths the surface, then another coat of glaze is applied to finish the job. For a deeper look, and longer wear, several coats of the clear glaze can be applied. Later, in areas that get more wear, as in front of a sink or range, or at a doorway, the surface can be renewed with another application of one or more coats of the glaze.

The first step in the application is to prepare the surface to be covered. If there are loose tiles on the floor, they should be nailed down. Loose laminate on a counter top should be reglued. If the floor is concrete, it also must be smoothed. Chipped and damaged areas should be leveled with latex patching materials. In cases where the floor of a kitchen is badly worn, it may be easier to nail down plywood or hardboard underlayment. In

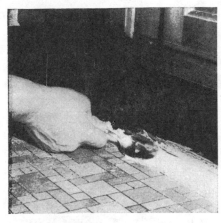

Surface preparation is important; it must be level and smooth, all loose material removed. Cove is of wood putty.

On ceramic tile, other slick surfaces, epoxy material is used. Fairly thick coating is spread over the surfaces.

Vinyl chips are self-leveling, tend to fall flat. On horizontal surfaces chips are tossed, allowed to fall like snow.

Complete and thorough masking is important to assure a neat job. Fixtures can be removed for easier job or masked.

Masking can be removed to permit easier sanding. Sand smooth and apply glaze coat.

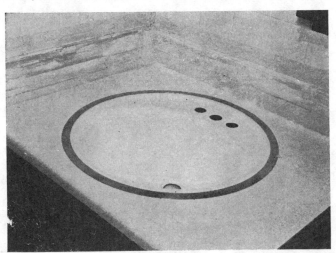

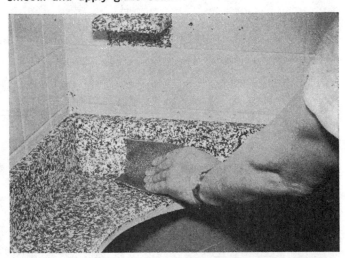

After base coat has set, excess flakes are brushed up, saved for reuse elsewhere. Shoe covers prevent dirt.

Inspect floor after flakes are brushed. Where coverage is insufficient, glaze area and "rechip." Glaze is final coat.

Glaze dries in about 45 min., then can be sanded, dust vacuumed up, final glaze coat applied.

bathrooms with ceramic floors, the tiles should be cemented firmly in place, and any missing tiles should be replaced with latex patching material.

All loose material should be vacuumed from the surface and any grease or wax should be removed. Although not absolutely necessary, a cove at the edges of a floor or countertop will make the surface much easier to clean and no dirt will collect in the corners. Wood putty is used to make the cove, it being shaped with the back of a spoon. Mask all areas that are not to be treated. The masking operation is shown clearly in the photos. Note in the bathroom that the upper row of tile is masked and it also is treated to match the floor and counter top.

On plastic laminate (Formica, Texolite, Micarta, etc.) as well as glazed ceramic tile, an epoxy-base material is applied, as it will adhere to the smooth surfaces. The material is applied with a roller, allowed to set for a few moments, then the flakes of color are tossed into the air and allowed to fall like snow. The flakes are largely self-leveling and will fall flat. When the glaze coat has set (epoxy takes a couple of hours, the regular urethane sets in 30 to 45 minutes), the surface is sanded lightly, if the dispersion of chips is satisfactory. If there are areas that seem to not have enough chips, another coat of glaze is applied in just those areas, and more chips are tossed over the surface. Loose chips or flakes are swept up and saved for use somewhere else. All dust is vacuumed from the surface and it is sanded lightly to remove any projecting flakes or roughness. A final coat of glaze is then applied. For a truly long-wearing surface several coats can be applied, which also will give the surface a depth of color that is truly beautiful.

The finished surface will have a gloss, but needs no waxing. Indeed, it is suggested that wax not be used. A light wiping with a damp cloth will remove most soiling.

The amazing material can be applied to metal surfaces, such as a diving board, as it will flex with the metal, rather than cracking. When the material is used on concrete walks, steps, patios, swimming-pool decks or other areas where rain could make the surface slick, white sand-blasting grit is tossed onto the partly-set glaze after the flakes of color are applied. The surface produced is nonskid, but still has the color and gloss that makes it truly attractive.

On lavatory allow final glaze coat to dry overnight. Fixtures then can be installed, and water will cause no problem.

CEILING BEAMS

If you have early-American furniture and decor in your home, you can add to the overall atmosphere by installing attractive ceiling beams. They are light in weight and easy to install, as opposed to real beams that are heavy, rather expensive and difficult to hang solidly and safely.

Planning

The first thing to decide if you want to install beams is to determine whether the beams will run the width or length of a room. Beams running the length of a room will make it appear longer and narrower. When run the width, beams will make a room seem wider but shorter. The next step is to figure the spacing for the beams. Generally they will be 30 to 36 inches apart. In the main, the beams should be spaced as though they actually were structural members that supported the ceiling. Thus, a small room will require only light beams, rather widely spaced. A larger room, of course, calls for larger beams, spaced more closely.

Installation

Nailers and hanger brackets (see drawing)

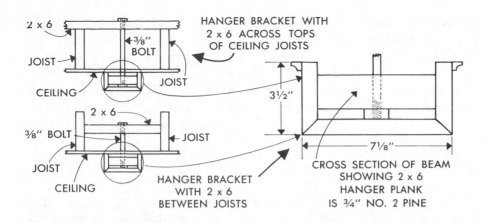

2 × 6

JOIST

CEILING

3/8" BOLT

HANGER BRACKET WITH 2 × 6 ACROSS TOPS OF CEILING JOISTS

JOIST

3/8" BOLT

JOIST

2 × 6

JOIST

CEILING

HANGER BRACKET WITH 2 × 6 BETWEEN JOISTS

3½"

7⅛"

CROSS SECTION OF BEAM SHOWING 2 × 6 HANGER PLANK IS ¾" NO. 2 PINE

Distress the beams to give "hand-hewn" look with axe, drawknife, files.

Nailers are lengths of 1 x 2 on the side walls, pieces of 2 x 4 or 2 x 6 on the ends of what will be the beams. Drill holes for lag-screw clearance.

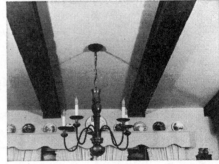

are the sole support for the fabricated beams, so they must be solidly attached so they will not loosen as the years pass. There should be a nailer at each end of each beam, and a hanger at the center. (If the beams are more than 12 feet long, two or more hangers are suggested.) Short lengths of 2 x 6 are ideal as nailers, as they provide generous nailing area, and can be drilled to accept lag screws that arc driven into the wall into the studs or headers.

Hanger brackets should be no less than 2 x 6 lumber, either running across the tops of the ceiling joists, or between them, depending on whether or not a finished floor is to be installed above or already exists above.

The three pieces of the beams can simply be butted together, but they will look much more authentic if the edges are mitered so the two lower edges of the beams are joined almost invisibly. Remember that beams butted against side walls will have only one lower edge, and require only one miter joint.

Because few rooms are square, and few walls are plumb, fit each beam in place separately. Glue and nail the beams together using 2-inch finishing nails. Countersink all nail heads. The assembled beams then can be returned to the shop and "distressed" to look genuine.

In the case of longer beams, it is better to assemble them in place after the component pieces are distressed. This is because it is necessary to assemble the beams around the supports and hangers, with a long 3/8-inch bolt supporting the 2 x 6 blocks that are hangers.

Stain the beams; one coat for light, two for dark. Two coats of clear lacquer are next, finally a coat of paste wax well buffed. Cove molding or quarter-round can be used against the ceiling and wall to seal those joints; especially if wall or ceiling is rough.

INSTALLING A SUSPENDED CEILING

If you are tired of looking at that rundown plaster ceiling with the hole, cracks and patches showing its age, then perhaps you should consider installing a suspended ceiling.

Planning

Take exact measurements of the room where the ceiling will be installed. Carefully measure any odd-shaped portions of the room. Next, transfer these measurements to graph paper, or bring the dimensions with you to a dealer who will be able to assist you in determining the materials you will need for the job.

Ceiling panels are available in 2-foot x 2-foot or 2-foot x 4-foot patterns. The materials required may be different depending upon the pattern you select. If you have chosen a 2x4 pattern you then may use the standard or reverse pattern. This is merely a matter of appearance and personal preference.

Sketch the layout for the ceiling on graph paper. The main tees should be drawn 4 feet apart and positioned in such a way that border patterns at the room edges are equal on both sides and at the same time as large as possible. It may be necessary to sketch more than one layout.

It is most important that the cross tees be spaced so the border panels at the ends of the room are equal and as large as possible. The 2x4 pattern will require cross tees 2 feet apart; the 2x2 pattern needs 2-foot cross tees added between the midpoints of the 4-foot cross tees.

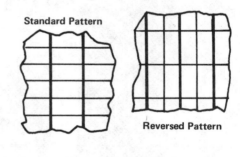

Standard Pattern   **Reversed Pattern**

Patterns for 2 x 4 panels.

If you will be adding built-in lighting, decide where these panels will be located and indicate them on your layout. Armed with your drawing, you should now be able to make a fair determination of the cost of materials.

Installing Wall Angles

Determine the exact height at which the ceiling is to be installed. If you are also installing recessed lights, allow a minimum of 6 inches of clearance between the old and the new ceilings. Install the appropriate lighting fixtures before any further work is done.

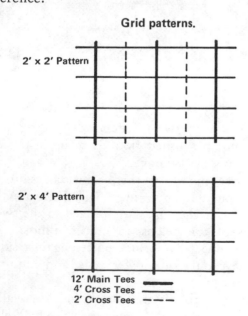

Grid patterns.

2' x 2' Pattern

2' x 4' Pattern

12' Main Tees
4' Cross Tees
2' Cross Tees

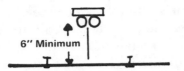

6" Minimum

Allow at least 6 inches of space if installing recessed lighting.

After determining the height of the new ceiling, use a level to draw a line completely around the room which will indicate the position of the wall angles. The bottom flange of the wall angle should sit on the line you have drawn. Fasten the wall angles firmly to the walls. Nail wall angles to studs or use screw anchors or other masonry fasteners on brick or masonry walls. Overlap the wall angles on inside corners; on outside corners miter the wall angles.

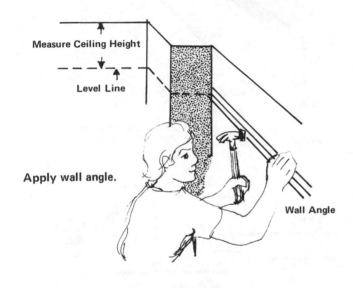

Measure Ceiling Height

Level Line

Apply wall angle.

Wall Angle

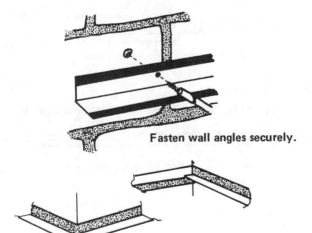

Fasten wall angles securely.

Suspension Wire Installation

If recessed lights are to be used, the wiring and lighting fixtures should be installed before the suspension wires for the tees are put into place.

Commonly used are two tube flourescent fixtures centered over a 2x4 panel with a luminous layin panel inserted instead of the regular ceiling tile.

The location of each main tee (which should always run at right angles to the joists in the room) can be indicated by stretching a tight line from the top edge of the wall angle on each side of the room at each point where the main tees are to be placed (refer to your drawing).

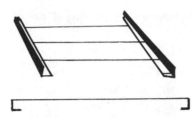

Stretch lines from tops of wall angles where main tees are to be placed.

Cut suspension wires to the proper length, that is, 12 inches longer than the distance between the old ceiling and the new guidelines string which indicates the position of each main tee.

The first suspension wire for each main tee should be located directly above the point where the first cross tee meets the main tee. Again, check your original sketch to determine this location.

Suspension wires should be securely fastened. Fasten them to the ceiling with screw eyes, screw hooks, nails or by drilling.

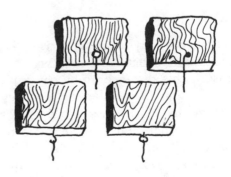

Methods of securing suspension wires.

231

Attach suspension wires every four feet along the level guideline. Pull on each wire to remove any kinks and then make a 90 degree bend where the suspension wire crosses the level line.

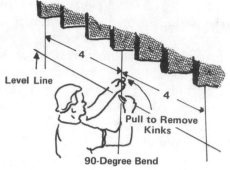

Connect suspension wires every 4 inches and bend.

Installing Main Tees

Most main tees are 12 feet long and have cross tee slots punched every 12 inches beginning 6 inches from each end.

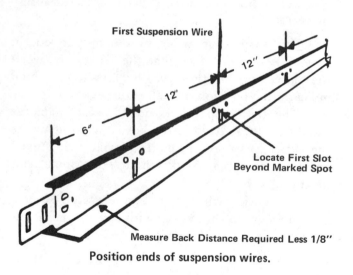

Position ends of suspension wires.

Using your layout sheet as a reference, determine the distance from the wall to the first tee. Measure this distance along the top flange of the main tee and locate the slot just beyond this point. From this slot measure back the same distance, less 1/8 inch and saw the main tee at that point. The 1/8 inch subtraction is for the wall angle thickness. Take into consideration whether or not the wall angles are square in positioning the cross tee slots.

If you are installing main tees in a room less than 12 feet across, cut the main tee to the exact measurement of the room; allow 1/8 inch for the thickness of the wall angle. If the room is wider than 12 feet, you can splice the main tees. Be sure to align them properly so that the suspension wires are correctly positioned.

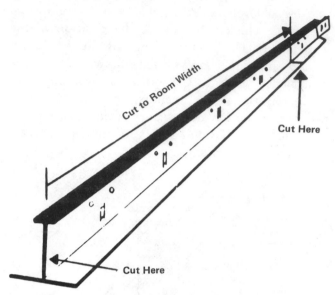

For a room less than 12 feet across, cut main tee to room width less 1/8 inch.

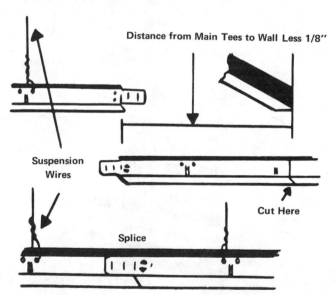

For rooms more than 12 feet across, splice main tees together.

Install the main tees; be sure to keep them level with the wall angle. Measure them with a long level at frequent intervals.

Align main tees with a level.

Cross Tee and Border Cross Tee Installation

Install cross tees by inserting the ends of the cross tees into the slots in the main tees. Refer to the manufacturer's instructions on how to attach them. The location of the cross tees will be determined by your selection of either 2x4 or 2x2 panels.

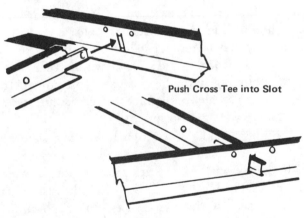

Insert cross tees into main tee slots.

The lock tab on the cross tee should be on the outside of the slot. Cross tees can usually be removed by depressing the lock tab with a screwdriver.

Install border cross tees between the wall angle and the last main tee. Measure from this last tee to the wall angle, allowing 1/8 inch for the thickness of the wall angle. Cut across tees and install by inserting the connector in the main tee and resting the cut edge on the wall angle.

Installing Panels

Ceiling panels can now be dropped into position by tilting them slightly, raising them through the framework, and then letting them drop into place. Border tiles must be cut to size. Using a sharp knife and working on a solid surface, cut the panel from the finished side. Use a straight-edge to ensure a clean cut.

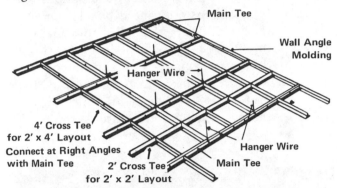

Tee arrangement for 2 x 4 and 2 x 2 patterns.

Tilt panel and drop into position.

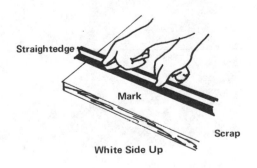

Cut border panels to proper size.

KEEP YOUR BASEMENT DRY

Water and excessive dampness in a basement often ruin furniture and other household goods and can also cause excessive humidity throughout the entire house. It provides a breeding place for germs, mosquitoes and other insects; promotes mildew and rusts tools; it may even contribute to depreciation of property value. Most serious basement water problems are caused by (1) porous or cracked walls and floors that allow outside water to seep in, and (2) backflow from overloaded sewers. Also, water may collect from condensation on coldwater pipes and on walls and floors during warm weather where humidity is high. Sometimes leaks develop in the water system.

Before.

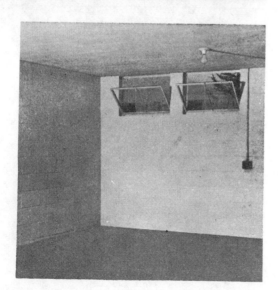

After.

Sealants for Masonry. In most cases it is possible to seal basement walls and floors from the inside effectively, even under conditions of severe water pressure. A quick-setting, cement-base putty is used to fill cracks and holes. One kind is especially formulated for use at joints subject to expansion and contraction, such as those between a basement floor and the walls. After plugging cracks and holes, a cement-base sealant is spread over the masonry surface. This, as well as the putty, anchors firmly in the pores of the masonry and prevents moisture penetration. A thinner finish coat in color can be added. Manufacturers of these products furnish detailed instructions on their use, which should be followed explicitly. The following details are based on information relating to one maker's products.

Surface Preparation. First you thoroughly clean the surfaces to which the waterproofing compounds are to be applied. Remove all loose dirt, defective cement, mortar and plaster droppings, efflorescence, oil, grease, whitewash, and at least 70 percent of adhering paint. You can chip off surplus cement, mortar and plaster. Scrub off paint, oil, soot and grease with a strong solution of household cleaning powder or caustic soda (1½ pounds of the latter per gallon of water). Always wear rubber gloves and a transparent face shield when scrubbing with these caustic solutions. After cleaning, rinse away all traces of the solution and the residue with a hose spray.

Filling Cracks and Holes. In sealing walls the first step is closing all cracks, holes and wall-to-floor joints with the quick-setting putty. Widen narrow cracks with a cold chisel so that the putty can be forced in deeply. Cracks not rough enough to anchor the putty should be undercut. Prepare only a small wad of putty about the size of an egg and use immediately because it sets in a few minutes which is indicated by its hardening and crumbling. When this occurs discard the putty in use and proceed with a fresh wad. Keep sides of cracks moist when pressing the putty in place for which you use a small trowel or putty knife. To fill large holes against water pressure apply the putty by hand, holding it in place until it sets. Build up the sides until they become small enough to insert a carrot-shaped plug of the putty.

When masonry-block walls hold considerable water it is advisable to drain them before starting to fill cracks. Drainage is accomplished by weep holes entering cores of blocks at floor level. The holes are drilled with a carbide-tipped bit in an electric drill or by means of a star drill and hammer. The weep holes are left open until 24 hours after the final application of sealing compound, at which time they are closed with carrot-shaped plugs and given two applications of sealer.

After a priming coat of sealer on the puttied areas, a heavy base coat is applied to lower portion of walls.

Water trapped inside of masonry blocks drained out through weep holes just above level of floor.

Application of second coat of the sealer over entire wall surface. Weep holes are plugged and coated last.

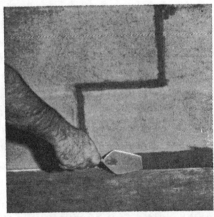

Quick-setting cement-base putty used to fill wall cracks and holes and joint between floor and walls.

Sealer and Finish Coats. To apply the sealer use a 6-inch tampico fiber brush—not a paint-brush. Or, you can use specially made 10- or 14-inch fiber brushes having long handles. In some cases the sealer is applied with a trowel in which case white silica sand is added as will be explained.

Dampen the wall at the repaired areas and apply a priming coat of the sealer. This prevents the puttied spots from showing up darker after the sealing has been completed. For basement walls subject to ordinary water pressure, brush on a heavy base coat up to about 30 inches above floor level, dampening the area to be coated. The base coat should be applied at the rate of 2 pounds per square yard. Be sure to keep the masonry surface damp just ahead of the sealer application. If the wall becomes dry or the sealer starts to pull during application, redampen the wall. Then apply a second coat of sealer. This goes over the entire wall at 1 pound per square yard. Following this you can apply a colored finish coat, ½ pounds per square yard, which will produce an extra-smooth surface.

For basement walls subject to severe water pressure, or where a smooth plastered surface is desired, brush sealer over the entire wall, 2 pounds per square yard, allow to dry for 12 hours, then trowel on sealer of plaster consistency at the rate of 10 pounds per square yard. To prepare sealer for troweling add and thoroughly mix clean, white silica sand in the proportion of 25 pounds per 50-pound bag of the sealer. Trowel to a smooth surface concealing all form marks and construction faults. A color finish coat can be added over this.

Basement Floors. Concrete floors that are in relatively good condition can be waterproofed similarly after a thorough cleaning, and filling of cracks and holes as previously explained. Brush on two coats of sealer, each at a minimum of 2 pounds per square yard. For smooth surface and color you can add a coat of the finish sealer.

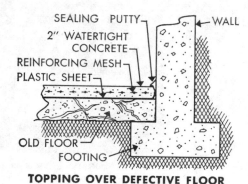

TOPPING OVER DEFECTIVE FLOOR

Badly cracked and broken floors should be either topped with a 2-inch layer of watertight concrete (1-2¼-3 mix with minimum amount of water for workability with trowel), or the floor should be replaced with watertight concrete. Topping entails complications such as raising floor drains to come flush with the higher floor surface. Replacement involves the breaking up and removal of the old floor. In either case a continuous sheet of polyethylene plastic of suitable thickness is first laid down as an additional precaution should cracks develop later. This is brought up at walls almost to the floor surface so that the joint can be sealed later with the sealing putty. Where the plastic is cut to fit around pipes and other projections, or where two pieces overlap, the joints are sealed with a special cement. Wire-mesh reinforcement for use in concrete floors is advisable

to prevent cracking. If water interferes with laying a floor it must be conveyed to a sump and pumped away, and the soil allowed to dry before laying the concrete.

Diversion of Water from Walls

Sometimes there's only occasional water leakage into a basement from a specific source that can be readily identified and eliminated. Then it may be possible to keep water out of the basement without the need of sealing the walls and floor. For example, basement window wells that are not provided with drains may accumulate enough

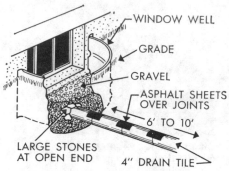

DRAINAGE OF WINDOW WELLS

water from rain or melting snow to flow over the window sills and into the basement. The solution is proper drainage of the wells. A drain-tile line is laid under the well and slopes downward away from the house for a distance of 6 to 10 feet. Gravel is substituted for earth in the well and about 6 inches below it. Large stones at the open end of the pipe will keep the gravel out. In case there is an existing drain line along the foundation footing, the gravel bed of a window well can be continued down to the drain line and a separate drain will not be required.

Another situation is that of gutter downspouts dispersing water along a foundation where it sinks into the ground and gets into a basement at the floor-to-wall joint, as well as through cracks in the wall, or seepage through a porous wall. By simply connecting the downspout to a plastic, vitrified-clay or cast-iron pipe, preferably buried, the water can be disposed of at some distance from the house at a lower level or into a dry well. The dry well may consist of concrete blocks set up to a cone shape so the inside diameter at bottom is about 40 inches.

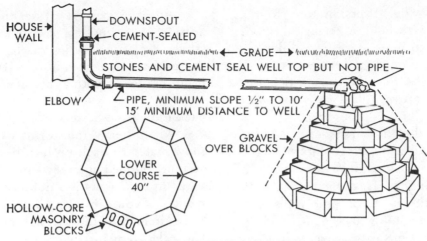

DIVERSION OF DOWNSPOUT WATER TO DRY WELL

A third instance is diversion of surface water running downhill toward a house. In this case a line of 6-inch drain tile is laid along the foundation footing. This may be completely effective in keeping water out of the basement. The drain line slopes to a lower level or empties into a dry well located not less than 15 feet from the house. The slope of the line should not be less than ½ inch in 10 or 12 feet.

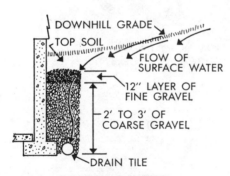

DIVERTING WATER FROM SLOPE TOWARD HOUSE

The drain tile is laid on undisturbed subsoil scraped down to the drainage slope. The pipe lengths are butted end to end and the joints covered with sheets of asphalt roofing to prevent the entrance of silt. These are held in place while the line is being covered with gravel or crushed stone to a depth of at least 2 feet, after which a layer of fine gravel and then topsoil is added to grade level.

Where subsoil is clay, the space between basement walls and surrounding clay, even when backfilled with soil, forms a reservoir which holds water and allows it to get into the basement. Frequently debris from construction is left in this space and is merely covered with topsoil. Subsequent rotting of the debris forms a sump at grade level. Cure for this situation is the same as previously discussed. The grade immediately adjoining a house should slope away from it for quick disposal of surface water, which is aided by a thick coat of turf. Sidewalks alongside a foundation wall should be slightly sloped for drainage to the far side. A flat area between two houses where water tends to collect can be drained.

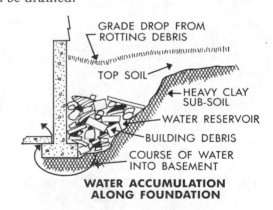

WATER ACCUMULATION ALONG FOUNDATION

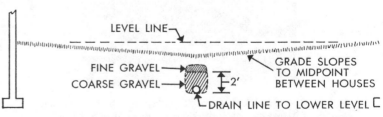

SWALE AND DRAINAGE BETWEEN ADJOINING HOUSES

237

The purpose of water diversion away from a foundation is not only to help in keeping it out of a basement but also to prevent structural damage to the house. Water in porous masonry walls creeps up by capillary action to the wood sills which may rot them if the sills are not laid on waterproof sill-sealing strips.

Houses built on filled-in marshland often have considerable trouble with wet basements when the water table rises above the basement floor level. Although thorough sealing of a basement can keep water out, new cracks in floor and walls may develop from settling and allow basement flooding. In such circumstances some home owners have resorted to automatic water control of the area immediately adjoining the house. This includes a drain line around the house conveying water to a sump pump which discharges it about 50 feet from the house.

Outside Waterproofing of Walls

When building a home having basement walls of masonry blocks, the walls can be sealed from the outside before the excavated space along them is back-filled. One method is to brush and trowel on sealer, same as for inside walls that are subject to severe water pressure, or to trowel on two coats of portland cement-plaster, each ¼-inch thick. The mix is proportioned to one sack of cement to 2½ cubic feet of damp mortar sand. The first coat is applied to a premoistened wall surface and is scratched to make it rough so that there will be good anchorage for the second coat. This can be applied the following day and troweled smoothly. It is kept moist for several days by sprinkling so it will dry slowly.

Portland-cement plaster being troweled on outside of newly erected masonry-block wall before back-filling.

Another method of sealing the wall on the outside is to apply a continuous layer of polyethylene plastic sheeting of the thickness used for this purpose. It comes in rolls 10 to 20 feet wide. Joints are sealed with a special cement.

Back Flow from Sewers

Where heavy rainstorms overload sewers and allow water to back up into basements, they may become flooded in a few minutes. Contaminated water in basements is a definite health hazard. To avoid this you can install a backwater valve in the house drain close to its outlet into the house sewer. The valve remains open when the water flow is toward the sewer but closes automatically when the flow is reversed. Most of these valves are made to accommodate a vertical length of pipe extending to floor level where it is capped. This arrangement makes the valve readily accessible for cleaning and repair.

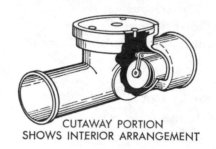

CUTAWAY PORTION SHOWS INTERIOR ARRANGEMENT

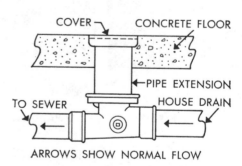

TYPICAL BACKWATER VALVE AND METHOD OF INSTALLATION

Condensation on Cold-Water Pipes

During warm weather when humidity is high, condensation-drip from cold-water pipes collects in puddles on the floor, and it may also collect on the adjacent walls. One way to avoid this trouble in basements that are kept closed to the entrance of humid air is to install an electric dehumidifier,

238

preferably one that is controlled automatically by means of a humidistat. Where humid air cannot be kept out of a basement, anti sweat coverings can be installed on cold-water pipes.

There are three kinds; flexible tape or strips

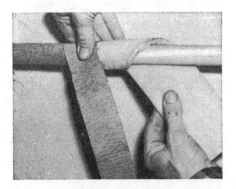

Fiber-glass insulation being wound on cold-water pipe and wrapped with vapor barrier to stop condensation.

Flexible tube of foam-type insulation with vapor barrier on outside surface comes in various sizes.

to wrap around the pipes, mastic for application with a brush or trowel, and flexible or rigid tubular jackets of various sizes. These coverings serve as insulation to reduce the transfer of cold from the pipe to the outer surface of the covering. They also have a vapor barrier that keeps moisture from penetrating to the pipe. The thickness of the insulation needed varies with the difference of temperature of the pipe and that of the surrounding air. It is important that the vapor barrier be continuous for maximum effectiveness.

Leaks in Water System

Leaks in a water system are infrequent. Instances of this are a defective water heater that requires replacement, worn washers or stem-packing of a water-heater drain or other valve. When water drips constantly from the overflow pipe that connects to the safety valve of a water heater the valve may need adjustment or replacement, or the heater thermostat may be set too high or be defective. Flexible hose connections to a washing machine as well as a flexible drain sump on many washers may deteriorate and develop leakage.

Basement Dampness

Being heavier than dry air, humid air tends to collect and remain in basements. Humidity is added by washing and drying of clothes as not all of it is removed by a dryer vent. Even though a basement has no standing water it may still be damp during warm weather in humid localities. The most practical solution for basement dampness is an electric dehumidifier as already mentioned. Keeping a basement dry will retard the formation of mold and mildew on paper, cloth, leather and wood.

7

EXTERIOR MAINTENANCE AND IMPROVEMENT

EXTERIOR MAINTENANCE AND IMPROVEMENT

7

BRICKS WITHOUT MORTAR ■ SEALANTS ■ POURING A CONCRETE SIDEWALK

WOOD WIDING ■ REROOFING ■ ABOUT CONCRETE BLOCKS ■ DRY PACK CONCRETE

WOOD DECAY ■ PROPER CONCRETE DEICERS ■ ALL ABOUT BRICK

LADDER SAFETY ■ CUTTING STONE ■ FENCES FOR YOUR HOME

USING CONCRETE ■ WOOD DECKS ■ BUILDING A FOUNTAIN ■ BUILDING A PATIO

LADDER SAFETY

Ladders, whether extension, straight or step, are indispensable to the do-it-yourself homeowner, especially for exterior work. With good maintenance and proper use a quality ladder will last for many years. Do not take short cuts in selecting, maintaining or using ladders.

Never use a damaged, bent or broken ladder, for obvious reasons. Never paint a ladder, since this can cover dangerous cracks or flaws.

Above all, a ladder must set firmly when being used. Each leg must be positioned firmly. The top of a straight ladder must rest against a solid surface. Set the bottom of a straight ladder out one-fourth the height of its support.

Always face a ladder when ascending or descending, and use only one rung at a time. Never reach beyond an easy arm's length.

Don't be tempted to move a ladder loaded down with tools and buckets. The results usually are spilled paint, hours of clean up and much muttering.

Step on the middle of each step or rung to assure proper weight distribution.

A stepladder should always be fully opened with the spreader or folding metal braces in a locked-down position. Never stand on the top step or pail shelf. The platform is only a shelf for tools or pails.

WOOD SIDING

Wood siding will keep any home attractive for many years to come. In fact, given reasonable care, wood siding will retain its beauty for centuries.

There are sound design and structural reasons, too, for using wood and wood-based materials for siding. It has a great flexibility and variety in patterns, sizes, and colors.

The hardheaded dollars-and-cents reasons are

Types of Wood Siding

Many kinds of wood siding based on lumber, plywood, and fiberboard are on the market today. All will give good service, provided each is used right. For houses, bevel siding is perhaps the most widely used. Drop siding and shiplap patterns are also used, especially on houses without sheathing. These patterns of siding are applied horizontally and tend to make a house appear lower and longer.

Vertical siding is increasingly popular on one-

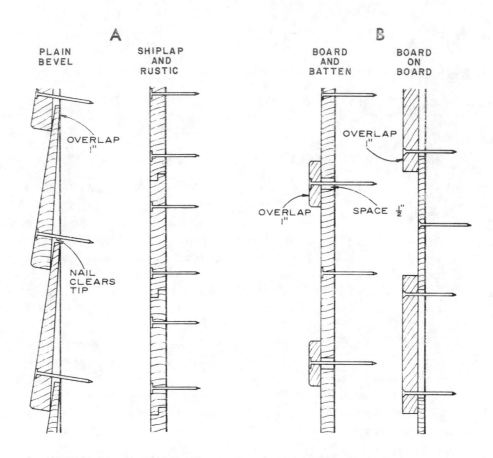

Patterns of wood siding and recommended nailing practices. A: horizontal application. B: vertical application.

wood's low initial cost and the ease and speed with which it can be sawed, fitted, and nailed into place. Other reasons are its fuel-saving value, due to the millions of tiny hollow fibers that make it a good insulator, and its natural resistance to weather.

Other reasons include wood's ability to hold a wide variety of finishes—clear ones that reveal and accentuate its natural beauty, stains that impart a rustic appearance, and paints of every conceivable color.

story houses. It consists of tongue-and-grooved boards or square-edged boards applied vertically, usually with narrow strips called battens nailed over the joints. Vertical patterns with smooth and rough-sawn surfaces are available in plywood of Douglas-fir, redwood, and western redcedar. Vertical siding tends to make a house appear taller.

The kind of siding chosen will depend on where the house is built, its price range, and the architectural effect wanted. A range of quality in lumber is available, from clean, smooth edge grained to rough, flat grained with knots and other characteristics that should be given special finishing treatments in accord with the effects wanted.

Paints last longer on edge-grained softwoods of low density that are low in swelling than on dense flat grained. Such flat-grained boards are better left rough sawn, and finished with a stain.

In painting flat-grained surfaces with broad bands of summerwood, special care should be given in selecting high-quality nonporous primers and topcoats that will protect the wood surface from excessive wetting with moisture (dew and rain).

Any wood surfaces such as those of plywood and fiberboards that are overlaid with resin-treated paper are excellent for painting. The overlay serves as a stabilizer against swelling from moisture.

Installation

Wood siding is simple to install. It is precision-manufactured to standard sizes, is easily cut, fitted, and fixed in place with ordinary tools.

Courses of horizontal siding should be spaced so that a single board runs continuously above and below windows and above doors without notching: Bevel siding 6 inches wide should have at least 1 inch of overlap between courses. Siding 8 inches or wider should overlap 1 to 1½ inches, depending on spacing required between window heights.

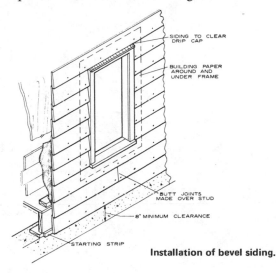

Installation of bevel siding.

Siding should be butted snugly and squarely against door and window casings, corner boards, and adjoining boards. (Corner boards should lie flat against the sheathing.) If metal corner covers are used, siding boards should be carefully cut to avoid leaving a hollow place under the corner cover where water could collect. Mitered corners should be precisely fitted for the same reason.

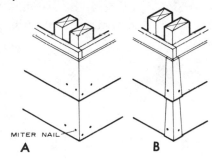

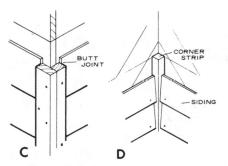

Recommended procedures for corners of siding: A, miter corners; B, metal corners; C, corner boards; D, interior corner.

To fasten siding in place, zinc-coated, aluminum, or other noncorrosive nails are recommended. Plain steel-wire nails, especially the large headed type that are designed for flush driving, make unslightly rust spots on most paints. Even small-headed plain steel nails, countersunk and puttied, are likely to spot the finish with rust. Natural finished siding is installed best with aluminum nails.

Nailing patterns for the various kinds of siding are very important for best performance, and should comply with the recommendations of the manufacturers.

Siding and Moisture

Wood siding is a part of the house; therefore, its performance is vitally affected by the rest of the structure.

Insulation, weatherstripping, and generally tight construction reduce fuel bills and make for comfort, but they may create some wintertime problems.

Water vapor formed within a house moves through the inner surfaces of the outer walls because of differences in temperature between the inside and outside. This water vapor condenses and collects as water or frost in the siding during the winter. With the return of warm weather in the spring, this moisture can—and often does—cause the exterior paint to blister. The problem has been further accentuated by air conditioning and by humidifying.

A number of measures can be taken to help keep moisture out of walls. One of the most effective is to put a good vapor barrier under the plaster, drywall, or paneling. Asphalt-coated paper, aluminum foil, and polyethylene film are good vapor barriers.

Rain and snow water must be kept out, too. Roof gutters must be sloped and have enough downspouts or they may overflow during rainstorms and let water seep into walls through joints in the siding. Attic floors should be well insulated and attic spaces ventilated so heat losses do not melt snow on roofs to produce dams and clog gutters.

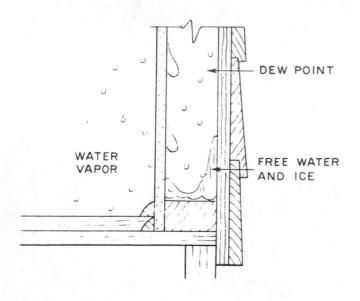

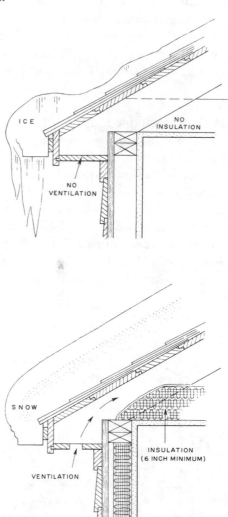

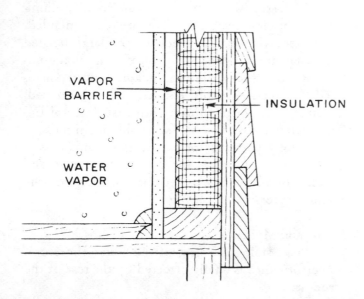

Vapor barriers avoid moisture problems in walls. Left, water vapor from inside house moved out through wall. When vapor met outside cold air, moisture condensed and froze. As outside temperatures rose in spring and summer, ice melted, and moisture was free to move through siding and destroy paint coating. Right, vapor barrier (on warm side of wall) has prevented moisture from getting into walls.

Snow and ice dams: Left, ice dams often build up on the overhang of roofs and in gutters and cause melting snow water to back up under shingles and under the facia board of closed cornices. Damage to ceilings inside and to paint outside results. Right, ice dams can be avoided by adequate ventilation and insulation.

Wide roof overhangs help in keeping moisture out. So too, does metal flashing in roof valleys, along dormers, and around chimneys. Window and door frames also need adequate cap flashing.

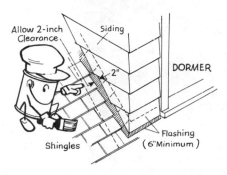

Metal flashing along dormers helps keep moisture out of siding; the flashing extends back of siding and under shingles.

A comparatively simple treatment for siding helps keep moisture out of walls. Siding can be dipped in a water-repellent preservative before it is installed or the water-repellent preservative can be brushed on after the siding is installed before it is painted. These preservatives are sold by lumber dealers and some paint stores. They contain fungicides, resins, and waxes (water repellent) that cause water to run off instead of penetrating into the wood at end and lap joints.

Finishes

The first finish on siding is the most important. It is the foundation for all subsequent finishes, and will probably remain there for the life of the house.

Selection of a finish must be made from two broad classes: (1) natural finishes and (2) paints. The natural finishes may be stains or preservatives. The choice will depend to a great extent on personal preference, with consideration of the advantages and disadvantages of each class of finish.

Natural Finishes. Natural-type finishes may either form a surface coat or penetrate the wood. Natural finishes that form a surface coating give a lustrous, even a glossy coating. These are chiefly spar varnishes. A really durable natural finish of this type has yet to be developed.

The penetrating natural finishes leave little or no continuous coating on the surface. Because there is no coating, there is no failure by blistering or peeling. These finishes are, therefore, ideally suited for rough and flat-grained surfaces that are difficult to paint effectively. Penetrating natural finishes include oil-base penetrating pigmented stains and water-repellent preservative finishes. Water-repellent preservatives penetrate wood readily and protect it from end staining, excessive cupping or twisting, and mildew. Wood finished in this manner will weather to a clean-buckskin or a light-tan color. Preservative-type finishes usually need refurbishing about every 2 years. Adding pigment to the water-repellent preservative will enhance the durability. Penetrating pigmented stains can be applied at any time over the water-repellent preservative treatment.

Good penetrating pigmented stains are inexpensive and much more durable than water-repellent preservative-type finishes. Stains penetrate and color wood, partially obscure the grain, but leave little or no surface film. Rough-sawn weathered wood and absorptive surfaces are especially suitable for stains. Good stains should last at least 5 years, and may last as long as 9 or 10. Even on planed surfaces, they will last at least as long as many paints before needing renewal.

House Paints. House paint is the most widely used finish for wood siding, and white is the most popular color. A good house paint should last at least 4 to 5 years before it must be renewed. See the chapter on Paints and Finishes for more information.

WOOD DECAY

Seasoned, properly used wood is a dependable building material. In properly designed houses that are well built and well maintained, decay causes little damage. Most damage can be avoided. Prevention is cheap; cure is sometimes costly.

Cause of Damage

Wood decay is caused by minute plants called fungi. These plants consist of microscopic threads that are visible to the naked eye only when many of them occur together. But it is easy to see the fruiting bodies of fungi, from which their spores are distributed. Some fungi merely discolor wood, but decay fungi destroy the fiber. Decayed wood is often dry in the final stages, but not while the decay is taking place, because fungi cannot work in dry wood. That is why there is no such thing as "dry rot," and why decay is a minor problem in the driest parts of the country.

Two species of fungi spread from moist soil

A decay fungus and its effect on wood. Fungi consist mainly of tiny threads that grow within the wood and can be seen there only with a microscope. In very moist air they may develop on the surface in sufficient quantity to be visible. The upper part of this piece of wood is softened and weakened, and the lower edge is cracked and nearly disintegrated. Decay fungi make no definite galleries like those cut by termites.

Fruiting bodies of different types of wood-rotting fungi. A, One of the bracket fungi common on softwoods exposed to rain. B, Upper and lower surfaces of a gill fungus. C, The crustlike fruiting body of a pore fungus. The microscopic spores which serve to spread these fungi to new locations are produced on the gills or pore surfaces on the under sides of the fruiting bodies.

or wood into dry wood by conducting water to wood through vinelike structures. Occasionally they cause great damage to buildings, but fortunately most fungi cannot conduct moisture in this way.

Fungi and termites may sometimes work in the same wood. Decay fungi soften the wood and, in the final stages, make it spongy or cause it to shrink or crack and crumble. None of the fungi produces the continuous, clear-cut tunnels or galleries characteristic of termite infestation.

Serious decay damage is most often due to one or more of the following errors in construction or maintenance:

1. Undrained soil and insufficient ventilation under basementless houses.
2. Wood such as grade stakes, concrete forms, or stumps left on or in soil under houses.
3. Wood parts of the house in direct contact with the soil, especially at dirt-filled porches.
4. Wood parts embedded in masonry near the ground.
5. Use of unseasoned and infected lumber.
6. Sheathing paper that is not sufficiently permeable to moisture vapor.
7. Inadequate flashing at windows, doors, and roof edges.
8. Poor joinery around windows and doors and at corners, and inadequate paint maintenance.
9. Lack of rain gutters, and roof without overhang.
10. Unventilated attics.
11. Roof leaks; leaks around shower-bathtub combinations, kitchen fixtures, and laundry rooms.
12. Failure to use preservatively treated or naturally durable wood where moisture cannot be controlled.

Moisture condensation on joists of a basementless house on a moist site. This occurs in cold weather and would in the end lead to decay. It can be avoided by ventilation or, at low cost, by covering the soil below with roll roofing.

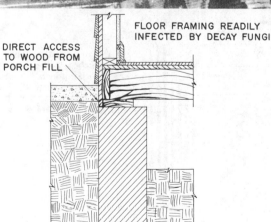

FLOOR FRAMING READILY INFECTED BY DECAY FUNGI

DIRECT ACCESS TO WOOD FROM PORCH FILL

A badly constructed porch with dirt fill. The most destruction of the decay fungi are likely to enter the house from soil contacts of the kind shown here.

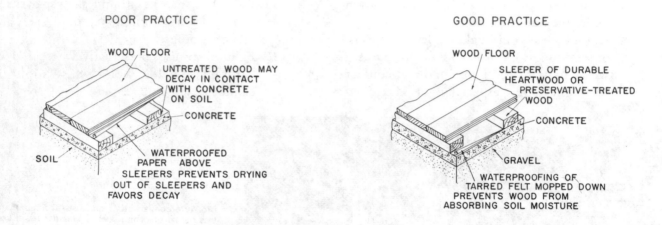

POOR PRACTICE

MOISTURE COLLECTS
UNDER POST FLUSH
WITH CONCRETE
FLOOR

POOR

WORSE

WORST

POST EMBEDDED IN CONCRETE

POST IN CONTACT WITH SOIL

FLOOR

GOOD PRACTICE

NONLOAD-CARRYING POST

GOOD

GOOD

FLOOR

FOOTING UNDER LOAD-BEARING
POST PREVENTS SETTLING

Wood posts on concrete basement floors.

POOR PRACTICE

WOOD FLOOR

UNTREATED WOOD MAY
DECAY IN CONTACT
WITH CONCRETE
ON SOIL

CONCRETE

SOIL

WATERPROOFED
PAPER ABOVE
SLEEPERS PREVENTS DRYING
OUT OF SLEEPERS AND
FAVORS DECAY

GOOD PRACTICE

WOOD FLOOR

SLEEPER OF DURABLE
HEARTWOOD OR
PRESERVATIVE-TREATED
WOOD

CONCRETE

GRAVEL

WATERPROOFING OF
TARRED FELT MOPPED DOWN
PREVENTS WOOD FROM
ABSORBING SOIL MOISTURE

Wood floors on concrete slabs. Waterproofing membranes may be placed either in, under, or on top of the slab.

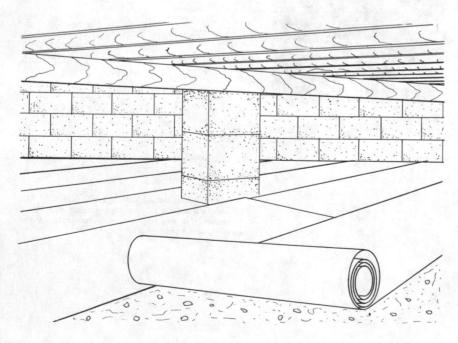

Roll roofing used to cover the soil under a house. Such a cover keeps the soil moisture from vaporizing into the air and then condensing on the sills and joists. Where roll roofing is used, the crawl-space ventilation, or most of them, can be safely closed during the winter.

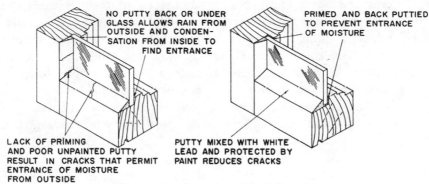

POOR PRACTICE — GOOD PRACTICE

NO PUTTY BACK OR UNDER GLASS ALLOWS RAIN FROM OUTSIDE AND CONDENSATION FROM INSIDE TO FIND ENTRANCE

PRIMED AND BACK PUTTIED TO PREVENT ENTRANCE OF MOISTURE

LACK OF PRIMING AND POOR UNPAINTED PUTTY RESULT IN CRACKS THAT PERMIT ENTRANCE OF MOISTURE FROM OUTSIDE

PUTTY MIXED WITH WHITE LEAD AND PROTECTED BY PAINT REDUCES CRACKS

Poor and good practices with window glass.

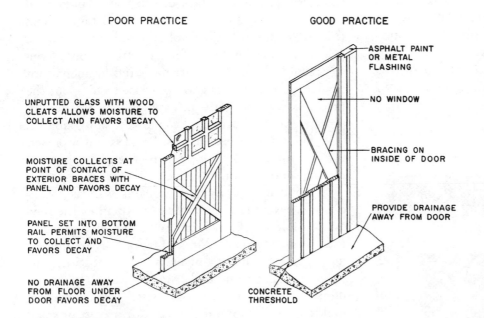

POOR PRACTICE — GOOD PRACTICE

ASPHALT PAINT OR METAL FLASHING

UNPUTTIED GLASS WITH WOOD CLEATS ALLOWS MOISTURE TO COLLECT AND FAVORS DECAY

NO WINDOW

MOISTURE COLLECTS AT POINT OF CONTACT OF EXTERIOR BRACES WITH PANEL AND FAVORS DECAY

BRACING ON INSIDE OF DOOR

PANEL SET INTO BOTTOM RAIL PERMITS MOISTURE TO COLLECT AND FAVORS DECAY

PROVIDE DRAINAGE AWAY FROM DOOR

NO DRAINAGE AWAY FROM FLOOR UNDER DOOR FAVORS DECAY

CONCRETE THRESHOLD

Poor and good practices in installing garage doors. If windows are installed, prime and back-putty before glazing and set cleats in putty mixed with white lead. Preservative treatment of the wood is often desirable.

Safeguards

To prevent decay, keep decay fungi from entering the lower part of the structure. Use dry wood as far as practicable, and build in a way that will keep wood dry most of the time. Spores or "seeds" of decay fungi are always present in the air; they can't be kept away from wood. But fungi can grow in wood only when it contains more than 10 percent moisture. Air-dry wood is regularly below this danger point.

Use Dry Lumber. Use only seasoned and sound lumber. Compared with green lumber, it has better nail-holding capacity, shrinks and warps less, and is safer from decay. During construction, store lumber off the ground and protect it from rain.

If only green material can be obtained, it should be open-piled on the job and allowed to dry as much as possible before it is used. The piles should be supported off the ground, the layers separated from each other by narrow strips of 1-inch dry lumber. Space the boards in each layer to let air move around them on all sides. If the piles cannot be put under cover, slope them toward one end. Overlap the boards in the top layer and extend them out at the front and back to keep rain off the boards beneath. Green lumber requires 60 days or more for thorough seasoning. But even a shorter period will do much to decrease the chance of decay.

Particularly avoid infected lumber that is wet. It is especially dangerous where the lumber is so enclosed that it cannot dry. Wood infected heavily by stain fungi should also be avoided, since it often contains decay fungi as well.

Protection Against Rain. Roofs with considerable overhang, both at eaves and gable ends, give more protection to the rest of the house than those with narrow overhang. In fact, a good roof overhang can do much to offset decay hazards in siding and around windows and doors. As a rule, an overhang of 12 inches is desirable for a 1-story house. In regions with heavy snow, flash the lower courses of shingles to keep melting snow from working into the walls. Gutters and downspouts are particularly desirable for houses without overhanging eaves. Flash horizontal wood surfaces or projections, including windows and doors, with a noncorroding metal.

In general, architectural frills or novel forms of construction should be studied carefully to determine whether they will provide entrance points or pockets in which moisture will remain long enough to let decay get started. Lumber takes water most readily through exposed ends, as in joints.

Southern pine sapwood joints cut open after 3 years of exposure to rain in Mississippi. The joint in the rail over the post at the left has admitted water and allowed decay. The continuous rail at the right has kept rain out and prevented decay. The discoloration in the post at right is simply iron stain from the nail.

Naturally Decay-Resistant Wood. The sapwood of all species of trees is susceptible to decay. Heartwood of most species, usually recognizable by its redder or darker color, is more durable. In Douglas-fir, southern pine, and white oak the heartwood is classed as moderately resistant. In tidewater red cypress, most cedars, and in redwood, it is highly resistant to decay and can even be used in contact with soil and semipermanent construction if there is no sapwood attached. However, even these woods do not have the decay resistance of wood fully impregnated with an effective preservative. The highly durable hardwoods, as black walnut, catalpa, Osage-orange, and the better varieties of black locust, are too hard or too scarce for general use in construction. Heartwood of resistant species is increasingly difficult to obtain and cannot be the principal reliance for safety in most house construction. Where preservative-treated lumber is not available for use, it is good practice to pick out the pieces containing only heartwood for use in sills, porches, outside steps, and the lowest siding boards.

Paint and Preservatives. Paint is not a preservative. However, it helps to prevent decay by protecting wood from intermittent wetting, especially if applied to ends and edges as well as to exposed faces and so maintained as to allow the fewest possible cracks at joints. When applied to wood that is not seasoned, it may favor decay by hindering further drying. Painting is not a substitute for good construction and maintenance. In warm moist climates or in rooms with very moist air, molds may develop on the paint or on dirt or small insects that adhere to it, and make it unsightly. Paints having low oil content and much zinc oxide are safest in this respect. On the gulf coast, where mildew is most common, fungicides to protect paint can be obtained from paint stores, with instructions for use. Many of the fungicides are highly poisonous, and should be used with caution. Observe the instructions on container labels.

To prevent decay, use treated wood for any members that are not likely to be properly protected against excessive moisture, unless heartwood of a highly resistant species is available. Sills or plates, sleepers, joists, beams, and girders in or on concrete, and exposed porches and steps are the members for which thorough preservative treatment can be most easily justified.

To be fully protected, wood must be deeply

impregnated with the preservative. This can be done best by treatment under pressure, using, when necessary, preservatives that permit painting. Less efficient but often adequate treatment can be given by so-called vacuum treatment or by heating wood and then soaking it in a cold preservative; for thin or short pieces, cold soaking is sufficient. Wood that is cut and fitted after treatment should be given a soaking or heavy brush treatment of the cut surfaces.

Wood can be given some protection from decay by more superficial treatments with preservatives, although chemicals added by dipping penetrate the wood of most species surprisingly little. Such treatment, while it is not dependable for wood exposed to severe conditions, can considerably increase the service life of wood that will be exposed to rain but not be in contact with the ground. Including water-repellent materials in the preservative formula makes the treatment more effective, particularly if the wood is to be left unpainted. Painting the wood after treatments of this type increases their effectiveness, especially if water repellents are not added.

It is even possible in some situations to give a somewhat effective treatment to uninfected wood already in place in a building, especially at joints and column ends. Ordinary brushing with preservatives does little, but heavy spraying or otherwise flooding a water-repellent preservative into joint areas can be helpful. Also, certain greaselike preservatives are being sold for this purpose. However, there are difficulties with these types of treatment. The parts of a building most likely to decay are not always easily reached, or if covered with a good paint coat will not take treatment. Moreover, a surface thoroughly treated with a solution or grease containing one of the heavier oils may not take paint for some months. It is much easier and better to treat the wood before it goes into construction; but treated or untreated, it should still be guarded against excessive moisture.

New Building Materials
Plywood and the various fiberboards used in

recent construction generally require the same precautions as lumber. Resin glues used in exterior-grade plywood are fungus-resistant but do not penetrate the wood enough to make it fungus-proof. With either fiberboard or plywood, joint construction should be carefully designed to prevent the entrance of rainwater. On edges of exposed plywood use a heavy coat of thick white-lead paint or other moisture-resistant coating. Avoid or flash horizontal joints or water tables on the outside of walls because they often let rain-water get in behind them. Use exterior grades of plywood not only in places exposed to rain but preferably also where the plywood is used as roof sheathing or over a crawl space beneath a house.

When heat insulation is used, the likelihood of moisture condensation and decay in the structure may be increased. To counteract this, place a vapor barrier between the insulating material and the inside of the house. Tight vapor barriers on the outer (cold) surface of the insulation increase the chance of decay.

Maintenance
A building frequently requires correction or compensation for shortcomings in the original construction. But even if the builder's job has been well done in every respect, inspection and continued care are needed.

No kind of house will long stand neglect. Rust stains around nail heads, paint peeling and blistering, paint discoloration at joints, and swelling and buckling of siding are some of the signs that moisture is not being controlled. Leaks in roofs, gutters, or plumbing and the clogging and overflow of gutters, downspouts, or drains can lead to wood decay. Cold pipes that "sweat" and moisten adjacent wood for long periods should be insulated. If ventilators under basementless houses are closed in winter, be sure to open them in early spring to lessen chances of decay. Do not allow soil, trash, firewood, or lumber to pile up against walls or sills. Likewise, do not raise the exterior grade to a level that brings it dangerously close to the wood.

REROOFING
Of the two major structural areas of a home, the roof and the foundation, it's the roof that

takes the worst beating. In the winter it's chilled from snow and freezing rain, gets brittle with cold, then thawed in the sun. At the same time, the underside of the roof is subjected to warmth and moisture from the inside of the house. In the summer the sun beats down on a roof, rains hammer at it and winds dry it out.

If a basement leaks, there can be damage and a lot of inconvenience. If a roof leaks, it can be a catastrophe, with every part of the house from roof to basement threatened.

What can you do? First, take a look at the roof every time you do your spring maintenance and repair. Are there loose and curled shingles? Shingles missing, valley surfaces that are drying out and cracking? You can apply roofing compound to worn areas, and use it to glue down loose shingles (asphalt type). Wooden shingles should be split and renailed. Wide cracks can be sealed with compound.

After a number of years the roof gets worn to the point where patching and fixing get out of

hand. You can see mildew, perhaps even rot, showing along the edges of the wooden portion of the roof. The rain gutters are full of debris; pieces of broken shingle, dirt, even gravel as in the case of the roof shown. You need a new roof, and there is no other answer.

Built-up roof with gravel is just 12 years old, but loose material fills rain gutters, tar paper is exposed.

Obvious sign of trouble are stains between decking boards near edge of the roof. Mildewed streaks indicate rotting.

At corner of roof damage is more extensive from underneath; boards have cracked, rot is splitting ends of planks.

Valley at intersection of two roofs is especially vulnerable. When old roofing was removed, rotting was exposed.

254

Corner of roof, where splitting showed on underside, is rotting badly. Leaves and debris from tree hastened damage.

What's the real story on reroofing? Can you do it yourself? Is it hard work? What is involved? What will it cost? Do you need help?

Estimating Costs

The first thing we learned was that the cost will be in the hundreds of dollars, rather than the thousands of dollars if you have it done.

Second, and another money-saver, if you have a low-pitched roof you can use shingles and avoid the cost of a hot-mopped, built-up roof, which only professionals can install. Almost any kind of shingles can be applied to a roof that has a 4-inch pitch or more. To determine your roof pitch, hold one end of a level on the roof, and angle it until it shows level. At a point 12 inches from the end of the level that touches the roof, measure down to the roof. The distance at that point, 2, 3, 5 inches, etc. is the pitch. Another way of describing roof pitch is by fractional numbers: a 1/3 pitch is 8 inches to the foot drop, a ¼ pitch is 6 inches and 1/6 pitch is 4 inches.

If a roof has a pitch of more than 2 inches, but less than 4 inches, you can use shingles of the type that have adhesive on the underside of the tabs. After this type shingle is installed, the heat of the sun softens the adhesive, and the tabs are firmly bonded to the shingle beneath. The adhesive holds so well that if you try to lift a shingle after the adhesive has been activated by the warmth of the sun, you will tear up the shingles, both the upper and lower one.

Preparation

If the old roof is in relatively good shape, you can apply new roofing right over it. The roof framing must be strong enough to support the added weight of the new roof; you usually can check this with the local building inspector. In most cases you will need a building permit; this can be done at the same time.

If you do apply a new roof over the old one, it's necessary to prepare the roof: curled shingles must be nailed down, missing shingles must be replaced to assure a flat, smooth surface. Wooden shingles that are curled and split have to be nailed down and any missing shingles must be replaced. All loose or protruding nails must be removed. If the shingles at the roof edges are badly weathered, remove enough to allow the application of a 1 x 4 or 1 x 6 board, and allow it to project beyond the edges of the roof deck the same amount as the wooden shingles did. Tapered feathering strips should be nailed along the butt edges of the courses of wooden shingles to provide a smooth surface to receive the new asphalt roofing.

Hardest part of job was removing old roofing material. Loose gravel was first swept off, but much remained.

All rotting boards were removed and replaced. At one corner of roof it was necessary to put in ten new 2 x 6 strips.

Where old asphalt shingles are to be covered, nail down or cut away all loose, curled or lifted shingles. Any loose or projecting nails should be pulled out. Any wood strips along the edges of the roof that are worn or weathered should be replaced. The old shingles are the underlayment, no felt is required.

With few exceptions, boards along the edge of a roof will require replacing. This is especially true of a low-pitch, built-up roof. In this case the raised "gravel stop" along the lower edges of the roof will catch and hold water, eventually causing rotting.

In some cases you can detect signs of this rotting by looking at the underside of the roof along the edges. If there is evidence of rotting, the old roof should be stripped off completely. Most built-up roofs will be over 2-inch decking. When you reroof your house it's a good idea to figure on spending some money for replacement lumber, beside the cost of the roofing itself.

It will be necessary to take down the rain gutters, and here again you may run into additional cost. Support straps or hangers for the gutters may be broken or badly rusted. Even some sections of the gutters may need replacing, as well as some downspouts.

After you have removed the rain gutters, and made necessary repairs to the existing roof, carefully sweep the roof to remove all debris. You don't want any material to be covered that would cause rotting, or that would break through the new roofing and cause a leak.

The next step is to install a sheetmetal angle (edging) along the edge of the roof. This metal assures that the edge of the roof is protected against damage, and that any water that runs back under the edges of the lowest shingle will simply contact the metal and run down and off. If there is no metal, the water is absorbed by the wood of the roof and you have the start of a rotting condition.

The lower (eaves) edge of the roof has the metal nailed to the deck, while the metal along the roof ends (raker) is applied over felt-paper underlayment. This assures that moisture will not get under the paper, even if wind-blown.

First step in reroofing is to nail on metal edge strip. Home owner here used old gravel guard, hammered it into L-shape.

The asphalt-saturated felt underlayment comes in rolls of 38 inches wide, with spacing marks on it for easy alignment and correct overlapping. While it is not critical to keep the felt aligned across the roof, as it is covered by the shingles, it does later make it easier to apply shingles, if the lines on the felt are straight and true.

The felt underlayment is held by as few fasteners as possible, which means a staple gun does the job quickly. You can run into problems, and a helper is a great asset for this operation. If you have a strip of felt only partially stapled and a gust of wind gets under one end, it can tear the full length loose, rolling and curling the paper while you make frantic efforts to hold it down. This can be a dangerous tactic, considering you are up on a roof, on a slanted surface with unsure footing. Rolling the paper a few feet at a time and stapling it well as you go along is the safest and surest method.

Felt-saturated underlayment (tar paper) was stapled to roof to seal it. Note lines on paper that speed alignment.

Underlayment is carried over ridge of roof to seal it. Top course of shingles also was run over the ridge and nailed.

Is the job of reroofing hard work? It's not easy, but the most difficult part is removing the old material, where that is necessary.

The next problem is that the moment you start removing the old roofing and expose the roof, you must start applying the felt. This prevents any damage if it should rain before you get the shingles installed.

Planning is important here. Figure how much old roofing you can remove in a day, while still allowing yourself time to staple on the felt before you quit. Generally it's best to figure on going from eaves edge to the ridge in one section. You then can install the felt up to and over the ridge. When you start on the other side of the roof you simply peel back that part of the felt overlapping the ridge, to permit removing the old roofing. When you apply the felt on the other side, replace the overlap, then overlap the ridge with felt from the other side. This gives you a double coverage over the ridge.

Edges of all shingles along edge of valley are cemented down to assure that water does not run under them.

Valleys where roofs join must handle a rush of water, so are double-thick. One layer has gravel face down.

Laying the Shingles

For the first course of shingles, turn them upside down, with the tabs facing toward the ridge. This provides a straight edge along the roof, plus a double thickness along the edge. The next course goes on top of the inverted course.

This double row of shingles along the edge helps reinforce this area, which already is well protected by the double thickness of saturated felt applied directly to the deck, and cemented together with roof compound up to a point 24 inches inside the wall line. This application system is especially important with roofs of low pitch.

After you have nailed on the first course of shingles, use a chalk line to snap a straight line for the next course. Professional roofers use a gauge on the head of their shingle hammer, to space one course from the next, but even they snap a chalk line every 5 courses or so, to be sure they stay in alignment.

Before applying shingles up to a valley, install strip material in the valley (roll roofing to match the shingles). Water runs to a valley from all parts of a roof, and the run-off here is especially heavy, so the roofing must be heavy at this point. The felt underlayment already is installed across the valley, then a strip of paper, gravel-side down, is nailed across the valley. This strip is 18 inches wide, cut from a 36-inch-wide strip.

A full-width strip, gravel-side up, then is nailed over the 18-inch piece. A chalk line is snapped the length of the valley, on each side, to mark where the shingles are cut. The valley should be 6 inches wide at the ridge, then taper out 1/8 inch per foot down to the roof edge. Which means for every 8-foot length of valley there is an additional 1 inch of width, ½ inch on each side of the valley center line. The upper corner of each shingle abutting the valley is cut off at an angle, to assure that water is not trapped under it. Additionally, each shingle is cemented to the valley strip to further assure water not getting under the shingles.

The ridge of the roof, after all courses of shingles have been applied, is sealed with overlapping pieces of shingle material (these ridge pieces can be purchased separately) or shingles with the tabs removed are overlapped the length of the ridge.

Squares of shingle material are bent over roof ridge, overlapped to seal it. With the job finished, aches go away.

Another aspect of roofing is flashing. When you strip off the old roofing and apply the saturated felt, check the flashing around chimneys, soil pipes, stacks, and the like. Replace metal flashing where necessary, or cover it with felt, after first applying a heavy coat of roofing compound. Shingles then are run up to the flashing and also sealed with compound. The felt and shingles are cut to fit around soil pipes, then flashed with compound.

Good heavy-duty roofing if properly applied will last 20 years or more. Expect some wood damage along the edges of the roof, so allow for the cost and time for installing the lumber. Determine what flashing will have to be replaced, or if it can be renovated with compound. Use the length of shingle nails specified for your roof application and apply the shingles as described by the manufacturer (on the shingle bundles).

Buy the shingles by the "square" which means 100 square feet, and the saturated felt the same way. Allow about 10 percent extra for waste in trimming and fitting.

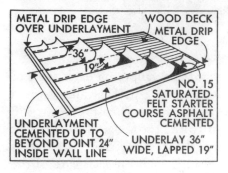

On low-slope roof metal edging is under the felt on the edges of roof, but over the felt along the raker edges.

Shingles on low-slope roof must be type with adhesive on tabs, or individual shingles must be cemented down.

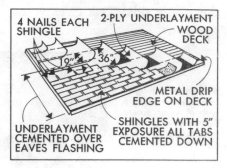

USING CONCRETE

Concrete home improvements can enhance the beauty and the value of your property. They can also make your routine lawn maintenance easier, your outdoor entertaining more enjoyable, and your housecleaning chores less burdensome from tracked-in dirt.

Materials

Ordinary tools and easily obtained materials are all that are needed for concrete work. You will usually have three options for obtaining concrete:

Buy ready mixed concrete.

Buy portland cement, sand and coarse aggregate and mix your own concrete.

Buy commercially dry-mixed concrete by the bag and merely mix with water.

Your choice depends on the size of the job and the amount of labor you wish to provide. In general, the more of your own labor, the less will be your out-of-pocket cost.

Forms for the concrete can be built with materials available from the local building materials dealer. Dimension lumber like 2 x 4's or 2 x 6's is used for more jobs. If large surfaces must be formed, like the sides of concrete steps, plywood is the most commonly used forming material. You should use either forming grade or exterior grade plywood that is undamaged by moisture. A light coat of oil on the forms will permit easier removal and help preserve the wood for possible reuse.

Reinforcing steel may or may not be needed. In general, flatwork such as sidewalks, patios, step-ping stones, and driveways requires no reinforcement if proper attention is paid to jointing. However, retaining walls and items subject to heavy loading will need to be reinforced.

Tools for doing concrete work consist of a strike-off board, a float of wood or light metal, a metal trowel, and edging tools.

Planning the Job

When planning the job, first calculate roughly the amount of concrete you'll need. Calculate the volume by multiplying length by width by thickness, all expressed in feet:

V (cubic feet) = L (feet) x W (feet) x T (feet).

Divide cubic feet by 27 to secure cubic yards. For flatwork, a simple rule for estimating the amount of concrete needed is: One cubic yard of concrete will cover about 300 square feet one inch thick, allowing for some waste. If the slab is 4 inches thick, a cubic yard will cover 300/4, or about 75 square feet.

Example: How much concrete will be needed to place a 2-foot 6-inch x 7-foot sidewalk 4 inches thick?

2½ x 7 = 17½ square feet.

One cubic yard 4 inches thick will place 300/4 = 75 square feet, 17½/75 = less than ¼. Thus, ¼ cubic yard is needed.

Most ready mix producers specify a minimum volume that they will deliver. This may be as little as one cubic yard (27 cubic feet). If your job requires an amount smaller than the minimum order, you may wish to investigate the other options described below. However, on larger jobs such as patios and driveways, ready mixed concrete usually is the best choice.

When you order ready mixed concrete, a good rule to follow is to ask for a mix that contains 550 pounds of cement (about six bags) to the cubic yard. Experience has shown this to be a durable mix for outdoor exposure. Also ask that the concrete be air entrained. Air entrainment gives hardened concrete increased resistance to salt action and cycles of freezing and thawing. It is good practice to tell the ready mix producer what you expect to build so that he can furnish the mix best suited to your job.

On jobs that you intend doing a piece at a time or where the quantity of concrete is less than the ready mix producer's minimum order, you may wish to mix your own. If you do so, remember that variations in proportions between batches will result in minor color differences in hardened concrete. Therefore, if the job is all one piece, such as a patio, try to do it in a continuous operation rather than spreading it over several days.

Hand-mixing in a mortar box or wheelbarrow is satisfactory only for very small jobs. It is difficult to get continuous-volume production by hand-mixing. Renting a small mixer will save back-breaking labor and make the job move more smoothly.

To mix one cubic yard of concrete you'll need:

    6 bags of portland cement
    1,250 pounds of concrete sand
    1,900 pounds of gravel or crushed stone
    About 30 gallons of water.

Sand and gravel vary, but a good mix to try for a starter is 1 part cement, 2¼ parts sand, and 3 parts gravel or crushed stone. The key to quality concrete is the proportion of water to cement. Plan to use about 5 gallons of water for each bag of

cement and keep this proportion constant. The amount of sand and gravel can be adjusted in later batches to get the workability desired.

Example: Determine the amount of materials to order for the 2-foot 6-inch x 7-foot x 4-inch sidewalk. You previously found that ¼ cubic yard of concrete was required, so you'll need:

    6/4 = 1½   Say 2 bags of cement.
    1,250/4 = 315   Say 325 pounds of sand.
    1,900/4 = 475   Say 500 pounds of gravel or crushed stone.

For jobs too small to order sand, gravel, and cement separately, you can buy bagged dry-mixed concrete at hardware stores and building materials dealers. Calculate the quantity of concrete needed; then find out the volume contained in each bag and determine the number of bags needed. Dry-mixed concrete needs only to be mixed with water, having been accurately proportioned in the factory.

The drawings show methods of forming for common jobs around the home. While 1-inch thick lumber can be used for forming, 2-inch lumber requires less bracing and is easier to keep in true alignment. A hint: Always err on the side of overbracing the forms. Once forms begin to bow from concrete pressure, it is virtually impossible to restore true alignment.

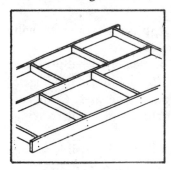
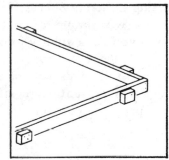

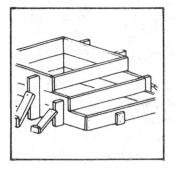
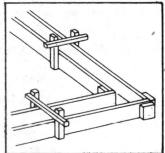

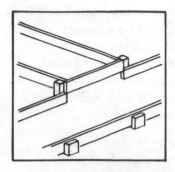

Forming for common concrete jobs. Precast work only.

Using Concrete Successfully

Two simple rules for placing concrete will help you get a quality job:

1. Place the concrete as near its final position as possible. This will save the labor of moving it and will prevent segregation of the mix. Compact or spade the concrete into the forms as it is being placed.

2. Work the surface as little as possible in the early stages. Overworking of concrete draws fine material to the surface and results in less durability. Strike the surface off to the desired level, moving the strike-off board across the surface as many times as needed. Smooth out irregularities with a float. Run an edger along the form boards. Cut dummy groove joints wherever needed. Then wait.

When the watery sheen has left the concrete surface, it is ready for final finishing. The first step is to use a wood or light metal float. On sidewalks, driveways, and steps this is often the final finish since it leaves a gritty slip-resistant finish. For smooth surfaces, use a steel trowel after the float. This finish is not commonly used on outdoor work since a troweled surface tends to be slippery when wet.

Here's a helpful hint: A gritty wood float finish hides irregularities better than a smooth surface. A beginner will often be better pleased with his work when the final finish is done with a wood float or a light brush drawn across the surface.

Concrete needs to be kept moist for several days after it has set. An economical way of curing is to cover the new concrete with a waterproof material such as polyethylene. This traps moisture in the concrete. Setting a sprinkler to keep the concrete continuously wet, or covering concrete with moist sand or burlap, also provides good curing. Hardness of the surface is greatly influenced by the length of time of moist curing.

Wherever possible, divide concrete into sections that are nearly square. Do this by cutting dummy groove joints in the fresh concrete to about one-fourth the concrete thickness. Then any cracks that form will tend to follow the straight dummy groove rather than be irregular. A 3-foot sidewalk would have dummy grooves at 3- to 4-foot intervals. A 10-foot driveway would have dummy grooves at 10- to 12-foot intervals.

A concrete slab should be separated from a foundation by putting expansion joint material along the foundation. This permits slight movement and avoids unsightly cracks along the wall.

Most concrete slabs are made at least 4 inches thick. This is thick enough for driveways that carry only autos and an occasional truck. Delivery trucks require a 6-inch thickness.

Stepping stones can be cast to any shape desired (like footprints) by removing sod, then carving the earth to the shape desired. Concrete is placed in the hole and finished. After concrete has hardened, the sod can be replaced.

With a little experience you can make concrete with an attractive decorative surface. The easiest way is to work colored stone into the surface of the fresh concrete. After the concrete is firm, but not fully set, wash the surface with water, using a stiff bristle brush. This will expose the colored aggregate.

You can precast flagstones, splash blocks, or other small items on any flat surface such as a garage floor. Place a layer of building paper, polyethylene, cardboard, or other bond breaker on the floor. Then build forms and place them over the bond breaker. Fill the forms with concrete and finish in the usual way. Precast items are usually made at least 2½ inches thick.

Precast flagstones are most easily set on a sand bed. One part portland cement mixed with 3 to 5 parts sand will result in a firmer bed than will sand alone. After the stones are set, washing the patio with water provides moisture that will permit the sand-cement bed to harden into a firm base.

A wide range of precast items for the home, lawn, and garden is available at local precast plants. These items are often available in a variety of colors that are impossible for the individual homeowner to produce. The precaster also can provide artistic designs more economically since his forms will be reused several times. Suggestions on how to handle and set the precast items can usually be obtained from the seller.

POURING A CONCRETE SIDEWALK

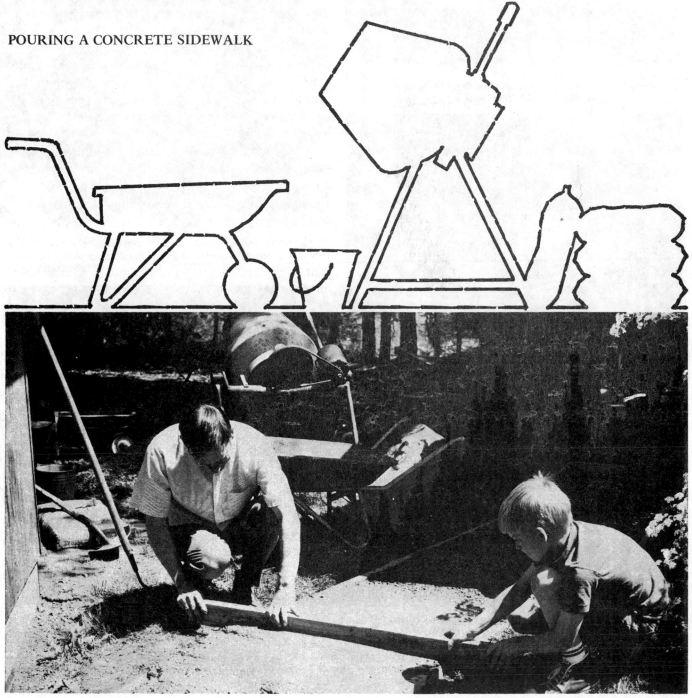

Lay out the walk with string and small stakes. Don't skimp on width; a few inches wider makes little difference in cost and work. Walks should be wider where youngsters play.

Forms are made of 2 x 4 material held by stakes cut from 1-in. stock. Make stakes 18 in. long, place one at each joint in form, and about every 2 ft. Level or slope forms.

Concrete is mixed in proportion of 1 cement, 2 sand and 3 gravel. For cubic yard you need 6¼ sacks of cement, ⅔ yard of sand, ¾ yard of gravel. 3 x 34-ft. sidewalk takes 1 yd.

Dig out the sod and soil 4 or 5 inches below ground level. Fill low spots with soil and tamp firmly and make bottom of excavation smooth and level. Remove any loose soil, grass.

If form is dug lower than 2 x 4s you can place an inch or so of gravel in the bottom for drainage in damp areas. Tamp this well and wet it down before pouring the concrete.

Materials for concrete are mixed with just enough water to make plastic, workable mix. Too dry and concrete will not work, and will crumble. Too much water, concrete is weak.

After concrete is worked with screed to level it (lead photo), wooden float is used to smooth surface. This finish is non-skid, good for bikes and roller skates, easily done.

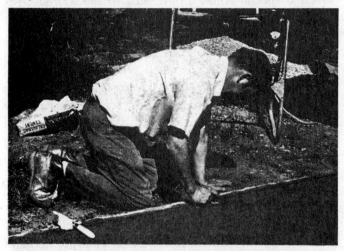
After floating, edger is used to finish edges of poured walk. Edger is used whether screed is flat or curved to produce an arched surface that sheds water in both directions.

As soon as edging is done, grooves are made across walk at intervals of about 3 ft. If walk cracks, it will usually be along these lines and will not easily show. Use straightedge guide.

If walk is to be used just for pedestrian traffic, and roller skating or bicycling will not be considered, then pattern surface with a straw broom (coarse) or hair broom (smooth).

For a really slick surface (seldom applied where people will be walking) use a steel trowel. Finished concrete will be slick when it is wet, but this surface is fine for inside.

ABOUT CONCRETE BLOCKS

Versatility of concrete masonry is vividly demonstrated by the range of sizes and shapes of units being manufactured today. Forty years ago, inventory of a typical block manufacturing plant consisted of less than 30 different sizes. Today, this figure exceeds 100 and the total number of different sizes, shapes and types manufactured across the country is well over 700.

Size

Units are made in sizes which range from one inch in thickness and in lengths up to 24 inches; they are solid or hollow and are made with dense and lightweight aggregates (materials).

The name designating various units has been fairly well standardized, and usually relates to the function in the wall.

Size of a concrete masonry unit is usually described by listing its thickness, or width first, followed by its height and then its length. Thus, a 4 x 8 x 16 block has a nominal width of 4 inches, height of 8 inches and length of 16 inches.

The nominal dimension includes ¾ inch allowed for the thickness of a standard mortar joint, so the actual dimensions of the well known 8-inch x 8-inch x 16-inch unit are manufactured as 7-5/8-inch x 7-5/8-inch x 15-5/8-inch.

American Society for Testing and Materials (ASTM) specifications permit a maximum variation in overall dimensions (length, width and height) of plus or minus 1/8 inch from the actual dimensions specified by the manufacturer. It is the usual practice, however, to manufacture the units within a tolerance of plus or minus 1/16 inch.

Although the industry has standardized on exterior dimensions of modular units, differences in thickness of face shells and webs, and size and number of cores for the same size hollow unit may exist between manufacturers. As an example, the 8 x 8 x 16 hollow unit may range from about 50 percent to 63 percent solid, depending upon the size and number of cores. These variations may result from the need to obtain properties such as fire resistance, sound insulations, and the like.

Appearance

Concrete masonry units offer a vast array of choices of natural faces and finishes for walls. These range from a wide variety that come at no extra cost to highly unusual, more expensive block for developing luxurious effects.

Concrete masonry may be used as veneer to produce a nonstructural masonry facing on a backing of wood, concrete, or masonry. The purpose may be protection, insulation or ornamentation. Units with tile-like faces, ground surfaces, or sculptured or other finished faces are often used. The veneer is ordinarily supported at its base and may be held to the wall with mortar, grout or steel anchors.

With skill in laying, block may be used to produce walls in which the block surface is left exposed on both sides, a practice that may introduce significant economy. It is often possible to make use of tile-faces or other decorative units to provide a special finish on one side of the wall and yet to leave the plain face exposed as an attractive finished surface on the other.

Nominal thicknesses of as little as 4 inches in interior walls may be used when necessary, provided the block meets all necessary requirements such as strength and sound resistance. Exterior walls may be exposed on both sides where thermal transmission requirements permit.

Texture in block is of interest in relation to its appearance, its sound absorption, and the ease with which the block may be painted or waterproofed.

Coarse textures provide better sound absorption than smooth textures. To satisfy the demand for coarse textured units the block manufacturer may use large coarse aggregate, a harsh aggregate grading, an angular aggregate, a dry or lean mix, or any combination of these which is needed to produce a quality product.

Fine textures also have decorative appeal. A mix containing mainly fine natural sand may give an appearance much like that of quarried limestone. Various degrees of smoothness can be achieved with any aggregate by changes in mix proportions. Fine textures may be less absorptive of sound but are also less absorptive of paint than coarse textures.

With some aggregates—whether normal weight or lightweight—surface grinding brings out great color and variety from units that would otherwise be nondecorative. Ground surfaces are also more accurately planed than molded surfaces, an advantage in the ease of making the wall plumb.

"Customized," or the "Architectural Facing" concrete masonry units, are designed and manufactured to provide the finished surface of a wall without the addition of opaque coatings or treatments which would appreciably change its appearance.

Design and Structural Qualities

Using these units, a wall may be built as an exterior or interior bearing or non-loadbearing wall. It may be designed of "through-wall" units where only one masonry unit comprises the wall section. The wall section may consist of architectural facing concrete masonry units as a veneer, backed up with concrete masonry or other materials. Or the units may be the facing portion of the structural composite or cavity wall.

The same variables that influence the performance of any masonry wall—units, mortar, workmanship, and construction details—must be given more thorough attention in the design and construction of a wall using architectural facing units. This is particularly true for exterior walls which will not receive painting or coating.

Fluted and scored, or ribbed, units provide the architect with raised striations that can be developed into many kinds of patterns. The accuracy that is achieved in machine production of these units makes it possible to produce the effect of long, continuous vertical straight lines, even when the block are laid in running bond.

Shadowall block, developed and introduced by the National Concrete Masonry Association, are units with recessed corners that may be put together in such limitless variety of patterns that this product has been called the "block of 1,000 faces." Interesting changing shadow effects can be obtained with such units when used on exteriors.

Irregular, slumped or overhanging surfaces can be used to produce rugged or rustic effects. Such block are made from mixes that are slightly wetter than normal so that they can be deformed, or slumped immediately after they have come out of the mold box of the machine.

Units with many of the characteristics of rough quarried stone are produced by lengthwise mechanical splitting of solid concrete block. A variety of sizes are available and special hollow block may also be used for splitting. Ribbed units, previously described, can be split to produce unusual effects.

Each individual block acquires its own distinctive texture in the splitting operation. By changes in aggregate, pigment and block size many different colors, textures and shapes become possible.

Split block is useful for entire walls on either the exterior or interior, as well as for fireplace facings, chimneys and planters. It has the same high durability and low maintenance cost as other concrete masonry units.

Open-faced block of many patterns is available for decorative uses, or for partially screening walls or yards from either the sun or outside viewers. This screen block is made in a wide variety of patterns and is useful, both indoors and out, for fences and carport walls, sun screens, curtain walls, room dividers, and veneers and friezes. Only a limited number of patterns may be available in a single locality.

Due to the fragile nature of screen walls, the use of steel reinforcement is recommended wherever it can be embedded in mortar joints, in bond beam courses, or grouted into continuous vertical or horizontal cells. Horizontal joint reinforcement, two No. 9 gauge wires or equivalent, placed 12 or 16 inches apart is recommended when screen wall units are laid in stack bond.

Block with colorful, hard, glossy, mar-resistant surfaces that resemble ceramic tile in appearance, durability, and ease of cleaning are produced by some manufacturers. Surfaces may be made of epoxy or polyester resins and may contain fine sand or other fillers. Ceramic or porcelainized glazes, mineral glazes and cement-like finishes have also been used.

Most of the variations discussed so far depend on the shape, size, configuration or texture of the block. The designer can achieve still further finished wall effects simply by varying the pattern in which the block are laid. Basically the patterns group themselves into several main classifications: running bond, stacked bond, coursed or patterned ashlar (various repeating patterns), diagonal bond, basket weave, and diagonal basket weave. Each classification includes various kinds of arrangements and the number can be enlarged by the use of various sizes of block, alone or in combinations.

In addition to its many other uses, concrete masonry can serve for such applications as retaining walls, swimming pool walls, patios, planters, and fences. Whenever a masonry wall is to be ex-

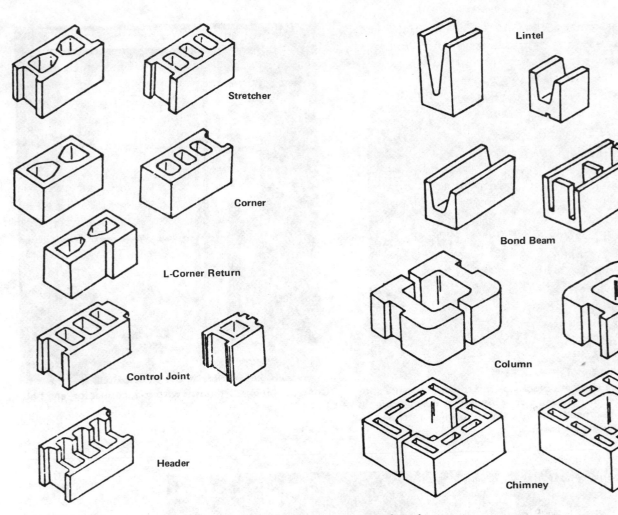

Stretcher

Corner

L-Corner Return

Control Joint

Header

Lintel

Bond Beam

Column

Chimney

The name usually refers to function.

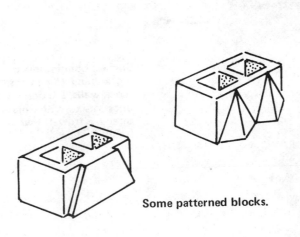

Some patterned blocks.

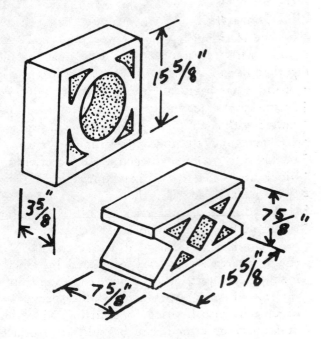

Typical screen block.

Dry stacking a concrete block column to fit between a door and a window or between two windows. A narrow column such as this one needs the additional strength provided by tie-down or reinforcing rods.

Concrete blocks tied down with rod, connector, and bolt in floor.

Surface bonding mix being applied to concrete block walls. Laborer applies mix with plasterer's trowel while holding a hawk.

posed to substantial lateral loads, such as from earth pressure, earthquakes or high winds, it should be properly reinforced with steel reinforcement and grout. Detailed information is available from the National Concrete Masonry Association or the local block manufacturer.

Rapid Assembly Systems

A number of rapid assembly systems have come into use in the past 20 years. These are systems designed for assembly by the unskilled or partially skilled. They include: 1. Tongue-and-groove interlocking systems that are assembled dry and then bonded together by grout that flows through horizontal and vertical channels. 2. Wedge shaped blocks that interlock and are self-aligning and self-plumbing. 3. Surface bonding application which involves stacking the block up without mortar and then trowelling both sides with a plaster containing strands of fiberglass, providing a waterproof wall with good lateral strength.

DRY-PACK CONCRETE

Concrete is a great material for home owners. It can be used for walks, driveways, patios, steps and other projects. It also is great for creating backaches and sore muscles when you mix it by hand in a wheelbarrow or on a driveway with a shovel. Using a powered mixer is considerably easier, but the wet mixture of sand, cement and gravel seems to get heavier with every batch and pouring a few square yards can be a bone-wrenching experience. Especially when you do a job in early spring before you have done enough exercise to at least limber up winter-softened muscles.

There is a method of "pouring" concrete that considerably reduces the labor, yet which produces a finished product that is probably stronger than most concrete mixed in the usual way.

Water is not mixed with the sand, gravel and cement; rather, the "dry" mix is placed, then the moisture is added after the material is leveled and tamped. The system was evolved by road engineers to get a repaired stretch of highway back in service as quickly as possible. The method proved to be extremely durable, and is now fairly standard in this type of repair work.

Basically the system consists of taking a sack of prepared (ready-mix) concrete that consists of the correct proportions of sand, gravel and cement and pouring it into place, tamping it solid, then carefully spraying it with a mist of water from a hose. Water is never allowed to accumulate on the surface of the dry mix, but when the visible water has been absorbed by the concrete, more can be added to assure a complete reaction between the various materials in the mix.

Water also can be flowed underneath the placed concrete, as it is drawn up through the dry mix. For faster action, water can be applied from both above and below.

Where to Use Dry-Pack Concrete

A number of "back-yard" projects are shown in the photos, where brick, stone and other materials were combined with the concrete to create beautiful surfaces. For such projects to be built by a home owner the following steps are required:

First, and this is an important step that too many builders overlook, the area where the project —walk, patio, ornamental surface, what have you— will be located must be stripped of sod, tree roots and all vegetation. If the soil is firm, or if you are adding to an existing hard surface, it probably is not necessary to use a form. If there is any doubt, if the soil appears to be soft enough to crumble after you pour in your concrete, then by all means put in a form. This can be 1-inch stock, if it will be supported by the soil adjacent to it. If the edge will be clear of the ground in any area, then use a 2 x 4 and support it with stakes driven into the ground. This is important because when using the dry-mix method you must tamp the poured mixture, and this heavy pounding can break down loose soil, or push over a form that is not strongly braced.

Examine the soil in the bottom of your excavation. If it is firm clay, it probably will support your concrete with no further preparation. If it is sandy or loamy, then tamp it firmly. A chunk of 2 x 6 or 2 x 8 spiked to a 2 x 4 handle is easy and inexpensive to make. Tamp the soil until it is firm and well compacted.

Now pour in enough clean sand to build up 1 to 2 inches. This means that the original excavation should be deep enough to allow for the sand, plus 3½ inches or more of concrete mix. If you are going to use pieces of rock, brick, even broken chunks of concrete, then make the excavation deep enough to allow for the pieces of material, plus the sand.

The next step is to place the pieces of material, keeping the tops level with the upper edges of your forms. Shim up the low pieces with bits of rock or other material, and pack sand firmly around them.

First step is to strip off sod, remove tree roots and vegetation. Use forms if necessary, tamp soil, add sand which is tamped, leveled and dampened thoroughly.

270

Second step is to place stones, bricks, pieces of broken concrete inside form, flush with top. Allow 1-in. space between objects and form. Pour in dry-mix concrete.

Last step is to sprinkle dry concrete mix with fine spray, add water every 20 minutes or so for 2 hours. Water can be added underneath, through sand. Season for 24 hours.

You are ready for the concrete mix now; but not quite. Pour out the bag of concrete mix into a wheelbarrow or on a concrete driveway. If you see streaks of gravel, sand or cement, it means you'd better mix the material. Use a light shovel and turn the material over a few times so the colors of the gray cement powder, the yellow sand and white gravel blend into one color.

Now shovel, or pour, the dry mix into your form, over the stones, bricks or whatever until it is almost level with these objects. Brush the mix off the objects, then carefully tamp the concrete mixture until it is solid. Add more mix and tamp again,

until your form is filled to the top with solidly packed concrete mixture. Be sure there is at least 1 inch between the objects and the edge of the form.

The final step is to lightly spray water over the surface of the packed concrete. Mist the water on the concrete until it almost stands on the surface, then stop! During the next two hours, add water again in the same manner. Do this every 20 minutes or so. After the 2 hours, wait 24 hours before the surface is used.

Here are the steps again:
1. Prepare area by digging out earth, removing plant and vegetable life.
2. Tamp soil solid, add 1 to 2 inches of sand, tamp and level, then dampen thoroughly to firm the sand and provide additional moisture for dry mix.
3. Arrange material (bricks, rocks, etc.), allowing at least 1 inch space between it and form.
4. Place dry-mix concrete, sweep, tamp, sweep, sprinkle with water every 20 minutes or so for 2 hours, then let set for 24 hours before using.

PROPER CONCRETE DEICERS

Some commercial products used by home owners to remove snow and ice from sidewalks and driveways may also damage the concrete.

Harmful amounts of ammonium nitrate or sulphates, used ordinarily in farm fertilizers, are contained in some deicing products now on the market. While these compounds are effective ice removers, they also can cause concrete to disintegrate or the surface to spall.

Shoppers are urged to check the contents of packaged deicers to be sure they contain no nitrate or sulphate compounds. Products that have either calcium chloride or sodium chloride as their main active ingredient generally are safe to use.

Of the two chemicals, sodium chloride, which is ordinary table salt, can damage lawns and shrubs. Calcium chloride will not damage vegetation, but can cause corrosion of metal. Which means if you use calcium chloride and it is splashed up on your car, wash it off as quickly as possible. This is true, of course, of almost any deicing chemical, as witness the damage to cars from materials used to clean ice and snow from roads.

The plain truth is that, as of now, there is no single product that is an effective deicer and also is completely safe to use near lawns and metal, such as porch railings.

Home owners should be especially careful with new concrete. A walk, drive, steps, porch or whatever should be dried out thoroughly, and go through at least one winter before any deicer, including salt, is used for it.

The best single precaution to assure maximum resistance to freeze-thaw damage and chemical attack is to use air-entrained concrete made with air-entraining admixture, has billions of tiny air bubbles that provide room for water to expand as it freezes. The result is less possibility of scaling or spalling as a result of freezing and thawing or from chemical attack.

If you are going to have a drive, walk, steps, porch, patio or other concrete surface replaced, check with a ready-mix concrete company about air-entrained material. It may cost a little more than regular concrete, but not nearly as much as replacing a complete structure of concrete.

ALL ABOUT BRICK

Brick can be used in a wide variety of ways in and around the home. These uses include fireplaces, floors, decorative walls, dividers and planters inside the home, and barbecues, patios, screen walls, retainer walls and tree wells outside the home. Choosing the right brick and using proper construction techniques are key factors in the success of any brick project.

A brick is defined as a small building unit, solid or cored not in excess of 25 percent, commonly in the form of a rectangular prism formed from clay or shale and fused by heat. The cores in some units have been introduced as an aid to uniform drying and burning of the clay and as a means of reducing the weight.

Other brick-like materials on the market today include concrete brick, plastic brick, fly ash brick, glass brick, sawdust brick and even cow dung brick. All of these materials have different engineering properties than the real clay brick. These different properties may or may not suit the need for which they are intended.

The Federal Trade Commission requires the manufacturer of any product sold as a brick but produced from a material other than clay to specifically preface it as concrete brick, plastic brick or whatever. Only a clay brick can be referred to generically as "brick."

If other than clay brick is used, the purchaser should be thoroughly aware of the limitations of its use and not expect the same results that would be achieved by the use of clay units. Unless otherwise stated, we will be referring to clay brick.

Two principal types of manufacturing techniques are used in the production of brick.

Molded brick is produced either by machine or hand molding techniques. A handmade appearance is achieved through the use of soft mud in the manufacturing process.

Extruded brick is produced by forcing stiff mud through a die. These bricks are usually cored and have a more machine-perfect appearance. Various textures are applied to the sides of the unit.

Both molded and extruded brick can be used in most applications in and around the house. Molded brick is usually more expensive than extruded brick, but many feel the handmade look is worth the additional cost.

Brick is available in over 10,000 different sizes, shapes, textures and colors. The final choice of the brick unit having the right combination of these qualities is usually an esthetic consideration of the purchaser. Certain qualities, however, may be more desirable for some applications than for others.

Sizes, Grades, and Mortars

Brick sizes are quoted as either a "nominal" or "actual" size. The nominal size is equal to the manufactured or actual size plus the thickness of the mortar joint for which the unit is designed.

For example, the standard modular brick has these actual dimensions: 3-5/8 inches thick, 2¼ inches high, and 7-5/8 inches long. Corresponding nominal dimensions for the same brick would be 4 inches, 2-2/3 inches and 8 inches. In this case a 3/8 inch mortar joint accounts for the difference.

All brick used in outdoor structures should be of an SW Grade. Used or salvaged brick should not be used unless they have been tested and meet SW Grade requirements. Type M or Type S mortar should be used.

Composition of these mortars by volume is as follows:

Type M
1 part portland cement
¼ part hydrated lime
3 parts sand

Type S
1 part portland cement
½ part hydrated lime
4½ parts sand

All joints should be completely filled with mortar. This is particularly important since outdoor structures will be exposed to extreme weather.

Another common brick used around the home is the paving brick. This brick unit does not have any coring and is available in various sizes. Typical patio or walkway paving brick is 3-5/8 inches thick by 7-5/8 inches long and 2¼ inches in height. A 4 inch by 8 inch unit is generally used when mortarless paving is desired. The bricks are tightly abutted to each other over a firm base. The 3-5/8 inch by 7-5/8 inch by 2¼ inch unit is more easily utilized if mortar joints are desired.

If mortarless paving is desired, brick units that are twice as long as they are wide permit the selection of a wider range of design patterns. Mortared paving should be placed on a rigid base such as a concrete slab.

Recommended is a membrane layer of roofing felt or polyethylene plastic directly beneath mortarless paving. This reduces the tendency toward staining, and prevents grass and weed growth in the joint between the units.

Mortarless paving can be done with semi-skilled labor or by the handyman around the house. This may result in significant cost savings.

Where to Use Brick

A brick fireplace or barbecue in conjunction with a patio will greatly enhance the livability of a back yard area.

For small yards a very simple barbecue grill can be constructed. To insure proper disposition of smoke, care should be taken in selection of the outdoor fireplace location. The fireplace should be

planned to face the prevailing breezes so that the smoke will blow away and the best draft will be provided. Fire brick should be selected for the firebox of an outdoor fireplace.

The simplest form of the barbecue grill can be built with brick by a handyman. Natural earth tones of brick make it ideal for this and other outdoor applications.

Other applications of brick outside the home include brick screen walls, planting boxes, edging, concealment structures, fences and retaining walls. Pierced brick screens offer beauty as well as privacy without loss of light or air. They can provide a handsome separation between a children's play area and the adults' terrace.

Planters can be constructed of a wide variety of designs. Care should be taken to provide drainage in the form of weep holes through the brick or a drain at the bottom. The inside face of the walls should be waterproofed with an asphalt coating to prevent efflorescence or staining on the outside face.

Brick edging may be used to define a lawn area. Small brick enclosures may be used to conceal undesirable items. These structures may either be pierced walls to provide ventilation as required in the case of an air conditioning unit, or solid walls which may be desirable in the case of trash cans. Brick fences can provide privacy and create a courtyard effect. This is particularly true for small lots such as townhouse lots.

One of the most frequent uses of brick in landscaping is in retaining walls. Applications of retaining walls are almost endless. A word of caution about retaining walls—they will function properly only if properly designed and constructed. They will be subject to the most severe conditions and, consequently, more care should be taken in their construction than for other brick structures.

Although brick used inside the home will be subject to virtually no deterioration, the texture of the face of the brick may be of concern in certain areas. Texture will vary from very smooth to very rough and include sand faced units and glazed brick.

A sand faced brick may not be desirable in areas where it will often be touched or rubbed. The sand will readily be rubbed off and may present a cleaning problem at floor level. Sand faced brick should never be used for flooring application.

A very rough textured brick will tend to snag clothes when the two come into contact. This type of texture, however, can produce an attractive wall if properly constructed.

Glazed brick can form a very striking wall. The typical glazed brick of the single-glaze type will cost about twice as much as an unglazed unit. Brilliant colors can be produced with a double glazed unit but this type of brick is seldom used, principally due to its cost—usually four to five times that of regular brick. Special ordering will probably be necessary.

Brick performs its functions of beauty and durability most noticeably when used on the exterior walls of the home. Brick is fire resistant and virtually maintenance free. It will not corrode, rot, split or warp. It can't be dented and it never has to be painted.

A unique characteristic of brick is its design flexibility. No other material can offer the designer the wide variety of colors, textures and patterns that can be incorporated into a house design as can brick. With proper design it can be used to bring out the stateliness of a traditional home as well as the natural look of a contemporary home.

Brick walls will usually cost a little more than walls of other materials. The walls, however, are only a small portion (between 5 and 10 percent) of the price of a house. The cost differential between brick and other wall types is, therefore, modest. This initial cost difference will be recovered by the owner in the form of lower maintenance cost.

Bricks that have their exposed face sealed with some type of sealer are not recommended for exterior use. Glazed brick would fall in this category. Sealed brick does not allow the wall to "breathe" and may result in spalling or flaking away of the face of the brick. The painting of brick is not recommended for this same reason.

In summary, brick can be used to form a structure that is durable, esthetically pleasing, and virtually maintenance free. The variety of colors, textures and patterns available with brick give it a design flexibility unsurpassed by other materials.

BRICKS WITHOUT MORTAR

A Sunday drive through your nearest new-housing development will surprise you with the "renaissance" brick is having. Never in its 9,000 year history has brick been put to wider or more varied use in the home. It's not unusual to find homes today that use brick in exposed interior walls, floors, patios, walks, garden walls, retaining walls, tree wells, lawn edgings, planters, play structures, fireplaces, hearths, benches, and even table-tops and swimming pools.

It's true that handling brick and mortar properly takes a bit of practice. But there are numerous ways in which brick can be used without mortar, and many homeowners have found that this clay building product is one of their best out-of-doors friends.

With a little time and patience almost any do-it-yourselfer can build a brick patio or walk. The first job is to level the area to be covered with bricks, and excavate at least five or six inches below the surface. Put down a sand bed at least two inches thick, and preferably thicker, and level and tamp the sand. It's usually best to provide a border of some kind; it can be of wood, or you can use bricks placed on end or on their sides.

With the sand bed prepared, you're ready to place the bricks. Be certain to use a brick that is burned hard to withstand exposure to the weather. There are three major patterns in which the brick can be laid. One is a "running" pattern, in which the units are simply lapped. Then there's the "basketweave," created by placing two brick units at right angles to two other units. Finally, there's the "herringbone" with each unit butted up to a unit placed at right angles. A chisel or brick "set" can be used to cut or break bricks. Once your brick is placed, finish the job by sweeping fine sand into the cracks between the bricks. The result will be a surface that will resist weathering and traffic, and will have a natural beauty that enhances any yard.

There are other ways to use brick without mortar that can cut down on your yard work. Brick makes an excellent edging for planting beds, trees and shrubs. Placed flat on the ground it will hold in mulch and provide a level surface on which to run a lawn mower, thus eliminating the need to hand clip grass around such areas.

You can also use brick to create neat, practical "pads" for such uses as a place to park bicycles, or sit garbage cans. In short, brick used without mortar can provide beauty and utility in your yard.

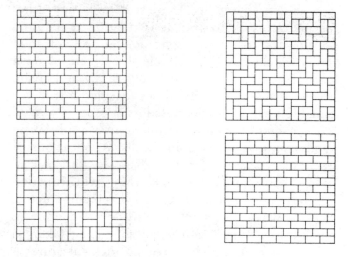

A few patterns available with the use of brick paving.

CUTTING STONE

If you would like to build a stone wall, fireplace, barbecue or other structure, and have access to a supply of sandstone or limestone (granite or other very hard stone cannot be worked easily by a do-it-your-selfer) there is no reason why you cannot do the job yourself.

Yes, there is some hard work involved, and you will be tired enough to sleep well at the end of a day of stone cutting, but the actual cutting and shaping of the stone is not at all difficult.

Very few tools are needed, and they can be purchased from a well-stocked hardware store, or through the catalog of a mail-order house. You

Stone can come in three or four-hundred-pound chunks, as did author's. On old rock it may be necessary to chip off corner to determine grain before cutting.

After grain has been determined, smaller stones can be opened like leaves of a book by just hammering along the grain lines. Resulting slabs will have relatively flat, smooth surfaces.

Rough-cut rocks then are laid out, both for ease of selection and to help estimate amount of stone needed to do particular job. These stones are further cut to rectangular shapes.

Necessary tools are shown in front of partially finished wall: trowels, stone hammer, rule, chisel and power saw. Note how blade is worn from use; it will cut many stones.

To cut rock to proper lengths and width, it first is scored with abrasive cut-off wheel in portable electric saw. This assures rock will break in proper place. Note face shield.

On end, cross-grain cuts, it takes careful work with hammer and chisel, with cut made on both surfaces of the stone to make a clean cut. (Author has shockproof wrist watch.)

For "rustic" or "primitive" look to stonework, the smooth cut made by the cut-off blade is removed by chiseling a line just behind the cut. Heavy cold chisel was used.

Finished wall is kept moist for several days to assure that mortar seasons properly. Mortar stains can be removed with dilute solution of hydrochloric acid, surface then flushed.

may already have a portable circular saw; you then need only an abrasive cut-off blade. You also will need a small sledge hammer or mason's hammer, two or three stone chisels, a cold chisel and a rule. You also need the usual tools for laying bricks or blocks: a large and a small trowel, a mortar box of some kind, a hoe to mix the mortar and a board (hawk) to carry the mortar to the job.

The main trick in cutting stone is to find the grain and use it to assure cutting fairly straight slabs that will be relatively smooth. The grain will be seen as light, parallel streaks running through the stone. With smaller chunks of rock—2 feet or less in length—you can use a chisel somewhat like

you might use an ice pick to cut ice. Find the line of the grain, then move the chisel along the line, tapping firmly. Repeat this operation back and forth along the line until the stone opens up.

For larger stones, first make a cut along the grain line with the abrasive wheel in the portable electric saw. The cut should be about ½ to 5/8 inch deep. This will require making several passes, each time setting the blade a little deeper. For all cutting with the saw, and for chiseling, protect your eyes with goggles or a face shield. The shield is more comfortable to wear, and offers protection from flying pieces of rock that might cut your face, as well as protecting your eyes.

After making the saw cut—on thick stones make a cut on both surfaces of the rock—drive two or more stone chisels into the cut. If driven firmly they will wedge in the cut. Move along, tapping on each chisel until the stone finally parts along the line. Yes, you will occasionally have a rough cut that does not follow the saw cut, but by and large the cuts will be good.

When you have to cut across the grain, you will have to make the saw cuts deeper, and use more chisels per length of cut.

As indicated in the drawing, there are various ways of cutting and laying stone. But since sandstone or limestone comes in layers, it looks best when cut in rectangular shapes. The ends of the stones can be cut neatly square, or irregular. On the surface of the stone you can take a small cold chisel and chip around the edges of the face so it has a rough look or it may be left flat as it comes from the first split. Loose splinters of stone should be removed from the face, and the saw mark should be chipped away to restore the natural look of the stone.

Soft stones tend to soak up a lot of water,

which will create dry mortar and make a poor bond, so the stones should be soaked in a tub of water several minutes before they are laid. Be sure there is no mud or dirt on the stones when they are positioned, as their porosity will permit the dirt to be drawn up through them and cause stains. These discolorations will take months or years of weathering before they no longer are visible. After the wall is finished, an application of clear silicone sealer will make it both water and stain proof.

Laying stones takes time. Check at the end of each day and remove excess mortar. Keep the walls wet to assure that the mortar sets, rather than just drying out. If you lay a stone veneer next to a brick or wooden wall, use metal ties to secure the walls together. (They can be purchased at building-material dealers that handle sand, gravel, cement, etc.) Ties also should be used at the corners of masonry walls to minimize cracking.

Your house will be more comfortable, look better, last longer and you will save hours of work and hundreds, if not thousands of dollars, in repairs.

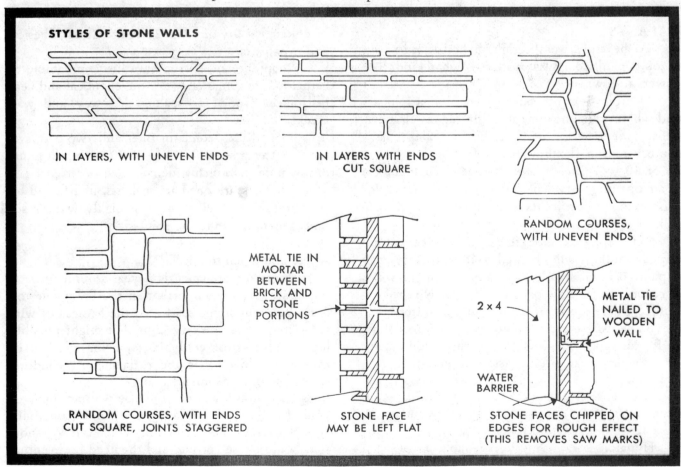

STYLES OF STONE WALLS

IN LAYERS, WITH UNEVEN ENDS

IN LAYERS WITH ENDS CUT SQUARE

RANDOM COURSES, WITH UNEVEN ENDS

RANDOM COURSES, WITH ENDS CUT SQUARE, JOINTS STAGGERED

METAL TIE IN MORTAR BETWEEN BRICK AND STONE PORTIONS

STONE FACE MAY BE LEFT FLAT

2 x 4

WATER BARRIER

METAL TIE NAILED TO WOODEN WALL

STONE FACES CHIPPED ON EDGES FOR ROUGH EFFECT (THIS REMOVES SAW MARKS)

Stone was used extensively in walls and landscaping of the front of this home, including steps that lead to lower level. Stonework and landscaping with plants blends home in with its natural surroundings.

SEALANTS

To be truly weathertight a house must have all joints caulked. The question is what kind? The answers follow:

Flexible Sealants have good elongation, are used where joint movement is limited, as elasticity is lost over a period of time. Butyl Sealants are a member of the flexible-sealant family, but have a life of 10 to 15 years. Most efficient when applied to an opening between two similar surfaces. Not recommended for joints deeper or wider than ¼ inch.

Acrylic Latex is flexible and an excellent all-purpose caulk. It adheres well to most surfaces, can be painted immediately after application. In white or colors, for inside or outside use. Not recommended where joints are continually in water.

Solvent-Base Acrylics come in various colors, are for all types of joints except those continually wet. Twenty-year life, must be heated for application.

Elastomeric Sealants have rubber-like consistency, come as one- and two-part formulations. One-part is best for home use.

Hypalon is elastomeric, available in selection of colors, has life of 15 to 20 years. Good adhesion and expansion.

Neoprene and Nitrile have life comparable to Hypalon, are remarkable for oil, chemical and heat resistance. Good for sealing driveway and wall cracks.

Polysulfides come in one- and two-part systems, better grades have life of 20 years, fill joints 3/8 inch deep, ¾ inch wide.

Silicones are one-part sealants, unaffected by temperature, last 20 years, are highly water-resistant, generally cannot be painted.

Where and When to Caulk

Home maintenance is a year-around project, but it's especially important in the fall when you must get your home ready for the ravages of winter. Time to caulk every joint that might possibly let in a draft of cold air, replacing cracked or broken window panes and reglazing any windows where the putty is missing.

Your home will not only be warmer and free of drafts, but you will save money on heating bills. A well-caulked joint will not let in rain or snow that could cause rotting, and the need for eventual replacement or repair of wooden parts.

While old-fashioned oil-base caulking compound still is available, we strongly recommend a modern material like latex caulking. This new material stays elastic under extremes of temperature and flexes with the expansion and contraction of a joint. It will last for years, rather than the few seasons the old oil-base will last. It will readily accept oil-base or latex paints, and can be applied to new wood without it first being primed.

One area often overlooked by a home owner is where wood meets masonry. This kind of joint is especially vulnerable to moisture entering to cause rotting. Be sure the joint is dry, then brush out any dirt or foreign material. Because such a joint generally is fairly wide, cut off the tip of the cartridge to create a wide ribbon of caulking. For most jobs you need cut the tip to produce only a narrow ribbon.

Important place to seal against moisture, but often overlooked, is joint between wood structure and adjacent masonry.

The same latex material is used around door and window frames, as well as where siding meets trim. It should be applied at about 60 degrees temperature, and never below 40 degrees.

Another place you might miss is around and on aluminum storm sash and doors, whether the combination type or single-duty units. Every corner will have a joint that should be sealed, and

Caulking can be purchased in "aluminum gray" for sealing joints in aluminum storm doors and windows.

there is a special caulking for the job that is available in an "aluminum-gray" color. This butyl-rubber sealant also comes in white, black and bronze to match the colors of various metals.

Flashing around chimneys is sealed with brushed on asphalt sealer; this can be repaired with tubes in compound.

Flashing around chimneys, as well as soil stacks that project through a roof, usually is sealed against the roof with a brushed-on asphalt sealer. Over the years this sealer will dry out and crack from exposure to sun and weather. It can readily be repaired from cartridges of asphalt-base caulking. If you haven't been on your roof in a few years, now would be a good time to check the various flashings. Have you checked the rain gutters lately? Even if they are fairly new there might be leaks in the end caps or the connectors. For these joints there is a special caulking that comes in cartridges for the home owner. All the products that are packaged in cartridges also can be purchased in bulk for bigger jobs.

Joints in rain gutters can be made watertight with a "gutter and lap sealer." Caulk end caps and connectors.

Do you have a greenhouse or cold frame with either glass or clear plastic where the glazing compound is breaking up? For places like this there is a translucent caulking that is waterproof and which will adhere tenaciously to both wood or metal frames, and to the glass or plastic.

Don't forget the inside of your home when you do your caulking: bathrooms are vulnerable to moisture damage, especially between tubs and tile

Unusual translucent caulking is used around frames of greenhouses and cold frames to seal glass.

and vanities and tile. For this application there are compounds that can be dispensed from a tube. The secret of a good job here is to be sure to remove any old material and wipe the surfaces with alcohol. The caulk then will adhere well, stays white, and is easily cleaned. It flexes with the movement of the fixture. Keep in mind that a bathtub may raise and lower as much as 1/8 inch when filled and emptied of water.

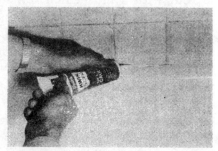

Tub-and-tile caulking comes in squeeze tube and is used around tubs and basins. Material is flexible.

Rope caulking is a material used mostly by professionals, such as installers of air conditioners. It is available, however, and a home owner can use it in the same manner to seal the cabinets of window and through-the-wall air conditioners. You simply unroll the caulking, break off the length needed and press it into place.

One important job too often ignored by a home owner is the maintenance of glazing in windows and doors. Old-fashioned putty dries and falls out and frequently it simply is painted over. Water can enter and cause rotting, the glass will be loose and cold air can enter.

Sharpen an old wood chisel and scrape out the old putty. If the wood looks dry and unpainted where the putty is removed, prime it. When it is dry, apply glazing compound. When the compound (and, it's no longer just "putty") has set, paint it. Storm sash also needs to have the glazing checked and replaced where necessary.

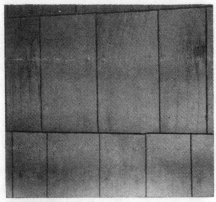

Weathered areas of paint were wire-brushed, projecting nails recessed. Paint that adhered made prime coat.

Crack in planting box can be caulked yearly, but only real cure is rebuilding entire brickwork.

Joints to be caulked should be painted first if paint has weathered away. After caulking sets, paint again.

Brickwork on chimney showed scaling, peeling paint; it was brushed off, painted. After two years, no peeling.

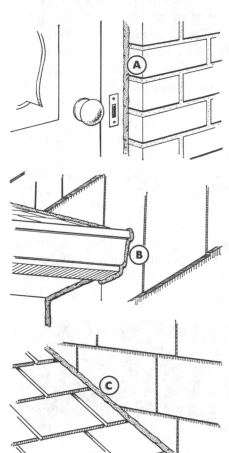

Letters mark areas that require caulking. Trim enamel is used for doors, windows, that require contrasting color.

This photo shows actual pieces of trim taken from house that was painted; no back-priming or caulking.

With all the caulking done, all the gutters sealed and the windows reglazed, now is the time to paint your house.

FENCES FOR YOUR HOME

Wood Fences

In today's growing communities privacy is a precious commodity, and enclosing property with fencing is usually the answer. Fencing not only serves as a privacy barrier, but can add beauty and charm to a home, and if designed for specific purposes, can make working or playing in the enclosed areas more enjoyable. Let's consider some variation in fencing. For protection from pets and wildlife you will need barriers they can't hurdle. A fence to control noise should be solid in the direction of the sound. A solid fence also provides protection against icy winter winds and prevents drifting snow from endangering plants and shrubs. You may have a wind or sun problem that is making pool-side unbearable. The solution may be a fence that's mostly openwork with just a small solid section for blocking out sun or wind from your favorite spot. Hiding that highway or roadside stand just past your property line is certainly the job for a fence, but don't shy away from one with openwork. Laced with a good crop of vines, it may be just the thing.

Now available to the home owner considering a fence is a line of components that can be assembled to create 1½ million different styles of fencing. Most unusual is that the fence is available at the cost of mass-produced ready-mades that offer fewer design variations. The fencing consists of modules available in eight patterns. These sections range in height from 1 to 3 feet, all are 3 feet long.

To install, you first check for grades, dips, concrete walks or obstacles in the path of the fence. Using a plot plan of your property determine your property lines. Compare your plot plan with your neighbor's to be sure there will be no differences. Although few communities insist that boundary fences be installed directly on the property line, it's a good precaution to set the fence 4 to 6 inches inside your property line.

Installation. When you are ready to start the installation, drive a wooden stake into the ground at one of the corners of your intended fence. Tying a mason's line to this, pull it taut and tie it to the stake at the next corner. Using the line as a guide, you should have no difficulty in setting your posts correctly. When inserting the post into the freshly dug hole, toss back just enough dirt to hold it upright while you check it for plumb with a level. Then tamp the remaining dirt solidly around the post.

Fence is aligned using mason's line tied taut between two stakes. Outside edges of posts are set against line.

Eight-foot sections of fencing are laid along mason's line prior to digging holes and installing posts.

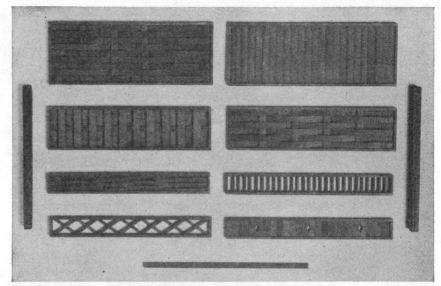

Fencing modules come in different patterns, making possible an almost endless variety of design combinations.

Use of post-hole digger saves time. Heaping dirt onto canvas square saves lawn. Post is inserted into hole, enough dirt is thrown back in to hold post. Post is checked for plumb. Remaining dirt is replaced and compacted.

Support bar is positioned into bracket, again checked for alignment. Galvanized-steel or aluminum nails are used.

Special bracket is attached to posts to position and hold support bar. Distance between posts is measured with bar, it is checked for level.

Fence sections are placed on support bar and modules stacked onto each other to achieve desired appearance.

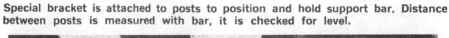

Sections are temporarily tacked until spacing and location proves out. Then line is plumbed and nailed permanently.

Drilling small pilot holes before installing gate hardware will minimize cracking and splitting of the wood.

If you are using posts that have not previously been "preservative-treated," then measure out about one-half cup of pentachlorophenol (available locally), and pour it into ground adjacent to and on all sides of the post. This poisons the soil so that fungus, termites, bacteria and other decay producing agents are killed.

It's good practice to install the fence sections as the posts are set. Position the sections of the fence in place before you tamp down the earth for the second post.

For "stepping" fence sections to conform to the contour of the land, install the first section, then position the adjacent section 1 inch off the ground on the high side of the slope.

Be sure the nails you use are large enough to hold securely, but not so large they split the wood. They should be galvanized-steel or preferably aluminum.

It's simple to determine the fence-post locations accurately as the bottom rail that supports the stacked modules may be used as a measuring stick. Lay it along the fence line and set posts at each end.

If your fence is to have a gate, it will require an opening 2½ inches wider than the gate itself to allow for hinges and latches.

Fiber Glass Fences

A combination of fiber glass panels and redwood framing offers one of the easiest and quickest ways to get beautiful outdoor privacy or protection from wind and sun. All it takes is a simple plan and ordinary hand tools.

Design possibilities are limited only by your budget and imagination. Fences can be in zig-zag or straight lines, panels can be arranged with corrugations horizontal or vertical, or alternated for interesting effects. Accordian and basket-weave designs are well within range of average carpentry skills. The panels cut easily with a wood-cutting saw, and can be fastened with screws or nails.

Redwood is known for its good looks and ability to resist weathering, and fiber glass requires no painting. Back-yard missiles such as baseballs just bounce off harmlessly. Normal rainfall and occasional spraying with a garden hose will keep the panels clean. Fiber glass is translucent so it lets in light, but keeps out harsh glare.

Before you decide where to build a fence or screen, it's a good idea to look over your property for good locations. Think about fence height, length and the effect you want to achieve. Check the view from neighboring yards and windows, your own included. Check the direction of prevailing winds, the direction of the sun's rays during the time the screened area will be most used.

Use stakes and string to outline your proposed fence and make a rough sketch of the overall plan. Show distances from existing structures and lot lines. In some localities fence regulations require the consent of neighbors and nearby lot owners. Check with your local building inspector.

When it comes to choosing fiber glass you will find there is little difference in cost between the lowest and highest grades. Since it takes no more time to put up the best-grade panel, it makes good sense to get the best quality you can find.

All fiber glass panels look pretty much alike; here are some tips on getting the best: weathering ability and resistance to surface erosion is largely determined by the quality, amount and degree of saturation of the acrylic resins used. Insist on a panel with the best-quality acrylic throughout, as well as the best light stabilizers. A pebbled surface is a sign of quality and means the surface will stay clean longer because of the washing action of rain, like a mountain stream over pebbles.

Fence posts should be 4 x 4s. If the soil is loose, make the holes oversize and pour concrete around the posts, sloping the top to shed water. Use coarse gravel under the posts to assure drainage.

With framing assembled, stop strips in place, panels are simply slipped in place, held with other stop strips.

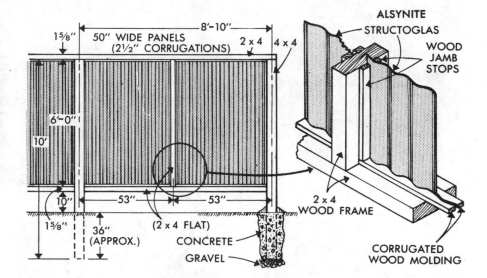

WOOD DECKS

The most versatile, and popular area of your home can be a wooden deck. Each deck takes on its own personality; if it is a high deck, it becomes a "balcony" with a sweeping view. A low deck can surround a swimming pool, edge a beautiful garden, provide a quiet place to sun, or a clean, dry playground for the youngsters. Barbecueing, dancing, partying, relaxing, reading or just sunning, all take on a new aspect when you do them on a beautiful deck you've built yourself.

Decks come in all shapes and sizes, from "minidecks" that are merely a small platform by a door, to wide decks that completely encircle the house for a variety of activities.

Building a sturdy deck should prove no problem to the determined do-it-yourselfer, even if he has no previous experience. However careful attention must be paid to all phases of the building and certain rules must be followed.

Planning

Because the deck will be a large portion of your total landscaping, a great deal of attention should be paid to preplanning to assure that the deck will be a functional as well as beautiful installation.

The first step is to determine where you wish the deck, what types of activity it will handle, and what size it will be. Using a 50 or 100-foot steel tape, measure off the area you wish to provide with a deck. It's not a bad idea to measure off your entire lot, carefully measuring the position of your house in relation to the lot. Then, using a scale ruler, draw a scale plan of your house and lot. Now that you have a good proportioned sketch of your property, you can play with deck ideas. Try them all; a semicircle, square, or an L-shape around one corner of the house. By using the scale ruler, cutting out the different shapes from small pieces of paper, and fitting them in place on the property sketch

Before: back yard is uninteresting, has small concrete slab at back door that is muddy, unusable after each rain.

After: wood deck makes back yard livable again. Family practically lives out on deck during summer months.

First step in construction of deck was to break up concrete slab, dig holes for supporting posts.

you'll get a good idea of what you wish the deck to include.

After you have determined what shape and size the deck is to be, the next step will be to acquire a building permit, and check on local zoning laws regarding building and/or property additions.

The next step is to design the deck to determine what kinds and sizes of material will be needed.

Decks are supported by posts which are set or anchored in a number of ways. The easiest, al-

though the least effective, is to simply dig a hole, set in the posts and tamp dirt back tightly into the hole. A much more solid post can be assured by pouring concrete in the hole around the post. Or you can pour concrete foundation blocks, and position the posts on these, anchoring the posts with metal straps or an anchor pin made of pipe. Deck support columns should be a minimum of 4 x 4 (dimensional).

The connecting beams can be either 4 x 4's, 2 x 6's or 2 x 8's, depending on the design of the deck. If you wish an extra strong deck, you can double up the beams, one on each side of each post.

The deck flooring should be weather-resistant 2 x 4's to minimize twisting and warping. Flatgrain lumber should be laid with the heart-wood side down. To determine this, examine the end of the stock; the circular arcs described by the grain should be in the shape of a rainbow, or with the arcs up.

Any nails used in the deck should be galvanized to prevent discoloration of the wood. Also any bolts should be coated with a rust-inhibiting paint before installing. All members of the deck in contact with, or close to, the ground should be soaked in a good wood preservative before installation.

Positioning and Inserting the Posts

After determining the size and shape of the

A small mixer making five gallons at a time is used to make the concrete needed for the post holes.

After cross beams are placed in position, cross bracing is installed, tops of supporting posts cut off level.

Straightedge is clamped into position along outer edge of deck and circular saw used to cut outer edge straight.

The posts are positioned in their holes using a string guide line, concrete poured around them, posts plumbed.

Window well presents a problem. Posts are set on each side of well to support a cutout around well.

Lengthwise beams are clamped into position on supporting posts, holes drilled, beam and post bolted together.

Deck flooring is placed in position, nailed down using galvanized nails. Thin wooden stick used to determine spacing.

Window well is fitted with a lift-up door that provides access to outside water faucet and hose storage.

deck, a line is tied to each corner of the house and to stakes to form a rectangle or other shape, the size of the deck. The lines must be level, as determined by using a string or line level.

The position of each supporting post is marked on the line by sticking on a piece of masking tape, then the post holes are dug. These holes should be deep enough to be below the frost line, and of a size to allow a good pour of concrete around the post.

Posts are not positioned next to the house. After determining the position of the deck in relation to the house, a 2 x 6 or 2 x 8 beam called a "ledge" is nailed to the house to support the deck.

After each post hole is dug the posts are rough-cut to length; they are left somewhat longer than the measurement from the bottom of the post hole to the deck-level string.

A batch of concrete is mixed for each post hole using an electric mixer such as the one shown, or by hand in a wheelbarrow.

The mix should be 1 part cement, 2 parts sand, 3 parts gravel and enough water to allow the mix to pour well. Each post is correctly positioned in its hole, against the leveled string, held plumb and the concrete mix poured around the post. You will have to tamp the concrete to settle it down in the hole and around the posts. Make sure the post is plumb in both directions before proceeding to the next post. When all posts have been set, the concrete is allowed to set for at least 24 hours before disturbing.

Laying the Deck

The stringers or beams are clamped in position on the post supports and nailed with galvanized nails, or bolted with ¼-inch lag bolts. The beams should be level in both directions, starting from the ledger attached to the building. After the beams are securely fastened to each post, a handsaw is used to square off the protruding portion of each post, flush with the beams.

The deck flooring is laid in place, and using galvanized nails, is nailed to each one of the beams or stringers. A piece of 1/8-inch stock is used as a spacer, or you can use a 10-penny nail for a gauge. Too many decks are built with wider spacing which is dangerous, causing people to stumble and fall. When all flooring boards for the deck are nailed in position, a straight board is clamped along each edge of the deck and a portable circular saw run along its edge to produce a finished edge.

You may wish to use a light stain-finish or even paint on your deck. But the easiest to maintain, is a nonfinished deck left to weather.

If building a deck from start to finish is somewhat more challenging than you wish to tackle, there is a prefabricated deck available which comes in 3 x 3 or 4 x 4-foot preassembled sections. These sections are made of a beautiful redwood and are designed to interlock without the need of nailing. The deck sections can be installed on level ground, over sand, gravel or even on an old and deteriorating concrete patio. Their design makes the finished deck completely flexible; you can add or subtract sections to build the deck to suit your needs. If you're renting or living in a mobile home and wish to move, just pick up your deck and take it with you.

The drawings illustrate typical deck construction details, including a high or "balcony deck." As each deck requires individual planning you will have to design your deck to suit your needs.

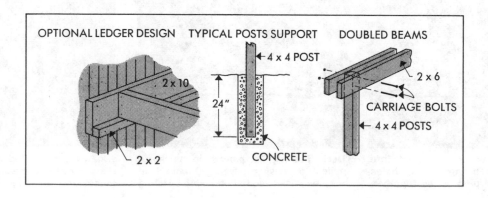

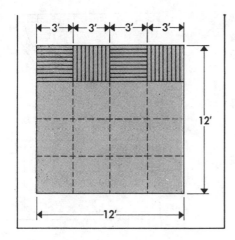

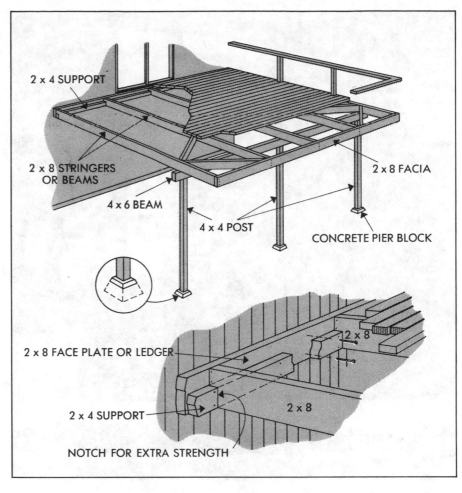

2 x 4 SUPPORT

2 x 8 STRINGERS OR BEAMS

4 x 6 BEAM

4 x 4 POST

2 x 8 FACIA

CONCRETE PIER BLOCK

2 x 8 FACE PLATE OR LEDGER

2 x 8

2 x 4 SUPPORT

2 x 8

NOTCH FOR EXTRA STRENGTH

BUILDING A FOUNTAIN

Any yard will be a more pleasant place with an attractive fountain and the musical sound of water splashing from basin to basin. At night the light shining through the glass blocks and the opening above the middle basin make the fountain an eye-catching focal point. The fountain can be located on a patio or in a corner of the yard that can be seen from the house.

If the fountain pictured is not of a design that is right for your yard or patio, you can readily modify the styling while still following the basic engineering. Keep in mind the basic idea of pump house and pool. No water-supply line is required, as the pump recirculates the same water over and over. You need only occasionally add water from a garden hose as it evaporates or splashes out under the influence of a brisk wind. With several basins and short drops for the water this should not be a major problem. If the fountain is a basic one, with a single stream of water falling from near the top, then you may have a splashing condition that will cause problems.

We used a pottery crock as the main fall for our fountain simply because it caught our eye in a "junk" shop. You can do something similar or make any substitution you find intriguing. You might even make a wooden bucket or use a ready-made figure of cast concrete. Even another basin could be used as the top fall. The main idea is to picture the project as you want it to be, before you start building. Check through your local second-hand stores and through the scrap pile in your workshop. You may have some items in the potting shed, such as broken bird baths or large ornamental clay pots, that can be utilized in the fountain structure.

The submersible pump used in the fountain shown was purchased for about $20. It will lift quite a volume of water over 10 feet. At a height of 5 feet it will pump 200 gallons per hour, which is an excellent flow for a fountain of this, or simi-

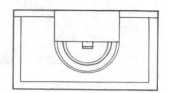

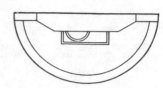

FLAGSTONE TOP (ALL VERSIONS)

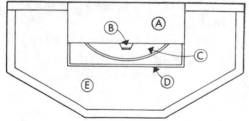

A — PUMP-HOUSE
B — WATERFALL OUTLET
C — UPPER BASIN
D — LOWER BASIN
E — POOL

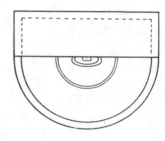

lar size. Installation is a snap, you just set the pump on the floor of the pump house and run a plastic hose up to the crock or other outlet. Water in the lower basin runs to the pump and is recirculated back to the top.

The best bet for an electrical supply is to come from an existing outside outlet, or run a wire from the basin or crawl space. The wire must be the underground type and is buried in a trench about a foot deep, minimizing any chance for a shovel to cut into it during garden or yard work. Bring the wire up through a length of ¾-inch pipe

that later will be secured by the pouring of the pump-house slab.

The base dimensions of the project fountain can be used as a starting point for your own fountain. The footing may seem oversize for what may end up as a low, lightweight wall, but overbuilding here is a safety factor. You don't want any wall cracks to show up later.

All the fountain details are shown. Study this drawing carefully before you begin construction. The overflow pipe F is necessary to maintain the water level when it rains. The water-passage pipe

G is almost optional, as water will flow from pool to pump house through the drain line, but since it is easy to install, add it anyway to assure a good flow of water.

If your soil is stable, you can trench it for use as forms for the footings. Otherwise, nail up simple forms from 1 x 8s or 1 x 10s and remove them after the concrete has set. Be sure before doing any of the concrete work that you have thoroughly soaked and tamped the soil. When you put in the steel reinforcing rods, make bends at the corners and T-shapes at intersections of walls. Wire all rod joints.

Make an assembly of the drain line, but do not install the short vertical pieces until after the line has been placed in the soil. The faucet and hose bib at the end of the drain line is a good idea, as all you then have to do to drain the pool for cleaning is to turn a valve. By connecting a hose to the drain you can water nearby plants so it won't be wasted.

The next step is to mix and pour the concrete for the base slabs. This is a regular one-cement, two-sand, three-gravel mix, well spread and tamped. Be sure to wet down both soil and footing walls and tamp well where base slab and footings meet. Work over the surface with a wooden float and remember that all surfaces must slope toward the drains. After the concrete has set for a half hour or so, smooth-finish the surface with a steel trowel.

Building up the walls is a standard bricklaying job, and unless you want a very formal appearance be casual with the work to create a rustic effect. The lines do not have to be exactly plumb and you can occasionally substitute a stone for a brick. Be sure to use mortar generously so all joints will be packed solidly. Soak bricks and stones before placing them, and as you go, "butter" the back sides of the walls with mortar. This is more or less a "stucco" job necessary for waterproofing the pool. Don't let the mortar get too set before smoothing the joints. The joints can be struck off in the standard manner with a joint tool, but a stiff-bristled brush used on the joints and stucco gives a good effect, and the operation required no great skill. A whisk broom works fine.

A heavy steel angle must be used to support any span across the lower walls. The angle is raised slightly above the walls so there will be a slope on the structure supported by the angle. The bottoms of the various basins should be level across the back, but slanted toward the basin in front to assure good drainage. The middle basin, which can be a piece of crockery, a crock cover, bird bath, etc. is mortared in place, and supported until the mortar sets.

A heavy bridge block is used above the middle basin to keep the weight of the wall off it. The opening also allows light to shine through from the pump house for an attractive night-time glow on the rippling water.

The crock used for the water discharge is located so the water falls directly in the center of the basin just below it. You also can control this somewhat by restricting the water line to reduce the flow of water and move the discharge back toward the wall of the fountain.

Another thought to keep in mind when building up the wall of the pump house: install the electrical fittings at the same time. Fasten the various junction boxes and light fixtures to strips of metal that can be slipped into the mortar joints. And, most important of all, receptacles and fixtures must be grounded! This means that the cable from the house or other electrical supply must have a third wire, and it must be grounded back at the service box in the house. The ground wire then is fastened to each junction box and receptacle, so that in the event of any short circuit anywhere in the system—and this is always a possibility in a very wet situation as around the fountain—there will be no shock hazard. For the same reason, use watertight fittings at all connections. These watertight fittings are used even in the pump house that is protected against the weather.

The pump house requires an access door. It is hinged to a frame that is preassembled and installed as the wall is built. About every third course of bricks, (measured on the frame) drive large nails through the frame and bend them so they will anchor in the mortar as the joints are made. Various shelves of rock can be included in the wall of the fountain, and pieces of statuary and figurines can be displayed to make the fountain more attractive. The top of the wall can be made as a planter box, if it is wide enough. The top of the pump house should be a single slab of stone to make this compartment water and weathertight.

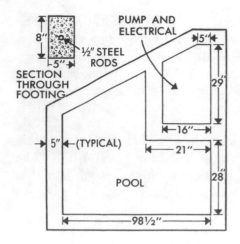

SECTION THROUGH FOOTING

8"
5"
1/2" STEEL RODS

PUMP AND ELECTRICAL

5"

29"

16"

21"

5" (TYPICAL)

28"

POOL

98½"

Pouring footing is first part of job; remove forms after 24 hours. Note cable up through pump-house base.

PUMP-HOUSE DRAIN
POOL DRAIN
OUTSIDE FAUCET FOR HOSE

90° ELBOW
TEE

Position drain line, add vertical stubs that are cut to length to permit base to slope down to them to drain.

A — FOOTING
B — BASE SLABS
C — POOL
D — PUMP-HOUSE
E — WATER LEVEL
F — 2" OVERFLOW PIPE
G — 2" WATER PIPE
H — DRAIN LINES
I — BURIAL CABLE
J — ¾" PIPE FOR WIRE
K — SUBMERSIBLE PUMP
L — PLASTIC PIPE

M — LOWER BASIN
N — MIDDLE BASIN
O — WATERFALL CROCK
P — BRIDGE BLOCKS
Q — OPENING OVER MIDDLE BASIN
R — FLAGSTONE
S — REFLECTOR-TYPE LIGHT
T — ON-OFF SWITCH
U — OUTLET BOX

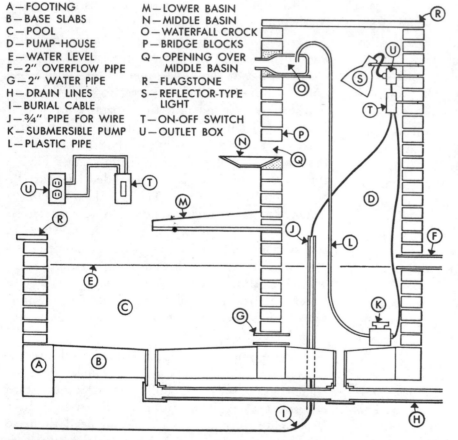

Build walls on footings, then build up entire pool area. Glass blocks let light from pump house reflect in pool.

The lower basin of the fountain may be lined with colorful rocks, even large chunks of glass, such as can be obtained from lapidary-supply houses.

Lighting, especially colored lamps, would be attractive, shining through the main discharge at the top and through the opening above the middle basin. This lighting would have to be planned ahead of time, and the fixtures located inside the pump house.

Seal the main basin of the fountain with waterproofing paint, of the type used to seal basement walls against moisture. It comes a standard white, but can be tinted with tubes of coloring to produce a number of attractive hues. Follow the instructions on using the sealer paint; in most cases

For rustic effect, use occasional stone in place of brick. Stone should be about brick size, soaked in water.

Any span across lower walls requires use of heavy angle for support. Blocks under angle are to provide slope.

Bottom of basin should be level across the back, but pitched uniformly to front to assure proper drainage.

Middle basin is a crock cover, another purchase from a "junk" store. Slope same as lower basin.

Note heavy bridge block above middle basin. Light in pump house shines through this opening onto water.

Situate main fall so water will hit in center of middle basin. You can control this somewhat by restricting hose.

Electric fixtures are set in wall as it is built up. Metal strips on back of boxes are mortared into the joints.

Frame of access door is built before wall is started. Nails through frame tie it to the mortar joints in the wall.

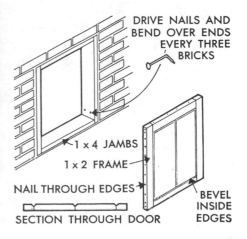

DRIVE NAILS AND BEND OVER ENDS EVERY THREE BRICKS

1 x 4 JAMBS

1 x 2 FRAME

NAIL THROUGH EDGES

BEVEL INSIDE EDGES

SECTION THROUGH DOOR

295

Finished door, assembled and installed. In your assembly you may wish a different style of paneling.

two coats will be required. Coloring the second coat will make it easy to see that you are covering the first coat completely. If you want the final coat to be white, then color the first coat.

Use a stiff-bristled brush and "scrub" the waterproofing paint into every mortar joint, any cracks that show in the lower concrete, and any joint between the brickwork and concrete. To assure maximum strength in the poured-concrete of the pool, the moment the concrete has set up, about 12 hours, fill the pool with water. Concrete that sets slowly, while covered with water, is at least 100 per cent stronger than concrete that sets up dry.

After the mortar has set between the bricks, and both bricks and mortar are thoroughly dry, coat the walls with a clear silicone sealer that can be brushed or sprayed onto the surfaces. This will minimize the problems with efflourescence, and in colder climates will help avoid damage caused by freezing and thawing of moisture in the mortar joints, and even in the somewhat porous bricks themselves.

BUILDING A PATIO

If you want your patio to be an outdoor "living room" you must look beyond the mere pouring of a concrete slab, or the setting of some blocks or slate in the ground. Instead of a fence, visualize a screen that in itself is attractive to look at and designed to create points of interest. Pri-

vacy, yes, but with the open feeling you want when you are outdoors.

Ideally, there should be a focal point, a main attraction, something that catches the eye; such as a fountain, rock garden, etc.

The screen is not expensive, being made of stock lumber which you can buy by the running foot. Figuring 4 x 4 posts, stringers and fence boards, the cost will be about $1 a running foot for the complete fence. This is figuring posts being set on 8-foot centers. The screen illustrated has posts about every 5 feet, which requires buying some extra material, but the cost increases only a little. The point is that the material is "utility" grade; it's the home craftsman's time and interest that transforms the ordinary lumber into a decorator-type patio screen.

The plaques can reflect your interests: bas-reliefs of cars can show interest in sports cars, trains can tell of your model-railroading hobby. If you are a wood carver, the plaques can be your own work, and there would be no better way to make the screen a creation of your own skills.

The patio surface can be precast blocks, slate, stone or poured concrete. The patio shown was of the latter material, redwood 2 x 4s on edge creating a grid, and also providing forms for the concrete that was reinforced with steel rods.

To build the screen you may, at some lumber yards, be able to buy board-fence by the foot. A "package" of this kind will include 4 x 4 posts, 2 x 4 stringers and 1 x 8 boards. This setup is for posts on 8-foot centers. Check your own layout; you may want the posts closer together. If you do, it later will be necessary to buy extra stringers and posts, but these can be purchased after you are sure how many feet of each you will need.

Posts and stringers should be preshaped. Notice that the intermediate posts are grooved on opposite faces, while the end posts are treated this way on just one side. Both the top and bottom stringers are grooved.

Because you are buying "rough" lumber you will become aware that all similar pieces are not exactly alike; dimensions may vary a bit. And, of course, 4 x 4s and 2 x 4s do not match those measurements. Before starting to groove and dado, pick the best side of each piece and mark it with chalk. Then, when you cut the full-length grooves, keep this marked face against the saw fence. The

Temporary cleats are nailed on posts to keep all their tops same level. They are plumbed, concrete poured.

Corner of finish frame shows simple, neat joint made by butting frame members, using finish nails, countersinking.

Spacer strips in grooves position top rails above stringers. As option, groove above top rail can be filled.

Concrete plaques are poured in shallow forms, reinforced with steel rods. These plaques give fence individuality.

One suggestion for plaques is to inset pottery jars or vases in which live or artificial flowers can be placed.

Plaster figures and plaques are inexpensive, can be set in concrete, then later antiqued to protect them.

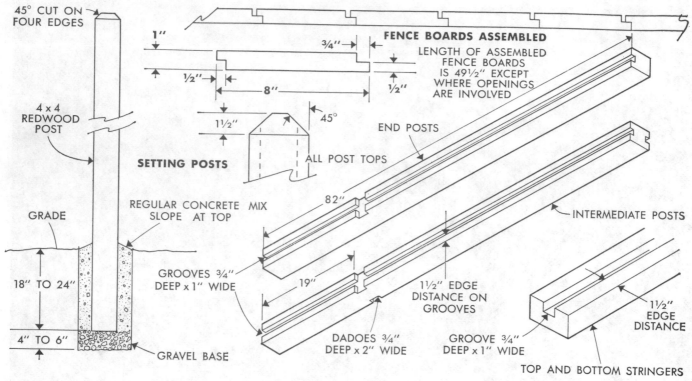

45° CUT ON FOUR EDGES

4 x 4 REDWOOD POST

SETTING POSTS

GRADE

REGULAR CONCRETE MIX SLOPE AT TOP

18" TO 24"

4" TO 6"

GRAVEL BASE

1"

1/2"

8"

3/4"

1/2"

1 1/2"

45°

ALL POST TOPS

FENCE BOARDS ASSEMBLED

LENGTH OF ASSEMBLED FENCE BOARDS IS 49 1/2" EXCEPT WHERE OPENINGS ARE INVOLVED

END POSTS

INTERMEDIATE POSTS

82"

19"

GROOVES 3/4" DEEP x 1" WIDE

1 1/2" EDGE DISTANCE ON GROOVES

DADOES 3/4" DEEP x 2" WIDE

GROOVE 3/4" DEEP x 1" WIDE

1 1/2" EDGE DISTANCE

TOP AND BOTTOM STRINGERS

SHAPE PIECE TO FILL GROOVE (OPTIONAL)

1" x 3" TOP RAIL

TOP STRINGER

FILLER 3/4" x 1" x 5"

POST-TOP DETAILS

Completed concrete plaque with vases is set in finished frame in fence, foliage is planted in them.

Plaster casting has been antiqued and given coating of glaze to weatherproof it. Bright colors can be used here.

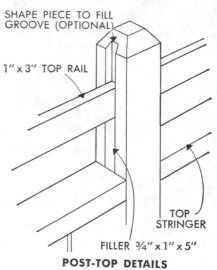

grooves will not be centered in the stock, but all will have the same edge distance, which is the important factor. Be generous on the plus side with the width of the grooves. There is no point in trying to make the boards a tight fit. And a spell of rainy weather could swell the boards enough to split the posts and stringers. Make the grooves 1/16 to 1/8 inch wider than necessary, and you will make sure of an easy assembly job.

Posts are set in the ground. Depending on your area, the frost line may require the posts to be set in the ground from 18 to 24 inches. In some

of the northern states this may be as much as 36 inches. This means you will require longer posts. There should be a minimum of 1 inch between the lower stringer and the ground, which will require cutting the 3/4 inch deep x 2-inch wide dado in the posts farther from the end than the 19 inch.

Dig all holes, put in the gravel base for draining, then slip in the posts. Next, cut stringers to length and nail in place with 16 d galvanized nails. When you set the posts and stringers, keep the chalk marks that denote the best faces toward the patio.

298

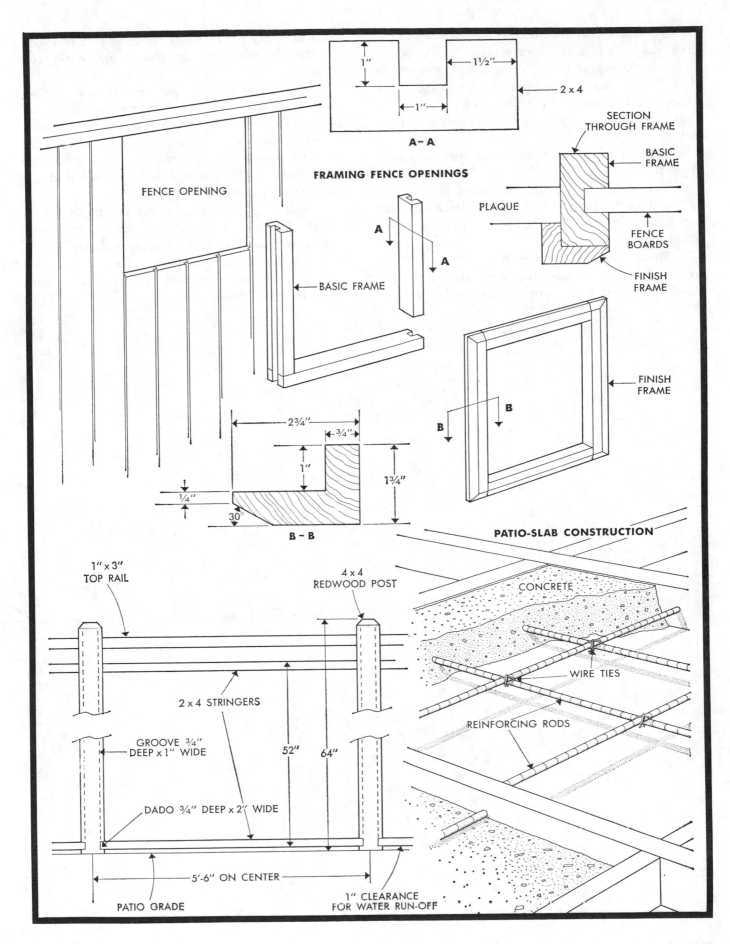

FRAMING FENCE OPENINGS

A-A

1"

1"

1½"

2 x 4

SECTION THROUGH FRAME

BASIC FRAME

PLAQUE

FENCE BOARDS

FINISH FRAME

FENCE OPENING

BASIC FRAME

A

A

B

B

B

B

FINISH FRAME

2¾"

¾"

1"

¼"

1¾"

30°

B - B

PATIO-SLAB CONSTRUCTION

CONCRETE

WIRE TIES

REINFORCING RODS

1" x 3" TOP RAIL

4 x 4 REDWOOD POST

2 x 4 STRINGERS

GROOVE ¾" DEEP x 1" WIDE

DADO ¾" DEEP x 2" WIDE

52"

64"

5'-6" ON CENTER

PATIO GRADE

1" CLEARANCE FOR WATER RUN-OFF

To assure that the tops of all posts are at the same height, use a temporary cleat on each post. After the posts and the bottom stringers are in place, check each post for plumb on two faces. Use temporary bracing on each post to keep it plumb, then pour the concrete. If your patio is large enough you can order ready-mix in a truck, and pour around the posts at the same time you pour the patio.

Details for the fence boards are just rabbets cut on diagonally-opposite corners. After assembly you have tight joints on the back of the screen and grooves on the front.

Total board width between posts is best determined by actual measurement. Best bet is to place one board in the center and to add boards toward each post. You then rip each end board to fit. The boards must be placed before the top stringer.

Where you have an opening, reduce the length of the boards. The basic-frame members are grooved like the stringers. The bottom piece, which is notched at each end and nailed down into the top edges of the fence boards. The two verticals are toe-nailed at the bottom and end-nailed down through the top stringer.

Shape up the material for the finish frame. Install the verticals first, then cut the two horizontals to exact length and nail them down.

The top rails, ripped from fence boards, are cut to fit between the posts and set on filler strips to assure a level line.

8

PLUMBING AND TEMPERATURE CONTROL

PLUMBING & TEMPERATURE CONTROL

8

FIRST AID FOR AERATORS ■ FUELS AND BURNERS ■ AUTOMATIC CONTROLS

TOOLS AND SPARE PARTS ■ FAUCET REPAIR ■ REPAIRING LEAKS IN PIPES AND TANKS

CLEARING CLOGGED DRAINS ■ FROZEN WATER PIPES ■ REPAIRING WATER CLOSETS

FROSTPROOF HYDRANTS ■ INSTALLING PLASTIC PIPE ■ WATER AIR HEATING

PLUMBING PRECAUTIONS ■ HOT-WATER AND STEAM HEATING ■ ELECTRIC HEATING

FURNACE CHECK-UP ■ AIR CONDITIONING ■ CONTROLLING HUMIDITY

SIMPLE PLUMBING REPAIRS

You can save money and avoid delays by making minor plumbing repairs yourself.

Jobs that you can do with a few basic tools include:

Repairing water faucets and valves.

Repairing leaks in pipes and tanks.

Thawing frozen pipes.

Repairing water closets.

Cleaning clogged drains.

Extensive plumbing repairs or alterations in the plumbing system usually require authorization from local authorities and possibly inspection of the completed work. Therefore such work should be done by a qualified or licensed plumber.

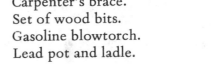

TOOLS AND SPARE PARTS

Basic tools that you should have on hand to make simple plumbing repairs include:

Wrenches, including pipe wrenches, in a range of sizes to fit the pipe, fittings, fixtures, equipment, and appliances in the system.

Screwdrivers in a range of sizes to fit the faucets, valves, and other parts of the system.

Ball peen hammer or a 12-or 16-ounce clawhammer.

Rubber force cup (plunger or "plumber's friend").

Cold chisel and center punch.

Cleanout auger ("snake").

Friction tape.

Adjustable pliers.

Additional tools required for more extensive plumbing repairs include:

Pipe vise.

Set of pipe threading dies and stocks.

Hacksaw and blades (blades should have 32 teeth per inch).

Pipe cutter, roller type.

Tapered reamer or half-round file.

Carpenter's brace.

Set of wood bits.

Gasoline blowtorch.

Lead pot and ladle.

Caulking tools.

Copper tube cutter with reamer (if you have copper tubing).

Always use the proper size wrench or screwdriver. Do not use pipe wrenches on nuts with flat surfaces; use an adjustable or open-end wrench. Do not use pipe wrenches on polished-surface tubings or fittings, such as found on plumbing fixtures; use a strap wrench. Tight nuts or fittings can sometimes be loosened by tapping lightly with a hammer or mallet.

When cutting pipe with a hacksaw, insert the pipe through a block of hard wood. A slot sawed in the block guides the saw during the cutting.

It should not be necessary to stock a large number of spare parts. Past plumbing troubles may give some indication as to the kind of parts most likely to be needed. Spare parts should include:

Faucet washers and packing.

One or two lengths of the most common type and size of piping in the plumbing system.

Several unions and gaskets or unions with ground surfaces.

Several couplings and elbows.

A few feet of pipe strap.

An extra hose connection.

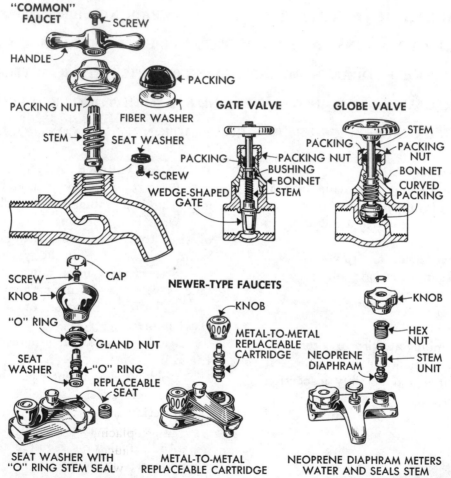

FAUCET REPAIR

No matter how fancy, all faucets do one thing—control the flow of water. Faucets and globe valves, the type of shutoff valves commonly used in home water systems, are very similar in construction and repair instructions given apply to both. However, faucets and valves come in a wide variety of styles.

Mixing faucets are found in sinks, laundry trays, and bathtubs and many are of the newer single-control variety. Mixing faucets regulate a mix of hot and cold water to produce the desired temperature. They are, in actuality, two separate units requiring independent repair.

All faucets have a valve of some sort, plus other moving parts that must be sealed to prevent water leakage. Other than cleaning out foreign matter or mineral deposits (and excluding the repair

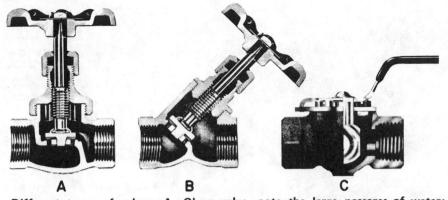

Different types of valves: A. Glove valve, note the large passages of water; B. Y-pattern glove valve, the flow is almost straight; C. Ball valve, straight flow; some makes are available with the port in the ball the same diameter as the pipe.

Repair kits are available to replace worn parts in single-control faucets, such as this "Delta" unit. Note strip in pliers.

of leaking pipes), replacing the seals and valve parts that have become worn or lost resiliency is the major part of faucet upkeep.

Disassembly and Replacement Parts

To make the job simple, it is necessary to know how to disassemble and reassemble the faucet and to know what parts need replacement or repair.

Hopefully you have saved the installation and maintenance sheets for complex faucets installed in your home. These sheets generally have "exploded" assembly drawings and information on getting special repair parts. You often can get this information from your dealer, if you don't have it. Common repair parts, O-rings, washers, spray hoses and even complete repair kits for popular faucets can be purchased at well-stocked hardware stores. If you don't have an instruction sheet, take the defective parts to the store with you to get replacements that fit.

Replacement knobs are available. If you need to replace one unit on a two-knob fixture, you may have to buy both knobs to get a match. Take along the old knob.

A badly worn or damaged faucet may require replacement. Measure the hole spacing on the old one to make sure the new one will fit.

Common faucets have a body fitted with a removable stem that has coarse threads. There is a washer on the end, and packing around the stem. "Frostproof" sill cocks are a variation of this design. Newer washer-type faucets employ an O-ring in place of the packing around the stem.

One of the newer "metal-to-metal" faucets uses a special-alloy valve cartridge that is replaced as a unit should leakage occur. Another type has a single, replaceable neoprenediaphram that seals not only across the seat, but also the stem.

Disassembly is generally the same. Remove the knob or handle first. Unscrew the bonnet, packing or gland nut. Unscrew the stem to get at the valve seat. Some faucets have threaded replaceable seats that are removed with an Allen wrench.

Single-control mixing faucets may have a lever, turn knob or T-handle which controls volume and temperature. There are three general types:

One style has either a ball that swivels in a cup-shaped seat, or a cup-shaped cap that swivels over a ball-shaped seat. Both employ spring-loaded cup-like seal seats to control water flow.

A second type employs a cam moved by a lever to contact the stems of spring-loaded valves.

A third type uses an O-ring-sealed spool that moves laterally and rotates to control flow and mixture. Replacing the spool is the usual repair for this kind of faucet.

Faucets with spray hoses will have a "diverter" valve, usually located under the swivel spout. It diverts water to the hose, rather than the spout. A slight spout flow is normal with most faucets. Movable spouts generally have O-rings to seal them.

Faucet disassembly often requires removing rather delicate, highly-polished parts and hidden screws. Knob screws may be hidden with friction-fit caps. They usually can be pried off with a knife blade. Some faucets have an Allen setscrew near

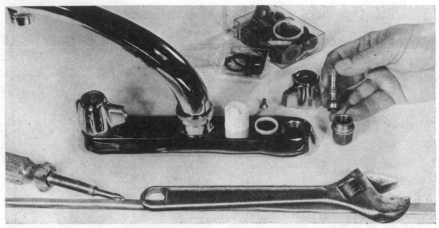

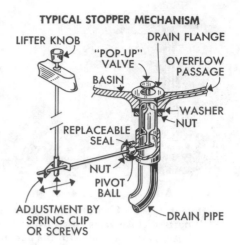

LIFTER KNOB — DRAIN FLANGE
"POP-UP" VALVE — OVERFLOW PASSAGE
BASIN
REPLACEABLE SEAL
WASHER
NUT
NUT
PIVOT BALL
ADJUSTMENT BY SPRING CLIP OR SCREWS
DRAIN PIPE

Newer washer-type faucets are likely to have some plastic parts and an O-ring, rather than packing to seal the stem against leaking.

"FROSTPROOF" SILL COCK

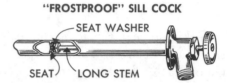

SEAT WASHER
SEAT — LONG STEM

ANGLE STOP

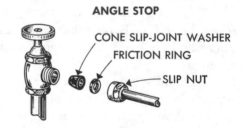

CONE SLIP-JOINT WASHER
FRICTION RING
SLIP NUT

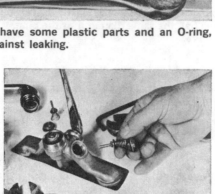

"Speakman" single-control units have unique valve cartridge that is quickly removed and replaced if faucet leaks.

Some "Sears Roebuck" one-lever valves depend on cam that tilts to open valves. Caps expose O-ring valves for cleaning.

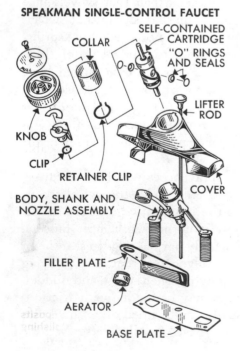

SPEAKMAN SINGLE-CONTROL FAUCET

COLLAR
SELF-CONTAINED CARTRIDGE
"O" RINGS AND SEALS
LIFTER ROD
KNOB
CLIP
RETAINER CLIP
BODY, SHANK AND NOZZLE ASSEMBLY
COVER
FILLER PLATE
AERATOR
BASE PLATE

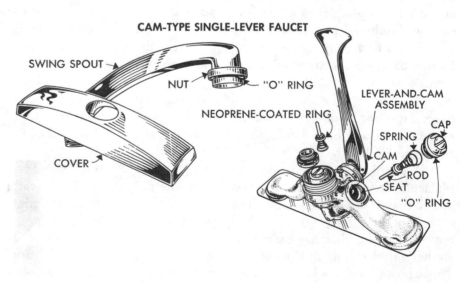

CAM-TYPE SINGLE-LEVER FAUCET

SWING SPOUT
NUT
"O" RING
NEOPRENE-COATED RING
LEVER-AND-CAM ASSEMBLY
CAP
SPRING
CAM
ROD
SEAT
"O" RING
COVER

"Peerless" single-control faucet has seals in dome that is covered with cup that is positioned by the handle.

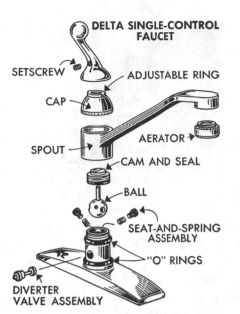

DELTA SINGLE-CONTROL FAUCET

SETSCREW
CAP
SPOUT
ADJUSTABLE RING
AERATOR
CAM AND SEAL
BALL
SEAT-AND-SPRING ASSEMBLY
"O" RINGS
DIVERTER VALVE ASSEMBLY

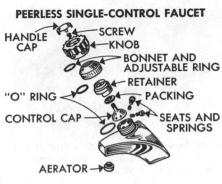

PEERLESS SINGLE-CONTROL FAUCET

HANDLE CAP
SCREW
KNOB
BONNET AND ADJUSTABLE RING
RETAINER
PACKING
"O" RING
CONTROL CAP
SEATS AND SPRINGS
AERATOR

the base of the handle.

To prevent damage to plated fixtures wrap wrenches and pliers with rubber.

Rubber seals and O-rings will leak if the metal surfaces are rough. Always replace abraded seals and smooth metal surfaces with crocus cloth.

Packing and sealants are handy to seal other faucet leaks. If a new dome packing is not immediately available, a temporary seal can be made by wrapping impregnated-string packing around the stem.

Pipe sealant can be used on fittings that are removed or replaced, to prevent leakage.

Common Problems

If a faucet drips when closed or vibrates ("sings" or "flutters") when opened, the trouble is usually the washer at the lower end of the spindle. If it leaks around the spindle when opened, new packing is needed. To replace the washer:

Shut off the water at the shutoff valve nearest the particular faucet.

Disassemble the faucet—the handle, packing nut, packing, and spindle, in that order. You may have to set the handle back on the spindle and use it to unscrew and remove the spindle.

Remove the screw and worn washer from the spindle. Scrape all the worn washer parts from the cup and install a new washer of the proper size.

Examine the seat on the faucet body. If it is nicked or rough, reface it. Hardware or plumbing-supply stores carry the necessary seat-dressing tool. Hold the tool vertically when refacing the seat.

Reassemble the faucet. Handles of mixing faucets should be in matched positions.

If a washer requires frequent replacement, it may be the wrong type or the seat may be rough and scoring the washer. Flat washers are used on seats having a crown or round ridge for the washer seat. Tapered or rounded washers are used with tapered seats. These seats may be replaced if worn or damaged.

Replaceable seats have either a square or hex shaped water passage for the seat removal tool. Seat dressing tools are available for non-replaceable seats.

Aerator screens may plug with deposits or foreign material. Clean them, or replace screw-on aerator completely.

Faucet-maintenance time is a good opportunity to routinely clean out the drain pipes to assure no residue.

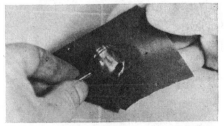

Remove imperfections, mineral deposits on movable faucet parts by polishing with fine crocus cloth. Rub lightly.

Spray-hose valves may drip due to material lodging in seat. Hoses may be purchased to replace leaking ones.

Replacement washers for standard faucets come in two types, conventional at right, nonrotating type at the left.

Damaged or worn nonreplaceable seats can be smoothed with tools that cut a new face. Faucet is cut to show tool.

Occasionally a faucet will be noisy when water is flowing. This may be due to a loose washer or worn threads on the stem and receiver, permitting the stem to vibrate or chatter. Pressing down on the handle will stop stem vibration but will not affect a loose washer.

Replacement stems are available; however, if the receiving threads are worn excessively a new stem would not eliminate the problem completely. In some faucets it is possible to replace the stem receiver, the stem, and the seat, thus restoring all normal wearing parts within the faucet.

Several new faucet designs aimed at easier operation, eliminating drip, and promoting long service life, are on the market. Instructions for repair may be obtained from dealers.

If a shower head drips, the supply valve has not been fully closed, or the valve needs repair.

After extended use and several repairs, some valves will no longer give tight shutoff and must be replaced. When this becomes necessary, it may be advisable to upgrade the quality with equipment having better flow characteristics and longer-life design and materials. In some cases, ball valves will deliver more water than globe valves. Some globe valves deliver more flow than others for identical pipe sizes. Y-pattern globe valves, in straight runs of pipe, have better flow characteristics than straight stop valves.

FAUCET-WASHER SIZE CHART

DIMENSION INSIDE WASHER IS ACTUAL SIZE, NUMBER BELOW IS TRADE SIZE.

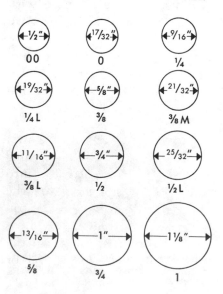

FAUCET TROUBLESHOOTING CHART

Problem	Probable Cause	Cure
Water leaks at spout	Washer worn, hard, damaged	Replace seal or washer
Water leaks at knob or lever	Stem packing or O-ring worn, hard, damaged	Replace packing or O-ring
Water leaks around swivel spout	O-ring worn, hard, damaged	Replace O-ring (s)
Lever or knob moves stiffly	Bonnet nut or adjusting ring too tight	Back off nut or ring slightly
Restricted water flow	Filter screen in aerator or faucet plugged	Clean or replace screen (s)
Faucet loose in fixture	Rubber or metal shank washer damaged Shank nut loose	Replace washer (s) Tighten nut
Closed stopper allows water to drain	Pop-up valve dirty Valve or drain damaged Lifter misadjusted	Remove and clean Smooth or replace Adjust to fully close
Supply line leaks	Nut (s) loose Slip-joint washer bad	Tighten nuts Replace washer
Twin-faucet knobs misaligned	Improper assembly Seats or seals worn	Close faucet, remove knobs, install aligned Replace parts
Spray hose drips	Hose-head valve not closing	Check for foreign material; replace head
Hose flow slight	Hose kinked or blocked Aerator or nozzle plugged Diverter valve defective	Replace hose or unit Clean or replace Clean or recondition
Leak at stopper lever	Lever nut loose Packing defective Pivot ball worn or damaged	Tighten nut Replace packing Replace ball and packing

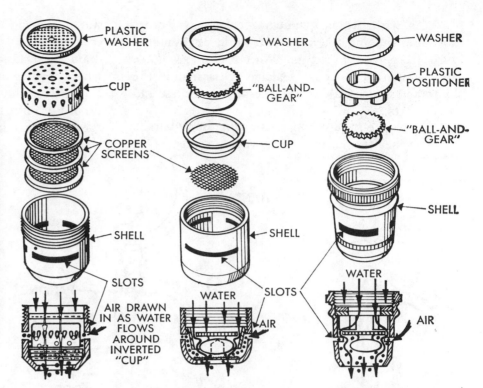

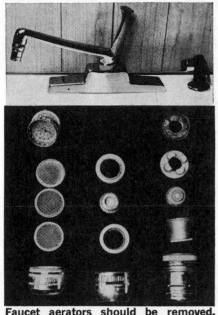

Faucet aerators should be removed, cleaned periodically. Three types of aerators are shown pulled apart.

FIRST AID FOR AERATORS

When the flow of water in a faucet becomes restricted, check the aerator before you call a plumber or start tearing out pipes.

Almost all modern faucets have this device, which is screwed onto the end to create a "soft" flow of water that will not readily splash or splatter when it hits a flat surface. There are a number of different types, all however, work on the same principle. The flow of water is routed through the aerator so that at one point the stream passes around a shaped member and must flow faster to do so. This faster flow creates a slight vacuum that pulls air into the stream of water, breaking it up into a sort of "foam."

If the aerator is only slightly plugged it sometimes is possible to clear it by removing it from the faucet and holding it under the stream from the faucet, upside down. This may flush out the tiny particles of rust and other debris that plug the narrow passages inside the aerator. If this "backflushing" does not clear the aerator, then it must be disassembled for cleaning. Servicing is simply a matter of taking them apart, keeping the parts in order, cleaning them and reassembling.

Another problem with any aerator is rust and corrosion, despite the fact that the inside components are brass, bronze or stainless steel. Small particles of steel will adhere, cause rust themselves,

and a form of galvanic action. Periodic cleaning of the aerators is the best insurance against trouble.

Liming caused by hard water and which you can see as a sediment in cooking pans, will also settle in aerators. If you find this deposit in an aerator, soak the parts in a mild acid such as vinegar, then scrub with a household scouring pad.

Good preventive maintenance requires that aerators be "backflushed" regularly.

FROSTPROOF HYDRANTS

Frostproof hydrants are basically faucets, although they may differ somewhat in design from ordinary faucets.

Two important features of a frostproof hydrant are: (1) The valve is installed under ground—below the frostline—to prevent freezing, and (2) the valve is designed to drain the water from the hydrant when the valve is closed.

The frostproof hydrant works as follows: When the handle is raised, the piston rises, opening the valve. Water flows from the supply pipe into the cylinder, up through the riser, and out the spout. When the handle is pushed down, the piston goes down, closing the valve and stopping the flow of water. Water left in the hydrant flows out the drain tube into a small gravel-filled dry well or drain pit.

As with ordinary faucets, leakage will probably be the most common trouble encountered with frostproof hydrants. Worn packing, gaskets, and washers can cause leakage. Disassemble the hydrant as necessary to replace or repair these and other parts.

Frostproof yard hydrants having buried drains can be health hazards. The vacuum created by water flowing from the hydrant may draw in contaminated water standing above the hydrant drain level. Such hydrants should be used only where positive drainage can be provided.

Frostproof wall hydrants are the preferred type. For servicing sprayers using hazardous chemicals, hydrants having backflow protection should be used.

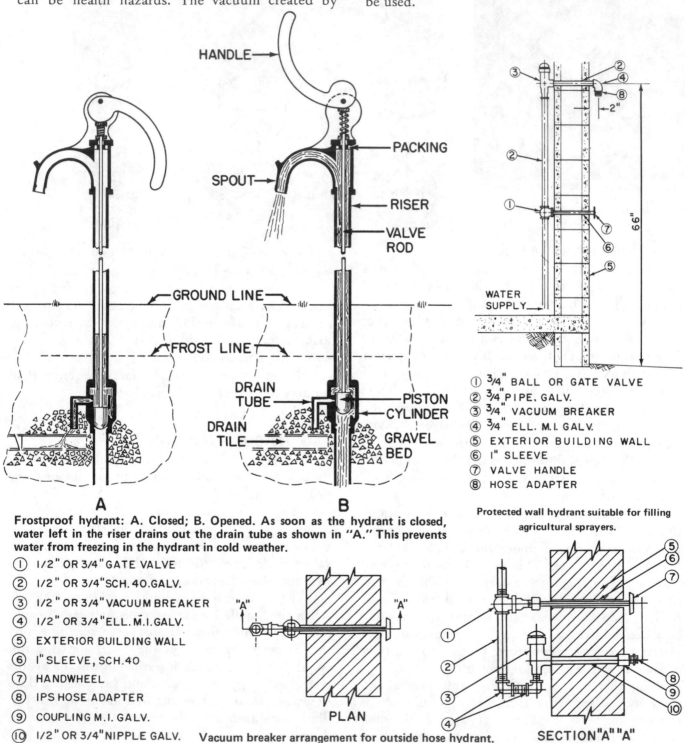

Frostproof hydrant: A. Closed; B. Opened. As soon as the hydrant is closed, water left in the riser drains out the drain tube as shown in "A." This prevents water from freezing in the hydrant in cold weather.

① 1/2" OR 3/4" GATE VALVE
② 1/2" OR 3/4" SCH. 40. GALV.
③ 1/2" OR 3/4" VACUUM BREAKER
④ 1/2" OR 3/4" ELL. M.I. GALV.
⑤ EXTERIOR BUILDING WALL
⑥ 1" SLEEVE, SCH. 40
⑦ HANDWHEEL
⑧ IPS HOSE ADAPTER
⑨ COUPLING M.I. GALV.
⑩ 1/2" OR 3/4" NIPPLE GALV.

① 3/4" BALL OR GATE VALVE
② 3/4" PIPE, GALV.
③ 3/4" VACUUM BREAKER
④ 3/4" ELL. M.I. GALV.
⑤ EXTERIOR BUILDING WALL
⑥ 1" SLEEVE
⑦ VALVE HANDLE
⑧ HOSE ADAPTER

Protected wall hydrant suitable for filling agricultural sprayers.

Vacuum breaker arrangement for outside hose hydrant.

REPAIRING LEAKS IN PIPES AND TANKS

Pipes

Leaks in pipes usually result from corrosion or from damage to the pipe. Pipes may be damaged by freezing, by vibration caused by machinery operating nearby, by water hammer, or by animals bumping into the pipe.

Corrosion. Occasionally waters are encountered that corrode metal pipe and tubing. (Some acid soils also corrode metal pipe and tubing.)

The corrosion usually occurs, in varying degrees, along the entire length of pipe rather than at some particular point. An exception would be where dissimilar metals, such as copper and steel, are joined.

Treatment of the water may solve the problem of corrosion. Otherwise, you may have to replace the piping with a type made of material that will be less subject to the corrosive action of the water.

It is good practice to get a chemical analysis of the water before selecting materials for a plumbing system. Your State college or university may be equipped to make an analysis; if not, you can have it done by a private laboratory.

Repairing Leaks. Pipes that are split by hard freezing must be replaced.

A leak at a threaded connection can often be stopped by unscrewing the fitting and applying a pipe joint compound that will seal the joint when the fitting is screwed back together.

Small leaks in a pipe can often be repaired with a rubber patch and metal clamp or sleeve.

This must be considered as an emergency repair job and should be followed by permanent repair as soon as practicable.

Large leaks in a pipe may require cutting out the damaged section and installing a new piece of pipe. At least one union will be required unless the leak is near the end of the pipe. You can make a temporary repair with plastic or rubber tubing. The tubing must be strong enough to withstand the normal water pressure in the pipe. It should be slipped over the open ends of the piping and fastened with pipe clamps or several turns of wire.

Vibration sometimes breaks solder joints in copper tubing, causing leaks. If the joint is accessible, clean and resolder it. The tubing must be dry before it can be heated to soldering temperature. Leaks in places not readily accessible usually require the services of a plumber and sometimes of both a plumber and a carpenter.

Tanks

Leaks in tanks are usually caused by corrosion. Sometimes, a safety valve may fail to open and the pressure developed will spring a leak.

While a leak may occur at only one place in the tank wall, the wall may also be corroded thin in other places. Therefore, any repair should be considered as temporary, and the tank should be replaced as soon as possible.

A leak can be temporarily repaired with a toggle bolt, rubber gasket, and brass washer. You may have to drill or ream the hole larger to insert the toggle bolt. Draw the bolt up tight to compress the rubber gasket against the tank wall.

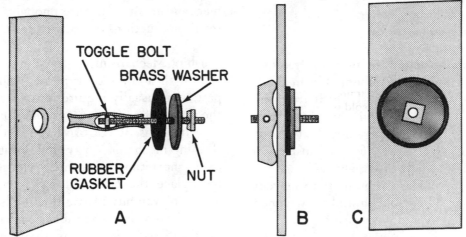

Closing a hole in a tank: A. The link of the toggle bolt is passed through the hole in the tank (hole is enlarged if necessary). B. Side view of tank edge (nut is drawn up tightly to compress washer and gasket against tank). C. Outside view of completed repair.

WATER HAMMER

Water hammer sometimes occurs when a faucet is suddenly closed. When the flow of water is suddenly stopped, its kinetic energy is expended against the walls of the piping. This causes the piping to vibrate, and leaks or other damage may result.

Water hammer may be prevented or its severity reduced by installing an air chamber just ahead of the faucet. The air chamber may be a piece of air-filled pipe or tubing, about 2 feet long, extending vertically from the pipe. It must be airtight.

An air chamber requires occasional replenishing of the air to prevent it from becoming water-logged—that is, full of water instead of air.

A properly operating hydropneumatic tank, such as the type used in individual water systems, serves as an air chamber, preventing or reducing water hammer.

FROZEN WATER PIPES

In cold weather, water may freeze in underground pipes laid above the frostline or in pipes in unheated buildings, in open crawl spaces under buildings, or in outside walls.

When water freezes it expands. Unless a pipe can also expand, it may rupture when the water freezes. Iron pipe and steel pipe do not expand appreciably. Copper pipe will stretch some, but does not resume its original dimensions when thawed out; repeated freezings will cause it to fail eventually. Flexible plastic tubing can stand repeated freezes, but it is good practice to prevent it from freezing.

Preventing Freezing

Pipes may be insulated to prevent freezing, but this is not a completely dependable method. Insulation does not stop the loss of heat from the pipe—merely slows it down—and the water may freeze if it stands in the pipe long enough at below-freezing temperature. Also, if the insulation becomes wet, if may lose its effectiveness.

Electric heating cable can be used to prevent pipes from freezing. The cable should be wrapped around the pipe and covered with insulation.

Thawing

Use of electric heating cable is a good method of thawing frozen pipe, because the entire heated length of pipe is thawed at one time.

Thawing pipe with a blowtorch can be dangerous. The water may get hot enough at the point where the torch is applied to generate sufficient steam under pressure to rupture the pipe. Steam from the break could severely scald you.

Thawing pipe with hot water is safer than thawing with a blowtorch. One method is to cover the pipe with rags and then pour the hot water over the rags.

When thawing pipe with a blowtorch, hot water, or similar methods, open a faucet and start thawing at that point. The open faucet will permit steam to escape, thus reducing the chance of the buildup of dangerous pressure. Do not allow the steam to condense and refreeze before it reaches the faucet.

Underground metal pipes can be thawed by passing a low-voltage electric current through them. The current will heat the entire length of pipe through which it passes. Both ends of the pipe must be open to prevent the buildup of steam pressure.

CAUTION: This method of thawing frozen pipe can be dangerous and should be done by an experienced person only. It cannot be used to thaw plastic tubing or other non-electricity-conducting pipe or tubing.

REPAIRING WATER CLOSETS

Water closets (commonly called toilets) vary in general design and in the design of the flushing mechanism. But they are enough alike that general repair instructions can suffice for all designs.

Flushing Mechanism

With a common type of flushing mechanism, parts that usually require repair are the flush valve, the intake (float) valve, and the float ball.

In areas of corrosive water, the usual copper flushing mechanism may deteriorate in a comparatively short time. In such cases, it may be advisable to replace the corroded parts with plastic parts. You can even buy plastic float balls.

Flush Valve. The rubber ball of the flush valve may get soft or out of shape and fail to seat properly. This causes the valve to leak. Unscrew the ball from the lift wire and install a new one.

The trip lever or lift wire may corrode and

fail to work smoothly, or the lift wire may bind in the guides. Disassemble and clean off corrosion or replace parts as necessary.

Most plumbing codes require a cutoff valve in the supply line to the flush tank, which makes it unnecessary to close down the whole system. If this valve was not installed, you can stop the flow of water by propping up the float with a piece of wood. Be careful not to bend the float rod out of alignment.

Intake (Float) Valve. A worn plunger washer in the supply valve will cause the valve to leak. To replace the washer:

Shut off the water and drain the tank.

Unscrew the two thumbscrews that hold the levers and push out the levers.

Lift out the plunger, unscrew the cup on the bottom, and insert a new washer. The washer is made of material such as rubber or leather.

Examine the washer seat. If nicked or rough, it may need refacing.

If the float-valve assembly is badly corroded, replace it.

Float Ball. The float ball may develop a leak and fail to rise to the proper position. (Correct water level is about 1 inch below the top of the overflow tube or enough to give a good flush.) If the ball fails to rise, the intake valve will remain open and water will continue to flow. Brass float balls can sometimes be drained and the leak sol-dered. Other types must be replaced. When working on the float ball, be careful to keep the rod aligned so that the ball will float freely and close the valve properly.

Bowl Removal

An obstruction in the water closet trap or leakage around the bottom of the water-closet bowl may require removal of the bowl. Follow this procedure:

Shut off the water.

Empty the tank and bowl by siphoning or sponging out the water.

Disconnect the water pipes to the tank.

Disconnect the tank from the bowl if the water closet is a two-piece unit. Set the tank where it cannot be damaged. Handle tank and bowl carefully; they are made of vitreous china or porcelain and are easily chipped or broken.

Remove the seat and cover from the bowl.

Carefully pry loose the bolt covers and remove the bolts holding the bowl to the floor flange. Jar the bowl enough to break the seal at the bottom. Set the bowl upside down on something that will not chip or break it.

Remove the obstruction from the discharge opening.

Place a new wax seal around the bowl horn and press it into place. A wax seal (or gasket) may be obtained from hardware or plumbing-supply stores.

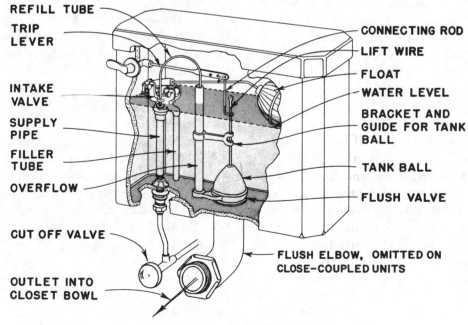

Water closet (toilet) flush tank.

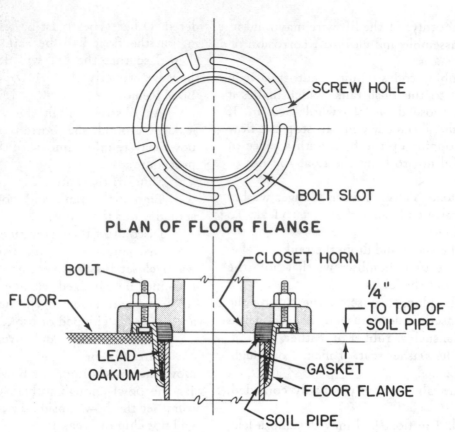

PLAN OF FLOOR FLANGE

SCREW HOLE

BOLT SLOT

CLOSET HORN

BOLT

FLOOR

¼"
TO TOP OF
SOIL PIPE

LEAD

OAKUM

GASKET

FLOOR FLANGE

SOIL PIPE

Connection of water closet to floor and soil pipe.

Set the bowl in place and press it down firmly. Install the bolts that hold it to the floor flange. Draw the bolts up snugly, but not too tight because the bowl may break. The bowl must be level. Keep a carpenter's level on it while drawing up the bolts. If the house has settled, leaving the floor sloping, it may be necessary to use shims to make the bowl set level. Replace the bolt covers.

Install the tank and connect the water pipes to it. It is advisable to replace all gaskets, after first cleaning the surfaces thoroughly.

Test for leaks by flushing a few times.

Install the seat and cover.

Tank "Sweating"

When cold water enters a water closet tank, it may chill the tank enough to cause "sweating" (condensation of atmospheric moisture on the outer surface of the tank). This can be prevented by insulating the tank to keep the temperature of the outer surface above the dew point temperature of surrounding air. Insulating jackets or liners that fit inside water-closet tanks and serve to keep the outer surface warm are available from plumbing-supply dealers.

CLEARING CLOGGED DRAINS

Drains may become clogged by objects dropped into them or by accumulations of grease, dirt, or other matter.

Fixture and Floor Drains

If the obstruction is in a fixture trap, usually the trap can be removed and cleared. If the obstruction is elsewhere in the pipe other means must be used.

Cleanout augers—long, flexible, steel cables commonly called "snakes"—may be run down drainpipes to break up obstructions or to hook onto and pull out objects. Augers are made in various lengths and diameters and are available at hardware and plumbing-supply stores. (In some cases, you may have to call a plumber, who will probably have a power-driven auger.)

Small obstructions can sometimes be forced down or drawn up by use of an ordinary rubber force cup (plunger or "plumber's friend").

Grease and soap clinging to a pipe can sometimes be removed by flushing with hot water. Lye or lye mixed with a small amount of aluminum shavings may also be used. When water is added to

314

the mixture, the violent gas-forming reaction and production of heat that takes place loosens the grease and soap so that they can be flushed away. Use cold water only. Chemical cleaners should not be used in pipes that are completely stopped up, because they must be brought into direct contact with the stoppage to be effective. Handle the material with extreme care and follow directions on the container. If lye spills on the hands or clothing, wash with cold water immediately. If any gets into the eyes, flush with cold water and call a doctor.

Sand, dirt, or clothing lint sometimes clogs floor drains. Remove the strainer and ladle out as much of the sediment as possible. You may have to carefully chip away the concrete around the strainer to free it. Flush the drain with clean water.

When drains have become partially clogged due to lack of water to transport all solids through them, large buckets or other containers should be used to flush them. Water should be poured fast enough to nearly fill the drain.

Occasional flushing of floor drains may prevent clogging.

CAUTION: Augers, rubber force cups, and other tools used in direct contact with sewage are subject to contamination. Do not later use them for work on your potable water supply system unless they have been properly sterilized.

Outside Drains

Roots growing through cracks or defective joints sometimes clog outside drains or sewers. You can clear the stoppage temporarily by using a root-cutting tool. However, to prevent future trouble, you should re-lay the defective portion of the line, using sound pipe and making sure that all joints are watertight.

If possible, sewer lines should be laid out of the reach of roots. But if this is impossible or impracticable, consider using impregnated fiber pipe which tends to repel roots.

INSTALLING PLASTIC PIPE

Easy to handle, time-saving, cost-saving, space-age plastic piping is rapidly taking over tasks previously handled by metal and other materials in applications inside and outside of the home. Among these are drain, waste and vent lines, water lines,

sewer lines, waterwell systems, lawn sprinklers, swimming-pool circulation lines and fountains, as well as gas distribution and chemical-waste systems, industrial and oil-field uses.

Just as the professional installers have, you will be surprised to find that plastic piping is non-corrosive, easier to handle and install and less expensive than other types of piping, and is available in all the usual sizes, types and varieties of pipe and fittings.

A true product of the space age, plastic piping has been thoroughly time-tested by rigid laboratory procedures and rigorous field tests. Thirty-year installations have been found to be performing satisfactorily. Most standards associations and codes associations recognize plastic piping; some city codes do not.

The most commonly used types of plastic pipe and fittings are ABS (acrylonitrile-butadiene-styrene), PE (polyehtylene), and PVC (polyvinyl chloride) for pressure applications such as transportation of water. ABS and PVC are used in DWV (drain, waste and vent) applications.

Installation of the plastic piping is similar to that of metal piping except that it's easier, quicker, less expensive. The procedure outlined here is designed to reflect recommendations of manufacturers as well as good practice in the field.

Because of variations from one area to another, no attempt has been made to follow any one particular plumbing code. Needless to say, the installer should always check the requirement of the local codes where they exist.

The installation procedure for both ABS-DWV and PVC-DWV is essentially the same, the preferred method of joining being solvent welding.

In assembling pipe and fittings, exercise care to establish proper grade and alignment before joining. Position the pipe and fittings so that identifying markings will be readily visible for inspection when installed.

Make sure all needed materials and tools are handy, including the specific solvent for type of piping. Methyl Ethyl Ketone Cleaner, clean rags, nonsynthetic paint brush, a saw with fine teeth, miter box, knife or file. Have the installation all set up with fittings marked for position or alignment before proceeding to joint make-up. Remember that the solvent weld has a fast setting time. Allow for thermal expansion by allowing freedom for the pipe to move with temperature changes. Don't pull or force the pipe into the line when assembling.

ABS and PVC-DWV should be supported just as any other piping system. Use metal or other approved hangers. Do not compress or distort the pipe. Ordinary plumber's tape or banding may be used when the pipe is suspended below floor systems. Vertical piping should be supported at mid-joint between the ceiling and floor. Secure branch fitting to the framing.

Make trench bottoms of compacted backfill so that no settlement can occur.

Use only ABS cement for ABS pipe and fittings and PVC cement for PVC; use only N.S.F.-approved piping.

Read the directions on the cans of solvent cement and Methyl Ethyl Ketone. Exercise normal caution in handling, as when using any flammable material.

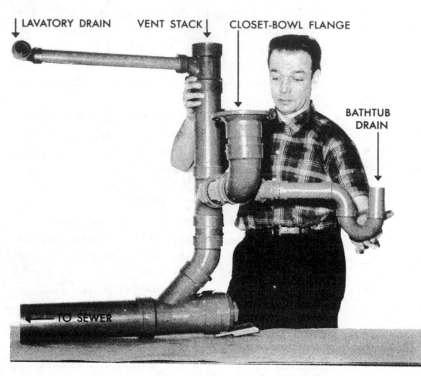

Plastic piping is cut using a handsaw and miter box. Do not use a standard wheel cutter. It will raise a flare on the end of the pipe which will scrape the cement from the joint.

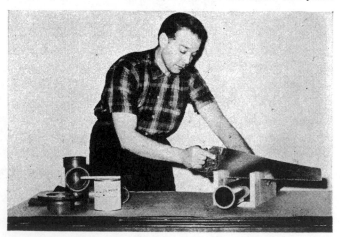

Or, use a Thin-Wheel Plastic-Pipe Cutter, making sure you cut the pipe square.

Remove any inside burrs with file or knife. Unremoved burrs may scrape lines in cement causing leaks around joints.

Wipe pipe clean with dry cloth. Be sure to remove all traces of dirt, moisture which could interfere with joining.

316

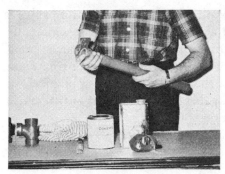

Remove the gloss from PVC piping by sandpapering, but without causing deep scores around the end.

For ABS, PVC piping first coat inside of the fitting socket.

Coat the outside of the pipe joining area, using a nonsynthetic brush.

Immediately assemble parts using quarter turn to spread cement.

Compression test revealed resiliency of plastic piping. Joint was mashed, showed no indications of cracking.

PLUMBING PRECAUTIONS

Polluted water or sewage may carry such diseases as typhoid fever and amoebic dysentery. If you do your own plumbing work, be sure that:

There are no leaks in drainpipes through which sewage gases can escape.

There are no cross connections between piping carrying water from different sources unless there can be reasonable certainty that all sources are safe and will remain safe.

There can be no back siphonage of water from plumbing fixtures or other containers into the water-supply system.

Once a pipe has become polluted, it may be difficult to free it of the pollution. For this reason, building codes do not permit the use of secondhand pipe. All initial piping and parts and subsequent replacements should be new.

Since a plumbing system will require service from time to time, shutoff valves should be installed at strategic locations so that an affected portion can be isolated (water flow to it cut off) with minimum disturbance to service in the rest of the system. Shutoff valves are usually provided on the water closet supply line, on the hot- and cold-water supply line to each sink, tub, and lava-

tory, and on the water heater supply line. Drain valves are usually installed for water-supply piping systems and for hot-water storage tanks.

A pressure-relief valve should be installed for the water heater storage tank to relieve pressure buildup in case of overheating.

EMERGENCIES

Below are emergencies that may occur and the action to take. The name, address, and phone number of a plumber who offers 24-hour service should be posted in a conspicuous place.

Burst Pipe or Tank. Immediately cut off the flow of water by closing the shutoff valve nearest to the break. Then arrange for repair.

Water Closet Overflow. Do not use water closet until back in working order. Check for and remove stoppage in closet bowl outlet, drain line from closet to sewer, or sewer to septic tank. If stoppage is due to root entry into pipe, repair of pipe at that point is recommended.

Rumbling Noise in Hot Water Tank. This is likely a sign of overheating which could lead to the development of explosive pressure. (Another indication of overheating is hot water backing up in the cold-water supply pipe.) Cut off the burner immediately. Be sure that the pressure-relief valve is operative. Then check (with a thermometer) the temperature of the water at the nearest outlet. If above that for which the gauge is set, check the thermostat that controls burner cutoff. If you cannot correct the trouble, call a plumber.

Cold House. If the heating system fails (or if you close the house and turn off the heat) when there is a chance of subfreezing weather, com-pletely drain the plumbing system. A drain valve is usually provided at the low point of the water supply piping for this purpose. A pump, storage tank, hot-water tank, water closet tank, water-treatment apparatus, and other water-system appliances or accessories should also be drained. Put antifreeze in all fixture and drain traps.

Hot-water and steam heating systems should also be drained when the house temperature may drop below freezing.

HOME HEATING

Different types of heating equipment and systems are available for heating the home. Considerations in selecting a unit or system include heating requirements, installation and maintenance costs, and heating costs. Heating-equipment dealers and contractors can assist in determining heating requirements and in selecting the most efficient and economical unit for your house.

For safety and efficiency, have a reputable contractor install your central heating system and inspect it once a year.

Reducing Heat Requirements

Much can be done to reduce the heat requirements in a house. This, in turn, can reduce heating costs and increase personal comfort.

New houses may be oriented so that the main rooms and the large windows in the rooms face south to receive maximum sunlight in the winter. (In summer, the sunlight may be shaded out by trees, wide eaves, shutters, awnings, or other natural or artificial shading.)

Tight construction also reduces heat requirements. Insulate ceilings and outside walls. Caulk and weatherstrip joints. Install storm sash or double- or triple-glazed windows to reduce heat loss through the windows. An old house should always be repaired and insulated before a new heating system is installed.

The chimney is a part of the heating plant; proper construction and maintenance are important. Chimneys should extend a minimum of 2 feet above the roof ridge. Keep flues clean and free from leaks.

WARM AIR HEATING

Area heating units, which include stoves, circulator heaters, and "pipeless" furnaces, are installed in the room or area to be heated. In central systems, the heating unit is located in the basement or other out-of-the-way place and heat is distributed through ducts.

Central heating systems are the most efficient and economical method of heating.

It is best to buy a heating unit designed specifically for the fuel to be used. Coal or wood burners can be converted to oil or gas but usually do not have sufficient heating surface for best efficiency.

Stoves, Circulator Heaters, and Pipeless Furnaces

Stoves are one of the simplest heating devices. Although they are cheaper than central heating systems, stoves are dirtier, require more attention, and heat less uniformly.

Wood- or coal-burning stoves without jackets heat principally by radiation. Jacketed stoves or circulator heaters heat mainly by convection and are available for burning the four common fuels—wood, coal, oil, or gas.

With proper arrangement of rooms and doors, a circulator heater can heat four or five small rooms, but in many instances heating will not be uniform. A small fan to aid circulation will increase efficiency. The distance from the heater to the center of each room to be heated, measured through the door opening, should be not more than about 18 feet. Doors must be left open; otherwise, grills or louvers are needed at the top and bottom of doors or walls for air circulation.

"Pipeless" furnaces may be used in smaller houses. They discharge warm air through a single register placed directly over the furnace.

Small gas-fired vertical heaters are sometimes recessed in the walls of the various rooms. Such

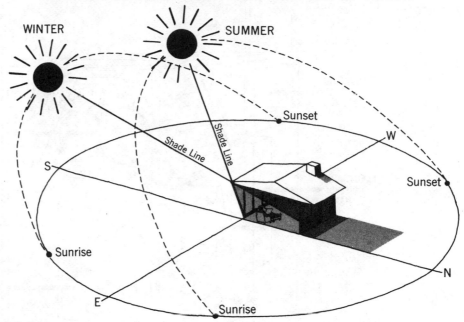

Solar orientation of a house to reduce heat requirements. Large glass areas face south to take advantage of the winter sun which strikes the earth at a lower angle than the summer sun.

units may be either manually or thermostatically controlled. Heater vents are carried up through the partitions to discharge the burned gases through a common vent extending through the roof.

Fireplaces

Fireplaces are used more for personal enjoyment than for heating efficiency. They are often used to supplement other heating equipment, to take the chill off the house when it is not cold enough to run the furnace, or for emergency heating when the central system fails.

Modified fireplaces are manufactured units, made of heavy metal and designed to be set in place and concealed by brickwork or other masonry construction. They are more efficient than ordinary fireplaces, because warm air is discharged from air ducts surrounding the fireplace. A fan in the duct system will improve the circulation.

Central Heating Systems

Forced-warm-air heating systems are more efficient and cost less to install than gravity warm air heating systems.

Forced-warm-air systems consist of a furnace, ducts, and registers. A blower in the furnace circulates the warm air to the various rooms through supply ducts and registers. Return grilles and ducts carry the cooled room air back to the furnace where it is reheated and recirculated.

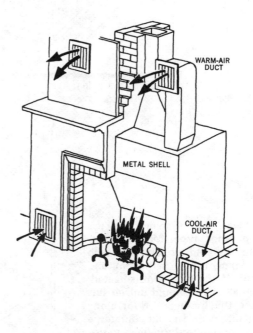

Modified fireplaces heat more efficiently than ordinary fireplaces. Cool air enters the inlets at the bottom, is heated by contact with the warm metal of the fireplace, rises by natural circulation, and is discharged through the outlets at the top. The outlets may be located in the wall of an adjacent room or a second-story room.

319

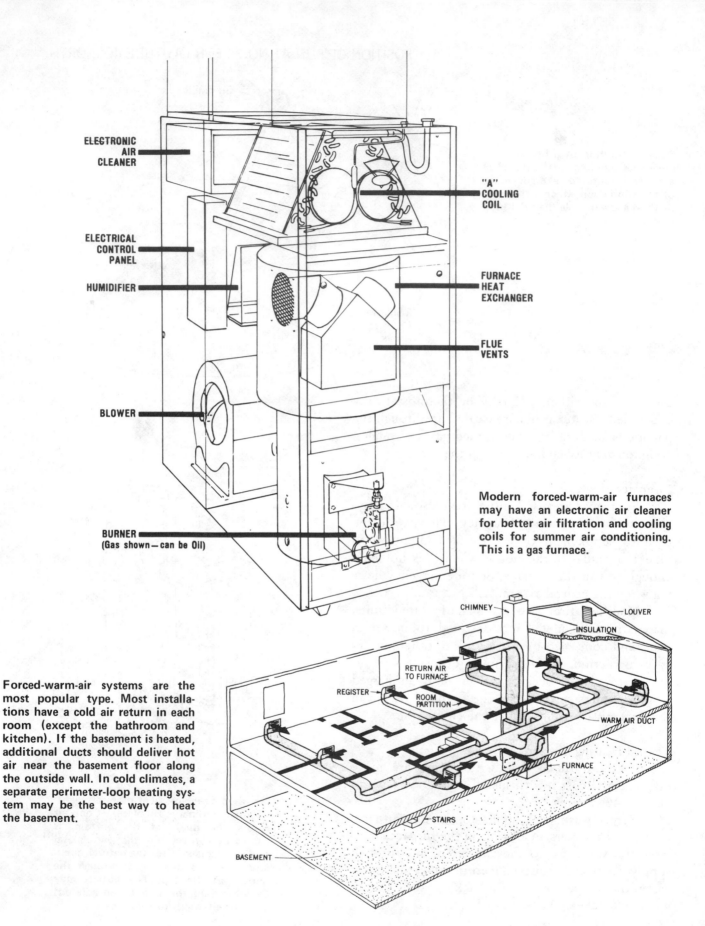

ELECTRONIC
AIR
CLEANER

ELECTRICAL
CONTROL
PANEL

HUMIDIFIER

BLOWER

BURNER
(Gas shown — can be Oil)

"A"
COOLING
COIL

FURNACE
HEAT
EXCHANGER

FLUE
VENTS

Modern forced-warm-air furnaces may have an electronic air cleaner for better air filtration and cooling coils for summer air conditioning. This is a gas furnace.

Forced-warm-air systems are the most popular type. Most installations have a cold air return in each room (except the bathroom and kitchen). If the basement is heated, additional ducts should deliver hot air near the basement floor along the outside wall. In cold climates, a separate perimeter-loop heating system may be the best way to heat the basement.

CHIMNEY

LOUVER

INSULATION

RETURN AIR
TO FURNACE

REGISTER

ROOM
PARTITION

WARM AIR DUCT

FURNACE

STAIRS

BASEMENT

Forced-warm-air systems heat uniformly and respond rapidly to changes in outdoor temperatures. They can be used in houses with or without basements—the furnace need not be below the rooms to be heated nor centrally located.

The warm air is usually filtered through inexpensive replaceable or washable filters. Electronic air cleaners can sometimes be installed in existing systems and are available on specially designed furnaces for new installations.

A humidifier may be added to the system to add moisture to the house air and avoid the discomfort and other disadvantages of a too-dry environment.

Warm-air supply outlets are preferably located along outside walls. They should be low in the wall, in the baseboard, or in the floor where air cannot blow directly on room occupants.

Most installations have a cold air return in each room. When supply outlets are along outside walls, return grilles should be along inside walls in the baseboard or in the floor. When supply outlets are along inside walls, return grilles should be along outside walls.

Centrally located returns work satisfactorily with perimeter-type heating systems. One return may be adequate in small houses. In larger or split-level houses, return grilles are generally provided for each level or group of rooms.

In the crawl-space plenum system, the entire crawl space is used as an air supply plenum or chamber. Heated air is forced into the crawl space and enters the rooms through perimeter outlets,

usually placed beneath windows, or through continuous slots in the floor adjacent to the outside wall. With tight, well-insulated crawl-space walls, this system can provide uniform temperatures throughout the house.

In houses without basements, horizontal furnaces that burn gas or oil may be installed in the crawl space or hung from ceiling joists in the utility room or adjoining garage. The gas furnaces may also be installed in attics. Allow adequate space for servicing the furnaces. Insulate attic furnaces and ducts heavily to prevent excessive heat loss.

Vertical gas or oil furnaces designed for installation in a closet or a wall recess or against a wall are popular especially in small houses. The counterflow type discharges the hot air at the bottom to warm the floor Some units provide discharge grilles into several rooms.

Upflow-type vertical furnaces may discharge the warm air through attic ducts and ceiling diffusers. Without return air ducts, these furnaces are less expensive, but also heat less uniformly.

Houses built on a concrete slab may be heated by a perimeter-loop heating system. Warm air is circulated by a counterflow type furnace through ducts cast in the outer edge of the concrete slab. The warm ducts heat the floor, and the warm air is discharged through floor registers to heat the room.

To prevent excessive heat loss, the edge of the slab should be insulated from the foundation walls and separated from the ground by a vapor barrier.

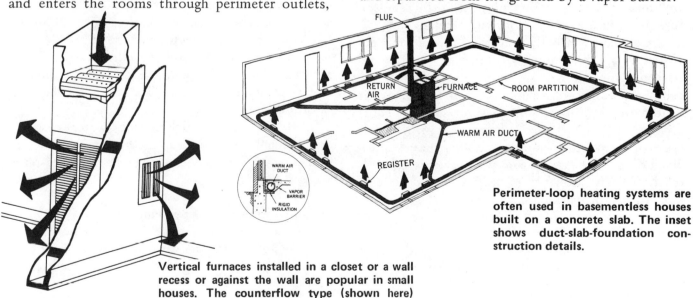

Vertical furnaces installed in a closet or a wall recess or against the wall are popular in small houses. The counterflow type (shown here) discharges the warm air at the bottom.

Perimeter-loop heating systems are often used in basementless houses built on a concrete slab. The inset shows duct-slab-foundation construction details.

HOT-WATER AND STEAM HEATING

Hot-water and steam heating systems consist of a boiler, pipes, and room heating units (radiators or convectors). Hot water or steam, heated or generated in the boiler, is circulated through the pipes to the radiators or convectors where the heat is transferred to the room air.

Boilers are made of cast iron or steel and are designed for burning coal, gas, or oil. Cast-iron boilers are more resistant to corrosion than steel ones. Corrosive water can be improved with chemicals. Proper water treatment can greatly prolong the life of steel boiler tubes.

Buy only a certified boiler. Certified cast-iron boilers are stamped "I-B-R" (Institute of Boiler and Radiator Manufacturers); steel boilers are stamped "SBI" (Steel Boiler Institute). Most boilers are rated (on the nameplate) for both hot water and steam. Contractors can advise on selecting a boiler.

Conventional radiators are set on the floor or mounted on the wall. The newer types may be recessed in the wall. Insulate behind recessed radiators with 1-inch insulation board, a sheet of reflective insulation, or both.

Radiators may be partially or fully enclosed in a cabinet. A full cabinet must have openings at top and bottom for air circulation. Preferred location for radiators is under a window.

Baseboard radiators are hollow or finned units that resemble and replace the conventional wood baseboard along outside walls. They will heat a well-insulated room uniformly, with little temperature difference between floor and ceiling.

Convectors usually consist of finned tubes enclosed in a cabinet with openings at the top and bottom. Hot water or steam circulates through the tubes. Air comes in at the bottom of the cabinet, is heated by the tubes, and goes out the top. Some units have fans for forced-air circulation. With this type of convector, summer cooling may be provided by adding a chiller and the necessary controls to the system. Convectors are installed against an outside wall or recessed in the wall.

Forced-Hot-Water Heating Systems

Forced-hot-water heating systems are recommended over the less efficient gravity hot-water-heating systems.

In a one-pipe system, one pipe or main serves for both supply and return. It makes a complete circuit from the boiler and back again. Two risers extend from the main to each room heating unit. A two-pipe system has two pipes or mains. One carries the heated water to the room heating units; the other returns the cooled water to the boiler.

A one-pipe system takes less pipe than a two-pipe system. However, in the one-pipe system, cooled water from each radiator mixes with the hot water flowing through the main, and each succeeding radiator receives cooler water.

Because water expands when heated, an expansion tank must be provided in the system. In an "open system," the tank is located above the highest point in the system and has an overflow pipe extending through the roof. In a "closed system," the tank is placed anywhere in the system, usually near the boiler. Half of the tank is filled with air, which compresses when the heated water expands. Higher water pressure can be used in a closed system than in an open one. Higher pressure raises the boiling point of the water.

With heating coils installed in the boiler or in a water heater connected to the boiler, a forced-hot-water system can be used to heat domestic water year-round. If you want to use your heating plant to heat domestic water, consult an experienced heating engineer about the best arrangement.

One boiler can supply hot water for several circulation heating systems. The house can be "zoned" so that temperatures of individual rooms or areas can be controlled independently. Remote areas such as a garage, workshop, or small greenhouse, can be supplied with controlled heat.

Gas- and oil-fired boilers for hot-water heating are compact and are designed for installation in a closet, utility room, or similar space, on the first floor if desired.

Electrically heated hydronic (water) systems are especially compact, and the heat exchanger, expansion tank, and controls may be mounted on a wall.

Steam Central-Heating Systems

Steam heating systems are not used as much as forced-hot-water or warm-air systems. For one thing, they are less responsive to rapid changes in heat demands.

One-pipe steam heating systems cost about as

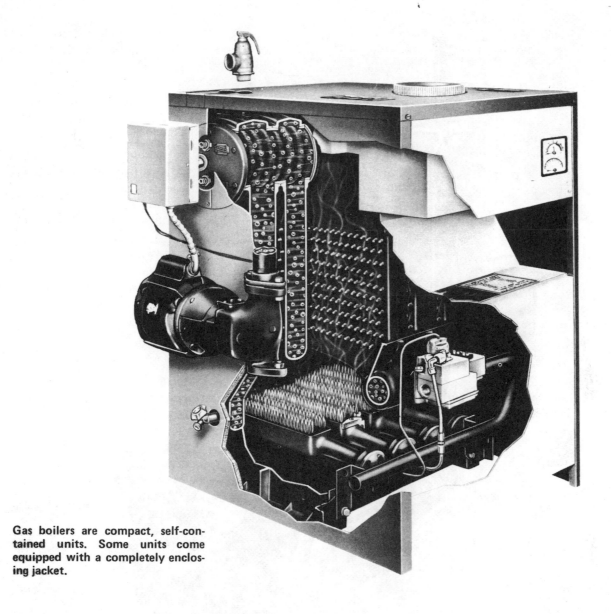

Gas boilers are compact, self-contained units. Some units come equipped with a completely enclosing jacket.

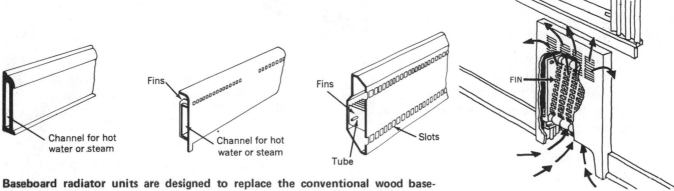

Fins

Channel for hot water or steam

Fins

Channel for hot water or steam

Tube

Fins

Slots

FIN

Baseboard radiator units are designed to replace the conventional wood baseboard. In the hollow types, *A* and *B,* water or steam flows directly behind the baseboard face. Heat from that surface is transmitted to the room. In the finned-tube type, the water or steam flows through the tube and heats the tube and the fins. Air passing over the tube and fins is heated and delivered to the room through the slots.

Convectors for hot water or steam heating are installed against the wall or recessed in the wall as shown.

Oil-fired boilers are also available with a completely enclosing jacket.

much to install as one-pipe hot-water systems. Two-pipe systems are more expensive.

The heating plant must be below the lowest room heating unit unless a pump is used to return the condensate to the boiler.

Radiant Panel Heating

Radiant panel heating is another method of heating with forced hot water or steam. It is also a method of heating with electricity.

Hot water or steam circulates through pipes concealed in the floor, wall, or ceiling. Heat is transmitted through the pipes to the surface of the floor, wall, or ceiling and then to the room by radiation and convection. No radiators are required —the floor, wall, or ceiling, in effect, act as radiators.

With radiant panel heating, rooms can be more comfortable at lower air temperatures than with other heating systems at higher air temperatures. Temperatures are generally uniform throughout the room.

Underfloor radiant panel heating systems are difficult to design. For instance, a carpeted or bare

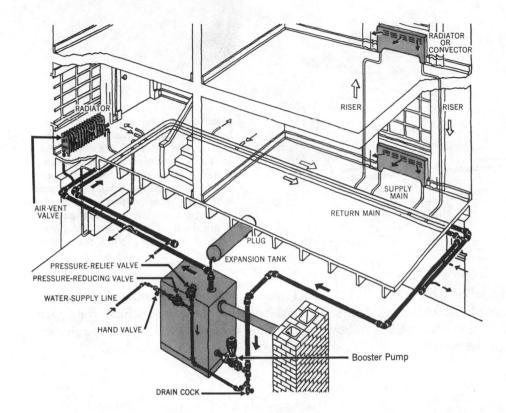

RADIATOR OR CONVECTOR

RISER

RISER

RADIATOR

SUPPLY MAIN

RETURN MAIN

AIR-VENT VALVE

PLUG

EXPANSION TANK

PRESSURE-RELIEF VALVE

PRESSURE-REDUCING VALVE

WATER-SUPPLY LINE

HAND VALVE

Booster Pump

DRAIN COCK

Two-pipe forced-hot-water systems have two supply pipes or mains. One supplies the hot water to the room heating units, and the other returns the cooled water to the boiler.

The heat exchanger, expansion tank, and controls for an electrically heated hydronic (water) system are compact enough to mount on a wall.

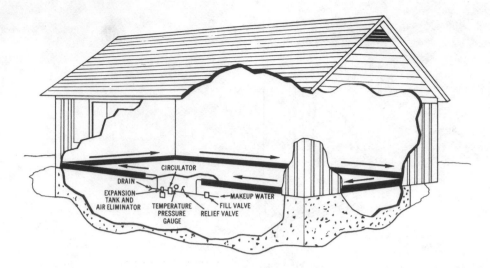

wood floor might be very comfortable while the ceramic-tiled bathroom floor or the plastic kitchen-floor covering might be too hot for bare feet. An experienced engineer should design the system.

ELECTRIC HEATING

Many types and designs of electric house-heating equipment are available. Some are (1) ceiling unit, (2) baseboard heater, (3) heat pump, (4) central furnace, (5) floor furnace, and (6) wall unit. All but the heat pump are of the resistance type. Resistance-type heaters produce heat the same way as the familiar electric radiant heater. Heat pumps are usually supplemented with resistance heaters.

Ceiling heat may be provided with electric heating cable laid back and forth on the ceiling surface and covered with plaster or a second layer of gypsum board. Other types of ceiling heaters include infrared lamps and resistance heaters with reflectors or fans.

Panel heating in poorly insulated ceilings is not practical unless you want to heat the space above the ceiling. Exterior wall panels require insulation behind them to reduce heat loss.

Baseboard heaters resemble ordinary wood baseboards and are often used under a large picture window in conjunction with ceiling heat.

The heat pump is a single unit that both heats and cools. In winter, it takes heat from the outdoor air to warm the house or room. In summer, it removes heat from the house or room and discharges it to the outside air. It uses less electricity to furnish the same amount of heat than does the resistance-type heater. Room air conditioners of the heat pump type are especially convenient in warmer climates where continuous heating is not needed or for supplemental heat in some areas of the house.

Electric heating cable is one of the different types of electric heating used.

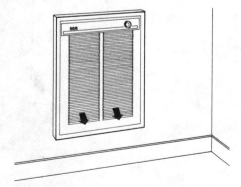

The better types of electrical wall heaters discharge the warm air from the bottom and circulate it by means of a fan.

Either heat pumps or furnaces with resistance heaters are used in forced-air central heating systems. They require ducts similar to those discussed for forced warm-air heating. Hot-water systems with resistance-type heaters are also available.

Wall units, either radiant or convection, or both, are designed for recessed or surface wall mounting. They come equipped with various types of resistance heating elements. The warm air may be circulated either by gravity or by an electric fan.

Each room heated by the equipment just described (with the exception of some central-heating systems) usually has its own thermostat and can be held at any desired temperature. Thermostats should be designed for long life and should be sensitive to change in temperature of ½ degree Farenheit, plus or minus.

FUELS AND BURNERS

The four fuels commonly used for home heating are wood, coal, oil, and gas. Electricity, though not a fuel, is being used increasingly.

Modern heating equipment is relatively efficient when used with the fuel for which it is designed. But, even with modern equipment, some fuels cost more than others to do the same job.

Comparing Fuel Costs

The therms of heat per dollar should not be the sole consideration in selecting the heating fuel. Installation cost, the efficiency with which each unit converts fuel into useful heat, and the insulation level of the house should also be considered. For example, electrically heated houses usually have twice the insulation thickness, particularly in the ceiling and floor, and, therefore, may require considerably less heat input than houses heated with fuel-burning systems. To compare costs for various fuels, efficiency of combustion and heat value of the fuel must be known.

Heating units vary in efficiency, depending upon the type, method of operation, condition, and location. Stoker-fired (coal) steam and hot-water boilers of current design, operated under favorable conditions, have 60 to 75 percent efficiency. Gas- and oil-fired boilers have 70 to 80 percent efficiency. Forced-warm-air furnaces, gas fired or oil fired with atomizing burner, generally provide about 80 percent efficiency. Oil-fired furnaces with pot-type burner usually develop not over 70 percent efficiency.

Wood. The use of wood requires more labor and more storage space than do other fuels. However, wood fires are easy to start, burn with little smoke, and leave little ash.

Most well-seasoned hardwoods have about half as much heat value per pound as does good coal. A cord of hickory, oak, beech, sugar maple, or rock elm weighs about 2 tons and has about the same heat value as 1 ton of good coal.

Coal. Two kinds of coal are used for heating homes—anthracite (hard) and bituminous (soft). Bituminous is used more often.

Anthracite coal sizes are standardized; bituminous coal sizes are not. Heat value of the different sizes of coal varies little, but certain sizes are better suited for burning in firepots of given sizes and depths.

Both anthracite and bituminous coal are used in stoker firing. Stokers may be installed at the front, side, or rear of a furnace or boiler. Leave space for servicing the stoker and for cleaning the furnace. Furnaces and boilers with horizontal heating surfaces require frequent cleaning, because fly ash (fine powdery ash) collects on these surfaces. Follow the manufacturer's instructions for operating stokers.

Oil. Oil is a popular heating fuel. It requires little space for storing and no handling, and it leaves no ash.

Two grades of fuel oil are commonly used for home heating. No. 1 is lighter and slightly more expensive than No. 2, but No. 2 fuel oil has higher heat value per gallon. The nameplate or guidebook that comes with the oil burner indicates what grade oil should be used. In general, No. 1 is used in pot-type burners, and No. 2 in gun- and rotary-type burners.

A competent serviceman should install and service an oil burner.

Oil burners are of two kinds—vaporizing and atomizing. Vaporizing burners premix the air and oil vapor. An automatic or handset valve regulates the amount of oil in the pot. Heat from the flame vaporizes the oil. In some heaters a pilot flame or electric arc ignites the oil pot when heat is required; in others the oil is ignited manually and burns continuously at any set fuel rate between high and low fire, until shut off. There are few

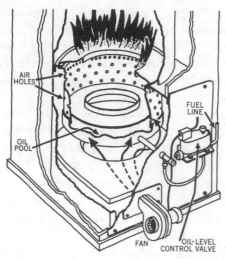

Vaporizing or pot-type oil burners are the least expensive type.

moving parts, and operation is quiet. Some pot-type burners can be operated without electric power.

Atomizing burners are of two general types—gun (or pressure) and rotary. The gun burner is by far the more popular type for home heating. It has a pump that forces the oil through a special atomizing nozzle. A fan blows air into the oil fog; and an electric spark ignites the mixture, which burns in a refractory-lined firepot.

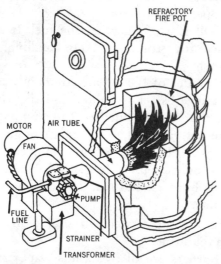

The gun or pressure type oil burner is the most popular for home central heating systems.

Gas. Gas is used in many urban homes and in some rural areas. It is supplied at low pressure to a burner head where it is mixed with the right amount of air for combustion.

A room thermostat controls the gas valve. A

pilot light is required. It may be lighted at the beginning of the heating season and shut off when heat is no longer required. However, if it is kept burning during nonheating seasons, condensation and rapid corrosion of the system will be prevented.

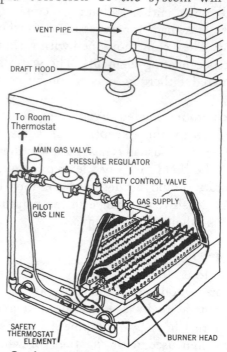

Gas burners vary in design, but all operate on much the same principle. The controls shown are essential for safe operation.

The pilot light should be equipped with a safety thermostat to keep the gas valve from opening if the pilot goes out; no gas can then escape into the room. (The pilot light of all automatic gas-burning appliances should be equipped with this safety device.)

Three kinds of gas—natural, manufactured, and bottled—are used. Bottled gas (usually propane) is sometimes called LPG (liquefied petroleum gas). Different gases have different heat values when burned. A burner adjusted for one gas must be readjusted when used with another gas.

Conversion gas burners may be used in boilers and furnaces designed for coal if they have adequate heating surfaces. Furnaces must be properly gastight. Conversion burners, as well as all other gas burners, should be installed by competent, experienced heating contractors who follow closely the manufacturer's instructions. Gas-burning equipment should bear the seal of approval of the American Gas Association.

Vent gas-burning equipment to the outdoors. Keep chimneys and smoke pipes free from leaks. Connect all electrical controls for gas-burning equipment on a separate switch so that the circuit can be broken in case of trouble. Gas-burning equipment should be cleaned, inspected, and correctly adjusted each year.

Bottled gas is heavier than air. If it leaks into the basement, it will accumulate at the lowest point and create an explosion hazard. When bottled gas is used, make sure that the safety control valve is so placed that it shuts off the gas to the pilot as well as to the burner when the pilot goes out.

Electricity. Electric heating offers convenience, cleanliness, evenness of heat, safety, and freedom from odors and fumes. No chimney is required in building a new house, unless a fireplace is desired.

For electric heating to be more competitive economically with other types of heating, houses should be well insulated and weatherstripped, should have double- or triple-glazed windows, and should be vapor sealed.

Some power suppliers will guarantee a maximum monthly or seasonal cost when the house is insulated and the heating system installed in accordance with their specifications.

The heating equipment should be only large enough to handle the heat load. Oversized equipment costs more and requires heavier wiring than does properly sized equipment.

AUTOMATIC CONTROLS

Each type of heating plant requires special features in its control system. But even the simplest control system should include high-limit controls to prevent overheating. Limit controls are usually recommended by the equipment manufacturer.

The high-limit control, which is usually a furnace or boiler thermostat, shuts down the fire before the furnace or boiler becomes dangerously or wastefully hot. In steam systems, it responds to pressure; in other systems, it responds to temperature.

Other controls insure that all operations take place in the right order. Room thermostats control the burner or stoker on forced systems. They are sometimes equipped with timing devices that can be set to change automatically the temperatures desired at night and in the daytime.

Since the thermostat controls the house temperature, it must be in the right place—usually on an inside wall. Do not put it near a door to the outside; at the foot of an open stairway; above a heat register, television, or lamp; or where it will be affected by direct heat from the sun. Check it with a good thermometer for accuracy.

Oil-Burner Controls

The oil-burner controls allow electricity to pass through the motor and ignition transformer and shut them off in the right order. They also stop the motor if the oil does not ignite or if the flame goes out. This is done by means of a stack

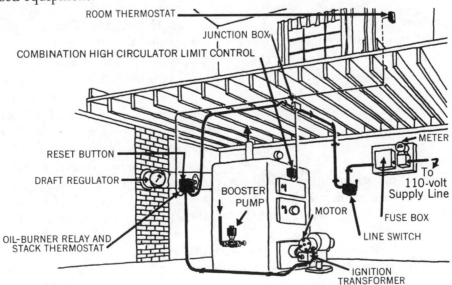

Controls for an oil burner for a forced-hot-water heating system.

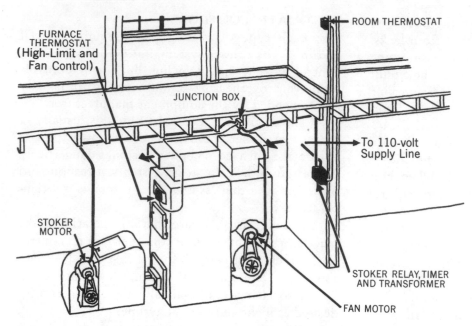

FURNACE THERMOSTAT (High-Limit and Fan Control)

ROOM THERMOSTAT

JUNCTION BOX

To 110-volt Supply Line

STOKER MOTOR

STOKER RELAY, TIMER AND TRANSFORMER

FAN MOTOR

Controls for a stoker-fired coal burner with a forced-warm-air heating system.

thermostat built into the relay. Without the protection of the stack thermostat or electric eye, a gun- or rotary-type burner could flood the basement with oil if it failed to ignite. With such protection, the relay allows the motor to run only a short time if the oil fails to ignite; then it opens the motor circuit and keeps it open until it is reset by hand.

In an oil burner with a forced-hot-water system, the boiler thermostat acts as high-limit control if the water in the boiler gets too hot.

Stoker-Fired Coal-Burner Controls

The control system for a coal stoker is much like that for an oil burner. However, an automatic timer is usually included to operate the stoker for a few minutes every hour or half hour to keep the fire alive during cool weather when little heat is required. In the stoker-control setup for a forced warm-air system, the furnace thermostat acts as high-limit and fan control.

Other Heating-System Controls

Warm-air, hot-water, or steam heat distribution systems may be controlled in many ways. If the furnace or boiler heats domestic water, more controls are needed.

In some installations of forced hot-water systems, especially with domestic-water hookups, a mixing valve is used. The water temperature of the boiler is maintained at some high, fixed value. Only

a portion of this high-temperature water is circulated through the heating system. Some of the water flowing through the radiators bypasses the boiler. The amount of hot water admitted is controlled by a differential thermostat operating on the difference between outdoor and indoor temperatures. This installation is more expensive than the more commonly used control systems, but it responds almost immediately to demands; and, although it cannot anticipate temperature changes, it is in a measure regulated by outside temperatures, which change earlier than do those indoors.

The flow of hot water to each part of a building can be separately controlled. This zoning can be used to maintain sleeping quarters at a lower temperature than living quarters. Electric heating is also well adapted to zoning.

FURNACE CHECK-UP

Minimize chances for a breakdown of your furnace in the middle of winter by spending a little time "tuning it up" for cold weather. First, make sure the filter is clean. If it is really dirty, don't try to clean it, but replace it. If you can't get the filter really clean, it quickly will get dirty again and the lowered efficiency of the furnace will cost you money in added fuel.

Even a brand-new filter will become clogged with dirt after about a month of operation, so it is recommended that filters be replaced about four times during the peak heating season. Some filters are sold in a "4-pack."

To tune the furnace, first check the blower motor. A few drops of oil, or a spoonful of grease in the cups will lubricate it for the season. The shaft of the blower also requires this lubrication.

The belt between the blower and motor should deflect from ¾ to 1 inch. Any more deflection means it is too loose and will slip and wear. Any tighter means the belt will cause wear on the bearings of the motor and blower.

Use a vacuum cleaner to remove dust and dirt from the blower compartment of the furnace, and clean all hot and cold-air registers in the house.

The register covers are easily removed, and the dust you take out will not get caught in the filter, nor blow into the house.

Forced-air systems used for both heating and cooling may have settings on duct dampers for summer and winter that should be adjusted. The blower may have two speeds; slow is for winter.

After you have done all these maintenance tasks, and you think the furnace is still not working properly, or if you smell fumes, call an authorized service man. The few dollars you spend could save your life or your house.

AIR CONDITIONING

Central Air Conditioning

You can install a central air conditioner, and every room in your house will have refreshingly cool, dehumidified air. Your family will be happy and comfortable during the day, and sleep soundly at night.

The secret of the low price is that you install the central air conditioner yourself, with a do-it-yourself kit that contains everything you need including precharged lines to run from the cooling coil in the furnace to the condenser located outside the house.

The first step in the installation is to get a survey booklet from the dealer or manufacturer, in which you write all the factors that affect the BTU gain or loss in your home: the size of the house, the number of windows and doors, the amount of insulation, its relationship to the sun and so on. These figures determine the size of the unit you will need. When this has been determined, you order the kit and it is delivered complete with installation instructions.

Installation. You first cut a hole in the furnace plenum (the instructions show various types of furnaces, and you check the one that is closest to your type to determine your setup), then enlarge it, using the furnished metal cover as a template to locate the hole for inserting the cooling coils, and for the sheet metal screws used to attach the cover plate.

You now can reach through the opening to install the telescoping support rods on which the coils will set. Over the rods are fitted four baffle plates (provided in the kit) that must be cut to fit. They assure that all air flows through the coils. To further assure airtightness, mastic is applied to all joints between the furnace plenum and the baffles, and a strip of mastic is applied to the baffles to seal the joint between the baffles and the coils. The coil unit next is inserted in the plenum and placed on the baffles. It is positioned so the condensate drain projects outside the plenum.

You now move outside where one of three methods is used to create a level platform for the condenser unit: poured concrete, precast patio blocks or concrete blocks. The condenser also has leveling devices at each corner, so it can be leveled if the slab or blocks are not exactly true, or if they later settle.

The precharged lines (they come in various

First step is to fill out survey form that determines BTU requirements of your house so proper unit can be selected.

Kit is complete, with all items necessary to install condenser and coil, plus tubing, etc. You must furnish platform.

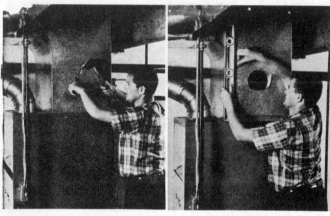

Hammer and screwdriver are used to start hole in bonnet, then tin snips are used to enlarge hole so you can see inside. Cover is used as template to locate screw holes.

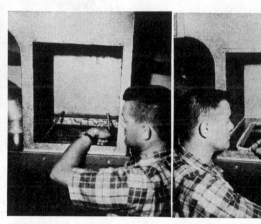

Telescoping support rods are inserted in bonnet, then baffle plates are fastened to them. Compound is used to seal all joints; strips also are located where cooling unit will rest.

Cooling coil is slipped into bonnet, placed over strips of sealing compound; drain must project.

Spring bender supplied in kit permits bending precharged tubing to make a neat job of this important task.

Drain trap and flexible tubing lead condensate to drain. This is simple gravity-flow device with no pump.

After condenser is set on level platform, precharged lines are connected to it with a wrench and job is done.

lengths, of 5-foot increments) next are attached to the cooling coils in the furnace and routed out to the condenser. To permit bending these rigid lines, a coil-spring bending device is included in the kit. These lines are simply attached and tightened with a wrench.

The electrical circuit required for the condenser must be 220 volts and, depending on the unit installed, a 30 or 40-ampere circuit breaker is required on the supply lines. In many areas this wiring must be done by a licensed electrician, so check with your local building authorities to be sure. Illegal wiring could bring a fine for improper installation, and your fire or home owner's insurance could be voided.

The shut-off switch for the condenser is built right in, which eliminates the need for adding extra junction boxes, and makes for a neat, and safe, installation.

A trap is installed on the condensate-drain line, to run moisture pulled from the air and condensed on the coils in the furnace, to any convenient drain. Be sure the drain is properly installed, as this water could cause rust and damage in the furnace if not properly drained away. Wiring is finished by installing a thermostat.

Room Air Conditioners

An air conditioner has four jobs to do in making you comfortable on a hot, humid day. It cools the air; it removes moisture from air; it filters out dust; and it circulates the air inside the room.

The compressor, a kind of pump, compresses the refrigerant gas, thereby raising its temperature

to about 210 degrees Fahrenheit. The hot gas is forced through the pipe and carried outside the room to the hot pipe coil. A fan blows outside air across the coil, cooling the gas to about 115 degrees and turning it into a liquid. Excess heat is discharged to the outdoor air. The refrigerant liquid is now forced through the pipe and back into the room through an expansion device, where it rapidly expands and drops sharply in temperature to a chill 45 degrees. The chilled refrigerant liquid flows to the cooling coils while the fan blows room air across the coils, through the filter, and into the room. In the process, the room air is both cooled and circulated.

As the air is cooled, it loses moisture, which collects on the cooling coils and then drips into a pan. From this indoor pan, water flows downhill through the tubing to the outdoor pan. Usually excess water is sprayed by the fan onto the hot pipe coils, where it evaporates and joins outdoor air. In the meantime, the refrigerant gas is warmed to 60 degrees by room air and travels through the pipe back to the compressor and starts the cycle over again.

Estimating Cooling Capacity. You can make a reasonably good estimate of your cooling needs by following this method:

Find the volume of the room by multiplying the width, length, and height, in feet.

Multiply the volume by 10 if the roof or attic is well insulated or if another room is above. If the room has many windows or an uninsulated ceiling or roof, multiply by 18.

Multiply this answer by 16 if the longest wall faces north; by 17 if it faces east; by 18 if it faces south; by 19 if it faces west.

Divide this answer by 60 to obtain BTU's per hour.

If you plan to cool several rooms, do a calculation for each room and then add the answers to find your total cooling needs.

Take your estimate with you when you go shopping for a conditioner. If you are using your own figures, you can ask the dealer to check them to see if you have analyzed the situation correctly. In the store, compare your estimate to the cooling capacities listed in BTU/hr units on the hang tags or labels on conditioners.

Select a machine that is close to your estimate—within 1,000 BTU/hr for smaller condi-

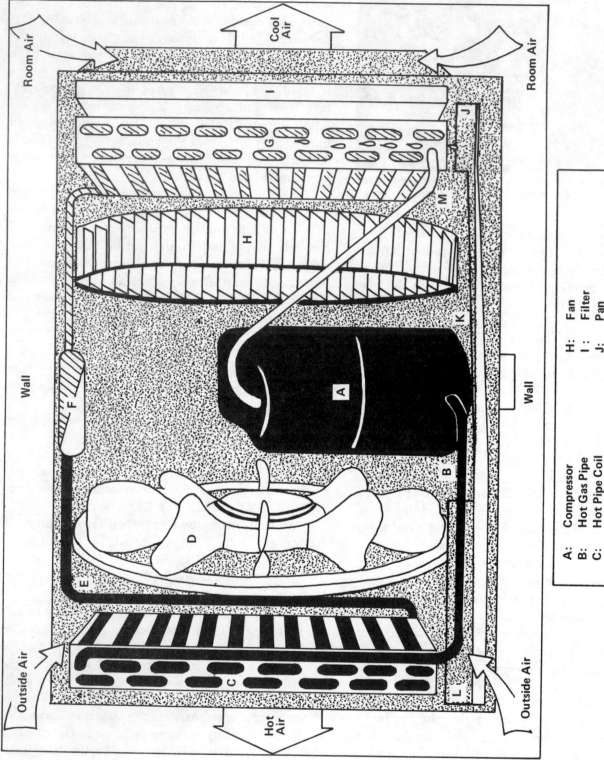

Room Air

Cool Air

Room Air

Wall

Wall

Outside Air

Outside Air

Hot Air

A: Compressor
B: Hot Gas Pipe
C: Hot Pipe Coil
D: Fan
E: Refrigerant Liquid Pipe
F: Expansion Device
G: Cooling Coils

H: Fan
I: Filter
J: Pan
K: Tubing to Outdoor Pan
L: Outdoor Pan
M: Refrigerant Gas
    Return Pipe

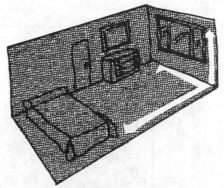

Height, width, and length of the area to be cooled.

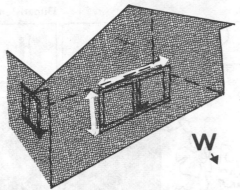

Number, sizes, and directions faced by windows.

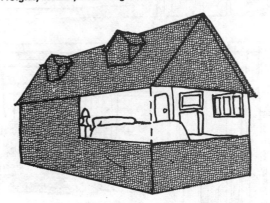

Location of space to be cooled within the building.

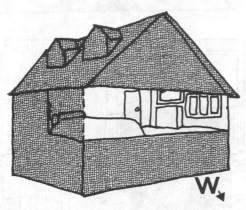

Direction of the longest side of the space to be cooled.

tioners or 2,000 or 3,000 BTU/hr for larger ones. A conditioner with too little cooling won't do the job on hot days; one with too much will keep the space cool but will not take out enough moisture to prevent it from feeling damp and uncomfortable.

Selection of Location, Dimensions, and Shape. The shape and dimensions of the room air conditioner you need depend on the shape and dimensions of the window where it will be installed. If the conditioner doesn't approximately fit the window selected, an exact, airtight installation will be difficult to achieve. If you do not have an airtight installation, the conditioner will never cool up to its rated capacity.

A window that faces north is the best place for your air conditioner because it is shaded most of the day. Don't install your conditioner in a window where outdoor airflow will be blocked by a nearby building or dense bushes.

Inside, avoid room corners or places where large pieces of furniture could hinder air circulation.

For a sash window, measure the width and height inside the frame when the window is open. Make sure the conditioner model you buy comes with side panels that will cover the full window width. If your window is 40 inches or more wide, you may have to pay for an accessory mounting kit.

For open casement and sliding windows, measure the width and height inside the frame when the window is open. Be sure the conditioner's mounting materials will extend the full height of the window opening. For a closed casement window, measure the width and height of the glass to be removed.

Sash windows, which slide up and down, accept conventional conditioners that are box shaped and wider than they are high. When such a conditioner is installed, the bottom window half rests on the top of the conditioner; panels fill in side space.

Casement windows, which swing back and forth like a door, and windows that slide horizontally usually require tall, narrow conditioners. Such conditioners are installed in windows left completely or partly open. For closed casement windows a specially shaped conditioner is available

Location. **Dimensions.** **Shape.**

that has a small front and is deep from front to back. It is installed by removing one or two small panes of glass and inserting the unit in the opening.

In some areas local laws or building regulations require that a conditioner must not project more than a certain distance from a building wall. Check to see if such rules apply to your home...

Note: When you are selecting a conditioner, see if the machine has a label that tells you how many inches it extends into and outside of the room from the mounting.

Home Wiring Capacities. Circuits in most houses and apartments supply electricity at about 115 volts and 15 amperes. Kitchens and laundry rooms may have circuits that supply 20 amperes. Before you buy a conditioner, find out the amperage of the outlet where the conditioner will be located. If you have any doubt about the amperage or voltage of the outlet, consult a licensed electrician.

Local Electrical Codes. In most of the United States conditioners that draw 7.5 amperes or less at

115 volts may be connected to household circuits; in some areas and buildings, conditioners with ratings up to 12 amperes may be plugged into 115-volt, single-outlet circuits; but nowhere should machines drawing more than 12 amperes be connected to 15-ampere 115-volt circuits.

To find out the electrical rating allowable for a conditioner connected to your home wiring, telephone the city or county engineer's office, a licensed electrician, or the local electric utility company. You can also consult a local air conditioner dealer. If you live in an apartment, check with the building manager before you purchase a conditioner.

Special High-Voltage Check. Any person considering buying a 208- or 230-volt conditioner should consult a qualified electrician, his dealer, or the local power company about the actual voltage delivered to his home. It may be anywhere from less than 200 volts to more than 240 volts.

Installation. If your conditioner is not big or unusually shaped, you should be able to do the mounting and sealing. But if the conditioner's electrical installation requires anything more complicated than putting a plug in a socket or changing a fuse, call a licensed electrician or get your dealer's assistance.

Mounting and Sealing. Small- and medium-size room air conditioners for open-window installations can be mounted, or fixed in place, by you and a helper. You should know how to use common tools and exactly follow instructions in the owner's manual that comes with the machine. Before you begin, inspect the window sill and frame to see that it is strong enough to support the conditioner when it is in place. A few additional pointers are:

Install the outside mounting feet or brackets before lifting the conditioner into the window—even to test its fit. Without the brackets the outdoor part of the machine will be unsupported.

Never lift a conditioner by yourself.

Never lift a machine by a plastic front panel; it is easily broken.

For sealing, again follow instructions in the owner's manual. If the seal is airtight, no daylight will show through the mounting or around the edges.

Connecting to Electrical Outlet. All room air conditioners come equipped with cords ending in three-prong plugs for connecting with grounded, three-hole electrical outlets. If your home has only two-hole outlets, have a three-hole outlet installed. You can either call a licensed electrician yourself or ask your conditioner dealer to provide this service.

With a three-hole, grounded outlet you and your home are protected if an electrical short circuit should develop in the machine; electricity would flow through the cord to the third hole in the outlet and from there through wiring to a metal bar buried in the earth outside the building. Without a grounded outlet a short circuit could give you a shock or start a fire.

Never remove the third prong from the conditioner plug. Adapter plugs for fitting three-prong plugs in two-hole outlets are not recommended. They may not provide adequate grounding.

Fusing the Circuit. A household circuit on which a room air conditioner is installed should have a circuit breaker or a special slow-blow fuse. A slow-blow fuse can be bought at most hardware stores and installed by anyone who can change an ordinary fuse. Always use a fuse with the same number of amperes as your old fuse; a larger size will not provide proper protection.

Extension Cords. Avoid the use of extension cords. If you must use one, buy a new, heavy-duty cord with a three-hole receptacle at one end and a three-prong plug at the other. Be sure that it matches the volts and amperes of your home air conditioner circuit and that it is safety inspected by a testing laboratory such as Underwriters' Laboratories, Inc. Buy one only as long as absolutely necessary; never buy one longer than 10 feet. If you use a cord, be sure it is firmly plugged in. Never put a cord where it will be walked on, pinched in a doorway, or exposed to heat. Inspect the cord frequently and buy a new one if you find any signs of wear.

Using Conditioner Controls. The thermostat should be left alone once you have found the temperature comfortable for you. However, you may set the thermostat for a slightly higher temperature if you plan to be away for several hours; the conditioner will quickly bring down the temperature when you return.

Air intakes or outlets should be kept closed unless specially needed. Open vents waste cool air.

Grilles should be set so that cool air flows up,

out, and away from the nearest wall to cover the whole room.

Fans should be set at high speed in hot weather to take full advantage of the conditioner's cooling capacity; in cool, moist weather they should be at low speed for less cooling and more moisture removal.

Lightening Conditioner Workload. Keep heat outside by closing all windows and doors to the conditioned space and sealing air leaks with weatherstripping or caulking. Keep storm windows on. Pull shades or drapes across windows during the day or put up outside awnings. If you have an attic, cool it with a ventilation fan. Prevent heat buildup inside during the hottest part of the day by turning off appliances and lights not in use. Try to cook main meals, take showers, and do washing and ironing in the morning or evening.

During low-voltage (brownout) situations, set the thermostat for a higher temperature. At low voltage a conditioner has lessened efficiency and must work harder for the same cooling. Leave the conditioner on all the time to distribute cooling work throughout the day unless municipal regulations on the use of electricity direct differently. If a severe brownout situation is announced, turn off the conditioner to avoid possible permanent damage to its motors.

Self-Service Care. Cleaning and protection of certain conditioner parts aids efficient, trouble-free cooling. It may prevent service calls and repairs. Be sure to unplug the conditioner before doing any home maintenance.

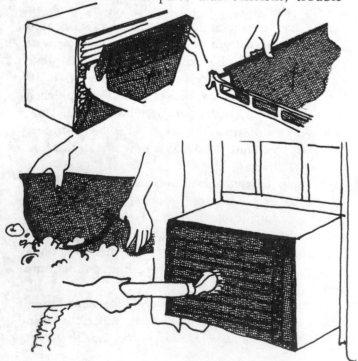

The filters should be cleaned or changed at least once a month to prevent dirt from collecting on the cooling coils and decreasing cooling efficiency. If you change filters, make sure the replacement is of the same material, quality, and thickness as the original.

Cooling coils on the outside of the conditioner should be protected in winter by a dust-proof and moistureproof cover, such as a plastic sheet. This will keep out windblown dirt and help prevent rusting caused by rain and snow.

Before you call a serviceman, be sure you really need him. Consider the following common problems:

Conditioner Won't Run: Check to see if the conditioner plug is firmly in its electrical outlet. Check for a blown fuse or a tripped circuit breaker. If you find either, unplug other appliances from the circuit before resetting the breaker or replacing the fuse.

Conditioner Doesn't Cool Enough: Vacuum clean, wash, or change the filter. Vacuum clean the cooling coils so they are free of dust and lint. Make sure that the window mounting has no air leaks. Close the conditioner exhaust and intake openings to prevent the escape of cool air. Set the thermostat for a lower room temperature. Set the fan on high speed if it is a hot day to bring room air past the cooling coils more frequently. Call your electric utility company to find out if there is temporary low voltage in your area. If there is, the efficiency of your conditioner may be lessened until voltage returns to normal. A repairman cannot help.

Conditioner Makes Strange Noises or Turns On and Off Rapidly: Vacuum clean, wash, or change the filter. Vacuum clean the cooling coils so they are free of dust and lint. Set the fan on high speed if the day is hot to bring room air past the cooling coils more frequently.

Conditioner Drips Water Inside Room: Vacuum clean, wash, or change the filter. Vacuum clean the cooling coils so they are free of dust and lint. Find out whether the outside temperature is lower than 70 degrees. If it is, turn the conditioner off until outside temperature is higher, or use the fan only setting.

CONTROLLING HUMIDITY

Let's start by defining "relative humidity:" this is the amount of water vapor in the air at a given temperature, as compared to what it would hold when completely saturated with water. For example, a relative humidity of 50 per cent means that there is half the possible amount of water vapor in the air. A relative humidity (RH) of 100 per cent is the point at which the air is saturated with vapor, and condensation will occur.

Warm air will hold a greater amount of water (not percentage) than cold air. Which is why air that is chilled by an air conditioner loses moisture, and there must be a condensate drain to handle this water. On a hot, humid day you are uncomfortable because there is little or no evaporation of perspiration from your skin. On a dry day, at the same temperature, you could be quite comfortable.

Conversely, in the winter you will be comfortable at a lower temperature if the humidity is about 40 per cent. If the humidity is lower than this, there will be evaporation of moisture from your skin and you could feel chilly at 75 or 80 degrees.

In the old days homes would be hot and humid in the summer, and wood warped and swelled with the humidity. In the winter the furnace would dry the air and wood dried, split and cracked; glue joints loosened in furniture. Pans of water were placed around the house in an attempt to increase humidity.

In today's tightly-built homes the situation is often reversed. Air conditioning in the summer dries the house and its contents, in the winter scaled-in water vapor causes all kinds of problems. For example, washing and rinsing 80 square feet of floor creates 2.4 pounds of water; drying 10 pounds of clothes in an automatic drier produces about 10 pounds of moisture; cooking three meals for a family of four puts almost 5 pounds of moisture into the air. Four people are responsible for introducing about 12 pounds of water into the air, and 88 pounds of moisture result from every 1,000 cubic feet of gas burned in range, furnace and hot-water tank.

Problem Spots

Warm, moist air tends to go toward cold, dry air, which means walls and windows. Damage at windows is readily noticeable; more serious problems often are hidden until damage occurs. This is a situation where there is no vapor barrier on the insulation. A break in the vapor barrier, even when the insulation has a barrier also can allow the moisture to pass through the plasterboard, insulation and onto the inner side of the siding. In cold weather it will freeze inside the sheathing or siding, then melt when the weather warms. This can cause serious rotting of the siding, sheathing and studding.

Blistered, peeling paint on the outside of the house very often indicates that there is no vapor barrier, and the moisture is simply lifting the paint off the wood. Where no vapor barrier exists, you can paint the inner surfaces of the outside walls with spar varnish or varnish-base enamel to provide a moisture seal. Water-base paint or wall covering can be applied over the seal.

If you have metal windows they must be insulated or cold is conducted to the inside to cause sweating. This is not stopped by storm sash over the glass part only. Inside storm sash is the answer. The lower part of the sash may have hinged inserts for ventilation and cutouts for window mechanisms.

To indicate the difference in various materials regarding heat loss: considering each material to be 1 inch thick and 1 foot square, with a difference of 32 degrees between inside and outside temperatures, wood will lose 25 BTUs per hour. Glass gives up 168 BTUs, steel 9,984 and aluminum 45,312 per hour.

The windows in a modern home may occupy up to 40 per cent of the total wall area, so storm sash is a must; it keeps in heat in winter, and keeps it out in summer.

The simplest way to determine the relative humidity in your home is to have a "weather center" that includes a hygrometer. If you don't have one, or have a scientific curiosity, you can make a sling psychrometer. It consists of two accurate thermometers on a base, one with the bulb left dry, the other with a wet bulb. When whirled in the air for 20 seconds the temperature of each is read immediately, the wet bulb first. This is done a few times to get two readings on the wet bulb that agree closely. These are compared with figures on a psychrometric table for the existing barometric pressure to determine relative humidity. Such

Rain gutters filled with leaves and debris may be the cause of water seeping into wall when ice dams form.

Opening fireplace damper will help reduce humidity by allowing moist air to escape up chimney. Don't overdo.

Excess dampness in uninsulated room above this one has condensed, seeped through floor and ruined this ceiling.

This bathroom window has lost the battle against humidity; showers and baths create damaging water vapor.

Poorly-closing door on the lint trap of a clothes drier can fill a room with water vapor. Renew gasket if needed.

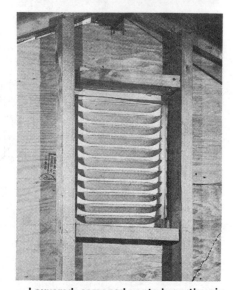

Louvered, screened vents keep the air moving in this unheated attic. Use at least two vents for cross ventilation.

Rain water around the foundation of a house will cause damp basement. Divert water away from house.

A dehumidifier will remove up to 20 pints of water from the air daily. A humidifier will add even more than this.

Cooking adds a lot of water vapor to air in home. Keep an exhaust fan running to draw this air out.

Exhaust fans can be used effectively in problem areas such as bathrooms, laundry rooms and kitchens.

Airing the home a few minutes each day by opening windows brings in cooler air that is drier, lowers the humidity.

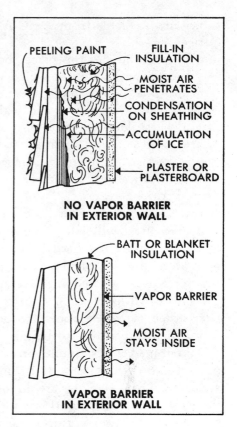

PEELING PAINT
FILL-IN INSULATION
MOIST AIR PENETRATES
CONDENSATION ON SHEATHING
ACCUMULATION OF ICE
PLASTER OR PLASTERBOARD

NO VAPOR BARRIER IN EXTERIOR WALL

BATT OR BLANKET INSULATION
VAPOR BARRIER
MOIST AIR STAYS INSIDE

VAPOR BARRIER IN EXTERIOR WALL

Storm sash creates a "dead-air" space between windows, which serves as insulation to eliminate "sweating."

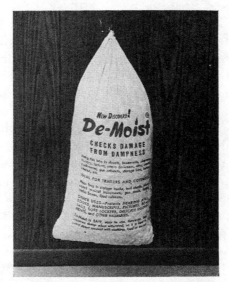

Low-cost dehumidifier is bag of silica-gel. Reusable "pebbles" will absorb twice their weight in water.

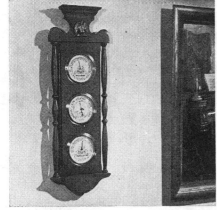

Home weather station is handy in determining relative humidity indoors. The ideal humidity is about 40 percent.

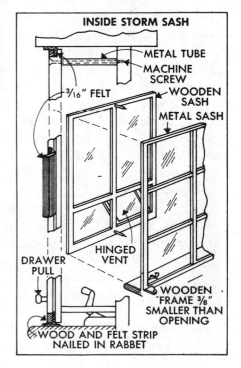

INSIDE STORM SASH

METAL TUBE
MACHINE SCREW
WOODEN SASH
METAL SASH
3/16" FELT
HINGED VENT
DRAWER PULL
WOODEN FRAME 3/8" SMALLER THAN OPENING
WOOD AND FELT STRIP NAILED IN RABBET

tables are available from the Government Printing Office.

In some homes the spaces between first-floor joists at the walls are not sealed with a vapor barrier, and this permits moist air from a basement or crawl space to get into the walls. These spaces should be sealed. Alternately, it sometimes is necessary to provide air circulation through walls to remove moist air. The air can go to an unheated attic that is well ventilated, or outdoors through a slotted cornice.

Lack of a vapor barrier on a ceiling under an unheated attic will allow moist air to reach and condense on roof boards. To prevent this condensation, provide plenty of ventilation in the attic. Screened, louvered vents at opposite ends of a gable roof will prevent this condensation problem. For other types of roofs, wooden dormer-type vents or metal vents can be installed. The area of the combined vents should provide 1 square foot of ventilation for every 300 square feet of floor area. When room ceilings are directly below rafters, the space between insulation and roof boards may be ventilated from cornices to continuous ridge vents or other venting arrangements. For flat and slightly sloping roofs, the vent area should be 1 foot for every 150 square feet of floor.

Where earth is frequently wet, crawl spaces are subject to excessive humidity. Air circulation often will dispose of the moist air. Vents in diagonally-opposite corners to take advantage of prevailing wind will help. The vent area of all vents should be 2 square feet per lineal feet of perimeter, plus one-half per cent of crawl-space area. If existing vents are inadequate an exhaust fan can be used. Ground moisture can be stopped with a layer of plastic sheeting placed on leveled earth and covered with 3 inches of sand. The foundation walls also should be water-proofed. Tiling outside the wall will drain away water that rises above the crawl-space floor.

As an alternate, the underside of the floor joists can be sealed with a vapor barrier, if pipes and heating ducts do not make this impractical. The barrier is sealed to pipes that pass through it. Joints in the plastic are overlapped and fastened to the joists lengthwise with slats.

Controlling Humidity

Day-to-day measures to control humidity include such home-maintenance tasks as keeping rain gutters clean. If they plug up in the winter and cause ice dams, water will back up under shingles and run down inside the attic and down through walls. Since moist air tries to reach cooler dry air, open the damper on a fireplace to allow the humid air to escape. Keep in mind that heat also escapes up the chimney, so don't leave the damper open too long.

Clothes driers, as previously stated, produce a tremendous amount of water vapor, so be sure the door over the lint trap is closed tightly. If the gasket is worn or damaged, replace it.

Check outside the house to make sure water from downspouts flows away from the house. Cast-concrete diverters may do the job, or plastic pipe can be used to route the water away from the foundation.

Inside the basement you may need a dehumidifier to lower the humidity. If your budget won't stand the cost of this mechanical device, then you can use silica gel. This substance has great affinity for moisture, and is sold in 1 and 5-pound bags that are hung in the lower half of the room where they will absorb twice their weight in water vapor. When the bag feels damp and about twice its original weight, the contents of the bag are dried in an oven and used again.

Where possible, install exhaust fans in problem areas, such as kitchen, laundry and bath.

In the winter a big help is to "air out" the house by opening windows slightly for a few minutes daily. To demonstrate how effective this cool air is in reducing humidity, consider that a small house of 9,600 cubic feet holds about 15 pounds of water at 80 degrees F. when the humidity is 100 per cent. The same amount of outdoor air at 40 degrees and 100 per cent humidity contains only about 4 pounds of water. If a complete air change is made, and the admitted air is heated to 80 degrees, the humidity will be about 25 per cent. This does not consider moisture that might be absorbed from household furnishings. When outside air has the same relative humidity as inside air, an exchange of air is not effective.

If you have a forced-air furnace, fresh air can be admitted through a 3-inch pipe connected to the cold-air return of the furnace. A damper in the pipe controls the amount of air admitted. This would generally eliminate the need for open-

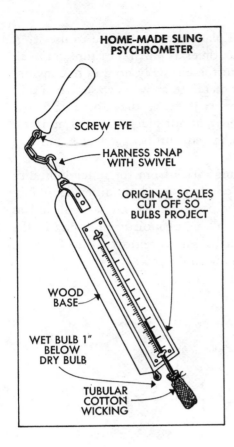

HOME-MADE SLING PSYCHROMETER

- SCREW EYE
- HARNESS SNAP WITH SWIVEL
- ORIGINAL SCALES CUT OFF SO BULBS PROJECT
- WOOD BASE
- WET BULB 1" BELOW DRY BULB
- TUBULAR COTTON WICKING

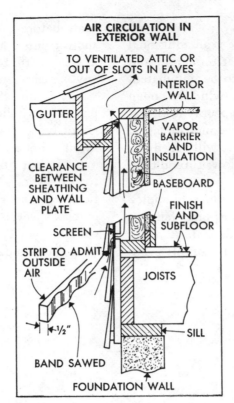

AIR CIRCULATION IN EXTERIOR WALL

- TO VENTILATED ATTIC OR OUT OF SLOTS IN EAVES
- GUTTER
- INTERIOR WALL
- VAPOR BARRIER AND INSULATION
- CLEARANCE BETWEEN SHEATHING AND WALL PLATE
- BASEBOARD
- SCREEN
- FINISH AND SUBFLOOR
- STRIP TO ADMIT OUTSIDE AIR
- JOISTS
- ½"
- SILL
- BAND SAWED
- FOUNDATION WALL

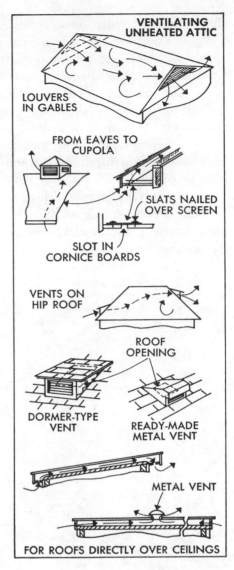

VENTILATING UNHEATED ATTIC

- LOUVERS IN GABLES
- FROM EAVES TO CUPOLA
- SLATS NAILED OVER SCREEN
- SLOT IN CORNICE BOARDS
- VENTS ON HIP ROOF
- ROOF OPENING
- DORMER-TYPE VENT
- READY-MADE METAL VENT
- METAL VENT
- FOR ROOFS DIRECTLY OVER CEILINGS

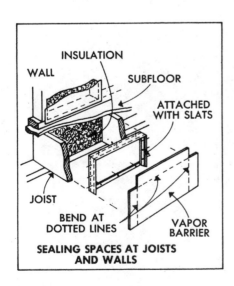

- INSULATION
- WALL
- SUBFLOOR
- ATTACHED WITH SLATS
- JOIST
- BEND AT DOTTED LINES
- VAPOR BARRIER

SEALING SPACES AT JOISTS AND WALLS

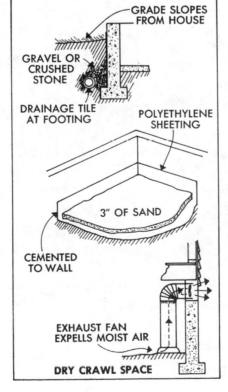

- GRADE SLOPES FROM HOUSE
- GRAVEL OR CRUSHED STONE
- POLYETHYLENE SHEETING
- DRAINAGE TILE AT FOOTING
- 3" OF SAND
- CEMENTED TO WALL
- EXHAUST FAN EXPELLS MOIST AIR

DRY CRAWL SPACE

As clearly indicated on these batts of insulation, the vapor barrier should always face toward inside of room.

ing windows to introduce fresh air.

If you have a new home there is an additional problem. Moisture in damp plaster, concrete and lumber may take several seasons to be eliminated. For this reason, keep basement windows open when practical, to allow the escape of moisture-laden air. If you have central air conditioning, a supply and return in the basement will speed the removal of moisture, and the windows should then not be opened.

Other very simple things to reduce humidity would be to replace washers in dripping faucets. Are house plants watered every day? Is it really necessary, or does much of the water simply evap-orate before the plants have a chance to use it? A shower puts four times as much moisture in the air as a tub bath; but there's really no way to convince anyone who's addicted to showers to soak in a tub!

Be sure the vent from the clothes dryer is properly installed, and not plugged. If the moist air is not being discharged outdoors it will be flowing into the house.

If your home varies from too much humidity to too little, a combination humidifier/dehumidifier might be the answer. One model will add as much as eleven gallons of moisture per day in the winter, then can be set to remove up to 20 pints of moisture a day in summer.

WORKING WITH METAL

METAL
WORKING

CUTTING METAL ■ BENDING AND FLARING METALLIC TUBING

REMOVING BROKEN BOLTS AND STUDS

POLISHING A FLAT METAL SURFACE ■ SOLDERING

CUTTING METAL

Many handtools and power tools have been designed for the specific purpose of cutting metals quickly and accurately.

Metal Cutting with Chisels

When struck with a heavy hammer, a cold chisel is capable of cutting metal. With chisel and hammer, you can cut wires, bars, rods and other shapes of metal and also cut off the heads of rivets and bolts.

Cutting Wire or Round Stock. Mark a guideline on the stock and place the work on the top face of an anvil or other suitable working surface. Place the cutting edge of the chisel on the mark in a vertical position and lightly strike the chisel with a hammer. Check the chisel mark for accuracy. Continue to strike the chisel until the cut is made. The last few blows of the hammer should be made lightly to avoid damage to the anvil, supporting surface, or to the chisel.

Heavy stock is cut in the same manner except that the cut is made halfway through the stock; the work is then turned over and the cut finished from the opposite side.

Removing a Rivet or Bolt Head. Hold the work in a heavy vise or secure it some other way so that the work will not move. Hold the cold chisel with one face of the bevel flat on the surface of the job. Strike the head of the chisel with the hammer as you loosely hold and guide the chisel.

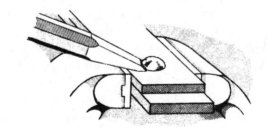

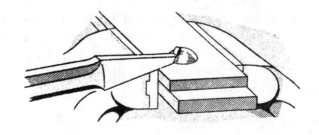

Cutting off a rivet head with a chisel.

347

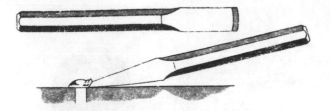

Cutting off a rivet head with a side cutting chisel.

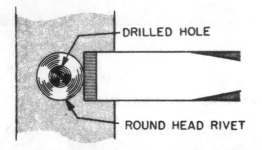

DRILLED HOLE

ROUND HEAD RIVET

Removing a rivet head in a hard to reach position.

To cut off a rivet head with a cape chisel, select a chisel of about the same size as the diameter of the rivet. Cut through the center of the rivet head, holding one face of the bevel flat on the surface of the job, and then sever the center of the head from the shank or body.

To cut off a rivet head with a side cutting chisel, place the chisel nearly flat on the surface of the work with its single bevel upwards. Drive the cutting edge under the edge of the rivet head just as you would if you were using a cold chisel.

The cutting edge of the chisel has a slight radius which will tend to prevent the corners from cutting undesirable grooves in the surface of the work.

To remove a rivet head when there is not room enough to swing a hammer with sufficient force to cut the rivet, first drill a hole about the size of the body of the rivet in and almost to the bottom of the rivet head. Then cut off the head with a cold chisel.

Metal Cutting with Drills

In drilling any metal, there are several general steps to be followed. First, mark the exact location of the hole. Second, secure the work properly. Then, use the correct cutting speed and appropriate cutting oil or other coolant, where applicable.

Finally, apply pressure on the drill properly. It is assumed that you have selected the correct drill size.

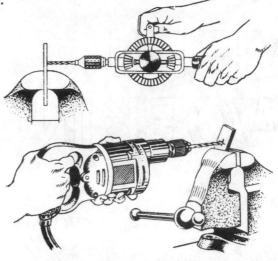

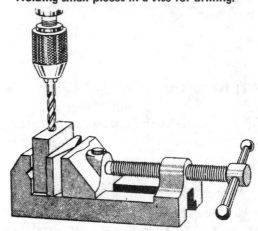

Holding small pieces in a vise for drilling.

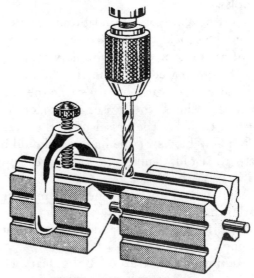

Holding work with a drill press vise.

Holding work in V-blocks.

Locating the Hole. The exact location of the hole must be marked with a center punch. The punch mark forms a seat for the drill point, thus ensuring accuracy. Without the punch mark, the drill may have a tendency to "walk off" before it begins to cut into the metal.

Holding the Work. Most work is held for drilling by some mechanical means such as a vise or clamps. It is mandatory that the work be well secured. If not, the work or stock may rotate at high speed or fly loose, and become a high speed projectile endangering all within range.

When drilling in small pieces with a hand held drill, it is best to hold the work in a vise so that the axis of the drill is horizontal. This position provides better control of the drilling operation and will tend to ensure a hole which will be square with the surface of the work.

When drilling in small pieces with a drill press, hold the work either in a drill press vise or between V-blocks. Caution: Be sure to fasten the drill press vise or V-block to the drill press table.

When using a drill press to drill holes in the end of round stock, place the stock in one of the V-grooves in the stationary jaw of the drill vise; these V-grooves will hold the work perpendicular to the table of the drill press. The drilled hole will then be parallel with the axis of the round stock.

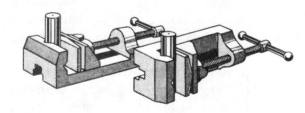

Holding work to drill holes in the end of round stock.

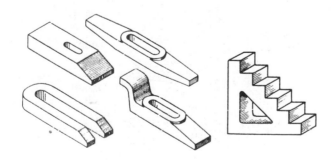

Step block and clamps.

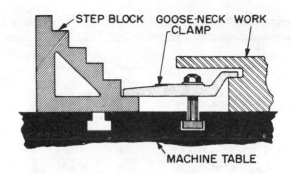

Holding work with step block and clamp for drilling.

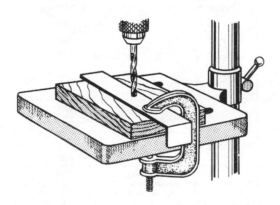

Drilling holes in large pieces can be accomplished by holding the work with a stepblock and clamps. (A piece of metal of suitable size, with a hole drilled near one end makes a suitable substitute for a clamp.)

When holding work with step blocks and clamps, you may use a gooseneck clamp. Notice that the body of the clamp is approximately parallel with the surface of the drill press table and that the bolt is held close to the work rather than close to the step block. This setup provides the most favorable mechanical advantage. Usually, two or more clamps are used on each setup.

If you are required to hold thin metal, place it on a block of wood to provide support directly beneath the intended hole. This support will also help minimize drill breakage when the feed pressure is applied. Secure the C-clamp and drill through the metal and into the wood. Stop drilling when wood chips appear to avoid damage to the drill table.

Speed Information. The correct cutting speed for metal drilling depends upon the type of metal and its properties plus the diameter and type of drill (high speed or carbon).

349

Diameter of Drill	Soft Metals 300 F.P.M.	Annealed Cast Iron 140 F.P.M.	Mild Steel 100 F.P.M.	Malleable Iron 90 F.P.M.	Hard Cast Iron 80 F.P.M.	Tool or Hard Steel 60 F.P.M.	Alloy Steel Cast Steel 40 F.P.M.
1/16 (No. 53 to 80)	18320	8554	6111	5500	4889	3667	2445
3/32 (No. 42 to 52)	12212	5702	4071	3666	3258	2442	1649
1/8 (No. 31 to 41)	9160	4278	3056	2750	2445	1833	1222
5/32 (No. 23 to 30)	7328	3420	2444	2198	1954	1465	977
3/16 (No. 13 to 22)	6106	2852	2037	1833	1630	1222	815
7/32 (No. 1 to 12)	5234	2444	1745	1575	1396	1047	698
1/4 (A to E)	4575	2139	1527	1375	1222	917	611
9/32 (G to K)	4071	1900	1356	1222	1084	814	542
5/16 (L, M, N)	3660	1711	1222	1100	978	733	489
11/32 (O to R)	3330	1554	1110	1000	888	666	444
3/8 (S, T, U)	3050	1426	1018	917	815	611	407
13/32 (V to Z)	2818	1316	939	846	752	563	376
7/16	2614	1222	873	786	698	524	349
15/32	2442	1140	814	732	652	488	326
1/2	2287	1070	764	688	611	458	306
9/16	2035	950	678	611	543	407	271
5/8	1830	856	611	550	489	367	244
11/16	1665	777	555	500	444	333	222
3/4	1525	713	509	458	407	306	204

Figures are for High-Speed Drills. The speed of Carbon Drills should be reduced one-half. Use drill speed nearest to figure given.

Drilling Hints. It is necessary to use a cutting oil to lubricate and cool the drill when drilling steel and wrought iron. Cast iron, aluminum, brass and other soft metals may be drilled dry, although at high drilling speeds it is advisable to use some medium to cool these metals. Compressed air, water, and lard oil are examples of such cooling media. Be sure to use goggles whenever you use compressed air.

Always apply pressure on a line which goes straight through the axis of the drill. (Side pressure will enlarge the hole and can break the drill.)

Keep the drill steady and apply enough pressure to keep it cutting. Too much pressure will overload the motor; too little pressure will merely cause the drill to "polish" instead of cut. This will quickly dull the cutting edges of the drill. You will know the pressure is correct when the drill bites continuously without overloading the drill motor.

When drilling large holes, do it in stages. A pilot hole is a good idea, since it serves as a guide for the larger drill and helps to increase accuracy.

Threads and Thread Cutting

Threads are helical ridges cut into screws, nuts, bolts, or the walls of a hole, so that the action of turning the screw, nut, or bolt gives it endwise as well as rotary motion.

Many thread types exist. These types include bolt threads, machine screw threads and pipe threads. Before we proceed with descriptions of thread cutting procedures, we must become familiar with the terminology to be used.

Thread Terminology. The outside diameter of a thread is known as the major diameter. The diameter across the roots of the thread is called the

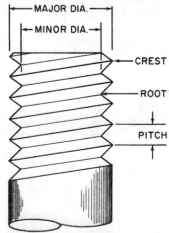

Thread terminology.

minor diameter. The pitch is defined as the distance from any point on the thread of a screw to the corresponding point on an adjacent thread. It is usually measured from crest to crest and is expressed by a specific quantity of threads per inch.

Tap Drill Determination. If a threaded hole is to be made in a piece of metal, a hole of suitable size must first be drilled. The hole must be somewhat smaller than the size of the bolt to be screwed into it. The resultant thread is known as a "75% thread" because the diameter of the hole is 75% of the difference between the major and minor diameters, subtracted from the major diameter.

When the tap hole is the right size, it is a little larger than the root diameter of the tap.

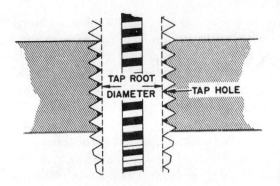

Proper size drilled hole for tapping.

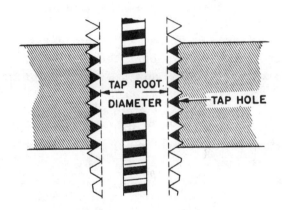

Oversize drilled hole for tapping.

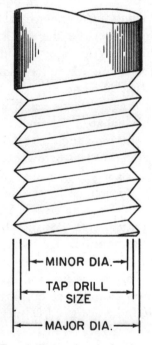

Tap drill size determination.

The tap will cut a thread in the work which is only 75 percent as deep as the thread on the tap. The other 25 percent of the depth of thread on the tap provides clearance between the tap hole and the root diameter of the tap. This makes tapping easier.

If the tap drill selected is oversize, the tap hole will be oversize, and the tap can cut only shallow threads in the work. With less than a full 75 percent depth of thread, stud or capscrew threads usually strip.

If the tap drill selected is undersize, the tap hole will be undersize, being perhaps equal to the

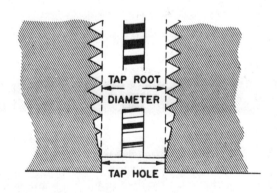

Undersize drilled hole for tapping.

root diameter of the tap. Then there will be no clearance, and the tap will turn hard, tear the threads, and probably break.

Cutting Internal Pipe Threads. Pipe threads are tapered threads to provide an airtight and liquidtight joint. A 3/8-inch machine thread tap and a 3/8-inch pipe thread tap are different. The 3/8-inch machine thread tap will cut machine threads in a hole so that a 3/8-inch cap screw, having the same thread can be screwed into the hole. The 3/8-inch pipe thread tap will cut pipe threads in a hole so that a 3/8-inch threaded pipe can be screwed into the hole. Pipe diameters are measured and given as inside diameters, and the wall thickness of the pipe must be taken into consideration.

The N.P.T., which formerly stood for National Pipe Thread, is still used as a carryover and now refers to the new name for the same thread, American Standard Taper Pipe Thread. This standard taper is ¾-inch per foot.

To cut internal pipe threads, drill a tap hole in the stock to be tapped and run the pipe tap into the tap hole. Notice that the first few threads on the pipe tap are ground away. This makes starting easier. Plenty of lard oil is the standard lubricant for steel. Tap copper and brass with no lubricant. The depth to which it is desirable to tap pipe threads is usually determined by turning the threaded pipe into the tapped hole for a trial. The last few threads on the pipe should still be visible when the pipe is drawn up tight in the tapped hole.

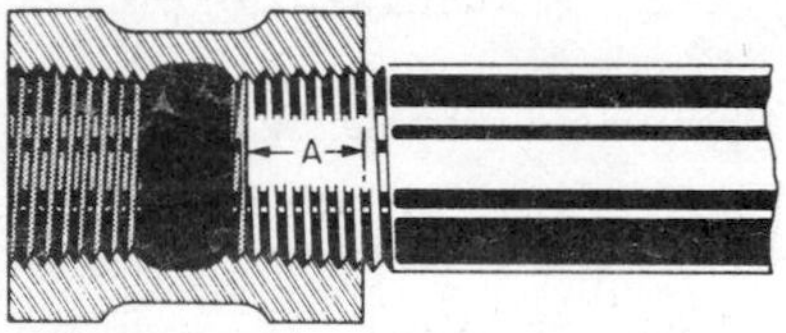

Size of Pipe, Inches	Dimension A, Inches	Size of Pipe, Inches	Dimension A, Inches	Size of Pipe, Inches	Dimension A, Inches
1/8	1/4	1 1/2	11/16	5	1 1/4
1/4	3/8	2	3/4	6	1 5/16
3/8	3/8	2 1/2	15/16	7	1 3/8
1/2	1/2	3	1	8	1 7/16
3/4	9/16	3 1/2	1 1/16	9	1 1/2
1	11/16	4	1 1/8	10	1 5/8
1 1/4	11/16	4 1/2	1 3/16	12	1 3/4

Length of thread on pipe required to make a tight joint.

The general practice in tapping holes for pipe threads is to drill the proper size tap hole and then start the pipe tap right into the tap hole. Some people recommend using a pipe reamer, especially when large deep holes are to be tapped. A pipe reamer has the same ¾ inch per foot taper as a pipe tap. A reamed pipe tap hole would have the same shape as the pipe tap, and therefore would make tapping easier and reduce wear on the tap.

Cutting External Pipe Threads. Usually, both ends of a pipe are threaded with external pipe threads. Notice, in all the figures showing pipe threads, that they are V-shaped. The standard ¾ inch taper per foot of pipe threads is equal to 1/16 inch per inch. Therefore, the taper of the threads on each side of the pipe is 1/32 inch taper per inch. This taper cannot be changed. This produces a tight joint. The angle between sides of the threads is 60 degrees and several threads on the end of the pipe are perfect threads. The next few have V-bottoms but flat tops, and the last few threads have both flat tops and bottoms. Each size of pipe has a certain number of threads per inch, built into the pipe taps and dies.

Adjustable pipe dies have a reference mark on each die which, when lined up with the corresponding reference mark on the die stock, will give a standard-size thread. You adjust the dies one way or the other from the reference mark to cut a thread with the fit you want.

To cut external threads on iron pipe, first determine its nominal size. Nominal size means the "name size" of the pipe such as 1/8-inch, ¾-inch, and so on. Except in the sizes below 1-inch, nominal sizes correspond closely to inside diameters. For 1-inch pipe and larger, measure the inside diameter (I.D.) with your rule, to the closest 1/32 inch, and you will have nominal size. For sizes below 1 inch, you can determine nominal size by measuring the outside diameter (O.D.) to the nearest 1/32 inch and reading the corresponding nominal size in the table. This method can also be employed for sizes 1-inch and above in lieu of the I.D. measurement.

Approximate O.D. of Standard Wrought Iron Pipe.

Nominal Size	Outside Diameter	Nominal Size	Outside Diameter
1/8	13/32	3 1/2	4
1/4	17/32	4	4 1/2
3/8	11/16	4 1/2	5
1/2	27/32	5	5 9/16
3/4	1 1/16	6	6 5/8
1	1 5/16	7	7 5/8
1 1/4	1 21/32	8	8 5/8
1 1/2	1 29/32	9	9 5/8
2	2 3/8	10	10 3/4
2 1/2	2 7/8	11	11 3/4
3	3 1/2	12	12 3/4

To begin cutting, put the die stock on the pipe so that the pipe passes through the guide and enters the tapered face of the pipe die. Turn the die stock clockwise for right-hand threads, applying pressure only when starting. It is not necessary to turn the die back and forth as you do when cutting machine threads. Pipe-threading dies can cut continuously because they cut only as many threads on the pipe as there are on the die itself and because there is plenty of room in a pipe die for the chips to escape. After the die has taken hold, it will feed itself. When cutting threads on steel pipe, apply lard oil to the pipe and die where the cutting is actually taking place. Continue turning until the end of the pipe has gone through the die and is flush with the near face.

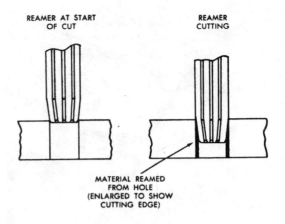

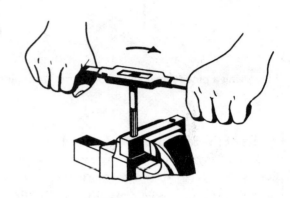

Reaming a hole with a straight hole reamer.

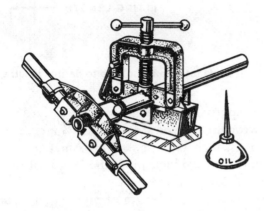

Threading an external pipe thread with a pipe die.

Reaming Operations

Reaming operations are jobs that smoothly enlarge drilled holes to an exact size and finish the hole at the same time. A hole that has been made by drilling is usually slightly oversize. This is quite satisfactory for holes in which bolts or rivets are placed. When greater accuracy and a smooth finish are required, the hole is first drilled undersize and then finished by reaming. Reamers are also used to remove burrs from the insides of pipe.

Straight Holes. A solid straight-hole reamer is used for most work, since it is the most accurate and rugged reamer. The straight-hole handreamer is turned by means of a tap wrench that is tightened on the square end of the reamer shank.

Secure the work in a vise so that the hole to be reamed is perpendicular to the top of the vise jaws. Position the reamer at the top of the hole. Straight-hole reamers have a slight taper at the end

Using a tap wrench to turn a hand reamer.

so that they will fit into the hole easily. Turn the wrench clockwise very slowly until the reamer is centered in the hole.

After the reamer is centered in the hole, turn the wrench clockwise with a steady firm pressure until the reamer has been turned all the way through the hole. When reaming steel, use cutting oil or machine oil to lubricate the tool. When reaming soft iron, do not lubricate the tool. To remove the reamer from the hole turn the wrench clockwise and raise the reamer simultaneously.

Note: Turning the wrench too fast or too slowly will cause the reamer to chatter, producing an unevenly reamed hole.

Burr Removal. After a piece of pipe has been cut, the ends should be reamed to remove the burr that is left on the inside of the pipe. This burr, if not removed, will restrict the flow of fluid in the pipe. Besides the pipe reamer you will need a vise to hold the pipe steady. After making sure the pipe is held firmly in the vise, insert the reamer in the end of the pipe and turn the handle. Rotate the

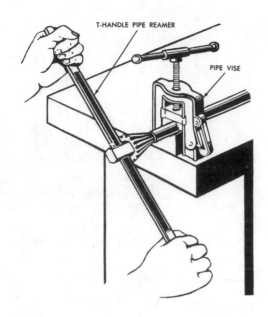

Using a pipe reamer to remove burrs from pipe.

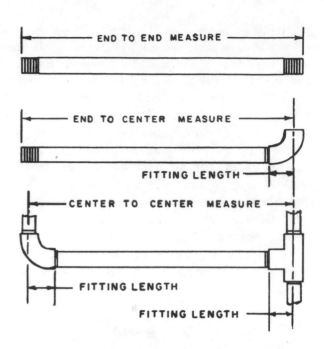

Proper methods for measuring pipe to desired lengths.

handle of the reamer clockwise in short even strokes until the burrs inside the cut piece of pipe are completely removed. Remove the reamer from the pipe by rotating it clockwise and reducing applied pressure.

Cutting Piping and Tubing

In performing certain tasks, you may need to cut pipe or tubing. The main difference between pipe and tubing lies in their wall thicknesses; pipe has thicker walls than tubing. Though pipe cutters are larger than tube cutters, they work on the same principle.

Pipe. You will probably cut more pipes made of iron than any other metal. These pipes must be cut to specific lengths. Before cutting a pipe to length, make sure you have the correct measurement.

The end-to-end method includes measuring the threaded portions of the pipe and measuring the pipe from end to end. The end-to-center method is used on a section of pipe that has a fitting screwed on one end only; measure from the free end of the pipe to the center of the fitting at the other end of the pipe. The center-to-center method is used when both ends of the pipe have fittings; measure from the center of one fitting to the center of the other fitting at the opposite end of the pipe.

The approximate length of thread on ½- and ¾-inch wrought iron or steel pipe is ¾ inch. On 1-, 1¼-, and 1½-inch pipe, it is approximately 1 inch long. On 2- and 2½-inch pipe, the length of thread is 1-1/8 and 1½ inches respectively.

To determine the length of pipe required, take the measurement of installation such as center to center of the pipe requiring two fittings. Measure the size of the fittings.

Subtract the total size of the two fittings from the installation measurement. Multiply the approximate thread length by 2 and add the result to the length obtained. This will give the length of pipe required.

After the length of the pipe has been determined, measure the pipe and mark the spot where the cut is to be made with a scriber or crayon. Lock the pipe securely in a pipe vise.

Inspect the cutter to make sure that there are no nicks or burrs in the cutting wheel. Open the jaws of the cutter by turning the handle counterclockwise. Position the cutter around the pipe at the marked point. Make sure the cutting wheel is exactly on the mark and close the jaws of the cutter lightly against the pipe by turning the cutter handle clockwise. After making contact, turn the cutter handle clockwise one-fourth of a turn more. This will put a bit on the pipe.

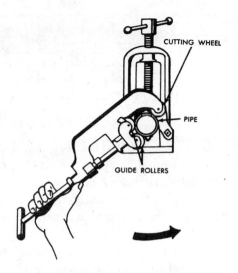

Cutting pipe with a pipe cutter.

Grasp the cutter handle and rotate the cutter as a whole one complete revolution, swinging it around the pipe.

Turn the cutter handle clockwise one-fourth of a turn more to take another bite on the pipe and rotate the cutter another complete revolution. Keep the cutter perpendicular to the pipe at all times or the wheel will not track properly. Repeat this operation until the pipe is cut. Remove the small shoulder on the outside of the pipe with a file and remove the burr on the inside with a reamer.

Tubing. Copper tubing is one kind of metallic tubing that you can cut readily with a tube cutter. To cut tubing, place the tube cutter with the cutting wheel on the mark where the cut is to be made. Move the cutting wheel into light contact with the tubing.

SCREW THE CUTTING WHEEL LIGHTLY AGAINST THE TUBING

ROTATE THE CUTTER KEEPING A SLIGHT PRESSURE AGAINST THE CUTTING WHEEL WITH THE SCREW ADJUSTMENT.
Steps in cutting tubing with a tube cutter.

Then swing the handle around the tubing as you feed the cutting wheel a little for each revolution by turning the screw adjustment. Different wall thicknesses, kinds, and diameters of metallic tubing require different feeds. The feed pressure is correct when it keeps the wheel cutting but does not flatten the tubing.

The design of some tubing cutters will permit cutting off a flared end close to the base of the flare. Place the flare in this groove so that the cutting wheel rides at the base of the flare. Then cut off the flare as you would cut tubing.

Burrs that form may be similar to those formed in pipe cutting. Remove the inside burr with the reamer attached to the tubing cutter opposite the handle. In some cases a three-cornered scraper, pocketknife blade, or round file may work better than the reamer. After reaming clean out the chips. Then remove any outside burr with a file.

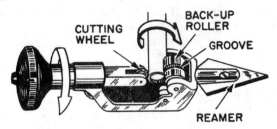

Cutting tubing close to the base of a flare.

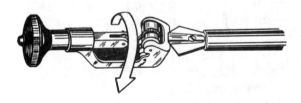

Reaming the burrs from a piece of tubing.

BENDING AND FLARING METALLIC TUBING

The objective in tube bending is to obtain a smooth bend without flattening the tube. Tube bending is usually accomplished with one of the tube benders discussed in this chapter. In an emergency, however, aluminum tubing under one-fourth of an inch in diameter may be bent by hand.

Spring Benders

External spring-type benders come in sizes to bend ¼-inch, 5/16-inch, 3/8-inch, 7/16-inch, ½-inch, and 5/8-inch outside-diameter soft copper, aluminum, and other soft metallic tubing.

To bend tubing with this type of bender, first select the size that will just slip over the size of tubing you want to bend. Then slip it over the tubing so that it centers at the middle of the proposed bend. Grasp the bender with both hands and make the bend.   The restraining action of the bender will prevent the tubing from collapsing at the bend and will produce a smooth curve. To remove the bender, grasp the belled end and pull it off the tubing.

Internal spring-type benders come in sizes to bend 3/8-inch, ½-inch, and 5/8-inch outside-diameter tubing. This type can be used when both ends of a length of tubing are flared and the external type cannot be applied. To bend tubing with an internal spring-type bender, select the proper size bender and slip it inside of the tubing. Insert it so that the center of its length is at the center of the proposed bend. Grasp the tubing with both hands and make the bend. If the bender sticks out of the end of the tubing, remove it by pulling it out. If not, remove it with a fish wire or other simple means.

Hand Tube Bender

The hand tube bender consists of four parts: handle, radius block (mandrel), clip, and slide bar. The radius block is marked in degrees of bend ranging from 0 to 180. The slide bar has a mark which is lined up with the zero mark on the radius block. The tube is inserted in the tool, and after lining up the marks, the slide bar is moved around until the mark on the slide bar reaches the desired degrees of bend on the radius block.

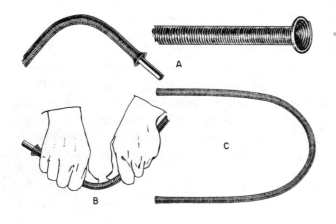

Bending tubing with spring type tube benders.

This type of bender is furnished in 3/16-inch, ¼-inch, 5/16-inch, 3/8-inch, and ½-inch sizes. For larger sizes of tubing similar mandrel-type benders are used. The only difference is that these larger benders are geared for greater mechanical advantage.

Flaring

Tube flaring is a method of forming the end of a tube into a funnel shape so that it can be held by a threaded fitting. A partially threaded flare nut is slipped over the tube, the end of the tube is flared, the flare is seated with the inside of the flare against the end of a fitting which has threads on the outside, and then the flare nut is screwed onto the fitting, pushing the outside of the flare against the seating surface of the fitting.

To flare the end of tubing, first check to see that it has been cut off squarely and has the burrs removed from both inside and outside. Remember to slip the flare nut on the tube before you make the flare. Open the flaring tool at the die which corresponds to the size of the tubing being flared. Insert the end of the tubing to protrude slightly above the top face of the die blocks. The amount by which the tubing extends above the blocks determines the finished diameter of the flare. The flare must be large enough so that it will seat properly against the fitting, but small enough so that the threads of the flare nut will slide over it. You determine the correct size by trial-and-error.

Then close the die block and secure the tool with the wing nut. Use the handle of the yoke to tighten the wing nut.

Place the yoke over the end of the tubing and tighten the handle to force the cone into the end of the tubing. The completed flare should be slightly visible above the face of the die blocks.

REMOVING BROKEN BOLTS AND STUDS

When the removal of a broken bolt or stud is required, flood the part being worked on with plenty of penetrating oil or oil of wintergreen. Time permitting, soak the area for several hours or overnight. A week's soaking may loosen a bolt which would otherwise have to be drilled out.

If enough of the broken piece protrudes take hold of it with vise-grip pliers and carefully try to ease it out. If the bolt cannot be turned, further soaking with penetrating oil may help. Or try removing the pliers and jarring the bolt with light

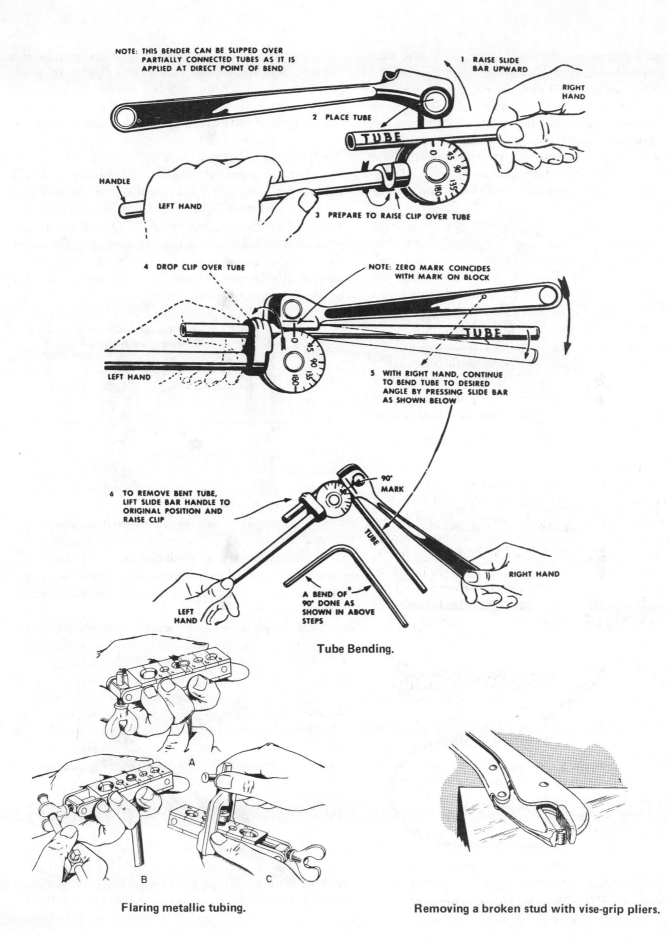

NOTE: THIS BENDER CAN BE SLIPPED OVER PARTIALLY CONNECTED TUBES AS IT IS APPLIED AT DIRECT POINT OF BEND

1 RAISE SLIDE BAR UPWARD

RIGHT HAND

2 PLACE TUBE

TUBE

HANDLE

LEFT HAND

3 PREPARE TO RAISE CLIP OVER TUBE

4 DROP CLIP OVER TUBE

NOTE: ZERO MARK COINCIDES WITH MARK ON BLOCK

LEFT HAND

TUBE

5 WITH RIGHT HAND, CONTINUE TO BEND TUBE TO DESIRED ANGLE BY PRESSING SLIDE BAR AS SHOWN BELOW

6 TO REMOVE BENT TUBE, LIFT SLIDE BAR HANDLE TO ORIGINAL POSITION AND RAISE CLIP

90° MARK

TUBE

A BEND OF 90° DONE AS SHOWN IN ABOVE STEPS

LEFT HAND

RIGHT HAND

Tube Bending.

A

B

C

Flaring metallic tubing.

Removing a broken stud with vise-grip pliers.

357

hammer blows on the top and around the sides. This may loosen the threads so that the bolt can then be removed with the vise-grip pliers.

If a bolt has been broken off flush with the surface, it is sometimes possible to back it out with light blows of a prick punch or center punch.

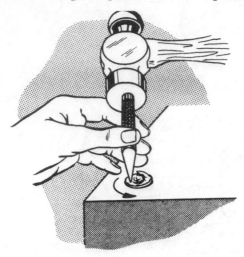

Removing a broken bolt with a prick punch.

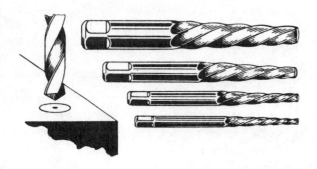

Screw and bolt extactors for removing broken studs.

However, if the bolt was broken due to rusting, this method will not remove it. If it cannot be removed by careful punching first on one side and then the other, a screw and bolt extractor may remove it.

When using this extractor, file the broken portion of the bolt to provide a smooth surface at the center for a punch mark, if possible. Then carefully center punch the exact center of the bolt.

If possible, drill through the entire length of the broken bolt. Then carefully work some pene-

trating oil through this hole so that it fills the cavity beneath the bolt and has a chance to work its way upwards from the bottom of the bolt. The more time you let the penetrating oil work from both ends of the broken bolt, the better are your chances of removing it.

When drilling a hole in a stud which has broken off below the surface of the piece which it was holding, a drill guide will center the drill and may be preferred rather than a center punch mark.

When the hole has been drilled, and additional penetrating oil has had time to soak, put the spiral end of the screw and bolt extractor into the hole. Set it firmly with a few light hammer blows and secure the tap wrench.

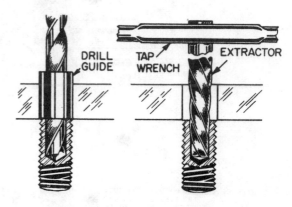

Removing a stud broken off below the surface.

Carefully try to pack the broken bolt out of the hole. Turn the extractor counterclockwise. (This type of extractor is designed for right hand threads only.).

A screw and bolt extractor can sometimes be used to remove an Allen head capscrew when the socket has been stripped by the Allen wrench.

When attempting this removal, carefully grind off the end of the extractor so that it will not bottom before the spiral has had a chance to take hold.

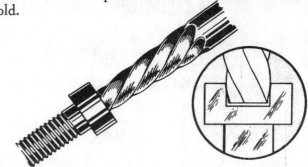

Removing an Allen head capscrew with a bolt extractor.

358

In doing this grinding operation, great care must be taken to keep the temperature of the extractor low enough so that the tip can be handled with the bare hands. If the hardness is drawn from the tip of the extractor by overheating during the grinding, the extractor will not take hold.

Removing a Broken Bolt and Retapping Hole

To remove a broken bolt and retap the hole, file the bolt smooth, if necessary, and center-punch it for drilling.

Then select a twist drill which is a little less than the tap-drill size for the particular bolt that has been broken. This drill will just about but not quite touch the crests of the threads in the threaded hole or the roots of the threads on the threaded bolt. Carefully start drilling at the center punch mark, crowding the drill one way or the other as necessary so that the hole will be drilled in the exact center of the bolt. The drill has now almost drilled the remaining part of the bolt away and will eventually break through the bottom of the bolt. When this happens, all that will remain of the bolt will be a threaded shell. With a prick punch or other suitable tool, chip out and remove the first 2 or 3 threads, if possible, at the top of the shell. Then carefully start a tapered tap into these several clean threads and continue tapping until the shell has been cut away and the original threads restored.

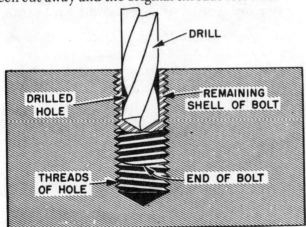

Removing a broken bolt and retapping hole to same size.

In cases where the identical size of capscrew or bolt is not necessary as a replacement, center-punch and drill out the old bolt with a drill larger than the broken bolt. Tap the hole first, and then finish it with a bottoming tap. Replace with a larger size capscrew or stud.

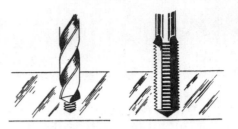

Removing broken bolt and retapping hole to larger size.

Removing a Broken Tap from a Hole

To remove a broken tap from a hole, generously apply penetrating oil to the tap, working it down through the four flutes into the hole. Then, if possible, grasp the tap across the flats with vise-grip pliers. Carefully ease the tap out of the hole, adding penetrating oil as necessary.

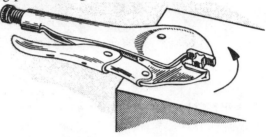

Removing a broken tap with vice-grip pliers.

If the tap has broken off at the surface of the work, or slightly below the surface of the work, the tap extractor may remove it. Again, apply a liberal amount of penetrating oil to the broken tap. Place the tap extractor over the broken tap and lower the upper collar to insert the four sliding prongs down into the four flutes of the tap. Then slide the bottom collar down to the surface of the work so that it will hold the prongs tightly against the body of the extractor. Tighten the tap wrench on the square shank of the extractor and carefully work the extractor and strike a few sharp blows with a small hammer and pin punch to jar the tap loose. Then reinsert the tap remover and carefully try to back the tap out of the hold.

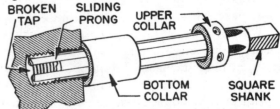

Removing a broken tap with a tap extractor.

Each size of tap will require its own size of tap extractor. Tap extractors come in the following sizes: ¼-inch, 5/16-inch, 3/8-inch, 7/16-inch, ½-inch, 9/16-inch, 5/8-inch, ¾-inch, 7/8-inch, and 1-inch.

When a tap extractor will not remove a broken tap, it is often possible to do so by the following method: Place a hex nut over the tap and weld the nut to the tap. Be sure to choose a nut with a hole somewhat smaller than the tap diameter to reduce the possibility of welding the nut and the tap to the job itself.

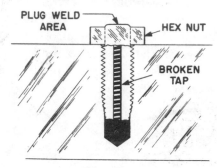

Using a plug weld to remove a broken tap.

POLISHING A FLAT METAL SURFACE

When polishing a flat metal surface, first draw file the surface. Then, when the best possible draw filed surface has been obtained, proceed with abrasive cloth, often called emery cloth. Select a grade of cloth suited to the draw filing. If the draw filing was well done only a fine cloth will be needed to do the polishing.

If your cloth is in a roll, and the job you are polishing is the size that would be held in a vise, tear off a 6- or 8-inch length of 1- or 2-inch width. If you are using sheets of abrasive cloth, tear off a strip from the long edge of the 8 by 11 sheet.

Wrap the cloth around the file and hold the file as you would for draw filing. Hold the end of the cloth in place with your thumb. In polishing, apply a thin film of lubricating oil on the surface being polished and use a double stroke with pressure on both the forward and backward strokes. Note that this is different from the drawfiling stroke in which you cut with the file in only one direction.

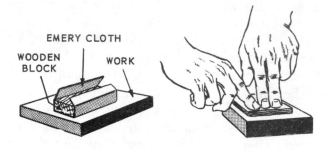

Alternate methods for polishing a flat metal surface.

SOLDERING

Soldering is a metal-joining process in which a lower melting-point metal (called solder) is heated to the point where it melts and wets the joint surface and then is allowed to solidify in place. To enable the solder to wet the surfaces readily and be drawn into fine cracks, the surfaces and the solder must be clean and free of oxide film. When necessary, the cleaning is done with chemicals or abrasives. One cleaning substance frequently used is called flux.

Copper, tin, lead, and brass are examples of readily solderable metals. Galvanized iron, stainless steel, and aluminum are difficult to solder and require the use of special techniques.

Soldering is a practical method of forming reliable electrical connections and is also used to make tight joints, such as lap seams of sheet metal, and to hold parts together physically. Soldered joints, however, do not support loads for long periods of time as well as welded joints do. Where load support is a governing factor, the usual practice calls for riveting, bolting, or using another means of fastening followed by sealing of the joints with solder.

In soldering the readily solderable metals, you only need the solder, a flux, and a heat source.

Solders

By definition, solders are joining materials or alloys that melt below 800 degrees F. They are available in various forms—wire, bar, ingot, paste and powder.

Fluxes

Soldering fluxes are agents which clean sol-

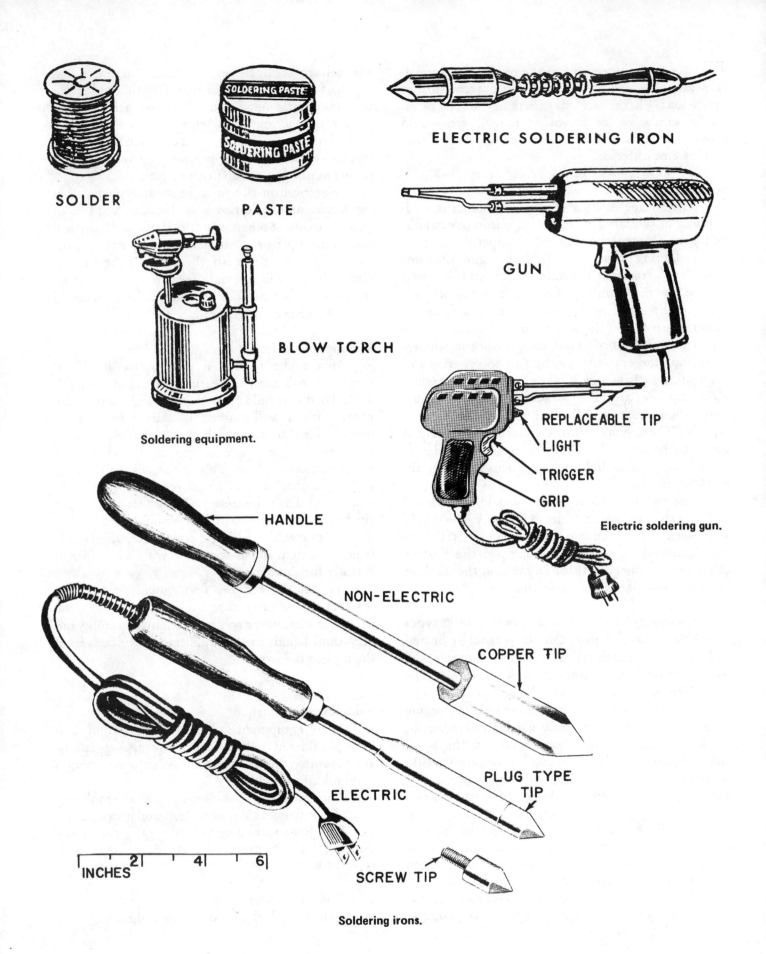

SOLDER

PASTE

ELECTRIC SOLDERING IRON

GUN

BLOW TORCH

Soldering equipment.

REPLACEABLE TIP

LIGHT

TRIGGER

GRIP

Electric soldering gun.

HANDLE

NON-ELECTRIC

COPPER TIP

ELECTRIC

PLUG TYPE TIP

INCHES 2 4 6

SCREW TIP

Soldering irons.

derable metals by removing the oxide film normally present on the metals and also prevent further oxidation. Fluxes are classified as noncorrosive, mildly corrosive, or corrosive, ranging from mild substances such as rosin to chemically active salts such as zinc chloride.

Soldering Tools

The source of heat for melting solder is a soldering gun (electric) or a soldering iron (electric or nonelectric), sometimes called a copper.

Soldering Gun. The soldering gun operates from any standard 115-volt outlet and is rated in size by the number of watts it consumes. All good quality soldering guns operate in a temperature range of 500 degrees to 600 degrees F. The important difference in gun sizes is not the temperature, but the capacity of the gun to generate and maintain a satisfactory soldering temperature while giving up heat to the joint soldered. The tip heats only when the trigger is depressed, and then very rapidly. These guns afford easy access to cramped quarters, because of their small tip. Most soldering guns have a small light that is focused on the tip working area.

The tip of a soldering gun should be removed occasionally to permit cleaning away the oxide scale which forms between the tip and metal housing. Removal of this oxide increases the heating efficiency of the gun. If for any reason the tip does become damaged, replaceable tips are available.

Soldering Irons. There are two general types of soldering irons in use. One is electrically heated and the other nonelectrically heated. The essential parts of both types are the tip and the handle. The tip is made of copper.

A nonelectric soldering iron is sized according to its weight. The commonly used sizes are the ¼-, ½-, ¾-, 1-, 1½-, 2-, and 2½-pound irons. The 3-, 4-, and 5-pound sizes are not used in ordinary work. Nonelectric irons have permanent tips and must be heated over an ordinary flame, or with a blowtorch.

The electric soldering iron transmits heat to the copper tip after the heat is produced by electric current which flows through a self-contained coil of resistance wire, called the heating element. Electric soldering irons are rated according to the number of watts they consume when operated at the voltage stamped on the iron. There are two types of tips on electric irons: plug tips which slip into the heater head and, which are held in place by a setscrew, and screw tips which are threaded, and which screw into or on the heater head. Some tips are offset and have a 90-degree angle for soldering joints that are difficult to reach.

Electric iron tips must be securely fastened in the heater unit. The tips must be clean and free of copper oxide. Sometimes the shaft oxidizes and causes the tip to stick in place. Remove the tip occasionally and scrape off the scale. If the shaft is clean, the tip will not only receive more heat from the heater-element, but it will facilitate removal when the time comes to replace the tip.

Tinning a Soldering Iron

If a soldering iron is new or has just been forced, it will need to be tinned (coated with solder). To do so hold it in the vise and "dress" the point with a well-chalked file. By "dressing" is meant filing to remove hammer marks resulting from the forging process and to round off the sharp corners slightly. This is not always required when a tinned iron is to be retinned. Inspection will reveal if it is necessary. Then heat the copper tip hot enough so that it will readily melt solder. Try melting solder with the copper frequently as it is being heated, and as soon as it will melt solder, it is ready for tinning.

To tin the copper, first quickly dip it into rosin or apply rosin core solder to the tip of the iron. The coating of solder is bright and shiny and very thin. It aids in the rapid transfer of heat from the iron to the work.

Soldering Procedure

Many equipment failures can be attributed to poorly soldered joints. The following suggestions are presented in an effort to assist in effecting a good job of soldering.

The parts to be soldered must be absolutely clean (free from oxide, corrosion and grease).

The joint should be prepared just prior to soldering since the prepared surfaces will soon corrode or become dirty if it remains exposed to the air.

The parts to be joined must be securely joined mechanically before any soldering is done.

A good, well-bonded connection is clean, shiny, and round.

Precautions

One sizzling burn experience is usually enough to breed a healthy respect for hot objects. When using a soldering iron or gun always bear in mind the following:

Electric soldering irons must not remain connected longer than necessary and must be kept away from flammable material.

In order to avoid burns, always assume that a soldering iron is hot.

Never rest a heated iron anywhere but on a metal surface or rack provided for this purpose. Faulty action on your part could result in fire, extensive damage, and serious injuries.

Never swing an iron to remove solder because the bits of solder that come off may cause serious skin or eye burns or ignite combustible materials in the work area.

When cleaning an iron, use a cleaning cloth or damp sponge, but DO NOT hold the cleaning cloth or sponge in your hand. Always place the cloth or damp sponge on a suitable surface and wipe the iron across it to prevent burning your hand.

Hold small soldering jobs with your pliers or a suitable clamping device. Never hold the work in your hand.

After completing the task requiring the use of a soldering iron, disconnect the power cord from the receptacle and, when the iron has cooled off, return it to its storage place. Do not throw irons into a toolbox. When storing irons for long periods of time, coat the shaft and all metal parts with rust-preventive compound and store in a dry place.

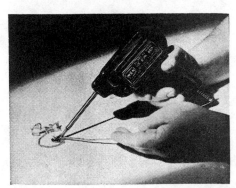

Application of various tips.

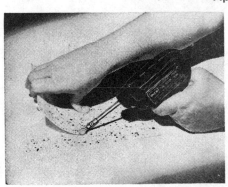

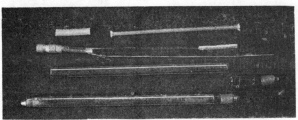

Disassembled tip.

Soldering guns and irons are readily available for the home craftsman at local hardware stores. They are popularly sold in kit form, usually containing a selection of tips for various applications.

The model shown has an automatic thermal control which permits the heating capacity of the tip to be changed by simply inserting another tip.

Some kits also contain additional special-purpose tips such as one that heats plastic tile to facilitate cutting and a "shoe-shaped" tip for steaming dents from wood or softening hard putty around window panes.

In this model, the secret of thermal control is in the special wire used in the tip. When the wire is cold, the current passes through it fairly easily and there is a heavy surge until the gun heats up. The hot wire now resists passage of the current, so the amount of electricity used is reduced, and the temperature of the tip of the gun levels off at this point. As the tip cools from use, resistance drops, current again flows and the temperature rises to the predetermined heat.

The versatility of this tool, as well as the simple, but highly effective automatic heat control, make it a valuable tool for any handyman.

FASTENING TECHNIQUES

FASTENING TECHNIQUES

10

SCREWS AND BOLTS ■ WOOD FASTENERS ■ RIVET TECHNIQUES

PLASTER, CONCRETE AND MASONRY FASTENERS

WOOD JOINERY ■ ADHESIVES

SCREWS AND BOLTS

Screws have many advantages for the home carpenter since they are more lasting and stronger than nails. It may be a bit more expensive to use screws rather than nails, but it may also be necessary for the best results. Screws provide more holding power; they are easily tightened to insure pieces being joined are secure; they are neater in appearance; and they can be removed without damage to the material. Common wood screws are made of stainless steel, aluminum, brass or unhardened steel. The steel may be bright in finish, blued, or zinc-, cadmium- or chrome-plated.

Wood screws are threaded from a gimlet point for approximately two-thirds of the length of the screw and have a slotted head for driving. They vary in length from ¼ to 6 inches. Screws up to 1 inch long increase in size by eighths of an inch; screws 1 to 3 inches long increase in size by quarters of an inch, and screws 3 to 6 inches long increase by half inches.

Screws also vary in diameter as well as length of shaft. Each length is made in a number of shaft sizes specified by an arbitrary number that represents no special measurement but indicates relative differences in diameter. Complete specifications for a screw include type, material, finish, length and screw size number. The screw size number indicates the wire gauge of the body, drill or bit size for the body hole, and drill or bit size for the starter hole.

Screw Shapes and Sizes

The selection of the best screw shape for use depends on the purpose it must serve. Following are some common shapes and sizes.

Flat Head. The most popular, this can be countersunk or screwed in until the head is flat with the surface of the stock, or slightly below the surface.

Oval Head. Although this type can be countersunk, and sunk to the rim, it often protrudes slightly.

Round Head. The head of this screw protrudes entirely and is somewhat decorative.

Fillister Head. The head is shaped like three checkers on top of each other so that it may be easily countersunk.

Pan Head. The head is shaped like an upside-down frying pan, narrower on the top, flat on top and bottom.

Truss or Stove Head. The head is wide and thin.

Headless. The slot is recessed into the shank.

Lentil Head. The head is shaped like a small

round candy.

Binding Head. This has slightly tapered sides and a rounded top.

Bung Head. This small head, not wider than the shank, is easily countersunk.

Drive. A steel spiral knurl (raised twirl) is hardened so that the screw can drive into soft metal.

Dovel. A wood screw with threads on both ends.

Winged. The head is wing shaped like a bolt so that it can be turned by hand.

Hanger Bolt. A wood screw on one end, a machine bolt on the other.

Screws vary in diameter, length and thread. The diameter is expressed in gauge numbers ranging from "0" which is equal to about 1/16 inch to "20", equal to about 29/64 inch. Lengths are specified in inches and fractions of an inch. Common lengths are ¼-, ½-, 5/8-, ¾-, 7/8- and 1-inch, and 1¼-, 1½-, 1¾-, 2-, 2¼-, 2½-, 3-, 4-, 4¼-, 5- and 6-inch screws. Each screw has a smooth portion be-

tween the head and the threads called the shank.

The screw slots most widely known are the straight slot and the Phillips cross slot. The Freason cross slot is similar to the Phillips, and the Pozzi drive has even more grooves, to permit maximum drive. Several other cross slots are also made. Each type of slot requires a different type of screwdriver, if the slot is not to be damaged. The bolt head has a special rosette head to prevent tampering.

Locks in the thread are created in some patented bolts and some screws. Nylock has a resilient nylon insert in its threaded section which wedges the screw tightly against the opposite threads. The Thredlock Screw has a bulge on one thread which resists removal. The Springtite has a coiled spring-lock washer. The Spin-Lok has locking teeth under the head that act like a ratchet. Some very large screws made without slots are known as lag bolts or lag screws and are turned with a wrench. Stock sizes range in length from 1-inch to 16-inch and from ¼- to 1-inch diameter.

Screw threads per inch.

Diameter		Threads Per Inch			
No.	Inch	Decimal Equivalent	NC	NF	EF
0	----	.0600	---	80	---
1	----	.0730	64	72	---
2	----	.0860	56	64	---
3	----	.0990	48	56	---
4	----	.1120	40	48	---
5	----	.1250	40	44	---
6	----	.1380	32	40	---
8	----	.1640	32	36	---
10	----	.1900	24	32	40
12	----	.2160	24	28	---
---	1/4	.2500	20	28	36
---	5/16	.3125	18	24	32
---	3/8	.3750	16	24	32
---	7/16	.4375	14	20	28
---	1/2	.5000	13	20	28
---	9/16	.5625	12	18	24
---	5/8	.6250	11	18	24
---	3/4	.7500	10	16	20
---	7/8	.8750	9	14	20
---	1	1.0000	8	14	20

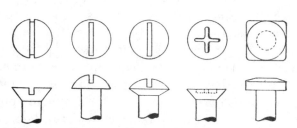

FLAT HEAD   ROUND HEAD   OVAL HEAD   PHILLIPS HEAD   LAG

Woodscrew heads.

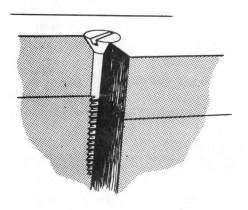

Using a woodscrew to hold two pieces of wood together.

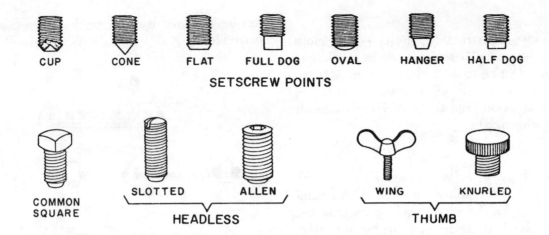

CUP CONE FLAT FULL DOG OVAL HANGER HALF DOG

SETSCREW POINTS

COMMON
SQUARE

SLOTTED ALLEN

HEADLESS

WING KNURLED

THUMB

Setscrews and thumb screws.

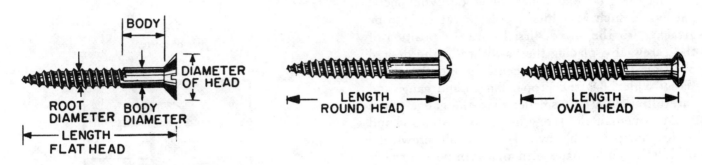

BODY

DIAMETER
OF HEAD

ROOT
DIAMETER BODY
DIAMETER

LENGTH
FLAT HEAD

LENGTH
ROUND HEAD

LENGTH
OVAL HEAD

Nomenclature and types of woodscrews.

COMMON

ROUND FLAT OVAL FILLISTER

WASHER SQUARE HEXAGON

SPECIAL

PHILLIPS FLAT HEAD
SPEC COUNTERSINK FLATHEAD
SPANNER FLATHEAD
ONE WAY SLOT FLATHEAD
SIDESLOT

SAME FOR ROUND, OVAL, AND FILLISTER HEADS

PHILLIPS BRAZIER
HEAD PHILLIPS WASHER
HEAD PYRAMID
HEAD SPECIAL BINDING
HEAD

HEXAGON HEAD HEXAGON
WASHER HEAD TWIN HEAD
WRENCH TYPE CLOCK HEAD

Machine screw and capscrew heads.

Bolts

For heavy construction, bolts offer more strength than screws. These are made in stock sizes in length from ¾-inch to 20-inch and from 3/16- to ¾-inch diameter. Those with round heads are known as carriage bolts and those with square heads are called machine bolts.

Using a Screw

To start a screw, make an entering hole with an awl or drill. Avoid tapping the screw with a hammer; this may split the wood and/or destroy the head of the screw. Unless a screw is properly started, it may enter at an angle or force the screw driver to slip off the groove and mar the wood. When metal hardware, such as a hinge, bolt or catch, is to be attached to the wood, first locate the position of the screws by placing the hardware in the desired position and marking the center point. Select the screw which has the proper length and gauge and carefully drill a hole smaller than the gauge of the screw (one-half the screw length on softwood and slightly deeper on hardwood). For small screws, the pilot hole can be made with an awl or with a nail.

The next step depends on the nature of the wood which is being joined. If both pieces are softwood, or the bottom piece is softwood, make a hole approximately as wide and as deep as the shank of the screw. Then bore additional area for countersinking a flat head or oval head, using a special countersink bit the exact size of the screwhead that is to go below the wood surface. If both pieces of stock, or the bottom, are hardwood, bore a hole through the top piece slightly narrower than the screw, and continue a hole of smaller diameter in the second piece. Always drill for one screw at a time.

In using a power drill, a special attachment makes it easy to drill an entrance hole, shank clearance and a head countersink in a single operation. These are made for many screw sizes.

When nails or screws are stored in boxes or cans, a sample should be taped to the outside of the container for identification purposes. Glass jars are even more preferable. When replacing a screw, you may find that it fits loosely and does not provide enough rigidity. If the fit is good, you can get additional grip by dipping the screw in glue or paint. If, however, the hole is too large, inserting a wooden match or toothpick can be helpful. Tight screws

can be loosened by soaking them in a few drops of peroxide.

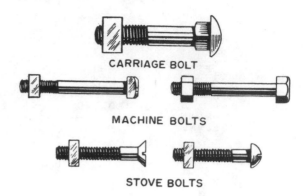

Types of bolts.

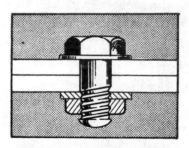

BOLT GRIP LENGTH CORRECT

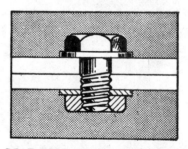

BOLT GRIP LENGTH TOO SHORT

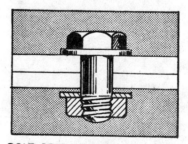

BOLT GRIP LENGTH TOO LONG

Correct and incorrect grip lengths.

OTHER WOOD FASTENERS

In addition to nails and screws, there are certain specialized devices for holding pieces of wood together. These include anchors, bolts, builders' hardware, metal wood connectors and wood joints. Special fasteners have been devised for many special purposes. A hand rail bolt has threads on both ends. Rings and plates are metal washers with special grooves or cuts that hold to the wood and prevent slipping. Mending plates are screwed to two connected pieces to provide a rigid support. Similarly, angle irons, T-irons, and corner-angled (L-shaped) irons provide reinforcement for special varied corners. The clamp nail, from ¼ to 6 inches long, is a newer type of joining device. It has two flanges that fit into sawed grooves in each end of a joint and are held with a drop of glue. Toothed rings are corrugated and toothed, and are made from 16 gauge plate low-carbon steel. They are used between two timber frames for light construction and are embedded into the contact faces of the joint members by means of pressure.

PLASTER, CONCRETE AND MASONRY FASTENERS

Special hardware is used for fastening into plaster, concrete and masonry. One group of items is inserted into a hole bored into the base. Into this an anchor or plug (usually of lead, sometimes of plastic) is inserted to receive a screw. Among these are the rawl pins, the star driving anchor, the Johnsen and Ackerman anchor, the lead shield and the expansion iron shield.

A second group is designed to hold onto an anchor by expanding. Among these is the toggle bolt, which is inserted flat into the hole and expands, butterfly-fashion, when tightened, and the molly expansion anchor. A third group includes a variety of clips, ties and tapped inserts.

Use molly screws or toggle bolts on a plastered wall where strength is needed to hold heavy pictures, mirrors, towel bars, etc.

Molly screws have two parts. To install, first make a small hole in the plaster and drive the casing in even with the wall surface. Tighten the screw to spread the casing in the back. Remove the screw and put it through the item you are hanging, into the casing, and tighten.

To install toggle bolts, drill a hole in the plaster large enough for the folded toggle to go through. Remove toggle. Put the bolt through towel bar or whatever you are hanging. Replace toggle. Push toggle through the wall and tighten with a screwdriver.

Plaster anchor screws should be used where you want to attach something to a concrete wall. To install, first make a small hole in the wall and drive the casing in even with the wall surface. Put screw through item and into the casing, and tighten.

NAILS

Nails achieve their fastening or holding power when they displace wood fibers from their original position. The pressure exerted against the nail by these fibers, as they try to spring back to their original position, provides the holding power.

The usual type of shank is round, but there are various special-purpose nails with other types of shanks. Nails with square, triangular, longitudinally grooved and spirally grooved shanks have a much greater holding power than smooth round wire nails of the same size.

The lengths of the most commonly used nails are designated by the "PENNY" system. The abbreviation for the word "penny" is the letter "d." Thus the expression "a 2d nail" means a two-penny nail. The penny sizes and corresponding length, and thicknesses (in gauge sizes) of the common nails are shown in the table. The thickness of a nail increases and the number of nails per pound decreases with the penny size.

Nails larger than 20d are called spikes and are generally designated by their length in inches (such as 5 inches or 6½ inches); nails smaller than 2d are designated in fractions of an inch instead of in the penny system.

Some Types of Nails

The brad and the finish nail both have a deep countersink head that is designed to be "set" below the surface of the work. These nails are used for interior and exterior trimwork where the nails are "set" and puttied to conceal their location. The casing nail is used for the same purpose, but because of its flat countersink head, may be driven flush and left that way.

The other nails shown are all flat-headed, without countersinks. One of these flat-headed nails (called the common nail) is one of the most widely used in general wood construction. Nails with large flat heads are used for nailing roof paper,

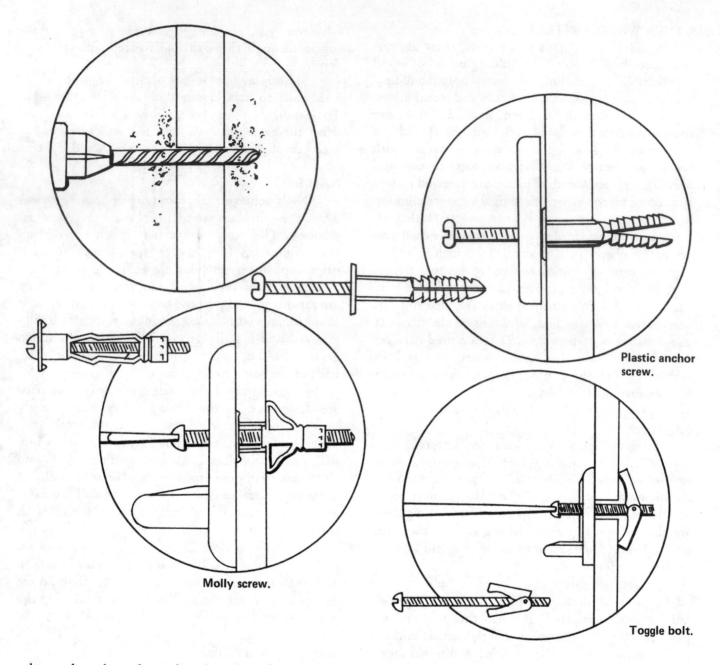

Plastic anchor screw.

Molly screw.

Toggle bolt.

plaster board, and similar thin or soft materials. Duplex or double-headed nails are used for nailing temporary structures, such as scaffolds, which are eventually to be dismantled. When using the double-headed nail it is driven to the lower head so that it can be easily drawn at a later time.

In addition to variations in their heads, nails vary at their points. The duller the point, the less the danger of splitting the wood. Blunt points appear on cut nails (for floors and shingles). These prevent wood from splitting because they cut their way through wood fibers. Blunt nails do not hold as well as sharp nails, however.

Another difference in nails occurs in the shank. The holding power of a nail varies directly with the amount of area in contact with the wood. Therefore, some nails are designed to have a maximum outside area. A square shank has more area than a round one. Some shanks have grooves and spirals, and even barbs, to give them more holding power. Other nail shanks are etched or coated. Etching triples the holding power of nails in soft or hard woods. Cement coated nails will hold from 75 to 100 percent stronger in softwoods than will un-coated nails. Among other specialized nails are resin-coated, copper-plated, brass-plated, tin-coated,

372

Common nail sizes.

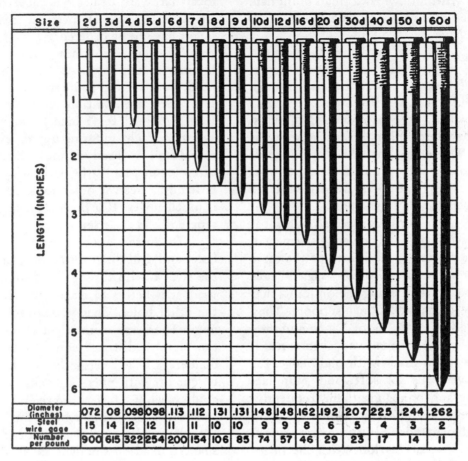

Size	2d	3d	4d	5d	6d	7d	8d	9d	10d	12d	16d	20d	30d	40d	50d	60d
Diameter (inches)	072	08	.098	098	.113	.112	131	.131	148	148	162	192	207	225	.244	.262
Steel wire gage	15	14	12	12	11	11	10	10	9	9	8	6	5	4	3	2
Number per pound	900	615	322	254	200	154	106	85	74	57	46	29	23	17	14	11

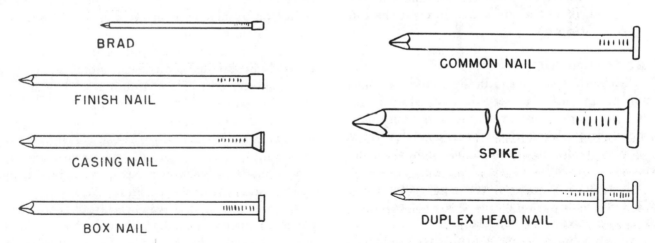

BRAD

FINISH NAIL

CASING NAIL

BOX NAIL

COMMON NAIL

SPIKE

DUPLEX HEAD NAIL

Nail varieties.

cadmium-plated, nickel-plated, chromium-plated, galvanized, blue, acid-etched, painted and japanned.

Nailing is considered the least sophisticated joining method and generally is used for work in which appearance is not too important and for quick fastening. A big danger in nailing is splitting the stock. Hardwoods, especially, resist nailing, and even some softwoods like Douglas fir, white cedar and eastern hemlock will split easily. You can reduce this danger by using a blunt nail, or by boring an entrance hole with an awl or a small blunt nail, or by dipping the nail in wax or grease or a heavy oil.

For holding small brads or tacks that are too small for the fingers to grip, use a heavy paper, cardboard, or a drinking straw. Slip the nail through the paper and hold the paper. For especially strong joining, anchor nailing is recommended. That is, driving the nails through both pieces of stock at opposite angles. Where the position of the boards makes it impossible to drive a nail in straight, "toe-nailing" can be used. Here nails are driven at an angle less than a right angle to the base.

One type of nail is purposely not straight. It is a piece of corrugated steel with one edge sharpened. When two flat pieces are to be joined at the same level, particularly mitre joints, these "wiggle" nails will do a creditable strengthening job on joints that are glued or have other additional support. They are available in depths of ¼, ½, or 1 inch and they can have as few as two or as many as seven corrugations. The wiggle nail is made with plain edges for hardwood and saw edges for softwood. Manufacturers of furniture and boxes use them frequently. They are inexpensive and will quickly and easily do a job that would otherwise require expert work. They are made in two styles: one with the ridges running parallel and the other with the ridges running at a slight angle to one another. The second type has a tendency to compress the material because the ridges and grooves are closer at the top than at the bottom.

RIVET TECHNIQUES

With new space-age adhesives and fasteners coming on the market every day, we often forget about one of the most versatile and easily used fasteners, rivets. Rivets have been used for years, and maybe you haven't noticed, but there are many new ones on the market.

Rivets have a way of being permanent, and that's their main advantage over screws, bolts, adhesives, etc. Rivets are especially good in applications where vibrations are a problem. You don't need to worry about their loosening up or coming unscrewed.

Types of Rivets and Installation

There is a wide range of different types of rivets available for general use. You will find your local hardware dealer has most of these in stock. Rivets of a special metal such as stainless steel might have to be ordered.

The most common types of rivets are the familiar soft iron ones. They are made in round-head, flathead and countersunk head.

They are available in a variety of diameters from 1/8 inch to ½ inch or more. Lengths begin about ¼ inch and run up to several inches. The roundhead is used in most instances. The head often forms part of the decorative design, but if the protruding head is objectional, the flathead profile is much lower. If a flush surface is desired, use the tapered-head style set in a countersunk hole.

To install a common iron rivet, locate the holes and drill them with a bit just large enough for the rivet to slip through. If several rivets are being used, it is better to install one rivet before drilling the other holes. Then you are sure of perfect alignment. The shank of the rivet should extend through the metal a distance equal to about 1½ times the diameter of the rivet. If the shank is too long, it can be cut off with pliers, a hacksaw, bolt nippers or a cold chisel. To fasten the rivet, hit the shank end a solid blow to expand it to fit the hole tightly. Then with light blows of the peen end of the hammer, shape a head on the rivet. Be sure to hold the head end against a solid piece of metal. If appearance is a factor, you can keep from flattening the head end by supporting it on a block of lead or a bar of solder or by placing it in the cup-shaped end of a rivet set held in a vise.

Tinner's rivets are another commonly used type. They are used on sheet metal such as tin plate, galvanized iron and aluminum. They are sold in a wide range of sizes and metals. The size is by weight: 2-pound tinner's rivets would weigh 2 pounds per thousand. For 26-Ga. galvanized iron, a 1-pound rivet is suggested. These rivets are commonly made in black iron but also in tinned iron, copper, stainless steel and aluminum.

There are several ways to install these rivets. Holes for the rivets can be punched over a chunk of lead or the end grain of a block of wood. On thicker metal you can drill the holes, being careful to locate them at least two rivet diameters from the edge of the metal. A third way uses the rivet to cut its own hole in the sheet metal. Select a rivet set with a hole into which the rivet slides easily. Put the rivet head down on a solid metal surface. Place

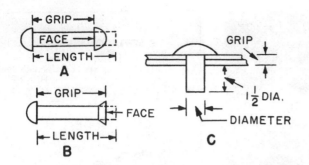

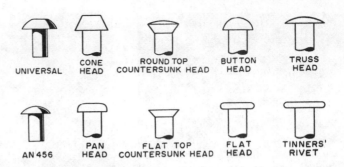

Showing what is meant by
"grip" of rivet.

Some common types of rivets.

UNIVERSAL CONE HEAD ROUND TOP COUNTERSUNK HEAD BUTTON HEAD TRUSS HEAD

AN 456 PAN HEAD FLAT TOP COUNTERSUNK HEAD FLAT HEAD TINNERS' RIVET

Guide for selecting rivet size
for sheet metal work.

Gauge of Sheet Metal	Rivet Size (weight in pounds per 1,000 rivets)
26	1
24	2
22	2 1/2
20	3
18	3 1/2
16	4

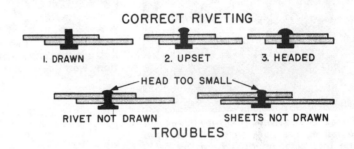

CORRECT RIVETING

1. DRAWN 2. UPSET 3. HEADED

HEAD TOO SMALL

RIVET NOT DRAWN SHEETS NOT DRAWN

TROUBLES

Correct and incorrect riveting.

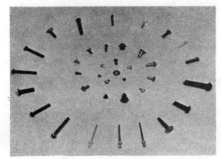

There are hundreds of types and sizes of rivets. Rivets can be purchased for use in soft iron, steel, copper, etc.

Tools for fastening with rivets includes a good electric drill, ball-peen hammer, punch and a rivet set.

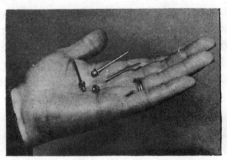

A squeeze rivet compresses and fastens when the gun handle is squeezed. The nail-like mandrel is discarded.

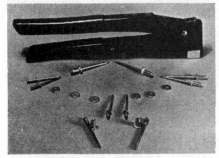

One type of specialized rivet is the "squeeze-type" made for use in a riveting gun. Primarily for sheet metal.

Two sizes of rivet sets are shown. The concave depression in the end is used to form a rounded end on the shank.

Leather, canvas, plastics and even wood can be riveted together using large, flat-head copper rivets with a washer.

375

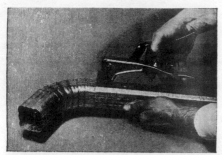

A typical use of the "squeeze-type" rivet. Ordinary riveting with punch and hammer and anvil would be impossible.

To make holes in sheet metal for riveting, use the proper size punch and position work over end grain of block.

Squeeze-type rivets after they have been installed. The rivet on the left is from the tool side, on right from the back.

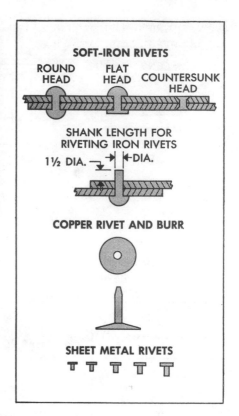

the metal over the rivet and the rivet set hole directly over the rivet. A tap with a hammer will punch the rivet through. Tap the rivet set again to squeeze the two pieces of metal together. Then set the rivet with a sharp blow from a hammer. Finally, shape the head with the cup-shaped depression of the rivet set.

Several kinds of rivets are useful for fastening leather, canvas, plastic and similar materials. The most common is the flathead style copper rivet that uses a washer or burr on the end to be riveted. This makes a bearing surface against resilient materials so the rivet cannot pull through. The large flathead pulls down flush with the surface on the opposite side.

The split rivet and the hollow rivet are also commonly used on leather. They do not have the holding power of the ones using a washer under the riveted end, but they do well for many jobs.

The popular squeeze-type rivet has become quite widely used. This is a special rivet applied with a tool or "gun" made for this type of rivet only. These rivets can be applied from the face surface without the necessity of supporting the back side of the rivet to form a head. Then the mandrel breaks off and is discarded. Rivets are made in 1/8- and 3/16-inch diameters and several lengths for dif-

ferent thicknesses of material. They are made in steel, aluminum and copper. Some are closed so that they can be used on vessels that must be watertight. When used on soft materials, backup plates (washers) are available.

Removing Rivets

We've been talking at length about selecting rivets and installing them. The next logical question is: How do you get them out in case your "permanent" fastening must be taken apart? Here's how: To remove common iron rivets, you can grind or file off the head flush with the surface and drive it out with a pin punch. Or, use a chisel to cut the rivet head. Once the head is gone, the rest is easy. To remove a countersunk rivet, drill out the head, then punch the remainder out.

To keep the drill bit from drifting when you drill out a rivet, use a sharp center punch to mark the center of the head of the rivet, to provide a "locater" for the bit. Use a variable-speed drill motor if you have one, and drill at slow speed to get started, then moderate speed until you have drilled just through the head. Generally the head will spin off, but a light tap with a chisel may be required.

Use a flat-end drift pin to remove rivets, not a

center punch. The latter may cause the rivet shank to expand and jam in the hole.

Pop rivets are easy to remove, just drill into the head with a 1/8-inch drill. The rivet will fall apart.

While a rivet set is not an absolute necessity for working with rivets, it does make the work faster and neater and the cost is moderate. Most large hardware stores will have them or can order them for you. Get one of a size for the rivets you use. It will have the correct size shank hole, and a proper diameter round depression for shaping the rivet heads.

WOOD JOINERY

For simplicity, let's divide joints into five classifications that define how and where a joint is used: Vertical Corner Joints, used to form the corners of such items as boxes, cabinet cases, etc. Horizontal Corner Joints, used in picture frames and to join the stiles and rails on doors, window frames, etc. Cross Joints, used when a flush joint is needed where two members cross each other. T-Joints, used to join members at a right angle, at other than a corner. Splices, used to connect the ends of two pieces, usually of narrow stock. Edge Joints, used to join the edges of two pieces, such as for making a table top.

Because the technique used in making each joint will vary, depending on whether the cutting is done with hand tools or radial-arm or table saw, we will not describe how to make each one. A study of each joint, and familiarity with your own particular tools will determine the method you use.

There are, however, some time and trouble-saving tips that apply to joining in general. One rule is: measure, make your first cuts so you allow a little extra stock, then make fine adjustments of your tools with following fine cuts, until you have the fit you want. To be strong, a joint must be cut correctly so it fits snugly togehter. Because so-called 1-inch stock actually measures 25/32 inch, and varies due to moisture content, it is almost impossible to locate a center or divide two pieces into thirds for a tight mortise-and-tenon joint using a rule and pencil.

As an example, if you are going to make tongue-and-groove joints, try it this way: set up your dado blade to a width approximately one-third the thickness of the stock. No matter how carefully you check and measure, chances are the cut for the groove is going to be slightly off center. So, make the cut in two passes, reversing the work on the second pass, so one cut is made with each side of the work riding against the fence with a radial-arm saw or table saw. The created groove is some odd fractional dimension in width, but is exactly on center. When you are ready to cut the tongues on the opposite edges, use one of the grooved pieces to guide your setup, but allow a little extra stock. Make your first passes, check for fit, then adjust to remove a little more stock. A couple of passes should create a really close fit.

To find the exact center for lap joints, make a series of cuts, each slightly deeper, on two pieces until they fit exactly. Save these scraps as gauges for your next job.

If you intend to do much joinery there are a few accessories that are worthwhile to have. One of the most valuable is a tenoning jig. This is simply an upright plate to which work can be clamped. The jig rides in the slot for the miter gauge on a table saw, and is adjustable laterally to position the work over the saw blade. End cuts on narrow stock that would be difficult become a snap. By using two stops, both pieces of a corner joint can be matched and cut at the same time, invaluable for such jobs as cutting the spline groove in a mitered corner. As in grooving, you save time and gain accuracy by reversing the stock and making a second cut.

Closed mortises can be made by hand, but you can do a quicker, more accurate job with a mortising chisel in a drill press. A shaper or a molding cutter-head on your saw is almost a must for cutting accurate glue points.

Vertical Corner Joints

The plain butt joint is about as simple as you can get. It is glued, nailed or screwed together and used where there is little stress. The rabbet joint is not tremendously strong, but somewhat better than a plain butt. It often is used in drawer backs and cabinet backs. The drawer-corner joint is the next step up, and often is used in quality furniture. The drawer-front joint is identical to the drawer-corner joint, but the edge overhangs the side to create a beveled flange. Often used in cabinetry where the edges of the sides are exposed, the miter joint is used extensively in plywood construction to con-

1. Tenoning jig rides in slot for miter gauge, simplifies cutting ends of stock.

3. For fast and accurate cutting of mortises, mortising chisel in drill press is an absolute must. Device "drills" square hole.

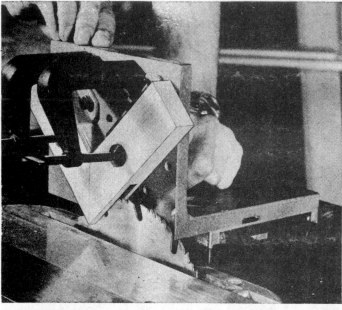

2. Using two stops on tenoning jig permits cutting both pieces of a corner joint, invaluable for cutting spline slot.

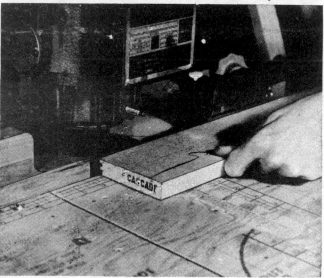

4. Cutting glue joints on edges of stock requires a shaper, or molding-head cutter in table or radial-arm saw as shown.

5. Butt joint is simplest of all joints, but the weakest; it is glued, nailed or screwed. 6. Rabbet joint is not very strong, but better than a simple butt. 7. Drawer-corner joint often is used in fine furniture is quite strong, with large glue surfaces. 8. Drawer-front joint is identical to drawer-corner joint, but has extended edge that overhangs the side to create a flange.

378

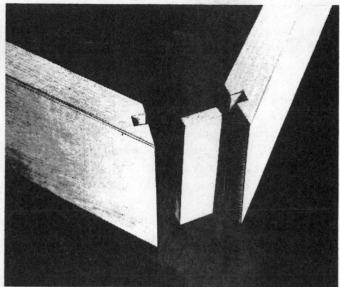

9. Often used in cabinetry when edges of the sides are exposed, the miter joint is used extensively for plywood.

10. A stronger miter is the splined or feathered miter. The spline can be solid stock or plywood, the latter stronger.

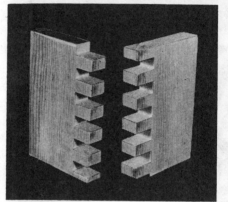

11. One of the strongest of all corner joints, the box-corner does require precise cutting for a proper fit.

12. A classic, and extremely strong is the dovetail joint, easily cut with a jig and router or bit in a drill press.

13. Jig for cutting dovetail cuts grooves and tongues in adjacent pieces in one simple operation with router.

ceal the core laminations. Used for the same purpose, but considerably stronger is the splined or feathered miter.

The finger or box-corner joint is one of the strongest corner joints, but is not often used because it requires precise cutting for a proper fit. It is handsome and should be considered for fine work. The dovetail-corner joint is the strongest joint of all, and although fairly intricate, can be cut with a jig used with drill press or router.

Horizontal Corner Joints

The corner lap joint is a simple but sturdy joint used in concealed framing, as in furniture. The lapped-miter joint is used for joining frames where a neater joint is desired.

Where a miter joint with added strength is required the wedge miter is employed. Generous gluing surfaces make this joint strong. The doweled-miter is another way of making a miter joint much stronger. Accurate location of the dowel holes is the only problem, and a doweling jig solves this.

Strongest of all the miter joints is the mitered-through tenon; it is used where the miter is to show on both sides of a strong joint. This joint creates a sort of "built-in" spline, but the spline is part of one member, thus the joint is really strong.

Make measurements accurately, use sharp saw blades and sharp tools when making joints. Your finished project will be only as strong as the joints in it.

Continuing with the five classes of joints (Vertical and Horizontal Corner Joints counting as one), there are three more that are in the first classification:

The through mortise-and-tenon is another very strong joint that often is found on the frames of cabinet doors. It also is used in wooden frames for screen and storm doors. Generally it is glued and nailed, bradded or stapled.

Where a strong, locked joint is required, and appearance is of secondary importance, the corner-locked mortise-and-tenon is used. In most cases, however, the home craftsman would settle for the through mortise-and-tenon rather than going to the extra cutting required to make the locked version of the joint.

The dowelled butt joint is another strong corner joint that gives a neat appearance from any side. At least two dowels should be used; a single dowel provides little resistance to a twisting force on the joint.

Cross Joints

Often found in framing work, the cross half-lap joint is used where a flat joint is needed at the crossing point of two members. When accurately cut the joint is scarcely visible, and with several gluing surfaces it is quite strong.

Splice Joints

The lap splice is a moderately strong splice that is made in the same way as other lap joints. Each member is rabbeted half-way through to create a flush surface on both sides of the joint.

Probably the strongest of all splice joints, the keyed lap splice, has several glue surfaces plus an insert that provides the key.

The bevel splice is more attractive and somewhat stronger than the plain lap splice. The beveled surfaces tend to lock when stress is placed endwise, and the gluing surfaces are larger than on a plain lap.

Interesting in appearance, yet quite simple to make, the forked butt splice is relatively strong and extremely handsome when used in an exposed area. Generous glue surfaces resist strains lengthwise of the stock, the bevels provide sideways strength.

14. Simple but sturdy is the corner-lap joint, often used in concealed framing in furniture, as in dust shields.

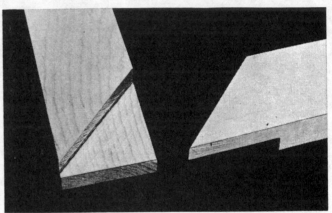

15. Where a neater joint is required in framing, the lapped-miter is employed. One side shows miter, the other is a butt.

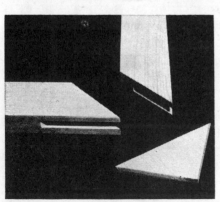

16. Much stronger than a plain miter is the wedge miter, where a triangular spline is fitted in grooves in the joint.

17. The doweled miter is another way of strengthening a miter; locating the dowels is the only problem.

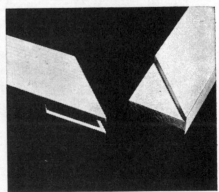

18. Strongest of all the miter joints is the mitered-through tenon where the "spline" is actualy part of one member.

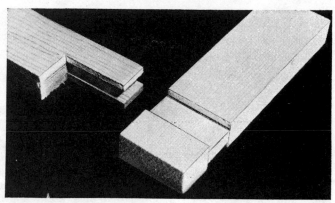

19. Through mortise-and-tenon is another very strong joint, often found on the frames of cabinet doors, dust partitions.

20. Where a strong locked joint is required, and appearance is not important, corner-locked mortise-and-tenon is used.

21. Neat in appearance and much stronger than regular butt joint is doweled butt joint; looks good from any side.

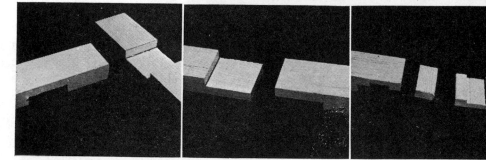

22. Often used in framing work, cross half-lap makes flat joint where two members cross.
23. A moderately strong joint is the lap splice, which is made in the same way as other lap joints. **24.** Probably the strongest of all splice joints is the keyed lap-splice. **25.** More attractive, stronger than plain lap is bevel splice.

26. Relatively simple to make, and strong and handsome when used in an exposed position is the forked butt-splice.

27. Often found in old furniture, the lapped dovetail serves as middle lap, but dovetail prevents upright pulling loose.

28. Used to join shelves to cabinet sides, sliding dovetail prevents loosening from shrinkage or warping. 29. Plain dado joint is most commonly used to secure shelves to supports. 30. Dado with shoulder is variation of plain dado, is used for same purposes; shelves, cross members. 31. Stopped dado has strength of dado, but neater appearance of butt.

T-Joints

Often found in old furniture, the lapped dovetail serves the same function as the middle lap joint except that the dovetail assures that the member at right angles will not be pulled loose. Accurate measuring and careful cutting are called for to make this joint neat and strong.

Frequently used in quality construction to join shelves to cabinet sides, the sliding dovetail adds strength and helps prevent ends from pulling loose due to shrinkage or warping of the stock. This joint can be made with a saw, but a router bit or dovetail blade will make the job a lot easier.

Most commonly used to secure shelves to supports or cabinet sides, the plain dado joint is neat and strong, is ideal when using plywood for cabinetry.

The dado with a shoulder is a variation of the plain dado joint, and is used for the same purposes. Because the dado is narrower, it does not weaken a panel quite as much as the full-width dado.

A version of the stopped dado often is used on shelving or framing where the strength of a dado joint is necessary, but the appearance of a common butt joint is desired. A straight router bit is used to cut this dado.

The "furniture" stopped dado frequently is used to join stringers to cross members on the interior framing in furniture construction. It is a strong joint and fast and easy to make, because the dado is made by dropping the workpiece over the saw blade.

The bridle joint is the strongest of all the T-joints. It is resistant to stress from any angle or direction.

The mortise-and-tenon joint has the combined advantages of strength plus the appearance from all sides of a plain butt joint. It also can be used as a corner joint and often is used for windows, door frames, etc.

Edge Joints

The tongue-and-groove joint is the most common of all the edge joints except for a plain butt. Probably its biggest use is joining sections of paneling together.

The edge joint with spline is another variation of the tongue-and-groove joint. Both edges are grooved and the spline serves as a tongue for both sides. This joint often is found in table tops where several boards are assembled edge-to-edge, as the end pattern of the splines and grooves is attractive and looks professional.

Glue joints are the ultimate method for joining several pieces of stock to form one wide board, because they not only provide a large amount of surface area for the glue to grip, but the beveled tongues and grooves assure perfect surface alignment between pieces. This is a joint best done on a shaper; make practice cuts on scrap stock until you have the correct setup, then keep samples of the joint for future duplications of the joints.

So, there they are; many joints from which to make a selection. Many are interchangeable and all do the job. Choose the one that best fits not only the requirements of the job, but also the tools in your shop.

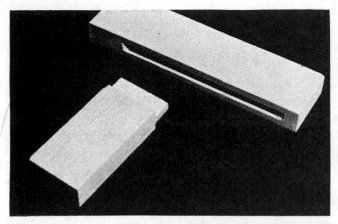

32. Sometimes called the "furniture" stopped dado, this joint is used on interior construction in furniture framing.

33. Strongest of all the T-joints is the bridle joint, which is resistant to strains from any angle, direction.

34. Combined advantages of great strength plus neat appearance from all sides makes mortise-and-tenon popular.

35. Tongue-and-groove joint is most common of edge joints, except for plain butt, fine for assembling panels.

36. Edge joint with spline is a variation of tongue-and-groove joint. Both edges are grooved to accept spline.

37. Glue joints are the ultimate in joining several pieces to form wide board; ample glue surfaces.

ADHESIVES

Because every home workshop handles a variety of materials other than wood, a good selection of adhesives is a must.

White glue (a vinyl-acetate emulsion) is the modern adhesive most home craftsmen use for wooden projects that are to be used indoors. It also is good for paper, leather, cloth and other relatively porous materials. While it is white when applied, it sets clear and will fill a joint that is not completely tight. Before it sets it can be cleaned away with warm water. It is moisture-resistant, but should not be used where moisture is a problem, as it will fail if in a constant-wet condition.

only what you can use in that period of time.

Contact cement (neoprene rubber and phenolic resins) gets its name from the fact that when spread on two surfaces and allowed to dry it will adhere only to itself; it bonds on contact. The rubber makes the quick "grab," the resins form a strong, long-lasting joint. Contact adhesive is used for applying plastic laminates to counter tops, cabinets and walls. No clamping is required. The latest formulations of contact adhesive are those for fastening wood veneers to wooden ground coats, even to metal surfaces. This simplifies veneering, eliminating the need for clamps and presses.

Hot-melt glue from electric gun can be used for wood, replacing resilient tiles and on most relatively porous materials.

U.S. Pylwood's Touch-N-Glue is a type of contact adhesive. Glue is applied, surfaces touched, separated 5 min.

Household Cement by Duro is made from clear resins, as are other adhesives of similar types used for jewelry.

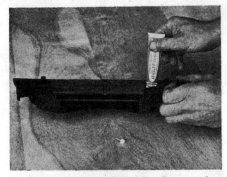

Modern glues made with clear resins have long life; early cements of this type tended to have short life.

Wilhold Glu-On is a "fastening adhesive," can be used on metal, glass, ceramics, non-porous materials.

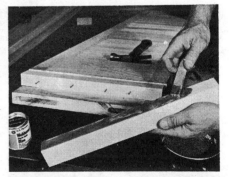

Plastic-resin glue is made by several companies. It has high water resistance, takes about 12 hrs. to set.

Plastic-resin glue (urea-formaldehyde) can be obtained as a powder to be mixed with water, or as a ready-mixed material. It has largely replaced the old animal-hide glues, is extremely moisture resistant so it can be used for boats, water skis, spars and masts. It is excellent for hardwood furniture. Before setting it can be cleaned away with warm water. The type that is mixed with water for use has a pot life of 3 or 4 hrs., so you mix

Fastening adhesive is similar to contact adhesive, except that it is thicker and does not require double-coating, as does the contact. It will adhere to metal, ceramics, masonry, glass, wood, leather and almost any clean, dry surface. It can be used to mount metal towel bars on glazed tile, house numbers on exterior masonry, fasten loosened gate hinges and repair downspouts and gutters. It is oil and water-resistant.

While most of the specialized adhesives are sold in "home-size" tubes, you can purchase larger quantities.

Material used for porcelain repair adheres strongly, stays white, withstands heat up to 400 deg. F.

Plastic Rubber repairs items of rubber, can be used for insulating and calking. Excellent for auto weatherstripping.

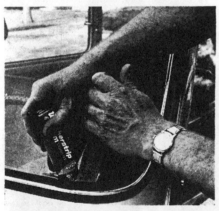

Weatherstrip and Trim Cement is transparent, seals weatherstripping on house and auto windows, radiator hoses.

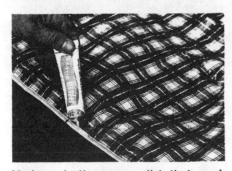

Modern plastics are so slick that most adhesives will not adhere. Special mender "welds" the material.

Handy-Patch kit contains a roll of Celastic, a material that is dipped in a liquid that "activates" it for repairing.

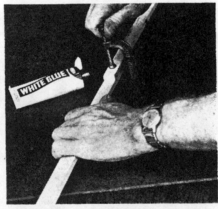

This White Glue is not water-base type generally used for woodworking, but has ketone solvent, this is flammable.

"Lock washer in a tube" keeps nuts and bolts from loosening under vibration, but will break free under wrench.

Contact Cement is familiar material in most workshops, is used for applying plastic laminates to counter tops.

"Liquid Solder" is quick, cold repair of metal items that might ordinarily require hot solder. Resists heat, water.

Water Putty is powder that is mixed with water to create paste that will adhere to wood, metal, plaster.

Stop-It tightens new or worn threaded connections so vibration will not loosen them; works on wood and metal.

There has been a great deal of publicity and misinformation spread about epoxy glues. These two-part adhesives will adhere almost anything to anything, but they have definite limitations. For example, they are much stronger than wood, but so are other adhesives, including the white glues. If this is true, and it is, then why go to the expense and bother of the two-part epoxies? They do best on hard materials like metal, stone, glass and concrete. They are too hard and brittle to do well on soft materials. Also, if two dissimilar materials, such as wood and metal, are joined, their varying rates of expansion due to heat and moisture will cause the joint to fail, as the adhesive will not flex with joint movement. One of the advantages of epoxies is that there is no solvent in them, so two hard materials can be clamped tightly together, with no worry about room for solvent evaporation.

For an extra-strong joint in wood, try an aliphatic resin, the next step up from a white glue. They are generally available where white glue is sold.

A clear household or "jewelry" cement, made from mitrate resins, is another useful adhesive. It is fast-drying, clear and long lasting. Much used for jewelry, it can be applied to most surfaces to create a strong joint.

Besides various kinds of adhesives for sticking things together, every home shop needs related materials, such as caulking and wood putty. Many types of caulking can be used to adhere such things as ceramic tiles to walls, while still being flexible enough for sealing the joint between your bathtub and a wall.

Next to your home, your car will require various kinds of adhesives for its maintenance. A leak around the windshield or window can be sealed with a "liquid rubber" or a regular weatherstrip sealer.

Chips in a porcelain sink or tub require another kind of adhesive that stays white and resists both heat and water.

Modern plastics are so slick that ordinary glues will not adhere; a special cement is required that actually melts the surface of the plastic to cause a fusing or welding of the material with a patch.

Powdered metal is used as reinforcement and to give color in two-part Epoxy Steel that can be used for metal.

Plastic Patch seals holes in beach balls, vihyl swimming and wading pools. Filler and Solder is plastic material for auto-body work that sets up quickly, stays flexible. Muffler Sealer assures tight joints in auto-exhaust system.

11

ELECTRICITY AND WIRING

ELECTRICITY AND WIRING

11

WIRING SYSTEMS ■ INTERIOR WIRING INSTALLATION ■ TOOLS AND SUPPLIES
TYPE OF CONNECTION ■ TYPES OF LAMPS ■ DANGER! ELECTRICAL SHOCK
SIGNS AND SYMBOLS ■ REPLACING A WORN OUT WALL SWITCH
REPLACING AN ELECTRIC PLUG ■ THREE-WAY SWITCHES ■ FOUR-WAY SWITCHES

Although it is desirable for you, the domestic handyman, to have some understanding of wiring systems, it is strongly recommended that most jobs involving electrical know-how be left to a qualified licensed electrician. The following is only intended to familiarize you with electrical supplies and systems.

In the latter portion of this chapter you will find specific information on a number of tasks which the educated handyman should have little or no difficulty in accomplishing.

SIGNS AND SYMBOLS

Symbols. The more common symbols and line conventions used in wiring plans are shown. These symbols enable precise location of any electrical equipment in a building from the study of a drawing.

Schematic Wiring Diagrams. Electrical plans show what items are installed, their approximate location, and the circuits to which they are connected. This is the form of wiring plans used most frequently in construction drawing. Single lines indicate the location of wires connecting the fixtures and equipment. Two conductors are indicated in a schematic diagram by a single line.

If there are more than two wires together, short parallel lines through the line symbols indicate the number of wires represented by the line. Connecting wires are indicated by placing a dot at the point of intersection. No dot is used where wires cross without connecting. You may encounter drawings in which the lines indicating the wiring have been omitted. In this type of drawing only the fixture and equipment symbols are shown; the location of the actual wiring is to be determined by an electrician. No actual dimensions or dimension lines are shown in electrical drawings. Location dimensions and spacing requirements are given in the form of notes or follow standard installation principles.

Drawing Notes. A list of drawing notes is ordinarily provided on a schematic wiring diagram to specify special wiring requirements.

Color Coding. The National Electrical Code requires that a grounded or neutral conductor be identified by an outer color of white or natural gray for Number 6 wire or smaller. For larger conductors the outer identification of white or natural gray may be used, or they should be identified by white markings at the terminals.   The ungrounded conductors of a circuit are identified with insula-

STANDARD ELECTRICAL SYMBOLS

ITEM	SYMBOL
WIRING CONCEALED IN CEILING OR WALL	————————
WIRING CONCEALED IN FLOOR	— — —
EXPOSED BRANCH CIRCUIT	– – – – –
BRANCH CIRCUIT HOME RUN TO PANEL BOARD (NO. OF ARROWS EQUALS NO. OF CIRCUITS, DESIGNATION IDENTIFIES DESIGNATION AT PANEL	A1 A3 ⟶⟶
THREE OR MORE WIRES (NO. OF CROSS LINES EQUALS NO. OF CONDUCTORS) TWO CONDUCTORS INDICATED IF NOT OTHERWISE NOTED)	―///―
INCOMING SERVICE LINES	▷
CROSSED CONDUCTORS, NOT CONNECTED	+ OR ⌷
SPLICE OR SOLDERED CONNECTION	● OR ⊥
CABLED CONNECTOR (SOLDERLESS)	■
WIRE TURNED UP	——————○
WIRE TURNED DOWN	——————●

tion colored black, red, and blue, used in that order, in two-, three-, or four-wire circuits, respectively. All circuit conductors of the same color are connected to the same ungrounded (hot) feeder conductor throughout the installation. A grounding conductor, used solely for grounding purposes, should be bare or have a green covering.

TYPES OF CONNECTIONS

Splices. A spliced wire must be as good a conductor as a continuous conductor. Though splices are permitted wherever accessible in wiring systems, they should be avoided whenever possible.

The best wiring practice (including open wiring systems) is to run continuous wires from the service box to the outlets. UNDER NO CONDITIONS SHOULD SPLICES BE PULLED THROUGH CONDUIT. SPLICES MUST BE PLACED IN APPROPRIATE ELECTRICAL BOXES.

Solderless Connectors. Connectors are sometimes used in place of splices because of their ease of installation. Since heavy wires are difficult to splice and solder properly, split-bolt connectors are commonly used for wire joining. Solderless connectors, popularly called wire nuts, are used for connecting small-gauge and fixture wires. One

ITEM	SYMBOL	ILLUSTRATION
LIGHTING OUTLETS* CEILING	○	
WALL		
FLUORESCENT FIXTURE		
CONTINUOUS ROW FLUORESCENT FIXTURE		
BARE LAMP FLUORESCENT STRIP		

*LETTERS ADDED TO SYMBOLS INDICATE SPECIAL TYPE OR USAGE

    J-JUNCTION BOX   R-RECESSED

    L-LOW VOLTAGE   X-EXIT LIGHT

ITEM	SYMBOL	ILLUSTRATION
RECEPTACLE OUTLETS** SINGLE OUTLET		
DUPLEX OUTLET		
QUADRUPLEX OUTLET		
SPECIAL PURPOSE OUTLET		
20-AMP, 250-VOLT OUTLET		

SINGLE FLOOR OUTLET
   (BOX AROUND ANY OF ABOVE
   INDICATES FLOOR OUTLET OF
   SAME TYPE)		

**LETTER G NEXT TO SYMBOL INDICATES GROUNDING TYPE

ITEM	SYMBOL	ILLUSTRATION
SWITCHES		
SINGLE POLE SWITCH	S	
DOUBLE POLE SWITCH	S_2	
THREE WAY SWITCH	S_3	
SWITCH AND PILOT LAMP	S_P	
CEILING PULL SWITCH	Ⓢ	
PANEL BOARDS AND RELATED EQUIPMENT		
PANEL BOARD AND CABINET		
SWITCHBOARD, CONTROL OR SUB-CONTROL POINT		
SERVICE SWITCH OR CIRCUIT BREAKER	▬ OR ▬ OR ⊗	
EXTERNALLY OPERATED DISCONNECT SWITCH		
MOTOR CONTROLLER	⊠ OR MC	
MISCELLANEOUS TELEPHONE	◀|	
THERMOSTAT	Ⓣ	
MOTOR	Ⓜ	

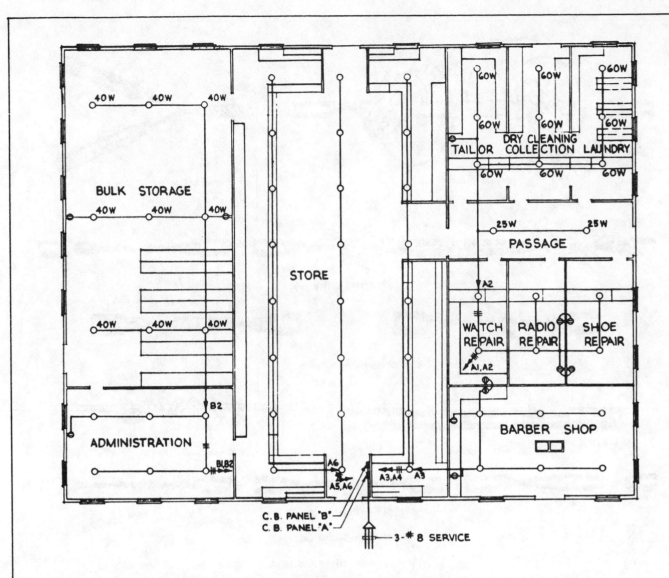

ELECTRICAL PLAN
SCALE NO. 1

GRAPHIC SCALES

0 5' 10' 15'

NO. 1

ELECTRICAL NOTES	
CONNECTED LOAD	
LIGHTING	5.15 KW
RECP EST	1.20 KW
TOTAL	6.35 KW
1. UNLESS OTHERWISE NOTED ON PLAN ALL LAMPS TO BE 100W.	
2. ALL 40, 60 & 100W LAMPS TO HAVE 8" CONICAL SHADES.	

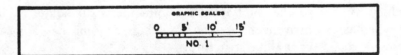

Typical wiring diagram.

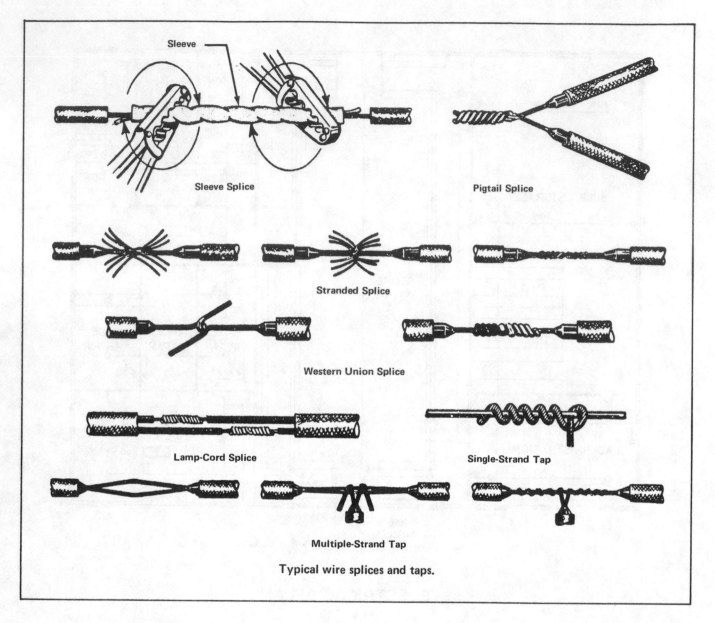

Sleeve

Sleeve Splice

Pigtail Splice

Stranded Splice

Western Union Splice

Lamp-Cord Splice

Single-Strand Tap

Multiple-Strand Tap

Typical wire splices and taps.

design consists of a funnel-shaped metal-spring insert molded into a plastic shell, into which the wires to be joined are screwed. The other type has a removable insert which contains a setscrew to clamp the wires. The plastic shell is screwed onto the insert to cover the joint.

Soldering. When a solderless connector is not used, the splice must be soldered before it is considered to be as good as the original conductor. The primary requirements for obtaining a good solder joint are a clean soldering iron, a clean joint, and a nonacid flux. These requirements are satisfied by the use of pure rosin on the joint or by the use of a rosin core solder.

To insure a good solder joint, the electric heated or copper soldering iron should be applied to the joint until the joint melts the solder by its own heat. A poorly soldered joint has a weak crystalline structure.

Dip soldering is a method of soldering frequently used by experienced electricians because of its convenience and relative speed for soldering pigtail splices.

Every soldered joint is covered with a coating of rubber, or varnished cambric. Friction tape replaces the wire insulation of the conductor. In taping a spliced solder joint the rubber or cambric tape is started on the tapered end of the wire insulation and advances toward the other end, with each succeeding wrap, by overlapping the windings.

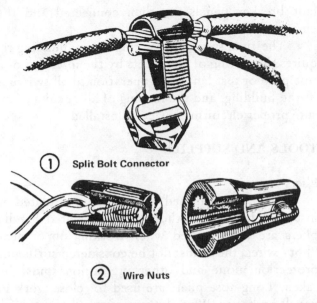

① Split Bolt Connector

② Wire Nuts

Solderless connectors.

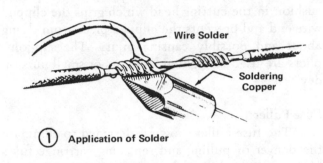

Wire Solder

Soldering Copper

① Application of Solder

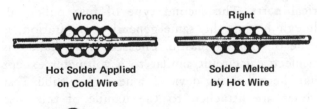

Wrong	Right
Hot Solder Applied on Cold Wire	Solder Melted by Hot Wire

② Right and Wrong Solder Joint

Soldering and solder joints.

This procedure is repeated from one end of the splice to the other until the original thickness has been restored. The joint is then covered with several layers of friction tape.

Though this method for taping joints is still considered to be standard, the plastic electrical tape, which serves as an insulation and a protective covering, should be used whenever available. This

tape materially reduces the time required to tape a joint and reduces the space needed by the joint because a satisfactory protective and insulation covering can be achieved with three-layer taping.

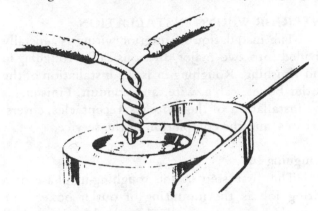

Dip soldering.

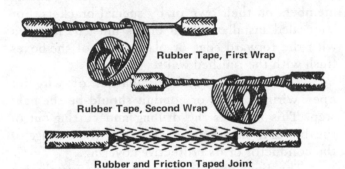

Rubber Tape, First Wrap

Rubber Tape, Second Wrap

Rubber and Friction Taped Joint

Rubber- and friction-tape insulating.

Insulation and Making Wire Connections

When attaching a wire to a switch or an electrical device or when splicing it to another wire, the wire insulation must be removed to bare the copper conductor. There is a right and wrong way to remove insulation. When the wire-stripping tool is applied at right angles to the wire, there is danger that the wire may be nicked and thus weakened. Therefore extreme caution must be used to make sure the wire is not nicked. To avoid nicks, the cut is made at an angle to the conductor. After the protective insulation is removed, the conductor is scraped or sanded thoroughly to remove all traces of insulation and oxide on the wire.

The correct method of attaching the trimmed wire to terminals is to be sure the wire loop is always inserted under the terminal screw so that tightening the screw tends to close the loop. The loop is made so that the wire insulation ends close to the terminal.

INTERIOR WIRING INSTALLATION

The installation of interior wiring is generally divided into two major divisions called roughing-in and finishing. Roughing-in is the installation of the outlet boxes, cable, wire, and conduit. Finishing is the installation of the switches, receptacles, covers, fixtures, and the completion of the service.

Roughing-In

The first step in the roughing-in phase of a wiring job is the mounting of outlet boxes. The mounting can be expedited if the locations of all boxes are first marked on the studs and joists of the building.

All the boxes are mounted on the building members on their own or by special brackets. For concealed installation, all boxes must be installed with the forward edge or plaster ring of the boxes flush with the finished walls.

The circuiting and installation of wire for open wiring, cable, or conduit should be the next step. This involves the drilling and cutting-out of the building members to allow for the passage of the conductor or its protective covering.

The final roughing-in step in the installation of conduit systems is the pulling-in of wires between boxes. This can also be included as the first step in the finishing phase and requires care in the handling of the wires to prevent the marring of finished wall or floor surfaces.

Finishing

The splicing of joints in the outlet and junction boxes and the connection of the bonding circuit is the initial step in the completion phase of a wiring job.

Upon completion of the first finishing step, the proper leads to the terminals of switches, ceiling and wall outlets, and fixtures are then installed.

The devices and their cover plates are then attached to the boxes. The fixtures are generally supported by the use of special mounting brackets called fixture studs or hickeys.

The service-entrance cable and fusing or circuit breaker panels are then connected and the circuits fused.

The final step in the wiring of any building requires the testing of all outlets by the insertion of a test prod or test lamp, the operation of all switches in the building, and the loading of all circuits to insure proper circuiting has been installed.

TOOLS AND SUPPLIES

Pliers

Pliers are furnished with either uninsulated or insulated handles. Although the insulated handle pliers are always used when working on or near "hot" wires, they must not be considered sufficient protection alone and other precautions must be taken. Long-nose pliers are used for close work in panels or boxes. Wire clippers are used to cut wire to size. One type of wire clippers has a plastic cushion in the cutting head which grips the clipped wire end and prevents the clipped piece from flying about and possibly causing injury. The slip-joint pliers are used to tighten locknuts or small nuts on devices.

Fuse Puller

The fuse puller shown is designed to eliminate the danger of pulling and replacing cartridge fuses by hand. It is also used for bending fuse clips, adjusting loose cutout clips, and handling live electrical parts. The second type of fuse puller, although having the same general configuration, is made of molded plastic. Encased in the handle is an electrical circuit similar to a voltmeter except that the indicating device is a neon glow tube. Test probes are attached to the handle of this fuse puller and may be used to determine if voltage is present in a circuit.

Screwdrivers

Screwdrivers are made in many sizes and tip shapes. Those used in electricity should have insulated handles. Generally, screwdrivers are used in attaching electrical devices to boxes and attaching wires to terminals. One variation of the screwdriver is the screwdriver bit which is held in a brace and used for heavy-duty work. For safe and efficient application, screwdriver tips should be kept square and properly tapered and should be selected to match the screw slot.

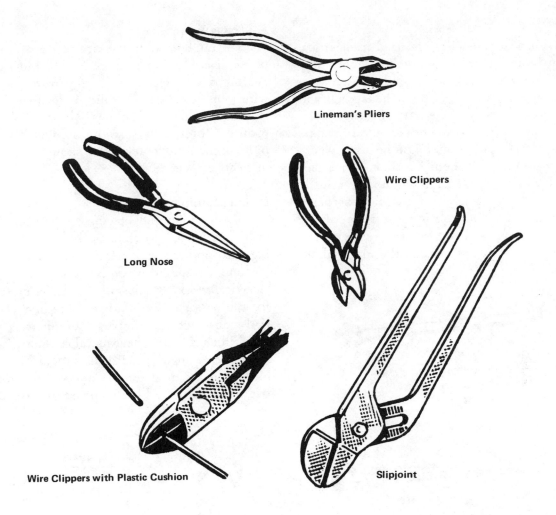

Lineman's Pliers

Wire Clippers

Long Nose

Wire Clippers with Plastic Cushion

Slipjoint

Pliers.

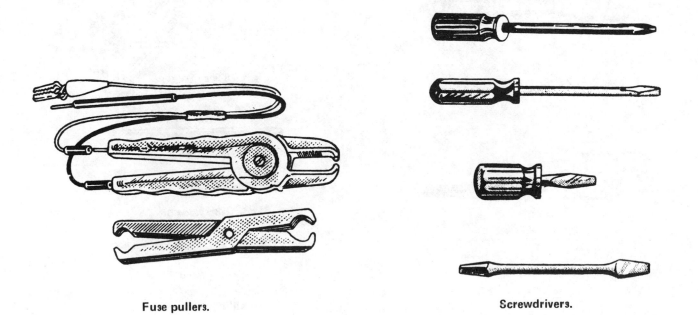

Fuse pullers.

Screwdrivers.

Wrenches

Four types of wrenches are used in electrical work. Adjustable open-end wrenches, commonly called crescent wrenches, open end, closed end, and socket wrenches are used on hexagonal and square fittings such as machine bolts, hexagon nuts, or conduit unions. Pipe wrenches are used for pipe and conduit work and should not be used where crescent, open end, closed end, or socket wrenches can be used. Their construction will not permit the application of heavy pressure on square or hexagonal material, and the continued misuse of the tool in this manner will deform the teeth on the jaw faces and mar the surfaces of the material being worked.

Open- and Box-End

Ratchet

Crescent

Pipe

Wrenches.

Soldering Equipment

A standard soldering kit consists of nonelectric or electric soldering irons or both, a blowtorch (for heating a nonelectric soldering iron and pipe or wire joints), a spool of solid tin-lead wire solder or flux core solder, and soldering paste. An alcohol or propane torch may also be used in place of the blowtorch. Acid core solder should never be used in electrical wiring.

Drilling Equipment

Drilling equipment consists of a brace, a joist-drilling fixture, an extension bit to allow for drilling into and through deep cavities, an adjustable bit, and a standard wood bit. These are required in electrical work to drill holes in building structures for the passage of conduit or wire in new or modified construction. Similar equipment is required for drilling holes in sheet-metal cabinets and boxes. In this case high speed drills should be used. Carbide drills are used for tile or concrete work. Electric power drills aid in this phase of an electrician's work.

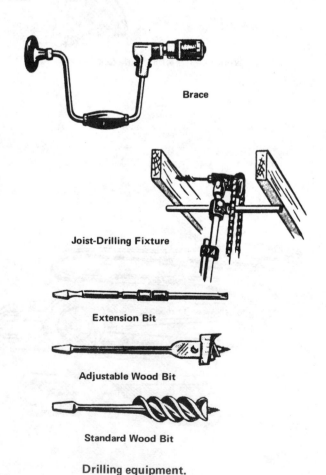

Brace

Joist-Drilling Fixture

Extension Bit

Adjustable Wood Bit

Standard Wood Bit

Drilling equipment.

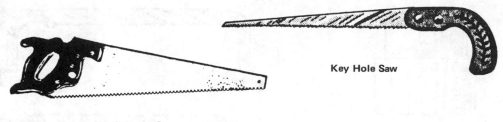

Crosscut Saw

Key Hole Saw

Chisel

Woodworking tools.

Woodworking Tools

The crosscut and keyhole saws and wood chisels are used to remove wooden structural members obstructing a wire or conduit run and to notch studs and joists to take conduit, cable, or box-mounting brackets. They are also used in the construction of wood-panel mounting brackets. The keyhole saw may again be used to cut openings in walls of existing buildings where boxes are to be added.

Metalworking Tools

The cold chisels and center punches shown, besides several other types of metalworking tools, are used when working on steel panels. The knock-out punch is used either in making or enlarging a hole in a steel cabinet or outlet box. The hacksaw is usually used by an electrician to cut conduit, cable, or wire too large for wire cutters. A light steady stroke of about 40 to 50 times a minute is best. A new blade should always be inserted with the teeth pointing away from the handle. The tension wingnut is tightened until the blade is rigid. Care must be taken because insufficient tension will cause the blade to twist and jam whereas too much tension will cause the blade to break. Blades have 14, 18, 24, and 32 teeth per inch. The best blade for general use is one having 18 teeth per inch. A blade with 32 teeth per inch is best for cutting thin material. The mill file shown in the figure is used in filing the sharp ends of cutoffs as a precaution against short circuits.

Masonry-Working Tools

An electrician should have several sizes of masonry drills in his tool kit. These normally are carbide-tipped and are used to drill holes in brick or concrete walls either for anchoring apparatus with expansion screws or for the passage of conduit or cable.

Conduit Threaders and Dies

Rigid conduit is normally threaded for installation. One type of conduit threader and dies is used in cutting pipe threads on conduit. The tapered pipe reamer is used to ream the inside edge of the conduit as a precaution against wire damage. The conduit cutter is used when cutting thin-wall conduit and has a tapered blade attachment for reaming the conduit ends.

Knives and Other Insulation-Stripping Tools

Wire and cable insulation should be stripped or removed with the proper tools. The knives and patented wire strippers are used to bare the wire of insulation before making connections. The scissors shown are used to cut insulation and tape. A multi-purpose tool designed to cut and skin wires, attach terminals, gauge wire, and cut small bolts may also be used. The armored-cable cutter may be used instead of a hacksaw in removing the armor from the electrical conductors at box entry or when cutting the cable to length.

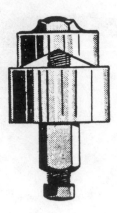

Knockout Punch

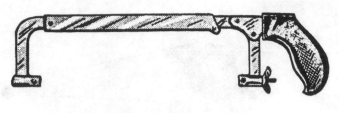

Hacksaw and Blade

Mill File

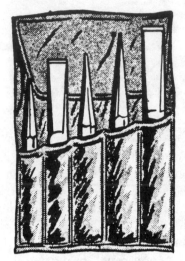

Cold Chisels and Punches

Metalworking tools.

Starr Drill

Power-Operated

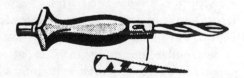

Drill Holding Wedge

Hand-Operated

Masonry drills.

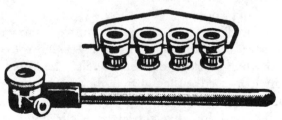

Conduit Threader

Conduit Reamer

Thin-Wall Conduit Cutter and Reamer

Conduit threader, reamers, and cutter.

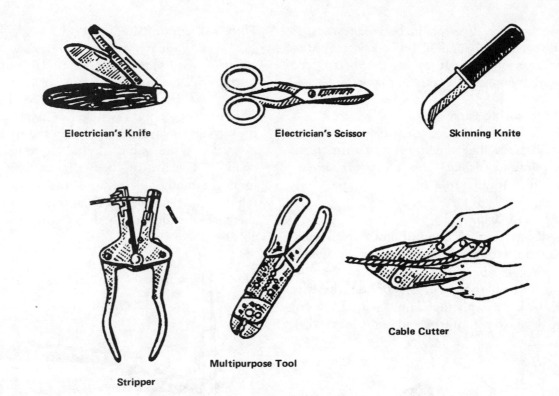

Electrician's Knife   Electrician's Scissor   Skinning Knife

Stripper   Multipurpose Tool   Cable Cutter

Insulation-stripping tools.

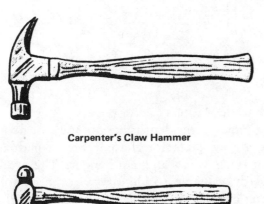

Carpenter's Claw Hammer

Machinist's Ball-Peen Hammer

Hammers.

Hammers

Hammers are used either in combination with other tools such as chisels or in nailing equipment to building supports. A carpenter's clawhammer and a machinist's ball peen hammer can both be advantageously used in electrical work.

Tape

Various types of tapes are used to replace insulation and wire coverings. Friction tape is a cotton tape impregnated with an insulating adhesive compound. It provides weather resistance and limited mechanical protection to a splice already insulated. Rubber or varnished cambric tape may be used as an insulator when replacing wire covering. Plastic electrical tape is made of a plastic material with adhesive on one face. It has replaced friction and rubber tape in the field for 120- and 208-volt circuits, and as it serves a dual purpose in taping joints, it is preferred over the former methods.

Fish Wire and Drop Chain

Fish Wire. Fish wires are used primarily to pull wires through conduits. Many pulls are quite difficult and require a fish-wire "grip" or "pull" to obtain adequate force on the wire in pulling. The fish wire is made of tempered spring steel about ¼-inch wide and is available in lengths to suit requirements. It is stiff enough to preclude bending under normal operation but can be pushed or pulled easily around the bends or conduit elbows.

Drop Chain. When pulling wires and cables in existing buildings, the electrician will normally employ a fish wire or drop chain between studs. A drop chain consists of small chain links attached to a lead or iron weight. It is used only to feed through wall openings in a vertical plane.

Ruler and Measuring Tape

As an aid in cutting conduit to exact size as well as in determining the approximate material quantities required for each job, electrical supplies should include a folding rule and a steel tape.

Wire Clamps and Grips

To pull wire through conduit and to pull open-wire installations tight, wire grip is an invaluable aid. The wire grip has been designed so that the harder the pull on the wire, the tighter the wire will be tripped. The splicing clamp is used to twist the wire pairs into a uniform and tight joint when making splices.

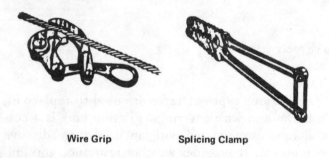

Wire Grip   Splicing Clamp

Wire grip and splicing clamp.

Extension Cord and Light

The extension light normally is supplied with a long extension cord and is used when normal building lighting has not been installed or is not functioning.

Rubber-Handle Guards

Extension light (without bulb).

Thin-Wall Conduit Impinger

When indenter type couplings and connectors are used with thin-wall conduit, an indenter tool (a thin-wall conduit impinger) must be used to attach these fittings permanently to the conduit. This tool has points which, when pressed against the fittings, form indentations in the fitting and are pressed into the wall of the tubing to hold it on the conduit. The use of these slip-on fittings and the impinger materially reduces the installation time required in electrical installations and thus reduces the cost of thin-wall conduit installations considerably.

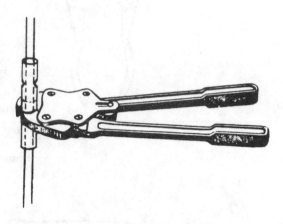

Thin-wall conduit impinger.

Wire Code Markers

Tapes with identifying numbers or nomenclature are available for the purpose of permanently identifying wires and equipment. These are particularly valuable to identify wires in complicated wiring circuits, in fuse circuit breaker panels, or in junction boxes.

WIRING SYSTEMS

There are many different wiring systems currently in use which vary in complexity from the simple-to-install open wiring to the more complex conduit systems. These various systems contain common components. This section describes these common or general use materials.

Electrical Conductors

Single Conductors. Electrical conductors that provide the paths for the flow of electric current generally consist of copper or aluminum wire or cable over which an insulating material is formed.

402

The insulating material insures that the path of current flow is through the conductor rather than through extraneous paths, such as conduits, water pipes, and so on. The wires or conductors are initially classified by type of insulation applied and wire gauge. The various types of insulation are in turn subdivided according to their maximum operating temperatures and nature of use.

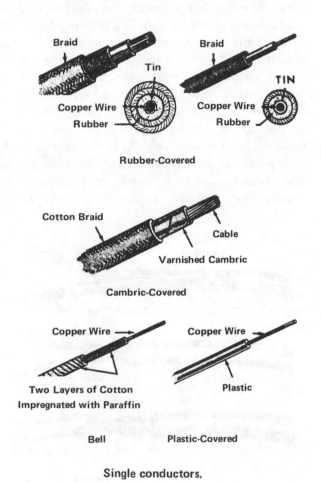

Single conductors.

Wire Sizes. The wire sizes are denoted by the use of the American Wire Gauge (AWG) standards. The largest gauge size is No. 0000. Wires larger than this are classified in size by their circular mil cross-sectional area. One circular mil is the area of a circle with a diameter of 1/1,000 of an inch. Thus, if a wire has a diameter of 0.10 inch or 100 mil, the cross sectional area is 100 x 100 or 10,000 circular mils. The most common wire sizes used in interior wiring are 14, 12, and 10 and they are usually of solid construction. Some characteristics of the numbering system are:

1. As the numbers become larger, the size of the wire decreases.

2. The sizes normally used have even numbers, e.g., 14, 12, and 10.

3. Numbers 8 and 6 wires, which are furnished either solid or stranded, or normally used for heavy-power circuits or as service-entrance leads to buildings. Wire sizes larger than these are used for extremely heavy loads and for poleline distributions.

Multiconductor Cables. There are many types of installations of electrical wiring where the use of individual conductors spaced and supported side by side becomes an inefficient as well as hazardous practice. For these installations, multiconductor cables have been designed and manufactured. Multiconductor cables consist of the individual conductors as outlined above, arranged in groups of two or more. An additional insulating or protective shield is formed or wound around the group of conductors. The individual conductors are color coded for proper identification. The description and use of each type of multiconductors are given below.

Armored cable, commonly referred to as BX, can be supplied either in two- or three-wire types and with or without a lead sheath. The wires in BX, matched with a bare equipment ground wire, are initially twisted together. This grouping, totaling three or four wires with the ground, is then wrapped in coated paper and a formed self-locking steel armor. The cable without a lead sheath is widely used for interior wiring under dry conditions. The lead sheath is required for installation in wet locations and through masonry or concrete building partitions where added protection for the copper conductor wires is required.

Nonmetallic sheathed cable consists of two or three rubber- or thermoplastic-insulated wires, each covered with a jute type of filler material which acts as a protective insulation against mishandling. This in turn is covered with an impregnated cotton braid. The cable is light in weight, simple to install, and comparatively low priced. It is used quite extensively in interior wiring, but is not approved for use in wet locations. A dual-purpose plastic sheathed cable with solid copper conductors can be used underground outdoors or indoors. It needs no conduit, and its flat shape and gray or ivory color make it ideal for surface wiring. It resists moisture,

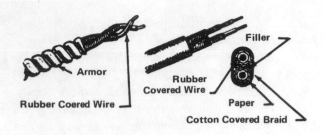

Metallic Armored Cable (BX)   Nonmetallic Sheathed Cable

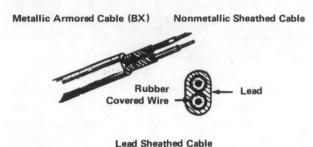

Lead Sheathed Cable

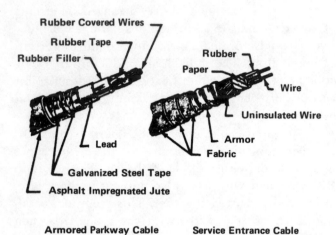

Armored Parkway Cable   Service Entrance Cable

Multiconductor cables.

acid, and corrosion and can be run through masonry or between studding.

Lead-covered cable consists of two or more rubber-covered conductors surrounded by a lead sheathing which has been extruded around it to permit its installation in wet and underground locations. Lead-covered cable can also be immersed in water or installed in areas where the presence of liquid or gaseous vapors would attack the insulation on other types.

Parkway cable provides its own protection from mechanical injury and therefore can be used for underground services by burying it in the ground without any protecting conduit. It normally consists of rubber-insulated conductors enclosed in a lead sheath and covered with a double spiral of

galvanized steel tape which acts as a mechanical protection for the lead. On top of the tape, a heavy braid of jute saturated with a waterproofing compound is applied for additional weather protection.

Cords. Many items using electrical power are either of the pendant, portable, or vibration type. In these cases the use of cords is authorized for delivery of power. These can be grouped and designated as either lamp, heater, or heavy-duty power cords. Lamp cords are supplied in many forms. The most common types are the single-paired rubber-insulated and twisted-paired cords. The twisted-paired cords consist of two cotton-wound conductors which have been covered with rubber and rewound with cotton braid. Heater cords are similar to this latter type except that the first winding is replaced by heat-resistant asbestos. Heavy-duty or hard-service cords are normally supplied with two or more conductors surrounded by cotton and rubber insulation. In manufacture,

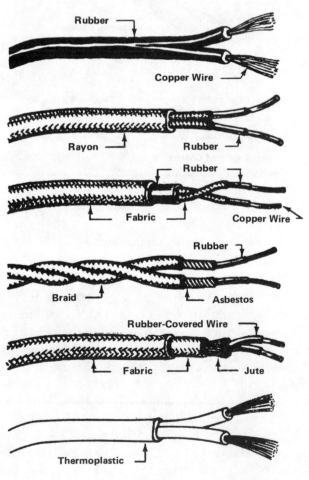

Types of flexible cords.

these are first twisted or stranded. The voids created in the twisting process are then filled with jute and the whole assembly covered with rubber. All cords, whether of this type or of the heater or lamp variety, have the conductors color coded for ease of identification.

Electrical Boxes

Design. Outlet boxes bind together the elements of a conduit or armored cable system in a continuous grounded system. They provide a means of holding the conduit in position, a space for mounting such devices as switches and receptacles, protection for the device, and space for making splices and connections.

Outlet boxes are manufactured in either sheet steel, porcelain, bakelite, or cast iron and are either round, square, octagonal, or rectangular.

The fabricated steel box is available in a number of different designs. For example, some boxes are of the sectional or "gang" variety, while others have integral brackets for mounting on studs and joists. Moreover, some boxes have been designed to receive special cover plates so that switches, receptacles, or lighting fixtures may be more easily installed. Other designs facilitate installation in plastered surfaces. Regardless of the design or material, they all should have sufficient interior volume to allow for the splicing of conductors or the making of connections. For this reason the allowable minimum depth of outlet boxes is limited to 1½ inches in all cases except where building-supporting members would have to be cut. In this case the minimum depth can be reduced to ½ inch.

Selection. The selection of boxes in an electrical system should be made in accordance with the maximum allowable conductor capacity for each type of box.

Outlet Boxes for Rigid and Thin-Wall Circuit and Armored Cable. Steel or cast iron outlet boxes are generally used with rigid and thin-wall conduit or armored cable. The steel boxes are either zinc- or enamel-coated, the zinc coating being preferred when installing conduit in wet locations. All steel boxes have "knockouts." These knockouts are indentations in the side, top, or back of an outlet box, sized to fit the standard diameters of conduit fittings or cable connectors. They usually can be removed with a small cold chisel or punch to facilitate entry into the box of the conduit or cable.

Boxes designed specifically for armored-cable use also have integral screw clamps located in the space immediately inside the knockouts and thus eliminate the need for cable connectors. This reduces the cost and labor of installation. Box covers are normally required when it is necessary to reduce the box openings, provide mounting lugs for electrical devices, or to cover the box when it is to be used as a junction.

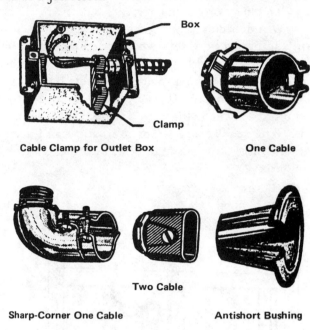

Cable Clamp for Outlet Box   **One Cable**

Two Cable

Sharp-Corner One Cable   **Antishort Bushing**

Armored-cable fittings.

Outlet Boxes for Nonmetallic Sheathed Cable and Open Wiring.

Steel. Steel boxes are also used for nonmetallic cable and open wiring. However, the methods of box entry are different from those for conduit and armored-cable wiring because the electrical conductor wires are not protected by a hard surface. The connectors and interior box clamps used in nonmetallic and open wiring are formed to provide a smooth surface for securing the cable rather than being the sharp-edged type of closure normally used.

Nonmetallic. Nonmetallic outlet boxes made of either porcelain or bakelite may also be used with open or nonmetallic sheathed wiring. Cable or wire entry is generally made by removing the knockouts of preformed weakened blanks in the boxes.

Special. In open wiring, conductors should normally be installed in a loom from the last support to the outlet box. Although all of the boxes described above are permissible for open wiring, a special loom box is available which has its back corners "sliced off" and allows for loom and wire entry at this sliced-off position.

Attachment Devices for Outlet Boxes. Outlet boxes which do not have brackets are supported by wooden cleats or bar hangers.

Wooden cleats. Wooden cleats are first cut to size and nailed between two wooden members. The boxes are then either nailed or screwed to these cleats through holes provided in their back plates.

Strap hangers. If the outlet box is to be mounted between studs, mounting straps are necessary. The readymade straps are handy and accommodate not only a single box, but a 2, 3, 4, or 5 gang box.

Bar hangers. Bar hangers are prefabricated to span the normal 16-inch and 24-inch joist and stud spacings and are obtainable for surface or recessed box installation. They are nailed to the joist or stud exposed faces. The supports for recessed boxes normally are called offset bar hangers.

Patented supports. When boxes have to be installed in walls that are already plastered, several patented supports can be used for mounting. These obviate the need for installing the boxes on wooden members and thus eliminate extensive chipping and replastering.

Knobs, Tubes, Cleats, Loom, and Special Connectors

Open wiring requires the use of special insulating supports and tubing to insure a safe installation. These supports, called knobs and cleats, are smooth-surfaced and made of porcelain. Knobs and

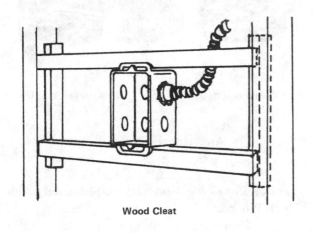

Wood Cleat

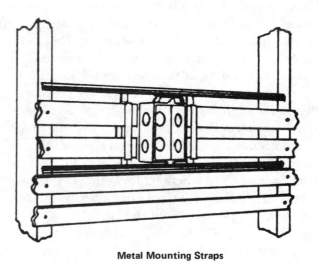

Metal Mounting Straps

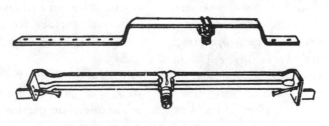

Bar Hangers

Typical box mountings.

cleats support the wires which are run singly or in pairs on the surface of the joists or studs in the buildings. Tubing or tubes, as they are called, protect the wires from abrasion when passing through wooden members. Insulation of loom of the "slip-on" type is used to cover the wires on box entry and at wire-crossover points. The term "loom" is applied to a continuous flexible tube woven of cambric material impregnated with varnish. At points where the type of wiring may change and where boxes are not specifically required, special open wiring to cable or conduit wiring connectors should be used. These connectors are threaded on one side to facilitate connection to a conduit and have holes on the other side to accommodate wire splices but are designed only to carry the wire to the next junction box.

Cable and Wire Connectors

Code requirements state that "Conductors shall be spliced or joined with splicing devices approved for the use or by brazing, welding, or soldering with a fusible metal or alloy. Soldered splices shall first be so spliced as to be mechanically and electrically secure without solder and then soldered." Soldering or splicing devices are used as added protection because of the ease of wiring and the high quality of connection of these devices. Assurance of high quality is the responsibility of the electrician who selects the proper size of connector relative to the number and size of wires.

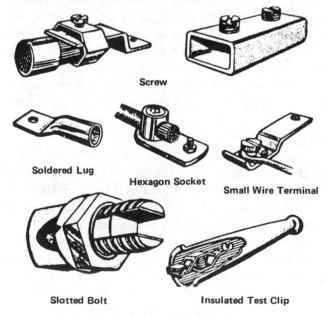

Screw

Soldered Lug

Hexagon Socket

Small Wire Terminal

Slotted Bolt

Insulated Test Clip

Cable and wire connectors.

Straps and Staples

All conduits and cables must be attached to the structural members of a building in a manner that will preclude sagging. The cables must be supported at least every 4½ feet for either a vertical or horizontal run and must have a support in the form of a strap or staple within 12 inches of every outlet box. Conduit-support spacings vary with the size and rigidity of the conduit.

Cable Staples. A very simple and effective method of supporting BX cables on wooden members is by the use of cable staples.

Insulating Staples. Bell or signal wires are normally installed in pairs in signal systems. The operating voltage and energy potential is so low in these installations (12 to 24 volts) that protective coverings such as conduit or loom are not required. To avoid any possibility of shorting in the circuit, they are normally supported on wood joists or studs by insulated staples.

Straps. Conduit and cable straps are supplied as either one-hole or two-hole supports and are formed to fit the contour of the specific material for which they are designed. The conduit and cable straps are attached to building materials by "anchors" designed to suit each type of supporting material. For example, a strap is attached to a wood stud or joist by nails or screws. Expanding anchors are used for box or strap attachment to cement or brick structures and also to plaster or plaster-substitute surfaces. Toggle and "molly" bolts are used where the surface wall is thin and has a concealed air space which will allow for the release of the toggle or expanding sleeve.

Receptacles, Fixtures, and Receptacle Covers

Portable appliances and devices are readily connected to an electrical supply circuit by means of an outlet called a receptacle. For interior wiring these outlets are installed either as single or duplex receptacles. Receptacles previously installed, and their replacements in the same box, may be two-wire receptacles. All others must be the three-wire type. The third wire on the three-wire receptacle is used to provide a ground lead to the equipment which receives power from the receptacle. This guards against dangers from current leakage due to faulty insulation or exposed wiring and helps prevent accidental shock. The receptacles are constructed to receive plug prongs either by a straight

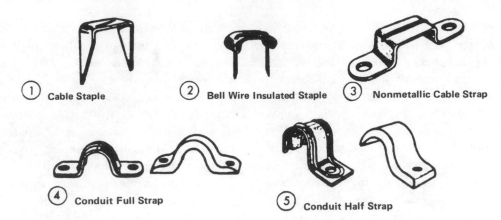

① Cable Staple   ② Bell Wire Insulated Staple   ③ Nonmetallic Cable Strap

④ Conduit Full Strap   ⑤ Conduit Half Strap

Straps and staples.

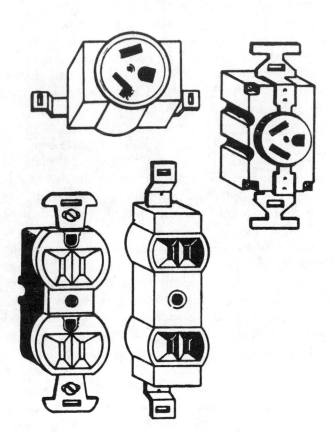

Types of wall receptacles.

push action or by a twist-and-turn push action. Fixtures are similar to receptacles but are used to connect the electrical supply circuit directly to lamps inserted in their sockets.

Knob-and-Tube Wiring. Receptacles with their entire enclosures made of some insulating material, such as bakelite, may be used without metal outlet boxes for exposed, open wiring or nonmetallic sheathed cable.

Conduit and Cable. The receptacles commonly used with conduit and cable installations are constructed with yokes to facilitate their installation in outlet boxes. In this case they are attached to the boxes by metal screws through the yokes, threaded into the box. Wire connections are made at the receptacle terminals by screws which are an integral part of the outlet. Receptacle covers made of either brass, steel, or nonmetallic materials are then attached to box and receptacle installations to afford complete closure at the outlets.

Surface Metal Raceways. These provide a quick inexpensive electrical wiring installation method since they are installed on the wall surface instead of inside the wall.

Surface metal raceway is basically of two types: one-piece construction or two-piece construction. When working with the one-piece construction type, the metal raceway is installed like conduit, then the wires are "pulled" to make the necessary electrical connections. If working with the two-piece construction type, the base piece is installed along the wiring run. Wiring is next laid in the base piece and held in place with clamps. After the wires are laid, the capping is snapped on and the job is complete.

A multioutlet system, with grounding inserts if desired, has outlets spaced every few inches so that several tools or pieces of equipment can be used simultaneously. An overfloor metal raceway system handles telephone and signal or power and light wiring where the circuits must be brought to locations in the middle of the floor area. These systems are all designed so that they can be installed independently of other wiring systems, or may be economically connected to existing systems.

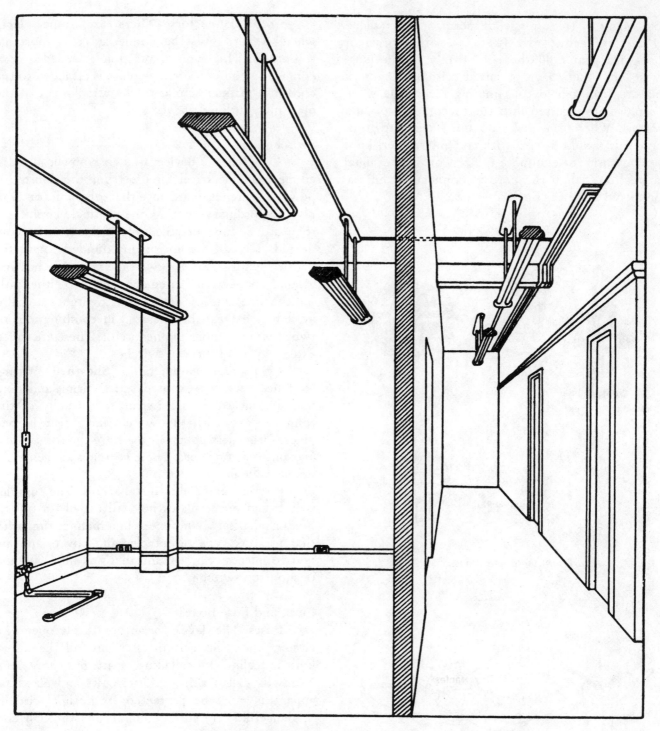

Surface metal raceways.

Plugs and Cord Connection

Plugs. Portable appliances and devices that are to be connected to receptacles have their electrical cords equipped with plugs that have prongs which mate with slots in the outlet receptacles. A three-prong plug can fit into a two-prong receptacle by using an adapter. If the electrical conductors connected to the outlet have a ground system, the lug on the lead wire of the adapter is connected to the center screw holding the receptacle cover to the box. Many of these plugs are permanently molded to the attached cords. There are other types of cord-grips that hold the cord firmly to the plug. Twist-lock plugs have patented prongs that catch and are firmly held to a mating receptacle when the plugs are inserted into the receptacle slots and twisted. Where the plugs do not have cord-grips, the cords should be tied with an Underwriters knot at plug entry to eliminate tension on the terminal connections when the cord is connected and disconnected from the outlet receptacle.

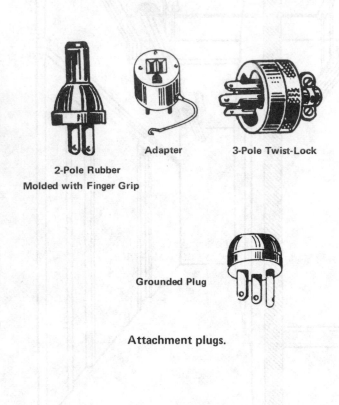

2-Pole Rubber Molded with Finger Grip

Adapter

3-Pole Twist-Lock

Grounded Plug

Attachment plugs.

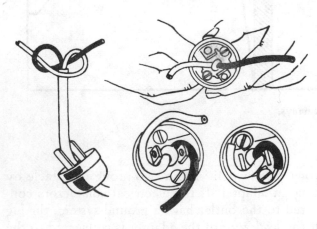

The Underwriters' knot.

Cord Connectors. There are some places where a cord must be connected to a portable receptacle. This type of receptacle, called a cord connector body or a female plug, is attached to the cord in a manner similar to the attachment of the male plug outlined above.

Switches and Covers

A switch is a device used to connect and disconnect an electrical circuit from the source of power. Switches may be either one-pole or two-pole for ordinary lighting or receptacle circuits. If they are of the one-pole type, they must be connected to break the hot or ungrounded conductor of the circuit. If of the two-pole type, the hot and ground connection can be connected to either pole on the line side of the switch. Switches are also available that can be operated in combinations of two, three, or more in one circuit. These are called three-way and four-way switches.

Open and Nonmetallic Sheathed Wiring. Switches used for exposed open wiring and nonmetallic sheathed cable wiring are usually of the tumbler type with the switch and cover in one piece. Other less common ones are the rotary-snap and pushbutton types. These switches are generally nonmetallic in composition.

Conduit and Cable Installations. The tumbler switch and cover plates normally used for outlet-box installation are mounted in a manner similar to that for box type receptacles and covers and are in two pieces. Foreign installations may still use pushbutton switches.

Fuses and Fuse Boxes

Fuses. The device for automatically opening a circuit when the current rises beyond the safety limit is technically called a cutout, but more commonly is called a fuse. All circuits and electrical apparatus must be protected from short circuits or dangerous overcurrent conditions through correctly rated fuses.

Standard. The cartridge type fuse is used for current rating above 30 amperes in interior wiring systems. The ordinary plug or screw type fuse is satisfactory for incandescent lighting or heating appliance circuits.

Special. On branch circuits, wherever motors are connected, time-lag fuses should be used instead of the standard plug or cartridge type fuse.

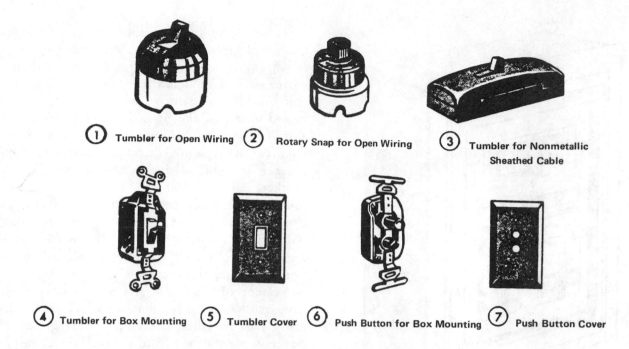

① Tumbler for Open Wiring ② Rotary Snap for Open Wiring ③ Tumbler for Nonmetallic Sheathed Cable

④ Tumbler for Box Mounting ⑤ Tumbler Cover ⑥ Push Button for Box Mounting ⑦ Push Button Cover

Switches and covers.

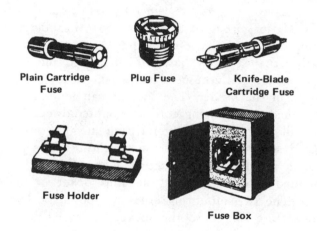

Plain Cartridge Fuse

Plug Fuse

Knife-Blade Cartridge Fuse

Fuse Holder

Fuse Box

Typical fuses and fuse box.

These fuses have self-compensating elements which maintain and hold the circuit in line during a momentary heavy ampere drain, yet cut out the circuit under normal short-circuit conditions. The heavy ampere demand normally occurs in motor circuits when the motor is started. Examples of such circuits are the ones used to power oil burners or air conditioners.

Fuse Boxes. As a general rule the fusing of circuits is concentrated at centrally located fusing or distribution panels.

Circuit Breaker Panels

Circuit breakers are devices resembling switches that trip or cut out the circuit in case of overamperage. They perform the same function as fuses and can be obtained with time-lag opening features similar to the special fuses. Based on their operation, they may be classified as a thermal, magnetic, or combination thermal-magnetic reaction type.

A thermal type circuit breaker has a bimetallic element integrally built within the breaker that responds only to fluctuations in temperature within the circuit. The element is made by bonding together two strips of dissimilar metal, each of which has a different coefficient of expansion. When a current is flowing in the circuit, the heat created by the resistance of the bimetallic element will expand each metal at a different rate causing the strip to bend. The element acts as a latch in the circuit as the breaker mechanism is adjusted so that the element bends just far enough under a specified current to trip the breaker and open the circuit.

A magnetic circuit breaker responds to changes in the magnitude of current flow. In operation an increased current flow will create enough magnetic force to "pull up" an armature, opening the circuit. The magnetic circuit breaker is usually

Typical circuit breaker box.

used in motor circuits for closer adjustment to motor rating while the circuit conductors are protected, as usual, by another circuit breaker.

The thermal-magnetic breaker, as the name implies, combines the features of the thermal and magnetic types. Practically all of the molded case circuit breakers used in lighting panelboards are of this type. The thermal element protects against overcurrents in the lower range and the magnetic element protects against the higher range usually occurring from short circuits.

During the last decade, circuit breakers have been used to a greater extent than fuses because they can be manually reset after tripping, whereas fuses require replacement. Fuses may easily be replaced with higher capacity ones that do not protect the circuit. This is difficult to do with circuit breakers. In addition they combine the functions of fuse and switch, and when tripped by overloads or short circuits, all of the ungrounded conductors of a circuit are opened simultaneously. Each branch circuit must have a fuse or circuit breaker protecting each ungrounded conductor. Some in-

stallations may or may not have a main breaker that disconnects everything. As a guide during installation, if it does not require more than six movements of the hand to open all the branch circuit breakers, a main breaker or switch is not required ahead of the branch-circuit breaker. However if more than six movements of the hand are required, a separate disconnecting main circuit breaker is required ahead of the branch-circuit breaker. Each 120-volt circuit requires a single-pole (one-pole) breaker to protect both ungrounded conductors. You can, however, place two single-pole breakers side by side, and tie the two handles together mechanically to give double-pole protection. Both handles can then be moved by a single movement of the hand. A two-pole breaker may have one handle or two handles which are mechanically tied together, but either one requires only one movement of the hand to break the circuit.

TYPES OF LAMPS
Lampholders and Sockets

Lamp sockets are generally screw-base units placed in circuits as holders for incandescent lamps. A special type of lampholder has contacts, rather than a screw base, which engage and hold the prongs of fluorescent lamps when they are rotated in the holder. The sockets can generally be attached to a hanging cord or mounted directly on a wall or ceiling in open wiring installations by using screws or nails in the mounting holes provided in the nonconducting material which is molded or formed around the lamp socket.

The two mounting holes in a porcelain lamp socket are spaced so the sockets may also be attached to outlet box "ears" or a plaster ring with machine screws. The screw threads molded or rolled in the ends of the lampholder sockets also facilitate their ready integration in other types of lighting fixtures such as table lamps, floor lamps, or hanging fixtures which have reflectors or decorative shades. In an emergency, a socket may also be used as a receptacle. The socket is converted to a receptacle by screwing in a female plug. One type of ceiling lampholder has a grounded outlet located on the side. Lamp sockets are produced in many different sizes and shapes.

Reflectors and Shades

Several types of reflectors and shades are used

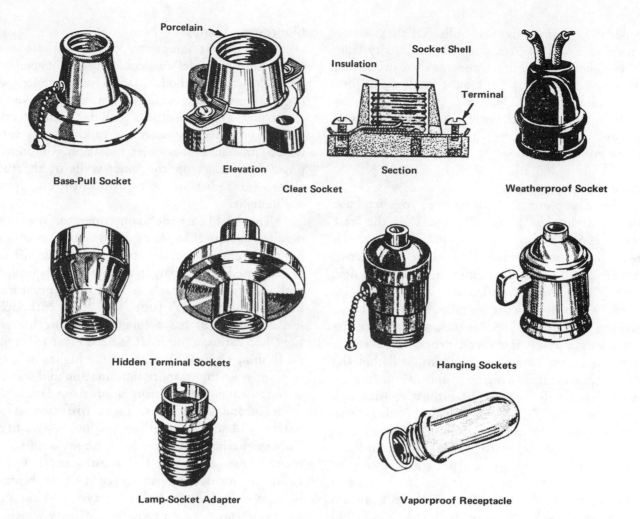

Base-Pull Socket

Porcelain

Elevation

Cleat Socket

Insulation

Socket Shell

Terminal

Section

Weatherproof Socket

Hidden Terminal Sockets

Hanging Sockets

Lamp-Socket Adapter

Vaporproof Receptacle

Lampholders and sockets.

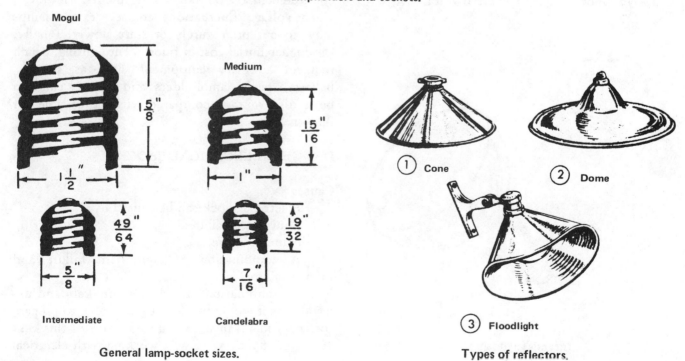

Mogul

Medium

$1\frac{5}{8}''$

$1\frac{1}{2}''$

$\frac{15}{16}''$

$1''$

$\frac{49}{64}''$

$\frac{5}{8}''$

$\frac{19}{32}''$

$\frac{7}{16}''$

Intermediate

Candelabra

General lamp-socket sizes.

① Cone

② Dome

③ Floodlight

Types of reflectors.

to focus the lighting effect of bulbs. Of these, some are used to flood an area with high intensity light and are called floodlights. Others, called spotlights, concentrate the useful light on a small area. Both floodlights and spotlights can come in two- or three-light clusters with swivel holders. They can be mounted on walls or posts or on spikes pushed into the ground.

Incandescent Lamps

The most common light source for general use is the incandescent lamp. Though it is the least efficient type of light, its use is preferred over the fluorescent type because of its low initial cost, ease of maintenance, convenience, and flexibility. Its flexibility and convenience is readily seen by the wide selection of wattage ratings that can be inserted in one type socket. Further, since its emitted candlepower is directly proportional to the voltage, a lower voltage application will dim the light. A high rated voltage application from a power source will increase its intensity. Although an incandescent light is economical, it is also inefficient because a large amount of the energy supplied to it is converted to heat rather than light. Moreover, it does not give a true light because the tungsten filament emits a great deal more red and yellow light than does the light of the sun. Incandescent lights are normally built to last 1,000 hours when operating at their rated voltage.

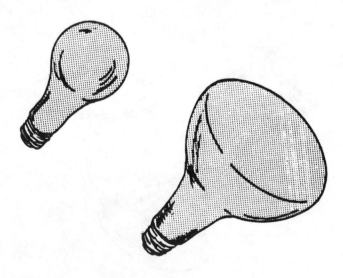

Incandescent lamps.

Fluorescent Lamps

Fluorescent lamps are either of the conventional "hot cathode" or "cold cathode" type.

The "hot cathode" lamp has a coiled wire type of electrode, which when heated gives off electrons. These electrons collide with mercury atoms, provided by mercury vapor in the tubes, which produces ultraviolet radiation. Fluorescent powder coatings on the inner walls of the tubes absorb this radiation and transform the energy into visible light.

The "cold cathode" lamp operates in a similar manner except that its electrode consists of a cylindrical tube. It receives its name because the heat is generated over a larger area and, therefore, the cathode does not reach as high a temperature as in the "hot cathode" tube. The "cold cathode" is less efficient but has a longer operating life than the "hot cathode" unit. It is used most frequently on flashing circuits. Because of the higher light output per watt input, more illumination and less heat is obtained per watt from fluorescent lamps than from incandescent ones. Light diffusion is also better, and surface brightness is lower. The life of fluorescent lamps is also longer compared to filament types. However, the fluorescent lamp, because of its design, cannot control its beam of light as well as the incandescent type and has a tendency to produce stroboscopic effects which are counteracted by phasing arrangements. Moreover, when voltage fluctuations are severe, the lamps may go out prematurely or start slowly. Finally, the higher initial cost in fluorescent lighting, which requires auxiliary equipment such as starters, ballasts, special lampholders, and fixtures can also be a disadvantage compared with other types of illumination.

DANGER! ELECTRICAL SHOCK

Causes

Electrical shock can be caused by:
Equipment failure.
Human failure.
A combination of equipment failure and human failure.

A combination of events so unlikely and unusual that it would be almost impossible to prepare for them in advance. Luckily accidents of this kind are rare. If they were not, working with electrical equipment would be extremely hazardous.

Equipment Failure. Seldom is electrical shock caused solely by equipment failure, but it can happen. To fit into this category, the equipment would have to be properly installed, tested for safety after installation, and used according to suitable safety precautions. The equipment failure would have to be completely unpredictable.

Human Failure. Human failures that can lead to electrical shock are:

Failure to observe the necessary safety precautions when using or working on equipment that would be perfectly safe if handled properly. A careless person might fail to test equipment to make sure that it is de-energized before working on it. He might not use proper care to avoid contact with equipment or conductors that were known to be energized.

Making improper modifications to equipment or using improper equipment.

Failure to make adequate repairs on equipment that has already caused nonfatal shocks.

Failure to test the insulation resistance and the completion of the ground connection after the equipment has been repaired.

Human failure perhaps is prevalent because people so often have a rather casual attitude toward the deadly potentialities of electrical circuits and equipment. A way has not been found to make electrical equipment that will not shock its users when it is improperly used.

Conditions for Shock

Two conditions must be satisfied for current to flow through a man:

The man must form part of a closed circuit in which current can flow.

Somewhere in the closed circuit there must be an electromotive force or a difference in potential to cause current flow.

To guard against electrical shock a person should see to it that the body never forms part of a closed circuit through which current can flow.

REPLACING AN ELECTRIC PLUG

The replacement of a worn electric plug is probably the most common electrical repair you will encounter. Damaged plugs should be replaced promptly as they may cause electrical shock or fire and impair the efficiency of the appliance.

Equipment

Tools needed for the repair are minimal. All you need purchase is a new plug; buy one with a UL label. A screwdriver and a knife complete the tools required.

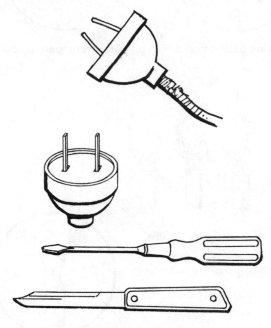

Tools you will need.

Replacement

First, cut the cord off at the damaged point. Do not attempt to repair the cord by taping. Taping is to be considered an emergency measure only. The worn section should be removed and the plug replaced as quickly as possible.

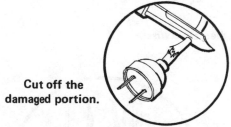

Cut off the damaged portion.

Slip the plug back on the cord. Now clip and separate the cord, tying it with an Underwriters' knot. Remove a half-inch of the insulation from the end of the wires, but take care not to cut any of the small wires. Twist the small wires together in a clockwise direction. Pull the knot firmly into the plug and then pull one wire around each terminal to the screw.

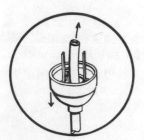

Slip plug back on cord.

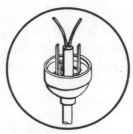

Clip and separate cord.

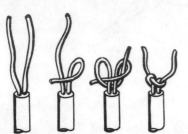

Make an Underwriters' knot.

Remove ½ inch insulation.

Twist wires together, clockwise.

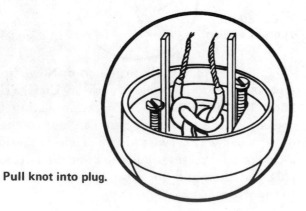

Pull knot into plug.

Wrap each wire around a screw, clockwise, Now tighten the screw. In order to be sure of a good connection, check to see that the insulation comes just to the screw, but not under it.

Replace the insulation cover back over the plug and the job is complete.

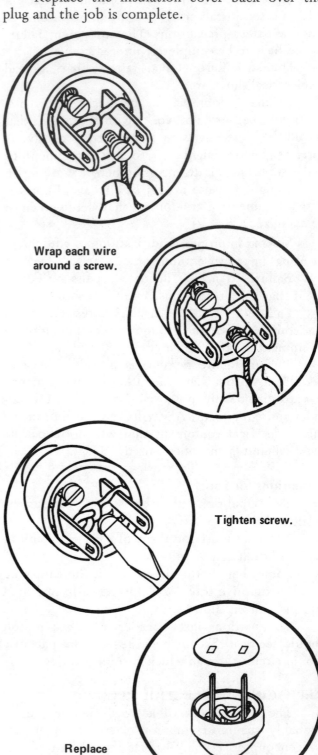

Wrap each wire around a screw.

Tighten screw.

Replace insulation cover.

REPLACING A WORN OUT WALL SWITCH

The first and most important step is to turn off the current. If you don't do this you may not be in any condition to complete the repair. Turn off the current by flipping off the circuit breaker or removing the fuse that controls the circuit to the switch.

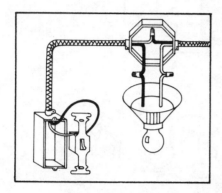

Wiring of a switch that controls a ceiling light.

Remove the cover plate by unscrewing its two screws. You will now have exposed the switch. Remove the top and bottom screws that hold the switch in the box. Gently pull out the switch to expose the two screws that connect the wires to the switch. You will note that one wire is black (or red) and the second wire is white. Usually, the white wire is the ground wire. However, if it is used as a "hot" line, it should be painted black at the end. This is a legal requirement and must be complied with for the purpose of your own safety. "Hot" wires must be either black or painted black.

Loosen the two screws holding the wires in place. This will enable you to remove the switch.

Do not tamper with any other wires you may

When installing a new switch, wrap the wires around the screws in a clockwise direction. Toggle should be "up."

find in the box except those connected to the switch. These wires may feed other lights or outlets and have nothing to do with this switch.

When installing the new switch, connect it in the same way as the old one. Make sure the switch will be in the "off" position when the toggle is down. If you replace the switch with a silent mercury-type switch, look for the word "TOP" stamped on the switch body and install the switch so this word appears on the top.

In making the wire connections, wrap the wires around the screw clockwise; tightening the screws will keep the wires wrapped around the shank of the screw.

THREE-WAY SWITCHES

Almost every home will have at least one pair of three-way switches to control a light from two locations. Sooner or later one of the switches will have to be replaced, and the trouble starts. You install what you know is a brand-new switch, but the system doesn't work properly: you can't turn the light off from both switches, or you can't turn it on from both locations.

The problem? While both switches are three-way units, their construction internally is different, and the external connectors are at different positions. The three-way switch actually is a single-pole, double-throw switch. One of the external connectors will be marked by being black (copper-coated in the Montgomery-Ward Mohican switch) and is indicated in the drawing of the four switches by a black dot. The black wire from the light is connected to this terminal on one of the switches, while the black (hot) wire from the power source is connected to this marked terminal on the other switch.

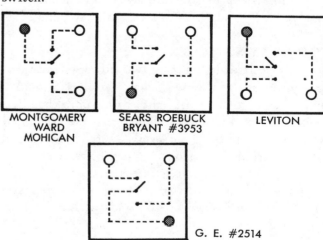

MONTGOMERY WARD MOHICAN

SEARS ROEBUCK BRYANT #3953

LEVITON

G. E. #2514

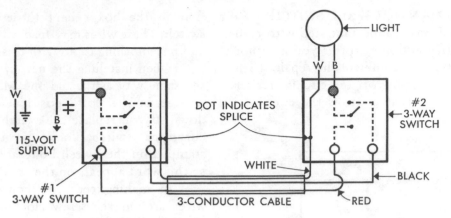

The white wire (neutral, or common ground) is run from the power source through both switches (by means of the white wire in the three-wire conductor used between the switches) to the light, as indicated in the drawing.

The red and black wires of the three-wire conductor are connected to the switches as indicated; the black to each righthand terminal, the red to each lefthand terminal. Thus, if you use two brands of switches, what is "right" of one actually is the bottom or top of another type. Keep these drawings handy when you are replacing three-way switches.

The action of a three-way switch is to transfer the red and black "traveler" wires so as to connect to a "hot" wire on the marked terminal. With switch 1 in the "up" position, the black traveler is hot. Closing switch 2 to "up" lights the lamp. Moving either switch down turns off the lamp. With switch 1 in the "down" position the red traveler is "hot" and moving switch 2 down lights the lamp. When the internal parts of both switches are up or down the lamp will be on, when not the same, the lamp is off.

This is the reason three-way switches are not marked "on" and "off" as are regular switches.

FOUR-WAY SWITCHES

To control lights from two different locations it is necessary to use two 3-way switches. Should it be necessary to control lights from more than two places, then 4-way switches must be combined with 3-way units. The 4-way switches are wired into the circuit between the 3-way units.

The 4-way switch is like a two-pole, double-throw switch. It has a pair of terminals opposite each other, with two on top and two on the bottom edges.

One drawing shows the 4-way switch is closed in the "down" position. Tracing the wires through the switch, the red and black wires enter and leave the switch with no change. Another drawing shows the 4-way switch closed in the "up" position. Tracing the wires through the switch in this configuration it will be noted that the red and black wires have been "swapped" with respect to the entering wires. The entering red wire now is connected to the black wire leaving the switch. Likewise, the entering black wire is now connected to the red wire leaving the switch.

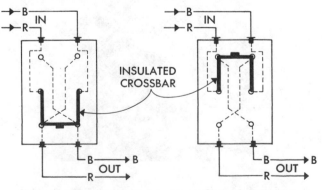

Closed in "down" position.   Closed in "up" position.

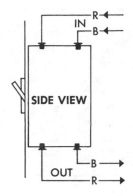

SIDE VIEW

IN
R
B

OUT
B
R

Two 3-way switches for convenient control of one light from two locations are also illustrated. This is the type setup often seen at the foot and head of a stairway, and also just inside doors on opposite sides of a large room where people would be entering or leaving from either door. An outdoor light might also be controlled by two such switches, one being in the house, the other on a patio or at the garage.

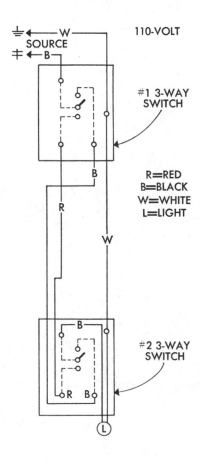

110-VOLT
SOURCE
W
B

#1 3-WAY SWITCH

B

R=RED
B=BLACK
W=WHITE
L=LIGHT

R

W

B

#2 3-WAY SWITCH

R   B

L

**Two 3-way switches control
one light from two locations.**

Two 3-way switches can be combined with a 4-way switch. This arrangement permits controlling a light from three different locations. Detail A shows the 4-way switch in the up position, while in Detail B the 4-way unit is in the down position. Dotted lines show the internal connections of the switches.

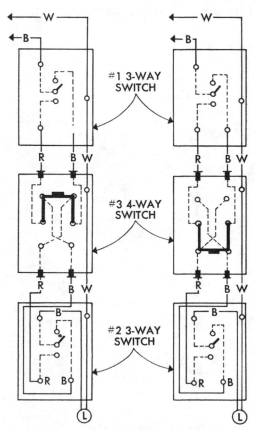

Combined 3-way and 4-way switches.

The red and black "traveler" wires connect together the 3-way and 4-way switches. The white (common) wire runs straight through the switches from the power source to the light. There are no breaks or disconnects in it.

The action of the 3-way switches and the 4-way switch is to transfer (swap) the red and black "traveler" wires as needed to light the lamp. This is done by operating any one of the switches, once the wiring job is completed. The following chart explains the action of the three switches. Reference is made to the internal positions of the switches, not necessarily to their external parts. These switches are not marked "on" or "off" because they can be either on or off in either the up or down position.

When wiring together the 3-way and 4-way switches, three-wire cable must be used. Do not use a two-wire cable with a twisted braid or sheathing with no insulation, as in cables that have a grounding circuit. In a grounding circuit, the bare conductor will never be "hot" unless there is a short circuit; in a circuit with 3-way and 4-way switches the white wire will always carry current.

Sw 1	Sw 3	Sw 2	Light
DOWN	DOWN	DOWN	ON
UP	UP	UP	OFF
UP	DOWN	DOWN	OFF
UP	UP	DOWN	ON
UP	DOWN	UP	ON
DOWN	DOWN	UP	OFF
DOWN	UP	UP	ON
DOWN	UP	DOWN	OFF

12

REMODELING

REMODELING 12

ADDING ON ROOMS ■ BATHROOM REMODELING ■ NEW BEDROOMS

BASEMENT REMODELING ■ ATTIC CONVERSION ■ BREEZEWAY CONVERSION

SCREENED–IN PORCH ■ GOURMET KITCHEN ■ BUILDING STAIRWAYS

ADDING ON ROOMS

A room addition begins with a need, progresses to an idea and is translated into a drawing. A drawing is required in order to obtain the necessary building permit. In most cases an accurate, although fairly rough drawing will be adequate.

After you have completed the drawing plans, you might find it helpful to make a scale model of the house showing the room addition so that you can consider what the completed project will look like.

Plans, or a working drawing, are necessary not only for a building permit, but they are invaluable in getting estimates. Your scale model can be of assistance here, too.

After you have obtained the building permit, you might require financing to either pay a contractor; if you are doing it yourself or contracting parts of the job, you will need funds to pay for building materials.

There are several possibilities open to you regarding the construction of the addition. One, you can hire a contractor to handle the entire job, or to complete only part of it, such as the shell. Two, you can act as your own contractor and hire the various craftsmen. Three, you can do it yourself.

As to financing with a contractor, shop care-fully. Two remodeling companies may quote the same finished price, but the financing cost with one may be several hundred dollars more than the other, with payments over the same period of time. In another instance, you might receive a range in bids from $5200 to $7200. However, the low bid may not include some feature you wish, such as a concrete patio attached to the new room.

Also, check with your local lumber yard for available pamphlets, booklets and information sheets on home remodeling. Your lumber dealer can also arrange for estimates on the cost of remodeling, and usually can recommend contractors who will do a good job at a reasonable cost. In all cases, be sure to get more than one estimate on building costs.

If you decide to be your own contractor you might be able to save considerable money. Get your own bids on labor and the costs of materials. Whereas contractor bids might range from $5200 to $7200, acting as your own contractor the cost might be as low as $4000.

Be sure to avoid two of the pitfalls present when doing your own contracting. One, make sure that the bid from each craftsman, or firm as in the case of a masonry contractor, is a set price. Two, the purchase of materials should be unrelated to the hiring of labor, and each contract so stipulated. This means that it is necessary for you to buy the material and pay for it when it is delivered. Delivery must also be scheduled to meet the working schedules of the various individuals or firms that are contracted to do the work.

Also consider the possibility of hiring a contractor to build the shell, which should include the foundation or basement, the walls with windows and doors, and the roof with roofing applied. You can then finish the inside of the room in complete comfort, no matter what the time of year.

The final option is to do the entire job yourself. If you are somewhat experienced in the various skills necessary to complete the job successfully, you can save a great deal of money. However, if you are not, it is suggested that you consider the other possibilities.

Hiring a contractor to do the entire job will be the most expensive. Contracting the job yourself will reduce the cost, but the least expensive way by far, is to do the work yourself. However, you will in effect, be trading off your time for the money you save.

In the following pages you will see specific examples of room addition jobs which should be of assistance to you in solving your own room addition problem.

ROOM ADDITION #1

The photos in this section show a typical room addition, from the foundation to the roof. You may want a basement under your room addition, but in the case shown, as in many homes, the existing basement was large enough for the needs, and the additional 10 to 20 per cent cost was not considered a worthwhile investment.

The photos show how a room can be built, and even if you do have a contractor put up the shell, they will give you some ideas of what to look for in a quality building. Note especially the care used in making the joint between the existing and new roof and the wall.

First step, unless basement is to be included, is to dig trench, pour footing, build foundation wall of concrete block.

Drain and water lines, plus pipes or tubing for gas supply, if required, are installed inside foundation, (roughed in).

Sill plate of 2 x 4s is fastened to foundation, then "box" of 2 x 8s is spiked to sills and to existing house wall.

Floor joists next are cut and fitted to rest on sill plates, butting snugly against box of 2 x 8s on foundation.

Sheets of plywood now are nailed to the floor joists to make a solid, flat floor. Sheet edges are butted tightly.

Most of the wall sections were built on the floor, then lifted into position. Headers for windows are included here.

Long wall of room addition was built in two sections, each then raised to vertical and spiked through floor to joists.

When wall section was not too big for two men to handle easily, plywood sheathing could be applied on floor.

Wall sections were held plumb, then spiked in place. Note that wire comes up through bottom of wall framing.

Framing of short wall, with headers for windows preinstalled, is finished after wall is erected, to check window height.

Partition in room starts with stud, plumbed and spiked to wall of existing house. Use level frequently to assure plumb.

Tops of walls and partitions are doubled up to create headers on which roof and ceiling beams will rest.

Because of shallow roof pitch, was no attic, so ceiling joists supported no weight; ends toe-nailed to framing.

Ridge pole is supported by two rafters, then the rest of the rafters were cut to length and spiked to wall and ridge.

End rafters are supported by vertical 2 x 4s notched to fit with outside faces flush with rafters, plywood attached.

Following style of existing house, back of roof is flush with rear wall, front has overhang. Rafters trimmed with saw.

End rafter next to house is spiked directly to it, flush with existing end rafter of house. Angle cut in place.

Room addition extended beyond front of house, requiring that wall fit into existing roof. Wall is absolutely level.

Roof of room addition was higher at front than that of house because of extending at front. Flashing is required.

Heavy calking is applied inside wall that rests on roof, 2 x 4 is bedded in calking, to assure a leakproof joint.

Battens are nailed over joints in plywood sheathing. For the best job "back-prime" all battens.

Joints between sheathing and windows are covered with battens. Back-priming is required here, calking would help.

Don't skimp on the roof covering. It takes a beating from wind, sun, rain and snow, should be the best quality.

With room addition pretty well along, it is apparent that small house will have a much bigger look with new room.

426

This was existing door in end wall of house; door is removed, now is entrance to utility room as next photo.

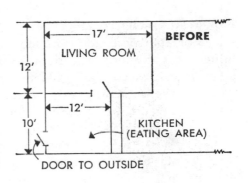

Washer, dryer, refrigerator-freezer and other appliances are in new utility room where they are handy, out of way.

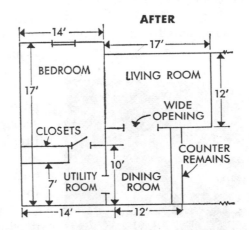

Large-size bedroom at front of room addition has two generous-size closets with sliding doors, room for chairs.

At opposite end of bedroom from closets are two windows, which face front. Note ample room for bed, dresser.

Extending new room forward of existing house provides break in wall to avoid long, uninteresting expanse of wall.

In original arrangement, kitchen-utility room was entered through door directly from living room; was no dining room.

Door from living room was removed, opening widened, and original kitchen now is dining room. Cabinets kept on wall.

ROOM ADDITION #2

For the room addition shown, it was determined that dropping the floor to ground level—a sloping yard was the problem—would be best. Keeping the room on level with the rest of the house would create a useless empty space under the room, and it would be high off the ground and look awkward. Dropping the room to ground level would permit changing a small den in the existing house into an attractive balcony overlooking the new room. An open-beamed ceiling, where the underside of the roof was the finished ceiling, assured a height sufficient for the balcony effect.

Construction started, of course, with the foundation. Its depth and width is determined by local building codes. Because the foundation is so important, the home owner builder checked carefully to be sure he was hiring the best contractor for this job. The footing is poured concrete, on which concrete-block foundation walls are laid plumb and level. It also was necessary to build a wall of block around one edge of the patio, as indicated, so it could be poured flush with the floor of the new room. Provision was made in the foundation of the room for the fireplace and hearth, and in the wall of the patio to provide access to a cleanout below the fireplace. Very careful planning is necessary to allow for these various construction factors. For this reason, unless the room addition is to be simply four walls and a roof, it may pay to hire an architect to draw up the plans. He will consider these various factors

and your subcontractors will not have to tear out some construction and rebuild it because of poor judgment in making up the plans.

Note that in one drawing there are vents installed in the foundation of the house, and an access door to permit storing ladders and other bulky items in the crawl space under the new room.

The floor joists and rough flooring are installed next. In this stage of construction allowance is made for the fireplace. The concrete patio is poured, a form next to the wall of the room providing for a deep footing for the fireplace, as well as an opening for an ash clean-out.

Standard construction, with 2 x 4s on 16-inch centers is used for the walls. Note, however, that a header is located over the wide openings for the sliding glass doors, and over the opening for the fireplace. "Cutting-in" the new roof to the old is a job for a skilled carpenter and, again, the home owner contractor made sure he selected the best for this job.

With the room well along it was time to remove the wall of the existing house. This is another job that calls for skill and care. Not only is it necessary to support the roof while removing this load-bearing wall, but all wires must be carefully removed and rerouted. Water and sewer lines also would have to be relocated if any were in the wall. A double 2 x 12 was used for the header that replaced the support of the wall. Columns cut from 4 x 4s and fitted between the floor of the balcony and the roof, provided additional support. Later, for safety and appearance, a wrought-iron railing was fitted between the columns.

A short stairway was built to lead down from the balcony to the new room, and another leads from the family room down to the existing basement. This ready access will permit future remodeling of the basement.

When the fireplace was completed, paneling was applied to the walls, and plasterboard to the ceiling (underside of the roof). All trim was fitted around windows and doors, and underlayment was nailed to the subflooring. Resilient tile was applied over the underlayment. All these operations could be done by a skilled home craftsman, which could mean a further saving in cost.

A small bay at the back of the room illustrates how a picture window should be located.

Shingle siding, to match that on the existing house was installed on the room addition, and asphalt shingles to match the house further tied the room addition to the home.

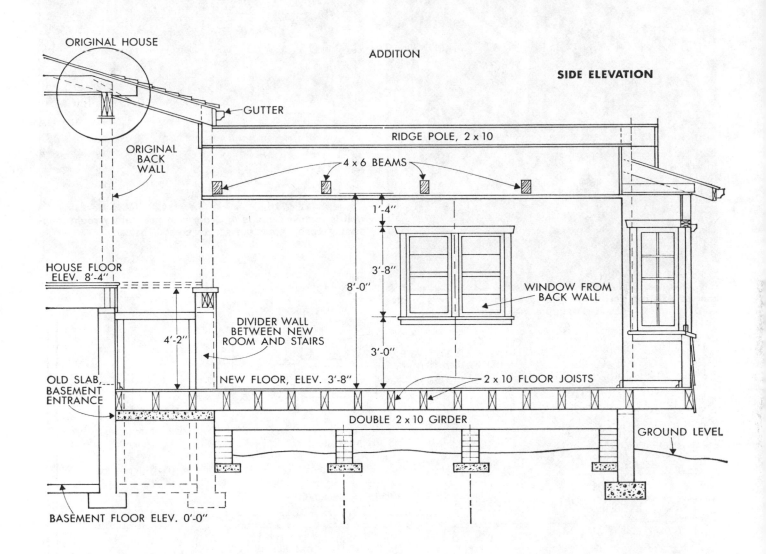

ORIGINAL HOUSE

ADDITION

SIDE ELEVATION

GUTTER

ORIGINAL BACK WALL

RIDGE POLE, 2 x 10

4 x 6 BEAMS

1'-4"

3'-8"

8'-0"

WINDOW FROM BACK WALL

HOUSE FLOOR ELEV. 8'-4"

DIVIDER WALL BETWEEN NEW ROOM AND STAIRS

4'-2"

3'-0"

OLD SLAB, BASEMENT ENTRANCE

NEW FLOOR, ELEV. 3'-8"

2 x 10 FLOOR JOISTS

DOUBLE 2 x 10 GIRDER

GROUND LEVEL

BASEMENT FLOOR ELEV. 0'-0"

Lowest cost foundation is footing with concrete blocks laid on it. Depth and width of footing meets local code.

Construction is standard, angled rafters butted against ridge board, "bird's mouth" notches fit over walls.

Looking through windows of house before wall is removed shows construction of roof and walls with sheathing.

Wall of existing house is stripped of sheathing and insulation, wiring is relocated, supporting beam installed.

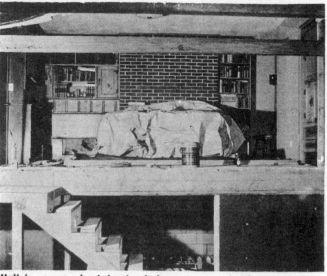

Wall is removed, stairs lead down to new family room, supporting beam is located across created balcony.

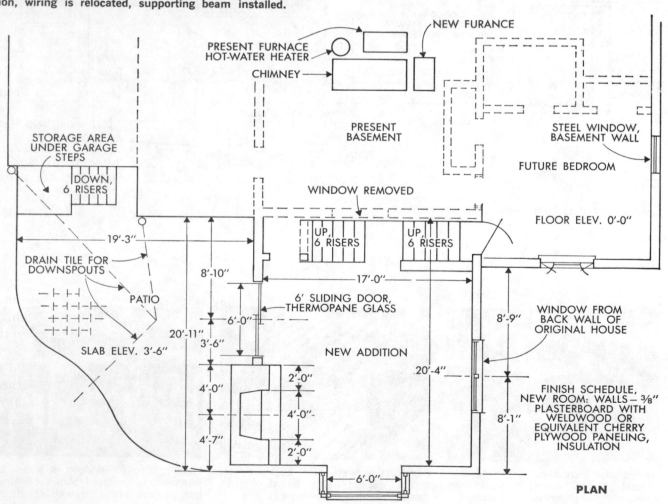

PRESENT FURNACE
HOT-WATER HEATER

NEW FURANCE

CHIMNEY

PRESENT BASEMENT

STEEL WINDOW, BASEMENT WALL

FUTURE BEDROOM

STORAGE AREA UNDER GARAGE STEPS

DOWN, 6 RISERS

WINDOW REMOVED

FLOOR ELEV. 0'-0''

19'-3''

UP, 6 RISERS

UP, 6 RISERS

DRAIN TILE FOR DOWNSPOUTS

PATIO

8'-10''

17'-0''

6' SLIDING DOOR, THERMOPANE GLASS

WINDOW FROM BACK WALL OF ORIGINAL HOUSE

8'-9''

6'-0''

3'-6''

20'-11''

SLAB ELEV. 3'-6''

NEW ADDITION

20'-4''

2'-0''

4'-0''

4'-0''

4'-7''

2'-0''

8'-1''

FINISH SCHEDULE, NEW ROOM: WALLS—3/8'' PLASTERBOARD WITH WELDWOOD OR EQUIVALENT CHERRY PLYWOOD PANELING, INSULATION

6'-0''

PLAN

Roof of addition ties neatly into existing house, patio door is in, opening is for fireplace.

Shingle siding to match that of the house is applied to room addition, will be stained to match.

ROOM ADDITION #3

Adding on a complete half a house might seem like an enormous undertaking, but it's not when you simply consider the project just an "oversize room."

In this situation a concrete block structure, formerly a dairy barn, was later converted to living quarters. The building just did not have enough room for the family, but remodeling a home while you live in it is one of the worst kinds of self-inflicted tortures.

So, the obvious solution was to build on rooms, space that would not be used until completed, while still living in the quarters that were cramped, but livable.

The first step in the project was to draw plans for the new section, including provision for utilizing the front wall of the existing structure. With this kind of remodeling you can let yourself go and plan rooms of a size that you really want, with conveniences you could not otherwise get. The master bedroom is a generous size, and the bathroom is right next to it. This is a complete bath, with tub and shower. The bathroom in the original structure was not changed, but a door was added to permit reaching it from the new family room at the back of the house. Thus, when guests are being entertained in the family room, they need not walk the length of the house to reach a bathroom.

Considerable time should be spent on the planning; once you get up the wood and masonry, changes are difficult, time-consuming and expensive to make. How about exposure? Will the sun shine in the windows too early in the morning, or will it overheat a room through large windows or a sliding-glass door?

What about traffic patterns? Do you have to walk through the living room to reach the kitchen with groceries? Do people walk directly into the living room from outside, bringing mud and dirt? Make sure you have an entry where shoes can be cleaned, raincoats can "drip-dry," overshoes can be removed and allowed to dry.

When you install the front-room door, don't forget to wire for a doorbell or chimes. It's a lot easier to run the wire between the joists and through the door frame during construction, than to fish wire and fight it after the wall is completed. And, don't forget lights at the front door; you may want to run a yard light from the same switch. In the latter case, allow for underground cable to the light.

In the construction shown it was decided to have a crawl space under the new section, as there was a full basement under the existing structure. An area somewhat more than 20 x 48 feet was excavated to below the frost line, the outline of the footings was marked with stakes and strings and the footings dug and poured.

When the footings—slightly wider than the

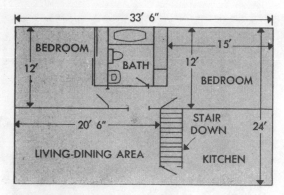

BEFORE

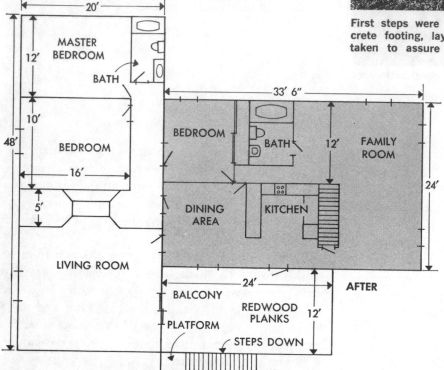

AFTER

First steps were digging out for crawl space, pouring concrete footing, laying up wall of concrete block. Care was taken to assure square corners, plumb foundation walls.

As soon as floor joists were installed and boxed in, sheets of plywood were nailed to them to create a sub floor.

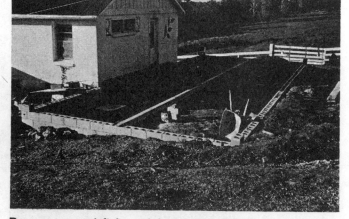

Recesses were left in end foundation walls to accept center beam. Small footings of concrete were poured to support columns on which center portion of beam rested.

With part of sub floor in place it was used to assemble wall sections that then were raised to vertical position.

432

concrete-block wall would be—had set, the concrete block was laid up. In the figuring for the footing, it was leveled so that the concrete-block wall, plus the floor joists, plus the sub and finished floor, would be flush with the floor of the existing building. Here again you had best do your planning and figuring before you do the work.

In the foundation wall shown, recesses were left in each end wall to accept a support beam made of three 2 x 12s spiked together. Three more supports were created for the beam down the center of the foundation by pouring footings, then laying-up concrete block and brick to the correct height.

Floor joists were next. With the use of the center support beam 10-foot lengths of 2 x 12 were used. These shorter beams were much easier to handle than would be 20-foot lengths, and less expensive. The joists were "boxed-in" by 2 x 12s across the front and back of the foundation.

Plywood was used for the subfloor, the 4 x 8-foot sheets (you can get 4 x 10 and 5 x 10-foot sheets in some areas) going down quickly and adding great strength to the structure.

With the subfloor for a working platform, sections of wall were built flat. Window openings were roughed-in, as were those for the door and the fireplace. Stock-size windows were used, and instructions with them showed the required rough openings. The same is true of the door; you can buy doors ready-hung in their frames ready for quick and simple installation.

The wall across the front of the house is 48 feet, which was much too long to be handled in one section, so the wall was built in two pieces. The builder and several friends then stood the sections upright, plumbed them and braced them temporarily in place. The end walls were built the same way, then raised in place.

One problem in building the walls flat is that they must be kept square. You need more than just a 2-foot square on the corners; it is necessary to measure the diagonals to make sure they are equal before nailing on the plywood sheathing. Once the plywood is attached there is practically no movement possible in the stud assembly.

If you are building in good weather, the next step is to build the interior partitions. In an area where weather is uncertain, or if you run into winter weather, you can install the ceiling joists

and build the roof to close in the structure. Interior partitions then are built on the floor and raised into position. This is somewhat more difficult with the ceiling joists in the way, but weather is the determining factor.

If you will use the attic space for storage (even a low attic can be used for this) be sure to frame in an opening for a "disappearing" stairway to permit access to the attic, or at least provide an opening that can be reached with the aid of a stepladder. Be sure, also, to apply insulation to the upper side of the trap door to the attic. An uninsulated sheet of plywood can create a downdraft of cold air in winter.

If you select a hip roof, as on the house shown, you probably will do well to hire a professional roof framer. These carpenters can lay out the rafters quickly and the roof structure can be assembled in a relatively short time. There are other jobs in building a house that may best be left to the professionals; and, in some cases, local building codes will require certain operations to be done by licensed professionals. Electrical work and plumbing are the two areas covered by most building codes.

Sheathing for the roof shown was plywood. Again, the larger sheets go on fast, and they provide tremendous strength to the roof, as well as keeping to a minimum the number of joints.

Provision must be made in the roof to provide ventilation for the attic space. Ventilated soffits under the roof overhang allow air to enter, but there must be outlets near the peak of the roof. These can be the low-profile type, or you may want the kind that rotates in the wind for more positive flow of air.

If your home, or addition, will include a fireplace you might, again, be better off to hire a professional. A chimney for a fireplace must include a smoke shelf, and a damper should be located in the throat just above the fireplace itself to seal out cold air when there is no fire.

The best method, of course, is to use a steel form and build the fireplace around it. These steel forms include a smoke shelf and damper, and the hollow form provides cold and hot-air openings so a room can be heated in mild weather. Some units even have provision for blowers to force the warmed air out into the room—sometimes through the back of the fireplace into an adjacent room.

Hip roof was choice for construction. You may need a carpenter for this operation; at least a well-detailed book.

Sheets of plywood were used for roof sheathing. They install quickly, add tremendous strength, create few seams.

Fireplace was built from rock dug up in a neighboring field. Not many builders have supply this convenient.

Massive fireplace is focal point of front of house. It was built by local fireplace mason to assure good burning.

Good insulation is a must in any construction. After insulation batts were in place, wiring was done.

All wiring for ceiling was done at same time as for walls, so switches, fixtures and junction boxes could be wired.

To assure solid construction and need for as few nails as possible, adhesive was applied to ceiling beams.

Nailing wallboard to ceiling can be a difficult job, but use of simple jigs made of lumber reduced work.

When exterior wall was framed to fit around fireplace, opening was temporarily closed with sheets of plywood.

With the shell of the house built—foundation, floors, walls and roofs—your next job is to install insulation. Here is no place to skimp. Ideally there should be 4 inches of insulation in the walls, 6 inches in the ceiling. In an unheated crawl space it will be necessary to install insulation on the underside of the floor. In the home shown, openings from the basement in the original building provided warm air that eliminated the need for insulation under the floor in the new crawl space.

When it comes to wiring, you have two choices as a do-it-yourselfer: before or after putting in the insulation. If you do the wiring before the insulation is stapled to the studs and joists you do have more room to drill holes and attach receptacle, switch and junction boxes. Drilling necessary holes before the insulation is put in is recommended. This assures you will not drill holes in, or tear, the paper on the insulation batts.

Putting in the wiring before the insulation means you will have to cut, stuff and fit the batts around the wiring, and it will take much more time. The method to use will be the one that works best for you; you may need both, depending on construction scheduling.

Putting up wallboard is best done with adhesive, plus a few nails. With this modern method there are fewer nails to give problems later, when they have to be tapped back in and recovered with spackle. A couple of jigs made from 2 x 4s, as shown in one photo, take a lot of the struggle out of attaching plasterboard to ceilings. Adhesive is used here also, with a few nails to hold the board

until the adhesive sets.

Plumbing is another project where professional help may be needed. If you are in an unincorporated area, or in a city that allows you to do your own work, you can rough-in the plumbing during the construction of the walls. Plastic pipe—if allowed in your city—is easy for the do-it-yourselfer to handle and join. It is ideal for waste, drain and vent lines, but may not be approved for hot-water lines. Some types can be used for cold water.

Wall studs in a bathroom should be 2 x 10s or 2 x 12s, both to permit routing the larger pipes through the wall, and to permit hiding them. Before installing wallboard, of course, check all lines to make sure there are no leaks. Tearing off plasterboard to get at a leaking joint can be a traumatic experience.

Brick and concrete block were used inside fireplace, but natural stone was used to face it inside.

Bathtub is in place, plumbing roughed-in for new bathroom in built-on section of the home. Tub should be covered.

Studs in wall of bathroom are 2 x 10s rather than 2 x 4s, to permit drilling holes for drain and vent lines.

NEW BEDROOM #1

When your family starts outgrowing the house and you don't want to move, or add on, the basement is the logical place to find more living space. You can create an extra bedroom for that growing teenager who needs a room of his own, or a quiet hobby or sewing room, even a guest room.

Minimum cost is the most appealing feature of a basement room. Second is the fact that you can do the building at any time of the year. The third advantage, too often overlooked by a harassed home owner, is the fact that you don't have to finish the whole basement! Close in only the space you need and ignore the rest of the basement. If the laundry room is there, and your workshop, simply close them off to create the new room.

In the situation shown, the bedroom was built immediately at the foot of the stairs leading down from the house. There is a disadvantage in that you must pass through the bedroom to get to the rest of the basement, but additional remodeling later will permit this room to be changed to a sort of entry to the rest of the basement; even a "living room" for the guest using the future bedroom.

In the case shown, the space was first closed in with standard 2 x 4 studding on 16-inch centers. The concrete outside walls were prepared for paneling by attaching furring strips with mastic and concrete nails. The walls of this particular basement were partly out of the ground, and absolutely dry. If there were any moisture problems, the walls would have been waterproofed first.

Special batt insulation just 5/8-inch thick now

Small window is calked, covered with insulation, aluminum foil, sealed with tape, covered with paneling.

Standard 2 x 4 studding forms two walls of new room, mastic used on floor plates; note large closet.

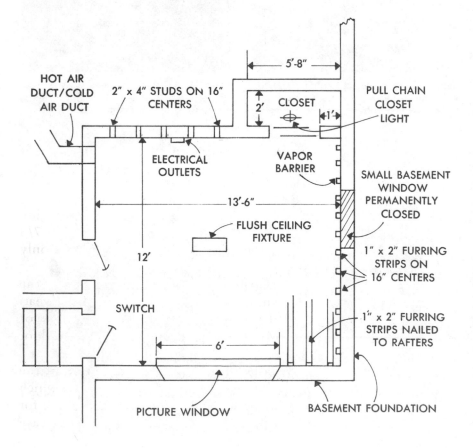

HOT AIR DUCT/COLD AIR DUCT

2" x 4" STUDS ON 16" CENTERS

5'-8"

2'

CLOSET

1'

PULL CHAIN CLOSET LIGHT

ELECTRICAL OUTLETS

VAPOR BARRIER

SMALL BASEMENT WINDOW PERMANENTLY CLOSED

13'-6"

FLUSH CEILING FIXTURE

1" x 2" FURRING STRIPS ON 16" CENTERS

12'

SWITCH

1" x 2" FURRING STRIPS NAILED TO RAFTERS

6'

PICTURE WINDOW

BASEMENT FOUNDATION

Focal point of room is large, airy window, which is framed to match the paneling and molding trim.

Furring strips are attached to concrete walls with 1½-in. concrete nails and builder's mastic.

Ceiling mastic and special clips hold 16-in. ceiling tiles in place. Furring strips are 8 in. apart.

Finished room is bright, attractive. Door on left leads upstairs; right one goes to basement. Note air ducts.

Window provides light and ventilation. Paneling is plastic-coated to resist wear-and-tear of active teenagers and guests.

is available for this type installation, readily fitting between the furring strips. It provides insulation, plus a vapor barrier. The barrier, of course, faces into the room, so that warm, moist air never contacts the cold concrete to cause condensation problems.

One large window in the basement shown was made a focal point for the room, as it overlooked the back yard. A smaller window was simply sealed with insulation and aluminum foil, then covered with paneling.

For the ceiling the furring strips were nailed on 8-inch centers to accept 16-inch tiles. These have additional support at the center by means of a metal clip, thus the 8-inch spacing for the furring.

All wiring now was done, both for receptacles in the walls and lights in the ceiling. No receptacles were installed on the outside walls, as the minimum depth for a receptacle box is about 1-7/8 inches and the furring plus the paneling is only about 1 inch.

Plastic-coated paneling was chosen for the room shown, because of its resistance to the wear-and-tear of an active teenager, plus its ease of cleaning. Matching molding was applied at floor and ceiling.

Vinyl-asbestos tile was put down before the lower molding was attached to the walls, which allowed leaving a small space along the edges for expansion. The tile also was chosen for its easy cleaning and long-wearing qualities.

Because this was to be a bedroom, generous closets were designed and built. Sliding doors require no room space for opening, and are an obvious choice for a small room.

Doors to the stairway and to the rest of the basement were regular hinged doors.

Because of the basement location, running hot and cold-air ducts to the room was relatively simple, and the openings into the room were designed into the walls and the registers bought along with the materials for the room.

Something to keep in mind when planning the room: if you do figure on further remodeling in the future, be sure to locate wiring, plumbing, heating, etc. so that it can be routed to the future rooms. For the same reason, be sure to locate doors properly so you don't have to remove them and replace them somewhere else when the remodeling begins.

NEW BEDROOM #2

A fully adequate bedroom can be built in a narrow space such as a playroom, no longer serving its original purpose, or an enclosed porch. The photos show two ends of a boy's room only 8 feet wide. A cabinet comprising drawers, shelving and a wardrobe closet occupies one end. Existing high windows required no alteration of position. At the other end, adjustable shelving on the walls permitted the trundle beds to be pushed into a corner.

The first step is to remove wallpaper, baseboard and other trim, installing whatever wiring and heating ducts or pipes may be necessary, then patching the plaster or wallboard to come flush with adjacent surfaces. Next, an uneven floor should be covered with underlayment if tile or sheet flooring is to be used.

The method of cabinet framing was selected because of its simplicity. Width dimensions are variable. Most of the framework consists of ¾-inch plywood and stock sizes of lumber. If a natural wood finish is desired, the exposed wood and plywood should match the wall planking. Rear rails and other rear horizontal framing pieces are mortised into the plywood sides and partitions. Corresponding rails and frame members across the front are similarly mortised except at the wardrobe closet. Its side is notched only for the toe space, ¾ inch less than the other partitions since it is ¾ inch narrower. The front rail is nailed to its edges, without mortising, as are the vertical trim pieces that conceal the plywood edge.

Although the height of 75 inches is given for the closet to accommodate a 6-foot door, it will be better, if there is an adjacent room door, to have the closet door the same height. Closet height then will be 2-3/8 inches more than that of the door. If desired, the closet can be extended to the ceiling, a plywood panel or planking filling the space above the door. Should ordinary plywood, not matching the wall planking, be used for the closet side, it can later be covered with planking.

After assembling the outside framework, the drawer supports are glued and nailed in place, pilot holes drilled for the finishing nails. These pieces are 2 inches wide to come flush with the under edges of the front and rear frame pieces, and project 3/8 inch above them; center them accurately. A filler strip flush with the edge of the cabinet end that adjoins a wall will prevent drawers from scraping on the wall. Thickness of this strip should be ¼ to ½ inch more than the planking.

Now the cabinet can be moved into the corner and the top rail is fastened with nails driven through the wallboard into the studs at four or five points. Glue-coated shims are driven under the lower edges of framing not in firm contact with the floor. Then the plywood top, which extends 1 inch beyond the front rail, is nailed down. A prop is wedged under unsupported portions of the rails while nailing. Later, just before applying wall planking, the cabinet top is covered with plastic laminate.

Cabinet shelving may be 3/8- or ¾-inch plywood glued and nailed to a frame of ¾-inch stock. The shelving is supported by cleats on the rear wall, on the side of the wardrobe closet and on the partition separating that shelving from the drawers. A cleat, centered on the underside of the top shelf, at the front, extends 3/8 inch to hold magnetic cabinet catches to be installed later.

The vertical trim and door-frame pieces for the closet can be installed now, followed by the door-frame pieces on the room wall, and the top of

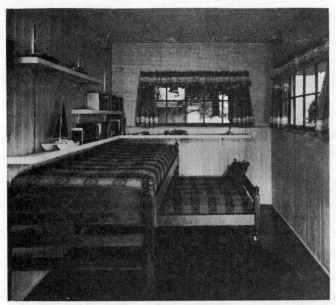

Trundle beds moved into corner and wall shelves that replace bookcases permit maximum utilization of floor space.

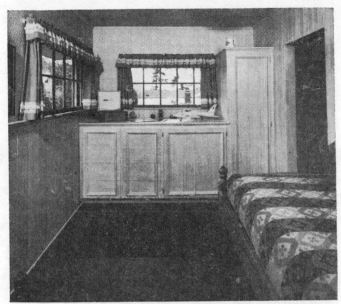

Cabinet at other end has spacious drawers, shelving and wardrobe closet. Molding serves as drawer and door pulls.

the closet. Should the piece on the room wall come directly over a stud, it is nailed to it, but this is not likely, and toggle bolts or other anchors will be needed for attachment to plaster or wallboard at points about 12 inches apart. If the wall is slightly uneven the door-frame piece should be shimmed so that it will be perfectly straight and parallel to the frame on the plywood wall. The thickness of this piece may be influenced by door width. The top end is notched for a neat fit of the top cross member. Edges of the top are concealed with molding. The cleat on the room wall supporting the top should be wide enough to take supports for the clothes-hanger rod.

Drawer fronts are ¾-inch stock rabbeted as shown or may be two pieces of 3/8-inch stock joined with glue and screws. The four rabbets on each drawer are of different widths. Those at the meeting ends of adjacent drawers are 1-13/16 inch wide while those at the outside ends are 1-5/8 inch wide. Edges of drawer fronts that are exposed when they are shut are slightly rounded. Drawer width X is 13/16 inch less than space between partitions for rollers and clearance. Length of drawer fronts is X plus 1-13/16 inch, which allows 1/16 inch clearance between meeting ends. A groove to take the plywood bottom is cut 3/16 inch deep in the front, sides and back, 3/8 inch above the lower edges. When assembling, the bottom is glued in the grooves to assure rigidity. The

recess in the back for the roller is cut before assembly. Each drawer has four rollers.

Molding is used instead of drawer pulls. After drilling holes through the drawer fronts for flat-head screws that just project into the molding ¼ or 3/8 inch, epoxy glue is applied to the molding and the screws are driven home to draw up the molding snugly.

The doors can be made of 3/8-inch plywood adhered to a frame of the same thickness with glue and screws. This plywood also should have a face veneer matching the drawer fronts and planking. Edges are slightly rounded to match the drawer fronts. At meeting edges of the doors, the frame and plywood come flush. The plywood projects 3/8 inch beyond the frame at the hinge edges and ¾ inch at top and bottom. Molding similar to that on the drawer fronts serves for door pulls.

Hanging the closet door completes the job except for the clothes-hangar rod and the shelf. A clearance of 1/16 inch is allowed at each edge of the door. You can use a ¾-inch plywood door that that is less than 18 inches wide. A prefabricated door, 1-3/8 inches thick, is better than plywood if the door opening is wider, as some warping is likely with plywood. The front of the door is fitted with the same molding used on the drawers and cabinet doors. Magnetic catches at the top and bottom will hold the door closed firmly.

In the case illustrated, the windowless walls

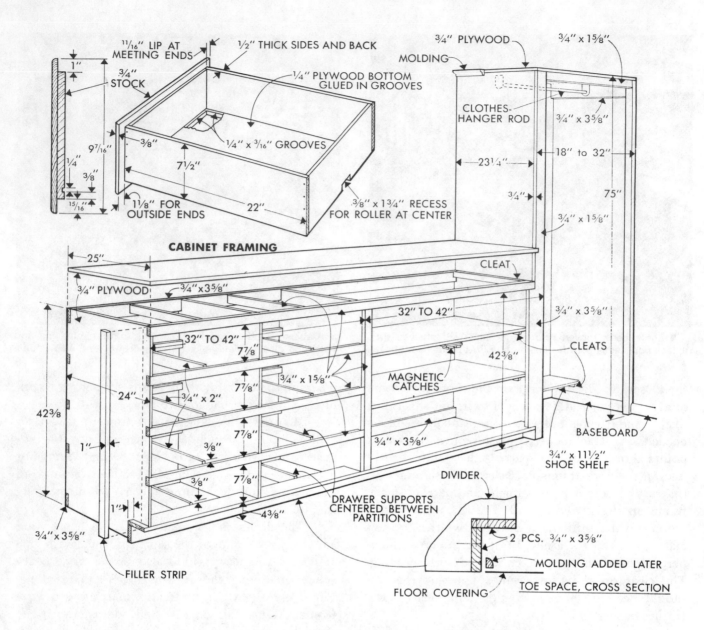

CABINET FRAMING

¹¹⁄₁₆″ LIP AT MEETING ENDS
1″
³⁄₄″ STOCK
½″ THICK SIDES AND BACK
¼″ PLYWOOD BOTTOM GLUED IN GROOVES
³⁄₄″ PLYWOOD
MOLDING
³⁄₄″ x 1⁵⁄₈″
9⁷⁄₁₆″
³⁄₈″
¼″ x ³⁄₁₆″ GROOVES
CLOTHES-HANGER ROD
³⁄₄″ x 3⁵⁄₈″
¼″
³⁄₈″
7½″
18″ to 32″
¹⁵⁄₁₆″
1¹⁄₈″ FOR OUTSIDE ENDS
22″
³⁄₈″ x 1³⁄₄″ RECESS FOR ROLLER AT CENTER
23¼″
³⁄₄″
75″
³⁄₄″ x 1⁵⁄₈″

25″
³⁄₄″ PLYWOOD
³⁄₄″ x 3⁵⁄₈″
CLEAT
³⁄₄″ x 3⁵⁄₈″
32″ TO 42″
32″ TO 42″
7⁷⁄₈″
42³⁄₈
24″
³⁄₄″ x 2″
³⁄₄″ x 1⁵⁄₈″
42³⁄₈″
MAGNETIC CATCHES
CLEATS
7⁷⁄₈″
³⁄₈″
³⁄₄″ x 3⁵⁄₈″
BASEBOARD
1″
7⁷⁄₈″
³⁄₈″
³⁄₄″ x 11½″ SHOE SHELF
1″
DIVIDER
³⁄₄″ x 3⁵⁄₈″
4³⁄₈″
DRAWER SUPPORTS CENTERED BETWEEN PARTITIONS
2 PCS. ³⁄₄″ x 3⁵⁄₈″
MOLDING ADDED LATER
FILLER STRIP
FLOOR COVERING
TOE SPACE, CROSS SECTION

were covered entirely with ¾-inch tongue-and-groove planking. This is adhered to the walls with a special adhesive applied with a gun. Each plank is checked for true vertical position and may require light tapping. On walls that have high windows, the planking is carried up to a horizontal strip ¾ inch wide and as thick as the planking. The top of this strip should come ½ inch below the windowsill if the ½-inch molding is to be added to serve as a sill. The strip should be uniformly straight and level, and the nails fastening it are driven into studs. The planking is pushed up to fit tightly against the strip by using a wedge for which a chisel will serve.

Short lengths of planking above the cabinet are applied after the top has been covered with plastic laminate.

Two types of molding are used to give a neat, finished appearance over the strip that tops the planking. Corner molding is used where walls meet the ceiling and a baseboard goes on at floor level. All the planking, the cabinet and the trim are sanded and finished natural to have a low luster. After the floor has been cleaned thoroughly it can be covered with tile, sheet flooring or carpeting, after which baseboard molding is applied and finished.

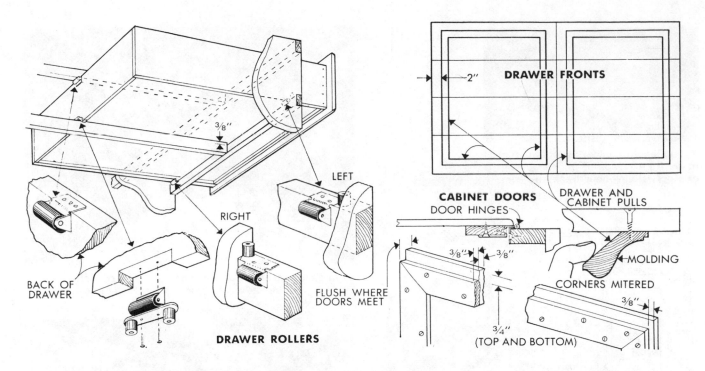

LEFT

RIGHT

FLUSH WHERE DOORS MEET

BACK OF DRAWER

DRAWER ROLLERS

2"

DRAWER FRONTS

CABINET DOORS

DOOR HINGES

DRAWER AND CABINET PULLS

3/8"   3/8"

MOLDING

CORNERS MITERED

3/8"

3/4"
(TOP AND BOTTOM)

3/8"

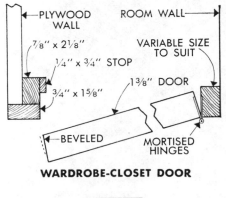

PLYWOOD WALL

ROOM WALL

7/8" x 2 1/8"

VARIABLE SIZE TO SUIT

1/4" x 3/4" STOP

1 3/8" DOOR

3/4" x 1 5/8"

BEVELED

MORTISED HINGES

WARDROBE-CLOSET DOOR

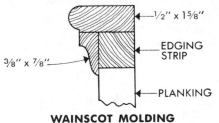

1/2" x 1 5/8"

EDGING STRIP

3/8" x 7/8"

PLANKING

WAINSCOT MOLDING

Using gun to apply ribbon of paneling adhesive to back of planking for firm attachment to plaster or wallboard.

As each plank is being adhered to wall it is gently tapped to the plumb position as indicated with a level.

BATHROOM REMODELING

The bathroom of your home is probably the only room in the house that is used every day by all members of the family. If you are thinking about remodeling your bathroom, the project examples that follow should give you some suggestions on how to plan for and achieve convenience and attractive appearance.

REMODELED BATHROOM

It may not be necessary to go to the expense of replacing major fixtures in a bathroom to give it a new and attractive appearance. The existing white fixtures (tub, lavatory and toilet) and cabinets can be retained and the room made to look completely new, with improved lighting and more storage space. During the remodeling job worn or

Full-length cabinet above lavatory is made from scraps of paneling, lengths of stock, sliding-door track and trim.

In this instance, door in wall that divided bath was extended to ceiling to create more light, spacious feeling.

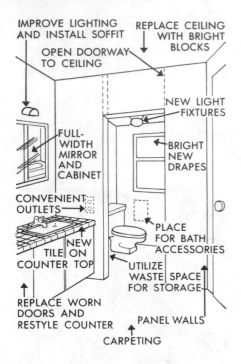

IMPROVE LIGHTING AND INSTALL SOFFIT

OPEN DOORWAY TO CEILING

REPLACE CEILING WITH BRIGHT BLOCKS

NEW LIGHT FIXTURES

FULL-WIDTH MIRROR AND CABINET

BRIGHT NEW DRAPES

CONVENIENT OUTLETS

NEW TILE ON COUNTER TOP

PLACE FOR BATH ACCESSORIES

UTILIZE WASTE SPACE FOR STORAGE

REPLACE WORN DOORS AND RESTYLE COUNTER

PANEL WALLS

CARPETING

Soffit is built above the tub and the lavatory, both for better lighting and for cozier feeling and appearance.

undesirable materials are replaced.

This means you must take a good look at the fixtures. If any of the major units are chipped, cracked or damaged so they cannot be repaired, they should be replaced now. If you wait until you finish the bathroom remodeling, then decide that the new surroundings have made a fixture look unsuitable, you will have a major project on your hands and much work will have to be redone. This would be false economy in time, money and materials. Take a good look! Perhaps one of the new epoxy spray paints can restore the fixture.

Planning Your Job

Bathrooms vary in shape considerably, and it is unlikely that your room will duplicate the one shown in this example. The ideas and improvements shown in these two versions, however, can be adapted to your situation with very little change.

First, thoroughly examine the room and the condition of the walls, floors, cabinets, counter tops and fixtures before making a rough sketch of how you want the finished job to appear. And, as previously stated, be sure of the condition of the major fixtures. Before you start is the time to replace them.

The styling shown is contemporary, but variations in wall paneling, counter top tile, mural design, cabinet hardware, curtain material, carpeting and light fixtures will make the design French provincial, early-American, Traditional or whatever you wish.

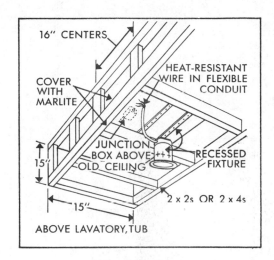

16" CENTERS

HEAT-RESISTANT WIRE IN FLEXIBLE CONDUIT

COVER WITH MARLITE

JUNCTION BOX ABOVE OLD CEILING

RECESSED FIXTURE

15"

15"

2 x 2s OR 2 x 4s

ABOVE LAVATORY, TUB

Ingenious metal clips are used to hold Hardboard panels directly to studs spaced close on soffit above tub.

Start the job by removing old materials from the walls and ceilings. Work on area you can handle conveniently.

Hardboard panels 16 in. wide are cut in short lengths and slipped behind moldings in places such as soffit.

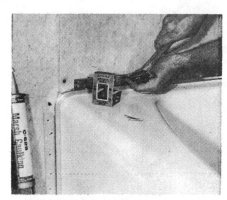

Special preformed metal moldings create a neat, watertight joint between the wall paneling and the tub contour.

Short lengths of 2 x 4 between wall studs create recess in which storage niche is formed from scraps of panel.

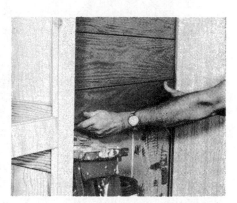

For variety, impression of length, paneling can be installed horizontally. Note roughed-in corner storage at left.

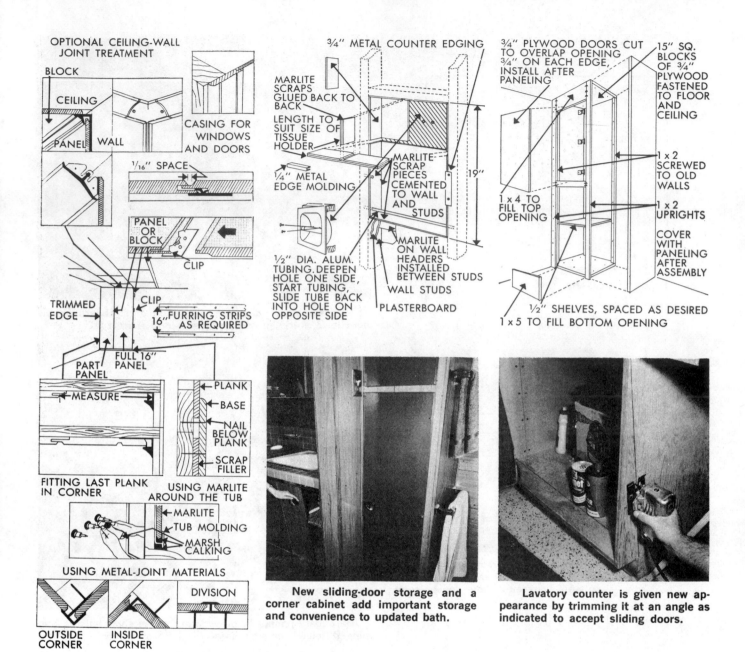

New sliding-door storage and a corner cabinet add important storage and convenience to updated bath.

Lavatory counter is given new appearance by trimming it at an angle as indicated to accept sliding doors.

Because a job this big can easily stretch over a period of several weeks, even months, during which time you will undoubtedly have to use the room, it is important to plan the work to cause minimum disruption at any given time.

Wiring

You may want to add lighting fixtures and convenience outlets as part of the remodeling; a shaver outlet near the lavatory counter, flush lights in the soffits and perhaps a vent fan. Check your local codes to make sure any wiring you do is safe in the high-moisture condition of the bathroom. Generally, flush lights should be installed with junction boxes and special heat-resistant wire. Shower lights should be gasketed fixtures designed especially for the purpose. All outlets and wall switches should be grounded. If you have any doubts about the wiring, hire a qualified electrician to do the job.

Paneling

In the bathroom shown the walls were previously finished in a combination of wood paneling, tile and painted plasterboard, all of which were worse for wear. The framing in the entire room had first been covered with plasterboard, which made a good base for the new materials. All the old panel-

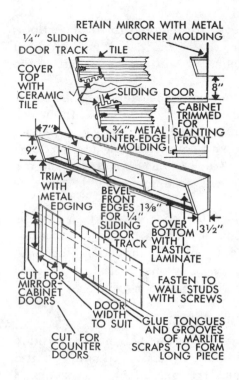

RETAIN MIRROR WITH METAL CORNER MOLDING
1/4" SLIDING DOOR TRACK
TILE
COVER TOP WITH CERAMIC TILE
SLIDING DOOR
8"
CABINET TRIMMED FOR SLANTING FRONT
3/4" METAL COUNTER-EDGE MOLDING
7"
9"
TRIM WITH METAL EDGING
BEVEL FRONT EDGES 1 3/8" FOR 1/4" SLIDING DOOR TRACK
COVER BOTTOM WITH PLASTIC LAMINATE
3 1/2"
CUT FOR MIRROR-CABINET DOORS
DOOR WIDTH TO SUIT
FASTEN TO WALL STUDS WITH SCREWS
CUT FOR COUNTER DOORS
GLUE TONGUES AND GROOVES OF MARLITE SCRAPS TO FORM LONG PIECE

When old tile on lavatory top is removed, all traces of old mastic must be scraped off before applying new tile.

Bright new ceramic tile is installed using ceramic-tile cement. Position and trim all pieces of tile before cementing.

Colored grouts are easily applied and wiped off with household sponge. Variety of colors add sparkle.

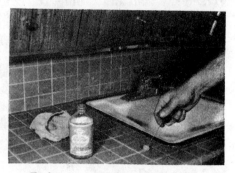

To keep grout clean and stain-free, seal it with special silicone-base sealer that is applied with cotton-swab.

Matching Marlite trim and new carpeting add final touch to modernized bathroom that now is luxurious.

ing and tile were removed and loose paint was scraped away. The same procedure can be used on plastered walls, as long as they are solid and smooth after loose paint and paper are removed. Horizontal furring strips spaced 16 inches apart should be used on new construction, and also will be required to plumb and true any crooked existing walls. When only short spaces are to be paneled as the face of the soffit, hardboard panels can be applied directly to the studs.

The Marlite panels used on the project shown are 3/4 inch thick with a textured wood grain and tongue-and-groove edges. The panels are 16 inches wide to match stud spacing and are random-grooved so joints look like grooves. No nails are used; the paneling is glued to the wall and held with special metal clips that hook into the joint grooves. The joint clips can be nailed directly through an existing plaster wall into the studs. A complete series of metal corners, edges and division molding are available, as are molded base and casing strips. The 16-inch panels also can be obtained in solid colors and patterns. Many of the designs are also made in 4 x 8-foot sheets as well as other sizes.

Because the 16-inch hardboard panels and deeply-textured design sheets are not recommended for high-moisture areas, as around a tub and shower, 1/8-inch Travertine marble-pattern sheet material was used at the ends of the tub, across the wall next to the tub, while a sheet of plain white was used on the soffit. This contrasted nicely with the wormy chestnut textured Marlite on the remainder of the walls and on the cabinet doors.

Special contoured moldings are supplied for fitting the material around the tub. Special mastic made by the panel manufacturer should be used to adhere the material to the walls, and a special caulking is required to assure watertight joints. These procedures are fully explained in the instruction material that is packed with the paneling.

Hardboard ceiling block comes in a variety of colors and patterns, is ¼ inch thick and 16 inches square. Each tile has tongue-and-groove edges for easy installation. The satin-finish plastic coating is easy to wipe clean.

If a narrow edge molding is to be used between the wall and ceiling, the ceiling blocks are installed first, then the wall paneling. If a clip-on cove molding is used, the wall paneling may be done first.

The ceiling blocks are glued and clipped in place much the same as the 16-inch wall panels. Wall paneling is started in a corner and worked around the room. Important installation details are shown.

Cabinet Work

Two cabinet jobs should be done as part of the paneling job: the convenience niche and the corner storage cabinet. The lavatory counter can be changed after the paneling is complete.

The convenience niche is made by facing a recess between two studs with scraps of paneling.

BASEMENT REMODELING

Conversion of wasted basement space is about the most economical way to get extra living area in a home. If you have a problem of water leakage or dampness in your basement, this must be eliminated before starting the conversion. A dry, warm room in a basement is as healthful a living space as any other part of a house.

LIVABLE BASEMENT

Planning

Start with a plan made to scale, ¼ or ½ inch to the foot. You'll find it convenient to use paper already crosslined in squares. Called "graph paper" it is available in stationery stores. Reproduce the basement floor plan, showing stairway, windows, heating plant, laundry equipment, etc. The posi-

Metal counter edge can be used for trim. A floor-to-ceiling cabinet can be made of ¾-inch plywood faced with paneling. It will appear as part of the wall.

A sliding-door, over-the-counter cabinet may be installed in conjunction with a full-width mirror. This unit is made of ¾-inch plywood. Edges are faced with counter edging and the doors slide in regular ¼-inch sliding-door track. The top may be covered with tile to match the lavatory counter.

By trimming the front edges of an existing counter you can achieve a matching slanting-front, sliding-door unit. Sliding doors for both cabinets are made by gluing pieces of paneling together, then cutting into door-size pieces.

Tile Laying

After scraping off the old mastic, position the tile and do any necessary trimming. After the tile is down, try one of the new colored grouting materials, and for maximum protection seal the grout.

Carpeting

Many of the new synthetic carpets are ideal for bathrooms. Installation with a rubber pad can be made directly over old floor tile. If the carpet is to be glued to the floor, it must be scrubbed thoroughly to remove the old wax.

tion of girders, pipes and ducts can be indicated by dotted lines, and girder posts by circles. Then, rule in the location of partitions you wish to install, and also the locations of electrical outlets and plumbing fixtures. If you need insulation, such as used in most house walls, indicate the added 4-inch thickness. Planning is influenced by the position and size of the furniture; also by built-in cabinets, benches, bunks, game equipment and other items. You may also have to make provisions for auxiliary heating equipment.

Level Floors

Many basements in newer homes have no floor drains, but most older basements have one or more. The slope of a floor toward a drain may be enough to interfere with the placement of furniture and also be inconvenient for walking. If the

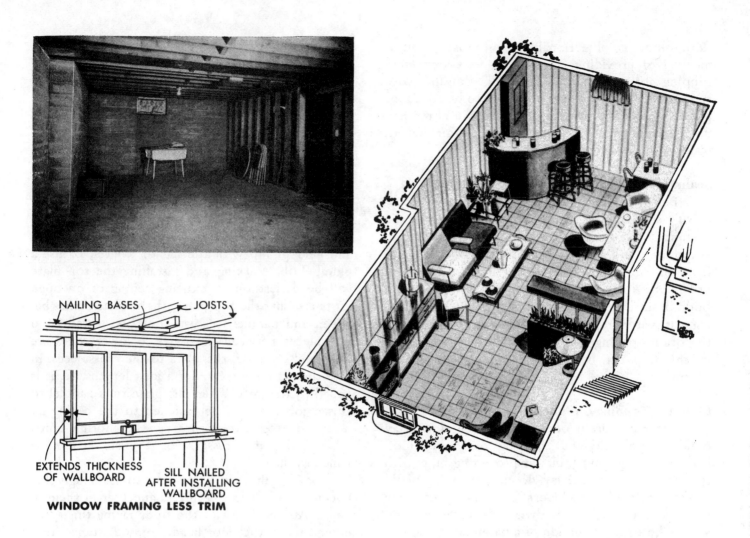

WINDOW FRAMING LESS TRIM

NAILING BASES   JOISTS

EXTENDS THICKNESS OF WALLBOARD   SILL NAILED AFTER INSTALLING WALLBOARD

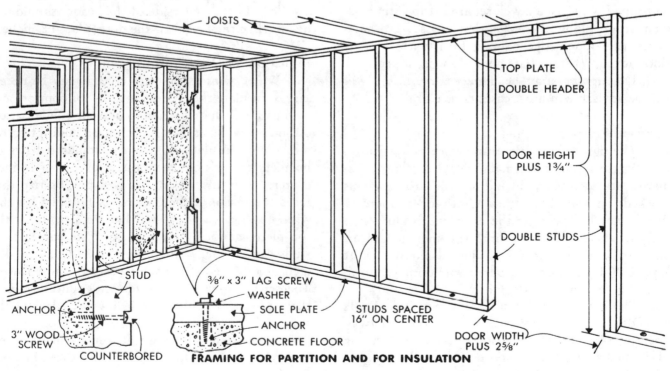

JOISTS

TOP PLATE
DOUBLE HEADER

DOOR HEIGHT PLUS 1¾"

DOUBLE STUDS

STUD

3/8" x 3" LAG SCREW
WASHER
SOLE PLATE
ANCHOR
CONCRETE FLOOR

ANCHOR

3" WOOD SCREW

COUNTERBORED

STUDS SPACED 16" ON CENTER

DOOR WIDTH PLUS 2⅝"

FRAMING FOR PARTITION AND FOR INSULATION

floor slope is objectionable, the most practical method of providing a level surface is a concrete topping not less than 2 inches thick. You may wish to top a floor only where a room is to be added, or possibly the entire basement floor. The latter may involve raising the heating plant, water heater, water softener and other items.

Sealing Floor Drains

Before a floor is topped, floor drains no longer of use should be sealed. This will prevent the entrance of sewer gas in case the water in the trap evaporates, and also will prevent backflow of water from an overloaded sewer if the house drain is not provided with a backwater valve. You can seal a floor drain by removing the perforated lid, pumping out water from the trap and then filling it and the drain opening with concrete. Let the concrete in the trap set before adding more to fill the opening.

Concrete Topping on Floor

After the drain opening has been closed, lay builders' polyethylene sheeting over the floor, sealing overlaps and joints at projecting pipes with special cement. Next, lay down reinforcing mesh, as used for walks and floors, then lay the concrete topping—a 1:2¼:3 mix with as little water as necessary. Where only a section of a basement floor is to be topped, you place a well secured stop form of 2-inch stock along the edge that crosses the basement, the upper edge coming flush with the new floor level. Where a basement floor is sloped only slightly, topping may be unnecessary, but it will still be advisable in most cases to seal drains.

Partition Framing

The figure shows the framework of a partition to separate a new room from the rest of the basement. Its position, including the doorway, is marked on the floor first. Width of a doorway should not be less than the door width plus 2-5/8 inches, which allows for jamb thickness and clearance, so that jambs can be adjusted plumb. Use at least a 30-inch door in a basement room, as furniture will be moved through it.

The partition sole plate consists of two 2 x 4s extending from opposite walls to the doorway opening. Mark off the location of studs at a spacing of 16 inches on center, and double studs on either side of the doorway. Make crosses at points to bore ½-inch holes for lag screws, one on either side of the doorway and others spaced 5 or 6 feet apart. Mark through these holes on the floor for drilling to take anchors for 3/8-inch lag screws. Holes in the floor are bored with a carbide-tipped bit in an electric drill. Fasten down the sole plate with 3/8 x 3-inch lag screws fitted with washers under the heads.

The top plate of a partition comes directly over the sole plate. Mark its position with the aid of a straight 2 x 4 set on or next to the sole plate and held plumb with the aid of a level, or use a plumb bob. Marking and installing the top plate will be easiest on an existing ceiling or on open joists crossing the top plate. If the plate comes between and parallel to joists you first install 2 x 6 crosspieces between the joists so lower edges are flush and then nail the plate to the crosspieces. In case the plate comes under a joist lengthwise, it is nailed to the joist. When the plate runs parallel to closed joists, it can be fastened to the ceiling by means of toggle or other type anchoring bolts. When the plate crosses closed joists, it can be nailed to them.

Saw each stud separately to fit snugly between the top and sole plates and toenail them in place. At the doorway the studs facing this space extend up to the floor header only. Distance from the floor to the underside of the header should not be less than the height of the door plus 1¾ inches.

Insulation for Outside Walls

Where winters are very cold it may be necessary to insulate the basement walls for comfort and to provide a vapor barrier to prevent condensation on masonry surfaces. A common and effective method of insulating is to use standard batts or blankets that fit between studs spaced on 16-inch centers. This insulation has a vapor barrier that faces the inside of the basement. Framing for this with 2 x 4 stock is erected like a partition. If the top plate cannot be fastened to joists, some of the studs can be anchored to the wall by means of 4½-inch wood screws or machine screws and anchors. The screw holes in the studs are counterbored so the screw heads will come below the edges of the studs.

When framing for insulation it will be necessary to extend window framing; also that of a door

Framing for planter shown. Overhead frame hides heating ducts, houses electric lights.

Screw-type nail driven into mortar of brick or concrete-block wall holds furring strips for panel application.

On cast-concrete walls, dowels driven snugly into drilled holes serve as anchors for nails holding furring.

Stapling is faster than nailing to attach soft ceiling tile to furring strips here crossing joists at right angle.

Tongue-and-groove edges of this wall paneling conceal clips that hold it in place on horizontal furring strips.

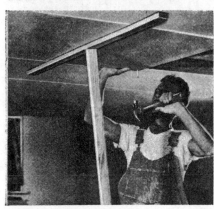

Large, unwieldy panel is held against joists for nailing after wedging prop between floor and panel.

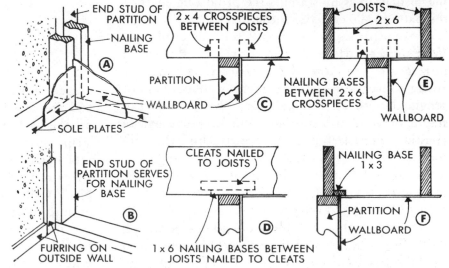

Nailing bases for wallboard, A where partition poins framing, B where it joins furring, C, D where it crosses joists, E between joists, F under joist.

449

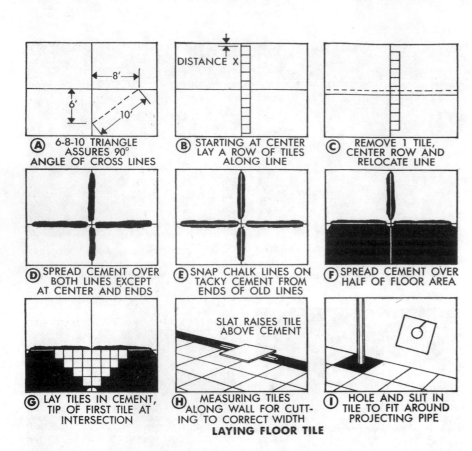

A 6-8-10 TRIANGLE ASSURES 90° ANGLE OF CROSS LINES

B STARTING AT CENTER LAY A ROW OF TILES ALONG LINE

C REMOVE 1 TILE, CENTER ROW AND RELOCATE LINE

D SPREAD CEMENT OVER BOTH LINES EXCEPT AT CENTER AND ENDS

E SNAP CHALK LINES ON TACKY CEMENT FROM ENDS OF OLD LINES

F SPREAD CEMENT OVER HALF OF FLOOR AREA

G LAY TILES IN CEMENT, TIP OF FIRST TILE AT INTERSECTION

H MEASURING TILES ALONG WALL FOR CUTTING TO CORRECT WIDTH

I HOLE AND SLIT IN TILE TO FIT AROUND PROJECTING PIPE

LAYING FLOOR TILE

Avoid getting cement between edges of floor tile by laying them in place without sliding them.

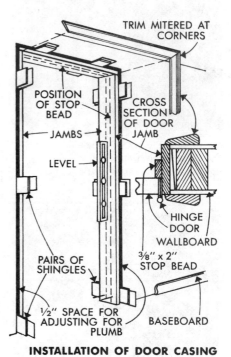

INSTALLATION OF DOOR CASING

if one is located in the wall. Details of doing this depend on the existing window and door installation. The illustration shows how this can be done for windows having wood frames. Be sure the window can be opened when framed in.

If there is any wiring to be done along the outside walls, such as for wall outlets and switches, this should be done before the insulation is put in place. The best and quickest method of fastening the insulation is by stapling the projecting edges of the batts to the edges of the studs.

Some types of wallboard serve as insulation. If this gives sufficient protection it is attached to furring strips on the walls, eliminating the more costly use of 2 x 4 stock. If the wallboard is not provided with an integral vapor barrier you can staple or cement aluminum foil or polyethylene sheeting over the furring before attaching the wallboard.

Furring Outside Walls

In case no insulation is required, the walls may be left as they are and painted for appearance. For a more luxurious effect, cover the walls with wallboard or planking to suit your taste and pocketbook. To attach this, 1 x 3 furring strips are ar-

ranged either vertically or horizontally on the wall and are spaced according to the recommendations of the wallboard manufacturer. Vertical furring strips spaced 16 inches on center are used for attachment of 4 x 8-foot panels. Usually furring strips can be held securely on brick and concrete-block walls by using 6 or 8d screw-type nails driven into mortar joints. Where the mortar is too hard for nail penetration, drill holes with a carbide-tipped masonry bit for snugly-fitting dowels to take the nails. The same method is used on poured-concrete walls. Where walls have been waterproofed, use specially designed devices to avoid breaking the seal.

It is important to have the surfaces of the furring strips in the same plane so the wallboard will be flat without humps or hollows. At low spots on the wall use shims, such as shingles, between it and the furring. High spots on the wall, such as caused by excess mortar, sometimes can be chipped down or the thickness of the furring reduced.

Hiding Pipes and Ducts

Groups of parallel pipes and heat ducts below joist level can be boxed in for better appearance. The example shows how 2 x 2 framing hides two projecting duct elbows and also encloses lights to illuminate the planter below it. The bottom of the enclosure later is fitted with a removable frosted glass. The finished arrangement is also shown. Adjustable outlets installed in hot-air ducts may be enough to furnish the extra heat for the basement room, thus eliminating the cost of a separate heating unit.

Where a group of parallel pipes is to be enclosed, it will be advisable to first cover cold-water pipes with anti-sweat covering since condensation-drip may leak through the enclosure and discolor it. Any valves in the pipe lines should be accessible by having removable panels. Where pipes are widely separated it may be possible to group them together in a single enclosure, which will take some plumbing work. Vertical pipes such as a soil-and-vent stack for a toilet may be enclosed in a similar fashion.

Electric Wiring

The time to have wiring done and plumbing installed in partitions is before they are covered with wallboard. In some instances it may be necessary to have pipes installed before a partition is framed. Although some home owners are capable of doing wiring and plumbing themselves, this work usually should be done by tradesmen, especially if it is subject to municipal approval.

Nailing Bases for Wallboard

When you are ready to apply wallboard examine all the framing carefully to see if edges of wallboard will cross open spaces where nailing bases should be provided. Examples of this are corners where partitions join outside-wall framing for insulation, or where they join furring, where the top plate of a partition crosses open joists, and where a partition is parallel to open joists, or comes directly under a joist.

Start by Covering Ceiling

There are many types of wallboards—hard and soft varieties in many sizes. Generally it is best practice to do the ceiling first, then the walls. Ceilings may be covered with 4 x 8-foot panels or with tiles. The latter are available in various sizes. When installing large panels they can be held in position for nailing by using a T-shape prop wedged between floor and ceiling.

Acoustic tile often is preferred for basement ceilings to reduce reverberations from the hard surfaces of the floor and walls. The tile may be nailed, stapled, cemented or held with clips. Some kinds are fitted in metal channels. When applied to an existing ceiling that is even and in good condition, a special mastic can be used. An uneven, cracked and broken ceiling usually requires furring strips for tile application. Furring is used across open joists for tiles smaller than 16 inches square. The latter size can be fastened to joists.

As a rule, tile application starts at the approximate center of a ceiling. To locate the starting point, measure to the walls to determine the width of the last tile row that is cut to fit. If this is too narrow, relocate the center point. This adjustment for tile width at walls is basically the same as for floor tile, as will be subsequently detailed. For ceiling tile a straight "starter strip" is nailed temporarily to the ceiling across either furring or joists to get the first row perfectly straight. Some irregularity may be noticed where cut tiles join walls, but this can be concealed with cove molding mitered at the corners.

Covering Walls

Panels of 4 x 8-foot size can be applied quickly and easily on partition framing or on vertical furring strips spaced 16 inches on centers. The vertical edges of the panel extend about halfway over the edges of studs or furring strips. Start nailing to intervening studs first, then to studs at the edges. It may be necessary to cut off the lower end of the panel so it will fit between the floor and ceiling, since many basements are not 8 feet high. There also are panels that are 16 and 32 inches wide, which can be similarly applied to studs and vertical furring strips. Where horizontal furring is recommended, spacing is important to obtain adequate reinforcement.

When nailing wallboard, use the type and size nail, and nail spacing, as suggested by the wallboard maker. Sometimes clips are used or the wallboard may be cemented to studs or furring. For fastening soft wallboards, staples often are used. Wallboard edges may be straight and are then butted together, or they may have tongue-and-groove edges that give a tighter fit and conceal nails or clips. Where nail heads are not so concealed they usually are sunk with a set, then filled to make them invisible.

For gypsum board (½-inch thickness recommended for basement walls and 3/8-inch for ceilings) the nail heads are sunken slightly, then "spotted" with hard-drying cement. The slightly recessed vertical edges are taped and cemented. When dry, the joint is sanded so it is concealed. There are special tapes for inside and outside corners.

Floor Tile

Vinyl or vinyl-asbestos floor tile in 9- or 12-inch squares and other sizes are popular for basement use. Asphalt tile also is used, as are other kinds. Some, however, are not suitable for concrete floors below grade level. Special moisture-proof, alkali-resistant cements are used. The floor should be smooth without ridges from troweling, free from oil and grease, and perfectly clean before applying tile.

To lay tile, snap two chalk lines at right angles to each other and crossing at the room's center. Getting the lines at a perfect right angle is important. Lay tiles along one line to opposite wall. If the spaces between the last tiles and the walls are less than one-half the width of a tile, remove one tile from the row, and rearrange the row so the tile-to-wall distances are about equal. Also, snap a new chalk line at the edge of the center tile, and eradicate the old line. Repeat this procedure to relocate the crossing line.

Now apply cement with a special notched trowel (having notches of size to suit the cement) over the lines except at the intersection point and at their ends.

Lay the first tile so its corner is exactly at the intersection of the lines and its edges aligned with them. Lay down a triangle of tiles from this point, proceeding until half of the floor has been covered. Lay the tiles down carefully to avoid sliding them into position, which will cause cement to get between the edges and prevent a tight fit. Set one edge of one already laid, corner to corner. You can stand or kneel on tiles already laid, but be careful not to move those near edges out of position. Tiles adjoining a wall usually must be cut to lesser width after measuring. The other half of the floor is laid in the same way. Where tile must fit around pipe, cut a hole and a slit.

Installing Door and Trim

The door casing of ¾-inch wood consists of three pieces cut so that when the top piece is nailed to the jambs there will be ½-inch space between the casing and the frame. The width of the casing is such that its edges come flush with the surface of the wallboard. Pairs of wood shingles are slid toward each other in the clearance space and adjusted so the jambs will be plumb, after which 8 or 10d finishing nails are driven through jambs and shingles. The top of the casing should come at perfect right angles to the sides. After nailing the casing, saw off the projecting ends of the shingles, avoiding damage to the casing.

Mark the door for height so it will have 1/16-inch clearance at the top and ¼-inch at the bottom, and cut off the surplus length from the lower cross-rail. The side of the door that is the straightest by sighting should be the latch edge. A slight warp at the hinge edge will be corrected by the center hinge. The latch edge of a door should be planed at a slight bevel toward the inside to clear the jamb. Tack stop beads in place temporarily to the jambs so the door will be flush with their edges. Place a strip of cardboard 1/16 inch thick on the top edge of the door, set it in position and secure it with shingle wedges at the bottom. Use a sharply-pointed pencil or knife edge to mark the hinge positions on both the door and the jambs. The top hinge should come about 6 inches below the top of the door, the bottom hinge about 12 inches above the floor; center the middle hinge between them. Mortises of exact size are cut in the door and jamb to take the hinge leaves snugly. If the mortises are cut accurately, you will be able to screw the hinge leaves in place, set the door up and insert the hinge pins. The stop beads on the jambs are mitered to the one at the top, then nailed on permanently with 5d finishing nails. After this you install the latch that usually is accompanied by installation instructions.

Casing trim is added to the door and also to the windows, and baseboard is nailed through the wallboard to studs and sole plate so it fits on the floor neatly. Corners of trim should be mitered for appearance.

ATTIC CONVERSION

Converting attic space into living quarters costs considerably less than adding an extra room to a house. One photo shows an efficient arrangement where a stairway enters an attic about midway from the side. Where a stairway enters at one end, as in the other photo, there may be only enough space for a hallway and closets or a bathroom.

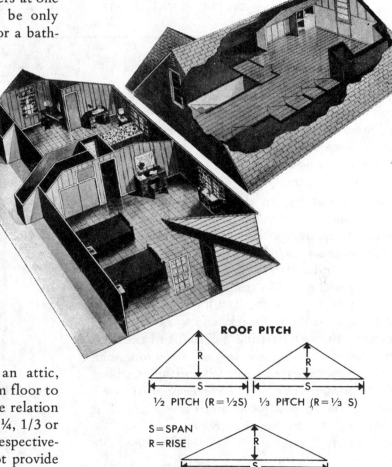

Typical attic before conversion; filled with odds and ends.

Planning

To determine the possibilities of an attic, measure its length, width and height from floor to roof ridge. Determine the roof pitch—the relation between rise (R) and span (S). When R is ¼, 1/3 or ½ of S, the roof has a ¼, 1/3 or ½ pitch respectively. Houses having ¼ pitch or less do not provide enough headroom for an attic conversion. Also, an attic having less rise than 8 feet will not be suitable. If your roof is 1/3 pitch or more there may be enough usable space as given in the table, which relates to 1/3 and ½ roof pitch.

Assuming your attic space is suitable, the next thing to do is get an architect's or contractor's advice on whether the joists are capable of taking the extra weight, particularly if a bathroom is included in your plans. For spans over 7 feet, 2 x 6 joists are not sufficient for supporting 40 pounds per square foot, the maximum allowance for residential struc-

ROOF PITCH

½ PITCH (R = ½S)   1/3 PITCH (R = 1/3 S)

S = SPAN
R = RISE

¼ PITCH (R = ¼ S)

tures. Joists of this size are intended to support the ceiling of the floor below rather than the weight of attic rooms and furniture. Joists supporting a bathroom should be strong enough to hold a weight of 60 to 70 pounds per square foot.

If joists are not strong enough, additional ones must be provided. Sometimes it is possible to

ATTIC WIDTH	FLOOR WIDTH WHEN SIDE WALL HEIGHT IS			CEILING WIDTH WHEN HEIGHT IS		
	4	5	6	7	8	9
FOR ⅓ PITCH ROOF						
24	12	9	0	3	0	0
26	14	11	8	5	2	0
28	16	13	10	7	4	1
30	18	15	12	9	6	3
FOR ½ PITCH ROOF						
20	12	10	8	6	4	2
22	14	12	10	8	6	4
24	16	14	12	10	8	6
26	18	16	14	12	10	8
28	20	18	16	14	12	10

nail joists of the same width to existing ones or install wider joists between existing ones. The latter arrangement will reduce vibration and sound to the rooms below. Checking on joist strength is not necessary if the house was built for subsequent addition of attic rooms.

Before starting on the work, make accurate plans to scale on cross-ruled paper, each square representing 1 square foot. Include partitions, doors, windows, stairway, chimney, soil stack, vent pipes and other details. Plan to have professionals do the wiring, plumbing and heating work unless you are fully competent to do so. Best location for a bathroom is close to the soil stack, and where pipes can be brought through existing partitions of the floor below. Avoid locating a bathroom on a long span of joists; rather locate it over supporting partitions below it. Sometimes it may be necessary to have a dormer for more headroom and floor space, or it may be needed to house a bathroom.

There are several types of dormers: The gable type gives some extra space, but not as much as a Dutch-colonial type. This can have a row of windows, its length being parallel to that of the house. Its appearance is as if part of the roof were pulled up to make room for two triangular end walls and a front wall. If you decide on a dormer, it should be built before you install the framework for the ceiling and partitions of the attic rooms.

Much of the waste space between side partitions and eaves can be used for storage space. Slid-ing doors here will give full access and are preferred to hinged doors that might interfere with best utilization of floor space.

Space beyond "knee" walls is utilized for storage: is fitted with shelves.

Construction

Usually an attic that is large enough for an extra room has a single-thickness floor and stairway leading to it. If there is no stairway, the space for one must be taken from a room below, at a spot where there will be sufficient headroom at attic level. Building a stairway is quite involved and most homeowners may prefer to have a contractor do the job. Three arrangements for stairways are shown. Where a turn is required, a landing always is preferable to a turn in the steps. If possible, avoid a stairway less than 3 feet wide.

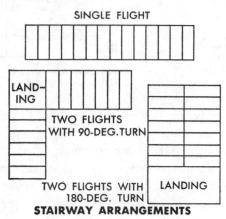

SINGLE FLIGHT

LANDING

TWO FLIGHTS WITH 90-DEG. TURN

TWO FLIGHTS WITH 180-DEG. TURN

LANDING

STAIRWAY ARRANGEMENTS

Location, shape and size of a stairwell (opening in the attic floor) are determined by the number of steps, tread width and riser height. Recommended tread widths is 10 to 10¾ inches, not including the distance it overlaps the riser below it. Riser height should be 6¾ to 7 inches. All risers should be the same height, treads the same width. Both tread width and riser height are subject to variation. Tread width, not including overlap, is found by dividing length of the stairwell in inches by the number of treads.

The stairwell must be adequately framed with double headers and one or more trimmers. The steps are supported by stringers that are notched or grooved to take the treads and risers. Center-to-center distance between stringers should not exceed 24 inches.

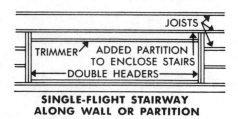

JOISTS

TRIMMER ADDED PARTITION TO ENCLOSE STAIRS

DOUBLE HEADERS

SINGLE-FLIGHT STAIRWAY ALONG WALL OR PARTITION

In case there is not enough space to build a permanent stairway, a "disappearing" stairway may be the answer.

Where wiring, plumbing, heating pipes or ducts are to be run under portions of the attic floor, and there is no existing floor, this part of the job is next, although part of the work must be done after ceiling and partition framing are in place. Some loose planks laid across joists of an unfloored attic will permit access to space between joists.

For subflooring you can use 5/8-inch plywood. Edges of panels that cross joists should be nailed to blocking spiked between the joists. Or, use standard floor boards, either with straight or tongue-and-groove edges. Although subfloor boards can be laid at right angles to the joists, a 45-degree angle will add to the rigidity of the house framing.

Before starting on ceiling and partition framing, or installing the insulation, vents should be provided for unused spaces on either side and above the planned rooms. This is to save on heat and prevent condensation in winter; to help keep rooms cool in summer. One of the drawings shows an arrangement at each end of a gable-type house. Roof vents near the eaves or else screened slots in the underside of the eaves may be preferred.

In all cases the vents should be screened to prevent the entrance of insects and birds. Vented spaces should be made accessible from the inside if possible, by means of removable panels in partitions and a trap door in the ceiling. Inlet vents are located at the lowest level of the space to be vented, outlet vents at the highest point. Total area of all screened inlet and outlet vents should be 1 square foot for every 100 square feet of floor area of space to be vented. Area of outlet vents should equal that of inlets.

There are many types of windows and installation details vary, therefore you may consider having a carpenter do this part of the work for the particular windows selected. All windows require framing that consists of headers and trimmers.

Ceiling joists and wall studs should be spaced 16 inches on centers. Nail the ceiling joists to rafters, as these usually are spaced this distance. The joists will replace existing rafter ties that may be below ceiling level. The ceiling height should not be less than 7 feet. Joists must be level and in the same horizontal plane. For spans of 7 feet or less you can use 2 x 4s, for longer spans, 2 x 6s. Frame an opening of adequate size for a trapdoor. Use headers and trimmers around a chimney. Most building codes stipulate a minimum clearance of

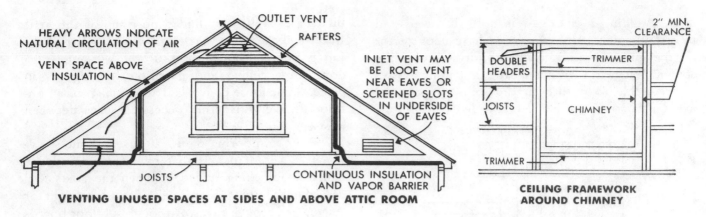

VENTING UNUSED SPACES AT SIDES AND ABOVE ATTIC ROOM

HEAVY ARROWS INDICATE NATURAL CIRCULATION OF AIR

VENT SPACE ABOVE INSULATION

OUTLET VENT

RAFTERS

INLET VENT MAY BE ROOF VENT NEAR EAVES OR SCREENED SLOTS IN UNDERSIDE OF EAVES

JOISTS

CONTINUOUS INSULATION AND VAPOR BARRIER

CEILING FRAMEWORK AROUND CHIMNEY

2" MIN. CLEARANCE

DOUBLE HEADERS

TRIMMER

JOISTS

CHIMNEY

TRIMMER

2 inches between chimney brickwork and any combustible material.

Room partitions consist of sole plates nailed to the floor, top plates fastened to rafters or to blocking between them, and studs toenailed to the plates, all 2 x 4s. To assure getting the top plates directly over the sole plates, use either a plumb bob or a straightedge with a level held against it. Partitions near eaves often are considerably less than 7 feet and are called "knee" partitions. Sole plate and studs are omitted at cabinet and closet-door locations. Storage space at eaves should be completely enclosed and insulated from the unused, vented spaces.

Framing of door openings consists of double studs at the sides and a header at the top. For the header use two lengths of 2 x 4 with a 3/8-inch spacer between them. Width and height of the open space for the door should be as indicated. A chimney can be concealed by partitions around it, or by enclosing it in a closet.

After ceiling and partition framing has been installed, examine all corners where ceiling and wallcovering materials are to meet. Provide nailing bases at all points where the edges of wallboard come over a void. Examples are shown. Matt or blanket type insulation fits between joists and rafters; it generally is stapled to their edges. This automatically places the vapor barrier to face inside as it should. The same material also is laid on the ceiling of the rooms below vented spaces. The back of access panels to the vented spaces can have aluminum foil and rigid insulating board attached to them.

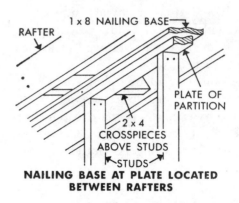

NAILING BASE AT PLATE LOCATED BETWEEN RAFTERS

RAFTER

1 x 8 NAILING BASE

PLATE OF PARTITION

2 x 4 CROSSPIECES ABOVE STUDS

STUDS

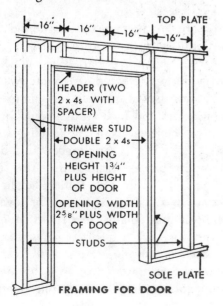

FRAMING FOR DOOR

TOP PLATE

16" 16" 16" 16"

HEADER (TWO 2 x 4s WITH SPACER)

TRIMMER STUD

DOUBLE 2 x 4s

OPENING HEIGHT 1¾" PLUS HEIGHT OF DOOR

OPENING WIDTH 2⅝" PLUS WIDTH OF DOOR

STUDS

SOLE PLATE

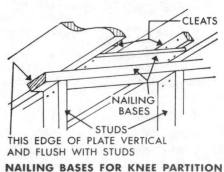

NAILING BASES FOR KNEE PARTITION

CLEATS

NAILING BASES

STUDS

THIS EDGE OF PLATE VERTICAL AND FLUSH WITH STUDS

Insulation, vapor barrier reduce heat loss in winter weather.

There are many types of wallboard and ceiling tile that come in various sizes and are applied in different ways. Some of these are prefinished. Ceiling tile smaller than 16 inches square requires furring strips, sometimes metal channels, across the joists. You can cover the ceiling as well as walls with 4 x 8-foot panels. Planking of random widths, some having tongue-and-groove edges, can be used on walls either vertically or horizontally. Vertical planking less than 16 inches wide requires furring strips nailed horizontally across the studs and spaced as recommended by the manufacturer.

If you use 4 x 8-foot panels of gypsum board, the 3/8-inch thickness is sufficient for ceilings and the ½-inch thickness for walls.

When applying any kind of wallboard or ceiling tile, follow the maker's recommendations in regard to fastening, which may call for nails of certain type and size, clips, staples or cement. Cove molding can be used where walls meet ceilings and edges of cut tiles are visible.

There's a wide choice of materials for finish floors—tile or various materials including vinyl, cork and wood, vinyl sheeting for wall-to-wall covering, and wood-strip flooring. Tile and sheeting can be applied directly over a 5/8-inch plywood subfloor, but for use over subfloor boards, the latter are first covered with 3/8-inch plywood or ¼-inch tempered-hardboard underlayment. The underlayment should be in good contact with the subfloor rather than merely bridging the ridges. An old, warped subfloor should be made even by nailing down any loose edges and sanding the entire surface. Sometimes insulating board is placed between the subfloor and underlayment to reduce sound transfer to rooms below. Cement is used for applying floor tile.

Planking is nailed or glued over horizontal furring strips on studs.

Underlayment provides smooth base for tile over rigid insulation.

BREEZEWAY CONVERSION

When one home owner needed additional living space he created it by closing in a breezeway that ran between his house and the garage. Many homes have such breezeways and, while they may be screened-in for summer, have little value for most of the year. In this particular case, the area had not been improved because there was only a partial roof. Because the area was in almost constant shade grass would not grow, and every rain

Before remodeling, kitchen was inadequate, garage was inconvenient, reached only by going outside the house. Kitchen windows facing garage received very little light, had view only of garage wall.

Dark, cramped corner of kitchen barely provided eating space for the family, none for relaxing.

Prior to change, breezeway was just a wasted space between the garage and the house, roof covered only part of the area, so it was not protected from weather.

made it a mud hole.

The space between house and garage measured 8 x 10 feet, which meant a room with 180 square feet could be built, and there would also be direct access to the garage from the house with no need to go outside. The wall of the house—the kitchen—and the wall of the garage would be used for two walls of the room, thus two more walls plus an extension of the roof would close in the room over a foundation. This is definitely an economical, and quick way of making additional living area.

Planning

The very first step is to make a working draw-

ing of the proposed room to present to the local building authorities so they will issue a building permit. The drawing should show the present structures, plus the added room. The foundation should be detailed; best to find out ahead of time how deep the footing and foundation wall should be, then show it on the plan. Wiring should be included, as well as any required ducts or pipes for heating. Elevations should show windows and doors to be included in the new construction. The building authorities also will tell you whether wiring and plumbing can be done by the home owner, or are required by code to be done by licensed professionals.

Construction

The first step in construction, as with any building, was the foundation. The siding (stucco in this case) was removed from the wall of the house to expose the existing foundation. Trenches were dug between the house and garage, and forms were built above them to meet the level of the house foundation. Siding on the garage was removed so the foundation could be poured against it. The floor of the garage was lower than that of the house. Depth of the foundation into the ground is determined by local code. If there is to be a crawl space, however, as is the case here, make the foundation deep enough to permit digging out to a

depth of 30 inches. This will permit a man to move under the floor should repairs be necessary.

A Franklin stove was to be used to heat this room, so a concrete slab was poured to provide a footing. The top of the slab was located to be flush with the finished floor of the room. A layer of brick later was applied to raise the stove above the floor. To assure a rigid, non-squeaking floor, four precast concrete piers were spaced down the center of the foundation the long way. Each was set in concrete to keep it in place, and the tops were leveled. Anchor bolts placed in the foundation when it was poured permitted bolting lengths of 2 x 6 for sills and 2 x 6 caps were bolted to the

Eating corner was replaced by wide door into new room. Door gives spacious look, light and air.

Exterior siding (texture 1-11 plywood siding) is extended across new addition on to kitchen wall to tie construction together. New coat of paint on entire house makes structure look as though it has always been the same shape and length.

Kitchen and cabinets were given coat of paint to create fresh appearance. Window over sink is removed, used for pass-through into new family room beyond wall.

459

Double 2 x 10 was spiked to 2 x 4s at side of opening to provide support over the wide door that was cut between the kitchen and the new room. Studs were shortened to fit above.

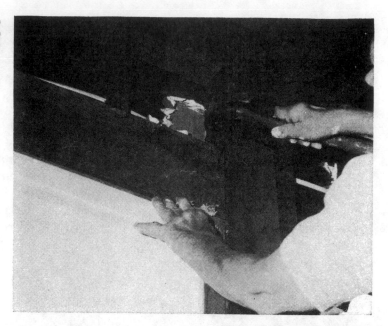

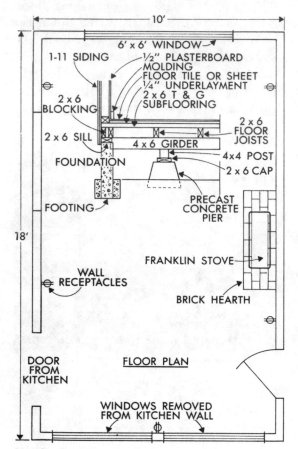

FLOOR PLAN

10'

6' x 6' WINDOW

1-11 SIDING
½" PLASTERBOARD
MOLDING
FLOOR TILE OR SHEET
¼" UNDERLAYMENT
2 x 6 T & G
SUBFLOORING

2 x 6
BLOCKING

2 x 6
FLOOR
JOISTS

2 x 6 SILL

4 x 6 GIRDER

4 x 4 POST

2 x 6 CAP

FOUNDATION

FOOTING

PRECAST
CONCRETE
PIER

18'

FRANKLIN STOVE

WALL
RECEPTACLES

BRICK HEARTH

DOOR
FROM
KITCHEN

WINDOWS REMOVED
FROM KITCHEN WALL

Simple floor plan was used to show location of windows, slab for Franklin stove, wiring.

Windows removed from wall of kitchen were fitted in new wall built to enclose breezeway. They are high to provide privacy, yet add light, spacious look.

piers. Blocks of a size slightly larger than the cross section of a 4 x 6 were nailed to the inside of the foundation forms, so that when the forms were striped away a recess about 2 inches deep was located inside each wall. The ends of a 4 x 6 girder now were fitted into these recesses, spanning the 18-foot length. Shingles were used to wedge the girder level and plumb so its upper edge was flush with the sills on the foundation. At each pier lengths of 4 x 4 were cut to fit between the pier caps and the underside of the girder. In some instances it might be necessary to wedge between the posts and caps to level the girder.

At this stage in construction the space inside the foundation was cleaned of all wood and debris and a vapor barrier of heavy plastic was installed. The plastic strips were overlapped 2 inches and run up the foundation walls about 6 inches. Floor joists next were positioned and spiked against the existing joists of the house to the girder and to a 2 x 6 spiked to the studs of the garage wall. Joists were 2 x 6s for the span involved, providing ample rigidity. As indicated, a 2 x 6 was located flush with the outside and inside edges of the sills; this "blocking" provided added support for the walls. To provide access to the crawl space a joist in one corner was cut out and boxed in to make an opening. Batt insulation was stapled to the undersides of the joists, vapor barrier up. Over the joists 2 x 6 tongue-and-groove subflooring (to match that of the original house) was nailed. A trap door was cut and fitted over the opening in the joists.

On the subfloor two walls assembled from 2 x 4s were erected. In the front wall two openings were cut to accept windows removed from the kitchen wall. In the back wall an opening was roughed out to received a 6 x 6-foot window purchased from a salvage company. The fascia board on the edge of the partial roof now was removed and extension rafters were spiked alongside the existing rafters and run over the top of the new wall. Over the rafters 2 x 6 tongue-and-groove decking was applied. Two louvers were installed on the back slope of the roof to assure adequate ventilation under the roof. A commercial roofer was hired to apply the tar paper, hot tar and gravel so roof matched that of the existing surfaces. If the roof had been wooden or composition shingles the home owner could have done the job himself.

A wide door was cut into the wall of the kitchen and headers installed above it. A smaller door was cut through the garage wall. These openings provided access to the new room, so siding now was applied to the new walls; in this case texture 1-11 plywood was used. Because the wall of the kitchen was offset from the rest of the house, all the stucco was removed and the new siding extended the full length of the offset. All wiring, switches and receptacles now were installed.

The room described was heated by a Franklin stove; if a room is to be heated by an existing furnace, ducts or piping should now be installed. Ceiling joists are next, although they could be installed before the roof was in place. Insulation now is stapled to walls and the ceiling. Plasterboard next was nailed to the ceiling joists. Two redwood beams—for appearance—were positioned against the ceiling, their ends supported on the headers over the windows. Walls next were covered with plasterboard. Taping the joints did give the home owner some problems. He used too much joint compound, a common failing with those not experienced at this job.

Windows now are installed and trimmed. The large door opening into the kitchen eliminated one of the kitchen-window openings, the other one over the sink is framed in, fitted with a wide stool and used as a pass-through from kitchen to the new room. The subfloor is covered with underlayment, either plywood or hardboard. The floor covering in the kitchen was not worn or damaged, so it was not removed. It was scrubbed thoroughly and all wax was removed, after which it was sanded to roughen the surface. This provided "tooth" for adhesive for the new floor covering. A slight difference in the floor levels between the kitchen and the new room was eliminated by shimming beneath the underlayment at the wide door with building felt. This brought the underlayment flush with the top of the floor covering in the kitchen. Sheet flooring now was cemented to the floor in the new room, and run on into the kitchen. This helped tie the two rooms together and made both of them seem larger.

Both the doors were now trimmed and a door was fitted into the smaller opening that led to the garage. Because the garage was not heated this was an exterior door, and it was completely weatherstripped. For this same reason insulation is stapled to the inside of the garage wall, vapor barrier toward the new room.

Because the garage floor was lower than the floor of the house, and of the new room, a step was fitted just outside the door to the garage. For safety sake, also, the door leading to the garage should open in toward the room. If the door opened into the garage a person might step through the door as they pushed it open, and fall and be hurt.

With all work done except for trimming between the walls and floor this was done next. The baseboard molding was cut to fit the four walls, then marked and removed. It was sealed and painted, then when the paint was dry was fastened to the wall with finishing nails. "Prefinishing" the molding eliminated the need for masking the floor and wall and permitted the job to be done much more quickly. The nail heads were recessed with a nail set, then covered with wood putty. A touch-up with a small brush finished the job.

The Franklin stove required a chimney, which was composed of prefabricated sections. An opening was cut in the roof and boxed in, then the roof jack was installed. An insulated plate also was fitted in the ceiling, to locate the pipe that connected the jack to the stove. This work actually is

Cozy wood fire in Franklin stove makes the room warm and intimate, there is ample space for eating. Room is ideal for informal entertaining, other family activities such as studying, working.

"Picture window" measuring 6 x 6 ft. looks out onto patio, makes room look and feel larger.

Window at left was in wall originally, the two on the right were taken from wall facing garage, installed in new outside wall. This window relocation saved a goodly amount of cash.

best done before the roofing and interior work are done, as the jack then can be sealed to the roof, and the plasterboard can be fitted around the ceiling plate.

Total cost of the remodeling was about $1500, figuring out to slightly less than $9 per square foot.

SCREENED-IN PORCH

If you are considering adding a screened-in porch to your home you might want to do as one home owner did to save time, money and labor,

Estimates from contractors ran as high as $3,300 for the job, so the home owner saved half the cost by doing the remodeling himself. The house looks, and is, bigger. It has more value, and most important, more room for the family. None of the work is beyond the capability of a do-it-yourself home owner.

and use pilings rather than a conventional footing and foundation. The pilings were 8-foot lengths of railroad ties that measure 6 x 8 inches. If ties are not available 6 x 6 timbers could be used, but the

After pilings are sawed off level, 4 x 8 timbers are placed on top, with one end resting on mud sill of existing house. Redwood decking is spaced maximum of ⅛ in. apart.

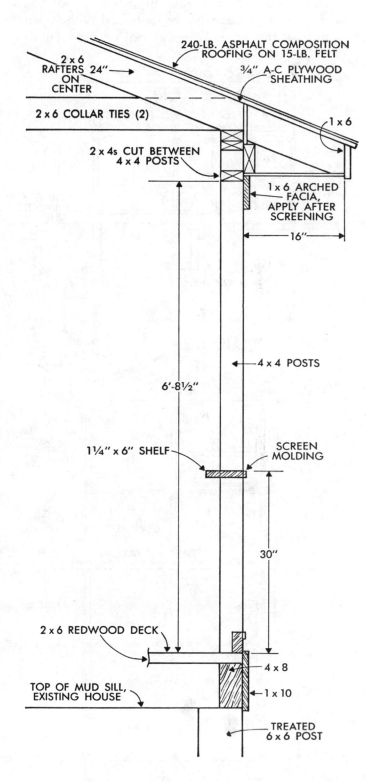

240-LB. ASPHALT COMPOSITION ROOFING ON 15-LB. FELT

2 x 6 RAFTERS 24" ON CENTER

¾" A-C PLYWOOD SHEATHING

2 x 6 COLLAR TIES (2)

1 x 6

2 x 4s CUT BETWEEN 4 x 4 POSTS

1 x 6 ARCHED FACIA, APPLY AFTER SCREENING

16"

4 x 4 POSTS

6'-8½"

1¼" x 6" SHELF

SCREEN MOLDING

30"

2 x 6 REDWOOD DECK

4 x 8

TOP OF MUD SILL, EXISTING HOUSE

1 x 10

TREATED 6 x 6 POST

lumber should be pressure-treated. Lengths of the piling will vary, of course, depending on the slope of the land, but at least 3 feet of each piling should be below ground level. Dig the holes so there is a minimum of 3 inches clearance all around so concrete can be poured to anchor the pilings. Plumb each post and hold it with two temporary braces before pouring the concrete. Height of the post above ground should be somewhat more than required. After the concrete is set, mark a level line and saw the posts to the correct height.

Height for level is determined by running a line from the top of the sill of existing house. Remove siding and sheathing at these points to permit inserting one end of each girder, as indicated. Note that the center line of posts are shorter by the height of a 4 x 6, these timbers being used for joists. They are hung on joist hangers, with their upper surfaces flush with the outside girders. Be sure that all upper surfaces are level and flush. Shim between pilings and girders or joists when necessary.

Installation of the 2 x 6 redwood decking is next. This structure was to be used in summer only, so the decking is spaced 1/8 inch. For an all-year room, the decking could be butted tightly, or plywood or hardboard underlayment could be nailed over the decking, with building felt between, on which resilient floor tiles could be cemented.

Walls are assembled from 4 x 4 "studs", with 2 x 4s at top and bottom. They can be nailed together on the floor, then raised in place. Temporarily brace the walls until the top double 2 x 4 is added to join the corners. To be sure of keeping the walls plumb, do not remove the braces until the roof framing is in place. Nail 2 x 4s on edge between the studs at the bottom, to provide a "ground" for the screen and molding.

Rafters are cut to create a pitch that will match the roof on the existing house. The roof is sheathed with ¾-inch A-C plywood, good side down. The underside of the plywood is the open ceiling of the room. Apply roofing material to match that on the existing home. Close in the end of the room with plywood, then cover it to match the siding of the house. Block in between the rafters on the tops of the walls to seal the wall. In the room shown, a boxed-in eaves was made to match that of the house.

Paint all surfaces before adding the screening.

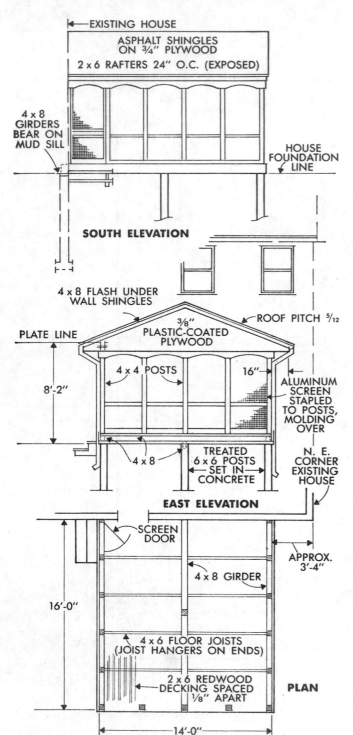

Walls are framed by using 2 x 4s for sills, with 4 x 4 "studs," capped by double 2 x 4s. Note temporary diagonal bracing; 2 x 4s spiked at corners keep walls plumb.

Roof is framed to match pitch of roof on existing house. Exposed eave end is sheathed with plywood, as is roof, then shingles to match house siding are nailed to plywood.

Structure is complete here except for screening. All members are painted before screen and molding are stapled in place, to simplify and speed job. Arches also must be installed.

464

This can be aluminum or plastic to keep maintenance to a minimum. Screening is stapled to the framing and the edges are covered with standard screen molding.

A door can be installed, as indicated. Note that in this installation a concrete stoop was simply covered over, no time or labor being spent to remove it. The plywood "scallops" over the individual screens were cut from plywood, and can be any pattern of your choice.

GOURMET KITCHEN

Typical of kitchens found in homes 30 to 60 years old, the one shown was simply ugly, poorly lighted and very inefficient.

The first step was to determine a plan that would best utilize every square inch of the room. A fairly large pantry had been converted by the previous owner into a very small, dark breakfast nook. Removal of the wall between the existing kitchen and this pantry was the first step in the project (after determining that the wall was not a load-bearing one). This operation increased the size of the kitchen by several square feet, and the adjacent dining room now was just a step through the kitchen door. Depending on the layout of the kitchen and dining room in your own remodeling project you might want to cut a "pass-through" in the wall. In the situation shown, the dining room was narrow enough to preclude the need for one.

The novice remodeler now emptied all the wall cabinets and tore them off the walls. Base cabinets, including the one containing the sink, were next.

Any kitchen remodeler should make provision for eating out at least a few days during the project; there is just no way to have meals without a sink, range and oven.

At this stage the remodeler had an empty room that was larger than the original. The remodeler now marked out on the floor and walls where each cabinet was to be located, as well as what it would contain, so it could be built to do the job.

Using this layout as a guide the home owner hired a plumber and electrician to modernize the wiring and piping. A small drain line from the sink was enlarged to handle the output of a garbage disposal unit that was to be included in the new sink. Lights over the sink and cabinets, as well as receptacles for appliances and disposal were roughed in. You might be able to handle the plumbing and wiring; remember our remodeler is a novice.

Cabinets

The home owner now went back to work, with the first project the base cabinets. A note here: professionals install the wall cabinets first, so they don't have to reach over the base cabinets later to make the installation of the wall cabinets. If you are in a hurry to get the kitchen back to usefulness, the base cabinets can come first, mainly because the sink is located in one of them. You can build all the base cabinets and fill them with the assorted items that have been sitting in corners and on tables and chairs around the house.

The tops of the base cabinets are sheets of ¾-inch plywood. You can install either plastic laminate, ceramic tile or a "seamless-flooring" over the plywood. Ceramic tile is the most expensive, and should be installed with mastic and a stain-resistant grout. The hole for the sink should be cut first in the case of the ceramic tile, while plastic laminate and the urethane-base plastic brush or roll-on material can be sawed after it has been applied. Get the sink first, then use the rim as a template, as per the instructions packed with the sink, to cut the proper size opening.

Hook up the plumbing and the disposal (or have it done) so you have a sink that can be used while the rest of the kitchen remodeling is done.

Cabinets in the kitchen shown were built in a fairly conventional manner but the choice of lumber was most unusual.

For most kitchen cabinets birch plywood is used, with white-pine plywood an occasional choice and white oak fast catching up, with the modern trend toward Spanish and Mediterranean decor. In the kitchen shown solid redwood was employed. A second difference was in the construction of the cabinet doors. While most such doors are shaped from hardwood plywood or with raised or sunken panels in hardwood frames, this builder utilized redwood. Strips of the lumber were edge-glued and cleated to make panels large enough for the doors. To minimize the problem of warping the

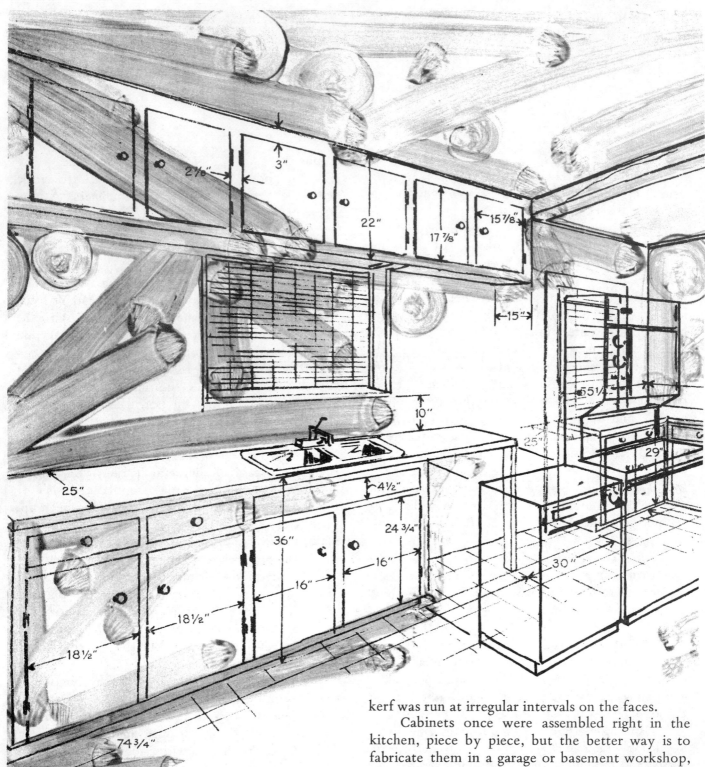

kerf was run at irregular intervals on the faces.

Cabinets once were assembled right in the kitchen, piece by piece, but the better way is to fabricate them in a garage or basement workshop, sizing them to fit a particular space in the kitchen, then carrying them to the kitchen for installation. Wooden shingles are use to level the cabinets, which are simply nailed to the wall. Any projecting shingles are trimmed flush, then a piece of trim is nailed down to cover any gap between

strips were arranged heartwood to sapwood, sapwood to heartwood, and so on. To give a bit of interest to the wide, flat surfaces of the doors, a saw

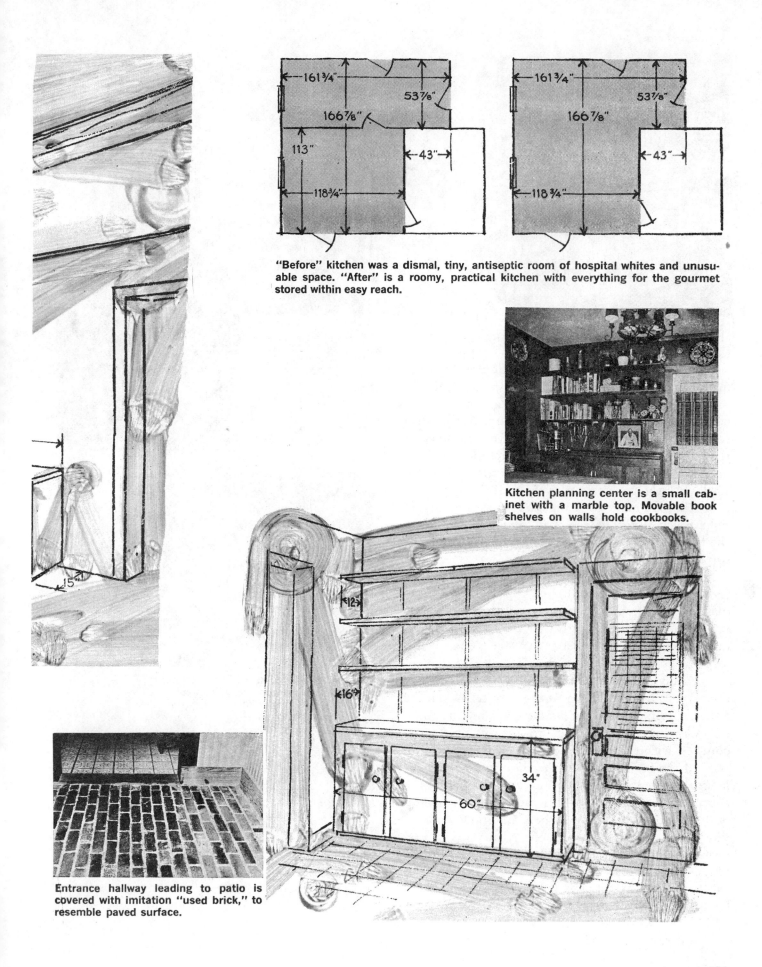

"Before" kitchen was a dismal, tiny, antiseptic room of hospital whites and unusuable space. "After" is a roomy, practical kitchen with everything for the gourmet stored within easy reach.

Kitchen planning center is a small cabinet with a marble top. Movable book shelves on walls hold cookbooks.

Entrance hallway leading to patio is covered with imitation "used brick," to resemble paved surface.

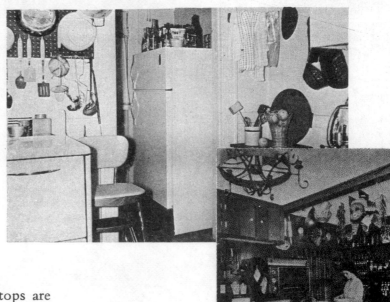

the floor and cabinet bottom. Counter tops are made separately and installed after the cabinet is in place. Drive screws up through the frame of the cabinet into the underside of the top. Cut the top so that it projects about ¼ inch beyond the edge of the cabinet, then nail a strip of ¾-inch plywood 1½ inches wide to the front edge. Keep the upper edge flush with the top surface of the top.

Tile, laminate or seamless coating are applied right to the edge of the strip, and can also be on the front of the attached strip, to give the look of a top that is 1½ inches thick.

To apply plastic laminate to the counter top (Formica, Micarta, etc.) first rip a strip of the material 1¾ inches wide on a radial-arm or table saw, using a plywood or other finetooth blade. A dull blade usually is better than a sharp one for this job.

Apply contact adhesive to the back of the laminate and to the edge of the counter. When the adhesive is dry, press the laminate against the counter allowing the top edge to project above the counter, with the lower edge flush with the bottom edge of the facing strip. Use a router with a straight laminate cutter to trim the material flush with the top of the counter. Or, you can use a belt sander with coarse paper. Smooth the laminate down until you just barely sand the counter top; this will remove any adhesive that has spilled or run onto the top. Next, cut a sheet of laminate to fit the top of the counter, leaving enough to allow a ¼-inch overhang, except at the back.

Using vinyl tile as a kitchen flooring makes it easy for the lady do-it-yourselfer to finish off her kitchen.

Again, brush contact adhesive on the back of the laminate and on the counter. When the adhesive is dry, cover the counter top with newspaper, leaving a ¼-inch strip of adhesive exposed at the back. Place the laminate on the counter, pressing the back edge into the adhesive; it will stick but still can be moved a bit to position it properly. Slide the newspapers out and roll the laminate in full contact with the adhesive; a cloth-covered rolling pin is good. A router with a laminate trimmer can be used to trim the projecting edges of the

The top of a combined glass-display and wine cabinet is enhanced with leaded glass panels in the redwood doors.

Bottom half of the cabinet provides for wine storage, as well as a serving counter and party-supplies storage.

laminate, or use a fine file. Wear safety glasses or a face shield to guard against flying slivers.

In the kitchen shown redwood was used on window and door casings, wall trim and ceiling beams. A wipe-on penetrating sealer was applied to the redwood, rather than the usual lacquer. The wood looks natural with no gloss, yet it is protected.

Unusual cooking utensils from around the world are displayed on perforated-hardboard panels spaced ¼ inch out from the walls to permit inserting the hooks.

BUILDING STAIRWAYS

Whether you are remodeling an existing room or adding on to your home, you may find it necessary to construct a new stairway.

In building a conventional indoor stairs, steps to an exterior deck or a "climbing area" that blends with a natural outdoor setting, there are basic considerations that apply to all projects that are meant to get you from one level to another.

All things considered, a gentle incline, or ramp, is probably the safest and easiest way to change altitude, but the shallow angle of such a slope makes it impractical except for some outdoor settings.

While 15 degrees is about right for a ramp, this won't work indoors, so we break up the slope into steps and this permits us to increase the angle to 30 or 35 degrees. Here we are talking about an almost ideal situation, considering the tread-riser relationship, and this seldom happens. We most often must figure angles between 20 and 50 degrees. Below 20 degrees you might just as well build a ramp. Above 50 degrees you can plan on a ladder or elevator.

The relationship between riser and tread is as important as the stair angle. No matter where or how you build a stairway, the normal total of riser height and tread depth should be about 17 or 18 inches. This means that the risers should be 7 inches or less; in some cases you may create treads that are so wide they require more than one stride.

In constructing a stairway you have two factors to work with, the total rise and the total run. Measure the height between the bottom and top floors and this is the total rise. Divide that figure by an ideal unit rise, 7 inches, and the result will indicate the number of unit risers you need. Forget any fraction, and use that figure to divide into the total rise and this will give you the actual unit rise.

To establish a starting point for the tread depth or unit run, subtract the unit rise from 18 inches. Now, multiply the result by the number of risers, minus one, and this will give you the total run. Under good conditions this arithmetic will work out all right, but should the answer prove impractical for the available space, a compromise must be made. You achieve a solution by changing the riser-tread relationship—subtracting from one to add to the other—so long as you remain within

Stair building is not the complicated job you might think, even for closed-in job if it is planned right.

Even rustic steps outdoors should be planned for comfort and safety. Risers are railroad ties, treads concrete.

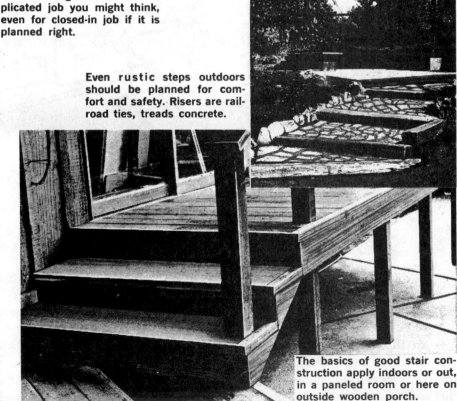

The basics of good stair construction apply indoors or out, in a paneled room or here on outside wooden porch.

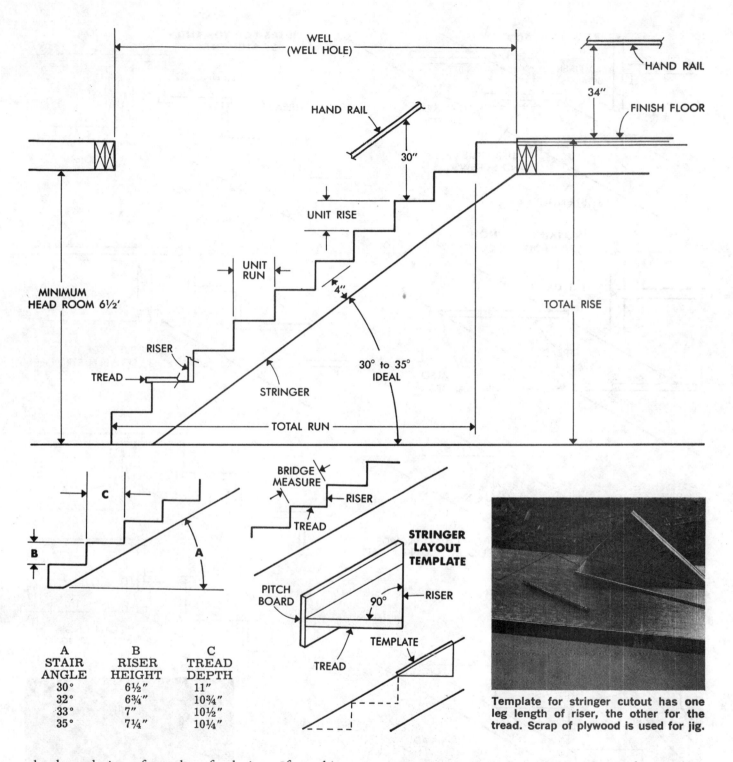

A STAIR ANGLE	B RISER HEIGHT	C TREAD DEPTH
30°	6½"	11"
32°	6¾"	10¾"
33°	7"	10½"
35°	7¼"	10¼"

Template for stringer cutout has one leg length of riser, the other for the tread. Scrap of plywood is used for jig.

the boundaries of good, safe design. If working with figures doesn't do the job for you, it's not far-fetched to draw a scaled layout of the situation. You might even bend up a piece of stiff cardboard to make a scale model. The more preplanning you do, the easier construction will be.

Remember that head room is important. Cracking your head on the overhead or having to stoop as you start up a stairway means the stairway was not planned well. The width of a stairway is determined by the use it will receive. For one-way traffic a width of 24 inches will do. For two people walking together, or for the passage of furniture, figure on a minimum of 36 inches. We would not recommend the 24-inch width for indoor stairs, and a local building code will probably dictate a

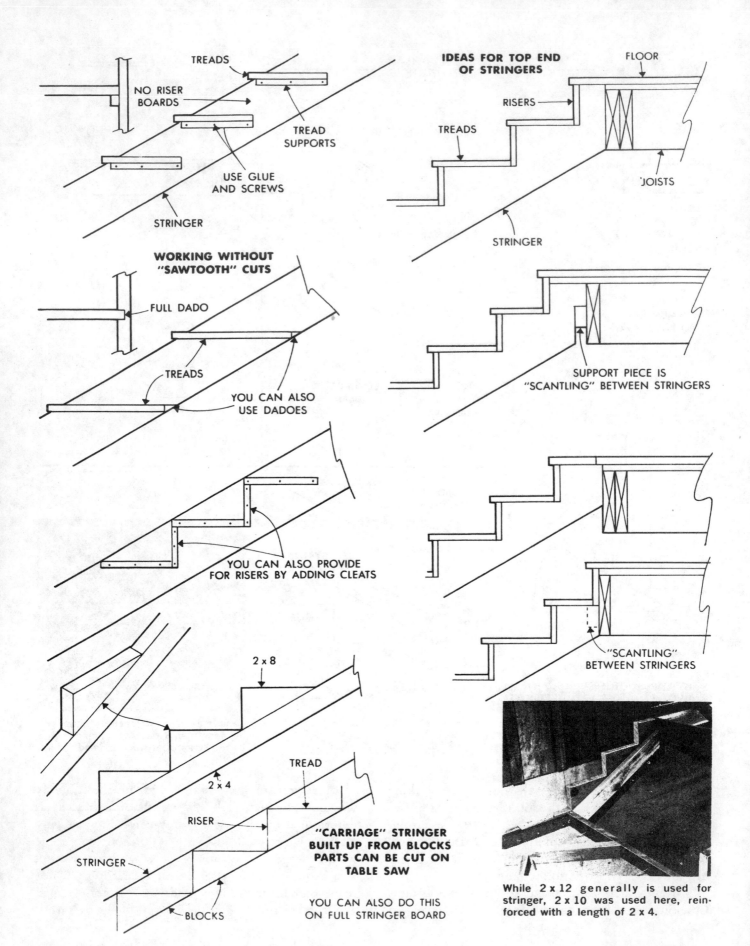

TREADS

NO RISER BOARDS

TREAD SUPPORTS

USE GLUE AND SCREWS

STRINGER

IDEAS FOR TOP END OF STRINGERS

FLOOR

RISERS

TREADS

JOISTS

STRINGER

WORKING WITHOUT "SAWTOOTH" CUTS

FULL DADO

TREADS

YOU CAN ALSO USE DADOES

SUPPORT PIECE IS "SCANTLING" BETWEEN STRINGERS

YOU CAN ALSO PROVIDE FOR RISERS BY ADDING CLEATS

"SCANTLING" BETWEEN STRINGERS

2 x 8

2 x 4

TREAD

RISER

STRINGER

BLOCKS

"CARRIAGE" STRINGER BUILT UP FROM BLOCKS PARTS CAN BE CUT ON TABLE SAW

YOU CAN ALSO DO THIS ON FULL STRINGER BOARD

While 2 x 12 generally is used for stringer, 2 x 10 was used here, reinforced with a length of 2 x 4.

greater width. If you have any doubt, check the local code.

Those components to which you attach the treads and risers are called stringers. They have saw-tooth cuts for the step parts and are set at the angle of the stairs. Their job is to provide parallel-to-the-floor bearing surfaces for the treads. Once you have established the tread-riser relationship, the layout on the stringer is quite simple.

The drawing indicates how to make a simple template that you can just trace around. A carpenter's square also can be used; just mark the unit rise on the tongue, the unit run on the blade. When these two points are adjusted to the edge of the stock, you mark around the corner of the square for the cutout pattern. When you measure between the legs of the notch on a straight line, then multi-ply this distance by the number of risers, you can determine the length required for the stringers. Add a few inches to play it safe.

Clamp the two stringers together and cut the notches with a handsaw, or portable electric saw and finish with a handsaw.

You can avoid the saw-tooth cuts by going along with one of the other ideas shown. A number of these designs are used on "utility" stairs, where riser boards are not used. One of the sketches shows how you can include vertical as well as horizontal cleats to provide nailing surfaces for risers. Another method is the "carriage" stringer. The advantage here is that you can cut the riser-tread blocks on a table saw.

Shown in another drawing are methods of attaching the upper ends of the stringers.

HOW TO FINISH OFF TREAD EDGES (NOSING)

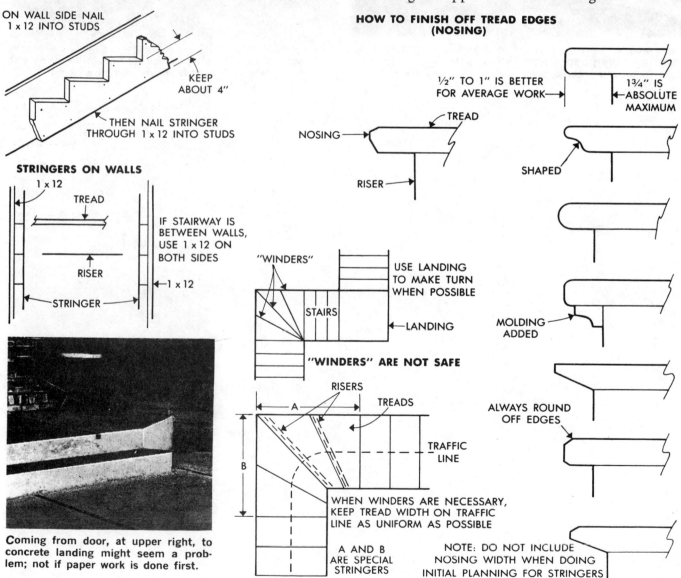

ON WALL SIDE NAIL 1 x 12 INTO STUDS

KEEP ABOUT 4"

THEN NAIL STRINGER THROUGH 1 x 12 INTO STUDS

STRINGERS ON WALLS

1 x 12
TREAD
RISER
STRINGER
1 x 12

IF STAIRWAY IS BETWEEN WALLS, USE 1 x 12 ON BOTH SIDES

Coming from door, at upper right, to concrete landing might seem a problem; not if paper work is done first.

"WINDERS"
STAIRS

USE LANDING TO MAKE TURN WHEN POSSIBLE
LANDING

"WINDERS" ARE NOT SAFE

RISERS
TREADS
A
B
TRAFFIC LINE

WHEN WINDERS ARE NECESSARY, KEEP TREAD WIDTH ON TRAFFIC LINE AS UNIFORM AS POSSIBLE

A AND B ARE SPECIAL STRINGERS

NOSING
TREAD
RISER

½" TO 1" IS BETTER FOR AVERAGE WORK

1¾" IS ABSOLUTE MAXIMUM

SHAPED

MOLDING ADDED

ALWAYS ROUND OFF EDGES

NOTE: DO NOT INCLUDE NOSING WIDTH WHEN DOING INITIAL PLANNING FOR STRINGERS

473

When attaching stringers to walls, first nail a 1 x 12 against the wall, driving the spikes into the studs. The stringer then is nailed to the 1 x 12 plate. A number of ways of finishing tread "nosings" are shown. Remember that this nosing dimension is not included in planning the tread depth.

Sometimes you don't have enough wall or floor space to provide a total run that relates safely to total rise. "Landings" are the answer here; platforms between stairs. "Winders" are to be avoided when possible, and when necessary, should be installed as shown.

The one series of photos shows how a simple stairway was designed and built; you can build stairways with the same methods of planning.

Using wooden landing on concrete improved appearance, kept tread-riser relationship.

To make landing feel solid, sleepers are set on concrete, filled in with concrete.

After concrete had set, 2-in. stock was nailed over sleepers, random lengths trimmed.

Stairway is complete here, except for finish trim to make it more attractive.

13

FURNITURE REPAIR AND FINISHING

FURNITURE REPAIR AND FINISHING

13

REMOVING WATER STAINS ■ REFINISHING WALNUT ■ EXOTIC WOODS ■ LACQUER

WATER-BASE STAINS ■ PENETRATING FINISHES ■ METALLIC POWDER STENCILING

RENOVATING A CHAIR ■ PAINT AND VARNISH REMOVAL ■ POLISHES AND WAXES

VARNISH ■ OIL-BASE STAINS ■ REFINISHING PRIMITIVES ■ ENAMELING FURNITURE

HOW TO CANE ANTIQUE CHAIRS ■ MARBLE-TOPPED FURNITURE ■ FINISH PATCHING

AEROSOL FINISHES ■ PAINTING A CHAIR ■ WOOD FILLERS ■ FINISHING TOYS

WATER-BASE STAINS

Water stains are just what they sound like: dyes or stains using water as a solvent. These stains have many advantages over other types, but are usually ignored by many finishers because of the skill required in applying them. Water stains are extremely transparent and brilliant and are best applied to fancy-figured woods. These stains are available in all the more common wood tones, as well as black, red, blue and yellow. If a darker or lighter shade of color is desired, merely mix in more

powder or add more water. Water stains also will not fade in strong sunlight, are deeply penetrating and are long lasting. A 1-ounce package of powder costs around 40 cents, and makes one quart of stain which will cover over 100 square feet of stock.

Applying wood stains correctly takes a bit of practice. Because they are quick drying they leave streaks and overlap areas. The water solvent of the stains also raises the wood grain, leaving a fuzzy, rough surface. Water stains cannot be applied over

Wood stains are available in all the most common wood tones, and may be intermixed to obtain special tones.

One package of powdered wood stain makes 1 qt. of finished stain. Is poured into a glass or plastic container.

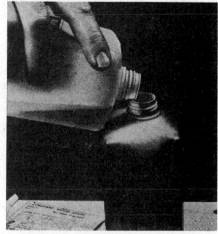

Hot water is poured into the container and shaken thoroughly to mix with the stain. Stain is highly concentrated.

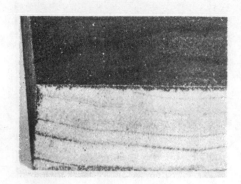

Much contemporary furniture is finished with penetrating sealer or oils. Night stand is walnut, ready to finish.

After surface is sanded as smooth as possible, stain is applied to even up color of wood. Let dry for 24 hours.

First coat of penetrating finish is applied. Wood surface is kept "wet" with finish for about an hour.

After finish has set for about an hour, excess sealer is wiped off with soft cloth that should be lint-free.

Last coat is applied, allowed to soak for an hour, excess wiped off, burnished with wax and steel wool.

surfaces that have been stripped for refinishing. The water will not penetrate through the oil-based materials left on the wood surface.

Water stains are mixed with hot water, testing the colors on a scrap of wood until the desired tone and shade is reached. The stain then is brushed onto the wood in a full, wet coat. Any surface to which water stains are applied must be sanded as smooth as possible, then wiped with a dry cloth. Oil from fingerprints will show up in the stain. As the stain is applied it is absorbed into the wood unevenly. Keep applying more stain to keep the wood surface wet, and with no dry spots. Then wipe off the surplus with a soft cloth. After the stain has set for 24 hours, smooth the raised grain and finish the wood surface.

OIL-BASE STAINS

Today everything is "easy-does-it," "quick-drying," etc. If you build, finish, or refinish furniture or cabinet work, sooner or later, you're going to run into a project made of several different types of wood, a tabletop with a light streak of sap wood running through it, or a similar problem. There is only one solution to these problems, one that is used quite often by professional cabinet-makers; a nonpenetrating oil stain. Because of their opaqueness and tendency to cloud the finish of some woods, nonpenetrating oil stains have fallen out of favor with many wood finishers. They are the only salvation in many cases, and should not be neglected.

This type of oil stain can be mixed, blended,

Nonpenetrating oil stains should be applied in a flowing, heavy coat with a clean, fine-bristle brush.

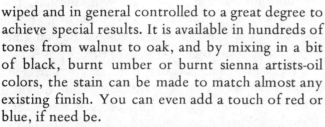

Nonpenetrating oil stain is basically heavy ground-pigments suspended in linseed oil, turpentine and other mediums.

Stain must be thoroughly stirred before each use, and during if kept open for any length of time. Pigments settle to bottom.

wiped and in general controlled to a great degree to achieve special results. It is available in hundreds of tones from walnut to oak, and by mixing in a bit of black, burnt umber or burnt sienna artists-oil colors, the stain can be made to match almost any existing finish. You can even add a touch of red or blue, if need be.

Controlling the stain tone after it has been applied is also an easy matter. If you wish a lighter stain, wipe the surplus stain off before it has a chance to dry thoroughly, (when it begins to glaze and dull over) or you can wipe it with a dry cloth.

To achieve a darker tone, you can wipe with a wet cloth dipped in stain, allow stain to dull thoroughly, then wipe lightly with a dry cloth, or even apply one light coat of stain, wiped almost immediately, then apply a fuller coat for double coverage.

Nonpenetrating stains are basically heavy ground-pigment suspended in a linseed-oil-turpentine solution, and you must thoroughly stir and mix the stain before each use. One good tip is to store the can upside down (with lid on tightly). This keeps the pigment from settling on the can bottom and hardening to the point that it's hard to stir.

When surface of applied oil stain begins to dull, surplus stain should be wiped from wood using a soft cloth.

Final wiping should be with the grain. By varying the pressure or drying time, lighter or darker tones can be achieved.

WHAT'S A SEALER?

It's the finish that makes the difference between a really top-notch project and one that's just so-so. And, quite often it's the use of a sealer that assures a really quality finish. All right, what's a sealer?

The old standby is shellac, thinned 50-50 with denatured alcohol. Any sealer should be ap-plied so thin that it does not show. Varnish thinned with turpentine or synthetic thinner is the next most common sealer. Either of these materials is applied before stain; this assures a more even absorption of the color. This is especially true on end grain.

Sealer is applied before filler on open-pored woods like oak, so excess filler is easily wiped off.

If you use nonpenetrating oil stain, a sealer must be used over it to prevent a brushed-on varnish coat from "lifting" it and creating a "muddy" appearance.

Modern sanding-sealer, usually with a vinyl base, is formulated to sand easily, yet not load up the sandpaper. Varnish, lacquer or other finish can be applied over it. It is excellent for woodwork in a home.

Sealers are used for painting; they are a must for such woods as fir plywood where hard and soft grain do not accept paint equally, which causes real problems. These "primer-sealers" are opaque as well as sealing, so they are ideal for such applications as covering water stains on a ceiling. Interior latex paint can't cover such stains, but the primer-sealer really seals in the stain, so the latex paint can be applied over the spot.

A specialty sealer is penetrating floor sealer, used for gymnasiums and other hardwood floors. It is both sealer and finish coat.

An even more special sealer is "lacquer sealer." It's not found in the average paint store, only those selling to professional finishers, cabinetmakers and the like. It is sprayed over stained and filled surfaces to provide an extra-smooth finish.

LACQUER

Lacquer is the finish preferred by furniture manufacturers and by top-notch cabinetmakers. When a clear lacquer is sprayed on wood—and it's available from a flat to a gloss finish—the result is a surface that is resistant to water, alcohol and abuse.

Clear lacquer also produces the least amount of color change in wood, as contrasted to other types of finishes.

A good lacquer finish does require that the wood surfaces be meticulously smooth. Use progressively finer grits of sandpaper, ending with the finest silicon-carbide open-coat paper. The next step is to seal the wood, either with a 50-50 mixture of thinner and lacquer or preferably with a special lacquer sanding-sealer. Apply the sealer in a full coat, but in a "dusting" spray. When the sealer is dry knock off raised grain and smooth the finish with very fine sandpaper. Wipe off the sanding dust with a tack cloth. The finish will now be a chalk-white color, but more lacquer will eliminate this.

Spraying lacquer always is thinned; go by the manufacturer's recommendations on the container, which may be as high as 35 to 50 per cent.

Lacquer and lacquer thinner are extremely flammable; and can be explosive. Shut down all flames: hot-water tank, furnace, gas range, etc., including the pilot lights for these appliances. Eliminate anything that could cause sparks or create static electricity. Use a fan to exhaust fumes outdoors.

Spray across the grain, then with it, moving steadily. Too close with the gun causes runs, too far can create "orange peel" as will low air pressure. Pin holes in the finish are due to not enough thinner, and "blushing" results from spraying on a humid day.

Buff down your final coat of lacquer with fine steel wool dipped in paste floor wax.

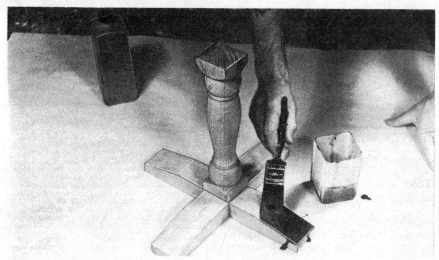

After the stain cools, it is shaken, then flowed onto the wood surface in a full, wet coat with a brush.

As the wood surface absorbs the stain, more is added until the surface stays wet, surplus is then removed.

After wood and stain have dried for at least 24 hrs., the whiskers raised by the water are removed with fine sandpaper.

Sewing stand of oak, ash and imbuya illustrate how water stain makes various woods the same general color.

Sanding sealer is applied in a thin coat on woodwork to assure smooth application of varnish to create fine finish.

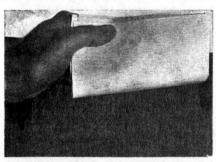

Sanding sealer is formulated so that sandpaper will not load up when the finish is smoothed.

Lacquer sealer is a "specialty" sealer used mostly by professionals who finish a large number of items.

Shellac is common sealer, used on end grain that is to be stained to prevent excess absorption.

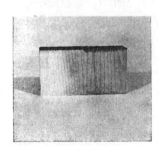

Two coats of shellac on one-half end grain at left; wood is sliced to show difference in penetration.

Shellac seals over non-penetrating oil stain, when varnish is to be applied as the final finish.

Varnish thinned half-and-half can be used as sealer. Use turpentine or recommended thinners.

Water stains on ceiling "bleed" through latex paint, can be hidden with primer-sealer, then paint.

Primer-sealer also is good on pine, fir, fir plywood to assure even application of paint.

First step in lacquering is to sand surfaces well, apply coat of sanding sealer.

Follow manufacturer's recommendations on proper amount of thinner.

Old-timers mixed thinner and lacquer by "feel." Should be slightly oily.

After lacquer and thinner have been mixed in required proportions they are poured into cup of sprayer.

When lacquer has dried for a couple of hours you can sand lightly. White appearance disappears with next coat.

After several (at least four) coats of lacquer, sanding between coats, buff with fine steel wool and paste wax.

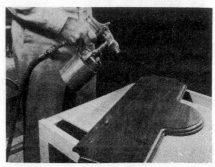

Lacquer is sprayed in light coats; you can apply coats over wet coats if you apply lightly so there are no runs.

VARNISH

Although some of the new "plastic" varnishes are getting close to being an "all-purpose" finish, the craftsman-finisher will do well to select a specific varnish suited for the particular job at hand. And that's where the problem comes in. There's a tremendous variety of varnishes on the market, and selecting the right one sometimes isn't easy.

Basically, there are two kinds of varnish, oleoresinous and synthetic. The oleoresinous varnishes are made of oils and natural resins. In manufacture, these natural resins are "cooked" to reduce them to a usable form.

On the other hand, synthetic-resin varnishes are manufactured by the reaction of various chemicals and are available in formulations according to the chemicals used.

Oleoresinous Varnishes

Oleoresinous varnishes are broken down into classifications according to their oil content and are called long, medium and short-oil varnishes. Spar and marine varnishes are the long-oil type. The increased amount of drying oil makes the film much tougher and elastic. The varnishes are very viscous and heavy-bodied, and dry slowly. Tung oil is added to make them water and weatherproof.

Floor and interior-trim varnishes are called medium-oil varnishes. They dry somewhat faster than the long-oil kinds, but are somewhat more elastic than short-oil types.

Furniture varnishes are classified as short-oil varnishes. They form a hard, brittle surface that can be polished to a high gloss. Because of the decreased amount of oils, they are thinner and penetrate the surface deeper. These varnishes, as well as the interior-trim varnishes, are available in regular-gloss or as a satin finish. The satin finish is achieved by adding flattening agents such as calcium, aluminum or zinc stearate.

Oleoresinous varnishes can be thinned with turpentine, naphtha or benzine.

Synthetic Varnishes

The wide variety of resins and multiple applications of synthetic varnishes makes them popular with industrial finishers, and some of the resins are available to the home craftsman.

Alkyd resins have somewhat better weathering properties and greater uniformity than oleoresinous varnishes.

Phenolic resins are thermosetting (cured by heat and pressure to an infusible state). They are industrially baked-on to produce bar and tabletops. In some cases they also are used on boats.

Amino resins are used in producing the pigmented white and light-colored baked-on finishes for appliances, and are not of much interest to the woodworker.

Acrylic resins are used primarily to coat metal (automotive finishes). They can be used to protect polished brass or aluminum from oxidizing.

Epoxy resin is one of the hardest coatings available. It is highly resistant to water and weathering so is used as a boat finish. However, in its clear state it will chalk and turn yellow. It comes in the familiar two parts that must be mixed together.

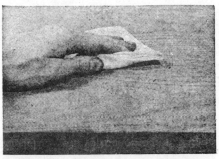

Always use a tack cloth before each varnish coat to remove the pieces of sanding grit and oil from your hands.

All varnishes should be strained before using. Strain just before using, with a ladies' nylon stocking.

Dip just the tip (about ½ in.) of the brush in the varnish. Lightly "strike" it against edge to remove excess.

In applying varnish try not to "brush out" any more than possible. Brush into previously-applied varnish.

Remove any lint or bubbles that remain, with the point of an artist's brush or a "ball of burnt varnish" on a stick.

After letting the first coat dry for at least two days, sand lightly with 6/0 garnet paper. Wipe with tack cloth.

After second coat, sand with 6/0 wet-or-dry sandpaper using Ivory soap and water as a protective "sludge."

After the final coat, apply paste wax with extra-fine steel wool. Allow to dry, then buff with a soft cloth.

Polyurethane is probably the synthetic resin most well-known to the average craftsman. It is one of the more versatile finishes and the closest to an "all-around" varnish. It is extremely mar-resistant and can be used indoors on floors and furniture. Because it is water and weather-resistant it can be used as an exterior finish. It dries quite transparent, retains its gloss for long periods and dries more rapidly than many other resins.

Although there is a great variety of varnishes, the technique of applying them is the same for all.

PENETRATING FINISHES

One of the easiest finishes to apply, and one that will consistently produce the best results for the home craftsman, is a penetrating sealer or oil. Penetrating sealers are just that, "penetrating" as opposed to the surface finishes, such as varnish or lacquer.

Penetrating finishes have several advantages over varnish and lacquer. They do not require "finesse" or skillful brush handling, nor do they require a dust-proof finishing room and lots of power-finishing equipment. You also don't have to sand between coats as on most other kinds of finishes. However this emphasizes proper preparation of the work surface before finish application, not during.

Because of an extremely low resin content, these finishes will not darken, crack, craze, check or peel. The finish wears down with the surface, so blemishes, dents and scratches do not show as on surface coatings such as varnish or lacquer.

Penetrating finishes will never completely take the place of surface-applied finishes, however they do play an important part in today's furniture finishing, and are fun and easy to use.

For the best application, the surface to be finished should be sanded as smooth as possible. Stain the surface the desired color, using either an oil-base stain, or one compatible with the brand of penetrating finish you wish to apply. Let dry for at least 24 hours. You can also apply a paste wood filler with stain if the wood is open-grain.

Apply the first coat of penetrating finish and let it thoroughly soak in, keeping the surface as "wet" as possible with finish. Let this "soak" for about an hour, then wipe off the surplus finish, burnish with a smooth cloth and let dry. Repeat the next day, and this time burnish with fine steel-wool and paste wax.

AEROSOL FINISHES

Sealers, stains, polyurethane varnish, epoxies, antiquing materials, multicolored paints, as well as specialty paints such as hammered-metal, wrinkle-finish, chalkboard and many others now are available in spray cans.

Because of the increasing demand for these easy-to-use products, paint companies are constantly researching for new and better products. Spray heads have been improved to give better spray patterns. New solvents and resins have speeded drying time, improved gloss, and reduced the possibility of sagging. There are smaller cans for those one-time small jobs, as well as more paint in the regular-size cans for better economy on bigger jobs.

With approximately half a pint of liquid in the regular 13 to 16 ounce spray can, aerosols may seem expensive. They represent, however, good values in other ways. They do a faster, smoother job than most of us can achieve with a brush, there are no brushes to buy, clean up and maintain, and the paint dries quicker. Some finishes like hammered and multicolor splatter cannot be achieved by brushing. Aerosols offer a saving of time and labor because you don't have to set up spray painting equipment.

There really is no mystery to the correct way of applying aerosol paints, although many of us simply pick up a container, spray and expect a perfect, professional finish. There are certain steps and methods that result in better finishes.

Whenever possible, position the work so the container can be held parallel to the surface being painted. Thoroughly shake the paint for about one minute. A paint temperature of 70 degrees provides the best internal pressure, viscosity, and drying rate.

Aerosol paints, as with compressor spraying, require safe practices. Always provide plenty of ventilation and wear a suitable mask to avoid breathing fumes and paint particles. Protect surrounding area from over-spray and avoid painting around open motors, open flames, stoves and furnaces.

Colored-opaque, clear, gloss, satin and flat materials make up the bulk of aerosol paints. Many are now alkyd or acrylic enamels although lacquers, polyurethane, varnish and shellac are available. Both alkyd and acrylic varieties offer good results and good coverage, but acrylics dry faster than most enamels.

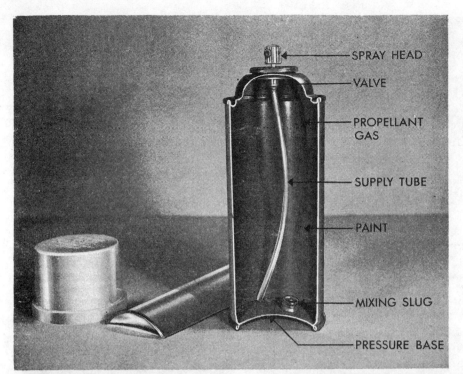

SPRAY HEAD

VALVE

PROPELLANT GAS

SUPPLY TUBE

PAINT

MIXING SLUG

PRESSURE BASE

Cutaway of aerosol can reveals secret of operation. Propellant gas pressure forces paint out of can when spray head is pressed. Note ballast in bottom.

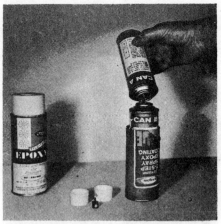

Hard, acid-resistant epoxy finishes come both as single-component aerosols and two-component type, which is mixed before use.

To spray a finish not available as an aerosol, use unit with separate propellant can and fluid jar. Propellant sprays several jars of fluid.

Metal objects can be repainted with special aerosols formulated for exterior metal. Loose paint should be removed, surface primed before use.

For easy spraying, try this snap-on spray can holder from Hyde Tools. Work revolves on lazy-susan bearing.

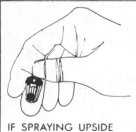

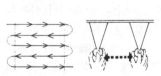

IF SPRAYING UPSIDE DOWN DOES NOT CLEAR NOZZLE, REMOVE SPRAY HEAD AND CLEAN NOTCH WITH THUMBNAIL

SEVERAL THIN COATS APPLIED IN SUCCESSIVE PASSES ARE BETTER THAN ONE HEAVY COAT WHICH WILL TEND TO SAG AND RUN. LAP EACH PASS ABOUT 1/3 OVER PREVIOUS PASS

TURNING CAN UPSIDE DOWN AND SPRAYING FOR AN INSTANT ASSURES USER CLEAR SPRAY HEAD FOR NEXT APPLICATION

Aerosols are excellent for sprucing up steel cabinets. Dark color adds subtle shading to edges after base coat.

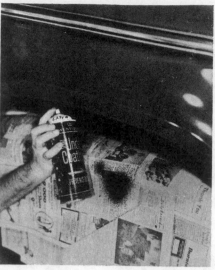

Heavy asphaltic aerosol simplifies job of undercoating to control rust and sound. Handy for undercoating repairs.

E-Pox-E spray enamels resist acids, alkalis, dirt and detergents. Is an excellent finish for appliances, fixtures.

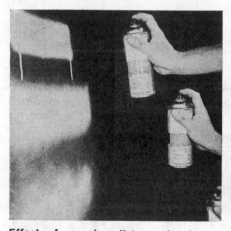

Effect of spraying distance is shown. Different products require different techniques. Always read instructions.

When spray is unhandy, spray liquid on card, use paper match as a small brush to apply on small scratches.

Clean and save spray heads from spent cans of solvent. They are handy when a head fails or gives poor pattern.

Lacquers, usually identified as such on the can, offer very rapid drying, but should not be used to coat over existing enamel finishes.

Polyurethane varnish, with its excellent wear resistance, high gloss (also available in satin), and rapid drying is excellent for clearcoating wood and metal.

Shellac in spray cans is a handy way to have this time-honored finish, good for its sealing and exceptional holdout qualities on wood, plaster, plywood and drywall. Spray at about 10 to 12 inches, avoiding high humidity. Second coat can be applied after about one hour.

Transparent, colored aerosols can be used to color-tone bare metal surfaces, glass, etc. Try the attractive shades of red, blue and green over burnished bare metal for attractive finishes.

Metallic and "glitter" paints usually contain bronze or aluminum powder or flakes suspended in varnish. Usual application distance is 4 to 5 inches. A thin bonding coat should be followed by a light full coat. The container must be shaken frequently to keep the heavy metal material in suspension.

Epoxies come as both two-component types, where you inject the contents of one container into the other, and modified-epoxy, single-component aerosols that are already mixed and ready to apply. These tough, glossy, acid and chemical-resistant materials are recommended for sinks, tanks, recoating appliances, etc. They do dry more slowly than regular enamel aerosols.

Aerosol primers that are compatible to the aerosol finishes are excellent materials to seal pores, cover imperfections, allow smooth sanding, and give the finish a tooth for best bonding. Some makers supply automotive primers in regular cans of fast-drying, color-matching material that can be wet-sanded and recoated with most automotive lacquers and synthetic enamels.

Rust-fighting aerosols fall into two categories—rust-inhibiting and rust-arresting. Most rust-inhibiting paints incorporate zinc chromate, a material that prevents oxidation, controlling rusting on a bare metal surface. Zinc chromate may be available in both primer and exterior finish materials.

Rust-arresting paints—usually primers, can be applied right over a badly rusted surface to arrest further rusting. These materials usually contain varnish and an animal-oil product.

On previously painted surfaces, wire-brush and sandpaper to remove blistered, peeled, or cracked paint. Spot-prime and allow plenty of drying time before finishing.

Heat-resisting aerosols are another specialty paint now on the market. Some will stand an almost unbelievable 1200 degrees. The other colors will take up to 650-800 degrees. It is interesting to see the coating adhering on red hot steel and retaining its color when the material cools. These coatings are also impervious to corrosion and salt spray, along with most solvents. It is necessary to thoroughly wire brush, or sand blast, the metal white before applying. After drying, the painted metal should be cured by heating in an oven, increasing the heat according to instructions. Fireplaces, lawnmower mufflers, engines, engine manifolds, headers, barbecues, furnaces, stoves, heaters, fire screens, etc., can usually be cured by carefully applying the heat of the normal application.

RUSTPROOF FINISHING

It used to be that the only rustproofing finishes available for use in the home shop were the familiar "red primer" or a can of aluminum paint.

Today, thanks to chemical research, there is a variety of "rustproofing" finishes offered, ranging from colorful high-gloss enamels containing fish oils to "exotic" plastic coatings that can be applied in the home shop. The advent of the aerosol spray can has even updated the old-time red primer and made it easier to use.

Any of the organic metal coatings such as paints, lacquers, plastics or epoxies require a primer of some sort to bond the coating to the metal surface. With some materials, the primer is included; with others, the primer must be applied separately.

Primers, which are made up of tiny flecks of metal suspended in a solvent, come in a variety of chemical formulas, the most popular ones remain the "zinc-chromate" and "red-lead" primers. For slightly rusted surfaces, you can use zinc chromate, but for heavily rusted or pitted surfaces, the red or "brown" primers are best.

These primers come in small aerosol spray cans for touch-up work or large 5-gallon cans for automotive repair shops. Most of the primers are available in small cans for brushing; however, in almost all cases a smoother job can be achieved by spraying the primer on the metal surface. It should be thinned according to the manufacturer's instructions for spraying. Properly mixed and sprayed primers are thin-bodied, and will run very easily, so they must be applied in thin "dusting" coats. Apply as many light coats as needed to cover the metal surface, then, when it is thoroughly dry, go over the primer surface with 400-grit superfine silicon-carbide paper.

First step is to remove old scale and rust with medium or coarse-grit emery cloth to prevent it from spreading.

Small areas can be touched up with a small spray can of rust-preventive metal primer. Use light dusting coats.

Several light coats are needed to cover rust spots, then steel wool lightly. Spray on metal enamel or acrylic paint.

Larger areas to be rustproofed require a larger spray gun to apply a good metal primer coat before the final finish.

There are some final finishes which contain primer materials. These are called rust-preventive or rust-inhibitive finishes and are designed primarily for indoor use or touch-up work, where the object will not receive much exposure to the elements. Read the label carefully before using and make sure you're using materials that will do the job you need.

Preparation is the most important factor in rustproofing a surface, whether primer is used or not. On a surface that is to be repainted or has rust on it, remove all the surface rust with coarse emery cloth. If the rust is heavy with lots of scale and pitted spots, go over the surface with a wire brush followed by medium-grit emery cloth.

There are other rust-stopping metal finishes on the market, among them a new penetrating oil in an aerosol can. It is excellent for use on fine machinery requiring close tolerances and is a great help to the home craftsman as well. Applied to the top of a rusted table saw and rubbed with steel wool, it will eventually give you a nice shiny table ready for action. Light sprays of the penetrating oil in the working parts of the saw will help to keep them free from rust.

To really protect the saw table surface, you can coat it with one of the new plastic coatings. These coatings not only prevent rust, but they become slicker with use, making the saw tabletop easier to work on.

Fingerprints are the worst enemy of metal finishes, as gunsmiths, dealers and owners will tell you. A light coat of rust-preventive oil will resist the corrosive action caused by the fingerprints. This same oil applied to your fine hand tools such as saws, carpenters' squares, even your steel tape, can protect them.

One of the most popular factory finishes for rustproofing was galvanizing. This required dipping the metal object such as roofing, guttering or plumbing pipe in a hot metal bath. Now you can galvanize metal objects at home from a spray can.

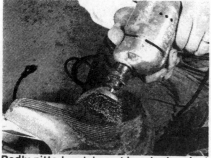

Badly pitted metal must be wire-brushed clean to produce a smooth paint-holding surface before applying primer.

Some metal finishes contain rust-stopping primers themselves; others have fish-oil vehicles to penetrate rust.

Old time "aluminum" rustproofing paints have been replaced by a variety of new and better rust-preventive paints.

"Cabinetmakers wax" is an excellent wax for antique furniture. Gives a fine "patina" to unsealed wood as well.

"Teak Foam" is especially formulated for cleaning oil-finished open-grain woods such as teak, walnut, rosewood.

Easy-to-use silicone dusting and cleaning waxes in aerosol containers are the most popular waxes today.

POLISHES AND WAXES

Polishes and waxes come in three forms: paste, liquid and aerosol. Paste wax is a concentrate used where protection is important, as on antiques, checked wood or soft leather. To improve checked wood surfaces, apply wax to a small area with fine steel wool, rubbing with the grain. Polish immediately while the wax is still moist.

Liquid polishes are available in several types. The familiar red-oil polish is formulated for wooden furniture and floors. It restores and polishes both light and dark wood. To use this polish, pour a few drops on a slightly damp cloth and apply with gentle strokes. Buff with a clean, dry cloth.

Another liquid polish, sold under many brand names, is "lemon-oil." It has yellow coloring and a lemon aroma, and is used the same as red-oil polish.

Cream polish is another type cleaner-polish. It is excellent for Danish-modern furniture or any dull or natural finish. It cleans without shining. Cream polish also can be used on "antiqued" finishes, laminated plastic, metal and vinyl surfaces. It is excellent for stainless steel, chrome and enameled wood.

"Kitchen waxes" are a liquid, but in heavy-duty form. They are made specially for cleaning and polishing in the kitchen.

The most popular polishes with the homemaker who is "easy-care" oriented are the aerosol "dusting" sprays. They are generally a formula of waxes and oils with silicones added. Many also have lemon oil. These waxes should be used sparingly, according to instructions. Usually they say to spray the furniture very lightly and evenly, then polish with a clean, dry cloth.

A streaked or dulled effect may result when an aerosol polish is used over an oil or paste-wax finish, or when liquid polish is used over wax. This can be corrected by complete removal of the polish with a cloth dampened in mineral spirits, then re-polishing to restore the finish.

All major aerosol polishes contain silicones. Some refinishers claim that varnish removal is difficult when silicone polishes have been used. Modern varnish removers have eliminated this problem to a large extent.

Never "dry-dust," as wiping a surface on which grit and dust have collected can cause minute scratches. Dust with wax to moisten the surface, and pick up grit without scratching.

There are wax finishes to produce the satiny patina important in finishing antiques or reproductions. You also can make your own wax finish: apply penetrating wood sealer to the raw wood and allow to set 10 minutes. Wipe off the surplus, let the sealer dry 24 hours. Rub lightly with steel wool, then apply paste wax with a steel-wood pad, rubbing with the grain. Buff shiny, then apply a second coat of wax with the cloth used for buffing.

For matching the right polish or wax to your particular finish, follow the recommendations in the chart.

Finish or Surface	Recommended Treatment
Wood—high luster (lacquer, varnish, etc.)	Dusting—Spray silicone wax Periodic cleaning—liquid polish (red oil) Protecting—paste wax
Wood—low luster (Danish-Modern Furniture)	Dusting—cream polish Periodic cleaning— oil cleansing foam
Wood—antiques	Paste wax
Wood—painted (antiqued)	Cream polish
Wood—unfinished	Wax finishes
Wood—worn finishes	Paste wax
Wood—checkered finishes	Paste wax
Wood—painted	Dusting—Spray silicone wax Periodic cleaning—"kitchen waxes" liquid polish Protecting—paste wax
Laminated plastic	Spray silicone wax Cream polish
Marble	Spray silicone wax
Metal and glass	Spray silicone wax Protecting metal—cream polish
Leather (sealed tabletops)	Same as wood, high-luster
Leather (dull or worn surfaces)	Paste wax
Leather upholstery	Paste wax Spray silicone wax
Vinyl upholstery	Dusting—Spray Silicone wax Periodic cleaning—"kitchen waxes" Protecting—cream polish.

FINISH PATCHING

No matter how well protected furniture will get dented and scratched, and many times the furniture won't get repaired because of the high cost involved or of finding someone to do the job.

Finish-patching is a method used by profes-

sional refinishers for repairing minor flaws, and with a little practice almost anyone can do their own furniture repairs.

You can make burn-in knives, as shown, or purchase them along with the stick shellac in all degrees of transparency and colors. You will need a

Burn-in knives can be purchased or "home-made" from hardened steel such as industrial hacksaw blades.

Source for heating knives can be electric knife oven, alcohol lamp, candle, small blow torch or hot plate.

It is good practice to wipe hot knife on rag each time before it is used; essential when working on blond finishes.

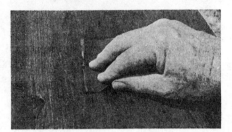

Pick up small amount of shellac on tip of knife. Remember, if shellac bubbles, the knife is too hot.

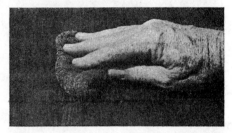

Drop melted shellac alongside the damaged area. Scratch to be patched here is white mark below knife tip.

Draw shellac into hole until level with surrounding finish. Smooth patch with wiping stroke of hot knife.

Sand patch with 360, wet-or-dry carbide paper and rubbing oil. Light touch is required to protect finish.

Polish patch with 4/0 steel wool to match sheen of surrounding finish. For higher gloss use rubbing compound.

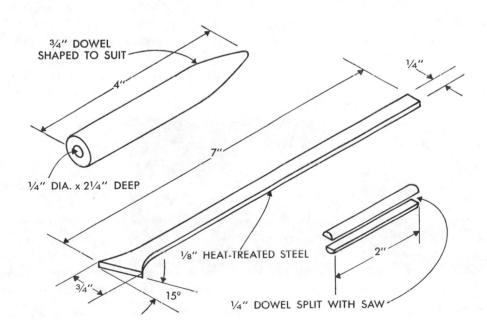

¾" DOWEL SHAPED TO SUIT

4"

¼" DIA. x 2¼" DEEP

7"

¼"

⅛" HEAT-TREATED STEEL

¾"

15°

2"

¼" DOWEL SPLIT WITH SAW

device for heating the knives, such as a knife-oven, alcohol lamp, candle, small blow torch, or hot plate. Also, you will need 4/0 steel wool, 360-grit, wet-or-dry paper, rubbing oil or a mixture of crude oil and mineral spirits or naphtha, rubbing compound and an assortment of old rags.

Clean the scratch or dent of any dust or finish particles. Wipe any soot off the heated knife and melt a small amount of shellac on the tip. If the shellac bubbles and boils, the knife is too hot; wipe it off, allow it to cool and start over again. Too hot a knife will scorch both shellac and finish. Drop the melted shellac alongside the damage and draw it into the edge of the hole with the opposite side of the knife. Repeat until the shellac is slightly above the surface of the surrounding finish. Then draw the knife rapidly across the patch and on both sides of it until the shellac is flush with the finish. The knife should be replaced with a heated knife as required. The stroke of the knife should be smooth, not contacting or leaving the surface abruptly. Using 360-paper dipped in rubbing oil, sand lightly and polish with 4/0 steel wool. For a high gloss, apply rubbing compound with a cheesecloth, then polish.

To avoid the bulls-eye appearance of a sharply defined hole such as a cigarette burn or deep gouge, scratch the ends of the hole with the grain and soften the finish with lacquer thinner. When this is dry, apply a thin layer of opaque shellac-stick matching the stained wood. Next, apply a layer of transparent shellac the color of finished wood and finally a layer of clear. With practice and experience you will develop the skill required to make a professional patch.

REMOVING WATER STAINS

Winter or summer, there are times when a frosty-cold drink really hits the spot. But that same sweating glass of goodness can make a white stain on the finish of fine furniture that is really tough to remove.

Ordinary furniture polish won't remove it, no matter how you rub. And hiding it with a plant or decorative item doesn't make it go away.

Prevention still is the best cure for water stains, which means when you refinish furniture, or apply finish to something you build yourself, use material that is stain resistant. Check the container of the finish you plan to use to see if it is stain resistant. If is isn't get something else.

One good method of prevention is to use a quality paste wax (not liquid polish) on a finish. If you see a stain quickly enough, a quick wipe will remove it, and you need just reapply the wax. Polish can be applied over the wax for a higher gloss. Lacquer is a good finish, if you top it with several coats of wax applied with fine steel wool.

Several methods can be used to remove white water stains, the method being determined by how deep the stain has penetrated. For light stains, sprinkle on cigarette or cigar ashes, then lightly rub with a soft cloth dipped in cooking oil, lemon oil or linseed oil. If there is just a trace of stain, wipe it with household ammonia. Immediately rinse with clear water, then wipe dry.

A harsher abrasive is table salt and oil; rub lightly. For stronger abrasion try rottenstone (at paint stores) with a cloth dipped in oil. A step rougher is pumice stone with an oiled cloth. Keep

Rottenstone is finer abrasive, pumice somewhat coarser; both are used with light oil. Rub lightly, blend spot.

In using any of the abrasive materials, use a folded cloth that makes a pad. This avoids concentrated rubbing.

After stain has been rubbed away, wipe entire surface with denatured alcohol, allow it to dry thoroughly.

the cloth in a soft pad so it does not concentrate the rubbing in one small area. Blend the spot into the rest of the surface.

After any of these operations, wipe the surface with alcohol, let dry, then apply paste wax.

Polish can be applied over the wax for a high gloss.

If the finish is thin, unfortunately, and you rub through it, the only solution is to strip the finish and redo the job. This time use a top-quality stain-resistant finishing material.

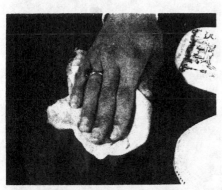
Final step in stain removal is to apply paste wax to the cleaned surface. Buff in well, then apply spray polish.

Best way to prevent water stains on furniture, when you make or refinish it, is to use a stain-resistant material.

Another good preventive "medicine" is to occasionally apply paste wax to a wood surface. Paste wax, not a liquid.

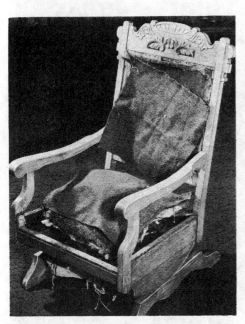

If it's loose in the joints, tap it apart, clean off the old glue and finish. Smooth and sand, make repairs.

Reassemble the chair, using a good grade of glue, clamping as per glue-maker's instructions.

As a short cut, old seat springs and padding were replaced with plywood panel and foam cushion.

RENOVATING AN OLD CHAIR

Is there an old chair tucked away in your attic? Have you noticed one in your neighbor's garage or among the jumble of sad looking furniture in a secondhand store? Take another look, a handsome heirloom may be masquerading as a piece of junk. After a Cinderella treatment by you it can proudly take its place as a comfortable, good-looking piece of furniture, a compliment-catcher and a source of satisfaction as the result of

Strips of wood inside seat frame support plywood panel so cushion will be in right position, replacing original.

Original webbing on back was left in place, but a sheet of ¾-in. foam padding is fitted behind it.

Sheet of hardboard covers back opening, being fastened with screws along sides. Top and bottom are free.

Strips of upholstery around seat edges hide unfinished wood. Material is wrapped around strips of cardboard.

Cushion of 4-in. foam is cut using template for plywood seat and it is covered with material. Material tacked to back.

time well spent. Our project was a platform rocker, but any chair responds to the same type of treatment.

The first step is to disassemble it by carefully tapping it apart at the joints. This permits cleaning off the old glue, making any necessary repairs, and simplifies stripping off the old finish with remover. The separate pieces are more easily sanded after the wood has dried than when the chair is assembled.

Reassemble the chair, using quality glue and clamping the various assemblies the length of time the glue manufacturer specifies. You can eliminate the reupholstery of spring-type cushions by using a piece of plywood to support a foam cushion.

The back can be padded also, utilizing the old webbing; you may have to replace the webbing. To hide the rough edges of the seat frame, tack cardboard strips over upholstery material, wrap the material up over the cardboard and tack it to the top of the frame. The seat cushion hides the upper edges of the material, as well as the tacks.

A real time and trouble-saver tip: refinish the chair before applying the upholstery.

HOW TO CANE ANTIQUE CHAIRS

Refinishing an old piece of furniture often is only one part of the job of putting it back in service. Often the seat and back should be caned to really finish the job.

Natural chair cane is imported from the Far East and is sold in hanks of 1,000 feet.

Each hank consists of many strips 15 to 20 feet long. Cane comes in different widths from fine-fine to wide; the latter is used for binding.

Cane is soaked in warm water for 5 or 10 minutes before it is used. You also need about a dozen short lengths of dowel, sharpened to fit in the holes in the chair. These hold the cane ends until they can be tied later. A pair of old scissors or diagonal-cutting pliers is required for cutting the tough cane, and a small sponge is needed to wet the cane in later steps.

In the first of the required seven steps, the strands can go either way, but the longer span usually is chosen. Start weaving in the center hole on one of the short sides, leaving 6 inches hanging free in back for later tying. Pin the cane to the center hole on the opposite side, go through the hole from front to back and up through the adjacent hole. The loop formed on the back between holes later is used for tying. Do not allow the cane to twist, and keep the shiny side out. Do not stretch, but simply pull out the slack. When the cane dries it becomes taut. Continue until all but the corner holes are filled, then return to the center and work towards the other side.

In the second step, the same process is repeated at right angles. The strands are not woven, but simply placed over the first. Repeat the first step for the third operation, but keep the strands to the right of those in step 1, not directly on top.

Weaving starts in the fourth step, with the strands going over and under steps 1 and 3, keeping parallel to, and below those, in step 2. The cane will pull through in one direction more smoothly than the other. Also, if you break a strand, go back to the last hole and peg or tie it.

After step 4 wet the caned area on both sides with a sponge dampened in warm water. Then, carefully force the pairs of cane together as tightly as possible, both vertically and horizontally.

The fifth step is a weaving step that goes diagonally. Start in a corner hole and weave over a pair, then under. It is important that the cane slides in the intersections; if it binds, remove the cane to the beginning step and weave the opposite way. For example, if you began by going under, then over, go over then under. If the cane binds, it will soon cut through at the intersections from the slight movement during use.

As you progress through the steps, tie the loose ends whenever there is available a loop between two holes in the back.

The sixth step is the same as the fifth, with the diagonal strands at the opposite angle. Again be sure the cane slips rather than binds at the intersections.

When all diagonal weaving is done, the cane is ready for binding. Use an awl to move the cane aside in the various holes so the strands can pass from a hole, around the binding and back to the

1. In first step cane is run long way (vertical here). Pegs hold ends.

2. In second step strands are run crossways to step one, not woven.

3. Strands in third step go over those in steps one and two.

same hole, then on to the next for a repeat. Keep the cane well moistened for weaving short angles.

When the binding is done, apply a couple of coats of thinned shellac and chair is ready for use.

Weaving starts in fourth step, new strand goes over and under vertical strands, below horizontal one.

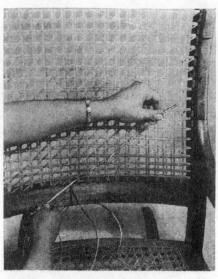

First diagonal strand is fifth step. It goes under vertical strands, over horizontal ones; slips easily.

In this step diagonal strand goes opposite to the previous step; this operation completes pattern of weave.

Loose ends are tied at back between loops of vertical strands. If tying is delayed, ends must be wet to tie.

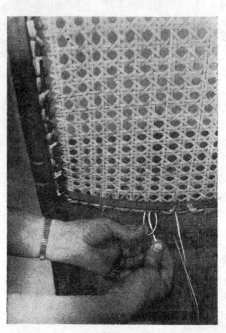

Binding is being applied. Tying strip goes in and out same hole, moves along back to next hole, then repeats.

PAINT AND VARNISH REMOVAL

The first step in the refinishing of used or remodeled furniture is usually the removal of old paint or varnish. Here are a few tips on how to make the job easier, faster, and more efficient.

There are three different methods you can use to remove old paint or varnish. The first method is to apply a chemical remover. This softens the paint so it can be scraped off or rinsed away with water. Another method commonly used for large areas is to sand the old paint off. The third and most difficult method is to apply heat to the old paint and scrape it off. Chemical removers are the fastest and the easiest and are therefore recommended for most types of furniture refinishing.

Chemical Removers

Chemical removers come in semi-paste and liquid forms. They are almost always sold as paint removers, but can be used as effectively to remove varnish. In addition to these two basic forms, chemical removers come in three different grades.

The best grade of chemical remover is the type that washes away with water. This eliminates much of the mess and hard work usually associated with refinishing furniture. This type of remover works quickly, cleans up easily, and is usually cheaper in the long run.

The next grade of remover often leaves a residue which must be sanded away. The manufacturer might claim it to be a little or no clean up remover, but if it doesn't specifically say "wash away," or "water wash," some residue will remain. Light sanding may be necessary to remove this residue.

The third grade of chemical remover contains a wax base. It will loosen the paint or varnish, but the wax must be removed with a paint thinner or solvent. These less expensive types of chemical removers are usually highly flammable.

Regardless of the type of chemical remover you decide to use, read the label thoroughly and follow the manufacturer's directions carefully. Do not use any type of chemical remover in an enclosed or poorly ventilated area.

How to Use Chemical Removers

Chemical removers can be harmful to the skin and eyes. Use them in a well ventilated area and with extreme caution. Always wear gloves to protect your hands and arms. Goggles are also recommended to protect your eyes from possible splashes of the chemical removers.

Liquid removers work best on flat, regular surfaces. Use the semi-paste removers on curved, carved, or irregular surfaces. This will prevent the problem of the remover dripping off the area to which it is applied.

If you are dealing with a flat surface, like a table or desk top, pour the remover directly from the can onto the flat surface. Cover the area completely and evenly. Don't be afraid to put on a good thick coat. Spread it evenly over the surface with a good brush. If you are using the liquid form

you can get good coverage by tilting the surface back and forth. Apply paint remover to small areas at a time. Cover only that space you can scrape or wash away before the remover dries.

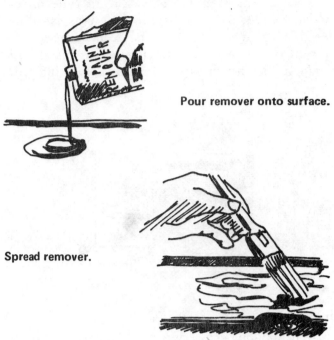

Pour remover onto surface.

Spread remover.

Most chemical removers should be left on for approximately 20 to 30 minutes. Before attempting to wash or scrape the entire area, test a small spot. Rub a gloved finger over the treated surface in a circular motion. If this cuts through to the wood surface the old paint has been sufficiently loosened by the remover. You can now begin to remove the loose paint. A medium grade steel wool, an abrasive scouring pad, or old rags can all be used.

Check to see that paint has been sufficiently loosened.

Steel wood helps to remove loosened paint.

If you used one of the less expensive types of remover you will also need to remove the old wax. You can do this with paint thinner or a solvent such as turpentine.

If you used the water wash up type of remover, the loosened paint can now be washed or hosed away. When the loosened paint has been removed, rinse the piece with clear water. Finish any rough spots with the steel wool or a scouring pad.

Hose off the paint and remover.

Removing Paint from Difficult Spots

It may be necessary to use a scraper or a blade to remove especially stubborn spots of paint or varnish. Don't hesitate to apply a second coat of remover if scraping is not effective.

You may need a scraper.

Apply a second coat if necessary.

Enamel may be especially difficult to remove. A second coat of chemical remover is usually required. It might even be necessary to apply a third coat to some spots if several layers of enamel have been applied to the piece.

Another common problem is an irregular surface. Curved surfaces, cut-out areas, and hard-to-reach spots are often a challenge for the do-it-yourselfer. With a little patience, however, even these difficult spots can be cleaned of all unwanted paint or varnish.

Removing paint from chair spindles, for example, is not easy. The best method is to apply a thick coat of semi-paste remover into the crack around each spindle. Use a regular brush and plenty of remover. Let it stand, remove, and reapply as necessary. Set the legs of the chair in metal containers or cans to collect any drips. Brush upward from the bottom of the legs and reuse any surplus remover.

Let remover soak in thoroughly.

Use a can to catch any surplus remover.

Plastic cleaning pads or copper scouring pads are excellent for use on carved areas. The scouring pad can be forced into these areas to remove old paint or varnish after it has been loosened by a chemical remover. Always rinse the surface well after the paint or varnish has been scoured off.

498

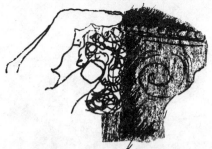

Steel wool helps to remove paint from carved areas.

Occasionally a scouring pad will not work in narrow grooves or slits. If this is your problem, use a stiff, narrow wire brush. Do not press too hard on the brush, however. If too much pressure is applied the wood which has been softened by the chemical remover may be permanently damaged.

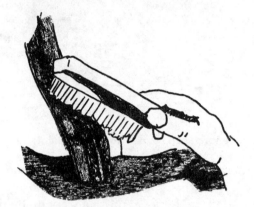

A small brush may be helpful in some spots.

Sometimes even a narrow brush will not fit into extremely narrow grooves or small holes. In this case, you may have to use a small stick to scrape the paint out of the grooves. A splintered piece of wood from a small board may be just what you need.

A small piece of wood is also a handy tool.

Turned legs, on tables and chairs, are also difficult spots. Use a twisted piece of rag or burlap like a shoeshine cloth to rub off the remover after it has set for about 20 minutes. This method usually works quickly and easily and eliminates most of the usual mess. A common kitchen-type scraper is another handy item for removing paint and varnish from difficult to reach areas.

Twisted burlap works well on turned legs.

Plug keyholes and hardware holes before using paint remover.

Hardware can be dipped in the remover.

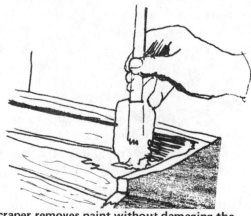

A kitchen scraper removes paint without damaging the softened wood.

Sanding

Any type of power or hand sander can be used to remove old paint or varnish from large, even surfaces. Power sanders are highly recommended for large jobs, but they should be used cautiously and with a light touch.

Special electric paint removers are available.

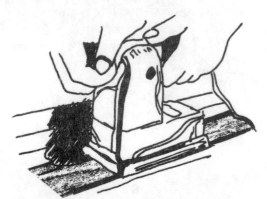

A power sander can be used for large jobs.

Sanding removes paint or varnish quickly and easily. It does have a big disadvantage, however, over both chemical removers and heat: it also removes some of the surface when it removes the paint. This makes sanding highly undersirable for removing paint from fine furniture, carved, or curved surfaces. Generally, sanding paint from a surface is not recommended except for extremely rough or large jobs.

If you do decide to sand, keep these points in mind. First, an open coat, coarse sandpaper must be used. Finer grain sandpapers clog up quickly. This makes them rather ineffective as paint removers.

Second, the item you are sanding must be thoroughly dusted or vacuumed to remove any particles which might cling to it when you apply the finish. If you are not careful you will wind up with a grainy or rough finish.

Third, use a light touch. Too much pressure on one spot will cause waves in the surface.

Heat

Old paint or varnish can also be removed with heat. The application of heat destroys the film in the old paint and facilitates scraping. Electric paint removers are available for removing paint or varnish by this method. A propane torch can also be used. Exercise extreme caution, however, if you use an open flame.

A propane torch can be used to remove paint.

Scrape the old paint away as soon as it is heated. A broad paint scraper is most effective when used to remove the paint right behind the torch or electric softener.

There is no open flame with an electric softener.

Never allow the flame from the torch to remain on one spot long enough to burn the wood. Keep the flame moving at all times. This will ensure that there will be no brown or dark spots caused by excessive heat.

Once you have successfully removed the old, unwanted paint or varnish you can proceed to refinish your item. The hard part of your job is over.

WOOD FILLERS

Finishing open-pored woods, such as ash, walnut and especially oak, requires the application of paste filler to create a smooth surface. Be careful when you buy filler and ask specifically for "paste filler." Too many products now on the market are "stain-fillers" or "sealer-fillers" and really are nothing more than sealers. They are fine for close-grained, fine-pored woods, but for oak and similar woods you want the ground-up quartz mixed with a vehicle, which is "paste" filler.

This filler can be mixed with stain (nonpenetrating oil stain only) to create a combination stain-filler. The filler is brushed on in a heavy coat, allowed to set until it dulls, then is wiped with burlap or other coarse cloth across the grain to pack it into the pores. Last step is to wipe with the grain. Allow the filler to dry as per the instructions on the container. Also mix and apply as described by the manufacturer.

You can stain first, then apply filler, but the stain must be sealed. The filler must be mixed with stain to match that already applied.

For special finishes, stain first, then apply natural filler, or filler mixed with white paint. This creates a "limed" or "silver oak" finish. Reversing the process, using stained filler on a light surface produces another "exotic" finish.

Black paint applied to open-grain ash shows clearly the pores and grains that would be filled flush with filler.

Mixing stain with filler makes "stain-filler" combination that both fills the wood and applies the color.

Paste filler must be mixed thoroughly before it is used; some types require thinning with linseed oil.

Brush on filler in full, wet coat, going with the grain. Brush firmly to force the filler into the grain.

REFINISHING WALNUT

Contrary to belief, refinishing furniture requires no complicated skills, and professional looking finishes may be obtained by anyone who follows certain steps and performs each operation as though it were the most important.

The first step in refinishing is to remove the old finish with a quality paint and varnish remover. Follow the directions given by the manufacturer for best results. Pieces of ¼- or 3/8-inch dowels about six or eight inches long, with their ends shaped as indicated, are used to remove residue from corners and carvings.

The second step is to wash the furniture thoroughly with lacquer thinner. In the case of open-grain wood, scrub the old filler out of the grain using a brass suede brush and lacquer thinner. When the old finish is removed, the stain in the filler is leached out.

If the furniture is nicked or scarred to the point that sanding cannot correct the faults (this is especially true of veneered surfaces) these scars should be patched with wood putty. An ordinary putty knife is too stiff, and will pull the patching material out of the holes, but a druggists' or cheese spatula makes an excellent patching knife. Grind off the rounded end of either of these flexible tools and use as you would a putty knife. If a hole is particularly deep, it is best to apply several layers of putty, with drying intervals between. The completed patch should be higher than the surrounding surface so that when it is sanded, it will be smooth and flush. When the patch is completed, check it for color match by moistening with turpentine or a turp substitute. If the colors match they will also match under the finish. If they don't match, dig out the patch and start over again. Sand with the grain and use progressively finer grits of sandpaper; 2/0 for rough sanding, 4/0 to remove the scratches left by 2/0, and 6/0 for final sanding. Do the final sanding by hand because you can feel when the surface has reached the desired smoothness.

Tools shaped from lengths of dowel are used to remove residual finish and filler from corners, hard-to-reach spots.

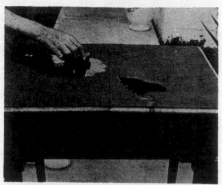

To get maximum depth to the new finish, old filler is scrubbed out of grain with lacquer thinner and suede brush.

Filler was removed from grain of walnut on right with lacquer thinner and brush. The walnut on the left was not treated.

After paint remover has been allowed to penetrate for a few minutes, finish and remover are moved to untreated area.

Remnants of finish and remover are removed from corners and carvings with a length of ⅜-in. dowel.

Table is carefully sanded. While sanders may be used for flat areas, hand-sanding preserves the patina of the old wood.

If an individual board has grain of varying colors, blend the two by using two pads of soft cloth, one dipped in non-grain-raising stain and the other in painters' alcohol (work in a well-ventilated area). Use the stain pad to darken the light wood and the alcohol pad to blend it into the darker wood. In the case of furniture that has a walnut body with birch, poplar, or gum legs or trim, use pigmented oil stain. Wipe it on the parts that are not walnut and remove the surplus with a cloth that has been dampened with turpentine, wiping with the grain. If the color is not dark enough, another coat of stain can be applied.

Walnut and many other open-grain woods require the use of paste wood filler, that can be pigmented. The filler, a silica base in linseed oil, is used to seal the open pores of the wood and bring out the grain. Filler is thinned to the consistency of thick paint and applied with a brush or cloth using strokes across and with the grain. It is then "padded" into the grain with a cloth pad using cir-cular strokes. When the filler dries it becomes dull. Wipe off the surplus with a coarse rag (burlap) across the grain. Any smears that are left on the surface should be wiped away with a soft cloth. The sharpened dowels previously used to clean up the remover now may be used to clean filler from difficult to reach areas. Allow the filler to dry 24 hours.

When the filler is thoroughly dry you can apply the finish. Lacquer finishes are the most popular, but others can be used effectively. In all instances the first or sealing coat should be sprayed on. Brushing a sealing material over filler and stain smears the surface.

If you are using lacquer the sealing coat should be lacquer sanding sealer. If you plan to use varnish, seal with varnish in an aerosol can.

Lacquer sanding sealer is ordinary lacquer with stearates or metallic soaps added to aid in sanding. In spraying lacquer, thinner should be added according to manufacturer's instructions,

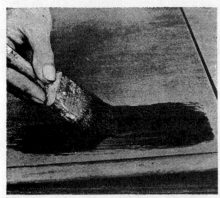

Filler is mixed according to manufacturer's directions, applied with brush or soft cloth, stroking with grain.

A coarse cloth (such as burlap) is used to scrub the filler into the grain. The padding is done in a circular motion.

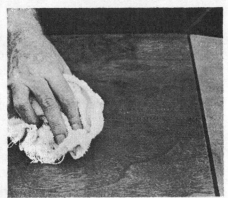

When filler dulls, surplus is wiped off across the grain with a coarse cloth. Remove smears carefully with cloth.

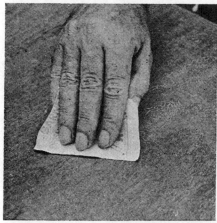

Sand sealer coat with 6/0 garnet paper. Even on sealer and finish, sand and rub with the grain.

Apply rubbing oil (paraffin oil) as a lubricant for final sanding to create glass-smooth surface.

Steel wool and rubbing oil are used rather than sandpaper on the moldings, details and rounded edges.

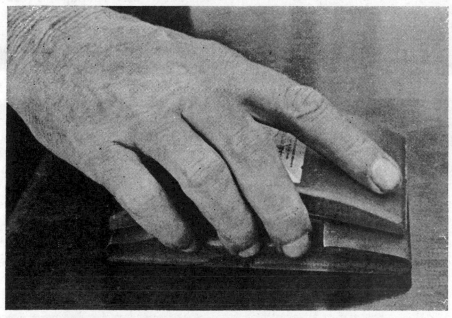

Rub flat area with fine grit silicon-carbide wet-or-dry paper using a rubber or felt-covered block. Rubbing oil (paraffin oil) is lubricant for sandpaper.

usually about 10 percent. Many professional finishers mix lacquer by rubbing it between their fingers and adding thinner as needed. It should have a slight oily feeling, but become tacky very quickly. Ordinary lacquer can be used as a sealing coat, but is harder to sand. If your first coat has a rough, sandy texture, either add thinner or reduce the air in relation to the volume of liquid passing through the spray nozzle. "Lacquer" guns mix the air externally, guns used for other materials such as enamels, mix the air and materials internally. A properly mixed lacquer will produce a "wet," but not heavy coating. When dry it should be barely visible. Practice on a piece of plywood until you achieve a smooth, wet coat with no runs or sags. Although correctly mixed and applied lacquer will not run easily, any runs that do appear should be allowed to dry, then be sanded off.

After the sealer has dried for at least two hours, sand with 6/0 garnet paper removing all the raised grain without cutting through to the bare wood.

The procedure for applying varnish is to flow a wet coat on with a fine quality natural-bristle or a tapered "flagged" synthetic bristle brush. Sand lightly when dry and repeat for two or three coats.

The procedure for spraying the finish coats of lacquer is the same as the sealer coat, except the lacquer is applied in somewhat heavier coats. These are still light as compared to varnish, and several of these coats will produce a deep finish. Two hours' drying time is usually adequate with light sanding between coats.

The materials needed to attain a "satin" finish are: 360-grit wet-or-dry silicon-carbide paper and paraffin (rubbing oil). The first step is to rub all flat surfaces with the 360 paper backed up with a rubber sanding block, using the rubbing oil as a lubricant. Most of the "orange peel" should be rubbed out by rubbing with the grain.

The final step is to rub all the molded edges and details (with the grain) with steel wool until all orange peel disappears.

If high gloss is desired, apply a generous coat of rubbing compound with a piece of cheesecloth that has been soaked in water and wrung out, then rub off the compound with a clean dry cloth turning it to provide a clean surface to the finish as you go. The finish should be smooth and extremely transparent.

REFINISHING PRIMITIVES

A "primitive" is a piece of furniture not old enough to be an antique, but with enough age to have a "personality." If this type of furniture is not too badly damaged, such as having been used for a workbench or chopping block, much of the "patina" (beauty achieved through age and countless polishing and rubbing) can be preserved when refinishing it.

In most cases primitives will be covered with several coats of paint or darkened finish, so the first step is to apply a generous coat of paint remover. Give the remover plenty of time to work, then use a dull putty knife to scrape off the loose finish. You may have to repeat this operation several times. When all the old finish has been removed, scrub the wood with fine steel wool and lacquer thinner. If you have been careful with the steel wool, the original stain and patina will still be in the wood, and you will not have to stain before applying a finish.

Apply a coat of lacquer sealer and allow it to dry overnight. After the sealer is dry lightly sand off any "whiskers" of wood that may have raised. Then apply several coats of brushing or spraying lacquer, lightly sanding between each. A thorough rubbing with fine steel wool will cut down the glossy highlights on the lacquer and give the finish the sheen of a fine old hand-rubbed surface.

If you have a primitive that is designed well, or just fits a certain corner of your room, but is too "rough" to finish as above you can apply a patina to it. Remove the finish as described previously then go a step further and sand down to the raw wood removing stain as well as finish.

Apply a "shading stain," a solution consisting of a small amount of brown maple nongrain-raising stain mixed with two parts clear lacquer and one part lacquer thinner. This can be sprayed or brushed on much like an "antique" glaze. Just remember to apply it with a light hand, and after the sealer coat.

A refinished primitive should not have a glossy, formal appearance, but should retain some evidence of its use and age.

Before: Typical of "primitives," this chest is not old enough to be an antique, but does have a character.

After: Refinished pine furniture looks more like the original finish might have if it had been cared for.

First step is to remove all old finish with paint remover, scraper and steel wool. May require several applications.

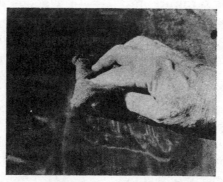

After scraping off all paint remover, scrub wood several times with lacquer thinner and fine steel wool.

Refinished primitive should have a clear finish, but should retain patina of time. Note inkstain, lower right.

PAINTING A CHAIR

Before starting the painting it's a good idea to wash all surfaces with a sponge and detergent and water. Note especially the arms and back where hands and arms have deposited body oils. For especially tough spots, use a household scouring pad. Let the chair stand overnight to be sure all moisture has dried before you do the painting.

When you paint a chair you can keep mess to a minimum, avoid wiping your arms on fresh paint and save time, by reversing the usual procedure of starting at the top and working down. Instead, turn the chair upside down on a table or workbench, with newspapers underneath to catch any drips or splatters, so it is at a convenient height. Next, tap push pins or small nails into the bottom of each leg.

Start painting at the bottom; the lower ends

of the legs and the rungs and the underside of the seat. When you have finished this part of the chair, Turn it right side up and stand it on the newspapers. The nails or pins will keep the legs up off the paper and the wet paint will not be marred.

You now can paint the arms and back of the chair, as well as the seat or any other part requiring refinishing. Look for any runs or sags created while painting the legs, and brush them lightly with a "dry" brush.

ENAMELING FURNITURE

One of the quickest and easiest ways to transform worn or unfinished pieces of furniture into dazzling delights is to apply a coat or two of enamel. Bright colors are the vogue now, so your imagination is the only limit to the effects you can create with your paintbrush.

Choosing the colors is your personal decision, but remember that only a quality enamel made by a reputable manufacturer is your assurance of easy application, good hiding power and a color-fast durable finish.

One of the most important steps in obtaining a successful enameling job is surface preparation. This will vary according to surface condition prior to painting. Wooden furniture in good condition requires only a good cleaning with odorless paint thinner to remove oil, wax or polish. Afterwards, sand lightly to dull the gloss of the old paint and provide a surface to which the new finish can adhere. If the wooden furniture is in poor condition, it should be completely stripped of its old finish: painting over a poor finish will simply repeat the

gouges, scratches and nicks, but in a brighter color! Use a good-quality paint remover and work in a well-ventilated area.

Fill any holes or cracks with wood putty and let dry thoroughly. Finally, sand as smooth as possible and apply an enamel undercoat. When this has dried, you are ready for the enamel topcoat.

Unfinished furniture usually is factory sanded. It's a good idea, however, to sand lightly before apply the undercoat. If you apply a second undercoat, sand lightly between coats.

To renew wrought iron and other metal furniture, clean thoroughly, then sand away rust. Prime the bare spots with metal primer, such as zinc chromate. When the primed areas are dry, apply the enamel. Do the same for aluminum furniture.

The final step is proper application: flow the enamel on with long, smooth strokes, with the grain. Don't reload the brush, but stroke across the grain, then, finally, with the grain. This method provides even coverage and picks up excess paint that might cause runs.

EXOTIC WOODS

Some of the most beautiful woods are teak, rosewood, amaranth, etc., but these woods are also some of the hardest-to-finish of woods. Their natural oils are retained even after they have been thoroughly dried and cured, and can cause all kinds of finishing troubles.

Regardless of the finish that is to be applied, the first step is to wash oily woods thoroughly with denatured alcohol (ordinary shellac thinner). Use a stiff-bristle brush and flood the area with alcohol. Repeat this operation at least two more

times, using clean alcohol each time. Allow the wood to air-dry between each alcohol bath. Don't heat it or set it in the sun to dry, as this will only force more oil to the surface.

After removing the oil from the wood surface, with the alcohol, the wood may be finished in one of several ways. Probably the easiest to apply is a penetrating oil finish. This type of finish provides a non-glossy look that compliments the beauty and grain of the wood. Several coats of finish should be applied, buffing each with a soft cloth.

Rosewood, Teak and other woods contain so much natural oil that they must be washed with denatured alcohol.

One of the best finishes for these woods is a good penetrating oil, applied liberally and buffed after each coat.

A wax finish can also be applied on oily woods. Apply several coats of paste floor wax, buffing with fine steel wool.

Clear lacquer can be applied to oily woods, but wood must be washed thoroughly with alcohol first.

Some woods have such large pores and open grain they require a sealer coat before the finish coat.

Or you can spray on a lacquer finish, but it must be applied in very thin coats. One unusual way of finishing these woods is to merely apply wax such as a good quality paste floor wax, buffing between coats with steel wool and buffing after the last coat with a soft cloth. A stainfiller should be used to fill the open pores first.

Varnish can be applied as a finish, but a thin wash-coat of sealer made up of thinned-down varnish or shellac must first be applied to the wood. This coat is then cut down to the wood surface by sanding and the final varnish coat applied.

METALLIC POWDER STENCILING

Although stenciling metallic powders onto furniture is an age-old craft, the beautiful, soft glow of the colors applied in a graceful design will add character to almost any furniture.

The first step is to design a pattern then cut a stencil from it. You can use the pattern shown, enlarging by the squares to fit your needs, or trace one from a pattern book such as found in any crafts store. If your pattern has overlapping or close fitting designs, you'll need at least two separate stencils. The stencils should be cut from a fairly heavy waxed-type paper or regular stencil paper. The surface to be stenciled is coated with

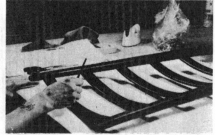

Stencil paper is laid over pattern and sharp razor knife used to carefully cut designs along lines.

Area to be stenciled is given a good coat of acrylic gold-leaf adhesive. Should be allowed to dry to tacky stage.

Stencil is positioned in place and taped down with masking tape. Pallet and brush are scraps of velvet.

½" SQS.

A piece of velvet is dipped in the fine metallic powder, excess shaken off then gently daubed over stencil.

When using two colors of powder on one stencil a small piece of stencil paper protects surrounding areas.

Stencil is carefully lifted off to reveal a beautiful shaded pattern. Stencils cleaned with alcohol may be reused.

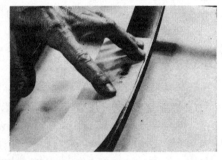

Most designs will require two or three stencils. Close-fitting patterns such as grape clusters require separate stencils.

Shading can be done, as well as blending of two colors, just by varying the amount of powders.

Be extremely careful not to move stencils around until design is covered, then remove carefully.

Result is a beautiful, glowing metallic design "Splatters" can be removed with dampened cotton swab.

Stenciled designs are covered with several coats of acrylic varnish to protect them from wear.

508

acrylic adhesive normally used for applying gold leaf, and allowed to dry to a "tacky" stage. The stencil then is taped in place, a piece of velvet dipped in a metallic powder and carefully rubbed over the stencil.

Place a practice card on the edge of a surface. Gently roll the brush through the paint, then wipe on a newspaper. Hold the ring and/or little finger along the edge to guide the brush, then lower it to the surface. When you start to run out of paint, lift the brush so the line goes to a point. Reload the brush and start back of the point.

With practice comes skill. Patterns can be made with stencils, or you may use decals. Do the striping by hand to keep the work as authentic as possible. You may have trouble making a straight line with a pencil, but you will be surprised at how easy it is to brush a straight line.

TORTOISESHELL FINISH

Even a plain piece of plywood takes on an exotic look with this finish that creates a "marbleized" or "tortoiseshell" appearance.

A top for a small table can be made by gluing together two 18-inch disks of ¾-inch fir plywood. The first step is to sand the surface to make it as smooth as possible. If there are any defects, fill them with wood putty.

The next step is to apply gesso. You may need as many as three applications. Sand each coat when it is dry before applying the next.

When the gesso is dry spray the surface olive green from a spray can. The gesso absorbs the paint so continue spraying (the spray paint dries in moments) until the surface no longer absorbs the paint and an even color is produced.

After the paint is dry brush on plain water. A couple of drops of liquid detergent will reduce surface tension for easier spreading. Into the water drop dry pigment powder—this can be any color—and spread it with a brush. When the color is well spread mix gold powder with alcohol and drip the mixture into the water-powder surface to create circles and abstract designs.

When this surface has dried, spray it with clear lacquer. The result is quite fabulous.

Gesso is applied next, to seal surface and permit further smoothing.

Use a forest or olive green as base coat.

Our project is top for small table, made by gluing together two 18-in. disks of ¾-in. plywood. First step is to sand.

When paint is dry, brush on water; this requires that surface is level. Use a drop of detergent to lower surface tension.

Into the water drop a small amount of dry pigment powder—burnt or raw umber—and spread it with a brush.

Spreading the pigment requires time because powder does not want to combine with water. Powder is oil-soluble.

When powder is spread so it pretty well covers the surface, drip an alcohol-gold powder mixture onto the wetted surface.

COLOR PATCHING

Color patching is based on a finishing method two centuries old called "French polish." For generations boiled linseed oil had been used as a finish for old furniture, and despite some disadvantages, there was no material to compete with it until shellac was imported from Asia. Although shellac had a tendency to lift previous coats, it was found that by dipping a cloth pad in shellac, then in linseed oil that it would be wiped or padded on to create a glossy, transparent finish.

Modern padding lacquers take the guesswork out of determining the correct blending of shellac and oil.

To use padding lacquers, apply a small amount to a cheesecloth, squeeze out the surplus, and wipe onto the surface, gradually contacting and leaving the surface, (somewhat like an airplane takeoff and landing).

Padding lacquers may be used to restore old finishes that are checking, crazing or have lost their transparency due to oxidation. First attempts with padding lacquer should be on a small surface such as an end table.

Brush on the first coat, softening the old finish to a semi-plastic state so it will flow together and fill the cracks and loosen the oxidation. When the first coat is no longer tacky, the actual hand padding is begun. The beginning strokes should be circular to knit the old finish together. (Remember to approach and leave the surface gradually.) Follow with a series of coats across the grain until all circular strokes are removed, then pad with the grain until all cross-grain strokes disappear. Let each application dry 15 or 20 minutes before the next coat.

This method can also be used as a complete finish on new wood, but it's necessary to apply more coats than when restoring an old finish.

Padding lacquers also may be used to "color-patch" marred or scratched finishes. For color-patching, padding lacquers are used with patching colors, of which there are two kinds; pigments or soluble aniline stains, both in powder forms. When pigment is used, the color remains the same regardless of how many applications, the patch becoming more opaque with added coats. When multiple applications of aniline stains are made the color gets darker and darker. Because the stains will penetrate and color the surrounding finish, they cannot be removed. On the other hand, the wrong shade of color pigment or a patch that is too opaque can be removed with a pad saturated with padding lacquer.

Other than this, color patching techniques are the same for both materials.

First pad a coat of finish on the area to be patched. Second, apply a small amount of pigment or stain into the area. Third, pad on another coat with the grain. Finally, to blend in the patch, pad a generous coat of finish over the entire area. Two or more colors can be blended between the fingers or on the patching surface, producing more realistic results.

To color-patch fine scratches, or where spots of finish have rubbed off edges, mix the proper color-patching pigment or stain, (somewhat on the light side), with padding lacquer and apply to the area with an artist's brush. When dry, pad a coat of finish over the repair.

In every instance of color patching; the final step is a generous application of padding lacquer

Dip cheesecloth into padding lacquer, squeeze out excess. Pad should be thoroughly moist, not overloaded.

Padding stokes should gradually contact and leave the surface. Pad should never stop or rest on the finish.

Roll patching pigment or stain between fingers until smooth, with no large particles, and pat into scratches.

with the grain. When this has dried thoroughly, sand lightly with 360-grit wet-or-dry paper and polish with 4/0 steel wood. In some cases, a light treatment of rubbing compound is necessary to match the gloss of the unrepaired or unrefinished spots. Or a high polish may be obtained by lightly wiping the surface with a lint-free cloth that has been dipped in alcohol. For a more satin finish, rub the finish with a felt pad dipped in oil and pumice stone.

An excellent way to practice color-patching techniques is on a piece of glass. When you can apply a color patch that is semi transparent and blends gradually to invisibility at the edges, you have truly mastered the art.

Coloring material is used like putty to fill blemishes. Color should be somewhat lighter than surrounding area.

Artist's brush dipped in mixture of patching pigment and padding lacquer is used in small areas.

After final coat is carefully padded on with the grain, sand patch lightly with 360-grit, wet-or-dry paper.

MARBLE-TOPPED FURNITURE

Genuine marble, a product of nature, comes in an almost endless variety of colors and veinings. Marble for shop use is available in either a polished or nonpolished finish. Normally you will find marble slabs from ½- to 1¼-inch thick.

Don't turn down a good buy because the marble you want is in three or four pieces, or has small missing corners. As long as no large pieces are missing, the slab can be made whole again with hardly a trace of the old break.

When you find a section of marble sized to fit your purpose, don't be concerned about the condition of its surface. Scratch away some of the dirt so you can see the true color. Then start your bargaining. Even bad pit marks, heavy scratches and massive staining can be removed.

After you've taken your piece of marble home, the first step is to inspect what you've got. Using a solution of dishwashing detergent and warm water, clean the surfaces, rinse and dry with a soft rag. Unless you're lucky, you will notice a number of blemishes, stains, scratches and even holes. This leads to the next step.

Smoothing the Surface

Start with 80-grit abrasive block. Applying moderate pressure, work the block back and forth

To inspect marble, wash with a solution of dishwashing detergent and warm water. Rinse and wipe dry with cloth.

If surface is very rough, pitted or with hollows, sand with an 80-grit abrasive block. Occasionally sprinkle with water.

The abrading process continues through 220 and 320-grits, but these stages can be done with power sander.

Remove organic stains with application of poultice made of facial tissues and 20-volume solution hydrogen peroxide.

Minute stains and scratches are removed with a final polishing. Start with 600-grit abrasive kept wet with water.

To detect an oil stain, dampen a piece of paper towel with cleaning fluid. Apply as poultice for removal of stain.

Rottenstone and water, mixed to a creamy paste, are scrubbed on marble for final step. Clean with warm water.

across the marble. Occasionally sprinkle with water to ease the friction. Take care not to rub too much in one area, since the coarse number 80-grit takes quite a bite. When the marble surface is relatively flat, change to a 120-grit.

The abrading process then continues through 220 and 320 grits, but these stages can be accomplished with a power sander or an electric drill with a disk sander mounted on a universal shaft. From time to time swab off the surface of the marble with warm water and a cellulose sponge.

Stop when minor scratches are still showing. The polishing process will remove these.

Stain Removal

Organic stains on marble are caused by tea, coffee, tobacco, wet bark, flowers and leached colors from paper or textiles. Usually you can identify this type of stain because it takes the shape of the staining object. Removal is easy through the application of a poultice made from facial tissues soaked in a 20-volume solution of hydrogen peroxide. Apply the soggy mass and cover with a plastic garment bag to prevent evaporation. Depending upon the depth of the stain, the process will require one to 48 hours.

To detect an oil stain, dampen a piece of blotting paper with cleaning fluid. Apply to the stained area, press down and remove. If the blotter absorbs some of the stain it is most likely oily in nature. Again treat with the tissue poultice—this time soaked with acetone. Acetone is available from your neighborhood druggist, but keep it away from wood finishes.

The Final Polish

Now the slab should have only a faint trace of staining and minute scratches. These will disappear during the polishing process. Using an abrasive disk of 600-grit, go over the entire surface. Sponge off with water and you should begin to see signs of a polish.

For the last step you'll need a quantity of rottenstone powder. Add enough water to about half a cup of the powder to make a creamy paste. Scrub the mixture into the marble using a felt pad on an orbital sander.

As you work, add water and powder to maintain consistency and sufficient abrasive action. After about five minutes, sponge off the surface with warm water and check the polish. Stand a book, with the jacket attached, on the marble. If you can read the printing on the jacket in the reflection, your job is done. A silicone spray wax will help the marble keep its shine.

Repairing Broken Marble

As long as you have all of the pieces, a broken marble slab can be repaired with hardly a trace. Assemble the pieces on a flat surface to check fit. Clean all edges thoroughly with acetone. From a marble dealer, obtain some polyester-resin in powder form and a small bottle of liquid catalyst. Two tablespoons of resin and 15 drops of catalyst will do a sizable repair job.

In making up a batch of cement, the amount of catalyst determines the setting time. For the two tablespoonsful -15 drops proportion allow 20 minutes of working time. Use a small paintbrush to coat the edges to be joined. After application, press the pieces together and remove excess cement with a putty knife. Clamping is unnecessary since weight of marble will maintain sufficient pressure.

Broken corners and holes call for another technique using marble dust and a resin cement. The mixture should be about the consistency of thick honey. It is poured into a wooden dam built around the broken corner. The wood is covered with wax paper. After overnight drying the wood forms are removed and the corners given an abrasive rubdown and final polishing.

FINISHING TOYS

Making toys for children, whether it's a brightly-colored dump truck, a hobbyhorse or a doll house, and watching the children's eyes light up with delight is one of the rewards of woodworking. But if you want to keep that happy gleam in their eyes, make sure the finish used is safe for them.

Every year, children all over the world become seriously ill from eating or chewing on paint-covered items. Usually, these are windowsills, woodwork or furniture that has been painted with old-fashioned lead-base paint. But in some cases, toys have been coated with dangerous materials by unsuspecting fathers and grandfathers.

You can be sure the toys and furniture you make have a safe nontoxic finish, by checking the label on the container carefully. It should clearly state that the paint or finish is free of lead pigment or can be used safely for children's toys and furniture. If it doesn't, don't use it!

Recent federal legislation requires all paints or finishing materials manufactured in the United States to be free of lead pigment, unless intended for use on such structures as bridges, piers, water towers, or ships. These paints contain red or gray lead and should not be used for metal toys.

When refinishing metal tricycles or wagons, use one of the new "primer-and-finish" coatings that contain safe rust-inhibitive agents.

Furniture and woodwork in children's rooms can be finished with enamels clearly stated for such use, or with clear spray lacquer. Most resin finishes such as varnishes, lacquers or penetrating oils are

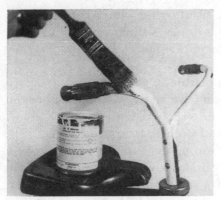

Metal toys should be finished with lead-free paints. Don't use those that contain red or gray lead pigments.

All children's toys should be sanded smooth; edges and corners rounded.

Subtle color can be added with poster colors or water-proof ink then varnish.

Salad bowl finish or penetrating-oil is a "safe" finish for any toddler's toys.

Safest finish is no finish at all, as youngsters will chew on most anything. Be sure small items are well sanded.

Bright-colored enamels used on toys should be lead-free and marked as safe for use on children's toys.

safe for use after they are dry.

Poster colors diluted with water and then coated with varnish are excellent for small toys. Latex paints also are fine, but they tend to produce a dirt-catching surface.

The best finish for toddler's toys is really no finish at all, but if you feel they must have a finish, use an oil or salad-bowl finish.

Preparing the surface of toys also is important, whether they are metal or wood. All sharp edges should be sanded smooth, free of splinters, and all corners rounded.

Most important: Check the label to be sure the finish is approved and safe for children's toys!

14

YOUR
SHOP

YOUR SHOP

SAWHORSES ■ PLANNING YOUR SHOP

HANDYMAN'S TOOL TOTER ■ APARTMENT WORKSHOP

PLANNING YOUR SHOP

Layout of a home workshop varies mostly with the following factors: 1. Operating area required by various power tools and equipment. 2. Shop space available. 3. Step-saving distances between tools and facilities most often used. 4. Location of doors and windows.

Shop Location

Often the basement is the only available space, although high humidity during summer months is a drawback, causing tools to rust. A dehumidifier can be used to overcome this problem. During cold weather the heating plant generally eliminates the humidity problem. Backflow of sewer lines through floor drains sometimes causes trouble but this can be prevented by installing a capped standpipe or a backflow valve in the drain. Humidity is generally less of a problem in a garage, except when a dripping car is driven in and parked. An attached, heated garage is best as this eliminates the need for a separate heater.

When a one-car garage is your only possibility it can provide sufficient workshop space when the car is parked outside temporarily. To accommodate the car inside, floor-type power tools can be pushed against one wall. An alternative is to build a carport so that neither car nor machines have to be moved. In this case you can substitute a wall with a window for the garage door, or at least seal all cracks along door edges to prevent heat loss during cold weather.

A two-car garage will accommodate a car while the shop is in use, except for occasional jobs that require more working area. If you desire still more space, explore the possibility of adding to a garage. In this case, a partition and a door between the car area and shop will help keep dust off the car.

A breezeway of adequate size between the house and garage can be enclosed to become a shop. Even a small 8 x 10-foot space can be made convenient. A layout in a room a few feet longer is also shown.

Power Tool Selection

Initial cost of power tools to serve a wide range of purposes can be kept relatively low by purchasing only a drill press and band saw. Besides its prime purpose for drilling, a drill press will also serve for grinding, buffing, polishing, sanding, scratch-brushing, routing, molding, dovetailing, hollow-chisel mortising, planing, paint mixing, light milling and light clamping. You can use it

Half of this two-car garage serves as workshop and photo darkroom. There are six power tools as listed in detail. For photo work, tight-fitting, weatherstripped "lids" of hardboard fit on window casings.

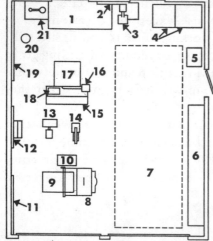

1—Bench, 33" x 72". 2—Small-supplies shelving. 3—Drill press on cabinet. 4—Clothes washer & dryer. 5—Heating fan. 6—Shelving, 18" x 144". 7—Space required for car. 9—Low storage chest. 10—Box for wood waste. 11—Garden-tool rack. 12—Large panels, stepladder. 13—Disk sander. 14—Band saw. 15—Wood lathe. 16—Scroll saw. 17—Card table. 18—Air compressor. 19—Hand-tool cabinet. 20—Waste can. 21—Photo enlarger.

This 14 x 17-ft. shop has seven power tools and a bench along one wall. Vise is on projecting T-section. Detail shows location of tools and facilities not included in photo such as grinder, sander, spray booth.

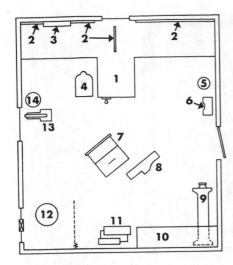

1—T-shaped bench, 28" x 14'. 2—Tool panels. 3—Small supplies shelving. 4—Drill press. 5—Waste can. 6—Grinder. 7—Table saw. 8—Jointer. 9—Lathe. 10—Overhead stock rack. 11—Combination disk-belt sander. 12—Spray booth. 13—Scroll saw. 14—Vacuum cleaner.

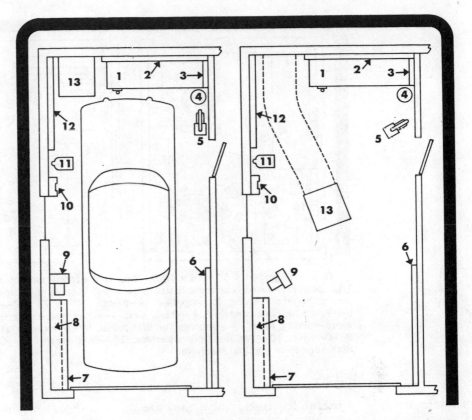

Combination one-car garage and workshop, size 11 x 23 ft., which houses five power tools without interfering with accommodation of car. Left drawing shows tools located along walls to provide space for car. Right drawing shows how they are pulled out for use when car is parked outside. 1—Bench, 27" x 8" 2—Hand-tool panel. 3—Small-supplies shelving. 4—Waste can. 5—Band saw. 6—Garden-tool rack. 7—Overhead stock rack. 8—Paint, supply shelving. 9—Disk sander. 10—Grinder. 11—Drill press. 12—Drill-press and saw-accessories shelving. 13—Combination saw-jointer.

for filing with special rotary files, or for driving a flexible shaft. Taping and scroll-sawing attachments also are available.

Besides making curved cuts, a band saw can make long ripping cuts accurately by using a fence clamped to the table. Crosscuts are limited to throat clearance. A band saw will cut much thicker stock (at slower speed) than can be cut on any other power saw. By installing a speed reducer and providing metal-cutting blades you can saw metal. By substituting an abrasive band you can sand edges neatly and get into tight corners that are impossible to reach with other power sanders.

Internal cutting can be done on a band saw that is equipped with a special saw-blade welder and grinder. However, the job of cutting, welding and grinding the blade for internal cuts must be done twice each time, which often takes longer than doing the work with a scroll saw or portable saber saw. Also, a welder-equipped band saw is a luxury item in the average home workshop.

A circular saw handles wide and long work beyond the capacity of a band saw. It also can be used for disk sanding, grinding, buffing, polishing, molding and will cut wide grooves when fitted with a dado cutter. For work to be edge-glued, a fine saw blade on a circular saw may eliminate need of a jointer.

A jointer not only produces matching smooth edges to be joined, but also serves as a planer to remove rough, uneven surfaces from stock of widths within the tool's capacity. A jointer also will do rabbeting. A thickness planer not only produces smooth surfaces on boards of widths within its capacity but it is the only tool that will accurately reduce the thickness of stock to desired smaller dimensions.

Although disk sanders and portable orbital

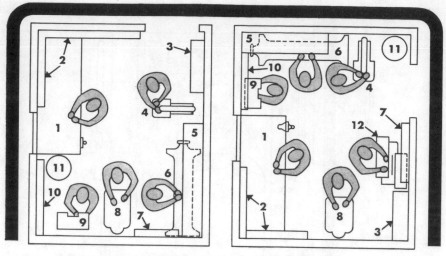

Two arrangements of an 8 x 10-ft. shop that accommodates four or five floor-type power tools for convenient use plus a 6-ft. bench, a cabinet for hand tools and adequate shelving for supplies. 1—Bench, 27" x 72". 2—Hand-tool panel. 3—Paint-supplies shelving. 4—Band saw. 5—Overhead stock rack. 6—Wood or metalworking lathe. 7—Shelves for drill-press, lathe accessories. 8—Drill press. 9—Grinder. 10—Small-supplies shelves. 11—Waste can. 12—Combination belt-disk sander or milling machine.

sanders are highly useful for many jobs, they are less satisfactory for fine finishing work, where sanding must be done with the wood grain, as can be done with belt sanders. A portable belt sander has a wide range of usefulness in any woodworking shop.

Combination power tools have a great advantage in conserving floor space. Such units provide several different tools, such as circular saw, band saw, jointer, drill press, sander and lathe, and the cost is much less than that of separate tools. The only disadvantage is that time is required to make the conversion from one tool to another.

Every shop should have a grinder, not only for removing and shaping metal, but especially for maintaining sharp edges on all cutting tools. It may be a separate unit or the work can be done on a drill press or circular saw equipped with a grinding wheel.

If you are especially interested in wood or metal turning, a suitable lathe with its accessories will be a necessary tool in your shop. To do much work with sheet metal, a bench-mounted shears, a bending brake, a slip roll for cylinders and a rotary machine for turning and beading are important tools. For precision machine-shop work in shaping metal, a milling machine or metalworking lathe with a milling attachment is indispensible.

For finishing with paint, lacquer or varnish, superior results will be achieved with a spray gun. This requires a booth from which fumes and suspended paint particles in the air are expelled outdoors with an exhaust fan. To keep a shop clean, a blower-suction type of vacuum cleaner is handy. A suitable box or bag can be attached to the chip outlet of a circular saw and jointer. A disk or belt sander should be provided with a suction fan connected to a bag, the fan operating while you sand.

Location of Tools and Facilities

Often the best location for a bench is against a wall, because rigidity is important. Besides sturdy construction, the rear legs of the bench can be anchored to wall studs with lag screws. A heavy machinist's vise may be located at the right end of the bench (as you face it) but a woodworker's vise goes at the left end, particularly for convenience in planing by hand. Perhaps you will want both. Butting the vise end of a bench into a corner restricts its usefulness. Therefore a vise position about midway between opposite walls is best. When possible a vise should be mounted over a bench leg for solidity when hammering. To save steps, a panel for hand tools should be close to the bench. A convenient, narrow tool cabinet is shown

This encourages keeping the bench top clear.

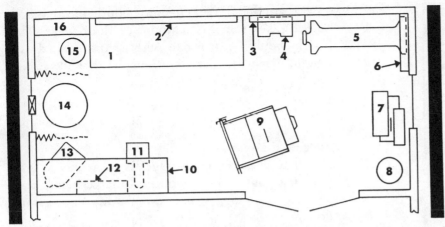

This 8 x 17-ft. shop provides adequate working space for table saw and jointer, making use of doorway for ripping long stock. 1—Bench, 27″ x 7′. 2—Hand-tool panel or cabinet. 3—Small-supplies shelving. 4—Grinder. 5—Lathe. 6—Lathe-accessories shelves. 7—Disk-belt sander. 8—Vacuum cleaner. 9—Table saw and jointer. 10—Overhead stock rack. 11—Band saw. 12—Drill-press accessories shelving. 13—Drill press. 14—Spray booth with tunrtable, pull-out curtains, exhaust fan. 15—Waste can. 16—Paint shelving.

Wood and metalworking shop in a 12 x 18-ft. room that also houses furnace and water heater. This layout can be modified for L-shaped room where furnace is not included. 1—Bench, 27″ x 72″. 2—Hand-tool panel or cabinet. 3—Drill-press accessories shelf. 4—Drill press. 5—Bench for sheet-metal tools; brake, slip roll, shears, etc. 6—Disk-belt sander. 7—Band saw. 8—Saw-accessories shelves. 9—Jointer (can be combined with saw). 10—Table saw. 11—Spray booth with turntable, curtain and fan. 12—Paint-supplies shelving. 13—Overhead stock rack. 14—Lathe. 15—Lathe and miller accessories shelving. 16—Milling machine. 17—Waste can. 18—Grinder. 19—Small-supplies shelving.

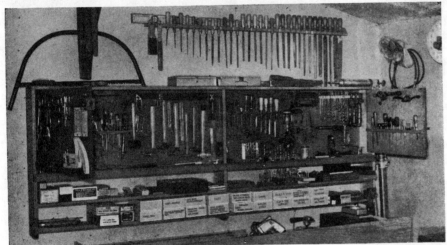

Hand-tool panel or cabinet close to bench saves many steps and helps avoid tool clutter on bench. Two hinged panels at ends of cabinet increase its capacity. Separate file rack above cabinet is within arm's reach.

Shelves for jars holding small items, such as nails and screws, should be within easy reach. A stock rack is not in constant use, so can be located anywhere as long as it does not interfere with the use of tools and facilities. It may be hung from the ceiling, high enough for sufficient head room.

A drill press is used frequently, so should be close to the bench. If at one end of the bench, place it so there is clearance for work extending from a vise. A grinder can be placed on the end of a bench, on a separate stand or on a wall shelf. A band saw must have clearance for ripping boards. The throat side can be quite close to a wall. On the opposite side there should be space for boards of which the ends are to be cut off.

A circular saw requires clearance on all sides at table level for ripping or crosscutting. Other tools and facilities of lesser height may be set in the clearance area except in front and on the left side where you handle stock. To support the free end of long work at table height of a band saw, circular saw, jointer or floor sander, provide a portable stand or horse having a roller that is adjustable for height.

A jointer and floor-type belt sander require working clearance for long stock at the front and back, but relatively small clearance on the left for the operator. Lathes can be backed close to walls,

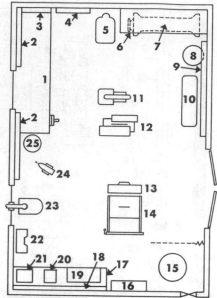

Well-equipped 12 x 18-ft. shop for wood, metal, ceramics and lapidary work. 1—Bench, 27" x 8'. 2—Hand-tool panel or cabinet. 3—Small supplies shelving. 4—Drill-press accessories shelving. 5—Drill press. 6—Overhead stock rack. 7—Woodworking lathe. 8—Vacuum cleaner. 9—Lathe-accessories shelving. 10—Metal-working lathe. 11—Band saw. 12—Combination disk-belt sander. 13—Jointer (may be combined with saw). 14—Table saw. 15—Spray booth with turntable, curtains, fan. 16—Paint-supplies shelving. 17—Lapidary bench. 18—Lapidary bench. 19—Lapidary saw, grinder and buffer. 20—Tumbler. 21—High-temperature oven for ceramics. 22—Grinder. 23—Forge. 24—Anvil. 25—Waste can.

as can grinders. A paint-spray booth located in a corner takes the least amount of floor space. The booth should be provided with a turntable, adjustable in height, to permit turning work while spraying it.

Suggested Layouts

The photos and the layouts given may help in planning your shop. If you make large items, plan an adequate exit, such as double doors (or garage door).

Illumination and Power Outlets

To avoid eye fatigue and contribute to greater accuracy, it is essential to have adequate illumination. Daylight from windows often is insufficient. Lamps should be located to avoid shadows in front of work. An overhead lamp placed just in front of the work and slightly to the left generally is best. A portable lamp can be placed to suit the worker.

Electric outlets should be located so cords will not interfere with either worker or machines. It's a good idea to have all machines on a separate circuit, properly fused, in a switchbox that can be locked to eliminate machine operation and possible accidents to children or unauthorized users of tools in your shop.

APARTMENT WORKSHOP

An old desk fitted with the right accessories can provide excellent working facilities for apartment dwellers. Accessories for the bench may vary according to your interests. You should have a device over the bench to store the most often used tools, a vise of some sort, soldering block, holsters for soldering gun and electric drill, clips for small tools such as the soldering pencil, and a multireceptacle line such as shown.

To convert an old desk to a workbench clean and repair it, smooth down the top and apply several coats of varnish. Cut a piece of perforated hardboard the length of the desk and either attach it to the wall over the desk or simply lean it against the wall resting on the desk. Plastic fixtures are

recommended for hanging the tools on the hardboard.

An auxiliary bench top is made to fit the top righthand drawer to keep the working space free and the drilling and soldering off the desk top. Attach a small vise to the auxiliary top.

One-half of a standard asbestos (6-inch x 6-inch) soldering block is mounted in a wooden frame as shown. The soldering clamps are alligator clips, which will hold all types and sizes of wire securely. The ends of the clips were flattened out and fastened to the wooden frame as shown.

The soldering pencil is held on the desk top with a spring clip. The remaining soldering block is used beneath it as a heat shield and solder stop.

The holster for the soldering gun is made of

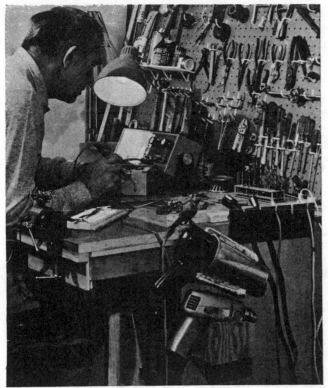

Hardboard with notches cut for cords, and identified with scraps of tape is combined with multireceptacle line.

Top drawer holds "lift-out" bench top used for small work. Holsters on side of bench are for drill and soldering gun.

Old desk is converted to apartment workbench. Added accessories provide more space and better working facilities.

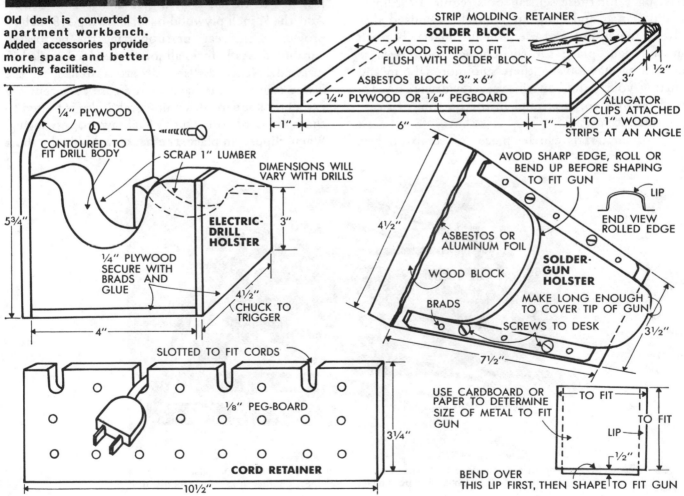

STRIP MOLDING RETAINER

SOLDER BLOCK

WOOD STRIP TO FIT FLUSH WITH SOLDER BLOCK

ASBESTOS BLOCK 3" x 6"

¼" PLYWOOD OR ⅛" PEGBOARD

½"

3"

1" 6" 1"

ALLIGATOR CLIPS ATTACHED TO 1" WOOD STRIPS AT AN ANGLE

¼" PLYWOOD

CONTOURED TO FIT DRILL BODY

SCRAP 1" LUMBER

DIMENSIONS WILL VARY WITH DRILLS

ELECTRIC-DRILL HOLSTER

3"

5¾"

¼" PLYWOOD SECURE WITH BRADS AND GLUE

4"

4½"

CHUCK TO TRIGGER

AVOID SHARP EDGE, ROLL OR BEND UP BEFORE SHAPING TO FIT GUN

LIP

END VIEW ROLLED EDGE

4½"

ASBESTOS OR ALUMINUM FOIL

WOOD BLOCK

BRADS

SOLDER-GUN HOLSTER

MAKE LONG ENOUGH TO COVER TIP OF GUN

SCREWS TO DESK

3½"

7½"

SLOTTED TO FIT CORDS

⅛" PEG-BOARD

CORD RETAINER

3¼"

10½"

USE CARDBOARD OR PAPER TO DETERMINE SIZE OF METAL TO FIT GUN

TO FIT

TO FIT

LIP

½"

BEND OVER THIS LIP FIRST, THEN SHAPE TO FIT GUN

sheet metal (coffee can, etc.). A wood block is cut to size as indicated and covered with asbestos sheet or aluminum foil as a heat shield. The holster should be long enough to prevent the hot tip from scorching the appliance cords hanging from the cord retainer.

A multireceptacle strip is fastened to the desk top and the appliance cords are connected to it when used. A peg-board or plywood cord retainer is cut as shown and screwed to the desk edge. The plugs are held in it when not in use. To avoid fumbling for the proper cord, plugs and slots in the retainer are identified as shown.

The holster for the electric drill is made of scrap stock to fit the contour of the drill body and fastened with glue and screws to the bench. It may be padded with strips of rubber if desired.

The desk drawers are used for small tools, tape, files and other items not on the board.

HANDYMAN'S TOOL TOTER

Have you ever crawled up onto the roof, or started some repair job around the house only to discover you didn't have the right tools and had to make one or more trips back to the workshop to hunt for a screwdriver, chisel, etc., you needed?

If it has happened to you very often, you've probably wished you had some sort of case to carry all the tools. This handyman's "footsaver" has space for the essential tools required for home maintenance and they are so well organized that after a few minutes of use, you automatically reach in the right place for the correct tool. Because everything has a place, there's no more jabbing and cutting your hands on chisels, screwdrivers or edge tools as you grope around in the bottom of a case for small items.

All materials can be pieces of scrap lumber, including the 1/8-inch perforated hardboard. The sides and front of the case are ¾-inch plywood and the base is ¼-inch plywood. After the sides are cut, holes are cut into the upper portions and a length of broom handle is inserted into the holes. The "handle" projects beyond one side, the projecting end is used to hold various rolls of tape. A metal pin in a blind hole holds the tape in place. The front piece is rabbeted on the ends as shown and fastened to the sides with glue and screws or nails. Add the ¼-inch plywood base, allowing 1/8 inch to project at the rear for supporting the perforated hardboard. As before, all joints are glued, nailed or screwed. Notched "shoes" are fastened to the lower edges of the back of the case to accept the carpenter's square. A small metal Z-clip is bolted to the hardboard to keep the hacksaw from swinging. When clipped in place, the hacksaw holds the short

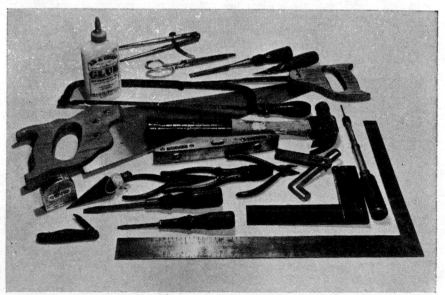

Shown are standard tools that fit into or on the case. Items that also fit into the case are spatula, rolls of tape, nailsets, punches, countersinks, and electric drill.

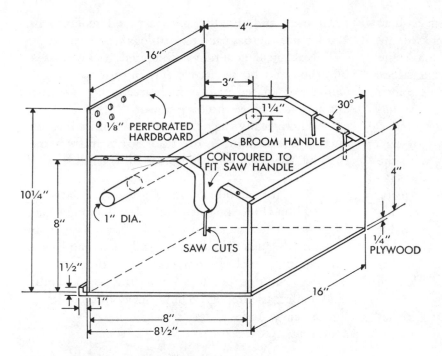

Tools are held on perforated hardboard by rugged plastic fixtures. Tape slips on handle, nailset, punches fit in drilled holes on top edges of case sides.

Front and back views show generous number of tools that fit into or on the back of the handy tool toter.

leg of the 2-foot square against the hardboard. Cut slots in the sides of the case for a handsaw and small square. Drill blind holes along the top edges of the sides for countersinks, punches, nailsets and pencils.

Snap the plastic clips into the perforated hardboard to locate the tools as desired.

Sanding and rounding the edges of the "toter" will prevent splinters and injury to hands, and a couple of coats of paint will improve the appearance of the case and protect the wood.

SAWHORSES

Sawhorses are a must for any building or remodeling work, and every workshop should have at least one pair. They are good scaffold supports for working or painting, and they are essential when laying out or cutting large sheets of plywood.

Two types of sawhorses are shown and described. One is quite light and easy to move around, but is sturdy and will support a fairly heavy load. The other type is built of heavier stock and will support almost any reasonable load you place on it. When cutting the various pieces, be sure to cut enough to make a pair of either type horse; a single unit is not much use, but three can be useful, as for plywood sheets. Two pair is better.

Either type sawhorse can be made in a short time, and with a minimum of tools. Legs of the lightweight horse are 1 x 4s. You can mark the angle on the ends by placing one leg of a 2-foot square at the 22-inch mark, the other at the 5-inch mark. Slide the square along the board 22 inches and mark again to create the angle for the second leg. Repeat twice more for the other pair of legs. The finished legs will be 22 inches long with the angle about 12 or 13 degrees. Separate the legs into pairs and chamfer them; be sure they are in pairs, with the chamfers facing. Two methods of cutting chamfers are possible, one is with a hatchet, and it is not really as crude as it seems (if you have a reasonable skill with the tool). It is, of course, quicker and more accurate to cut the angles on a table saw. Don't forget to make a right and left.

Nail the legs on the 2 x 4 tops about 4 inches from each end. Finally, measure and nail on the 1 x 4 braces across each pair of legs.

No finish generally is applied to sawhorses, but they can be painted if left outdoors. Use galvanized or coated nails, which are both rust-resistant and have better holding power.

Where really rugged support is required, as for cutting 2-inch lumber for floor joists, rafters and the like, these heavy-duty horses fill the bill.

The top member is an "I-beam" created by assembling three lengths of 2 x 4 and spiking them together. The legs also are 2 x 4s, but no angles are cut on the ends. The legs are spiked to the I-beam top about 4 inches from each end. Braces across the legs are located just under the top assembly and nailed to the legs. These heavy-duty units are quite heavy, and will stay in place.

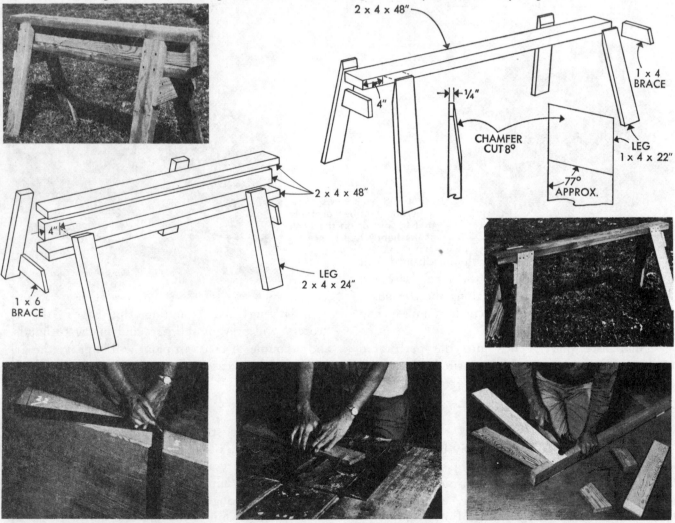

One way to mark correct angles: place 2-ft. square on board with 22-in. mark and 5-in. mark as shown.

Leg can be mitered on table saw, with miter gauge set at 12 degrees. Total length of leg is 22-in.

Legs are nailed to 2 x 4 tops about 4 in. from each end. Be sure leg end lines up flush with top of 2 x 4; use enough nails.

526

WEIGHTS AND MEASURES

TEMPERATURE

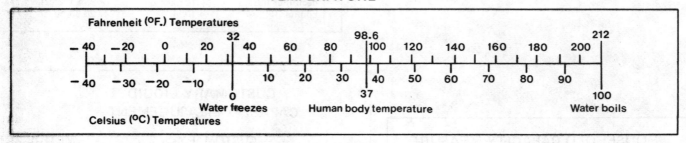

METRIC CONVERSIONS

IF YOU KNOW:	MULTIPLY BY:	TO FIND:	IF YOU KNOW:	MULTIPLY BY:	TO FIND:
Length and Distance			**Surface or Area**		
inches	25	millimeters	square inches	6.5	square centimeters
feet	30	centimeters	square feet	0.09	square meters
yards	0.9	meters	square yards	0.83	square meters
miles	1.6	kilometers	square miles	2.6	square kilometers
millimeters	0.04	inches	acres	0.4	hactares
centimeters	0.4	inches	square centimeters	0.16	square inches
meters	1.1	yards	square meters	1.2	square yards
kilometers	0.6	miles	square kilometers	0.4	square miles
			hectares	2.4	acres
Volume and Capacity					
ounces (fluid)	30	cubic centimeters	**Weight and Mass**		
pints	0.47	liters			
quarts	0.95	liters	ounces	28	grams
gallons	3.8	liters	pounds	0.45	kilograms
cubic centimeters	0.034	ounces (fluid)	tons	0.9	metric tons
liters	2.1	pints	grams	0.035	ounces
liters	1.06	quarts	kilograms	2.2	pounds
liters	0.26	gallons	metric tons	1.1	tons
Temperature					
degrees Fahrenheit	0.55 (after subtracting 32)	degrees Celsius	degrees Celsius	1.8 (then add 32)	degrees Fahrenheit

527

VOLUME MEASUREMENT

CUSTOMARY		METRIC
1 cubic inch (cu. in.)		= 16.387 cm^3
1 cubic foot (cu. ft.)	= 1,728 cu. in.	= 0.0283 m^3
1 cubic yard (cu. yd.)	= 27 cu. ft.	= 0.7646 m^3

METRIC		CUSTOMARY
1 cubic millimeter (mm^3)		= 0.00006 cu. in.
1 cubic centimeter (cm^3)	= 1,000 mm^3	= 0.0610 cu. in.
1 cubic decimeter (dm^3)	= 1,000 cm^3	= 0.0353 cu. ft.
1 cubic meter (m^3)	= 1,000 dm^3	= 1.3079 cu. yd.
1 cubic dekameter (dam^3)	= 1,000 m^3	= 1,307.9 cu. yd.
1 cubic hectometer (hm^3)	= 1,000 dam^3	= 1,307,9000 cu. yd.

METRIC CAPACITY MEASURE

METRIC		CUSTOMARY
1 milliliter (ml)		= 0.0610 cu. in.
1 centiliter (cl)	= 10 ml	= 0.6102 cu. in.
1 deciliter (dl)	= 10 cl	= 6.1025 cu. in.
1 liter (l)	= 10 dl	61.025 cu. in.
		or 1.057 liquid qt.
		or 0.908 dry.
		610.25 cu. in.
		6,102.50 cu. in.
1 dekaliter (dal)	= 10 l	35.315 cu. ft.
1 hectoliter (hl)	= 10 dal	or 264.178 gal.
1 kiloliter (kl)	= 10 hl	or 28.38 bu.

HOUSEHOLD CAPACITY MEASURE

CUSTOMARY		METRIC	
1 teaspoon		= 1/6 fl. oz.	= 4.9 ml
1 tablespoon	= 3 teaspoons	= 1/2 fl. oz.	= 14.8 ml
1 cup	= 16 tablespoons	8 fl. oz.	= 236.6 ml
1 pint	= 2 cups	16 fl. oz.	= 473.2 ml
1 quart	= 2 pints	= 32 fl. oz.	= 946.4 ml
1 gallon	= 4 quarts	= 128 fl. oz.	= 3.785 l

CUSTOMARY LIQUID CAPACITY MEASUREMENT

CUSTOMARY			METRIC
1 gill (gi.)		= 7.219 cu. in.	= 0.1183 l
1 pint (pt.)	= 4 gi.	= 28.875 cu. in.	= 0.4732 l
1 quart (qt.)	= 2 pt.	= 57.75 cu. in.	= 0.9463 l
1 gallon (gal.)	= 4 qt.	= 231 cu. in.	= 3.7853 l
1 barrel (liquids) (bbl.)	= 31.5 gal.	= 4.21 cu. ft.	= 119.24 l
1 barrel (petroleum (bbl.)	= 42 gal.	= 5.61 cu. ft.	= 158.98 l

IMPERIAL	CUSTOMARY		METRIC
1 imperial quart	= 1.2009 U.S. qt.	= 69.355 cu. in.	= 1.13649 l
1 imperial gallon	= 1.2009 U.S. gal.	= 277.420 cu. in.	= 4.54596 l

CUSTOMARY DRY CAPACITY MEASUREMENT

CUSTOMARY			METRIC
1 pint (pt.)		= 33.600 cu. in.	= 550.60 cm^3
1 quart (qt.)	= 2 pt.	= 67.20 cu. in.	= 1,101.21 cm^3
1 peck (pk.)	= 8 qt.	= 537.61 cu. in.	= 8,809.85 cm^3
1 bushel (bu.)	= 4 pk.	= 2,150.42 cu. in.	= 0.035239 m^3
1 barrel (bbl.)		= 4.08 cu. ft.	= 0.115627 m^3

IMPERIAL	CUSTOMARY		METRIC
1 imperial dry quart	= 1.032 U.S. qt.	= 69.354 cu. in.	= 1,136.5 cm^3
1 imperial bushel	= 1.032 U.S. bu.	= 1.284 cu. ft.	= 0.03636 m^3

METRIC WEIGHT

AVOIRDUPOIS

1 milligram (mg)		=	0.0154 gr.
1 centigram (cg)	= 10 mg	=	0.1543 gr.
1 decigram (dg)	= 10 cg	=	1.5432 gr.
1 gram (g)	= 10 dg	=	15.4323 gr.
1 dekagram (dag)	= 10 g	=	0.3527 oz.
1 hectogram (hg)	= 10 dag	=	3.5274 oz.
1 kilogram (kg)	= 10 hg	=	2.2046 lb.
1 quintal (q)	= 100 kg	=	220.46 lb.
1 metric ton (M.T.)	= 10 q or 1,000 kg	=	2,204.62 lb.

AVOIRDUPOIS WEIGHT

		METRIC	
1 grain (gr.)		=	0.0648 g
1 dram (dr.)	= 27.34375 gr.	=	1.7718 g
1 ounce (oz.)	= 16. dr.	=	28.3495 g
1 pound (lb.)	= 16 oz.	=	453.5924 g or 0.4536 kg
1 hundredweight (cwt.)	= 100 lb.	=	45.3592 kg
1 short ton (s.t.)	= 2,000 lb.	=	907.18 kg or 0.9072 M.T.

WOOD MEASUREMENTS

CUSTOMARY		METRIC
1 board foot (bd. ft.)	= 144 cu. in. (1 ft. x 1 ft. x 1 in.)	= .00236 m³
1 cord foot (cd. ft.)	= 16 cu. ft. (4 ft. x 4 ft. x 1 ft.)	= .4528 m³
1 cord (cd.)	= 8 cd. ft. (4 ft. x 4 ft. x 8 ft.)	= 3.625 m³

METRIC		CUSTOMARY
1 stere	1 m³	1.3079 cu. yd. or 0.2759 cord

LENGTH AND DISTANCE

CUSTOMARY		METRIC
1 inch (in.)		= 2.54 cm
1 foot (ft.)	= 12 in.	= 30.48 cm
1 yard (yd.)	= 3 ft.	= 0.9144 m
1 rod (rd.)	= 5½ yd.	= 5.0292 m
1 furlong (fur.)	= 40 rd. or 1/8 mi.	= 201.168 m
1 statute mile (mi.)	= 5,280 ft.	= 1.6093 km
1 league	= 3 mi.	= 4.8280 km

METRIC		CUSTOMARY
1 millimeter (mm)		= 0.03937 in.
1 centimeter (cm)	= 10 mm	= 0.3937 in.
1 decimeter (dm)	= 10 cm	= 3.937 in.
1 meter (m)	= 10 dm	= 39.37 in.
1 dekameter (dam)	= 10 m	= 393.7 in.
1 hectometer (hm)	= 10 dam	= 328.0833 ft.
1 kilometer (km)	= 10 hm	= 0.62137 mi.

SURFACE OR AREA

CUSTOMARY		METRIC
1 square inch (sq. in.)		= 6.4516 cm²
1 square foot (sq. ft.)	= 144 sq. in.	= 0.0929 m²
1 square yard (sq. yd.)	= 9 sq. ft.	= 0.8361 m²
1 square rod (sq. rd.)	= 30¼ sq. yd.	= 25.293 m²
1 acre (A.)	= 160 sq. rd.	= 0.4047 ha
1 square mile (sq. mi.)	= 640 A.	= 258.998 ha. or 2.5899 km²

METRIC		CUSTOMARY
1 square millimeter (mm²)		= 0.002 sq. in.
1 square centimeter (cm²)	= 100 mm²	= 0.1549 sq. in.
1 square decimeter (dm²)	= 100 cm²	= 15.499 sq. in.
1 square meter (m²)	= 100 dm²	= 1.549 sq. in.
1 square dekameter (dam²)	= 100 m²	= 119.6 sq. yd.
1 square hectometer (hm²)	= 100 dam²	= 2.4710 A
1 square kilmometer (km²)	= 100 hm²	= 247.104 A or 0.3861 sq. mi.

METRIC LAND MEASUREMENT

METRIC		CUSTOMARY
1 centiare (ca)		= 1.549 sq. in.
1 are (a)	= 100 ca	= 119.6 sq. yd.
1 hectare (ha)	= 100 a	= 2.4710 A
1 square kilometer (km²)	= 100 ha	or 0.3861 sq. mi.

INDEX